W9-CKB-973

811.3
Whi   Whittier, John
            Greenleaf

            The poetical
            works of Whittier

DATE DUE

MAR 1 4 1985		
MAR 1 4 1901		

Freeman Branch
Harris County Public
Library

HERE

hc
p   FM

HARRIS COUNTY PUBLIC LIBRARY

HOUSTON, TEXAS

The
Poetical Works
of
Whittier

The
Poetical Works
of
Whittier

Cambridge Edition

With a New Introduction
by Hyatt H. Waggoner

Houghton Mifflin Company Boston

Copyright © 1975 by Houghton Mifflin Company
All rights reserved. No part of this work may be
reproduced or transmitted in any form by any means,
electronic or mechanical, including photocopying and
recording, or by any information storage or retrieval
system, without permission in writing from the publisher.

Library of Congress Cataloging in Publication Data

Whittier, John Greenleaf, 1807–1892.
    The poetical works of Whittier.

    Text of the Cambridge ed. of 1894, which was
edited by H. E. Scudder and published under title:
The complete poetical works of John Greenleaf
Whittier.
    Includes indexes.
    I. Title.
PS3250.F75   811'.3   75-25974
ISBN 0-395-21599-4

Printed in the United States of America

V 10 9 8 7 6 5 4 3 2

EDITOR'S NOTE

THE TEXT of this edition is that of the Cambridge Edition of 1894, edited by Horace E. Scudder, which in turn was an expansion of the earlier Riverside Edition which Whittier himself saw through the press and for which he revised poems and wrote an Introduction and Notes to the poems. The new edition retained Whittier's arrangement and notes, but added the poems in *At Sundown*, published after the appearance of the earlier edition, and a few other poems not formerly included. The headnotes and the notes at the end of the volume were for the most part copies or abridgments of those used in the Riverside Edition, but a few were added containing facts brought to light after Whittier's death. These are distinguished by being enclosed in brackets.

In the present edition, the Cambridge Edition's "Biographical Sketch" and the Chronological Listing of all of Whittier's poems have been replaced by the present editor's Introduction and a Chronology of the principal events in Whittier's life and work.

HYATT H. WAGGONER

CONTENTS

CONTENTS

INTRODUCTION

LIKE the other "Schoolroom Poets" of the nineteenth century, Whittier came of old New England stock, but unlike the others he had little formal education and, socially speaking, came from what were then called "humble origins." He was born in the farmhouse in the eastern section of Haverhill that the first American Whittier, the poet's great-great-grandfather, had built in 1688, when he was already sixty-eight, to replace an earlier dwelling. The male Whittiers were hardy and long-lived. The five-generation period between the birth of Thomas, the immigrant from England, and the death of the poet covered two hundred and seventy-two years. Thomas was reputed to have been a "giant" in size and strength but his tall, thin, seemingly "frail" descendant outlived him and all his other direct male ancestors.

The poet's Quaker faith was also an inheritance. Thomas had risked his Puritan contemporaries' displeasure by protesting the persecution of the Quakers, and his son Joseph, the poet's great-grandfather, married a Quaker and adopted the faith, which came down to the poet to become for him a treasured birthright. The material inheritance, the ancestral farm, proved to be of little value to the young poet-to-be, who sought out easier ways to make a living. John Whittier, the poet's father, had never been able to pay off the farm's mortgage, no matter how thrifty he was or how long and hard he worked, and the poet sold the place a few years after his father's death. The great popular success of "Snow-Bound" in 1866, in which an incident in life on the farm is lovingly recalled, brought the poet the first financial security he had ever known, so that the homestead that had provided four generations with only a meager living may be said to have paid off at last after all, in a way none of those who had worked its indifferent soil could have foreseen.

The youthful William Lloyd Garrison and others tried to persuade the future poet to leave the farm and get the further education they saw as necessary if he were to develop his precocious literary talents. Whittier's father has sometimes been blamed for not immediately falling in with the idea, but there is no need to suppose that the father's reluctance to lose the help of one of his two sons arose only, or even chiefly, from a distrust of literature. Clearly, he needed all the help he could get to support the group pictured in "Snow-Bound." (When he first speaks in the poem it is to put the boys to work: "Boys, a path!") John Greenleaf's leaving the farm, first for a brief period at Haverhill Academy, then for newspaper editing and politics, however right the decision was for the future poet and for our literature, could be seen as amounting in effect to a desertion of the father. It may be significant in this relation that the father is the only character in the poem portrayed with no overt expressions of tenderness or sympathy to match those given the mother, the sisters, the aunt, the uncle, the schoolmaster, and even the half-insane relative who mingled inexplicable wrath with her piety.

Young Whittier's fierce ambition to "rise in the world" above his humble origins, to attain real distinction of some sort, was satisfied for a while with ever more prestigious editorships of weekly newspapers and with the extravagant praises heaped by other newspaper editors on the poems he proved capable of writing by the score. But politics soon came to seem to offer a surer road to greater fame, and for some years in the 1830's he centered his hopes on a conventional political career, with some success but with finally disappointing results. In Abolitionism he found, with Garrison's help once again, a cause that would at last permit him to pursue his ambition to be recognized, to put to good use his literary talents, and to square his "worldly" efforts with his Quaker conscience. Was not Abolition at once a moral cause and a political movement with a great need for adherents who could with equal facility produce prose tracts and polemical poems? The cause of freedom for the slaves seemed to Whittier a holy one, worth dedicating his life to even if it entailed periodic spells of nervous and physical exhaustion. That it also brought him into contact with an ever-widening circle of well-known public figures and reform-minded writers and provided him with a national, if partisan, audience for the works of his pen must have made it seem that the promptings of conscience and the workings of destiny were in singular harmony.

All this is not to cast doubt either on the sincerity of Whittier's devotion to his great cause or the degree to which he had internalized the values of his Quaker religious heritage. It is simply to see him as the human being he was, ambitious, conscientious, and probably, judging by the frequency of the illnesses that would now be considered psychosomatic, torn by neurotic conflicts. All his life he was attracted by, attractive to, and tended and protected by women, yet there was always some "good reason" why he could never marry. Only in the last part of his very long life did he achieve relatively good health and serenity. That Whittier suffered from a neurotic attachment to the Eden lost at puberty is clear enough. But the neuroses that caused him so much pain and distress he turned into a source of strength when he dealt with them creatively in his poetry. Without them, there might indeed have been no "Snow-Bound."

Anticipating Whitman later and Mark Twain later still, Whittier came from a literate but not a literary family, was chiefly self-educated, and began his writing career with productions that give us no reason to take them very seriously as literature. (Unlike Whitman's and Mark Twain's early journalism, Whittier's early poems are of course *intended* as "literature." Unlike Mark Twain's early journalism, they show no flashes of undeveloped genius, only a very considerable fluency or verbal aptitude.) In the end, Whittier gained full acceptance and respect in the dominant literary circles of his day — indeed, by the end of the century popular veneration of the man and his work probably exceeded even that accorded Longfellow — but it was never entirely clear whether it was the man, the work, or the message that made him finally a revered American institution and his birthdays national events. As the life presents the paradox of the gentle, devout Quaker who was intensely ambitious for the world's recognition, until recognition came to him, so the literary career confronts us with a whole series of paradoxes.

Whittier was inspired to attempt the writing of verses by his introduction to the poetry of Burns, whose situation seemed to him to parallel his own: a "peasant" writer who wrote, from outside sophisticated literary conventions, celebrations of the "commonplace." Yet his earliest, uncollected, newspaper poems are not at all like those of Burns but attempt, with surprising success in many cases, in view of the writer's age and background, to be like those of Byron and Scott and are full of the kinds of "literary" flourishes Burns had eschewed. His work began to exhibit qualities that make it possible to call him without complete inappropriateness "the American Burns" only after a dozen years or so of imitative "literary" writing and nearly two decades of effective polemical versifying had brought him sufficient prominence to allow him to cease striving for either political or literary fame and to write just as he wished about what meant most to him. The later verse is never imitative even when it is most self-indulgent and flat.

R. P. Warren has suggested that Whittier's long schooling in the art of writing effective verse polemics prepared him to become the poet who could finally write "Telling the Bees" and "Snow-Bound," verse written to the *point*, controlled by the subject, free of imitative conventional flourishes. The suggestion seems to me to contain a very valuable insight but perhaps to need a little qualification if it is not to seem to explain too much. True, there is an important sense in which Whittier may be said to have become a memorable poet by turning away from "literature" (as he knew it), but it is also true that when he ceased to imitate other poets, he developed no really clear conception of what literary ideal his own work should aim at. He began to write his best poems in the 1850's, when his withdrawal from an active part in political life was nearly complete, yet the bulk of his work from then until the end of his life continued to be characterized by organizational looseness, long-windedness, and a general lack of purely *stylistic* distinction. Except in his very best poems, he continued to present the paradox of the often moving and impressive poet who writes best when "style" doesn't count and the "poetry" doesn't matter.

Insofar as we concern ourselves only with Whittier's reputation in his own age, this paradox of "the style-less poet" seems fairly easily resolved. His early attempts at versifying in the manner of Byron and Scott won him recognition, to be sure, but the country newspaper editors who detected enormous literary promise in the verses they printed so gladly and often praised so extravagantly were comparing the unknown youngster's work with the average level of the newspaper verse of the day, much of it produced by "that damned mob of scribbling women" referred to by Hawthorne as *his* chief competitors for popular attention. (But whereas Hawthorne expressed his contempt for their melodramatic and sentimental gush, Whittier sincerely admired and often rivaled it.) Even later famous reformers like the young Garrison could hardly be counted on to arrive at an objective *literary* judgment of the quality of Whittier's early work. The amazing thing of course was that the almost "unlettered" farm boy wrote as polished and correct imitations of British poets as he did. When it was found that he could produce a tract as effective as "Justice and Expediency," a pamphlet written at Garrison's suggestion designed to arouse the conscience of the nation concerning the evils of slavery, and a verse polemic as eloquent, however marred for the contemporary reader it may be by its regional self-righteousness, as "Massachusetts to Virginia," those involved in the great crusade realized that they had found their most effective literary warrior. Whittier's earliest recognition must be largely discounted because of its source, and his later, Abolitionist-period, fame was partisan — which does not at all mean that none of his antislavery poems have poetic merit as the kinds of poems they frankly are but only that the national recognition they gained the poet can be explained in terms that have little to do with literary values, insofar as those can be distinguished from the values associated with politics, reform, and moral zeal.

Beginning in the sixties, with poems like "Barbara Frietchie," Whittier began to be a poetic spokesman, at first for the mood of the whole North (not just the Abolitionists, who had always been a minority), then for the whole country as it determined to forget the recent traumatic strife, idealized rapidly disappearing agrarian simplicities and the simpler virtues, and tried to resolve "the warfare of science with theology" with a "deeds, not creeds" religion. Providentially, it would seem, much that was most important in Whittier's background and experience had prepared him to become the spokesman for the postwar national mood. His had always been a relatively "creedless" religion, so that the hymns he wrote could and did find their way into many of the main-line Protestant hymnals. He did not need the spectacle of the commercial and industrial jungle of the Gilded Age and later to teach him the redemptive qualities of domesticity: his beloved mother and sisters, who nursed and nurtured him as long as they lived, had made the healing power of the family circle a reality to him. From the beginning of his career, he had believed in progress as well as in God, not identifying the two but seeing no conflict between them either. And he had come naturally by the blend of nostalgia, antiquarianism, and didacticism that marks his attitude toward the past.

Whittier, in short, didn't have to catch up with a changing age. After the Civil War, the age caught up with Whittier. His family history and religious values, his boyhood experiences and youthful struggles for recognition, his long participation in the great political drama that culminated in the tragic conflict of the Civil War, and his determination to preserve the essence of his inherited faith while still keeping his mind open to facts that seemed to make it ever more difficult to do so, all prepared him to speak for a transitional age whose religious and agrarian values were threatened from every side.

The precipitous decline in Whittier's reputation in the first half of our century was predictable. To a considerable extent writers in the early decades of the century defined themselves by their opposition to the writers the preceding age had most cherished. When Modernist poetic practice was codified in New Critical theory, it came to seem axiomatic that poetry in which irony and paradox, condensation, and intricate verbal complexities culminating sometimes in seven types of ambiguity were conspicuously absent could not possibly be taken seriously. To detect traces of didacticism or sentimentality in a poet seemed to make any further consideration of his work unnecessary.

Now that the Modernist conceptions of the qualities "good" poetry must always have are beginning to seem as dated as Whittier's own, it should be possible to reach a more just estimate of his achievement than either his later contemporaries or his more recent detractors achieved. It seems to me that the contemporary reader whose taste is sufficiently catholic to permit him to enjoy both Pope and Wordsworth, both Whitman and Eliot, is likely to decide that from the five hundred or so double-column pages of Whittier's collected verse he can cull several dozen poems, some of them of considerable length, that are rewarding to read or reread. This would be a small percentage of all that Whittier wrote, to be sure, but greater poets than he have written too much, and this is enough for a not too slender volume, enough to keep alive his reputation as a poet of the second rank whose best work deserves to be remembered and read.

Since readers who know only the most frequently anthologized poems may find even so limited and qualified a claim for Whittier's poetic achievement as this exaggerated, I shall make all the concessions that still seem necessary before going on to try to make a case for his best work.

To begin with, when Whittier writes at his average level, his verse is not just old-fashioned, it is likely to strike us as almost the exact opposite of the kind of poetry that most readers today, even those of us who would reject the idea that "a poem should not mean but be" is an adequate test of poetic merit, have come to like. If James's idea that what is stated is not literature and what is literature is not stated is the whole truth, then most of Whittier's poetry is not literature. It states, emphatically. It aims to convey truth and to influence moral attitudes. It is relaxed, ruminative, placid, unambiguous, most typically, "thin." It is almost never dramatic even when it deals, as it so often does, with people, and irony is generally confined to the unread poems of reform. In the classroom most of the poetry is, unfortunately, useful in a way that does Whittier's memory no good: it illustrates what Eliot meant by the concept of the "dissociation of sensibility." (But so, of course, does a great deal of good poetry from other periods besides the nineteenth century.) Anthology pieces like "The Barefoot Boy" have become children's classics, but we are likely to feel that the absence in them of any sign of the critical intelligence at work is fatal.

A symptom, if not perhaps one of the causes, of what is all too evidently, from our point of view, Whittier's weakness as a poet may be seen in his own taste in poetry. He extravagantly admired, not some of the really fine poems that Long-fellow wrote, but "The Psalm of Life," declaring it "worth more than all the dreams of Shelley, and Keats, and Wordsworth." He thought highly of the poetry of Lydia Maria Child, Grace Greenwood, and Alice and Phoebe Cary, who were, he thought, "richly gifted." He found in their verse the same unselfish dedication to the best causes that made *Uncle Tom's Cabin*, in his opinion, one of the noblest works of the century and that prompted his tribute to "sweet Eva" beginning, "Dry the tears for holy Eva,/ With the blessed angels leave her." To say that Whittier's moral sense had a greater hand in shaping his literary judgments than his aesthetic sense is to indulge in understatement. Nevertheless, Whittier's own self-estimate in "Proem" as an "untaught" versifier whose only claim to fame is that he put his verse, such as it was, to work in the service of duty and offered it at freedom's shrine, is too modest.

Whittier's post-Civil War contemporaries valued him most as a religious poet, and I think we shall have to also, if we are to continue to read him as he deserves to be read. He is, I think, one of a rather small number of religious poets in America whose work is still readable as poetry and not just as devotional exercise. The impression we are likely to get from some of the modern biographical treatments of Whittier, that his Quaker faith was a kind of side-issue, a personal foible having little to do with his dedication to progressive causes in an age of reform, could hardly be further from the truth.

One large section of the final edition of his poetry arranged by Whittier himself is labeled "Religious Poems," but most of his best poetry might very appropriately have been so labeled, and much of his best religious poetry is to be found in other sections of his book, in "Poems of Nature," for instance, and "Anti-Slavery Poems" and "Poems Subjective and Reminiscent." Paradoxically, it might be said that Whittier's poetry is often most effectively religious when it is not explicitly "religious poetry," and that his poems of nature and reform are seldom memorable except when they are informed by a strongly religious feeling. The very flat songs of labor are a case in point, and many of the poems of nature written after the Civil War are another. Only when the objects of nature serve as "attendant angels to the house of prayer" do the nature poems generally rise much above the level of the honest and conscientious. In short, the well-known hymns like "Dear Lord and Father of Mankind" express a feeling that is almost never absent from the best poetry but seldom well expressed directly.

Whittier shared, of course — both as a devout Quaker and as a man of his time and place — the tendency of nineteenth-century Protestantism to reduce religion to a matter of feeling and action in good causes, to deny the validity of religious *thought* and create a "religion of the heart." Anti-intellectualism frequently makes the positive religious affirmations in his poetry seem sentimental. His deep piety and his detestation of "the husks of creed" often combine to produce mere emphatic exhortations to faith instead of successful communications of religious thought or experience. But when he writes not of faith as such but of what he sees as the Christian demand for justice and love, he speaks with passion, with fire, and often with a fine control. Whittier's conscience was not just sensitive, it was informed, grounded in and directed by a deep understanding of the whole gospel that he never, despite the doubts that troubled him, ceased to hold up as the controlling image in his life. He fully anticipated the Social Gospel movement on its positive side without falling into its religious negativism. He saw formal creeds separating men and repudiated them for this and other reasons, but he felt that an untheological Biblical faith could draw men together and constituted the only unanswerable argument for reform.

Some of the finest invective poetry ever written in America resulted from his feeling of what was demanded by his faith. He was always particularly outraged by religious hypocrisy and cant, by "official piety" in consort with moral insensitiveness. He was, of course, sometimes merely provincial and sectarian in his condemnation of the churches, as when, in an early poem, he speaks of the "evil" faith of Rome, or when, more frequently, he is roused to indignation by any form of worship more "outward" than silent meditation and prayer. But he writes at his best, and his best in this area is very good, when he excoriates the "church-goers" who condone slavery and injustice, the "clerical oppressors" whose "faith" never issues in "works," or the church in whose name some of the most terrible crimes have been committed.

His authentic voice comes through to us very clearly, and without suffering by comparison with any other poet in America in the nineteenth century, in such poems as "Clerical Oppressors," "Official Piety," "The Gallows," "Lines on the Portrait of a Celebrated Publisher," "Letter: From a Missionary of the Methodist Episcopal Church South, in Kansas, to a Distinguished Politician," and "On a Prayer-book: With Its Frontispiece, Ary Scheffer's 'Christus Consolator,' Americanized by the Omission of the Black Man." The voice here is angry, even outraged, but never self-righteous or shrill or merely moralistic. Here for once Whittier is even capable of a kind of humor, as he registers the gap between word and deed and explores the characteristics of a "dead" faith. The result is a group of jeremiads that often rise to thoroughly effective satire and usually contain at least a few lines of memorable invective. When he returned to the theme in the poems written after the Civil War, it continued to inspire him to some of his best writing. Here's a sample from the Prelude to "Among the Hills":

Church-goers, fearful of the unseen Powers,
But grumbling over pulpit-tax and pew-rent,
Saving, as shrewd economists, their souls
And winter pork with the least possible outlay
Of salt and sanctity; in daily life
Showing as little actual comprehension
Of Christian charity and love and duty,
As if the Sermon on the Mount had been
Outdated like a last year's almanac . . .

This, I submit, is good didactic poetry — terse, pointed, memorable. Though it is above Whittier's average performance in its succinctness, there is a good deal more like it. To dismiss Whittier's poems of reform as versified propaganda, as we have tended to do, is easier if we have not read them than if we have. In Whittier's best work we have an expression of the religious conscience at its purest and best. If all the reformers of the age had had Whittier's humility and his faith and vision, Hawthorne might not have been moved to satirize reformism in *The Blithedale Romance* nor would James in *The Bostonians*. Whittier's antislavery poems are not irrelevant to us because legal slavery no longer exists, nor is their relevance simply a function of the fact that the fight for justice and freedom and brotherhood is never ended. The poems themselves supply the explanation of their continuing vitality: they are not propaganda verse so much as they are visions of the great society, the city of God on earth, and denunciations of all that hinders its arrival.

Whittier was less blind to the full range and complexity of human experience, even in his poems dedicated to his great cause, than reformers in any age generally are. Over against the demands of conscience for reform, on the one hand, he felt what he once called, in Hawthornesque terms, the brotherhood of guilt in "secret sin." "Guilt shapes the terror," he acknowledged, in a mood that did not often find so overt an expression but that generally qualified the moralizing. The recognition of tragedy is seldom wholly absent for long from his finest verse. At his best the optimism is not fatuous or the moralizing shallow. More than once he counselled "the lesson of endurance," that the sensitive conscience might not be blunted but be "taught by suffering."

The same Biblical faith that is ultimately responsible for keeping his poems of reform from being glib also keeps his best nature poetry from falling very often into the clichés of late romantic primitivism. His view of nature was consistent with his view of man and man's destiny. True, he tended usually to idealize New England scenery and he had an unfailing taste for the picturesque that makes us feel how necessary the modern revolt from the picturesque to the "antipoetic" was. But he repeatedly dissociated himself from any "cult of nature shaming man." It seems to me undeniable that his conservative Quaker faith preserved both his humanism and his sense of the urgency of the need for moral decision and commitment. Starting with the interest in and feeling for nature that was the gift of his period, he tried, with only intermittent success to be sure, to read nature as revelation, and saw, unfailingly, a vision of "our common earth a holy ground." When nature seemed most undecipherable as revelation, he turned with undiminished hope to the accomplishment of the vision.

"Sweeter than the song of birds / Is the thankful voice." Responsive to what he once called "the sacramental mystery of the woods," but with no intellectual tools to help him to interpret the sacrament except in the most general terms, he was often troubled by nature's "silence." Though he believed that nature was God's handiwork, he knew that his own "unanointed eyes," as he once called them, gave him no special visionary powers. He was closer to Hawthorne in this respect than to Emerson: he found surer support for his religious "trust" in the family circle around the hearth and in the "magnetic chain" of human sympathy and love than in nature's hieroglyphic. He never wavered in his conviction that man is "more than his abode, / The inward life than Nature's raimant more," as he says, a little awkwardly, in "Monadnock from Wachuset." His frequent withdrawals to nature were both means of communion with God and preparations for a return to man.

Perhaps the aspect of the thought in Whittier's poems that most dates them today is the unfailing faith in progress. When he writes of progress in the abstract, that is, of Progress, the result is usually no better than "The Psalm of Life." On this subject Whittier had no guide but what he once called the "moral steam-enginery" of his age. But these passages are easy to winnow out, and they are not a good enough reason for forgetting the rest of his work. Whittier had more hope than we generally have in this unhopeful age, in both the strict Pauline and the Quaker sense. But though we find it difficult to respond readily to cheerful writing, we ought to recognize that Whittier is, at his best at any rate, saved from the inanities of a too easy faith by his belief that social progress and individual redemption are not unrelated and that neither is automatic or inevitable. He knew that man had to choose, and that choice was not easy or success guaranteed. His lifelong devotion to "liberal" causes can only be fully understood when we realize the extent to which he was "conservative" — in the only viable sense of the term. The "eternal step of Progress" that resounds through his poetry is finally reducible to faith in God's finding willing hands to do His work. We need not share this faith to agree that it is not inane or necessarily unintelligent. As Whittier said of himself, "He reconciled as best he could / Old faith and fancies new."

When all this has been said in his defense, we are, to be sure, still left with a sense that Whittier at his best was a successful poet in spite of himself, in spite of some of his most significant ideas and attitudes. With at least a part of his mind he did not finally believe in poetry. His work aspires, Quakerwise, to silence. His attitude toward poetry was as ambivalent as his attitude toward nature: could nature be trusted to lead us to God, could words be trusted to communicate? He quite evidently distrusts the symbol even while he is using it, and often explicitly undercuts it.

Fundamentally Whittier distrusted the whole symbolizing process. He wanted to see nature as sacramental and often felt that he had succeeded, but he was repeatedly disturbed by the feeling that "the hollow sky is sad with silentness." His profound distrust of the "cumberings" of form and creed in religion is parallel with and related to his distrust of the symbol in poetry. Aspiring, as he said, to the "deepest of all mysteries, silence," much of his verse *tells* us to have no confidence in the intellect or in mere forms, tells us in flat, prosaic, intellectual statements with no imaginative flesh on their abstract bones. This is one of the reasons why we should reread the antislavery poems today. In them Whittier's imagination was energized by moral fervor and often found the adequate symbol. On the subjects to which he responded most deeply, the strength of his feeling carried him beyond distrust of symbolization, but his ideas on the subject never wavered and were never qualified: "The outward symbols disappear / For him whose inward sight is clear."

Perhaps. But then I suppose we shall have no poetry, or at least none but abstractly didactic verse written in purely denotative language. Whittier could never quite rid himself of the suspicion that this would be no great loss, despite his real respect for the older poets who excelled, he felt, in ways in which he was weakest. "The world will have its idols, / And flesh and sense their sign." Aesthetic theory and practice in Whittier's work are more obviously related to his fundamental religious convictions than they are in the work of most of his contemporaries. "Let sense be dumb, let flesh retire." It is not surprising that though it urges transcendence of the material and the formal, the bulk of his work fails to transcend univocal statement and mechanical form.

But of course "the bulk of the work" of most poets of the second rank fails to please after the poetic fashions and cultural milieu that partially shaped it have passed. For Whittier's best poems — and there are more of them than it has recently been fashionable to think — no apologies at all need to be made. They offer us fresh perceptions and feelings available only to Whittier, with his background, his sensibility, and his faith, but perceptions and feelings so expressed that they can become ours too, enlarging the circles of our awareness and responsiveness. In style, they are plain, direct, unadorned — but it has often been observed that the final triumph of style is that it should disappear as style. Their versification is traditional, but so is the versification of most of our nineteenth and many of our best twentieth century poets.

"Whittier's best poems," I say, need no defense today. But which poems are they? There is general agreement that "Telling the Bees" is one of them, and it seems clear enough that "Snow-Bound" is not only unique in our poetic heritage but deserves to be called "great." Probably few if any readers today would place among the best the favorites of his own age, "The Barefoot Boy" and "Barbara Frietchie," but what about "Among the Hills," "The Pennsylvania Pilgrim," or "The Tent on the Beach"? The present edition of Whittier's complete poetical works allows each reader to make his own selection — and it seems unlikely that any two readers would choose exactly the same poems.*

Whittier's claim for himself was typical of the man, modest and just and true. "What I had I gave." Clearly, what he had was not a major poetic talent, but it was well worth the giving, and no one else in his time or since was equipped to give it, for we have had no other poet with just his heritage, his experience, and his inward life. Indeed, to a sympathetic reader, it may well seem that Whittier's religious trust — his faith in the providence of a God who moves in mysterious ways, His wonders to perform — was justified by Whittier's own career. For without the fierce early ambitions, so clearly at odds with the parental voice of conscience, without the leaving of the farm where his help was needed, without the years of struggle for the great cause (and his recognition that his motives were mixed: for the cause, for self?), without the nervous exhaustions and the terrible headaches, he might well have ended by becoming just another Lydia Sigourney, an undistinguished sentimental versifier, instead of what he did become, a minor but authentic and unreplaceable voice in our poetry.

HYATT H. WAGGONER

*The following poems seem to me to offer the best basis for a defense of Whittier's achievement as a poet. They are at any rate the ones I have had chiefly in mind in making the claim that a significant number of his poems are still rewarding to read. It seems to me that many of the least known of them are better than many of those that are most commonly anthologized. I list them in the order which Whittier gave them in his final arrangement: "The New Wife and the Old," "Telling the Bees," "The Double-Headed Snake of Newbury," "Mabel Martin," "The Prophecy of Samuel Sewall," "Among the Hills" (the whole poem, but especially the Prelude), "The Pennsylvania Pilgrim," "The Fruit-Gift," "The Old Burying-Ground," "The River Path," "Monadnock from Wachuset," "A Summer Pilgrimage," "Ichabod," "The Tent on the Beach," "Abraham Davenport," "Clerical Oppressors," "Massachusetts to Virginia," "The Christian Slave," "Lines on the Portrait . . . ," "Official Piety," "The Haschish," "Letter from a Missionary . . . ," "The Panorama," "On a Prayer-Book," "My Namesake," "Snow-Bound," "Laus Deo," "Trust," "Trinitas," "Our Master."

CHRONOLOGY OF WHITTIER'S LIFE

1807   Born December 17 in Haverhill, Massachusetts, on the farm remembered in "Snow-Bound," to John and Abigail Hussey Whittier, the second of four children. The Whittiers came to New England in 1638 and the first Whittier had, in his old age, personally built the house in which Whittier was born. The birthplace, and Whittier's later Amesbury home, are now open to the public.

1814–15   Begins to attend the short winter terms of the district school.

1821   One of his teachers introduces him to the poetry of Burns and he begins to write verses himself.

1826   Sister Mary sends "The Exile's Departure," an imitation of Scott, to the *Newburyport Free Press*, whose editor, the young William Lloyd Garrison, publishes it and seeks out the author to encourage him to get an education and develop his literary talents.

1826–27   Thus encouraged, Whittier sends out many poems to local newspapers, which accept more than eighty of them. The works of Scott and Byron seem to have furnished the models for these fluent, "correct," and often florid verses in which Whittier has found neither his own voice nor his own subjects. When preparing the notes for his definitive edition late in life, Whittier described one of them as suggesting "the idea of a big Indian in his war-paint strutting about in Sir Walter Scott's plaid."

1827–28   Supports himself by shoemaking and schoolteaching for two terms at Haverhill Academy, completing his formal education.

1829   Edits the Boston weekly newspaper, *The American Manufacturer*, a position obtained for him by Garrison. Supports Clay and high tariffs and attacks Jackson and populist democracy.

1830   Edits the *Essex Gazette* (Haverhill), a less prestigious position which enables him to live at home. His father dies.

1830–32   Edits the important *New England Review* in Hartford for some eighteen months. Nervous and physical exhaustion force his resignation and second return to the farm. Publishes *Legends of New England*, his first book, a mixture of prose and verse aimed at showing that "New-England is rich in traditionary lore . . ."; he later deprecates the work and refuses to permit its reprinting. Hoping for a career in politics, he is elected to the state convention of the National Republican party and unsuccessfully seeks office as a Whig.

1833   Urged by Garrison, joins the Anti-Slavery party and is a delegate to the first meeting of the American Anti-Slavery Convention. Begins to write Abolitionist verses and publishes *Justice and Expediency*, a powerful anti-slavery tract.

1835   Elected to the Massachusetts legislature. Continues to live at home and oversee the management of the farm. Edits the *Haverhill Gazette*.

1836   Sells the farm and moves with his mother and sisters to nearby Amesbury, where he continues to live until his last years.

1837   Works actively for the Abolitionist cause in New York and Philadelphia. A collection of his Abolitionist verses, *Poems Written during the Progress of the Abolition Question in the United States*, appears in print.

1838   Publishes the first authorized collection of his poetry, *Poems*. Edits the *Pennsylvania Freeman*.

1839   Breaks with Garrison over the issue of Abolitionist tactics and helps to found the Liberty party, which he hopes will find for the antislavery cause a wider political base than Garrison's radical Abolitionism.

1840   Resigns the editorship of the *Pennsylvania Freeman* in ill health and returns home for good. Begins his gradual withdrawal from political activism.

1843   The publication of *Lays of My Home* suggests the renewal of his early interest in regional and historic subjects for his verse.

1844–45   Edits the *Middlesex Standard* in Lowell.

1846   Publishes *Voices of Freedom*.

1847   Becomes a corresponding editor of the *National Era*, which serves as the chief outlet for his poetry and prose for the next decade. Publishes *Super-Naturalism in New-England*, which Hawthorne, reviewing the volume, finds somewhat deficient in imagination.

1849   Publishes *Margaret Smith's Journal*.

1850   Publishes *Songs of Labor*, *Poetical Works*, and *Old Portraits and Modern Sketches*. During the 1850s writes many of his best poems, including "Telling the Bees," "Skipper Ireson's Ride," and "The Double-Headed Snake of Newbury," signaling his beginnings to find his poetic role as "the poet of the commonplace" and of New England's past. Persuades Charles Sumner to run for the Senate. After Sumner's election, the shift of Whittier's poetic energies from the political to the personal and legendary becomes still more pronounced.

1857   With the founding of the *Atlantic Monthly*, he is assured for the first time of a wide reading public in the company of the period's most respected authors. Mother dies.

1860   Publishes *Home Ballads*. Sister Mary dies.

1864   Sister Elizabeth dies. A niece, also named Elizabeth, moves into the Amesbury home to look after him. With the Emancipation Proclamation and the Union victory in the Civil War, he feels that the cause of freedom has been won and he may rest from his reforming labors.

1866   *Snow-Bound*, his masterpiece, is an immense popular success and gives him financial security for the first time.

1867   *The Tent on the Beach, and Other Poems* is a national bestseller.

1869   *Among the Hills, and Other Poems* makes explicit his decision to "lay aside grave themes, and idly turn / The leaves of memory's sketch-book." Writes an increasing number of religious and devotional poems.

1870   *Ballads of New England.*

1872   *The Pennsylvania Pilgrim, and Other Poems*, containing 'The Brewing of Soma," the final stanzas of which, beginning "Dear Lord and Father of Mankind," have become Whittier's best-known hymn.

1886   Harvard grants him an honorary LL.D., a somewhat belated acknowledgment that his age had come to think of the "uneducated farm boy" and one-time "radical" reformer as belonging in the company of Harvard-educated Emerson, Lowell, and Holmes and Bowdoin-educated, Harvard-associated Longfellow.

1888–89 Houghton Mifflin Co., the country's most distinguished publishing house of the period, issues a definitive edition of his poetry and prose in seven volumes.

1890   Privately prints his last book, *At Sundown.*

1892   Dies September 7 at Hampton Falls, New Hampshire and is buried in the family plot in Amesbury, where in his boyhood his family had regularly attended Friends' Meeting.

AUTHOR'S INTRODUCTION

THE edition of my poems published in 1857 contained the following note by way of preface : —

"In these volumes, for the first time, a complete collection of my poetical writings has been made. While it is satisfactory to know that these scattered children of my brain have found a home, I cannot but regret that I have been unable, by reason of illness, to give that attention to their revision and arrangement which respect for the opinions of others and my own afterthought and experience demand.

"That there are pieces in this collection which I would 'willingly let die,' I am free to confess. But it is now too late to disown them, and I must submit to the inevitable penalty of poetical as well as other sins. There are others, intimately connected with the author's life and times, which owe their tenacity of vitality to the circumstances under which they were written, and the events by which they were suggested.

"The long poem of 'Mogg Megone' was in a great measure composed in early life; and it is scarcely necessary to say that its subject is not such as the writer would have chosen at any subsequent period."

After a lapse of thirty years since the above was written, I have been requested by my publishers to make some preparation for a new and revised edition of my poems. I cannot flatter myself that I have added much to the interest of the work beyond the correction of my own errors and those of the press, with the addition of a few heretofore unpublished pieces, and occasional notes of explanation which seemed necessary. I have made an attempt to classify the poems under a few general heads, and have transferred the long poem of "Mogg Megone" to the Appendix, with other specimens of my earlier writings. I have endeavored to affix the dates of composition or publication as far as possible.

In looking over these poems I have not been unmindful of occasional prosaic lines and verbal infelicities, but at this late day I have neither strength nor patience to undertake their correction.

Perhaps a word of explanation may be needed in regard to a class of poems written between the years 1832 and 1865. Of their defects from an artistic point of view it is not necessary to speak. They were the earnest and often vehement expression of the writer's thought and feeling at critical periods in the great conflict between Freedom and Slavery. They were written with no expectation that they would survive the occasions which called them forth: they were protests, alarm signals, trumpet-calls to action, words wrung from the writer's heart, forged at white heat, and of course lacking the finish and careful word-selection which re-flection and patient brooding over them might have given. Such as they are, they belong to the history of the Anti-Slavery movement, and may serve as way-marks of its progress. If their language at times seems severe and harsh, the monstrous wrong of Slavery which provoked it must be its excuse, if any is needed. In at-tacking it, we did not measure our words. "It is," said Garrison, "a waste of politeness to be courteous to the devil." But in truth the contest was, in a great measure, an impersonal one, — hatred of slavery and not of slave-masters.

> "No common wrong provoked our zeal,
> The silken gauntlet which is thrown
> In such a quarrel rings like steel."

Even Thomas Jefferson, in his terrible denunciation of Slavery in the "Notes on Virginia," says: "It is impossible to be temperate and pursue the subject of Slavery."

After the great contest was over, no class of the American people were more ready, with kind words and deprecation of harsh retaliation, to welcome back the revolted States than the Abolitionists; and none have since more heartily rejoiced at the fast increasing prosperity of the South.

Grateful for the measure of favor which has been accorded to my writings, I leave this edition with the public. It contains all that I care to republish, and some things which, had the matter of choice been left solely to myself, I should have omitted.

J. G. W.

[Written to introdu

I LOVE t
Which softly me
    The songs
    Arcadian Si
Sprinkling our noon

    Yet, vainly in m
To breathe their marvell
    I feel them, as the
    In silence feel the
And drink with glad, still li

    The rigor of a frozen cl
The harshness of an untaught ea
    The jarring words of one
    Beat often Labor's hurried
Or Duty's rugged march through st

    Of mystic beauty, dreamy grace
No rounded art the lack supplies ;
    Unskilled the subtle lines to trace,
    Or softer shades of Nature's face,
I view her common forms with unanointed

    Nor mine the seer-like power to show
The secrets of the heart and mind ;
    To drop the plummet-line below
    Our common world of joy and woe,
A more intense despair or brighter hope to find.

    Yet here at least an earnest sense
Of human right and weal is shown ;
    A hate of tyranny intense,
    And hearty in its vehemence,
As if my brother's pain and sorrow were my own.

    O Freedom! if to me belong
Nor mighty Milton's gift divine,
    Nor Marvell's wit and graceful song,
    Still with a love as deep and strong
As theirs, I lay, like them, my best gifts on thy shrine!

AMESBURY, 11th mo., 1847.

NARRATIVE AND LEGENDARY POEMS

THE VAUDOIS TEACHER

This poem was suggested by the account given of the manner in which the Waldenses disseminated their principles among the Catholic gentry. They gained access to the house through their occupation as peddlers of silks, jewels, and trinkets. "Having disposed of some of their goods," it is said by a writer who quotes the inquisitor Rainerus Sacco, "they cautiously intimated that they had commodities far more valuable than these, inestimable jewels, which they would show if they could be protected from the clergy. They would then give their purchasers a Bible or Testament; and thereby many were deluded into heresy."

The poem, under the title *Le Colporteur Vaudois*, was translated into French by Professor G. de Felice, of Montauban, and further naturalized by Professor Alexandre Rodolphe Vinet, who quoted it in his lectures on French literature, afterwards published. It became familiar in this form to the Waldenses, who adopted it as a household poem. An American clergyman, J. C. Fletcher, frequently heard it when he was a student, about the year 1850, in the theological seminary at Geneva, Switzerland, but the authorship of the poem was unknown to those who used it. Twenty-five years later, Mr. Fletcher, learning the name of the author, wrote to the moderator of the Waldensian synod at La Tour, giving the information. At the banquet which closed the meeting of the synod, the moderator announced the fact, and was instructed in the name of the Waldensian church to write to me a letter of thanks. My letter, written in reply, was translated into Italian and printed throughout Italy.

"O LADY fair, these silks of mine are beautiful and rare, —
The richest web of the Indian loom, which beauty's queen might wear;
And my pearls are pure as thy own fair neck, with whose radiant light they vie;
I have brought them with me a weary way, — will my gentle lady buy?"

The lady smiled on the worn old man through the dark and clustering curls
Which veiled her brow, as she bent to view his silks and glittering pearls;
And she placed their price in the old man's hand and lightly turned away,
But she paused at the wanderer's earnest call, — "My gentle lady, stay!

"O lady fair, I have yet a gem which a purer lustre flings,
Than the diamond flash of the jewelled crown on the lofty brow of kings;
A wonderful pearl of exceeding price, whose virtue shall not decay,
Whose light shall be as a spell to thee and a blessing on thy way!"

The lady glanced at the mirroring steel where her form of grace was seen,
Where her eye shone clear, and her dark locks waved their clasping pearls between;
"Bring forth thy pearl of exceeding worth, thou traveller gray and old,
And name the price of thy precious gem, and my page shall count thy gold."

The cloud went off from the pilgrim's brow, as a small and meagre book,
Unchased with gold or gem of cost, from his folding robe he took!
"Here, lady fair, is the pearl of price, may it prove as such to thee!
Nay, keep thy gold — I ask it not, for the word of God is free!"

The hoary traveller went his way, but the gift he left behind
Hath had its pure and perfect work on that highborn maiden's mind,
And she hath turned from the pride of sin to the lowliness of truth,

And given her human heart to God in its
   beautiful hour of· youth !

And she hath left the gray old halls, where
   an evil faith had power,
The courtly knights of her father's train,
   and the maidens of her bower ;
And she hath gone to the Vaudois vales by
   lordly feet untrod,
Where the poor and needy of earth are
   rich in the perfect love of God !

THE FEMALE MARTYR

Mary G——, aged eighteen, a "Sister of
Charity," died in one of our Atlantic cities,
during the prevalence of the Indian cholera,
while in voluntary attendance upon the sick.

"BRING out your dead !" The midnight
   street
   Heard and gave back the hoarse, low
      call ;
Harsh fell the tread of hasty feet,
Glanced through the dark the coarse white
   sheet,
   Her coffin and her pall.
"What — only one !" the brutal hack-man
   said,
As, with an oath, he spurned away the dead.

How sunk the inmost hearts of all,
   As rolled that dead-cart slowly by,
With creaking wheel and harsh hoof-fall !
The dying turned him to the wall,
   To hear it and to die !
Onward it rolled ; while oft its driver
   stayed,
And hoarsely clamored, "Ho ! bring out
   your dead."

It paused beside the burial-place ;
   "Toss in your load !" and it was done.
With quick hand and averted face,
Hastily to the grave's embrace
   They cast them, one by one,
Stranger and friend, the evil and the just,
Together trodden in the churchyard dust !

And thou, young martyr ! thou wast there ;
   No white-robed sisters round thee trod,
Nor holy hymn, nor funeral prayer
Rose through the damp and noisome air,
   Giving thee to thy God ;

Nor flower, nor cross, nor hallowed taper
   gave
Grace to the dead, and beauty to the grave !

Yet, gentle sufferer ! there shall be,
   In every heart of kindly feeling,
A rite as holy paid to thee
As if beneath the convent-tree
   Thy sisterhood were kneeling,
At vesper hours, iike sorrowing angels,
   keeping
Their tearful watch around thy place of
   sleeping.

For thou wast one in whom the light
   Of Heaven's own love was kindled well ;
Enduring with a martyr's might,
Through weary day and wakeful night,
   Far more than words may tell :
Gentle, and meek, and lowly, and unknown,
Thy mercies measured by thy God alone !

Where manly hearts were failing, where
   The throngful street grew foul with death,
O high-souled martyr ! thou wast there,
Inhaling, from the loathsome air,
   Poison with every breath.
Yet shrinking not from offices of dread
For the wrung dying, and the unconscious
   dead.

And, where the sickly taper shed
   Its light through vapors, damp, confined,
Hushed as a seraph's fell thy tread,
A new Electra by the bed
   Of suffering human-kind !
Pointing the spirit, in its dark dismay,
To that pure hope which fadeth not away.

Innocent teacher of the high
   And holy mysteries of Heaven !
How turned to thee each glazing eye,
In mute and awful sympathy,
   As thy low prayers were given ;
And the o'er-hovering Spoiler wore, the
   while,
An angel's features, a deliverer's smile !

A blessed task ! and worthy one
   Who, turning from the world, as thou,
Before life's pathway had begun
To leave its spring-time flower and sun,
   Had sealed her early vow ;
Giving to God her beauty and her youth,
Her pure affections and her guileless truth

Earth may not claim thee. Nothing here
　Could be for thee a meet reward ;
Thine is a treasure far more dear :
Eye hath not seen it, nor the ear
　Of living mortal heard
The joys prepared, the promised bliss
　above,
The holy presence of Eternal Love !

Sleep on in peace. The earth has not
　A nobler name than thine shall be.
The deeds by martial manhood wrought,
The lofty energies of thought,
　The fire of poesy,
These have but frail and fading honors ;
　thine
Shall Time unto Eternity consign.

Yea, and when thrones shall crumble
　down,
　And human pride and grandeur fall,
The herald's line of long renown,
The mitre and the kingly crown, —
　Perishing glories all !
The pure devotion of thy generous heart
Shall live in Heaven, of which it was a
　part.

EXTRACT FROM "A NEW ENG-
LAND LEGEND"

Originally a part of the author's *Moll Pitcher*.

How has New England's romance fled,
　Even as a vision of the morning !
Its rites foredone, its guardians dead,
Its priestesses, bereft of dread,
　Waking the veriest urchin's scorning !
Gone like the Indian wizard's yell
　And fire-dance round the magic rock,
Forgotten like the Druid's spell
　At moonrise by his holy oak !
No more along the shadowy glen
Glide the dim ghosts of murdered men ;
No more the unquiet churchyard dead
Glimpse upward from their turfy bed,
　Startling the traveller, late and lone ;
As, on some night of starless weather,
They silently commune together,
　Each sitting on his own head-stone !
The roofless house, decayed, deserted,
Its living tenants all departed,
No longer rings with midnight revel
Of witch, or ghost, or goblin evil ;

No pale blue flame sends out its flashes
Through　creviced　roof　and　shattered
　　sashes !
The witch-grass round the hazel spring
May sharply to the night-air sing,
But there no more shall withered hags
Refresh at ease their broomstick nags,
Or taste those hazel-shadowed waters
As beverage meet for Satan's daughters ;
No more their mimic tones be heard,
The mew of cat, the chirp of bird,
Shrill blending with the hoarser laughter
Of the fell demon following after !
The cautious goodman nails no more
A horseshoe on his outer door,
Lest some unseemly hag should fit
To his own mouth her bridle-bit ;
The goodwife's churn no more refuses
Its wonted culinary uses
Until, with heated needle burned,
The witch has to her place returned !
Our witches are no longer old
And wrinkled beldames, Satan-sold,
But young and gay and laughing creatures,
With　the　heart's　sunshine　on　their　fea-
　　tures ;
Their sorcery — the light which dances
Where the raised lid unveils its glances ;
Or that low-breathed and gentle tone,
　The music of Love's twilight hours,
Soft, dream-like, as a fairy's moan
　Above her nightly closing flowers,
Sweeter than that which sighed of yore
Along the charmed Ausonian shore !
Even she, our own weird heroine,
Sole Pythoness of ancient Lynn,
　Sleeps　calmly　where　the　living　laid
　　her ;
And the wide realm of sorcery,
Left by its latest mistress free,
　Hath found no gray and skilled invader.
So perished Albion's " glammarye,"
　With him in Melrose Abbey sleeping,
His charmed torch beside his knee,
That even the dead himself might see
　The magic scroll within his keeping.
And now our modern Yankee sees
Nor omens, spells, nor mysteries ;
And naught above, below, around,
Of life or death, of sight or sound,
　Whate'er its nature, form, or look,
Excites his terror or surprise, —
All seeming to his knowing eyes
Familiar as his " catechise,"
　Or " Webster's Spelling-Book."

THE DEMON OF THE STUDY

THE Brownie sits in the Scotchman's room,
 And eats his meat and drinks his ale,
And beats the maid with her unused broom,
 And the lazy lout with his idle flail ;
But he sweeps the floor and threshes the
 corn,
And hies him away ere the break of dawn.

The shade of Denmark fled from the sun,
 And the Cocklane ghost from the barn-
 loft cheer,
The fiend of Faust was a faithful one,
 Agrippa's demon wrought in fear,
And the devil of Martin Luther sat
By the stout monk's side in social chat.

The Old Man of the Sea, on the neck of
 him
 Who seven times crossed the deep,
Twined closely each lean and withered
 limb,
 Like the nightmare in one's sleep.
But he drank of the wine, and Sindbad
 cast
The evil weight from his back at last.

But the demon that cometh day by day
 To my quiet room and fireside nook,
Where the casement light falls dim and
 gray
On faded painting and ancient book,
Is a sorrier one than any whose names
Are chronicled well by good King James.

No bearer of burdens like Caliban,
 No runner of errands like Ariel,
He comes in the shape of a fat old man,
 Without rap of knuckle or pull of bell ;
And whence he comes, or whither he goes,
I know as I do of the wind which blows.

A stout old man with a greasy hat
 Slouched heavily down to his dark, red
 nose,
And two gray eyes enveloped in fat,
 Looking through glasses with iron bows.
Read ye, and heed ye, and ye who can,
Guard well your doors from that old man !

He comes with a careless " How d' ye do ? "
 And seats himself in my elbow-chair ;
And my morning paper and pamphlet new
 Fall forthwith under his special care,
And he wipes his glasses and clears his
 throat,
And, button by button, unfolds his coat.

And then he reads from paper and book,
 In a low and husky asthmatic tone,
With the stolid sameness of posture and
 look
 Of one who reads to himself alone ;
And hour after hour on my senses come
That husky wheeze and that dolorous hum.

The price of stocks, the auction sales,
 The poet's song and the lover's glee,
The horrible murders, the seaboard gales,
 The marriage list, and the *jeu d'esprit*,
All reach my ear in the self-same tone, —
I shudder at each, but the fiend reads on !

Oh, sweet as the lapse of water at noon
 O'er the mossy roots of some forest tree,
The sigh of the wind in the woods of June,
 Or sound of flutes o'er a moonlight sea,
Or the low soft music, perchance, which
 seems
To float through the slumbering singer's
 dreams,

So sweet, so dear is the silvery tone,
 Of her in whose features I sometimes look,
As I sit at eve by her side alone,
 And we read by turns, from the self-same
 book,
Some tale perhaps of the olden time,
Some lover's romance or quaint old rhyme.

Then when the story is one of woe, —
 Some prisoner's plaint through his dun-
 geon-bar,
Her blue eye glistens with tears, and low
 Her voice sinks down like a moan afar ;
And I seem to hear that prisoner's wail,
And his face looks on me worn and pale.

And when she reads some merrier song,
 Her voice is glad as an April bird's,
And when the tale is of war and wrong,
 A trumpet's summons is in her words,
And the rush of the hosts I seem to hear,
And see the tossing of plume and spear !

Oh, pity me then, when, day by day,
 The stout fiend darkens my parlor door ;
And reads me perchance the self-same lay
 Which melted in music, the night before,

From lips as the lips of Hylas sweet,
And moved like twin roses which zephyrs
    meet !

I cross my floor with a nervous tread,
  I whistle and laugh and sing and shout,
I flourish my cane above his head,
  And stir up the fire to roast him out ;
I topple the chairs, and drum on the pane,
And press my hands on my ears, in vain !

I 've studied Glanville and James the wise,
  And wizard black-letter tomes which treat
Of demons of every name and size
  Which a Christian man is presumed to
    meet,
But never a hint and never a line
Can I find of a reading fiend like mine.

I 've crossed the Psalter with Brady and
    Tate,
  And laid the Primer above them all,
I 've nailed a horseshoe over the grate,
  And hung a wig to my parlor wall
Once worn by a learned Judge, they say,
At Salem court in the witchcraft day !

" *Conjuro te, sceleratissime,*
  Abire ad tuum locum ! " — still
Like a visible nightmare he sits by me, —
  The exorcism has lost its skill ;
And I hear again in my haunted room
The husky wheeze and the dolorous hum !

Ah ! commend me to Mary Magdalen
  With her sevenfold plagues, to the
    wandering Jew,
To the terrors which haunted Orestes when
  The furies his midnight curtains drew,
But charm him off, ye who charm him can,
That reading demon, that fat old man !

THE FOUNTAIN

On the declivity of a hill in Salisbury, Essex
County, is a fountain of clear water, gushing
from the very roots of a venerable oak. It is
about two miles from the junction of the
Powow River with the Merrimac.

TRAVELLER ! on thy journey toiling
  By the swift Powow,
With the summer sunshine falling
  On thy heated brow,

Listen, while all else is still,
To the brooklet from the hill.

Wild and sweet the flowers are blowing
  By that streamlet's side,
And a greener verdure showing
  Where its waters glide,
Down the hill-slope murmuring on,
Over root and mossy stone.

Where yon oak his broad arms flingeth
  O'er the sloping hill,
Beautiful and freshly springeth
  That soft-flowing rill,
Through its dark roots wreathed and bare,
Gushing up to sun and air.

Brighter waters sparkled never
  In that magic well,
Of whose gift of life forever
  Ancient legends tell,
In the lonely desert wasted,
And by mortal lip untasted.

Waters which the proud Castilian
  Sought with longing eyes,
Underneath the bright pavilion
  Of the Indian skies,
Where his forest pathway lay
Through the blooms of Florida.

Years ago a lonely stranger,
  With the dusky brow
Of the outcast forest-ranger,
  Crossed the swift Powow,
And betook him to the rill
And the oak upon the hill.

O'er his face of moody sadness
  For an instant shone
Something like a gleam of gladness,
  As he stooped him down
To the fountain's grassy side,
And his eager thirst supplied.

With the oak its shadow throwing
  O'er his mossy seat,
And the cool, sweet waters flowing
  Softly at his feet,
Closely by the fountain's rim
That lone Indian seated him.

Autumn's earliest frost had given
  To the woods below
Hues of beauty, such as heaven

Lendeth to its bow ;
And the soft breeze from the west
Scarcely broke their dreamy rest.

Far behind was Ocean striving
　With his chains of sand ;
Southward, sunny glimpses giving,
　'Twixt the swells of land,
Of its calm and silvery track,
Rolled the tranquil Merrimac.

Over village, wood, and meadow
　Gazed that stranger man,
Sadly, till the twilight shadow
　Over all things ran,
Save where spire and westward pane
Flashed the sunset back again.

Gazing thus upon the dwelling
　Of his warrior sires,
Where no lingering trace was telling
　Of their wigwam fires,
Who the gloomy thoughts might know
Of that wandering child of woe ?

Naked lay, in sunshine glowing,
　Hills that once had stood
Down their sides the shadows throwing
　Of a mighty wood,
Where the deer his covert kept,
And the eagle's pinion swept !

Where the birch canoe had glided
　Down the swift Powow,
Dark and gloomy bridges strided
　Those clear waters now ;
And where once the beaver swam,
Jarred the wheel and frowned the dam.

For the wood-bird's merry singing,
　And the hunter's cheer,
Iron clang and hammer's ringing
　Smote upon his ear ;
And the thick and sullen smoke
From the blackened forges broke.

Could it be his fathers ever
　Loved to linger here ?
These bare hills, this conquered river, —
　Could they hold them dear,
With their native loveliness
Tamed and tortured into this ?

Sadly, as the shades of even
　Gathered o'er the hill,

While the western half of heaven
　Blushed with sunset still,
From the fountain's mossy seat
Turned the Indian's weary feet.

Year on year hath flown forever,
　But he came no more
To the hillside on the river
　Where he came before.
But the villager can tell
Of that strange man's visit well.

And the merry children, laden
　With their fruits or flowers, —
Roving boy and laughing maiden,
　In their school-day hours,
Love the simple tale to tell
Of the Indian and his well.

PENTUCKET

The village of Haverhill, on the Merrimac, called by the Indians Pentucket, was for nearly seventeen years a frontier town, and during thirty years endured all the horrors of savage warfare. In the year 1708, a combined body of French and Indians, under the command of De Chaillons, and Hertel de Rouville, the infamous and bloody sacker of Deerfield, made an attack upon the village, which at that time contained only thirty houses. Sixteen of the villagers were massacred, and a still larger number made prisoners. About thirty of the enemy also fell, and among them Hertel de Rouville. The minister of the place, Benjamin Rolfe, was killed by a shot through his own door. In a paper entitled *The Border War of 1708*, published in my collection of *Recreations and Miscellanies*, I have given a prose narrative of the surprise of Haverhill.

How sweetly on the wood-girt town
The mellow light of sunset shone !
Each small, bright lake, whose waters still
Mirror the forest and the hill,
Reflected from its waveless breast
The beauty of a cloudless west,
Glorious as if a glimpse were given
Within the western gates of heaven,
Left, by the spirit of the star
Of sunset's holy hour, ajar !

Beside the river's tranquil flood
The dark and low-walled dwellings stood,
Where many a rood of open land
Stretched up and down on either hand,

With corn-leaves waving freshly green
The thick and blackened stumps between.
Behind, unbroken, deep and dread,
The wild, untravelled forest spread,
Back to those mountains, white and cold,
Of which the Indian trapper told,
Upon whose summits never yet
Was mortal foot in safety set.

Quiet and calm without a fear
Of danger darkly lurking near,
The weary laborer left his plough,
The milkmaid carolled by her cow ;
From cottage door and household hearth
Rose songs of praise, or tones of mirth.
At length the murmur died away,
And silence on that village lay.
— So slept Pompeii, tower and hall,
Ere the quick earthquake swallowed all,
Undreaming of the fiery fate
Which made its dwellings desolate !

Hours passed away.   By moonlight sped
The Merrimac along his bed.
Bathed in the pallid lustre, stood
Dark cottage-wall and rock and wood,
Silent, beneath that tranquil beam,
As the hushed grouping of a dream.
Yet on the still air crept a sound,
No bark of fox, nor rabbit's bound,
Nor stir of wings, nor waters flowing,
Nor leaves in midnight breezes blowing.

Was that the tread of many feet,
Which downward from the hillside beat ?
What forms were those which darkly stood
Just on the margin of the wood ?
Charred tree-stumps in the moonlight dim,
Or paling rude, or leafless limb ?
No, — through the trees fierce eyeballs
    glowed,
Dark human forms in moonshine showed,
Wild from their native wilderness,
With painted limbs and battle-dress !

A yell the dead might wake to hear
Swelled on the night air, far and clear ;
Then smote the Indian tomahawk
On crashing door and shattering lock ;
Then rang the rifle-shot, and then
The shrill death-scream of stricken men, —
Sank the red axe in woman's brain,
And childhood's cry arose in vain.
Bursting through roof and window came,
Red, fast, and fierce, the kindled flame,

And blended fire and moonlight glared
On still dead men and scalp-knives bared.

The morning sun looked brightly through
The river willows, wet with dew.
No sound of combat filled the air,
No shout was heard, nor gunshot there ;
Yet still the thick and sullen smoke
From smouldering ruins slowly broke ;
And, on the greensward many a stain,
And, here and there, the mangled slain,
Told how that midnight bolt had sped
Pentucket, on thy fated head !

Even now the villager can tell
Where Rolfe beside his hearthstone fell,
Still show the door of wasting oak,
Through which the fatal death-shot broke,
And point the curious stranger where
De Rouville's corse lay grim and bare ;
Whose hideous head, in death still feared,
Bore not a trace of hair or beard ;
And still, within the churchyard ground,
Heaves darkly up the ancient mound,
Whose grass-grown surface overlies
The victims of that sacrifice.

THE NORSEMEN

In the early part of the present century, a
fragment of a statue, rudely chiselled from
dark gray stone, was found in the town of
Bradford. on the Merrimac. Its origin must
be left entirely to conjecture. The fact that
the ancient Northmen visited the northeast
coast of North America and probably New
England, some centuries before the discovery
of the western world by Columbus, is now very
generally admitted.

GIFT from the cold and silent Past !
A relic to the present cast,
Left on the ever-changing strand
Of shifting and unstable sand,
Which wastes beneath the steady chime
And beating of the waves of Time !
Who from its bed of primal rock
First wrenched thy dark, unshapely block ?
Whose hand, of curious skill untaught,
Thy rude and savage outline wrought ?

The waters of my native stream
Are glancing in the sun's warm beam ;
From sail-urged keel and flashing oar
The circles widen to its shore ;

And cultured field and peopled town
Slope to its willowed margin down.
Yet, while this morning breeze is bringing
The home-life sound of school-bells ring-
   ing,
And rolling wheel, and rapid jar
Of the fire-winged and steedless car,
And voices from the wayside near
Come quick and blended on my ear, —
A spell is in this old gray stone,
My thoughts are with the Past alone !

A change ! — The steepled town no more
Stretches along the sail-thronged shore ;
Like palace-domes in sunset's cloud,
Fade sun-gilt spire and mansion proud :
Spectrally rising where they stood,
I see the old, primeval wood ;
Dark, shadow-like, on either hand
I see its solemn waste expand ;
It climbs the green and cultured hill,
It arches o'er the valley's rill,
And leans from cliff and crag to throw
Its wild arms o'er the stream below.
Unchanged, alone, the same bright river
Flows on, as it will flow forever !
I listen, and I hear the low
Soft ripple where its waters go ;
I hear behind the panther's cry,
The wild-bird's scream goes thrilling by,
And shyly on the river's brink
The deer is stooping down to drink.

But hark ! — from wood and rock flung back,
What sound comes up the Merrimac ?
What sea-worn barks are those which throw
The light spray from each rushing prow ?
Have they not in the North Sea's blast
Bowed to the waves the straining mast ?
Their frozen sails the low, pale sun
Of Thulë's night has shone upon ;
Flapped by the sea-wind's gusty sweep
Round icy drift, and headland steep.
Wild Jutland's wives and Lochlin's daugh-
   ters
Have watched them fading o'er the waters,
Lessening through driving mist and spray,
Like white-winged sea-birds on their way !

Onward they glide, — and now I view
Their iron-armed and stalwart crew ;
Joy glistens in each wild blue eye,
Turned to green earth and summer sky.
Each broad, seamed breast has cast aside
Its cumbering vest of shaggy hide ;

Bared to the sun and soft warm air,
Streams back the Northmen's yellow hair.
I see the gleam of axe and spear,
A sound of smitten shields I hear,
Keeping a harsh and fitting time
To Saga's chant, and Runic rhyme ;
Such lays as Zetland's Scald has sung,
His gray and naked isles among ;
Or muttered low at midnight hour
Round Odin's mossy stone of power.
The wolf beneath the Arctic moon
Has answered to that startling rune ;
The Gael has heard its stormy swell,
The light Frank knows its summons well ;
Iona's sable-stoled Culdee
Has heard it sounding o'er the sea,
And swept, with hoary beard and hair,
His altar's foot in trembling prayer !

'T is past, — the 'wildering vision dies
In darkness on my dreaming eyes !
The forest vanishes in air,
Hill-slope and vale lie starkly bare ;
I hear the common tread of men,
And hum of work-day life again ;
The mystic relic seems alone
A broken mass of common stone ;
And if it be the chiselled limb
Of Berserker or idol grim,
A fragment of Valhalla's Thor,
The stormy Viking's god of War,
Or Praga of the Runic lay,
Or love-awakening Siona,
I know not, — for no graven line,
Nor Druid mark, nor Runic sign,
Is left me here, by which to trace
Its name, or origin, or place.
Yet, for this vision of the Past,
This glance upon its darkness cast,
My spirit bows in gratitude
Before the Giver of all good,
Who fashioned so the human mind,
That, from the waste of Time behind,
A simple stone, or mound of earth,
Can summon the departed forth ;
Quicken the Past to life again,
The Present lose in what hath been,
And in their primal freshness show
The buried forms of long ago.
As if a portion of that Thought
By which the Eternal will is wrought,
Whose impulse fills anew with breath
The frozen solitude of Death,
To mortal mind were sometimes lent,
To mortal musings sometimes sent,

To whisper — even when it seems
But Memory's fantasy of dreams —
Through the mind's waste of woe and sin,
Of an immortal origin !

FUNERAL TREE OF THE SOKOKIS

Polan, chief of the Sokokis Indians of the country between Agamenticus and Casco Bay, was killed at Windham on Sebago Lake in the spring of 1756. After the whites had retired, the surviving Indians " swayed " or bent down a young tree until its roots were upturned, placed the body of their chief beneath it, and then released the tree, which, in springing back to its old position, covered the grave. The Sokokis were early converts to the Catholic faith. Most of them, prior to the year 1756, had removed to the French settlements on the St. François.

AROUND Sebago's lonely lake
There lingers not a breeze to break
The mirror which its waters make.

The solemn pines along its shore,
The firs which hang its gray rocks o'er,
Are painted on its glassy floor.

The sun looks o'er, with hazy eye,
The snowy mountain-tops which lie
Piled coldly up against the sky.

Dazzling and white ! save where the
       bleak,
Wild winds have bared some splintering
       peak,
Or snow-slide left its dusky streak.

Yet green are Saco's banks below,
And belts of spruce and cedar show,
Dark fringing round those cones of snow.

The earth hath felt the breath of spring,
Though yet on her deliverer's wing
The lingering frosts of winter cling.

Fresh grasses fringe the meadow-brooks,
And mildly from its sunny nooks
The blue eye of the violet looks.

And odors from the springing grass,
The sweet birch and the sassafras,
Upon the scarce-felt breezes pass.

Her tokens of renewing care
Hath Nature scattered everywhere,
In bud and flower, and warmer air.

But in their hour of bitterness,
What reck the broken Sokokis,
Beside their slaughtered chief, of this ?

The turf's red stain is yet undried,
Scarce have the death-shot echoes died
Along Sebago's wooded side;

And silent now the hunters stand,
Grouped darkly, where a swell of land
Slopes upward from the lake's white sand

Fire and the axe have swept it bare,
Save one lone beech, unclosing there
Its light leaves in the vernal air.

With grave, cold looks, all sternly mute,
They break the damp turf at its foot,
And bare its coiled and twisted root.

They heave the stubborn trunk aside,
The firm roots from the earth divide, —
The rent beneath yawns dark and wide.

And there the fallen chief is laid,
In tasselled garb of skins arrayed,
And girded with his wampum-braid.

The silver cross he loved is pressed
Beneath the heavy arms, which rest
Upon his scarred and naked breast.

'T is done : the roots are backward sent,
The beechen-tree stands up unbent,
The Indian's fitting monument !

When of that sleeper's broken race
Their green and pleasant dwelling-place,
Which knew them once, retains no trace ;

Oh, long may sunset's light be shed
As now upon that beech's head,
A green memorial of the dead !

There shall his fitting requiem be,
In northern winds, that, cold and free,
Howl nightly in that funeral tree.

To their wild wail the waves which break
Forever round that lonely lake
A solemn undertone shall make !

And who shall deem the spot unblest,
Where Nature's younger children rest,
Lulled on their sorrowing mother's breast ?

Deem ye that mother loveth less
These bronzed forms of the wilderness
She foldeth in her long caress ?

As sweet o'er them her wild-flowers blow,
As if with fairer hair and brow
The blue-eyed Saxon slept below.

What though the places of their rest
No priestly knee hath ever pressed, —
No funeral rite nor prayer hath blessed ?

What though the bigot's ban be there,
And thoughts of wailing and despair,
And cursing in the place of prayer !

Yet Heaven hath angels watching round
The Indian's lowliest forest-mound, —
And they have made it holy ground.

There ceases man's frail judgment ; all
His powerless bolts of cursing fall
Unheeded on that grassy pall.

O peeled and hunted and reviled,
Sleep on, dark tenant of the wild !
Great Nature owns her simple child !

And Nature's God, to whom alone
The secret of the heart is known, —
The hidden language traced thereon ;

Who from its many cumberings
Of form and creed, and outward things,
To light the naked spirit brings ;

Not with our partial eye shall scan,
Not with our pride and scorn shall ban,
The spirit of our brother man !

ST. JOHN

The fierce rivalry between Charles de La
Tour, a Protestant, and D'Aulnay Charnasy, a
Catholic, for the possession of Acadia, forms
one of the most romantic passages in the history
of the New World. La Tour received aid in sev-
eral instances from the Puritan colony of Mas-
sachusetts. During one of his voyages for the
purpose of obtaining arms and provisions for
his establishment at St. John, his castle was
attacked by D'Aulnay, and successfully de-
fended by its high-spirited mistress. A second
attack however followed in the fourth month,
1647, when D'Aulnay was successful, and the
garrison was put to the sword. Lady La Tour
languished a few days in the hands of her ene-
my, and then died of grief.

"To the winds give our banner !
    Bear homeward again ! "
Cried the Lord of Acadia,
    Cried Charles of Estienne !
From the prow of his shallop
    He gazed, as the sun,
From its bed in the ocean,
    Streamed up the St. John.

O'er the blue western waters
    That shallop had passed,
Where the mists of Penobscot
    Clung damp on her mast.
St. Saviour had looked
    On the heretic sail,
As the songs of the Huguenot
    Rose on the gale.

The pale, ghostly fathers
    Remembered her well,
And had cursed her while passing,
    With taper and bell ;
But the men of Monhegan,
    Of Papists abhorred,
Had welcomed and feasted
    The heretic Lord.

They had loaded his shallop
    With dun-fish and ball,
With stores for his larder,
    And steel for his wall.
Pemaquid, from her bastions
    And turrets of stone,
Had welcomed his coming
    With banner and gun.

And the prayers of the elders
    Had followed his way,
As homeward he glided,
    Down Pentecost Bay.
Oh, well sped La Tour !
    For, in peril and pain,
His lady kept watch,
    For his coming again.

O'er the Isle of the Pheasant
    The morning sun shone,
On the plane-trees which shaded
    The shores of St. John.

"Now, why from yon battlements
　Speaks not my love !
Why waves there no banner
　My fortress above ? "

Dark and wild, from his deck
　St. Estienne gazed about,
On fire-wasted dwellings,
　And silent redoubt ;
From the low, shattered walls
　Which the flame had o'errun,
There floated no banner,
　There thundered no gun !

But beneath the low arch
　Of its doorway there stood
A pale priest of Rome,
　In his cloak and his hood.
With the bound of a lion,
　La Tour sprang to land,
On the throat of the Papist
　He fastened his hand.

"Speak, son of the Woman
　Of scarlet and sin!
What wolf has been prowling
　My castle within? "
From the grasp of the soldier
　The Jesuit broke,
Half in scorn, half in sorrow,
　He smiled as he spoke :

"No wolf, Lord of Estienne,
　Has ravaged thy hall,
But thy red-handed rival,
　With fire, steel, and ball !
On an errand of mercy
　I hitherward came,
While the walls of thy castle
　Yet spouted with flame.

"Pentagoet's dark vessels
　Were moored in the bay,
Grim sea-lions, roaring
　Aloud for their prey."
"But what of my lady ? "
　Cried Charles of Estienne.
"On the shot-crumbled turret
　Thy lady was seen :

"Half-veiled in the smoke-cloud,
　Her hand grasped thy pennon,
While her dark tresses swayed
　In the hot breath of cannon !

But woe to the heretic,
　Evermore woe !
When the son of the church
　And the cross is his foe !

"In the track of the shell,
　In the path of the ball,
Pentagoet swept over
　The breach of the wall !
Steel to steel, gun to gun,
　One moment, — and then
Alone stood the victor,
　Alone with his men !

"Of its sturdy defenders,
　Thy lady alone
Saw the cross-blazoned banner
　Float over St. John."
"Let the dastard look to it ! "
　Cried fiery Estienne,
"Were D'Aulnay King Louis,
　I 'd free her again ! "

"Alas for thy lady !
　No service from thee
Is needed by her
　Whom the Lord hath set free ;
Nine days, in stern silence,
　Her thraldom she bore,
But the tenth morning came,
　And Death opened her door ! "

As if suddenly smitten
　La Tour staggered back ;
His hand grasped his sword-hilt,
　His forehead grew black.
He sprang on the deck
　Of his shallop again.
"We cruise now for vengeance !
　Give way ! " cried Estienne.

"Massachusetts shall hear
　Of the Huguenot's wrong,
And from island and creekside
　Her fishers shall throng !
Pentagoet shall rue
　What his Papists have done,
When his palisades echo
　The Puritan's gun ! "

Oh, the loveliest of heavens
　Hung tenderly o'er him,
There were waves in the sunshine,
　And green isles before him ;

But a pale hand was beckoning
  The Huguenot on ;
And in blackness and ashes
  Behind was St. John !

THE CYPRESS–TREE OF CEYLON

Ibn Batuta, the celebrated Mussulman trav-
eller of the fourteenth century, speaks of a
cypress-tree in Ceylon, universally held sacred
by the natives, the leaves of which were said
to fall only at certain intervals, and he who
had the happiness to find and eat one of them
was restored, at once, to youth and vigor.   The
traveller saw several venerable Jogees, or saints,
sitting silent and motionless under the tree.

THEY sat in silent watchfulness
  The sacred cypress-tree about,
And, from beneath old wrinkled brows,
  Their failing eyes looked out.

Gray Age and Sickness waiting there
  Through weary night and lingering
    day, —
Grim as the idols at their side,
  And motionless as they.

Unheeded in the boughs above
  The song of Ceylon's birds was sweet ;
Unseen of them the island flowers
  Bloomed brightly at their feet.

O'er them the tropic night-storm swept,
  The thunder crashed on rock and hill ;
The cloud-fire on their eyeballs blazed,
  Yet there they waited still !

What was the world without to them ?
  The Moslem's sunset-call, the dance
Of Ceylon's maids, the passing gleam
  Of battle-flag and lance ?

They waited for that falling leaf
  Of which the wandering Jogees sing :
Which lends once more to wintry age
  The greenness of its spring.

Oh, if these poor and blinded ones
  In trustful patience wait to feel
O'er torpid pulse and failing limb
  A youthful freshness steal ;

Shall we, who sit beneath that Tree
  Whose healing leaves of life are shed,

In answer to the breath of prayer,
  Upon the waiting head —

Not to restore our failing forms,
  And build the spirit's broken shrine,
But on the fainting soul to shed
  A light and life divine —

Shall we grow weary in our watch,
  And murmur at the long delay ?
Impatient of our Father's time
  And His appointed way ?

Or shall the stir of outward things
  Allure and claim the Christian's eye,
When on the heathen watcher's ear
  Their powerless murmurs die ?

Alas ! a deeper test of faith
  Than prison cell or martyr's stake,
The self-abasing watchfulness
  Of silent prayer may make.

We gird us bravely to rebuke
  Our erring brother in the wrong, —
And in the ear of Pride and Power
  Our warning voice is strong.

Easier to smite with Peter's sword
  Than "watch one hour " in humbling
    prayer.
Life's " great things," like the Syrian lord,
  Our hearts can do and dare.

But oh ! we shrink from Jordan's side,
  From waters which alone can save;
And murmur for Abana's banks
  And Pharpar's brighter wave.

O Thou, who in the garden's shade
  Didst wake Thy. weary ones again,
Who slumbered at that fearful hour
  Forgetful of Thy pain ;

Bend o'er us now, as over them,
  And set our sleep-bound spirits free,
Nor leave us slumbering in the watch
  Our souls should keep with Thee !

THE EXILES

The incidents upon which the following bal-
lad has its foundation occurred about the year
1660. Thomas Macy was one of the first, if

not the first white settler of Nantucket. The
career of Macy is briefly but carefully outlined
in James S. Pike's *The New Puritan*.

THE goodman sat beside his door,
  One sultry afternoon,
With his young wife singing at his side
  An old and goodly tune.

A glimmer of heat was in the air, —
  The dark green woods were still ;
And the skirts of a heavy thunder-cloud
  Hung over the western hill.

Black, thick, and vast arose that cloud
  Above the wilderness,
As some dark world from upper air
  Were stooping over this.

At times the solemn thunder pealed,
  And all was still again,
Save a low murmur in the air
  Of coming wind and rain.

Just as the first big rain-drop fell,
  A weary stranger came,
And stood before the farmer's door,
  With travel soiled and lame.

Sad seemed he, yet sustaining hope
  Was in his quiet glance,
And   peace,   like   autumn's   moonlight,
    clothed
  His tranquil countenance, —

A look, like that his Master wore
  In Pilate's council-hall:
It told of wrongs, but of a love
  Meekly forgiving all.

" Friend !   wilt   thou   give   me   shelter
    here ? "
  The stranger meekly said ;
And, leaning on his oaken staff,
  The goodman's features read.

" My life is hunted, — evil men
  Are following in my track ;
The traces of the torturer's whip
  Are on my aged back ;

" And much, I fear, 't will peril thee
  Within thy doors to take
A hunted seeker of the Truth,
  Oppressed for conscience' sake."

Oh, kindly spoke the goodman's wife,
  " Come in, old man ! " quoth she,
" We will not leave thee to the storm,
  Whoever thou mayst be."

Then came the aged wanderer in,
  And silent sat him down ;
While all within grew dark as night
  Beneath the storm-cloud's frown.

But while the sudden lightning's blaze
  Filled every cottage nook,
And with the jarring thunder-roll
  The loosened casements shook,

A heavy tramp of horses' feet
  Came sounding up the lane,
And half a score of horse, or more,
  Came plunging through the rain.

" Now, Goodman Macy, ope thy door, —
  We would not be house-breakers ;
A rueful deed thou 'st done this day,
  In harboring banished Quakers."

Out looked the cautious goodman then,
  With much of fear and awe,
For there, with broad wig drenched with
    rain,
  The parish priest he saw.

" Open thy door, thou wicked man,
  And let thy pastor in,
And give God thanks, if forty stripes
  Repay thy deadly sin."

" What seek ye ? " quoth the goodman ;
  " The stranger is my guest ;
He is worn with toil and grievous wrong,—
  Pray let the old man rest."

" Now, out upon thee, canting knave ! "
  And strong hands shook the door.
" Believe me, Macy," quoth the priest,
  " Thou 'lt rue thy conduct sore."

Then kindled Macy's eye of fire :
  " No priest who walks the earth,
Shall pluck away the stranger-guest
  Made welcome to my hearth."

Down from his cottage wall he caught
  The matchlock, hotly tried
At Preston-pans and Marston-moor,
  By fiery Ireton's side ;

Where Puritan, and Cavalier,
  With shout and psalm contended;
And Rupert's oath, and Cromwell's prayer,
  With battle-thunder blended.

Up rose 'he ancient stranger then :
  "My spirit is not free
To bring the wrath and violence
  Of evil men on thee ;

" And for thyself, I pray forbear,
  Bethink thee of thy Lord,
Who healed again the smitten ear,
  And sheathed His follower's sword.

" I go, as to the slaughter led.
  Friends of the poor, farewell ! "
Beneath his hand the oaken door
  Back on its hinges fell.

" Come forth, old graybeard, yea and nay,"
  The reckless scoffers cried,
As to a horseman's saddle-bow
  The old man's arms were tied.

And of his bondage hard and long
  In Boston's crowded jail,
Where suffering woman's prayer was
      heard,
  With sickening childhood's wail,

It suits not with our tale to tell ;
  Those scenes have passed away ;
Let the dim shadows of the past
  Brood o'er that evil day.

" Ho, sheriff ! " quoth the ardent priest,
  " Take Goodman Macy too ;
The sin of this day's heresy
  His back or purse shall rue."

" Now, goodwife, haste thee ! " Macy cried.
  She caught his manly arm ;
Behind, the parson urged pursuit,
  With outcry and alarm.

Ho ! speed the Macys, neck or naught, —
  The river-course was near ;
The plashing on its pebbled shore
  Was music to their ear.

A gray rock, tasselled o'er with birch,
  Above the waters hung,
And at its base, with every wave,
  A small light wherry swung.

A leap — they gain the boat — and there
  The goodman wields his oar ;
" Ill luck betide them all," he cried,
  " The laggards on the shore."

Down through the crashing underwood,
  The burly sheriff came : —
" Stand, Goodman Macy, yield thyself ;
  Yield in the King's own name."

" Now out upon thy hangman's face ! "
  Bold Macy answered then, —
" Whip women, on the village green,
  But meddle not with men."

The priest came panting to the shore,
  His grave cocked hat was gone ;
Behind him, like some owl's nest, hung
  His wig upon a thorn.

" Come back ! come back ! " the parson cried,
  " The church's curse beware."
"Curse, an thou wilt," said Macy, " but
  Thy blessing prithee spare."

" Vile scoffer ! " cried the baffled priest,
  " Thou 'lt yet the gallows see."
" Who 's born to be hanged will not be
      drowned,"
  Quoth Macy, merrily ;

" And so, sir sheriff and priest, good-by ! "
  He bent him to his oar,
And the small boat glided quietly
  From the twain upon the shore.

Now in the west, the heavy clouds
  Scattered and fell asunder,
While feebler came the rush of rain,
  And fainter growled the thunder.

And through the broken clouds, the sun
  Looked out serene and warm,
Painting its holy symbol-light
  Upon the passing storm.

Oh, beautiful ! that rainbow span,
  O'er dim Crane-neck was bended ;
One bright foot touched the eastern hills,
  And one with ocean blended.

By green Pentucket's southern slope
  The small boat glided fast ;
The watchers of the Block-house saw
  The strangers as they passed.

That night a stalwart garrison
  Sat shaking in their shoes,
To hear the dip of Indian oars,
  The glide of birch canoes.

The fisher-wives of Salisbury —
  The men were all away —
Looked out to see the stranger oar
  Upon their waters play.

Deer Island's rocks and fir-trees threw
  Their sunset-shadows o'er them,
And Newbury's spire and weathercock
  Peered o'er the pines before them.

Around the Black Rocks, on their left,
  The marsh lay broad and green ;
And on their right with dwarf shrubs
    crowned,
  Plum Island's hills were seen.

With skilful hand and wary eye
  The harbor-bar was crossed ;
A plaything of the restless wave,
  The boat on ocean tossed.

The glory of the sunset heaven
  On land and water lay ;
On the steep hills of Agawam,
  On cape, and bluff, and bay.

They passed the gray rocks of Cape Ann,
  And Gloucester's harbor-bar ;
The watch-fire of the garrison
  Shone like a setting star.

How brightly broke the morning
  On Massachusetts Bay !
Blue wave, and bright green island,
  Rejoicing in the day.

On passed the bark in safety
  Round isle and headland steep ;
No tempest broke above them,
  No fog-cloud veiled the deep.

Far round the bleak and stormy Cape
  The venturous Macy passed,
And on Nantucket's naked isle
  Drew up his boat at last.

And how, in log-built cabin,
  They braved the rough sea-weather ;
And there, in peace and quietness,
  Went down life's vale together ;

How others drew around them,
  And how their fishing sped,
Until to every wind of heaven
  Nantucket's sails were spread

How pale Want alternated
  With Plenty's golden smile ;
Behold, is it not written
  In the annals of the isle ?

And yet that isle remaineth
  A refuge of the free,
As when true-hearted Macy
  Beheld it from the sea.

Free as the winds that winnow
  Her shrubless hills of sand,
Free as the waves that batter
  Along her yielding land.

Than hers, at duty's summons,
  No loftier spirit stirs,
Nor falls o'er human suffering
  A readier tear than hers.

God bless the sea-beat island !
  And grant forevermore,
That charity and freedom dwell
  As now upon her shore !

THE KNIGHT OF ST. JOHN

ERE down yon blue Carpathian hills
  The sun shall sink again,
Farewell to life and all its ills,
  Farewell to cell and chain !

These prison shades are dark and cold,
  But, darker far than they,
The shadow of a sorrow old
  Is on my heart alway.

For since the day when Warkworth wood
  Closed o'er my steed, and I,
An alien from my name and blood,
  A weed cast out to die, —

When, looking back in sunset light,
  I saw her turret gleam,
And from its casement, far and white,
  Her sign of farewell stream,

Like one who, from some desert shore,
  Doth home's green isles descry,

And, vainly longing, gazes o'er
　The waste of wave and sky ;

So from the desert of my fate
　I gaze across the past ;
Forever on life's dial-plate
　The shade is backward cast !

I 've wandered wide from shore to shore,
　I 've knelt at many a shrine ;
And bowed me to the rocky floor
　Where Bethlehem's tapers shine ;

And by the Holy Sepulchre
　I 've pledged my knightly sword
To Christ, His blessed Church, and her,
　The Mother of our Lord.

Oh, vain the vow, and vain the strife !
　How vain do all things seem !
My soul is in the past, and life
　To-day is but a dream !

In vain the penance strange and long,
　And hard for flesh to bear ;
The prayer, the fasting, and the thong,
　And sackcloth shirt of hair.

The eyes of memory will not sleep, —
　Its ears are open still ;
And vigils with the past they keep
　Against my feeble will.

And still the loves and joys of old
　Do evermore uprise ;
I see the flow of locks of gold,
　The shine of loving eyes !

Ah me ! upon another's breast
　Those golden locks recline ;
I see upon another rest
　The glance that once was mine.

"O faithless priest ! O perjured knight !"
　I hear the Master cry ;
"Shut out the vision from thy sight,
　Let Earth and Nature die.

" The Church of God is now thy spouse,
　And thou the bridegroom art ;
Then let the burden of thy vows
　Crush down thy human heart ! "

In vain !　This heart its grief must know,
　Till life itself hath ceased,

And falls beneath the self-same blow
　The lover and the priest !

O pitying Mother ! souls of light,
　And saints and martyrs old !
Pray for a weak and sinful knight,
　A suffering man uphold.

Then let the Paynim work his will,
　And death unbind my chain,
Ere down yon blue Carpathian hill
　The sun shall fall again.

CASSANDRA SOUTHWICK

In 1658 two young persons, son and daughter
of Lawrence Southwick of Salem, who had
himself been imprisoned and deprived of nearly
all his property for having entertained Quakers
at his house, were fined for non-attendance at
church.　They being unable to pay the fine, the
General Court issued an order empowering
"the Treasurer of the County to sell the said
persons to any of the English nation of *Virginia*
or *Barbadoes*, to answer said fines."　An at-
tempt was made to carry this order into execu-
tion, but no shipmaster was found willing to
convey them to the West Indies.

To the God of all sure mercies let my bless-
　　ing rise to-day,
From the scoffer and the cruel He hath
　　plucked the spoil away ;
Yea, He who cooled the furnace around the
　　faithful three,
And tamed the Chaldean lions, hath set
　　His handmaid free !

Last night I saw the sunset melt through
　　my prison bars,
Last night across my damp earth-floor fell
　　the pale gleam of stars ;
In the coldness and the darkness all through
　　the long night-time,
My grated casement whitened with au-
　　tumn's early rime.

Alone, in that dark sorrow, hour after hour
　　crept by ;
Star after star looked palely in and sank
　　adown the sky ;
No sound amid night's stillness, save that
　　which seemed to be
The dull and heavy beating of the pulses
　　of the sea ;

All night I sat unsleeping, for I knew that
on the morrow
The ruler and the cruel priest would mock
me in my sorrow,
Dragged to their place of market, and bar-
gained for and sold,
Like a lamb before the shambles, like a
heifer from the fold !

Oh, the weakness of the flesh was there, —
the shrinking and the shame ;
And the low voice of the Tempter like
whispers to me came :
"Why sit'st thou thus forlornly," the
wicked murmur said,
"Damp walls thy bower of beauty, cold
earth thy maiden bed ?

"Where be the smiling faces, and voices
soft and sweet,
Seen in thy father's dwelling, heard in the
pleasant street ?
Where be the youths whose glances, the
summer Sabbath through,
Turned tenderly and timidly unto thy
father's pew ?

"Why sit'st thou here, Cassandra ? — Be-
think thee with what mirth
Thy happy schoolmates gather around the
warm, bright hearth ;
How the crimson shadows tremble on fore-
heads white and fair,
On eyes of merry girlhood, half hid in
golden hair.

"Not for thee the hearth-fire brightens,
not for thee kind words are spoken,
Not for thee the nuts of Wenham woods
by laughing boys are broken ;
No first-fruits of the orchard within thy
lap are laid,
For thee no flowers of autumn the youth-
ful hunters braid.

"O weak, deluded maiden ! — by crazy
fancies led,
With wild and raving railers an evil path
to tread ;
To leave a wholesome worship, and teach-
ing pure and sound,
And mate with maniac women, loose-
haired and sackcloth bound, —

"Mad scoffers of the priesthood, who mock
at things divine,

Who rail against the pulpit, and holy
bread and wine ;
Sore from their cart-tail scourgings, and
from the pillory lame,
Rejoicing in their wretchedness, and glory-
ing in their shame.

"And what a fate awaits thee ! — a sadly
toiling slave,
Dragging the slowly lengthening chain of
bondage to the grave !
Think of thy woman's nature, subdued in
hopeless thrall,
The easy prey of any, the scoff and scorn
of all ! "

Oh, ever as the Tempter spoke, and feeble
Nature's fears
Wrung drop by drop the scalding flow of
unavailing tears,
I wrestled down the evil thoughts, and
strove in silent prayer,
To feel, O Helper of the weak ! that Thou
indeed wert there !

I thought of Paul and Silas, within Phi-
lippi's cell,
And how from Peter's sleeping limbs the
prison shackles fell,
Till I seemed to hear the trailing of an
angel's robe of white,
And to feel a blessed presence invisible to
sight.

Bless the Lord for all his mercies ! — for
the peace and love I felt,
Like dew of Hermon's holy hill, upon my
spirit melt ;
When "Get behind me, Satan !" was the
language of my heart,
And I felt the Evil Tempter with all his
doubts depart.

Slow broke the gray cold morning ; again
the sunshine fell,
Flecked with the shade of bar and grate
within my lonely cell ;
The hoar-frost melted on the wall, and up-
ward from the street
Came careless laugh and idle word, and
tread of passing feet.

At length the heavy bolts fell back, my
door was open cast,
And slowly at the sheriff's side, up the
long street I passed ;

I heard the murmur round me, and felt,
    but dared not see,
How, from every door and window, the
    people gazed on me.

And doubt and fear fell on me, shame
    burned upon my cheek,
Swam earth and sky around me, my trem-
    bling limbs grew weak:
"O Lord! support thy handmaid; and
    from her soul cast out
The fear of man, which brings a snare,
    the weakness and the doubt."

Then the dreary shadows scattered, like a
    cloud in morning's breeze,
And a low deep voice within me seemed
    whispering words like these :
"Though thy earth be as the iron, and thy
    heaven a brazen wall,
Trust still His loving-kindness whose
    power is over all."

We paused at length, where at my feet
    the sunlit waters broke
On glaring reach of shining beach, and
    shingly wall of rock ;
The merchant-ships lay idly there, in hard
    clear lines on high,
Tracing with rope and slender spar their
    network on the sky.

And there were ancient citizens, cloak-
    wrapped and grave and cold,
And grim and stout sea-captains with
    faces bronzed and old,
And on his horse, with Rawson, his cruel
    clerk at hand,
Sat dark and haughty Endicott, the ruler
    of the land.

And poisoning with his evil words the
    ruler's ready ear,
The priest leaned o'er his saddle, with
    laugh and scoff and jeer ;
It stirred my soul, and from my lips the
    seal of silence broke,
As if through woman's weakness a warn-
    ing spirit spoke.

I cried, "The Lord rebuke thee, thou
    smiter of the meek,
Thou robber of the righteous, thou trampler
    of the weak !
Go light the dark, cold hearth-stones, — go
    turn the prison lock

Of the poor hearts thou hast hunted, thou
    wolf amid the flock ! "

Dark lowered the brows of Endicott, and
    with a deeper red
O'er Rawson's wine-empurpled cheek the
    flush of anger spread ;
"Good people," quoth the white-lipped
    priest, " heed not her words so wild,
Her Master speaks within her, — the Devil
    owns his child ! "

But gray heads shook, and young brows
    knit, the while the sheriff read
That law the wicked rulers against the poor
    have made,
Who to their house of Rimmon and idol
    priesthood bring
No bended knee of worship, nor gainful
    offering.

Then to the stout sea-captains the sheriff,
    turning, said, —
"Which of ye, worthy seamen, will take
    this Quaker maid ?
In the Isle of fair Barbadoes, or on Vir-
    ginia's shore,
You may hold her at a higher price than
    Indian girl or Moor."

Grim and silent stood the captains ; and
    when again he cried,
"Speak out, my worthy seamen ! " — no
    voice, no sign replied ;
But I felt a hard hand press my own, and
    kind words met my ear, —
"God bless thee, and preserve thee, my
    gentle girl and dear ! "

A weight seemed lifted from my heart, a
    pitying friend was nigh, —
I felt it in his hard, rough hand, and saw it
    in his eye ;
And when again the sheriff spoke, that
    voice, so kind to me,
Growled back its stormy answer like the
    roaring of the sea, —

"Pile my ship with bars of silver, pack
    with coins of Spanish gold,
From keel-piece up to deck-plank, the
    roomage of her hold,
By the living God who made me ! — I
    would sooner in your bay
Sink ship and crew and cargo, than bear
    this child away ! "

"Well answered, worthy captain, shame on
    their cruel laws ! "
Ran through the crowd in murmurs loud
    the people's just applause.
"Like the herdsman of Tekoa, in Israel of
    old,
Shall we see the poor and righteous again
    for silver sold ? "

I looked on haughty Endicott ; with wea-
    pon half-way drawn,
Swept round the throng his lion glare of
    bitter hate and scorn ;
Fiercely he drew his bridle-rein, and turned
    in silence back,
And sneering priest and baffled clerk rode
    murmuring in his track.

Hard after them the sheriff looked, in bit-
    terness of soul ;
Thrice smote his staff upon the ground,
    and crushed his parchment roll.
"Good friends," he said, " since both have
    fled, the ruler and the priest,
Judge ye, if from their further work I be
    not well released."

Loud was the cheer which, full and clear,
    swept round the silent bay,
As, with kind words and kinder looks, he
    bade me go my way ;
For He who turns the courses of the stream-
    let of the glen,
And the river of great waters, had turned
    the hearts of men.

Oh, at that hour the very earth seemed
    changed beneath my eye,
A holier wonder round me rose the blue
    walls of the sky,
A lovelier light on rock and hill and stream
    and woodland lay,
And softer lapsed on sunnier sands the
    waters of the bay.

Thanksgiving to the Lord of life ! to Him
    all praises be,
Who from the hands of evil men hath set
    his handmaid free ;
All praise to Him before whose power the
    mighty are afraid,
Who takes the crafty in the snare which
    for the poor is laid !

Sing, O my soul, rejoicingly, on evening's
    twilight calm

Uplift the loud thanksgiving, pour forth
    the grateful psalm ;
Let all dear hearts with me rejoice, as did
    the saints of old,
When of the Lord's good angel the rescued
    Peter told.

And weep and howl, ye evil priests and
    mighty men of wrong,
The Lord shall smite the proud, and lay
    His hand upon the strong.
Woe to the wicked rulers in His avenging
    hour !
Woe to the wolves who seek the flocks to
    raven and devour !

But let the humble ones arise, the poor in
    heart be glad,
And let the mourning ones again with
    robes of praise be clad.
For He who cooled the furnace, and
    smoothed the stormy wave,
And tamed the Chaldean lions, is mighty
    still to save !

THE NEW WIFE AND THE OLD

    The following ballad is founded upon one of
the marvellous legends connected with the fa-
mous General M——, of Hampton, New Hamp-
shire, who was regarded by his neighbors as a
Yankee Faust, in league with the adversary.
I give the story, as I heard it when a child,
from a venerable family visitant.

DARK the halls, and cold the feast,
Gone the bridemaids, gone the priest.
All is over, all is done,
Twain of yesterday are one !
Blooming girl and manhood gray,
Autumn in the arms of May !

Hushed within and hushed without,
Dancing feet and wrestlers' shout ;
Dies the bonfire on the hill ;
All is dark and all is still,
Save the starlight, save the breeze
Moaning through the graveyard trees ;
And the great sea-waves below,
Pulse of the midnight beating slow.

From the brief dream of a bride
She hath wakened, at his side.
With half-uttered shriek and start, —
Feels she not his beating heart ?

And the pressure of his arm,
And his breathing near and warm?

Lightly from the bridal bed
Springs that fair dishevelled head,
And a feeling, new, intense,
Half of shame, half innocence,
Maiden fear and wonder speaks
Through her lips and changing cheeks.

From the oaken mantel glowing,
Faintest light the lamp is throwing
On the mirror's antique mould,
High-backed chair, and wainscot old,
And, through faded curtains stealing,
His dark sleeping face revealing.

Listless lies the strong man there,
Silver-streaked his careless hair;
Lips of love have left no trace
On that hard and haughty face;
And that forehead's knitted thought
Love's soft hand hath not unwrought.

"Yet," she sighs, "he loves me well,
More than these calm lips will tell.
Stooping to my lowly state,
He hath made me rich and great,
And I bless him, though he be
Hard and stern to all save me!"

While she speaketh, falls the light
O'er her fingers small and white;
Gold and gem, and costly ring
Back the timid lustre fling, —
Love's selectest gifts, and rare,
His proud hand had fastened there.

Gratefully she marks the glow
From those tapering lines of snow;
Fondly o'er the sleeper bending,
His black hair with golden blending,
In her soft and light caress,
Cheek and lip together press.

Ha! — that start of horror! why
That wild stare and wilder cry,
Full of terror, full of pain?
Is there madness in her brain?
Hark! that gasping, hoarse and low,
"Spare me, — spare me, — let me go!"

God have mercy! — icy cold
Spectral hands her own enfold,
Drawing silently from them

Love's fair gifts of gold and gem.
"Waken! save me!" still as death
At her side he slumbereth.

Ring and bracelet all are gone,
And that ice-cold hand withdrawn;
But she hears a murmur low,
Full of sweetness, full of woe,
Half a sigh and half a moan:
"Fear not! give the dead her own!"

Ah! — the dead wife's voice she knows!
That cold hand whose pressure froze,
Once in warmest life had borne
Gem and band her own hath worn.
"Wake thee! wake thee!" Lo, his eyes
Open with a dull surprise.

In his arms the strong man folds her,
Closer to his breast he holds her;
Trembling limbs his own are meeting,
And he feels her heart's quick beating:
"Nay, my dearest, why this fear?"
"Hush!" she saith, "the dead is here!"

"Nay, a dream, — an idle dream."
But before the lamp's pale gleam
Tremblingly her hand she raises.
There no more the diamond blazes,
Clasp of pearl, or ring of gold, —
"Ah!" she sighs, "her hand was cold!"

Broken words of cheer he saith,
But his dark lip quivereth,
And as o'er the past he thinketh,
From his young wife's arms he shrinketh;
Can those soft arms round him lie,
Underneath his dead wife's eye?

She her fair young head can rest
Soothed and childlike on his breast,
And in trustful innocence
Draw new strength and courage thence;
He, the proud man, feels within
But the cowardice of sin!

She can murmur in her thought
Simple prayers her mother taught,
And His blessed angels call,
Whose great love is over all;
He, alone, in prayerless pride,
Meets the dark Past at her side!

One, who living shrank with dread
From his look, or word, or tread,

Unto whom her early grave
Was as freedom to the slave,
Moves him at this midnight hour,
With the dead's unconscious power !

Ah, the dead, the unforgot !
From their solemn homes of thought,
Where the cypress shadows blend
Darkly over foe and friend,
Or in love or sad rebuke,
Back upon the living look.

And the tenderest ones and weakest,
Who their wrongs have borne the meekest,
Lifting from those dark, still places,
Sweet and sad-remembered faces,
O'er the guilty hearts behind
An unwitting triumph find.

THE BRIDAL OF PENNACOOK

Winnepurkit, otherwise called George, Sachem of Saugus, married a daughter of Passaconaway, the great Pennacook chieftain, in 1662. The wedding took place at Pennacook (now Concord, N. H.), and the ceremonies closed with a great feast. According to the usages of the chiefs, Passaconaway ordered a select number of his men to accompany the newly married couple to the dwelling of the husband, where in turn there was another great feast. Some time after, the wife of Winnepurkit expressing a desire to visit her father's house was permitted to go, accompanied by a brave escort of her husband's chief men. But when she wished to return, her father sent a messenger to Saugus, informing her husband, and asking him to come and take her away. He returned for answer that he had escorted his wife to her father's house in a style that became a chief, and that now if she wished to return, her father must send her back, in the same way. This Passaconaway refused to do, and it is said that here terminated the connection of his daughter with the Saugus chief. — Vide MORTON's *New Canaan.*

WE had been wandering for many days
Through the rough northern country. We
    had seen
The sunset, with its bars of purple cloud,
Like a new heaven, shine upward from the
    lake
Of Winnepiseogee ; and had felt
The sunrise breezes, midst the leafy isles
Which stoop their summer beauty to the lips

Of the bright waters. We had checked our
    steeds,
Silent with wonder, where the mountain
    wall
Is piled to heaven ; and, through the narrow
    rift
Of the vast rocks, against whose rugged feet
Beats the mad torrent with perpetual roar,
Where noonday is as twilight, and the
    wind
Comes burdened with the everlasting moan
Of forests and of far-off waterfalls,
We had looked upward where the summer
    sky,
Tasselled with clouds light-woven by the
    sun,
Sprung its blue arch above the abutting
    crags
O'er-roofing the vast portal of the land
Beyond the wall of mountains. We had
    passed
The high source of the Saco ; and bewil-
    dered
In the dwarf spruce-belts of the Crystal
    Hills,
Had heard above us, like a voice in the
    cloud,
The horn of Fabyan sounding ; and atop
Of old Agioochook had seen the mountains
Piled to the northward, shagged with
    wood, and thick
As meadow mole-hills, — the far sea of
    Casco,
A white gleam on the horizon of the east ;
Fair lakes, embosomed in the woods and
    hills ;
Moosehillock's mountain range, and Kear-
    sarge
Lifting his granite forehead to the sun !

And we had rested underneath the oaks
Shadowing the bank, whose grassy spires
    are shaken
By the perpetual beating of the falls
Of the wild Ammonoosuc. We had tracked
The winding Pemigewasset, overhung
By beechen shadows, whitening down its
    rocks,
Or lazily gliding through its intervals,
From waving rye-fields sending up the
    gleam
Of sunlit waters. We had seen the moon
Rising behind Umbagog's eastern pines,
Like a great Indian camp-fire ; and its
    beams

At midnight spanning with a bridge of
silver
The Merrimac by Uncanoonuc's falls.

There were five souls of us whom travel's
chance
Had thrown together in these wild north
hills :
A city lawyer, for a month escaping
From his dull office, where the weary eye
Saw only hot brick walls and close thronged
streets ;
Briefless as yet, but with an eye to see
Life's sunniest side, and with a heart to
take
Its chances all as godsends ; and his brother,
Pale from long pulpit studies, yet retaining
The warmth and freshness of a genial heart,
Whose mirror of the beautiful and true,
In Man and Nature, was as yet undimmed
By dust of theologic strife, or breath
Of sect, or cobwebs of scholastic lore ;
Like a clear crystal calm of water, taking
The hue and image of o'erleaning flowers,
Sweet human faces, white clouds of the
noon,
Slant starlight glimpses through the dewy
leaves,
And tenderest moonrise. 'T was, in truth,
a study,
To mark his spirit, alternating between
A decent and professional gravity
And an irreverent mirthfulness, which often
Laughed in the face of his divinity,
Plucked off the sacred ephod, quite un-
shrined
The oracle, and for the pattern priest
Left us the man. A shrewd, sagacious
merchant,
To whom the soiled sheet found in Craw-
ford's inn,
Giving the latest news of city stocks
And sales of cotton, had a deeper meaning
Than the great presence of the awful
mountains
Glorified by the sunset ; and his daughter,
A delicate flower on whom had blown too
long
Those evil winds, which, sweeping from
the ice
And winnowing the fogs of Labrador,
Shed their cold blight round Massachusetts
Bay,
With the same breath which stirs Spring's
opening leaves

And lifts her half-formed flower-bell on its
stem,
Poisoning our seaside atmosphere.

It chanced
That as we turned upon our homeward
way,
A drear northeastern storm came howling
up
The valley of the Saco ; and that girl
Who had stood with us upon Mount Wash-
ington,
Her brown locks ruffled by the wind which
whirled
In gusts around its sharp, cold pinnacle,
Who had joined our gay trout-fishing in the
streams
Which lave that giant's feet ; whose laugh
was heard
Like a bird's carol on the sunrise breeze
Which swelled our sail amidst the lake's
green islands,
Shrank from its harsh, chill breath, and
visibly drooped
Like a flower in the frost. So, in that
quiet inn
Which looks from Conway on the moun-
tains piled
Heavily against the horizon of the north,
Like summer thunder-clouds, we made our
home :
And while the mist hung over dripping
hills,
And the cold wind-driven rain-drops all
day long
Beat their sad music upon roof and pane,
We strove to cheer our gentle invalid.

The lawyer in the pauses of the storm
Went angling down the Saco, and, returning,
Recounted his adventures and mishaps ;
Gave us the history of his scaly clients,
Mingling with ludicrous yet apt citations
Of barbarous law Latin, passages
From Izaak Walton's Angler, sweet and
fresh
As the flower-skirted streams of Stafford-
shire,
Where, under aged trees, the southwest
wind
Of soft June mornings fanned the thin,
white hair
Of the sage fisher. And, if truth be told,
Our youthful candidate forsook his ser-
mons,

His commentaries, articles and creeds,
For the fair page of human loveliness,
The missal of young hearts, whose sacred
    text
Is music, its illumining, sweet smiles.
He sang the songs she loved ; and in his
    low,
Deep, earnest voice, recited many a page
Of poetry, the holiest, tenderest lines
Of the sad bard of Olney, the sweet songs,
Simple and beautiful as Truth and Nature,
Of him whose whitened locks on Rydal
    Mount
Are lifted yet by morning breezes blowing
From the green hills, immortal in his lays.
And for myself, obedient to her wish,
I searched our landlord's proffered library :
A well-thumbed Bunyan, with its nice
    wood pictures
Of scaly fiends and angels not unlike them ;
Watts' unmelodious psalms ; Astrology's
Last home, a musty pile of almanacs,
And an old chronicle of border wars
And Indian history. And, as I read
A story of the marriage of the Chief
Of Saugus to the dusky Weetamoo,
Daughter of Passaconaway, who dwelt
In the old time upon the Merrimac,
Our fair one, in the playful exercise
Of her prerogative, — the right divine
Of youth and beauty, — bade us versify
The legend, and with ready pencil sketched
Its plan and outlines, laughingly assigning
To each his part, and barring our excuses
With absolute will. So, like the cavaliers
Whose voices still are heard in the Romance
Of silver-tongued Boccaccio, on the banks
Of Arno, with soft tales of love beguiling
The ear of languid beauty, plague-exiled
From stately Florence, we rehearsed our
    rhymes
To their fair auditor, and shared by turns
Her kind approval and her playful cen-
    sure.

It may be that these fragments owe alone
To the fair setting of their circum-
    stances, —
The associations of time, scene, and audi-
    ence, —
Their place amid the pictures which fill up
The chambers of my memory. Yet I trust
That some, who sigh, while wandering in
    thought,
Pilgrims of Romance o'er the olden world,

That our broad land, — our sea-like lakes
    and mountains
Piled to the clouds, our rivers overhung
By forests which have known no other
    change
For ages than the budding and the fall
Of leaves, our valleys lovelier than those
Which the old poets sang of, — should but
    figure
On the apocryphal chart of speculation
As pastures, wood-lots, mill-sites, with the
    privileges,
Rights, and appurtenances, which make up
A Yankee Paradise, unsung, unknown,
To beautiful tradition ; even their names,
Whose melody yet lingers like the last
Vibration of the red man's requiem,
Exchanged for syllables significant,
Of cotton-mill and rail-car, will look kindly
Upon this effort to call up the ghost
Of our dim Past, and listen with pleased ear
To the responses of the questioned Shade.

I. THE MERRIMAC

O child of that white-crested mountain
    whose springs
Gush forth in the shade of the cliff-eagle's
    wings,
Down whose slopes to the lowlands thy
    wild waters shine,
Leaping gray walls of rock, flashing
    through the dwarf pine ;

From that cloud-curtained cradle so cold
    and so lone,
From the arms of that wintry-locked mother
    of stone,
By hills hung with forests, through vales
    wide and free,
Thy mountain - born brightness glanced
    down to the sea !

No bridge arched thy waters save that
    where the trees
Stretched their long arms above thee and
    kissed in the breeze :
No sound save the lapse of the waves on
    thy shores,
The plunging of otters, the light dip of oars.

Green-tufted, oak-shaded, by Amoskeag's
    fall
Thy twin Uncanoonucs rose stately and tall,

Thy Nashua meadows lay green and un-
  shorn,
And the hills of Pentucket were tasselled
  with corn.

But thy Pennacook valley was fairer than
  these,
And greener its grasses and taller its trees,
Ere the sound of an axe in the forest had
  rung,
Or the mower his scythe in the meadows
  had swung.

In their sheltered repose looking out from
  the wood
The bark-builded wigwams of Pennacook
  stood ;
There glided the corn-dance, the council-
  fire shone,
And against the red war-post the hatchet
  was thrown.

There the old smoked in silence their pipes,
  and the young
To the pike and the white-perch their baited
  lines flung ;
There the boy shaped his arrows, and there
  the shy maid
Wove her many-hued baskets and bright
  wampum braid.

O Stream of the Mountains ! if answer of
  thine
Could rise from thy waters to question of
  mine,
Methinks through the din of thy thronged
  banks a moan
Of sorrow would swell for the days which
  have gone.

Not for thee the dull jar of the loom and
  the wheel,
The gliding of shuttles, the ringing of
  steel ;
But that old voice of waters, of bird and of
  breeze,
The dip of the wild-fowl, the rustling of
  trees !

II. THE BASHABA

Lift we the twilight curtains of the Past,
  And, turning from familiar sight and
    sound,

Sadly and full of reverence let us cast
  A glance upon Tradition's shadowy
    ground,
Led by the few pale lights which, glimmer-
    ing round
  That dim, strange land of Eld, seem
    dying fast ;
And that which history gives not to the eye,
The faded coloring of Time's tapestry,
Let Fancy, with her dream-dipped brush,
  supply.

Roof of bark and walls of pine,
Through whose chinks the sunbeams
  shine,
Tracing many a golden line
  On the ample floor within ;
Where, upon that earth-floor stark,
Lay the gaudy mats of bark,
With the bear's hide, rough and dark,
  And the red-deer's skin.

Window-tracery, small and slight,
Woven of the willow white,
Lent a dimly checkered light ;
  And the night-stars glimmered down,
Where the lodge-fire's heavy smoke,
Slowly through an opening broke,
In the low roof, ribbed with oak,
  Sheathed with hemlock brown.

Gloomed behind the changeless shade
By the solemn pine-wood made ;
Through the rugged palisade,
  In the open foreground planted,
Glimpses came of rowers rowing,
Stir of leaves and wild-flowers blowing,
Steel-like gleams of water flowing,
  In the sunlight slanted.

Here the mighty Bashaba
Held his long-unquestioned sway,
From the White Hills, far away,
  To the great sea's sounding shore ;
Chief of chiefs, his regal word
All the river Sachems heard,
At his call the war-dance stirred,
  Or was still once more.

There his spoils of chase and war,
Jaw of wolf and black bear's paw,
Panther's skin and eagle's claw,
  Lay beside his axe and bow ;
And, adown the roof-pole hung,
Loosely on a snake-skin strung,

In the smoke his scalp-locks swung
　　Grimly to and fro.

Nightly down the river going,
Swifter was the hunter's rowing,
When he saw that lodge-fire glowing
　　O'er the waters still and red ;
And the squaw's dark eye burned brighter,
And she drew her blanket tighter,
As, with quicker step and lighter,
　　From that door she fled.

For that chief had magic skill,
And a Panisee's dark will,
Over powers of good and ill,
　　Powers which bless and powers which
　　　　ban ;
Wizard lord of Pennacook,
Chiefs upon their war-path shook,
When they met the steady look
　　Of that wise dark man.

Tales of him the gray squaw told,
When the winter night-wind cold
Pierced her blanket's thickest fold,
　　And her fire burned low and small,
Till the very child abed,
Drew its bear-skin over head,
Shrinking from the pale lights shed
　　On the trembling wall.

All the subtle spirits hiding
Under earth or wave, abiding
In the caverned rock, or riding
　　Misty clouds or morning breeze ;
Every dark intelligence,
Secret soul, and influence
Of all things which outward sense
　　Feels, or hears, or sees, —

These the wizard's skill confessed,
At his bidding banned or blessed,
Stormful woke or lulled to rest
　　Wind and cloud, and fire and flood ;
Burned for him the drifted snow,
Bade through ice fresh lilies blow,
And the leaves of summer grow
　　Over winter's wood !

Not untrue that tale of old !
Now, as then, the wise and bold
All the powers of Nature hold
　　Subject to their kingly will ;
From the wondering crowds ashore,
Treading life's wild waters o'er,

As upon a marble floor,
　　Moves the strong man still.

Still, to such, life's elements
With their sterner laws dispense,
And the chain of consequence
　　Broken in their pathway lies ;
Time and change their vassals making,
Flowers from icy pillows waking,
Tresses of the sunrise shaking
　　Over midnight skies.

Still, to th' earnest soul, the sun
Rests on towered Gibeon,
And the moon of Ajalon
　　Lights the battle-grounds of life ;
To his aid the strong reverses
Hidden powers and giant forces,
And the high stars, in their courses,
　　Mingle in his strife !

III. THE DAUGHTER

The soot-black brows of men, the yell
　　Of women thronging round the bed,
The tinkling charm of ring and shell,
　　The Powah whispering o'er the dead !
All these the Sachem's home had known,
　　When, on her journey long and wild
To the dim World of Souls, alone,
In her young beauty passed the mother of
　　his child.

Three bow-shots from the Sachem's
　　dwelling
They laid her in the walnut shade,
Where a green hillock gently swelling
　　Her fitting mound of burial made.
There trailed the vine in summer hours,
　　The tree-perched squirrel dropped his
　　shell, —
On velvet moss and pale-hued flowers,
Woven with leaf and spray, the softened
　　sunshine fell !

The Indian's heart is hard and cold,
　　It closes darkly o'er its care,
And formed in Nature's sternest mould,
　　Is slow to feel, and strong to bear.
The war-paint on the Sachem's face,
　　Unwet with tears, shone fierce and red,
And still, in battle or in chase,
Dry leaf and snow-rime crisped beneath his
　　foremost tread.

Yet when her name was heard no more,
　And when the robe her mother gave,
And small, light moccasin she wore,
　Had slowly wasted on her grave,
Unmarked of him the dark maids sped
　Their sunset dance and moonlit play ;
No other shared his lonely bed,
No other fair young head upon his bosom
　　lay.

A lone, stern man.　Yet, as sometimes
　The tempest-smitten tree receives
From one small root the sap which climbs
　Its topmost spray and crowning leaves,
So from his child the Sachem drew
　A life of Love and Hope, and felt
His cold and rugged nature through
　The softness and the warmth of her young
　　being melt.

A laugh which in the woodland rang
　Bemocking April's gladdest bird, —
A light and graceful form which sprang
　To meet him when his step was
　　heard, —
Eyes by his lodge-fire flashing dark,
　Small fingers stringing bead and shell
Or weaving mats of bright-hued bark, —
With these the household-god had graced
　his wigwam well.

Child of the forest ! strong and free,
　Slight-robed, with loosely flowing hair,
She swam the lake or climbed the tree,
　Or struck the flying bird in air.
O'er the heaped drifts of winter's moon
　Her snow-shoes tracked the hunter's
　　way ;
And dazzling in the summer noon
The blade of her light oar threw off its
　shower of spray !

Unknown to her the rigid rule,
　The dull restraint, the chiding frown,
The weary torture of the school,
　The taming of wild nature down.
Her only lore, the legends told
　Around the hunter's fire at night ;
Stars rose and set, and seasons rolled,
Flowers bloomed and snow-flakes fell, un-
　questioned in her sight.

Unknown to her the subtle skill
　With which the artist-eye can trace
In rock and tree and lake and hill

The outlines of divinest grace ;
Unknown the fine soul's keen unrest,
　Which sees, admires, yet yearns alway ;
Too closely on her mother's breast
To note her smiles of love the child of Na-
　ture lay !

It is enough for such to be
　Of common, natural things a part,
To feel, with bird and stream and tree,
　The pulses of the same great heart ;
But we, from Nature long exiled,
　In our cold homes of Art and Thought
Grieve like the stranger-tended child,
Which seeks its mother's arms, and sees
　but feels them not.

The garden rose may richly bloom
　In cultured soil and genial air,
To cloud the light of Fashion's room
　Or droop in Beauty's midnight hair ;
In lonelier grace, to sun and dew
　The sweetbrier on the hillside shows
Its single leaf and fainter hue,
Untrained and wildly free, yet still a sister
　rose !

Thus o'er the heart of Weetamoo
　Their mingling shades of joy and ill
The instincts of her nature threw ;
　The savage was a woman still.
Midst outlines dim of maiden schemes,
　Heart-colored prophecies of life,
Rose on the ground of her young dreams
The light of a new home, the lover and the
　wife.

IV. THE WEDDING

Cool and dark fell the autumn night,
But the Bashaba's wigwam glowed with
　light,
For down from its roof, by green withes
　hung,
Flaring and smoking the pine-knots swung.

And along the river great wood-fires
Shot into the night their long, red spires,
Showing behind the tall, dark wood,
Flashing before on the sweeping flood.

In the changeful wind, with shimmer and
　shade,
Now high, now low, that firelight played,

On tree-leaves wet with evening dews,
On gliding water and still canoes.

The trapper that night on Turee's brook,
And the weary fisher on Contoocook,
Saw over the marshes, and through the pine,
And down on the river, the dance-lights
    shine.

For the Saugus Sachem had come to woo
The Bashaba's daughter Weetamoo,
And laid at her father's feet that night
His softest furs and wampum white.

From the Crystal Hills to the far southeast
The river Sagamores came to the feast ;
And chiefs whose homes the sea-winds shook
Sat down on the mats of Pennacook.

They came from Sunapee's shore of rock,
From the snowy sources of Snooganock,
And from rough Coös whose thick woods
    shake
Their pine-cones in Umbagog Lake.

From Ammonoosuc's mountain pass,
Wild as his home, came Chepewass ;
And the Keenomps of the hills which throw
Their shade on the Smile of Manito.

With pipes of peace and bows unstrung,
Glowing with paint came old and young,
In wampum and furs and feathers arrayed,
To the dance and feast the Bashaba made.

Bird of the air and beast of the field,
All which the woods and the waters yield,
On dishes of birch and hemlock piled,
Garnished and graced that banquet wild.

Steaks of the brown bear fat and large
From the rocky slopes of the Kearsarge ;
Delicate trout from Babboosuck brook,
And salmon speared in the Contoocook ;

Squirrels which fed where nuts fell thick
In the gravelly bed of the Otternic ;
And small wild-hens in reed-snares caught
From the banks of Sondagardee brought ;

Pike and perch from the Suncook taken,
Nuts from the trees of the Black Hills
    shaken,
Cranberries picked in the Squamscot bog,
And grapes from the vines of Piscataquog :

And, drawn from that great stone vase
    which stands
In the river scooped by a spirit's hands,
Garnished with spoons of shell and horn,
Stood the birchen dishes of smoking corn.

Thus bird of the air and beast of the field,
All which the woods and the waters yield,
Furnished in that olden day
The bridal feast of the Bashaba.

And merrily when that feast was done
On the fire-lit green the dance begun,
With squaws' shrill stave, and deeper hum
Of old men beating the Indian drum.

Painted and plumed, with scalp-locks flow-
    ing,
And red arms tossing and black eyes glow-
    ing,
Now in the light and now in the shade
Around the fires the dancers played.

The step was quicker, the song more shrill,
And the beat of the small drums louder still
Whenever within the circle drew
The Saugus Sachem and Weetamoo.

The moons of forty winters had shed
Their snow upon that chieftain's head,
And toil and care and battle's chance
Had seamed his hard, dark countenance.

A fawn beside the bison grim, —
Why turns the bride's fond eye on him,
In whose cold look is naught beside
The triumph of a sullen pride ?

Ask why the graceful grape entwines
The rough oak with her arm of vines ;
And why the gray rock's rugged cheek
The soft lips of the mosses seek :

Why, with wise instinct, Nature seems
To harmonize her wide extremes,
Linking the stronger with the weak,
The haughty with the soft and meek !

V. THE NEW HOME

A wild and broken landscape, spiked with
    firs,
  Roughening the bleak horizon's northern
    edge ;

Steep, cavernous hillsides, where black hem-
    lock spurs
And sharp, gray splinters of the wind-
    swept ledge
Pierced the thin-glazed ice, or bristling rose,
Where the cold rim of the sky sunk down
    upon the snows.

And eastward cold, wide marshes stretched
    away,
    Dull, dreary flats without a bush or tree,
O'er-crossed by icy creeks, where twice a
    day
    Gurgled the waters of the moon-struck
      sea ;
And faint with distance came the stifled
    roar,
The melancholy lapse of waves on that low
    shore.

No cheerful village with its mingling
    smokes,
    No laugh of children wrestling in the
      snow,
No camp-fire blazing through the hillside
    oaks,
    No fishers kneeling on the ice below ;
Yet midst all desolate things of sound and
    view,
Through the long winter moons smiled
    dark-eyed Weetamoo.

Her heart had found a home ; and freshly
    all
    Its beautiful affections overgrew
Their rugged prop. As o'er some granite
    wall
    Soft vine-leaves open to the moistening
      dew
And warm bright sun, the love of that
    young wife
Found on a hard cold breast the dew and
    warmth of life.

The steep, bleak hills, the melancholy
    shore,
    The long, dead level of the marsh be-
      tween,
A coloring of unreal beauty wore
    Through the soft golden mist of young
    love seen.
For o'er those hills and from that dreary
    plain,
Nightly she welcomed home her hunter
    chief again.

No warmth of heart, no passionate burst of
    feeling
    Repaid her welcoming smile and parting
    kiss,
No fond and playful dalliance half con-
    cealing,
    Under the guise of mirth, its tenderness ;
But, in their stead, the warrior's settled
    pride,
And vanity's pleased smile with homage
    satisfied.

Enough for Weetamoo, that she alone
    Sat on his mat and slumbered at his side ;
That he whose fame to her young ear had
    flown
    Now looked upon her proudly as his
    bride ;
That he whose name the Mohawk trembling
    heard
Vouchsafed to her at times a kindly look
    or word.

For she had learned the maxims of her
    race,
    Which teach the woman to become a
    slave,
And feel herself the pardonless disgrace
    Of love's fond weakness in the wise and
    brave, —
The scandal and the shame which they
    incur,
Who give to woman all which man re-
    quires of her.

So passed the winter moons. The sun at
    last
    Broke link by link the frost chain of the
    rills,
And the warm breathings of the southwest
    passed
    Over the hoar rime of the Saugus hills ;
The gray and desolate marsh grew green
    once more,
And the birch-tree's tremulous shade fell
    round the Sachem's door.

Then from far Pennacook swift runners
    came,
    With gift and greeting for the Saugus
    chief ;
Beseeching him in the great Sachem's
    name,
    That, with the coming of the flower and
    leaf,

The song of birds, the warm breeze and
   the rain,
Young Weetamoo might greet her lonely
   sire again.

And Winnepurkit called his chiefs together,
   And a grave council in his wigwam met,
Solemn and brief in words, considering
   whether
   The rigid rules of forest etiquette
Permitted Weetamoo once more to look
Upon her father's face and green-banked
   Pennacook.

With interludes of pipe-smoke and strong
   water,
   The forest sages pondered, and at length
Concluded in a body to escort her
   Up to her father's home of pride and
     strength,
Impressing thus on Pennacook a sense
Of Winnepurkit's power and regal conse-
   quence.

So through old woods which Aukeetamit's
   hand
   A soft and many-shaded greenness lent,
Over high breezy hills, and meadow land
   Yellow with flowers, the wild procession
     went,
Till, rolling down its wooded banks between,
A broad, clear, mountain stream, the Merri-
   mac was seen.

The hunter leaning on his bow undrawn,
   The fisher lounging on the pebbled shores,
Squaws in the clearing dropping the seed-
   corn,
   Young children peering through the
     wigwam doors,
Saw with delight, surrounded by her train
Of painted Saugus braves, their Weetamoo
   again.

VI. AT PENNACOOK

The hills are dearest which our childish
   feet
Have climbed the earliest ; and the streams
   most sweet
Are ever those at which our young lips
   drank
Stooped to their waters o'er the grassy
   bank.

Midst the cold dreary sea-watch, Home's
   hearth-light
Shines round the helmsman plunging
   through the night ;
And still, with inward eye, the traveller
   sees
In close, dark, stranger streets his native
   trees.

The home-sick dreamer's brow is nightly
   fanned
By breezes whispering of his native land,
And on the stranger's dim and dying eye
The soft, sweet pictures of his childhood
   lie.

Joy then for Weetamoo, to sit once more
A child upon her father's wigwam floor !
Once more with her old fondness to beguile
From his cold eye the strange light of a
   smile.

The long, bright days of summer swiftly
   passed,
The dry leaves whirled in autumn's rising
   blast,
And evening cloud and whitening sunrise
   rime
Told of the coming of the winter-time.

But vainly looked, the while, young Weeta-
   moo
Down the dark river for her chief's canoe ;
No dusky messenger from Saugus brought
The grateful tidings which the young wife
   sought.

At length a runner from her father sent,
To Winnepurkit's sea-cooled wigwam went ;
"Eagle of Saugus, — in the woods the dove
Mourns for the shelter of thy wings of
   love."

But the dark chief of Saugus turned aside
In the grim anger of hard-hearted pride ;
"I bore her as became a chieftain's
   daughter,
Up to her home beside the gliding water.

"If now no more a mat for her is found
Of all which line her father's wigwam
   round,
Let Pennacook call out his warrior train,
And send her back with wampum gifts
   again."

Came a troop with broadswords swinging,
Bits and bridles sharply ringing,
    Loose and free and froward ;
Quoth the foremost, " Ride him down !
Push him ! prick him ! through the town
    Drive the Quaker coward ! "

But from out the thickening crowd
Cried a sudden voice and loud :
    " Barclay ! Ho ! a Barclay ! "
And the old man at his side
Saw a comrade, battle tried,
    Scarred and sunburned darkly ;

Who with ready weapon bare,
Fronting to the troopers there,
    Cried aloud : " God save us,
Call ye coward him who stood
Ankle deep in Lützen's blood,
    With the brave Gustavus ? "

" Nay, I do not need thy sword,
Comrade mine," said Ury's lord ;
    " Put it up, I pray thee :
Passive to His holy will,
Trust I in my Master still,
    Even though He slay me.

" Pledges of thy love and faith,
Proved on many a field of death,
    Not by me are needed."
Marvelled much that henchman bold,
That his laird, so stout of old,
    Now so meekly pleaded.

" Woe 's the day ! " he sadly said,
With a slowly shaking head,
    And a look of pity ;
" Ury's honest lord reviled,
Mock of knave and sport of child,
    In his own good city !

" Speak the word, and, master mine,
As we charged on Tilly's line,
    And his Walloon lancers,
Smiting through their midst we 'll teach
Civil look and decent speech
    To these boyish prancers ! "

" Marvel not, mine ancient friend,
Like beginning, like the end,"
    Quoth the Laird of Ury ;
" Is the sinful servant more
Than his gracious Lord who bore
    Bonds and stripes in Jewry ?

" Give me joy that in His name
I can bear, with patient frame,
    All these vain ones offer ;
While for them He suffereth long,
Shall I answer wrong with wrong,
    Scoffing with the scoffer ?

" Happier I, with loss of all,
Hunted, outlawed, held in thrall,
    With few friends to greet me,
Than when reeve and squire were seen,
Riding out from Aberdeen,
    With bared heads to meet me.

" When each goodwife, o'er and o'er,
Blessed me as I passed her door ;
    And the snooded daughter,
Through her casement glancing down,
Smiled on him who bore renown
    From red fields of slaughter.

" Hard to feel the stranger's scoff,
Hard the old friend's falling off,
    Hard to learn forgiving ;
But the Lord His own rewards,
And His love with theirs accords,
    Warm and fresh and living.

" Through this dark and stormy night
Faith beholds a feeble light
    Up the blackness streaking ;
Knowing God's own time is best,
In a patient hope I rest
    For the full day-breaking ! "

So the Laird of Ury said,
Turning slow his horse's head
    Towards the Tolbooth prison,
Where, through iron gates, he heard
Poor disciples of the Word
    Preach of Christ arisen !

Not in vain, Confessor old,
Unto us the tale is told
    Of thy day of trial ;
Every age on him who strays
From its broad and beaten ways
    Pours its seven-fold vial.

Happy he whose inward ear
Angel comfortings can hear,
    O'er the rabble's laughter ;
And while Hatred's fagots burn,
Glimpses through the smoke discern
    Of the good hereafter.

Knowing this, that never yet
Share of Truth was vainly set
  In the world's wide fallow ;
After hands shall sow the seed,
After hands from hill and mead
  Reap the harvests yellow.

Thus, with somewhat of the Seer,
Must the moral pioneer
  From the Future borrow ;
Clothe the waste with dreams of grain,
And, on midnight's sky of rain,
  Paint the golden morrow !

THE ANGELS OF BUENA VISTA

A letter-writer from Mexico during the Mexican war, when detailing some of the incidents at the terrible fight of Buena Vista, mentioned that Mexican women were seen hovering near the field of death, for the purpose of giving aid and succor to the wounded. One poor woman was found surrounded by the maimed and suffering of both armies, ministering to the wants of Americans as well as Mexicans with impartial tenderness.

SPEAK and tell us, our Ximena, looking
  northward far away,
O'er the camp of the invaders, o'er the Mexican array,
Who is losing ? who is winning ? are they
  far or come they near ?
Look abroad, and tell us, sister, whither
  rolls the storm we hear.

" Down the hills of Angostura still the storm
  of battle rolls ;
Blood is flowing, men are dying ; God have
  mercy on their souls ! "
Who is losing ? who is winning ?   " Over
  hill and over plain,
I see but smoke of cannon clouding through
  the mountain rain. "

Holy Mother ! keep our brothers ! Look,
  Ximena, look once more.
" Still I see the fearful whirlwind rolling
  darkly as before,
Bearing on, in strange confusion, friend and
  foeman, foot and horse,
Like some wild and troubled torrent sweeping down its mountain course."

Look forth once more, Ximena ! " Ah ! the
  smoke has rolled away ;

And I see the Northern rifles gleaming down
  the ranks of gray.
Hark ! that sudden blast of bugles ! there
  the troop of Minon wheels ;
There the Northern horses thunder, with
  the cannon at their heels.

" Jesu, pity ! how it thickens ! now retreat
  and now advance !
Right against the blazing cannon shivers
  Puebla's charging lance !
Down they go, the brave young riders ;
  horse and foot together fall ;
Like a ploughshare in the fallow, through
  them ploughs the Northern ball."

Nearer came the storm and nearer, rolling
  fast and frightful on !
Speak, Ximena, speak and tell us, who has
  lost, and who has won ?
" Alas ! alas ! I know not ; friend and foe
  together fall,
O'er the dying rush the living : pray, my
  sisters, for them all !

" Lo ! the wind the smoke is lifting.
  Blessed Mother, save my brain !
I can see the wounded crawling slowly out
  from heaps of slain.
Now they stagger, blind and bleeding ; now
  they fall, and strive to rise ;
Hasten, sisters, haste and save them, lest
  they die before our eyes !

" O my heart's love ! O my dear one ! lay
  thy poor head on my knee ;
Dost thou know the lips that kiss thee ?
  Canst thou hear me ? canst thou
  see ?
O my husband, brave and gentle ! O my
  Bernal, look once more
On the blessed cross before thee ! Mercy !
  mercy ! all is o'er ! "

Dry thy tears, my poor Ximena ; lay thy
  dear one down to rest ;
Let his hands be meekly folded, lay the cross
  upon his breast ;
Let his dirge be sung hereafter, and his
  funeral masses said ;
To-day, thou poor bereaved one, the living
  ask thy aid.

Close beside her, faintly moaning, fair and
  young, a soldier lay,

Torn with shot and pierced with lances,
  bleeding slow his life away ;
But, as tenderly before him the lorn Ximena
  knelt,
She saw the Northern eagle shining on his
  pistol-belt.

With a stifled cry of horror straight she
  turned away her head ;
With a sad and bitter feeling looked she
  back upon her dead ;
But she heard the youth's low moaning, and
  his struggling breath of pain,
And she raised the cooling water to his
  parching lips again.

Whispered low the dying soldier, pressed
  her hand and faintly smiled ;
Was that pitying face his mother's ? did
  she watch beside her child ?
All his stranger words with meaning her
  woman's heart supplied ;
With her kiss upon his forehead, "Mother !"
  murmured he, and died !

" A bitter curse upon them, poor boy, who
  led thee forth,
From some gentle, sad-eyed mother, weep-
  ing, lonely, in the North ! "
Spake the mournful Mexic woman, as she
  laid him with her dead,
And turned to soothe the living, and bind
  the wounds which bled.

Look forth once more, Ximena !   " Like a
  cloud before the wind
Rolls the battle down the mountains, leav-
  ing blood and death behind ;
Ah ! they plead in vain for mercy ; in the
  dust the wounded strive ;
Hide your faces, holy angels !   O thou
  Christ of God, forgive ! "

Sink, O Night, among thy mountains ! let
  the cool, gray shadows fall ;
Dying brothers, fighting demons, drop thy
  curtain over all !
Through the thickening winter twilight,
  wide apart the battle rolled,
In its sheath the sabre rested, and the can-
  non's lips grew cold.

But the noble Mexic women still their holy
  task pursued,
Through that long, dark night of sorrow,
  worn and faint and lacking food.

Over weak and suffering brothers, with a
  tender care they hung,
And the dying foeman blessed them in a
  strange and Northern tongue.

Not wholly lost, O Father ! is this evil
  world of ours ;
Upward, through its blood and ashes, spring
  afresh the Eden flowers ;
From its smoking hell of battle, Love and
  Pity send their prayer,
And still thy white-winged angels hover
  dimly in our air !

THE LEGEND OF ST. MARK

" This legend [to which my attention was
called by my friend Charles Sumner], is the
subject of a celebrated picture by Tintoretto,
of which Mr. Rogers possesses the original
sketch.   The slave lies on the ground, amid a
crowd of spectators, who look on, animated by
all the various emotions of sympathy, rage,
terror ; a woman, in front, with a child in her
arms, has always been admired for the lifelike
vivacity of her attitude and expression.   The
executioner holds up the broken implements ;
St. Mark, with a headlong movement, seems to
rush down from heaven in haste to save his
worshipper.   The dramatic grouping in this
picture is wonderful ; the coloring, in its gor-
geous depth and harmony, is, in Mr. Rogers's
sketch, finer than in the picture." — MRS.
JAMESON's Sacred and Legendary Art, i. 154.

THE day is closing dark and cold,
  With roaring blast and sleety showers ;
And through the dusk the lilacs wear
  The bloom of snow, instead of flowers.

I turn me from the gloom without,
  To ponder o'er a tale of old ;
A legend of the age of Faith,
  By dreaming monk or abbess told.

On Tintoretto's canvas lives
  That fancy of a loving heart,
In graceful lines and shapes of power,
  And hues immortal as his art.

In Provence (so the story runs)
  There lived a lord, to whom, as slave,
A peasant-boy of tender years
  The chance of trade or conquest gave.

Forth-looking from the castle tower,
  Beyond the hills with almonds dark,

The straining eye could scarce discern
  The chapel of the good St. Mark.

And there, when bitter word or fare
  The service of the youth repaid,
By stealth, before that holy shrine,
  For grace to bear his wrong, he prayed.

The steed stamped at the castle gate,
  The boar-hunt sounded on the hill ;
Why stayed the Baron from the chase,
  With looks so stern, and words so ill ?

" Go, bind yon slave ! and let him learn,
  By scath of fire and strain of cord,
How ill they speed who give dead saints
  The homage due their living lord ! "

They bound him on the fearful rack,
  When, through the dungeon's vaulted
    dark,
He saw the light of shining robes,
  And knew the face of good St. Mark.

Then sank the iron rack apart,
  The cords released their cruel clasp,
The pincers, with their teeth of fire,
  Fell broken from the torturer's grasp.

And lo ! before the Youth and Saint,
  Barred door and wall of stone gave
    way;
And up from bondage and the night
  They passed to freedom and the day !

O dreaming monk ! thy tale is true ;
  O painter ! true thy pencil's art ;
In tones of hope and prophecy,
  Ye whisper to my listening heart !

Unheard no burdened heart's appeal
  Moans up to God's inclining ear ;
Unheeded by his tender eye,
  Falls to the earth no sufferer's tear.

For still the Lord alone is God !
  The pomp and power of tyrant man
Are scattered at his lightest breath,
  Like chaff before the winnower's fan.

Not always shall the slave uplift
  His heavy hands to Heaven in vain.
God's angel, like the good St. Mark,
  Comes shining down to break his
    chain !

O weary ones ! ye may not see
  Your helpers in their downward flight;
Nor hear the sound of silver wings
  Slow beating through the hush of night !

But not the less gray Dothan shone,
  With sunbright watchers bending low
That Fear's dim eye beheld alone
  The spear-heads of the Syrian foe.

There are, who, like the Seer of old,
  Can see the helpers God has sent,
And how life's rugged mountain-side
  Is white with many an angel tent !

They hear the heralds whom our Lord
  Sends down his pathway to prepare ;
And light, from others hidden, shines
  On their high place of faith and prayer.

Let such, for earth's despairing ones,
  Hopeless, yet longing to be free,
Breathe once again the Prophet's prayer :
  "Lord, ope their eyes, that they may
    see ! "

KATHLEEN

This ballad was originally published in my
prose work, *Leaves from Margaret Smith's Jour-
nal*, as the song of a wandering Milesian school-
master. In the seventeenth century, slavery
in the New World was by no means confined to
the natives of Africa. Political offenders and
criminals were transported by the British gov-
ernment to the plantations of Barbadoes and
Virginia, where they were sold like cattle in the
market. Kidnapping of free and innocent
white persons was practised to a considerable
extent in the seaports of the United Kingdom.

O NORAH, lay your basket down,
  And rest your weary hand,
And come and hear me sing a song
  Of our old Ireland.

There was a lord of Galaway,
  A mighty lord was he ;
And he did wed a second wife,
  A maid of low degree.

But he was old, and she was young,
  And so, in evil spite,
She baked the black bread for his kin,
  And fed her own with white.

She whipped the maids and starved the
    kern,
  And drove away the poor ;
" Ah, woe is me ! " the old lord said,
  " I rue my bargain sore ! "

This lord he had a daughter fair,
  Beloved of old and young,
And nightly round the shealing-fires
  Of her the gleeman sung.

" As sweet and good is young Kathleen
  As Eve before her fall ; "
So sang the harper at the fair,
  So harped he in the hall.

" Oh, come to me, my daughter dear !
  Come sit upon my knee,
For looking in your face, Kathleen,
  Your mother's own I see ! "

He smoothed and smoothed her hair
    away,
  He kissed her forehead fair ;
" It is my darling Mary's brow,
  It is my darling's hair ! "

Oh, then spake up the angry dame,
  " Get up, get up," quoth she,
" I 'll sell ye over Ireland,
  I 'll sell ye o'er the sea ! "

She clipped her glossy hair away,
  That none her rank might know,
She took away her gown of silk,
  And gave her one of tow,

And sent her down to Limerick town
  And to a seaman sold
This daughter of an Irish lord
  For ten good pounds in gold.

The lord he smote upon his breast,
  And tore his beard so gray;
But he was old, and she was young,
  And so she had her way.

Sure that same night the Banshee howled
  To fright the evil dame,
And fairy folks, who loved Kathleen,
  With funeral torches came.

She watched them glancing through the
    trees,
  And glimmering down the hill ;

They crept before the dead-vault door,
  And there they all stood still !

" Get up, old man ! the wake-lights shine ! '
  " Ye murthering witch," quoth he,
" So I 'm rid of your tongue, I little care
  If they shine for you or me."

" Oh, whoso brings my daughter back,
  My gold and land shall have ! "
Oh, then spake up his handsome page,
  " No gold nor land I crave !

" But give to me your daughter dear,
  Give sweet Kathleen to me,
Be she on sea or be she on land,
  I 'll bring her back to thee."

" My daughter is a lady born,
  And you of low degree,
But she shall be your bride the day
  You bring her back to me."

He sailëd east, he sailëd west,
  And far and long sailed he,
Until he came to Boston town,
  Across the great salt sea.

" Oh, have ye seen the young Kathleen,
  The flower of Ireland ?
Ye 'll know her by her eyes so blue,
  And by her snow-white hand ! "

Out spake an ancient man, " I know
  The maiden whom ye mean ;
I bought her of a Limerick man,
  And she is called Kathleen.

" No skill hath she in household work,
  Her hands are soft and white,
Yet well by loving looks and ways
  She doth her cost requite."

So up they walked through Boston town,
  And met a maiden fair,
A little basket on her arm
  So snowy-white and bare.

" Come hither, child, and say hast thou
  This young man ever seen ? "
They wept within each other's arms,
  The page and young Kathleen.

" Oh give to me this darling child,
  And take my purse of gold."

"Nay, not by me," her master said,
"Shall sweet Kathleen be sold.

"We loved her in the place of one
The Lord hath early ta'en ;
But, since her heart's in Ireland,
We give her back again!"

Oh, for that same the saints in heaven
For his poor soul shall pray,
And Mary Mother wash with tears
His heresies away.

Sure now they dwell in Ireland ;
As you go up Claremore
Ye 'll see their castle looking down
The pleasant Galway shore.

And the old lord's wife is dead and gone,
And a happy man is he,
For he sits beside his own Kathleen,
With her darling on his knee.

THE WELL OF LOCH MAREE

Pennant, in his *Voyage to the Hebrides*, describes the holy well of Loch Maree, the waters of which were supposed to effect a miraculous cure of melancholy, trouble, and insanity.

CALM on the breast of Loch Maree
A little isle reposes ;
A shadow woven of the oak
And willow o'er it closes.

Within, a Druid's mound is seen,
Set round with stony warders ;
A fountain, gushing through the turf,
Flows o'er its grassy borders.

And whoso bathes therein his brow,
With care or madness burning,
Feels once again his healthful thought
And sense of peace returning.

O restless heart and fevered brain,
Unquiet and unstable,
That holy well of Loch Maree
Is more than idle fable !

Life's changes vex, its discords stun,
Its glaring sunshine blindeth,
And blest is he who on his way
That fount of healing findeth !

The shadows of a humbled will
And contrite heart are o'er it ;
Go read its legend, "TRUST IN GOD,"
On Faith's white stones before it.

THE CHAPEL OF THE HERMITS

The incident upon which this poem is based is related in a note to Bernardin Henri Saint Pierre's *Etudes de la Nature*.

"We arrived at the habitation of the Hermits a little before they sat down to their table, and while they were still at church. J. J. Rousseau proposed to me to offer up our devotions. The hermits were reciting the Litanies of Providence, which are remarkably beautiful. After we had addressed our prayers to God, and the hermits were proceeding to the refectory, Rousseau said to me, with his heart overflowing, 'At this moment I experience what is said in the gospel: *Where two or three are gathered together in my name, there am I in the midst of them.* There is here a feeling of peace and happiness which penetrates the soul.' I said, 'If Fénelon had lived, you would have been a Catholic.' He exclaimed, with tears in his eyes, 'Oh, if Fénelon were alive, I would struggle to get into his service, even as a lackey!'"

In my sketch of Saint Pierre, it will be seen that I have somewhat antedated the period of his old age. At that time he was not probably more than fifty. In describing him, I have by no means exaggerated his own history of his mental condition at the period of the story. In the fragmentary Sequel to his *Studies of Nature*, he thus speaks of himself: "The ingratitude of those of whom I had deserved kindness, unexpected family misfortunes, the total loss of my small patrimony through enterprises solely undertaken for the benefit of my country, the debts under which I lay oppressed, the blasting of all my hopes, — these combined calamities made dreadful inroads upon my health and reason. . . . I found it impossible to continue in a room where there was company, especially if the doors were shut. I could not even cross an alley in a public garden, if several persons had got together in it. When alone, my malady subsided. I felt myself likewise at ease in places where I saw children only. At the sight of any one walking up to the place where I was, I felt my whole frame agitated, and retired. I often said to myself, 'My sole study has been to merit well of mankind; why do I fear them?'"

He attributes his improved health of mind and body to the counsels of his friend, J. J. Rousseau. "I renounced," says he, "my books.

I threw my eyes upon the works of nature,
which spake to all my senses a language which
neither time nor nations have it in their power
to alter. Thenceforth my histories and my
journals were the herbage of the fields and
meadows. My thoughts did not go forth pain-
fully after them, as in the case of human
systems; but their thoughts, under a thousand
engaging forms, quietly sought me. In these
I studied, without effort, the laws of that Uni-
versal Wisdom which had surrounded me from
the cradle, but on which heretofore I had be-
stowed little attention."

Speaking of Rousseau, he says: "I derived
inexpressible satisfaction from his society.
What I prized still more than his genius was
his probity. He was one of the few literary
characters, tried in the furnace of affliction, to
whom you could, with perfect security, confide
your most secret thoughts. . . . Even when he
deviated, and became the victim of himself or
of others, he could forget his own misery in
devotion to the welfare of mankind. He was
uniformly the advocate of the miserable.
There might be inscribed on his tomb these
affecting words from that Book of which he
carried always about him some select passages,
during the last years of his life: *His sins,
which are many, are forgiven, for he loved
much.*"

"I DO believe, and yet, in grief,
I pray for help to unbelief;
For needful strength aside to lay
The daily cumberings of my way.

"I 'm sick at heart of craft and cant,
Sick of the crazed enthusiast's rant,
Profession's smooth hypocrisies,
And creeds of iron, and lives of ease.

"I ponder o'er the sacred word,
I read the record of our Lord;
And, weak and troubled, envy them
Who touched His seamless garment's
    hem;

"Who saw the tears of love He wept
Above the grave where Lazarus slept;
And heard, amidst the shadows dim
Of Olivet, His evening hymn.

"How blessed the swineherd's low estate,
The beggar crouching at the gate,
The leper loathly and abhorred,
Whose eyes of flesh beheld the Lord!

"O sacred soil His sandals pressed!
Sweet fountains of His noonday rest!

O light and air of Palestine,
Impregnate with His life divine!

"Oh, bear me thither! Let me look
On Siloa's pool, and Kedron's brook;
Kneel at Gethsemane, and by
Gennesaret walk, before I die!

"Methinks this cold and northern night
Would melt before that Orient light;
And, wet by Hermon's dew and rain,
My childhood's faith revive again!"

So spake my friend, one autumn day,
Where the still river slid away
Beneath us, and above the brown
Red curtains of the woods shut down.

Then said I, — for I could not brook
The mute appealing of his look, —
"I too am weak, and faith is small,
And blindness happeneth unto all.

"Yet sometimes glimpses on my sight,
Through present wrong, the eternal right;
And, step by step, since time began,
I see the steady gain of man;

"That all of good the past hath had
Remains to make our own time glad,
Our common daily life divine,
And every land a Palestine.

"Thou weariest of thy present state;
What gain to thee time's holiest date?
The doubter now perchance had been
As High Priest or as Pilate then!

"What thought Chorazin's scribes? What
    faith
In Him had Nain and Nazareth?
Of the few followers whom He led
One sold Him, — all forsook and fled.

"O friend! we need nor rock nor sand,
Nor storied stream of Morning-Land;
The heavens are glassed in Merrimac, —
What more could Jordan render back?

"We lack but open eye and ear
To find the Orient's marvels here;
The still small voice in autumn's hush,
Yon maple wood the burning bush.

"For still the new transcends the old,
In signs and tokens manifold;

Slaves rise up men ; the olive waves,
With roots deep set in battle graves !

"Through the harsh noises of our day
A low, sweet prelude finds its way ;
Through clouds of doubt, and creeds of
    fear,
A light is breaking, calm and clear.

"That song of Love, now low and far,
Erelong shall swell from star to star !
That light, the breaking day, which tips
The golden-spired Apocalypse !"

Then, when my good friend shook his head,
And, sighing, sadly smiled, I said :
"Thou mind'st me of a story told
In rare Bernardin's leaves of gold."

And while the slanted sunbeams wove
The shadows of the frost-stained grove,
And, picturing all, the river ran
O'er cloud and wood, I thus began : —

In Mount Valerien's chestnut wood
The Chapel of the Hermits stood ;
And thither, at the close of day,
Came two old pilgrims, worn and gray.

One, whose impetuous youth defied
The storms of Baikal's wintry side,
And mused and dreamed where tropic day
Flamed o'er his lost Virginia's bay.

His simple tale of love and woe
All hearts had melted, high or low ; —
A blissful pain, a sweet distress,
Immortal in its tenderness.

Yet, while above his charmëd page
Beat quick the young heart of his age,
He walked amidst the crowd unknown,
A sorrowing old man, strange and lone.

A homeless, troubled age, — the gray
Pale setting of a weary day ;
Too dull his ear for voice of praise,
Too sadly worn his brow for bays.

Pride, lust of power and glory, slept ;
Yet still his heart its young dream kept,
And, wandering like the deluge-dove,
Still sought the resting-place of love.

And, mateless, childless, envied more
The peasant's welcome from his door
By smiling eyes at eventide,
Than kingly gifts or lettered pride.

Until, in place of wife and child,
All-pitying Nature on him smiled,
And gave to him the golden keys
To all her inmost sanctities.

Mild Druid of her wood-paths dim !
She laid her great heart bare to him,
Its loves and sweet accords ; — he saw
The beauty of her perfect law.

The language of her signs he knew,
What notes her cloudy clarion blew ;
The rhythm of autumn's forest dyes,
The hymn of sunset's painted skies.

And thus he seemed to hear the song
Which swept, of old, the stars along ;
And to his eyes the earth once more
Its fresh and primal beauty wore.

Who sought with him, from summer
    air,
And field and wood, a balm for care,
And bathed in light of sunset skies
His tortured nerves and weary eyes ?

His fame on all the winds had flown ;
His words had shaken crypt and throne ;
Like fire on camp and court and cell
They dropped, and kindled as they fell.

Beneath the pomps of state, below
The mitred juggler's masque and show,
A prophecy, a vague hope, ran
His burning thought from man to man.

For peace or rest too well he saw
The fraud of priests, the wrong of law,
And felt how hard, between the two,
Their breath of pain the millions drew.

A prophet-utterance, strong and wild,
The weakness of an unweaned child,
A sun-bright hope for human-kind,
And self-despair, in him combined.

He loathed the false, yet lived not true
To half the glorious truths he knew ;
The doubt, the discord, and the sin,
He mourned without, he felt within.

Untrod by him the path he showed,
Sweet pictures on his easel glowed
Of simple faith, and loves of home,
And virtue's golden days to come.

But weakness, shame, and folly made
The foil to all his pen portrayed ;
Still, where his dreamy splendors shone,
The shadow of himself was thrown.

Lord, what is man, whose thought, at times,
Up to Thy sevenfold brightness climbs,
While still his grosser instinct clings
To earth, like other creeping things !

So rich in words, in acts so mean ;
So high, so low ; chance-swung between
The foulness of the penal pit
And Truth's clear sky, millennium-lit !

Vain, pride of star-lent genius ! — vain,
Quick fancy and creative brain,
Unblest by prayerful sacrifice,
Absurdly great, or weakly wise !

Midst yearnings for a truer life,
Without were fears, within was strife ;
And still his wayward act denied
The perfect good for which he sighed.

The love he sent forth void returned ;
The fame that crowned him scorched and
        burned,
Burning, yet cold and drear and lone, —
A fire-mount in a frozen zone !

Like that the gray-haired sea-king passed,
Seen southward from his sleety mast,
About whose brows of changeless frost
A wreath of flame the wild winds tossed.

Far round the mournful beauty played
Of lambent light and purple shade,
Lost on the fixed and dumb despair
Of frozen earth and sea and air !

A man apart, unknown, unloved
By those whose wrongs his soul had moved,
He bore the ban of Church and State,
The good man's fear, the bigot's hate !

Forth from the city's noise and throng,
Its pomp and shame, its sin and wrong,
The twain that summer day had strayed
To Mount Valerien's chestnut shade.

To them the green fields and the wood
Lent something of their quietude,
And golden-tinted sunset seemed
Prophetical of all they dreamed.

The hermits from their simple cares
The bell was calling home to prayers,
And, listening to its sound, the twain
Seemed lapped in childhood's trust again.

Wide open stood the chapel door ;
A sweet old music, swelling o'er
Low prayerful murmurs, issued thence, —
The Litanies of Providence !

Then Rousseau spake : " Where two or
        three
In His name meet, He there will be ! "
And then, in silence, on their knees
They sank beneath the chestnut-trees.

As to the blind returning light,
As daybreak to the Arctic night,
Old faith revived ; the doubts of years
Dissolved in reverential tears.

That gush of feeling overpast,
" Ah me ! " Bernardin sighed at last,
" I would thy bitterest foes could see
Thy heart as it is seen of me !

" No church of God hast thou denied ;
Thou hast but spurned in scorn aside
A bare and hollow counterfeit,
Profaning the pure name of it !

" With dry dead moss and marish weeds
His fire the western herdsman feeds,
And greener from the ashen plain
The sweet spring grasses rise again.

" Nor thunder-peal nor mighty wind
Disturb the solid sky behind ;
And through the cloud the red bolt rends
The calm, still smile of Heaven descends !

" Thus through the world, like bolt and
        blast,
And scourging fire, thy words have passed.
Clouds break, — the steadfast heavens re-
        main ;
Weeds burn, — the ashes feed the grain !

" But whoso strives with wrong may find
Its touch pollute, its darkness blind ;

And learn, as latent fraud is shown
In others' faith, to doubt his own.

" With dream and falsehood, simple trust
And pious hope we tread in dust ;
Lost the calm faith in goodness, — lost
The baptism of the Pentecost !

" Alas ! — the blows for error meant
Too oft on truth itself are spent,
As through the false and vile and base
Looks forth her sad, rebuking face.

" Not ours the Theban's charmëd life ;
We come not scathless from the strife !
The Python's coil about us clings,
The trampled Hydra bites and stings !

" Meanwhile, the sport of seeming chance,
The plastic shapes of circumstance,
What might have been we fondly guess,
If earlier born, or tempted less.

" And thou, in these wild, troubled days,
Misjudged alike in blame and praise,
Unsought and undeserved the same
The skeptic's praise, the bigot's blame ; —

" I cannot doubt, if thou hadst been
Among the highly favored men
Who walked on earth with Fénelon,
He would have owned thee as his son ;

" And, bright with wings of cherubim
Visibly waving over him,
Seen through his life, the Church had
 seemed
All that its old confessors dreamed."

" I would have been," Jean Jacques re-
 plied,
" The humblest servant at his side,
Obscure, unknown, content to see
How beautiful man's life may be !

" Oh, more than thrice-blest relic, more
Than solemn rite or sacred lore,
The holy life of one who trod
The foot-marks of the Christ of God !

" Amidst a blinded world he saw
The oneness of the Dual law ;
That Heaven's sweet peace on Earth be-
 gan,
And God was loved through love of man.

" He lived the Truth which reconciled
The strong man Reason, Faith, the child ;
In him belief and act were one,
The homilies of duty done ! "

So speaking, through the twilight gray
The two old pilgrims went their way.
What seeds of life that day were sown,
The heavenly watchers knew alone.

Time passed, and Autumn came to fold
Green Summer in her brown and gold ;
Time passed, and Winter's tears of snow
Dropped on the grave-mound of Rousseau.

" The tree remaineth where it fell,
The pained on earth is pained in hell ! "
So priestcraft from its altars cursed
The mournful doubts its falsehood nursed.

Ah ! well of old the Psalmist prayed,
" Thy hand, not man's, on me be laid ! "
Earth frowns below, Heaven weeps above,
And man is hate, but God is love !

No Hermits now the wanderer sees,
Nor chapel with its chestnut-trees ;
A morning dream, a tale that 's told,
The wave of change o'er all has rolled.

Yet lives the lesson of that day ;
And from its twilight cool and gray
Comes up a low, sad whisper, "Make
The truth thine own, for truth's own
 sake.

" Why wait to see in thy brief span
Its perfect flower and fruit in man ?
No saintly touch can save ; no balm
Of healing hath the martyr's palm.

" Midst soulless forms, and false pretence
Of spiritual pride and pampered sense,
A voice saith, ' What is that to thee ?
Be true thyself, and follow Me ! '

" In days when throne and altar heard
The wanton's wish, the bigot's word,
And pomp of state and ritual show
Scarce hid the loathsome death below, —

" Midst fawning priests and courtiers foul,
The losel swarm of crown and cowl,
White-robed walked François Fénelon,
Stainless as Uriel in the sun !

" Yet in his time the stake blazed red,
The poor were eaten up like bread :
Men knew him not ; his garment's hem
No healing virtue had for them.

" Alas ! no present saint we find ;
The white cymar gleams far behind,
Revealed in outline vague, sublime,
Through telescopic mists of time !

" Trust not in man with passing breath,
But in the Lord, old Scripture saith ;
The truth which saves thou mayest not
    blend
With false professor, faithless friend.

" Search thine own heart. What paineth
    thee
In others in thyself may be ;
All dust is frail, all flesh is weak ;
Be thou the true man thou dost seek !

" Where now with pain thou treadest,
    trod
The whitest of the saints of God !
To show thee where their feet were set,
The light which led them shineth yet.

" The footprints of the life divine,
Which marked their path, remain in thine ;
And that great Life, transfused in theirs,
Awaits thy faith, thy love, thy prayers ! "

A lesson which I well may heed,
A word of fitness to my need ;
So from that twilight cool and gray
Still saith a voice, or seems to say.

We rose, and slowly homeward turned,
While down the west the sunset burned ;
And, in its light, hill, wood, and tide,
And human forms seemed glorified.

The village homes transfigured stood,
And purple bluffs, whose belting wood
Across the waters leaned to hold
The yellow leaves like lamps of gold.

Then spake my friend : " Thy words are
    true ;
Forever old, forever new,
These home-seen splendors are the same
Which over Eden's sunsets came.

" To these bowed heavens let wood and
    hill
Lift voiceless praise and anthem still ;
Fall, warm with blessing, over them,
Light of the New Jerusalem !

" Flow on, sweet river, like the stream
Of John's Apocalyptic dream !
This mapled ridge shall Horeb be,
Yon green-banked lake our Galilee !

" Henceforth my heart shall sigh no more
For olden time and holier shore ;
God's love and blessing, then and there,
Are now and here and everywhere."

TAULER

Tauler, the preacher, walked, one au-
    tumn day,
Without the walls of Strasburg, by the
    Rhine,
Pondering the solemn Miracle of Life ;
As one who, wandering in a starless night,
Feels momently the jar of unseen waves,
And hears the thunder of an unknown sea,
Breaking along an unimagined shore.

And as he walked he prayed. Even the
    same
Old prayer with which, for half a score of
    years,
Morning, and noon, and evening, lip and
    heart
Had groaned : " Have pity upon me, Lord !
Thou seest, while teaching others, I am
    blind.
Send me a man who can direct my steps ! "

Then, as he mused, he heard along his
    path
A sound as of an old man's staff among
The dry, dead linden-leaves ; and, looking
    up,
He saw a stranger, weak, and poor, and
    old.

" Peace be unto thee, father ! " Tauler
    said,
" God give thee a good day ! " The old
    man raised
Slowly his calm blue eyes. " I thank thee,
    son ;
But all my days are good, and none are ill."

Wondering thereat, the preacher spake again,
"God give thee happy life." The old man smiled,
"I never am unhappy."

                    Tauler laid
His hand upon the stranger's coarse gray sleeve :
"Tell me, O father, what thy strange words mean.
Surely man's days are evil, and his life
Sad as the grave it leads to." "Nay, my son,
Our times are in God's hands, and all our days
Are as our needs ; for shadow as for sun,
For cold as heat, for want as wealth, alike
Our thanks are due, since that is best which is ;
And that which is not, sharing not His life,
Is evil only as devoid of good.
And for the happiness of which I spake,
I find it in submission to His will,
And calm trust in the holy Trinity
Of Knowledge, Goodness, and Almighty Power."

Silently wondering, for a little space,
Stood the great preacher ; then he spake as one
Who, suddenly grappling with a haunting thought
Which long has followed, whispering through the dark
Strange terrors, drags it, shrieking, into light :
"What if God's will consign thee hence to Hell ? "

"Then," said the stranger, cheerily, "be it so.
What Hell may be I know not ; this I know, —
I cannot lose the presence of the Lord.
One arm, Humility, takes hold upon
His dear humanity ; the other, Love,
Clasps His Divinity. So where I go
He goes; and better fire-walled Hell with Him
Than golden-gated Paradise without."

Tears sprang in Tauler's eyes. A sudden light,
Like the first ray which fell on chaos, clove

Apart the shadow wherein he had walked
Darkly at noon. And, as the strange old man
Went his slow way, until his silver hair
Set like the white moon where the hills of vine
Slope to the Rhine, he bowed his head and said :
"My prayer is answered. God hath sent the man
Long sought, to teach me, by his simple trust,
Wisdom the weary schoolmen never knew."

So, entering with a changed and cheerful step
The city gates, he saw, far down the street,
A mighty shadow break the light of noon,
Which tracing backward till its airy lines
Hardened to stony plinths, he raised his eyes
O'er broad façade and lofty pediment,
O'er architrave and frieze and sainted niche,
Up the stone lace-work chiselled by the wise
Erwin of Steinbach, dizzily up to where
In the noon-brightness the great Minster's tower,
Jewelled with sunbeams on its mural crown,
Rose like a visible prayer. "Behold ! " he said,
"The stranger's faith made plain before mine eyes.
As yonder tower outstretches to the earth
The dark triangle of its shade alone
When the clear day is shining on its top,
So, darkness in the pathway of Man's life
Is but the shadow of God's providence,
By the great Sun of Wisdom cast thereon ;
And what is dark below is light in Heaven."

THE HERMIT OF THE THEBAID

O STRONG, upwelling prayers of faith,
  From inmost founts of life ye start, —
The spirit's pulse, the vital breath
  Of soul and heart !

From pastoral toil, from traffic's din,
  Alone, in crowds, at home, abroad,
Unheard of man, ye enter in
  The ear of God.

Ye brook no forced and measured tasks,
  Nor weary rote, nor formal chains ;

The simple heart, that freely asks
    In love, obtains.

For man the living temple is :
    The mercy-seat and cherubim,
And all the holy mysteries,
    He bears with him.

And most avails the prayer of love,
    Which, wordless, shapes itself in deeds,
And wearies Heaven for naught above
    Our common needs.

Which brings to God's all-perfect will
    That trust of His undoubting child
Whereby all seeming good and ill
    Are reconciled.

And, seeking not for special signs
    Of favor, is content to fall
Within the providence which shines
    And rains on all.

Alone, the Thebaid hermit leaned
    At noontime o'er the sacred word.
Was it an angel or a fiend
    Whose voice he heard ?

It broke the desert's hush of awe,
    A human utterance, sweet and mild ;
And, looking up, the hermit saw
    A little child.

A child, with wonder-widened eyes,
    O'erawed and troubled by the sight
Of hot, red sands, and brazen skies,   .
    And anchorite.

" What dost thou here, poor man ?   No
        shade
    Of cool, green palms, nor grass, nor
        well,
Nor corn, nor vines."   The hermit said :
    " With God I dwell.

" Alone with Him in this great calm,
    I live not by the outward sense ;
My Nile his love, my sheltering palm
    His providence."

The child gazed round him. " Does God
        live
    Here only ?—where the desert's rim
Is green with corn, at morn and eve,
    We pray to Him.

" My brother tills beside the Nile
    His little field ; beneath the leaves
My sisters sit and spin, the while
    My mother weaves.

" And when the millet's ripe heads fall,
    And all the bean-field hangs in pod,
My mother smiles, and says that all
    Are gifts from God.

" And when to share our evening meal,
    She calls the stranger at the door,
She says God fills the hands that deal
    Food to the poor."

Adown the hermit's wasted cheeks
    Glistened the flow of human tears ;
" Dear Lord ! " he said, " Thy angel speaks,
    Thy servant hears."

Within his arms the child he took,
    And thought of home and life with men ;
And all his pilgrim feet forsook
    Returned again.

The palmy shadows cool and long,
    The eyes that smiled through lavish
        locks,
Home's cradle-hymn and harvest-song,
    And bleat of flocks.

" O child ! " he said, " thou teachest me
    There is no place where God is not ;
That love will make, where'er it be,
    A holy spot."

He rose from off the desert sand,
    And, leaning on his staff of thorn,
Went with the young child hand in hand,
    Like night with morn.

They crossed the desert's burning line,
    And heard the palm-tree's rustling fan,
The Nile-bird's cry, the low of kine,
    And voice of man.

Unquestioning, his childish guide
    He followed, as the small hand led
To where a woman, gentle-eyed,
    Her distaff fed.

She rose, she clasped her truant boy,
    She thanked the stranger with her eyes ;
The hermit gazed in doubt and joy
    And dumb surprise.

And lo ! — with sudden warmth and light
  A tender memory thrilled his frame ;
New-born, the world-lost anchorite
  A man became.

" O sister of El Zara's race,
  Behold me ! — had we not one mother ? "
She gazed into the stranger's face :
  " Thou art my brother ! "

" O kin of blood ! Thy life of use
  And patient trust is more than mine ;
And wiser than the gray recluse
  This child of thine.

" For, taught of him whom God hath
      sent,
  That toil is praise and love is prayer,
I come, life's cares and pains content
  With thee to share."

Even as his foot the threshold crossed
  The hermit's better life began ;
Its holiest saint the Thebaid lost,
  And found a man !

MAUD MULLER

The recollection of some descendants of a
Hessian deserter in the Revolutionary war bear-
ing the name of Muller doubtless suggested
the somewhat infelicitous title of a New Eng-
land idyl. The poem had no real foundation
in fact, though a hint of it may have been found
in recalling an incident, trivial in itself, of a
journey on the picturesque Maine seaboard
with my sister some years before it was writ-
ten. We had stopped to rest our tired horse
under the shade of an apple-tree, and refresh
him with water from a little brook which
rippled through the stone wall across the road.
A very beautiful young girl in scantest sum-
mer attire was at work in the hay-field, and as
we talked with her we noticed that she strove
to hide her bare feet by raking hay over them,
blushing as she did so, through the tan of her
cheek and neck.

MAUD MULLER on a summer's day
Raked the meadow sweet with hay.

Beneath her torn hat glowed the wealth
Of simple beauty and rustic health.

Singing, she wrought, and her merry glee
The mock-bird echoed from his tree.

But when she glanced to the far-off town,
White from its hill-slope looking down,

The sweet song died, and a vague unrest
And a nameless longing filled her breast, —

A wish that she hardly dared to own,
For something better than she had known.

The Judge rode slowly down the lane,
Smoothing his horse's chestnut mane.

He drew his bridle in the shade
Of the apple-trees, to greet the maid,

And asked a draught from the spring that
      flowed
Through the meadow across the road.

She stooped where the cool spring bubbled
      up,
And filled for him her small tin cup,

And blushed as she gave it, looking down
On her feet so bare, and her tattered gown.

" Thanks ! " said the Judge ; " a sweeter
      draught
From a fairer hand was never quaffed."

He spoke of the grass and flowers and trees,
Of the singing birds and the humming bees ;

Then talked of the haying, and wondered
      whether
The cloud in the west would bring foul
      weather.

And Maud forgot her brier-torn gown,
And her graceful ankles bare and brown ;

And listened, while a pleased surprise
Looked from her long-lashed hazel eyes.

At last, like one who for delay
Seeks a vain excuse, he rode away.

Maud Muller looked and sighed : " Ah me !
That I the Judge's bride might be !

" He would dress me up in silks so fine,
And praise and toast me at his wine.

" My father should wear a broadcloth coat ;
My brother should sail a painted boat.

"I'd dress my mother so grand and gay,
And the baby should have a new toy each
    day.

"And I'd feed the hungry and clothe the
    poor,
And all should bless me who left our door."

The Judge looked back as he climbed the
    hill,
And saw Maud Muller standing still.

"A form more fair, a face more sweet,
Ne'er hath it been my lot to meet.

"And her modest answer and graceful air
Show her wise and good as she is fair.

"Would she were mine, and I to-day,
Like her, a harvester of hay;

"No doubtful balance of rights and wrongs,
Nor weary lawyers with endless tongues,

"But low of cattle and song of birds,
And health and quiet and loving words."

But he thought of his sisters, proud and
    cold,
And his mother, vain of her rank and gold.

So, closing his heart, the Judge rode on,
And Maud was left in the field alone.

But the lawyers smiled that afternoon,
When he hummed in court an old love-
    tune;

And the young girl mused beside the well
Till the rain on the unraked clover fell.

He wedded a wife of richest dower,
Who lived for fashion, as he for power.

Yet oft, in his marble hearth's bright glow,
He watched a picture come and go;

And sweet Maud Muller's hazel eyes
Looked out in their innocent surprise.

Oft, when the wine in his glass was red,
He longed for the wayside well instead;

And closed his eyes on his garnished rooms
To dream of meadows and clover-blooms.

And the proud man sighed, with a secret
    pain,
"Ah, that I were free again!

"Free as when I rode that day,
Where the barefoot maiden raked her hay."

She wedded a man unlearned and poor,
And many children played round her door.

But care and sorrow, and childbirth pain,
Left their traces on heart and brain.

And oft, when the summer sun shone hot
On the new-mown hay in the meadow lot,

And she heard the little spring brook fall
Over the roadside, through the wall,

In the shade of the apple-tree again
She saw a rider draw his rein;

And, gazing down with timid grace,
She felt his pleased eyes read her face.

Sometimes her narrow kitchen walls
Stretched away into stately halls;

The weary wheel to a spinnet turned,
The tallow candle an astral burned,

And for him who sat by the chimney lug,
Dozing and grumbling o'er pipe and mug,

A manly form at her side she saw,
And joy was duty and love was law.

Then she took up her burden of life again,
Saying only, "It might have been."

Alas for maiden, alas for Judge,
For rich repiner and household drudge!

God pity them both! and pity us all,
Who vainly the dreams of youth recall.

For of all sad words of tongue or pen,
The saddest are these: "It might have
    been!"

Ah, well! for us all some sweet hope lies
Deeply buried from human eyes;

And, in the hereafter, angels may
Roll the stone from its grave away!

MARY GARVIN

FROM the heart of Waumbek Methna, from
    the lake that never fails,
Falls the Saco in the green lap of Conway's
    intervales ;
There, in wild and virgin freshness, its
    waters foam and flow,
As when Darby Field first saw them, two
    hundred years ago.

But, vexed in all its seaward course with
    bridges, dams, and mills,
How changed is Saco's stream, how lost its
    freedom of the hills,
Since travelled Jocelyn, factor Vines, and
    stately Champernoon
Heard on its banks the gray wolf's howl,
    the trumpet of the loon !

With smoking axle hot with speed, with
    steeds of fire and steam,
Wide-waked To-day leaves Yesterday be-
    hind him like a dream.
Still, from the hurrying train of Life, fly
    backward far and fast
The milestones of the fathers, the land-
    marks of the past.

But human hearts remain unchanged : the
    sorrow and the sin,
The loves and hopes and fears of old, are to
    our own akin ;
And if, in tales our fathers told, the songs
    our mothers sung,
Tradition wears a snowy beard, Romance
    is always young.

O sharp-lined man of traffic, on Saco's
    banks to-day !
O mill-girl watching late and long the
    shuttle's restless play !
Let, for the once, a listening ear the work-
    ing hand beguile,
And lend my old Provincial tale, as suits,
    a tear or smile !

The evening gun had sounded from gray
    Fort Mary's walls ;
Through the forest, like a wild beast,
    roared and plunged the Saco's
    falls.

And westward on the sea-wind, that damp
    and gusty grew,
Over cedars darkening inland the smokes
    of Spurwink blew.

On the hearth of Farmer Garvin, blazed
    the crackling walnut log ;
Right and left sat dame and goodman, and
    between them lay the dog,

Head on paws, and tail slow wagging, and
    beside him on her mat,
Sitting drowsy in the firelight, winked and
    purred the mottled cat.

"Twenty years !" said Goodman Garvin,
    speaking sadly, under breath,
And his gray head slowly shaking, as one
    who speaks of death.

The goodwife dropped her needles : "It is
    twenty years to-day,
Since the Indians fell on Saco, and stole our
    child away."

Then they sank into the silence, for each
    knew the other's thought,
Of a great and common sorrow, and words
    were needed not.

"Who knocks ?" cried Goodman Garvin.
    The door was open thrown ;
On two strangers, man and maiden, cloaked
    and furred, the firelight shone.

One with courteous gesture lifted the bear-
    skin from his head ;
"Lives here Elkanah Garvin?" "I am
    he," the goodman said.

"Sit ye down, and dry and warm ye, for
    the night is chill with rain"
And the goodwife drew the settle, and
    stirred the fire amain.

The maid unclasped her cloak-hood, the
    firelight glistened fair
In her large, moist eyes, and over soft folds
    of dark brown hair.

Dame Garvin looked upon her : "It is
    Mary's self I see !
Dear heart !" she cried, "now tell
    me, has my child come back to
    me ?"

"My name indeed is Mary," said the
stranger sobbing wild ;
"Will you be to me a mother? I am
Mary Garvin's child !

"She sleeps by wooded Simcoe, but on her
dying day
She bade my father take me to her kinsfolk
far away.

"And when the priest besought her to do
me no such wrong,
She said, 'May God forgive me! I have
closed my heart too long.

"'When I hid me from my father, and shut
out my mother's call,
I sinned against those dear ones, and the
Father of us all.

"'Christ's love rebukes no home-love,
breaks no tie of kin apart ;
Better heresy in doctrine, than heresy of
heart.

"'Tell me not the Church must cen-
sure : she who wept the Cross be-
side
Never made her own flesh strangers, nor
the claims of blood denied ;

"'And if she who wronged her parents,
with her child atones to them,
Earthly daughter, Heavenly Mother! thou
at least wilt not condemn !'

"So, upon her death-bed lying, my blessed
mother spake ;
As we come to do her bidding, so receive
us for her sake."

"God be praised !" said Goodwife Garvin,
"He taketh, and He gives ;
He woundeth, but He healeth ; in her
child our daughter lives !"

"Amen !" the old man answered, as he
brushed a tear away,
And, kneeling by his hearthstone, said, with
reverence, "Let us pray."

All its Oriental symbols, and its Hebrew
paraphrase,
Warm with earnest life and feeling, rose
his prayer of love and praise.

But he started at beholding, as he rose
from off his knee,
The stranger cross his forehead with the
sign of Papistrie.

"What is this?" cried Farmer Garvin.
"Is an English Christian's home
A chapel or a mass-house, that you make
the sign of Rome ?"

Then the young girl knelt beside him, kissed
his trembling hand, and cried :
"Oh, forbear to chide my father ; in that
faith my mother died !

"On her wooden cross at Simcoe the dews
and sunshine fall,
As they fall on Spurwink's graveyard ; and
the dear God watches all !"

The old man stroked the fair head that
rested on his knee ;
"Your words, dear child," he answered,
"are God's rebuke to me.

"Creed and rite perchance may differ, yet
our faith and hope be one.
Let me be your father's father, let him be
to me a son."

When the horn, on Sabbath morning,
through the still and frosty air,
From Spurwink, Pool, and Black Point,
called to sermon and to prayer,

To the goodly house of worship, where, in
order due and fit,
As by public vote directed, classed and
ranked the people sit ;

Mistress first and goodwife after, clerkly
squire before the clown,
From the brave coat, lace-embroidered, to
the gray frock, shading down ;

From the pulpit read the preacher, "Good-
man Garvin and his wife
Fain would thank the Lord, whose kind-
ness has followed them through
life,

"For the great and crowning mercy, that
their daughter, from the wild,
Where she rests (they hope in God's peace),
has sent to them her child ;

"And the prayers of all God's people they
    ask, that they may prove
Not unworthy, through their weakness, of
    such special proof of love."

As the preacher prayed, uprising, the aged
    couple stood,
And the fair Canadian also, in her modest
    maidenhood.

Thought the elders, grave and doubting,
    "She is Papist born and bred ; "
Thought the young men, " 'T is an angel in
    Mary Garvin's stead ! "

THE RANGER

Originally published as *Martha Mason; a
Song of the Old French War.*

ROBERT RAWLIN ! — Frosts were falling
When the ranger's horn was calling
    Through the woods to Canada.
Gone the winter's sleet and snowing,
Gone the spring-time's bud and blowing,
Gone the summer's harvest mowing,
    And again the fields are gray.
    Yet away, he 's away !
Faint and fainter hope is growing
    In the hearts that mourn his stay.

Where the lion, crouching high on
Abraham's rock with teeth of iron,
    Glares o'er wood and wave away,
Faintly thence, as pines far sighing,
Or as thunder spent and dying,
Come the challenge and replying,
    Come the sounds of flight and fray.
    Well-a-day ! Hope and pray !
Some are living, some are lying
    In their red graves far away.

Straggling rangers, worn with dangers,
Homeward faring, weary strangers
    Pass the farm-gate on their way ;
Tidings of the dead and living,
Forest march and ambush, giving,
Till the maidens leave their weaving,
    And the lads forget their play.
    "Still away, still away ! "
Sighs a sad one, sick with grieving,
    " Why does Robert still delay ! "

Nowhere fairer, sweeter, rarer,
Does the golden-locked fruit bearer

Through his painted woodlands stray,
Than where hillside oaks and beeches
Overlook the long, blue reaches,
Silver coves and pebbled beaches,
    And green isles of Casco Bay ;
Nowhere day, for delay,
With a tenderer look beseeches,
    "Let me with my charmed earth stay."

On the grain-lands of the mainlands
Stands the serried corn like train-bands,
    Plume and pennon rustling gay ;
Out at sea, the islands wooded,
Silver birches, golden-hooded,
Set with maples, crimson-blooded,
    White sea-foam and sand-hills gray,
    Stretch away, far away,
Dim and dreamy, over-brooded
    By the hazy autumn day.

Gayly chattering to the clattering
Of the brown nuts downward pattering,
    Leap the squirrels, red and gray.
On the grass-land, on the fallow,
Drop the apples, red and yellow ;
Drop the russet pears and mellow,
    Drop the red leaves all the day.
    And away, swift away,
Sun and cloud, o'er hill and hollow
    Chasing, weave their web of play.

"Martha Mason, Martha Mason,
Prithee tell us of the reason
    Why you mope at home to-day :
Surely smiling is not sinning ;
Leave your quilling, leave your spinning ;
What is all your store of linen,
    If your heart is never gay ?
    Come away, come away !
Never yet did sad beginning
    Make the task of life a play."

Overbending till she 's blending
With the flaxen skein she 's tending
    Pale brown tresses smoothed away
From her face of patient sorrow,
Sits she, seeking but to borrow,
From the trembling hope of morrow,
    Solace for the weary day.
    "Go your way, laugh and play ;
Unto Him who heeds the sparrow
    And the lily, let me pray."

"With our rally rings the valley, —
Join us ! " cried the blue-eyed Nelly ;

"Join us!" cried the laughing May,
"To the beach we all are going,
And, to save the task of rowing,
West by north the wind is blowing,
  Blowing briskly down the bay!
  Come away, come away!
Time and tide are swiftly flowing,
  Let us take them while we may!

"Never tell us that you'll fail us,
Where the purple beach-plum mellows
  On the bluffs so wild and gray.
Hasten, for the oars are falling;
Hark, our merry mates are calling;
Time it is that we were all in,
  Singing tideward down the bay!"
  "Nay, nay, let me stay;
Sore and sad for Robert Rawlin
  Is my heart," she said, "to-day."

"Vain your calling for Rob Rawlin!
Some red squaw his moose-meat's broiling,
  Or some French lass, singing gay;
Just forget as he's forgetting;
What avails a life of fretting?
If some stars must needs be setting,
  Others rise as good as they."
  "Cease, I pray; go your way!"
Martha cries, her eyelids wetting;
  "Foul and false the words you say!"

"Martha Mason, hear to reason!
Prithee, put a kinder face on!"
  "Cease to vex me," did she say;
"Better at his side be lying,
With the mournful pine-trees sighing,
And the wild birds o'er us crying,
  Than to doubt like mine a prey;
  While away, far away,
Turns my heart, forever trying
  Some new hope for each new day.

"When the shadows veil the meadows,
And the sunset's golden ladders
  Sink from twilight's walls of gray,—
From the window of my dreaming,
I can see his sickle gleaming,
Cheery-voiced, can hear him teaming
  Down the locust-shaded way;
  But away, swift away,
Fades the fond, delusive seeming,
  And I kneel again to pray.

"When the growing dawn is showing,
And the barn-yard cock is crowing,

And the horned moon pales away:
From a dream of him awaking,
Every sound my heart is making
Seems a footstep of his taking;
  Then I hush the thought, and say,
  'Nay, nay, he's away!'
Ah! my heart, my heart is breaking
  For the dear one far away."

Look up, Martha! worn and swarthy,
Glows a face of manhood worthy:
  "Robert!" "Martha!" all they say.
O'er went wheel and reel together,
Little cared the owner whither;
Heart of lead is heart of feather,
  Noon of night is noon of day!
  Come away, come away!
When such lovers meet each other,
  Why should prying idlers stay?

Quench the timber's fallen embers,
Quench the red leaves in December's
  Hoary rime and chilly spray.
But the hearth shall kindle clearer,
Household welcomes sound sincerer,
Heart to loving heart draw nearer,
  When the bridal bells shall say:
  "Hope and pray, trust alway;
Life is sweeter, love is dearer,
  For the trial and delay!"

THE GARRISON OF CAPE ANN

FROM the hills of home forth looking, far
    beneath the tent-like span
Of the sky, I see the white gleam of the
    headland of Cape Ann.
Well I know its coves and beaches to the
    ebb-tide glimmering down,
And the white-walled hamlet children of
    its ancient fishing-town.

Long has passed the summer morning, and
    its memory waxes old,
When along yon breezy headlands with a
    pleasant friend I strolled.
Ah! the autumn sun is shining, and the
    ocean wind blows cool,
And the golden-rod and aster bloom around
    thy grave, Rantoul!

With the memory of that morning by the
    summer sea I blend

A wild and wondrous story, by the younger
 Mather penned,
In that quaint *Magnalia Christi*, with all
 strange and marvellous things,
Heaped up huge and undigested, like the
 chaos Ovid sings.

Dear to me these far, faint glimpses of the
 dual life of old,
Inward, grand with awe and reverence ;
 outward, mean and coarse and
 cold ;
Gleams of mystic beauty playing over dull
 and vulgar clay,
Golden-threaded fancies weaving in a web
 of hodden gray.

The great eventful Present hides the
 Past ; but through the din
Of its loud life hints and echoes from the
 life behind steal in ;
And the lore of home and fireside, and the
 legendary rhyme,
Make the task of duty lighter which the
 true man owes his time.

So, with something of the feeling which
 the Covenanter knew,
When with pious chisel wandering Scot-
 land's moorland graveyards through,
From the graves of old traditions I part
 the blackberry-vines,
Wipe the moss from off the headstones,
 and retouch the faded lines.

Where the sea-waves back and for-
 ward, hoarse with rolling pebbles,
 ran,
The garrison-house stood watching on the
 gray rocks of Cape Ann ;
On its windy site uplifting gabled roof and
 palisade,
And rough walls of unhewn timber with
 the moonlight overlaid.

On his slow round walked the sentry, south
 and eastward looking forth
O'er a rude and broken coast-line, white
 with breakers stretching north, —
Wood and rock and gleaming sand-drift,
 jagged capes, with bush and tree,
Leaning inland from the smiting of the
 wild and gusty sea.

Before the deep-mouthed chimney, dimly
 lit by dying brands,
Twenty soldiers sat and waited, with their
 muskets in their hands ;
On the rough-hewn oaken table the venison
 haunch was shared,
And the pewter tankard circled slowly
 round from beard to beard.

Long they sat and talked together, —
 talked of wizards Satan-sold ;
Of all ghostly sights and noises, — signs
 and wonders manifold ;
Of the spectre-ship of Salem, with the dead
 men in her shrouds,
Sailing sheer above the water, in the loom of
 morning clouds ;

Of the marvellous valley hidden in the
 depths of Gloucester woods,
Full of plants that love the summer, —
 blooms of warmer latitudes ;
Where the Arctic birch is braided by the
 tropic's flowery vines,
And the white magnolia-blossoms star the
 twilight of the pines !

But their voices sank yet lower, sank to
 husky tones of fear,
As they spake of present tokens of the
 powers of evil near ; —
Of a spectral host, defying stroke of steel
 and aim of gun ;
Never yet was ball to slay them in the
 mould of mortals run !

Thrice, with plumes and flowing scalp-locks,
 from the midnight wood they
 came, —
Thrice around the block-house march-
 ing, met, unharmed, its volleyed
 flame ;
Then, with mocking laugh and gesture,
 sunk in earth or lost in air,
All the ghostly wonder vanished, and the
 moonlit sands lay bare.

Midnight came ; from out the forest moved
 a dusky mass that soon
Grew to warriors, plumed and painted,
 grimly marching in the moon.
"Ghosts or witches," said the captain,
 "thus I foil the Evil One !"
And he rammed a silver button, from his
 doublet, down his gun.

Once again the spectral horror moved the
    guarded wall about ;
Once again the levelled muskets through
    the palisades flashed out,
With that deadly aim the squirrel on his
    tree-top might not shun,
Nor the beach-bird seaward flying with his
    slant wing to the sun.

Like the idle rain of summer sped the harm-
    less shower of lead.
With a laugh of fierce derision, once again
    the phantoms fled ;
Once again, without a shadow on the sands
    the moonlight lay,
And the white smoke curling through it
    drifted slowly down the bay !

" God preserve us ! " said the captain ;
    " never mortal foes were there ;
They have vanished with their leader,
    Prince and Power of the air !
Lay aside your useless weapons ; skill and
    prowess naught avail ;
They who do the Devil's service wear their
    master's coat of mail ! "

So the night grew near to cock-crow, when
    again a warning call
Roused the score of weary soldiers watch-
    ing round the dusky hall :
And they looked to flint and priming, and
    they longed for break of day ;
But the captain closed his Bible : " Let us
    cease from man, and pray ! "

To the men who went before us, all the un-
    seen powers seemed near,
And their steadfast strength of courage
    struck its roots in holy fear.
Every hand forsook the musket, every head
    was bowed and bare,
Every stout knee pressed the flag-stones, as
    the captain led in prayer.

Ceased thereat the mystic marching of the
    spectres round the wall,
But a sound abhorred, unearthly, smote the
    ears and hearts of all, —
Howls of rage and shrieks of anguish !
    Never after mortal man
Saw the ghostly leaguers marching round
    the block-house of Cape Ann.

So to us who walk in summer through the
    cool and sea-blown town,

From the childhood of its people comes the
    solemn legend down.
Not in vain the ancient fiction, in whose
    moral lives the youth
And the fitness and the freshness of an un
    decaying truth.

Soon or late to all our dwellings come the
    spectres of the mind,
Doubts and fears and dread forebodings,
    in the darkness undefined ;
Round us throng the grim projections of the
    heart and of the brain,
And our pride of strength is weakness, and
    the cunning hand is vain.

In the dark we cry like children ; and no
    answer from on high
Breaks the crystal spheres of silence, and
    no white wings downward fly ;
But the heavenly help we pray for comes to
    faith, and not to sight,
And our prayers themselves drive backward
    all the spirits of the night !

THE GIFT OF TRITEMIUS

TRITEMIUS of Herbipolis, one day,
While kneeling at the altar's foot to pray
Alone with God, as was his pious choice,
Heard from without a miserable voice,
A sound which seemed of all sad things to
    tell,
As of a lost soul crying out of hell.

Thereat the Abbot paused ; the chain
    whereby
His thoughts went upward broken by that
    cry ;
And, looking from the casement, saw below
A wretched woman, with gray hair a-flow,
And withered hands held up to him, who
    cried
For alms as one who might not be denied.

She cried, " For the dear love of Him who
    gave
His life for ours, my child from bondage
    save, —
My beautiful, brave first-born, chained with
    slaves
In the Moor's galley, where the sun-smit
    waves
Lap the white walls of Tunis ! " — " What
    I can

I give," Tritemius said, "my prayers." —
    "O man
Of God!" she cried, for grief had made
    her bold,
"Mock me not thus; I ask not prayers,
    but gold.
Words will not serve me, alms alone suffice;
Even while I speak perchance my first-
    born dies."

"Woman!" Tritemius answered, "from
    our door
None go unfed, hence are we always poor;
A single soldo is our only store.
Thou hast our prayers; — what can we
    give thee more?"

"Give me," she said, "the silver candle-
    sticks
On either side of the great crucifix.
God well may spare them on His errands
    sped,
Or He can give you golden ones instead."

Then spake Tritemius, "Even as thy
    word,
Woman, so be it! (Our most gracious
    Lord,
Who loveth mercy more than sacrifice,
Pardon me if a human soul I prize
Above the gifts upon his altar piled!)
Take what thou askest, and redeem thy
    child."

But his hand trembled as the holy alms
He placed within the beggar's eager palms;
And as she vanished down the linden shade,
He bowed his head and for forgiveness
    prayed.

So the day passed, and when the twilight
    came
He woke to find the chapel all aflame,
And, dumb with grateful wonder, to be-
    hold
Upon the altar candlesticks of gold!

SKIPPER IRESON'S RIDE

In the valuable and carefully prepared *His-
tory of Marblehead*, published in 1879 by
Samuel Roads, Jr., it is stated that the crew
of Captain Ireson, rather than himself, were
responsible for the abandonment of the dis-
abled vessel. To screen themselves they
charged their captain with the crime. In view
of this the writer of the ballad addressed the
following letter to the historian: —

OAK KNOLL, DANVERS, 5 *mo.* 18, 1880.

MY DEAR FRIEND; I heartily thank thee
for a copy of thy *History of Marblehead*. I
have read it with great interest and think good
use has been made of the abundant material.
No town in Essex County has a record more
honorable than Marblehead; no one has done
more to develop the industrial interests of our
New England seaboard, and certainly none
have given such evidence of self-sacrificing
patriotism. I am glad the story of it has been
at last told, and told so well. I have now no
doubt that thy version of Skipper Ireson's
ride is the correct one. My verse was founded
solely on a fragment of rhyme which I heard
from one of my early schoolmates, a native of
Marblehead.
I supposed the story to which it referred dated
back at least a century. I knew nothing of
the participators, and the narrative of the ballad
was pure fancy. I am glad for the sake of
truth and justice that the real facts are given in
thy book. I certainly would not knowingly do
injustice to any one, dead or living.
    I am very truly thy friend,
        JOHN G. WHITTIER.

OF all the rides since the birth of time,
Told in story or sung in rhyme, —
On Apuleius's Golden Ass,
Or one-eyed Calender's horse of brass,
Witch astride of a human back,
Islam's prophet on Al-Borák, —
The strangest ride that ever was sped
Was Ireson's, out from Marblehead!
    Old Floyd Ireson, for his hard heart,
    Tarred and feathered and carried in a
        cart
    By the women of Marblehead!

Body of turkey, head of owl,
Wings a-droop like a rained-on fowl,
Feathered and ruffled in every part,
Skipper Ireson stood in the cart.
Scores of women, old and young,
Strong of muscle, and glib of tongue,
Pushed and pulled up the rocky lane,
Shouting and singing the shrill refrain:
    "Here's Flud Oirson, fur his horrd
        horrt,
    Torr'd an' futherr'd an' corr'd in a
        corrt
    By the women o' Morble'ead!"

Wrinkled scolds with hands on hips,
Girls in bloom of cheek and lips,
Wild-eyed, free-limbed, such as chase
Bacchus round some antique vase,
Brief of skirt, with ankles bare,
Loose of kerchief and loose of hair,
With conch-shells blowing and fish-horns'
    twang,
Over and over the Mænads sang :
    "Here 's Flud Oirson, fur his horrd
        horrt,
    Torr'd an' futherr'd an' corr'd in a corrt
    By the women o' Morble'ead ! "

Small pity for him ! — He sailed away
From a leaking ship in Chaleur Bay, —
Sailed away from a sinking wreck,
With his own town's-people on her deck !
"Lay by ! lay by ! " they called to him.
Back he answered, "Sink or swim !
Brag of your catch of fish again ! "
And off he sailed through the fog and
    rain !
    Old Floyd Ireson, for his hard heart,
    Tarred and feathered and carried in a
        cart
    By the women of Marblehead !

Fathoms deep in dark Chaleur
That wreck shall lie forevermore.
Mother and sister, wife and maid,
Looked from the rocks of Marblehead
Over the moaning and rainy sea, —
Looked for the coming that might not
    be !
What did the winds and the sea - birds
    say
Of the cruel captain who sailed away ? —
    Old Floyd Ireson, for his hard heart,
    Tarred and feathered and carried in a
        cart
    By the women of Marblehead !

Through the street, on either side,
Up flew windows, doors swung wide ;
Sharp-tongued spinsters, old wives gray,
Treble lent the fish-horn's bray.
Sea-worn grandsires, cripple-bound,
Hulks of old sailors run aground,
Shook head, and fist, and hat, and cane,
And cracked with curses the hoarse re-
    frain :
    "Here 's Flud Oirson, fur his horrd horrt,
    Torr'd an' futherr'd an' corr'd in a corrt
    By the women o' Morble'ead ! "

Sweetly along the Salem road
Bloom of orchard and lilac showed.
Little the wicked skipper knew
Of the fields so green and the sky so blue.
Riding there in his sorry trim,
Like an Indian idol glum and grim,
Scarcely he seemed the sound to hear
Of voices shouting, far and near :
    "Here 's Flud Oirson, fur his horrd
        horrt,
    Torr'd an' futherr'd an' corr'd in a corrt
    By the women o' Morble'ead ! "

"Hear me, neighbors ! " at last he cried, —
"What to me is this noisy ride ?
What is the shame that clothes the skin
To the nameless horror that lives within ?
Waking or sleeping, I see a wreck,
And hear a cry from a reeling deck !
Hate me and curse me, — I only dread
The hand of God and the face of the dead ! "
    Said old Floyd Ireson, for his hard heart,
    Tarred and feathered and carried in a
        cart
    By the women of Marblehead !

Then the wife of the skipper lost at sea
Said, "God has touched him ! why should
    we ! "
Said an old wife mourning her only son,
"Cut the rogue's tether and let him run ! "
So with soft relentings and rude excuse,
Half scorn, half pity, they cut him loose,
And gave him a cloak to hide him in,
And left him alone with his shame and
    sin.
    Poor Floyd Ireson, for his hard heart,
    Tarred and feathered and carried in a
        cart
    By the women of Marblehead !

THE SYCAMORES

Hugh Tallant was the first Irish resident of
Haverhill, Mass. He planted the buttonwood
trees on the bank of the river below the village
in the early part of the seventeenth century.
Unfortunately this noble avenue is now nearly
destroyed.

IN the outskirts of the village,
    On the river's winding shores,
Stand the Occidental plane-trees,
    Stand the ancient sycamores.

One long century hath been numbered,
  And another half-way told,
Since the rustic Irish gleeman
  Broke for them the virgin mould.

Deftly set to Celtic music,
  At his violin's sound they grew,
Through the moonlit eves of summer,
  Making Amphion's fable true.

Rise again, thou poor Hugh Tallant!
  Pass in jerkin green along,
With thy eyes brimful of laughter,
  And thy mouth as full of song.

Pioneer of Erin's outcasts,
  With his fiddle and his pack;
Little dreamed the village Saxons
  Of the myriads at his back.

How he wrought with spade and fiddle,
  Delved by day and sang by night,
With a hand that never wearied,
  And a heart forever light, —

Still the gay tradition mingles
  With a record grave and drear,
Like the rollic air of Cluny
  With the solemn march of Mear.

When the box-tree, white with blossoms,
  Made the sweet May woodlands glad,
And the Aronia by the river
  Lighted up the swarming shad,

And the bulging nets swept shoreward,
  With their silver-sided haul,
Midst the shouts of dripping fishers,
  He was merriest of them all.

When, among the jovial huskers,
  Love stole in at Labor's side,
With the lusty airs of England
  Soft his Celtic measures vied.

Songs of love and wailing lyke-wake,
  And the merry fair's carouse;
Of the wild Red Fox of Erin
  And the Woman of Three Cows,

By the blazing hearths of winter,
  Pleasant seemed his simple tales,
Midst the grimmer Yorkshire legends
  And the mountain myths of Wales.

How the souls in Purgatory
  Scrambled up from fate forlorn,
On St. Keven's sackcloth ladder,
  Slyly hitched to Satan's horn.

Of the fiddler who at Tara
  Played all night to ghosts of kings;
Of the brown dwarfs, and the fairies
  Dancing in their moorland rings!

Jolliest of our birds of singing,
  Best he loved the Bob-o-link.
"Hush!" he'd say, "the tipsy fairies!
  Hear the little folks in drink!"

Merry-faced, with spade and fiddle,
  Singing through the ancient town,
Only this, of poor Hugh Tallant,
  Hath Tradition handed down.

Not a stone his grave discloses;
  But if yet his spirit walks,
'T is beneath the trees he planted,
  And when Bob-o-Lincoln talks;

Green memorials of the gleeman!
  Linking still the river-shores,
With their shadows cast by sunset,
  Stand Hugh Tallant's sycamores!

When the Father of his Country
  Through the north-land riding came,
And the roofs were starred with banners,
  And the steeples rang acclaim, —

When each war-scarred Continental,
  Leaving smithy, mill, and farm,
Waved his rusted sword in welcome,
  And shot off his old king's-arm, —

Slowly passed that august Presence
  Down the thronged and shouting street:
Village girls as white as angels
  Scattering flowers around his feet.

Midway, where the plane-tree's shadow
  Deepest fell, his rein he drew:
On his stately head, uncovered,
  Cool and soft the west-wind blew.

And he stood up in his stirrups,
  Looking up and looking down
On the hills of Gold and Silver
  Rimming round the little town, —

On the river, full of sunshine,
  To the lap of greenest vales
Winding down from wooded headlands,
  Willow-skirted, white with sails.

And he said, the landscape sweeping
  Slowly with his ungloved hand,
"I have seen no prospect fairer
  In this goodly Eastern land."

Then the bugles of his escort
  Stirred to life the cavalcade :
And that head, so bare and stately,
  Vanished down the depths of shade.

Ever since, in town and farm-house,
  Life has had its ebb and flow ;
Thrice hath passed the human harvest
  To its garner green and low.

But the trees the gleeman planted,
  Through the changes, changeless stand ;
As the marble calm of Tadmor
  Mocks the desert's shifting sand.

Still the level moon at rising
  Silvers o'er each stately shaft ;
Still beneath them, half in shadow,
  Singing, glides the pleasure craft ;

Still beneath them, arm-enfolded,
  Love and Youth together stray ;
While, as heart to heart beats faster,
  More and more their feet delay.

Where the ancient cobbler, Keezar,
  On the open hillside wrought,
Singing, as he drew his stitches,
  Songs his German masters taught,

Singing, with his gray hair floating
  Round his rosy ample face, —
Now a thousand Saxon craftsmen
  Stitch and hammer in his place.

All the pastoral lanes so grassy
  Now are Traffic's dusty streets ;
From the village, grown a city,
  Fast the rural grace retreats.

But, still green, and tall, and stately,
  On the river's winding shores,
Stand the Occidental plane-trees,
  Stand Hugh Tallant's sycamores.

THE PIPES AT LUCKNOW

An incident of the Sepoy mutiny.

PIPES of the misty moorlands,
  Voice of the glens and hills ;
The droning of the torrents,
  The treble of the rills !
Not the braes of bloom and heather,
  Nor the mountains dark with rain,
Nor maiden bower, nor border tower,
  Have heard your sweetest strain !

Dear to the Lowland reaper,
  And plaided mountaineer, —
To the cottage and the castle
  The Scottish pipes are dear ; —
Sweet sounds the ancient pibroch
  O'er mountain, loch, and glade ;
But the sweetest of all music
  The pipes at Lucknow played.

Day by day the Indian tiger
  Louder yelled, and nearer crept ;
Round and round the jungle-serpent
  Near and nearer circles swept.
"Pray for rescue, wives and mothers, —
  Pray to-day !" the soldier said ;
"To-morrow, death's between us
  And the wrong and shame we dread."

Oh, they listened, looked, and waited,
  'Till their hope became despair ;
And the sobs of low bewailing
  Filled the pauses of their prayer.
Then up spake a Scottish maiden,
  With her ear unto the ground :
"Dinna ye hear it ? — dinna ye hear it ?
  The pipes o' Havelock sound !"

Hushed the wounded man his groaning ;
  Hushed the wife her little ones ;
Alone they heard the drum-roll
  And the roar of Sepoy guns.
But to sounds of home and childhood
  The Highland ear was true ; —
As her mother's cradle-crooning
  The mountain pipes she knew.

Like the march of soundless music
  Through the vision of the seer,
More of feeling than of hearing,
  Of the heart than of the ear,
She knew the droning pibroch,

She knew the Campbell's call :
"Hark ! hear ye no MacGregor's,
  The grandest o' them all ! "

Oh, they listened, dumb and breathless,
  And they caught the sound at last ;
Faint and far beyond the Goomtee
  Rose and fell the piper's blast !
Then a burst of wild thanksgiving
  Mingled woman's voice and man's ;
"God be praised ! — the march of Have-
    look !
  The piping of the clans ! "

Louder, nearer, fierce as vengeance,
  Sharp and shrill as swords at strife,
Came the wild MacGregor's clan-call,
  Stinging all the air to life.
But when the far-off dust-cloud
  To plaided legions grew,
Full tenderly and blithesomely
  The pipes of rescue blew !

Round the silver domes of Lucknow,
  Moslem mosque and Pagan shrine,
Breathed the air to Britons dearest,
  The air of Auld Lang Syne.
O'er the cruel roll of war-drums
  Rose that sweet and homelike strain ;
And the tartan clove the turban,
  As the Goomtee cleaves the plain

Dear to the corn-land reaper
  And plaided mountaineer, —
To the cottage and the castle
  The piper's song is dear.
Sweet sounds the Gaelic pibroch
  O'er mountain, glen, and glade ;
But the sweetest of all music
  The Pipes at Lucknow played !

TELLING THE BEES

A remarkable custom, brought from the Old
Country, formerly prevailed in the rural dis-
tricts of New England. On the death of a
member of the family, the bees were at once
informed of the event, and their hives dressed
in mourning. This ceremonial was supposed
to be necessary to prevent the swarms from
leaving their hives and seeking a new home.
[The scene is minutely that of the Whittier
homestead.]

HERE is the place ; right over the hill
  Runs the path I took ;

You can see the gap in the old wall still,
  And the stepping-stones in the shallow
    brook.

There is the house, with the gate red-
    barred,
  And the poplars tall ;
And the barn's brown length, and the cattle-
    yard,
  And the white horns tossing above the
    wall.

There are the beehives ranged in the
    sun ;
  And down by the brink
Of the brook are her poor flowers, weed-
    o'errun,
  Pansy and daffodil, rose and pink.

A year has gone, as the tortoise goes,
  Heavy and slow ;
And the same rose blows, and the same
    sun glows,
  And the same brook sings of a year
    ago.

There 's the same sweet clover-smell in the
    breeze ;
  And the June sun warm
Tangles his wings of fire in the trees,
  Setting, as then, over Fernside farm.

I mind me how with a lover's care
  From my Sunday coat
I brushed off the burrs, and smoothed my
    hair,
  And cooled at the brookside my brow
    and throat.

Since we parted, a month had passed, —
  To love, a year ;
Down through the beeches I looked at last
  On the little red gate and the well-sweep
    near.

I can see it all now, — the slantwise rain
  Of light through the leaves,
The sundown's blaze on her window-pane,
  The bloom of her roses under the eaves.

Just the same as a month before, —
  The house and the trees,
The barn's brown gable, the vine by the
    door, —
  Nothing changed but the hives of bees.

Before them, under the garden wall,
  Forward and back,
Went drearily singing the chore-girl small,
  Draping each hive with a shred of black.

Trembling, I listened : the summer sun
  Had the chill of snow ;
For I knew she was telling the bees of
  one
Gone on the journey we all must go !

Then I said to myself, " My Mary weeps
  For the dead to-day :
Haply her blind old grandsire sleeps
  The fret and the pain of his age away."

But her dog whined low ; on the doorway
  sill,
With his cane to his chin,
The old man sat ; and the chore-girl still
  Sung to the bees stealing out and in.

And the song she was singing ever since
  In my ear sounds on : —
" Stay at home, pretty bees, fly not hence !
  Mistress Mary is dead and gone ! "

THE SWAN SONG OF PARSON AVERY

In Young's *Chronicles of Massachusetts Bay from 1623 to 1636* may be found Anthony Thacher's *Narrative of his Shipwreck.* Thacher was Avery's companion and survived to tell the tale. Mather's *Magnalia,* III. 2, gives further *Particulars of Parson Avery's End,* and suggests the title of the poem.

WHEN the reaper's task was ended, and the
  summer wearing late,
Parson Avery sailed from Newbury, with
  his wife and children eight,
Dropping down the river-harbor in the
  shallop " Watch and Wait."

Pleasantly lay the clearings in the mellow
  summer-morn,
With the newly planted orchards dropping
  their fruits first-born,
And the home-roofs like brown islands
  amid a sea of corn.

Broad meadows reached out seaward the
  tided creeks between,

And hills rolled wave-like inland, with
  oaks and walnuts green ; —
A fairer home, a goodlier land, his eyes
  had never seen.

Yet away sailed Parson Avery, away where
  duty led,
And the voice of God seemed calling, to
  break the living bread
To the souls of fishers starving on the
  rocks of Marblehead.

All day they sailed : at nightfall the
  pleasant land-breeze died,
The blackening sky, at midnight, its starry
  lights denied,
And far and low the thunder of tempest
  prophesied !

Blotted out were all the coast - lines,
  gone were rock, and wood, and
  sand ;
Grimly anxious stood the skipper with the
  rudder in his hand,
And questioned of the darkness what was
  sea and what was land.

And the preacher heard his dear ones,
  nestled round him, weeping sore :
" Never heed, my little children ! Christ
  is walking on before
To the pleasant land of heaven, where the
  sea shall be no more."

All at once the great cloud parted, like a
  curtain drawn aside,
To let down the torch of lightning on the
  terror far and wide ;
And the thunder and the whirlwind together
  smote the tide.

There was wailing in the shallop, woman's
  wail and man's despair,
A crash of breaking timbers on the rocks
  so sharp and bare,
And, through it all, the murmur of Father
  Avery's prayer.

From his struggle in the darkness with the
  wild waves and the blast,
On a rock, where every billow broke above
  him as it passed,
Alone, of all his household, the man of
  God was cast.

There a comrade heard him praying, in the
pause of wave and wind :
" All my own have gone before me, and I
linger just behind ;
Not for life I ask, but only for the rest Thy
ransomed find !

" In this night of death I challenge the
promise of Thy word ! —
Let me see the great salvation of which
mine ears have heard ! —
Let me pass from hence forgiven, through
the grace of Christ, our Lord !

" In the baptism of these waters wash
white my every sin,
And let me follow up to Thee my house-
hold and my kin !
Open the sea-gate of Thy heaven, and let
me enter in ! "

When the Christian sings his death-song,
all the listening heavens draw near,
And the angels, leaning over the walls of
crystal, hear
How the notes so faint and broken swell to
music in God's ear.

The ear of God was open to His servant's
last request ;
As the strong wave swept him downward
the sweet hymn upward pressed,
And the soul of Father Avery went, singing,
to its rest.

There was wailing on the mainland, from
the rocks of Marblehead ;
In the stricken church of Newbury the notes
of prayer were read ;
And long, by board and hearthstone, the
living mourned the dead.

And still the fishers outbound, or scudding
from the squall,
With grave and reverent faces, the ancient
tale recall,
When they see the white waves breaking
on the Rock of Avery's Fall !

THE DOUBLE–HEADED SNAKE OF NEWBURY

" Concerning yᵉ Amphisbæna, as soon as I
received your commands, I made diligent in-
quiry: . . . he assures me yᵗ it had really two
heads, one at each end ; two mouths, two stings
or tongues." —Rᴇᴠ. Cʜʀɪsᴛᴏᴘʜᴇʀ Tᴏᴘᴘᴀɴ *to*
Cᴏᴛᴛᴏɴ Mᴀᴛʜᴇʀ.

Fᴀʀ away in the twilight time
Of every people, in every clime,
Dragons and griffins and monsters dire,
Born of water, and air, and fire,
Or nursed, like the Python, in the mud
And ooze of the old Deucalion flood,
Crawl and wriggle and foam with rage,
Through dusk tradition and ballad age.
So from the childhood of Newbury town
And its time of fable the tale comes down
Of a terror which haunted bush and brake,
The Amphisbæna, the Double Snake !

Thou who makest the tale thy mirth,
Consider that strip of Christian earth
On the desolate shore of a sailless sea,
Full of terror and mystery,
Half redeemed from the evil hold
Of the wood so dreary, and dark, and old,
Which drank with its lips of leaves the dew
When Time was young, and the world was
new,
And wove its shadows with sun and moon,
Ere the stones of Cheops were squared and
hewn.
Think of the sea's dread monotone,
Of the mournful wail from the pine-wood
blown,
Of the strange, vast splendors that lit the
North,
Of the troubled throes of the quaking earth,
And the dismal tales the Indian told,
Till the settler's heart at his hearth grew
cold,
And he shrank from the tawny wizard
boasts,
And the hovering shadows seemed full of
ghosts,
And above, below, and on every side,
The fear of his creed seemed verified ; —
And think, if his lot were now thine own,
To grope with terrors nor named nor known,
How laxer muscle and weaker nerve
And a feebler faith thy need might serve ;
And own to thyself the wonder more
That the snake had two heads, and not a
score !

Whether he lurked in the Oldtown fen
Or the gray earth-flax of the Devil's Den,
Or swam in the wooded Artichoke,

Or coiled by the Northman's Written Rock,
Nothing on record is left to show ;
Only the fact that he lived, we know,
And left the cast of a double head
In the scaly mask which he yearly shed.
For he carried a head where his tail should
be,
And the two, of course, could never agree,
But wriggled about with main and might,
Now to the left and now to the right ;
Pulling and twisting this way and that,
Neither knew what the other was at.

A snake with two heads, lurking so near !
Judge of the wonder, guess at the fear !
Think what ancient gossips might say,
Shaking their heads in their dreary way,
Between the meetings on Sabbath-day !
How urchins, searching at day's decline
The Common Pasture for sheep or kine,
The terrible double-ganger heard
In leafy rustle or whir of bird !
Think what a zest it gave to the sport,
In berry-time, of the younger sort,
As over pastures blackberry-twined,
Reuben and Dorothy lagged behind,
And closer and closer, for fear of harm,
The maiden clung to her lover's arm ;
And how the spark, who was forced to stay,
By his sweetheart's fears, till the break of
day,
Thanked the snake for the fond delay !

Far and wide the tale was told,
Like a snowball growing while it rolled.
The nurse hushed with it the baby's cry ;
And it served, in the worthy minister's eye,
To paint the primitive serpent by.
Cotton Mather came galloping down
All the way to Newbury town,
With his eyes agog and his ears set wide,
And his marvellous inkhorn at his side ;
Stirring the while in the shallow pool
Of his brains for the lore he learned at
school,
To garnish the story, with here a streak
Of Latin and there another of Greek :
And the tales he heard and the notes he
took,
Behold ! are they not in his Wonder-Book ?

Stories, like dragons, are hard to kill.
If the snake does not, the tale runs still
In Byfield Meadows, on Pipestave Hill.
And still, whenever husband and wife

Publish the shame of their daily strife,
And, with mad cross-purpose, tug and strain
At either end of the marriage-chain,
The gossips say with a knowing shake
Of their gray heads, "Look at the Double
Snake !
One in body and two in will,
The Amphisbæna is living still ! "

MABEL MARTIN

A HARVEST IDYL

Susanna Martin, an aged woman of Ames-
bury, Mass., was tried and executed for the
alleged crime of witchcraft. Her home was in
what is now known as Pleasant Valley on the
Merrimac, a little above the old Ferry way,
where, tradition says, an attempt was made to
assassinate Sir Edmund Andros on his way
to Falmouth (afterward Portland) and Pema-
quid, which was frustrated by a warning timely
given. Goody Martin was the only woman
hanged on the north side of the Merrimac
during the dreadful delusion. The aged wife
of Judge Bradbury, who lived on the other side
of the Powow River, was imprisoned and would
have been put to death but for the collapse of
the hideous persecution.

The substance of the poem which follows
was published under the name of *The Witch's
Daughter*, in *The National Era* in 1857. In
1875 my publishers desired to issue it with illus-
trations, and I then enlarged it and otherwise
altered it to its present form. The principal
addition was in the verses which constitute
Part I.

PROEM

I CALL the old time back : I bring my
lay
In tender memory of the summer day
When, where our native river lapsed away,

We dreamed it over, while the thrushes
made
Songs of their own, and the great pine-trees
laid
On warm noonlights the masses of their
shade.

And *she* was with us, living o'er again
Her life in ours, despite of years and
pain, —
The Autumn's brightness after latter rain.

Beautiful in her holy peace as one
Who stands, at evening, when the work is
    done,
Glorified in the setting of the sun !

Her memory makes our common landscape
    seem
Fairer than any of which painters dream ;
Lights the brown hills and sings in every
    stream ;

For she whose speech was always truth's
    pure gold
Heard, not unpleased, its simple legends
    told,
And loved with us the beautiful and old.

I. THE RIVER VALLEY

Across the level tableland,
    A grassy, rarely trodden way,
    With thinnest skirt of birchen spray

And stunted growth of cedar, leads
    To where you see the dull plain fall
    Sheer off, steep-slanted, ploughed by all

The seasons' rainfalls. On its brink
    The over-leaning harebells swing,
    With roots half bare the pine-trees cling ;

And, through the shadow looking west,
    You see the wavering river flow
    Along a vale, that far below

Holds to the sun, the sheltering hills
    And glimmering water-line between,
    Broad fields of corn and meadows green,

And fruit-bent orchards grouped around
    The low brown roofs and painted eaves,
    And chimney-tops half hid in leaves.

No warmer valley hides behind
    Yon wind-scourged sand-dunes, cold and
        bleak ;
    No fairer river comes to seek

The wave-sung welcome of the sea,
    Or mark the northmost border line
    Of sun-loved growths of nut and vine.

Here, ground-fast in their native fields,
    Untempted by the city's gain,
    The quiet farmer folk remain

Who bear the pleasant name of Friends,
    And keep their fathers' gentle ways
    And simple speech of Bible days ;

In whose neat homesteads woman holds
    With modest ease her equal place,
    And wears upon her tranquil face

The look of one who, merging not
    Her self-hood in another's will,
    Is love's and duty's handmaid still.

Pass with me down the path that winds
    Through birches to the open land,
    Where, close upon the river strand

You mark a cellar, vine o'errun,
    Above whose wall of loosened stones
    The sumach lifts its reddening cones,

And the black nightshade's berries shine,
    And broad, unsightly burdocks fold
    The household ruin, century-old.

Here, in the dim colonial time
    Of sterner lives and gloomier faith,
    A woman lived, tradition saith,

Who wrought her neighbors foul annoy,
    And witched and plagued the country-
        side,
    Till at the hangman's hand she died.

Sit with me while the westering day
    Falls slantwise down the quiet vale,
    And, haply ere yon loitering sail,

That rounds the upper headland, falls
    Below Deer Island's pines, or sees
    Behind it Hawkswood's belt of trees

Rise black against the sinking sun,
    My idyl of its days of old,
    The valley's legend, shall be told.

II. THE HUSKING

It was the pleasant harvest-time,
    When cellar-bins are closely stowed,
    And garrets bend beneath their load,

And the old swallow-haunted barns, —
    Brown-gabled, long, and full of seams
    Through which the moted sunlight
        streams,

And winds blow freshly in, to shake
  The red plumes of the roosted cocks,
  And the loose hay - mow's scented
    locks, —

Are filled with summer's ripened stores,
  Its odorous grass and barley sheaves,
  From their low scaffolds to their eaves.

On Esek Harden's oaken floor,
  With many an autumn threshing worn,
  Lay the heaped ears of unhusked corn.

And thither came young men and maids,
  Beneath a moon that, large and low,
  Lit that sweet eve of long ago.

They took their places ; some by chance,
  And others by a merry voice
  Or sweet smile guided to their choice.

How pleasantly the rising moon,
  Between the shadow of the mows,
  Looked on them through the great elm-
    boughs !

On sturdy boyhood, sun-embrowned,
  On girlhood with its solid curves
  Of healthful strength and painless nerves!

And jests went round, and laughs that
    made
  The house-dog answer with his howl,
  And kept astir the barn-yard fowl ;

And quaint old songs their fathers sung
  In Derby dales and Yorkshire moors,
  Ere Norman William trod their shores ;

And tales, whose merry license shook
  The fat sides of the Saxon thane,
  Forgetful of the hovering Dane, —

Rude plays to Celt and Cimbri known,
  The charms and riddles that beguiled
  On Oxus' banks thé young world's
    child, —

That primal picture-speech wherein
  Have youth and maid the story told,
  So new in each, so dateless old,

Recalling pastoral Ruth in her
  Who waited, blushing and demure,
  The red-ear's kiss of forfeiture.

III. THE WITCH'S DAUGHTER

But still the sweetest voice was mute
  That river-valley ever heard
  From lips of maid or throat of bird ;

For Mabel Martin sat apart,
  And let the hay-mow's shadow fall
  Upon the loveliest face of all.

She sat apart, as one forbid,
  Who knew that none would condescend
  To own the Witch-wife's child a friend.

The seasons scarce had gone their round,
  Since curious thousands thronged to see
  Her mother at the gallows-tree ;

And mocked the prison-palsied limbs
  That faltered on the fatal stairs,
  And wan lip trembling with its prayers !

Few questioned of the sorrowing child,
  Or, when they saw the mother die,
  Dreamed of the daughter's agony.

They went up to their homes that day,
  As men and Christians justified :
  God willed it, and the wretch had died !

Dear God and Father of us all,
  Forgive our faith in cruel lies, —
  Forgive the blindness that denies !

Forgive thy creature when he takes,
  For the all-perfect love Thou art,
  Some grim creation of his heart.

Cast down our idols, overturn
  Our bloody altars ; let us see
  Thyself in Thy humanity !

Young Mabel from her mother's grave
  Crept to her desolate hearth-stone,
  And wrestled with her fate alone ;

With love, and anger, and despair,
  The phantoms of disordered sense,
  The awful doubts of Providence !

Oh, dreary broke the winter days,
  And dreary fell the winter nights
  When, one by one, the neighboring
    lights

Went out, and human sounds grew still,
  And all the phantom-peopled dark
  Closed round her hearth-fire's dying
    spark.

And summer days were sad and long,
  And sad the uncompanioned eves,
  And sadder sunset-tinted leaves,

And Indian Summer's airs of balm ;
  She scarcely felt the soft caress,
  The beauty died of loneliness !

The school-boys jeered her as they passed,
  And, when she sought the house of prayer,
  Her mother's curse pursued her there.

And still o'er many a neighboring door
  She saw the horseshoe's curvèd charm,
  To guard against her mother's harm :

That mother, poor and sick and lame,
  Who daily, by the old arm-chair,
  Folded her withered hands in prayer ; —

Who turned, in Salem's dreary jail,
  Her worn old Bible o'er and o'er,
  When her dim eyes could read no more !

Sore tried and pained, the poor girl kept
  Her faith, and trusted that her way,
  So dark, would somewhere meet the day.

And still her weary wheel went round
  Day after day, with no relief :
  Small leisure have the poor for grief.

IV. THE CHAMPION

So in the shadow Mabel sits ;
  Untouched by mirth she sees and hears,
  Her smile is sadder than her tears.

But cruel eyes have found her out,
  And cruel lips repeat her name,
  And taunt her with her mother's shame.

She answered not with railing words,
  But drew her apron o'er her face,
  And, sobbing, glided from the place.

And only pausing at the door,
  Her sad eyes met the troubled gaze
  Of one who, in her better days,

Had been her warm and steady friend,
  Ere yet her mother's doom had made
  Even Esek Harden half afraid.

He felt that mute appeal of tears,
  And, starting, with an angry frown,
  Hushed all the wicked murmurs down.

" Good neighbors mine," he sternly said,
  " This passes harmless mirth or jest ;
  I brook no insult to my guest.

" She is indeed her mother's child,
  But God's sweet pity ministers
  Unto no whiter soul than hers.

" Let Goody Martin rest in peace ;
  I never knew her harm a fly,
  And witch or not, God knows — not I.

" I know who swore her life away ;
  And as God lives, I 'd not condemn
  An Indian dog on word of them."

The broadest lands in all the town,
  The skill to guide, the power to awe,
  Were Harden's ; and his word was law.

None dared withstand him to his face,
  But one sly maiden spake aside:
  " The little witch is evil-eyed !

" Her mother only killed a cow,
  Or witched a churn or dairy-pan ;
  But she, forsooth, must charm a man ! "

V. IN THE SHADOW

Poor Mabel, homeward turning, passed
  The nameless terrors of the wood,
  And saw, as if a ghost pursued,

Her shadow gliding in the moon ;
  The soft breath of the west-wind gave
  A chill as from her mother's grave.

How dreary seemed the silent house !
  Wide in the moonbeams' ghastly glare
  Its windows had a dead man's stare !

And, like a gaunt and spectral hand,
  The tremulous shadow of a birch
  Reached out and touched the door's low
    porch,

As if to lift its latch ; hard by,
  A sudden warning call she heard,
  The night-cry of a boding bird.

She leaned against the door ; her face,
  So fair, so young, so full of pain,
  White in the moonlight's silver rain.

The river, on its pebbled rim,
  Made music such as childhood knew ;
  The door-yard tree was whispered
    through

By voices such as childhood's ear
  Had heard in moonlights long ago ;
  And through the willow-boughs below

She saw the rippled waters shine ;
  Beyond, in waves of shade and light,
  The hills rolled off into the night.

She saw and heard, but over all
  A sense of some transforming spell,
  The shadow of her sick heart fell.

And still across the wooded space
  The harvest lights of Harden shone,
  And song and jest and laugh went
    on.

And he, so gentle, true, and strong,
  Of men the bravest and the best,
  Had he, too, scorned her with the
    rest ?

She strove to drown her sense of wrong,
  And, in her old and simple way,
  To teach her bitter heart to pray.

Poor child ! the prayer, begun in faith,
  Grew to a low, despairing cry
  Of utter misery : " Let me die !

" Oh ! take me from the scornful eyes,
  And hide me where the cruel speech
  And mocking finger may not reach !

" I dare not breathe my mother's name :
  A daughter's right I dare not crave
  To weep above her unblest grave !

" Let me not live until my heart,
  With few to pity, and with none
  To love me, hardens into stone.

" O God ! have mercy on Thy child,
  Whose faith in Thee grows weak and
    small,
  And take me ere I lose it all ! "

A shadow on the moonlight fell,
  And murmuring wind and wave became
  A voice whose burden was her name.

VI. THE BETROTHAL

Had then God heard her ?   Had He
    sent
  His angel down ?   In flesh and blood,
  Before her Esek Harden stood !

He laid his hand upon her arm :
  " Dear Mabel, this no more shall be ;
  Who scoffs at you must scoff at me.

" You know rough Esek Harden well ;
  And if he seems no suitor gay,
  And if his hair is touched with gray,

" The maiden grown shall never find
  His heart less warm than when she
    smiled,
  Upon his knees a little child ! "

Her tears of grief were tears of joy,
  As, folded in his strong embrace,
  She looked in Esek Harden's face.

" O truest friend of all ! " she said,
  " God bless you for your kindly thought,
  And make me worthy of my lot ! "

He led her forth, and, blent in one,
  Beside their happy pathway ran
  The shadows of the maid and man.

He led her through his dewy fields,
  To where the swinging lanterns glowed,
  And through the doors the huskers
    showed.

" Good friends and neighbors ! " Esek said
  " I 'm weary of this lonely life ;
  In Mabel see my chosen wife !

" She greets you kindly, one and all ;
  The past is past, and all offence
  Falls harmless from her innocence.

" Henceforth she stands no more alone ;
  You know what Esek Harden is ; —
  He brooks no wrong to him or his.

" Now let the merriest tales be told,
  And let the sweetest songs be sung
  That ever made the old heart young !

" For now the lost has found a home ;
  And a lone hearth shall brighter burn,
  As all the household joys return ! "

Oh, pleasantly the harvest-moon,
  Between the shadow of the mows,
  Looked on them through the great elm-
    boughs !

On Mabel's curls of golden hair,
  On Esek's shaggy strength it fell ;
  And the wind whispered, " It is well ! "

THE PROPHECY OF SAMUEL SEWALL

The prose version of this prophecy is to be
found in Sewall's *The New Heaven upon the
New Earth*, 1697, quoted in Joshua Coffin's
History of Newbury. Judge Sewall's father,
Henry Sewall, was one of the pioneers of New-
bury.

UP and down the village streets
Strange are the forms my fancy meets,
For the thoughts and things of to-day are
    hid,
And through the veil of a closèd lid
The ancient worthies I see again :
I hear the tap of the elder's cane,
And his awful periwig I see,
And the silver buckles of shoe and knee.
Stately and slow, with thoughtful air,
His black cap hiding his whitened hair,
Walks the Judge of the great Assize,
Samuel Sewall the good and wise.
His face with lines of firmness wrought,
He wears the look of a man unbought,
Who swears to his hurt and changes not ;
Yet, touched and softened nevertheless
With the grace of Christian gentleness,
The face that a child would climb to kiss !
True and tender and brave and just,
That man might honor and woman trust.

Touching and sad, a tale is told,
Like a penitent hymn of the Psalmist old,
Of the fast which the good man lifelong
    kept
With a haunting sorrow that never slept,
As the circling year brought round the time
Of an error that left the sting of crime,
When he sat on the bench of the witchcraft
    courts,
With the laws of Moses and Hale's Reports,
And spake, in the name of both, the word
That gave the witch's neck to the cord,
And piled the oaken planks that pressed
The feeble life from the warlock's breast !
All the day long, from dawn to dawn,
His door was bolted, his curtain drawn ;
No foot on his silent threshold trod,
No eye looked on him save that of God,
As he baffled the ghosts of the dead with
    charms
Of penitent tears, and prayers, and psalms,
And, with precious proofs from the sacred
    word
Of the boundless pity and love of the Lord,
His faith confirmed and his trust renewed
That the sin of his ignorance, sorely rued,
Might be washed away in the mingled flood
Of his human sorrow and Christ's dear
    blood !

Green forever the memory be
Of the Judge of the old Theocracy,
Whom even his errors glorified,
Like a far-seen, sunlit mountain-side
By the cloudy shadows which o'er it glide !
Honor and praise to the Puritan
Who the halting step of his age outran,
And, seeing the infinite worth of man
In the priceless gift the Father gave,
In the infinite love that stooped to save,
Dared not brand his brother a slave !
" Who doth such wrong," he was wont to
    say,
In his own quaint, picture-loving way,
" Flings up to Heaven a hand-grenade
Which God shall cast down upon his head ! "

Widely as heaven and hell, contrast
That brave old jurist of the past
And the cunning trickster and knave of
    courts
Who the holy features of Truth distorts, —
Ruling as right the will of the strong,
Poverty, crime, and weakness wrong ;
Wide-eared to power, to the wronged and
    weak
Deaf as Egypt's gods of leek ;

Scoffing aside at party's nod
Order of nature and law of God ;
For whose dabbled ermine respect were
  waste,
Reverence folly, and awe misplaced ;
Justice of whom 't were vain to seek
As from Koordish robber or Syrian Sheik !
Oh, leave the wretch to his bribes and sins ;
Let him rot in the web of lies he spins !
To the saintly soul of the early day,
To the Christian judge, let us turn and
  say :
" Praise and thanks for an honest man ! —
Glory to God for the Puritan ! "

I see, far southward, this quiet day,
The hills of Newbury rolling away,
With the many tints of the season gay,
Dreamily blending in autumn mist
Crimson, and gold, and amethyst.
Long and low, with dwarf trees crowned,
Plum Island lies, like a whale aground,
A stone's toss over the narrow sound.
Inland, as far as the eye can go,
The hills curve round like a bended bow ;
A silver arrow from out them sprung,
I see the shine of the Quasycung ;
And, round and round, over valley and
  hill,
Old roads winding, as old roads will,
Here to a ferry, and there to a mill ;
And glimpses of chimneys and gabled
  eaves,
Through green elm arches and maple
  leaves, —
Old homesteads sacred to all that can
Gladden or sadden the heart of man,
Over whose thresholds of oak and stone
Life and Death have come and gone !
There pictured tiles in the fireplace show,
Great beams sag from the ceiling low,
The dresser glitters with polished wares,
The long clock ticks on the foot-worn stairs,
And the low, broad chimney shows the
  crack
By the earthquake made a century back.
Up from their midst springs the village
  spire
With the crest of its cock in the sun afire ;
Beyond are orchards and planting lands,
And great salt marshes and glimmering
  sands,
And, where north and south the coast-lines
  run,
The blink of the sea in breeze and sun !

I see it all like a chart unrolled,
But my thoughts are full of the past and
  old,
I hear the tales of my boyhood told ;
And the shadows and shapes of early days
Flit dimly by in the veiling haze,
With measured movement and rhythmic
  chime
Weaving like shuttles my web of rhyme.
I think of the old man wise and good
Who once on yon misty hillsides stood,
(A poet who never measured rhyme,
A seer unknown to his dull-eared time,)
And, propped on his staff of age, looked
  down,
With his boyhood's love, on his native town,
Where, written as if on its hills and plains,
His burden of prophecy yet remains,
For the voices of wood, and wave, and wind
To read in the ear of the musing mind : —

" As long as Plum Island, to guard the
  coast
As God appointed, shall keep its post ;
As long as a salmon shall haunt the deep
Of Merrimac River, or sturgeon leap ;
As long as pickerel swift and slim,
Or red-backed perch, in Crane Pond swim ;
As long as the annual sea-fowl know
Their time to come and their time to go ;
As long as cattle shall roam at will
The green grass meadows by Turkey Hill ;
As long as sheep shall look from the side
Of Oldtown Hill on marshes wide,
And Parker River, and salt-sea tide ;
As long as a wandering pigeon shall search
The fields below from his white-oak perch,
When the barley-harvest is ripe and shorn,
And the dry husks fall from the standing
  corn ;
As long as Nature shall not grow old,
Nor drop her work from her doting hold,
And her care for the Indian corn forget,
And the yellow rows in pairs to set ; —
So long shall Christians here be born,
Grow up and ripen as God's sweet corn ! —
By the beak of bird, by the breath of frost,
Shall never a holy ear be lost,
But, husked by Death in the Planter's
  sight,
Be sown again in the fields of light ! "

The Island still is purple with plums,
Up the river the salmon comes,
The sturgeon leaps, and the wild-fowl feeds

On hillside berries and marish seeds, —
All the beautiful signs remain,
From spring-time sowing to autumn rain
The good man's vision returns again !
And let us hope, as well we can,
That the Silent Angel who garners man
May find some grain as of old he found
In the human cornfield ripe and sound,
And the Lord of the Harvest deign to
    own
The precious seed by the fathers sown !

THE RED RIVER VOYAGEUR

[Suggested by reading the following passage
in *Minnesota and its Resources*, by J. Wesley
Bond: "As I pass slowly along the lonely
road that leads me from thee, Selkirk, mine
eyes do turn continually to gaze upon thy smil-
ing, golden fields, and thy lofty towers, now
burnished with the rays of the departing sun,
while the sweet vesper bell reverberates afar
and strikes so mournfully pleasant upon mine
ear. I feel satisfied that, though absent thou-
sands of weary miles, my thoughts will always
dwell on thee with rapturous emotions." At
midnight, with the last stroke of the clock
ushering in the 17th of December, 1891, the
84th anniversary of Whittier's birth, the bells
of St. Boniface rang a joyous peal.]

Out and in the river is winding
  The links of its long, red chain,
Through belts of dusky pine-land
  And gusty leagues of plain.

Only, at times, a smoke-wreath
  With the drifting cloud-rack joins, —
The smoke of the hunting-lodges
  Of the wild Assiniboins !

Drearily blows the north-wind
  From the land of ice and snow ;
The eyes that look are weary,
  And heavy the hands that row.

And with one foot on the water,
  And one upon the shore,
The Angel of Shadow gives warning
  That day shall be no more.

Is it the clang of wild-geese ?
  Is it the Indian's yell,
That lends to the voice of the north-wind
  The tones of a far-off bell ?

The voyageur smiles as he listens
  To the sound that grows apace ;
Well he knows the vesper ringing
  Of the bells of St. Boniface.

The bells of the Roman Mission,
  That call from their turrets twain,
To the boatman on the river,
  To the hunter on the plain !

Even so in our mortal journey
  The bitter north-winds blow,
And thus upon life's Red River
  Our hearts, as oarsmen, row.

And when the Angel of Shadow
  Rests his feet on wave and shore,
And our eyes grow dim with watching
  And our hearts faint at the oar,

Happy is he who heareth
  The signal of his release
In the bells of the Holy City,
  The chimes of eternal peace !

THE PREACHER

George Whitefield, the celebrated preacher,
died at Newburyport in 1770, and was buried
under the church which has since borne his
name.

Its windows flashing to the sky,
Beneath a thousand roofs of brown,
Far down the vale, my friend and I
Beheld the old and quiet town ;
The ghostly sails that out at sea
Flapped their white wings of mystery ;
The beaches glimmering in the sun,
And the low wooded capes that run
Into the sea-mist north and south ;
The sand-bluffs at the river's mouth ;
The swinging chain-bridge, and, afar,
The foam-line of the harbor-bar.

Over the woods and meadow-lands
A crimson-tinted shadow lay,
Of clouds through which the setting day
Flung a slant glory far away.
It glittered on the wet sea-sands,
It flamed upon the city's panes,
Smote the white sails of ships that wore
Outward or in, and glided o'er
The steeples with their veering vanes !

Awhile my friend with rapid search
O'erran the landscape. "Yonder spire
Over gray roofs, a shaft of fire ;
What is it, pray ?" — "The Whitefield
    Church !
Walled about by its basement stones,
There rest the marvellous prophet's bones."
Then as our homeward way we walked,
Of the great preacher's life we talked ;
And through the mystery of our theme
The outward glory seemed to stream,
And Nature's self interpreted
The doubtful record of the dead ;
And every level beam that smote
The sails upon the dark afloat
A symbol of the light became,
Which touched the shadows of our blame
With tongues of Pentecostal flame.

Over the roofs of the pioneers
Gathers the moss of a hundred years ;
On man and his works has passed the
    change
Which needs must be in a century's range.
The land lies open and warm in the sun,
Anvils clamor and mill-wheels run, —
Flocks on the hillsides, herds on the plain,
The wilderness gladdened with fruit and
    grain !
But the living faith of the settlers old
A dead profession their children hold ;
To the lust of office and greed of trade
A stepping-stone is the altar made.
The Church, to place and power the door,
Rebukes the sin of the world no more,
Nor sees its Lord in the homeless poor.
Everywhere is the grasping hand,
And eager adding of land to land ;
And earth, which seemed to the fathers
    meant
But as a pilgrim's wayside tent, —
A nightly shelter to fold away
When the Lord should call at the break of
    day, —
Solid and steadfast seems to be,
And Time has forgotten Eternity !

But fresh and green from the rotting roots
Of primal forests the young growth shoots ;
From the death of the old the new proceeds,
And the life of truth from the rot of creeds:
On the ladder of God, which upward leads,
The steps of progress are human needs.
For His judgments still are a mighty deep,
And the eyes of His providence never sleep:

When the night is darkest He gives the
    morn ;
When the famine is sorest, the wine and
    corn !

In the church of the wilderness Edwards
    wrought,
Shaping his creed at the forge of thought ;
And with Thor's own hammer welded and
    bent
The iron links of his argument,
Which strove to grasp in its mighty span
The purpose of God and the fate of man !
Yet faithful still, in his daily round
To the weak, and the poor, and sin-sick
    found,
The schoolman's lore and the casuist's art
Drew warmth and life from his fervent
    heart.
Had he not seen in the solitudes
Of his deep and dark Northampton woods
A vision of love about him fall ?
Not the blinding splendor which fell on
    Saul,
But the tenderer glory that rests on them
Who walk in the New Jerusalem,
Where never the sun nor moon are known,
But the Lord and His love are the light
    alone !
And watching the sweet, still countenance
Of the wife of his bosom rapt in trance,
Had he not treasured each broken word
Of the mystical wonder seen and heard ;
And loved the beautiful dreamer more
That thus to the desert of earth she bore
Clusters of Eshcol from Canaan's shore ?

As the barley-winnower, holding with pain
Aloft in waiting his chaff and grain,
Joyfully welcomes the far-off breeze
Sounding the pine-tree's slender keys,
So he who had waited long to hear
The sound of the Spirit drawing near,
Like that which the son of Iddo heard
When the feet of angels the myrtles
    stirred,
Felt the answer of prayer, at last,
As over his church the afflatus passed,
Breaking its sleep as breezes break
To sun-bright ripples a stagnant lake.

At first a tremor of silent fear,
The creep of the flesh at danger near,
A vague foreboding and discontent,
Over the hearts of the people went.

All nature warned in sounds and signs :
The wind in the tops of the forest pines
In the name of the Highest called to prayer,
As the muezzin calls from the minaret stair.
Through ceilëd chambers of secret sin
Sudden and strong the light shone in ;
A guilty sense of his neighbor's needs
Startled the man of title-deeds ;
The trembling hand of the worldling shook
The dust of years from the Holy Book ;
And the psalms of David, forgotten long,
Took the place of the scoffer's song.

The impulse spread like the outward course
Of waters moved by a central force ;
The tide of spiritual life rolled down
From inland mountains to seaboard town.

Prepared and ready the altar stands
Waiting the prophet's outstretched hands
And prayer availing, to downward call
The fiery answer in view of all.
Hearts are like wax in the furnace ; who
Shall mould, and shape, and cast them
    anew ?
Lo ! by the Merrimac Whitefield stands
In the temple that never was made by
    hands, —
Curtains of azure, and crystal wall,
And dome of the sunshine over all —
A homeless pilgrim, with dubious name
Blown about on the winds of fame ;
Now as an angel of blessing classed,
And now as a mad enthusiast.
Called in his youth to sound and gauge
The moral lapse of his race and age,
And, sharp as truth, the contrast draw
Of human frailty and perfect law ;
Possessed by the one dread thought that
    lent
Its goad to his fiery temperament,
Up and down the world he went,
A John the Baptist crying, Repent !

No perfect whole can our nature make ;
Here or there the circle will break ;
The orb of life as it takes the light
On one side leaves the other in night.
Never was saint so good and great
As to give no chance at St. Peter's gate
For the plea of the Devil's advocate.
So, incomplete by his being's law,
The marvellous preacher had his flaw ;
With step unequal, and lame with faults,
His shade on the path of History halts.

Wisely and well said the Eastern bard :
Fear is easy, but love is hard, —
Easy to glow with the Santon's rage,
And walk on the Meccan pilgrimage ;
But he is greatest and best who can
Worship Allah by loving man.

Thus he, — to whom, in the painful stress
Of zeal on fire from its own excess,
Heaven seemed so vast and earth so small
That man was nothing, since God was all, —
Forgot, as the best at times have done,
That the love of the Lord and of man are one.

Little to him whose feet unshod
The thorny path of the desert trod,
Careless of pain, so it led to God,
Seemed the hunger-pang and the poor man's
    wrong,
The weak ones trodden beneath the strong.
Should the worm be chooser ? — the clay
    withstand
The shaping will of the potter's hand ?

In the Indian fable Arjoon hears
The scorn of a god rebuke his fears :
"Spare thy pity !" Krishna saith ;
"Not in thy sword is the power of death !
All is illusion, — loss but seems ;
Pleasure and pain are only dreams ;
Who deems he slayeth doth not kill ;
Who counts as slain is living still.
Strike, nor fear thy blow is crime ;
Nothing dies but the cheats of time ;
Slain or slayer, small the odds
To each, immortal as Indra's gods !"

So by Savannah's banks of shade,
The stones of his mission the preacher laid
On the heart of the negro crushed and rent,
And made of his blood the wall's cement ;
Bade the slave-ship speed from coast to
    coast,
Fanned by the wings of the Holy Ghost ;
And begged, for the love of Christ, the gold
Coined from the hearts in its groaning hold.
What could it matter, more or less
Of stripes, and hunger, and weariness ?
Living or dying, bond or free,
What was time to eternity ?

Alas for the preacher's cherished schemes !
Mission and church are now but dreams ;
Nor prayer nor fasting availed the plan
To honor God through the wrong of man.

Of all his labors no trace remains
Save the bondman lifting his hands in
 chains.
The woof he wove in the righteous warp
Of freedom-loving Oglethorpe
Clothes with curses the goodly land,
Changes its greenness and bloom to sand ;
And a century's lapse reveals once more
The slave-ship stealing to Georgia's shore.
Father of Light ! how blind is he
Who sprinkles the altar he rears to Thee
With the blood and tears of humanity !

He erred : shall we count His gifts as
 naught ?
Was the work of God in him unwrought ?
The servant may through his deafness err,
And blind may be God's messenger ;
But the errand is sure they go upon, —
The word is spoken, the deed is done.
Was the Hebrew temple less fair and good
That Solomon bowed to gods of wood ?
For his tempted heart and wandering feet,
Were the songs of David less pure and
 sweet ?
So in light and shadow the preacher went,
God's erring and human instrument ;
And the hearts of the people where he
 passed
Swayed as the reeds sway in the blast,
Under the spell of a voice which took
In its compass the flow of Siloa's brook,
And the mystical chime of the bells of gold
On the ephod's hem of the priest of old, —
Now the roll of thunder, and now the awe
Of the trumpet heard in the Mount of Law.

A solemn fear on the listening crowd
Fell like the shadow of a cloud.
The sailor reeling from out the ships
Whose masts stood thick in the river-slips
Felt the jest and the curse die on his lips.
Listened the fisherman rude and hard,
The calker rough from the builder's yard ;
The man of the market left his load,
The teamster leaned on his bending goad,
The maiden, and youth beside her, felt
Their hearts in a closer union melt,
And saw the flowers of their love in bloom
Down the endless vistas of life to come.
Old age sat feebly brushing away
From his ears the scanty locks of gray ;
And careless boyhood, living the free
Unconscious life of bird and tree,
Suddenly wakened to a sense

Of sin and its guilty consequence.
It was as if an angel's voice
Called the listeners up for their final choice ;
As if a strong hand rent apart
The veils of sense from soul and heart,
Showing in light ineffable
The joys of heaven and woes of hell !
All about in the misty air
The hills seemed kneeling in silent prayer;
The rustle of leaves, the moaning sedge,
The water's lap on its gravelled edge,
The wailing pines, and, far and faint,
The wood-dove's note of sad complaint, —
To the solemn voice of the preacher lent
An undertone as of low lament ;
And the rote of the sea from its sandy coast,
On the easterly wind, now heard, now lost,
Seemed the murmurous sound of the judg-
 ment host.

Yet wise men doubted, and good men wept,
As that storm of passion above them swept,
And, comet-like, adding flame to flame,
The priests of the new Evangel came, —
Davenport, flashing upon the crowd,
Charged like summer's electric cloud,
Now holding the listener still as death
With terrible warnings under breath,
Now shouting for joy, as if he viewed
The vision of Heaven's beatitude !
And Celtic Tennant, his long coat bound
Like a monk's with leathern girdle round,
Wild with the toss of unshorn hair,
And wringing of hands, and eyes aglare,
Groaning under the world's despair !
Grave pastors, grieving their flocks to lose,
Prophesied to the empty pews
That gourds would wither, and mushrooms
 die,
And noisiest fountains run soonest dry,
Like the spring that gushed in Newbury
 Street,
Under the tramp of the earthquake's feet,
A silver shaft in the air and light,
For a single day, then lost in night,
Leaving only, its place to tell,
Sandy fissure and sulphurous smell.
With zeal wing-clipped and white-heat cool,
Moved by the spirit in grooves of rule,
No longer harried, and cropped, and
 fleeced,
Flogged by sheriff and cursed by priest,
But by wiser counsels left at ease
To settle quietly on his lees,
And, self-concentred, to count as done

The work which his fathers well begun,
In silent protest of letting alone,
The Quaker kept the way of his own, —
A non-conductor among the wires,
With coat of asbestos proof to fires.
And quite unable to mend his pace
To catch the falling manna of grace,
He hugged the closer his little store
Of faith, and silently prayed for more.
And vague of creed and barren of rite,
But holding, as in his Master's sight,
Act and thought to the inner light,
The round of his simple duties walked,
And strove to live what the others talked.

And who shall marvel if evil went
Step by step with the good intent,
And with love and meekness, side by side,
Lust of the flesh and spiritual pride ? —
That passionate longings and fancies vain
Set the heart on fire and crazed the brain ?
That over the holy oracles
Folly sported with cap and bells ?
That goodly women and learned men
Marvelling told with tongue and pen
How unweaned children chirped like birds
Texts of Scripture and solemn words,
Like the infant seers of the rocky glens
In the Puy de Dome of wild Cevennes :
Or baby Lamas who pray and preach
From Tartar cradles in Buddha's speech ?

In the war which Truth or Freedom wages
With impious fraud and the wrong of ages,
Hate and malice and self-love mar
The notes of triumph with painful jar,
And the helping angels turn aside
Their sorrowing faces the shame to hide.
Never on custom's oilèd grooves
The world to a higher level moves,
But grates and grinds with friction hard
On granite boulder and flinty shard.
The heart must bleed before it feels,
The pool be troubled before it heals ;
Ever by losses the right must gain,
Every good have its birth of pain ;
The active Virtues blush to find
The Vices wearing their badge behind,
And Graces and Charities feel the fire
Wherein the sins of the age expire ;
The fiend still rends as of old he rent
The tortured body from which he went.

But Time tests all. In the over-drift
And flow of the Nile, with its annual gift,

Who cares for the Hadji's relics sunk ?
Who thinks of the drowned - out Coptic
    monk ?
The tide that loosens the temple's stones,
And scatters the sacred ibis-bones,
Drives away from the valley-land
That Arab robber, the wandering sand,
Moistens the fields that know no rain,
Fringes the desert with belts of grain,
And bread to the sower brings again.
So the flood of emotion deep and strong
Troubled the land as it swept along,
But left a result of holier lives,
Tenderer mothers and worthier wives.
The husband and father whose children fled
And sad wife wept when his drunken tread
Frightened peace from his roof-tree's shade,
And a rock of offence his hearthstone made,
In a strength that was not his own began
To rise from the brute's to the plane of
    man.
Old friends embraced, long held apart
By evil counsel and pride of heart ;
And penitence saw through misty tears,
In the bow of hope on its cloud of fears,
The promise of Heaven's eternal years, —
The peace of God for the world's an-
    noy, —
Beauty for ashes, and oil of joy !

Under the church of Federal Street,
Under the tread of its Sabbath feet,
Walled about by its basement stones,
Lie the marvellous preacher's bones.
No saintly honors to them are shown,
No sign nor miracle have they known ;
But he who passes the ancient church
Stops in the shade of its belfry-porch,
And ponders the wonderful life of him
Who lies at rest in that charnel dim.
Long shall the traveller strain his eye
From the railroad car, as it plunges by,
And the vanishing town behind him search
For the slender spire of the Whitefield
    Church ;
And feel for one moment the ghosts of
    trade,
And fashion, and folly, and pleasure laid,
By the thought of that life of pure intent,
That voice of warning yet eloquent,
Of one on the errands of angels sent.
And if where he labored the flood of sin
Like a tide from the harbor-bar sets in,
And over a life of time and sense
The church-spires lift their vain defence,

As if to scatter the bolts of God
With the points of Calvin's thunder-rod, —
Still, as the gem of its civic crown,
Precious beyond the world's renown,
His memory hallows the ancient town !

THE TRUCE OF PISCATAQUA

In the winter of 1675–76, the Eastern Indians, who had been making war upon the New Hampshire settlements, were so reduced in numbers by fighting and famine that they agreed to a peace with Major Waldron at Dover ; but the peace was broken in the fall of 1676. The famous chief, Squando, was the principal negotiator on the part of the savages. He had taken up the hatchet to revenge the brutal treatment of his child by drunken white sailors, which caused its death.

It not unfrequently happened during the Border wars that young white children were adopted by their Indian captors, and so kindly treated that they were unwilling to leave the free, wild life of the woods ; and in some instances they utterly refused to go back with their parents to their old homes and civilization.

RAZE these long blocks of brick and stone,
These huge mill-monsters overgrown ;
Blot out the humbler piles as well,
Where, moved like living shuttles, dwell
The weaving genii of the bell ;
Tear from the wild Cocheco's track
The dams that hold its torrents back ;
And let the loud-rejoicing fall
Plunge, roaring, down its rocky wall ;
And let the Indian's paddle play
On the unbridged Piscataqua !
Wide over hill and valley spread
Once more the forest, dusk and dread,
With here and there a clearing cut
From the walled shadows round it shut ;
Each with its farm-house builded rude,
By English yeoman squared and hewed,
And the grim, flankered block-house bound
With bristling palisades around.
So, haply shall before thine eyes
The dusty veil of centuries rise,
The old, strange scenery overlay
The tamer pictures of to-day,
While, like the actors in a play,
Pass in their ancient guise along
The figures of my border song :
What time beside Cocheco's flood
The white man and the red man stood,
With words of peace and brotherhood ;

When passed the sacred calumet
From lip to lip with fire-draught wet,
And, puffed in scorn, the peace-pipe's smoke
Through the gray beard of Waldron broke,
And Squando's voice, in suppliant plea
For mercy, struck the haughty key
Of one who held, in any fate,
His native pride inviolate !

" Let your ears be opened wide !
He who speaks has never lied.
Waldron of Piscataqua,
Hear what Squando has to say !

" Squando shuts his eyes and sees,
Far off, Saco's hemlock-trees.
In his wigwam, still as stone,
Sits a woman all alone,

" Wampum beads and birchen strands
Dropping from her careless hands,
Listening ever for the fleet
Patter of a dead child's feet !

" When the moon a year ago
Told the flowers the time to blow,
In that lonely wigwam smiled
Menewee, our little child.

" Ere that moon grew thin and old,
He was lying still and cold ;
Sent before us, weak and small,
When the Master did not call !

" On his little grave I lay ;
Three times went and came the day,
Thrice above me blazed the noon,
Thrice upon me wept the moon.

" In the third night-watch I heard,
Far and low, a spirit-bird ;
Very mournful, very wild,
Sang the totem of my child.

" ' Menewee, poor Menewee,
Walks a path he cannot see :
Let the white man's wigwam light
With its blaze his steps aright.

" ' All-uncalled, he dares not show
Empty hands to Manito :
Better gifts he cannot bear
Than the scalps his slayers wear.'

"All the while the totem sang,
Lightning blazed and thunder rang ;
And a black cloud, reaching high,
Pulled the white moon from the sky.

"I, the medicine-man, whose ear
All that spirits hear can hear, —
I, whose eyes are wide to see
All the things that are to be, —

"Well I knew the dreadful signs
In the whispers of the pines,
In the river roaring loud,
In the mutter of the cloud.

"At the breaking of the day,
From the grave I passed away ;
Flowers bloomed round me, birds sang
    glad,
But my heart was hot and mad.

"There is rust on Squando's knife
From the warm, red springs of life ;
On the funeral hemlock-trees
Many a scalp the totem sees.

"Blood for blood ! But evermore
Squando's heart is sad and sore ;
And his poor squaw waits at home
For the feet that never come !

"Waldron of Cocheco, hear !
Squando speaks, who laughs at fear ;
Take the captives he has ta'en ;
Let the land have peace again !"

As the words died on his tongue,
Wide apart his warriors swung ;
Parted, at the sign he gave,
Right and left, like Egypt's wave.

And, like Israel passing free
Through the prophet-charmëd sea,
Captive mother, wife, and child
Through the dusky terror filed.

One alone, a little maid,
Middleway her steps delayed,
Glancing, with quick, troubled sight,
Round about from red to white.

Then his hand the Indian laid
On the little maiden's head,
Lightly from her forehead fair
Smoothing back her yellow hair.

"Gift or favor ask I none ;
What I have is all my own :
Never yet the birds have sung,
'Squando hath a beggar's tongue.'

"Yet for her who waits at home,
For the dead who cannot come,
Let the little Gold-hair be
In the place of Menewee !

"Mishanock, my little star !
Come to Saco's pines afar ;
Where the sad one waits at home,
Wequashim, my moonlight, come !"

"What !" quoth Waldron, "leave a
    child
Christian-born to heathens wild ?
As God lives, from Satan's hand
I will pluck her as a brand !"

"Hear me, white man !" Squando cried ;
"Let the little one decide.
Wequashim, my moonlight, say,
Wilt thou go with me, or stay ?"

Slowly, sadly, half afraid,
Half regretfully, the maid
Owned the ties of blood and race, —
Turned from Squando's pleading face.

Not a word the Indian spoke,
But his wampum chain he broke,
And the beaded wonder hung
On that neck so fair and young.

Silence-shod, as phantoms seem
In the marches of a dream,
Single-filed, the grim array
Through the pine-trees wound away.

Doubting, trembling, sore amazed,
Through her tears the young child gazed
"God preserve her !" Waldron said ;
"Satan hath bewitched the maid !"

Years went and came. At close of day
Singing came a child from play,
Tossing from her loose-locked head
Gold in sunshine, brown in shade.

Pride was in the mother's look,
But her head she gravely shook,
And with lips that fondly smiled
Feigned to chide her truant child.

Unabashed, the maid began :
" Up and down the brook I ran,
Where, beneath the bank so steep,
Lie the spotted trout asleep.

" ' Chip !' went squirrel on the wall,
After me I heard him call,
And the cat-bird on the tree
Tried his best to mimic me.

" Where the hemlocks grew so dark
That I stopped to look and hark,
On a log, with feather-hat,
By the path, an Indian sat.

" Then I cried, and ran away ;
But he called, and bade me stay ;
And his voice was good and mild
As my mother's to her child.

" And he took my wampum chain,
Looked and looked it o'er again ;
Gave me berries, and, beside,
On my neck a plaything tied."

Straight the mother stooped to see
What the Indian's gift might be.
On the braid of wampum hung,
Lo ! a cross of silver swung.

Well she knew its graven sign,
Squando's bird and totem pine ;
And, a mirage of the brain,
Flowed her childhood back again.

Flashed the roof the sunshine through,
Into space the walls outgrew ;
On the Indian's wigwam-mat,
Blossom-crowned, again she sat.

Cool she felt the west-wind blow,
In her ear the pines sang low,
And, like links from out a chain,
Dropped the years of care and pain.

From the outward toil and din,
From the griefs that gnaw within,
To the freedom of the woods
Called the birds, and winds, and floods.

Well, O painful minister !
Watch thy flock, but blame not her,
If her ear grew sharp to hear
All their voices whispering near.

Blame her not, as to her soul
All the desert's glamour stole,
That a tear for childhood's loss
Dropped upon the Indian's cross.

When, that night, the Book was read,
And she bowed her widowed head,
And a prayer for each loved name
Rose like incense from a flame,

With a hope the creeds forbid
In her pitying bosom hid,
To the listening ear of Heaven
Lo ! the Indian's name was given.

MY PLAYMATE

[When written, this poem bore the title
Eleanor, and when first printed *The Playmate*.]

THE pines were dark on Ramoth hill,
  Their song was soft and low ;
The blossoms in the sweet May wind
  Were falling like the snow.

The blossoms drifted at our feet,
  The orchard birds sang clear ;
The sweetest and the saddest day
  It seemed of all the year.

For, more to me than birds or flowers,
  My playmate left her home,
And took with her the laughing spring,
  The music and the bloom.

She kissed the lips of kith and kin,
  She laid her hand in mine :
What more could ask the bashful boy
  Who fed her father's kine ?

She left us in the bloom of May :
  The constant years told o'er
Their seasons with as sweet May morns,
  But she came back no more.

I walk, with noiseless feet, the round
  Of uneventful years ;
Still o'er and o'er I sow the spring
  And reap the autumn ears.

She lives where all the golden year
  Her summer roses blow ;
The dusky children of the sun
  Before her come and go.

There haply with her jewelled hands
  She smooths her silken gown, —
No more the homespun lap wherein
  I shook the walnuts down.

The wild grapes wait us by the brook,
  The brown nuts on the hill,
And still the May-day flowers make sweet
  The woods of Follymill.

The lilies blossom in the pond,
  The bird builds in the tree,
The dark pines sing on Ramoth hill
  The slow song of the sea.

I wonder if she thinks of them,
  And how the old time seems, —
If ever the pines of Ramoth wood
  Are sounding in her dreams.

I see her face, I hear her voice ;
  Does she remember mine ?
And what to her is now the boy
  Who fed her father's kine ?

What cares she that the orioles build
  For other eyes than ours, —
That other hands with nuts are filled,
  And other laps with flowers ?

O playmate in the golden time !
  Our mossy seat is green,
Its fringing violets blossom yet,
  The old trees o'er it lean.

The winds so sweet with birch and fern
  A sweeter memory blow ;
And there in spring the veeries sing
  The song of long ago.

And still the pines of Ramoth wood
  Are moaning like the sea, —
The moaning of the sea of change
  Between myself and thee !

COBBLER KEEZAR'S VISION

This ballad was written on the occasion of a
Horticultural Festival. Cobbler Keezar was a
noted character among the first settlers in the
valley of the Merrimac.

THE beaver cut his timber
  With patient teeth that day,

The minks were fish-wards, and the crows
  Surveyors of highway, —

When Keezar sat on the hillside
  Upon his cobbler's form,
With a pan of coals on either hand
  To keep his waxed-ends warm.

And there, in the golden weather,
  He stitched and hammered and sung ;
In the brook he moistened his leather,
  In the pewter mug his tongue.

Well knew the tough old Teuton
  Who brewed the stoutest ale,
And he paid the goodwife's reckoning
  In the coin of song and tale.

The songs they still are singing
  Who dress the hills of vine,
The tales that haunt the Brocken
  And whisper down the Rhine.

Woodsy and wild and lonesome,
  The swift stream wound away,
Through birches and scarlet maples
  Flashing in foam and spray, —

Down on the sharp-horned ledges
  Plunging in steep cascade,
Tossing its white-maned waters
  Against the hemlock's shade.

Woodsy and wild and lonesome,
  East and west and north and south ;
Only the village of fishers
  Down at the river's mouth ;

Only here and there a clearing,
  With its farm-house rude and new,
And tree-stumps, swart as Indians,
  Where the scanty harvest grew.

No shout of home-bound reapers,
  No vintage-song he heard,
And on the green no dancing feet
  The merry violin stirred.

" Why should folk be glum," said Keezar,
  " When Nature herself is glad,
And the painted woods are laughing
  At the faces so sour and sad ? "

Small heed had the careless cobbler
  What sorrow of heart was theirs

Who travailed in pain with the births of
      God,
And planted a state with prayers, —

Hunting of witches and warlocks,
    Smiting the heathen horde, —
One hand on the mason's trowel,
    And one on the soldier's sword !

But give him his ale and cider,
    Give him his pipe and song,
Little he cared for Church or State,
    Or the balance of right and wrong.

" 'T is work, work, work," he muttered, —
    "And for rest a snuffle of psalms ! "
He smote on his leathern apron
    With his brown and waxen palms.

" Oh for the purple harvests
    Of the days when I was young !
For the merry grape-stained maidens,
    And the pleasant songs they sung !

" Oh for the breath of vineyards,
    Of apples and nuts and wine !
For an oar to row and a breeze to blow
    Down the grand old river Rhine ! "

A tear in his blue eye glistened,
    And dropped on his beard so gray.
" Old, old am I," said Keezar,
    " And the Rhine flows far away ! "

But a cunning man was the cobbler ;
    He could call the birds from the
        trees,
Charm the black snake out of the
        ledges,
    And bring back the swarming bees.

All the virtues of herbs and metals,
    All the lore of the woods, he knew,
And the arts of the Old World mingled
    With the marvels of the New.

Well he knew the tricks of magic,
    And the lapstone on his knee
Had the gift of the Mormon's goggles
    Or the stone of Doctor Dee.

For the mighty master Agrippa
    Wrought it with spell and rhyme
From a fragment of mystic moonstone
    In the tower of Nettesheim.

To a cobbler Minnesinger
    The marvellous stone gave he, —
And he gave it, in turn, to Keezar,
    Who brought it over the sea.

He held up that mystic lapstone,
    He held it up like a lens,
And he counted the long years coming
    By twenties and by tens.

" One hundred years," quoth Keezar,
    " And fifty have I told :
Now open the new before me,
    And shut me out the old ! "

Like a cloud of mist, the blackness
    Rolled from the magic stone,
And a marvellous picture mingled
    The unknown and the known.

Still ran the stream to the river,
    And river and ocean joined ;
And there were the bluffs and the blue sea-
        line,
    And cold north hills behind.

But the mighty forest was broken
    By many a steepled town,
By many a white-walled farm-house,
    And many a garner brown.

Turning a score of mill-wheels,
    The stream no more ran free ;
White sails on the winding river,
    White sails on the far-off sea.

Below in the noisy village
    The flags were floating gay,
And shone on a thousand faces
    The light of a holiday.

Swiftly the rival ploughmen
    Turned the brown earth from their shares;
Here were the farmer's treasures,
    There were the craftsman's wares.

Golden the goodwife's butter,
    Ruby her currant-wine ;
Grand were the strutting turkeys,
    Fat were the beeves and swine.

Yellow and red were the apples,
    And the ripe pears russet-brown,
And the peaches had stolen blushes
    From the girls who shook them down.

And with blooms of hill and wildwood,
  That shame the toil of art,
Mingled the gorgeous blossoms
  Of the garden's tropic heart.

"What is it I see?" said Keezar:
  "Am I here, or am I there?
Is it a fête at Bingen?
  Do I look on Frankfort fair?

"But where are the clowns and puppets,
  And imps with horns and tail?
And where are the Rhenish flagons?
  And where is the foaming ale?

"Strange things, I know, will happen, —
  Strange things the Lord permits;
But that droughty folk should be jolly
  Puzzles my poor old wits.

"Here are smiling manly faces,
  And the maiden's step is gay;
Nor sad by thinking, nor mad by drink-
    ing,
  Nor mopes, nor fools, are they.

"Here's pleasure without regretting,
  And good without abuse,
The holiday and the bridal
  Of beauty and of use.

"Here's a priest and there is a Quaker,
  Do the cat and dog agree?
Have they burned the stocks for ovenwood?
  Have they cut down the gallows-tree?

"Would the old folk know their children?
  Would they own the graceless town,
With never a ranter to worry
  And never a witch to drown?"

Loud laughed the cobbler Keezar,
  Laughed like a school-boy gay;
Tossing his arms above him,
  The lapstone rolled away.

It rolled down the rugged hillside,
  It spun like a wheel bewitched,
It plunged through the leaning willows,
  And into the river pitched.

There, in the deep, dark water,
  The magic stone lies still,
Under the leaning willows
  In the shadow of the hill.

But oft the idle fisher
  Sits on the shadowy bank,
And his dreams make marvellous pictures
  Where the wizard's lapstone sank.

And still, in the summer twilights,
  When the river seems to run
Out from the inner glory,
  Warm with the melted sun,

The weary mill-girl lingers
  Beside the charmèd stream,
And the sky and the golden water
  Shape and color her dream.

Fair wave the sunset gardens,
  The rosy signals fly;
Her homestead beckons from the cloud,
  And love goes sailing by.

AMY WENTWORTH

TO WILLIAM BRADFORD

As they who watch by sick-beds find relief
Unwittingly from the great stress of grief
And anxious care, in fantasies outwrought
From the hearth's embers flickering low, or
    caught
From whispering wind, or tread of passing
    feet,
Or vagrant memory calling up some sweet
Snatch of old song or romance, whence or
    why
They scarcely know or ask, — so, thou and I,
Nursed in the faith that Truth alone is
    strong
In the endurance which outwearies Wrong,
With meek persistence baffling brutal force,
And trusting God against the universe, —
We, doomed to watch a strife we may not
    share
With other weapons than the patriot's
    prayer,
Yet owning, with full hearts and moistened
    eyes,
The awful beauty of self-sacrifice,
And wrung by keenest sympathy for all
Who give their loved ones for the living wall
'Twixt law and treason, — in this evil day
May haply find, through automatic play
Of pen and pencil, solace to our pain,
And hearten others with the strength we
    gain.

I know it has been said our times require
No play of art, nor dalliance with the lyre,
No weak essay with Fancy's chloroform
To calm the hot, mad pulses of the storm,
But the stern war-blast rather, such as sets
The battle's teeth of serried bayonets,
And pictures grim as Vernet's.   Yet with
    these
Some softer tints may blend, and milder
    keys
Relieve the storm-stunned ear.   Let us
    keep sweet,
If so we may, our hearts, even while we eat
The bitter harvest of our own device
And half a century's moral cowardice.
As Nürnberg sang while Wittenberg defied,
And Kranach painted by his Luther's side,
And through the war-march of the Puritan
The silver stream of Marvell's music ran,
So let the household melodies be sung,
The pleasant pictures on the wall be hung, —
So let us hold against the hosts of night
And slavery all our vantage-ground of light.
Let Treason boast its savagery, and shake
From its flag-folds its symbol rattlesnake,
Nurse its fine arts, lay human skins in tan,
And carve its pipe-bowls from the bones of
    man,
And make the tale of Fijian banquets dull
By drinking whiskey from a loyal skull, —
But let us guard, till this sad war shall cease,
(God grant it soon !) the graceful arts of
    peace :
No foes are conquered who the victors teach
Their vandal manners and barbaric speech.

And while, with hearts of thankfulness, we
    bear
Of the great common burden our full share,
Let none upbraid us that the waves entice
Thy sea-dipped pencil, or some quaint de-
    vice,
Rhythmic and sweet, beguiles my pen away
From the sharp strifes and sorrows of to-
    day.
Thus, while the east-wind keen from Lab-
    rador
Sings in the leafless elms, and from the shore
Of the great sea comes the monotonous roar
Of the long-breaking surf, and all the sky
Is gray with cloud, home-bound and dull, I
    try
To time a simple legend to the sounds
Of winds in the woods, and waves on peb-
    bled bounds, —

A song for oars to chime with, such as might
Be sung by tired sea-painters, who at night
Look from their hemlock camps, by quiet
    cove
Or beach, moon-lighted, on the waves they
    love.
(So hast thou looked, when level sunset
    lay
On the calm bosom of some Eastern bay,
And all the spray-moist rocks and waves
    that rolled
Up the white sand-slopes flashed with ruddy
    gold.)
Something it has — a flavor of the sea,
And the sea's freedom — which reminds of
    thee.
Its faded picture, dimly smiling down
From the blurred fresco of the ancient
    town,
I have not touched with warmer tints in
    vain,
If, in this dark, sad year, it steals one
    thought from pain.

Her fingers shame the ivory keys
    They dance so light along ;
The bloom upon her parted lips
    Is sweeter than the song.

O perfumed suitor, spare thy smiles !
    Her thoughts are not of thee ;
She better loves the salted wind,
    The voices of the sea.

Her heart is like an outbound ship
    That at its anchor swings ;
The murmur of the stranded shell
    Is in the song she sings.

She sings, and, smiling, hears her praise
    But dreams the while of one
Who watches from his sea-blown deck
    The icebergs in the sun.

She questions all the winds that blow,
    And every fog-wreath dim,
And bids the sea-birds flying north
    Bear messages to him.

She speeds them with the thanks of men
    He perilled life to save,
And grateful prayers like holy oil
    To smooth for him the wave.

Brown Viking of the fishing-smack !
Fair toast of all the town ! —
The skipper's jerkin ill beseems
The lady's silken gown !

But ne'er shall Amy Wentworth wear
For him the blush of shame
Who dares to set his manly gifts
Against her ancient name.

The stream is brightest at its spring,
And blood is not like wine ;
Nor honored less than he who heirs
Is he who founds a line.

Full lightly shall the prize be won,
If love be Fortune's spur ;
And never maiden stoops to him
Who lifts himself to her.

Her home is brave in Jaffrey Street,
With stately stairways worn
By feet of old Colonial knights
And ladies gentle-born.

Still green about its ample porch
The English ivy twines,
Trained back to show in English oak
The herald's carven signs.

And on her, from the wainscot old,
Ancestral faces frown, —
And this has worn the soldier's sword,
And that the judge's gown.

But, strong of will and proud as they,
She walks the gallery floor
As if she trod her sailor's deck
By stormy Labrador !

The sweetbrier blooms on Kittery-side,
And green are Eliot's bowers ;
Her garden is the pebbled beach,
The mosses are her flowers.

She looks across the harbor-bar
To see the white gulls fly ;
His greeting from the Northern sea
Is in their clanging cry.

She hums a song, and dreams that he,
As in its romance old,
Shall homeward ride with silken sails
And masts of beaten gold !

Oh, rank is good, and gold is fair,
And high and low mate ill ;
But love has never known a law
Beyond its own sweet will !

THE COUNTESS

TO E. W.

I inscribed this poem to Dr. Elias Weld of
Haverhill, Massachusetts, to whose kindness I
was much indebted in my boyhood. He was
the one cultivated man in the neighborhood.
His small but well-chosen library was placed at
my disposal. He is the "wise old doctor" of
Snow-Bound.
Count François de Vipart with his cousin
Joseph Rochemont de Poyen came to the
United States in the early part of the present
century. They took up their residence at
Rocks Village on the Merrimac, where they
both married. The wife of Count Vipart was
Mary Ingalls, who, as my father remembered
her, was a very lovely young girl. Her wed-
ding dress, as described by a lady still living,
was "pink satin with an overdress of white lace,
and white satin slippers." She died in less than
a year after her marriage. Her husband re-
turned to his native country. He lies buried in
the family tomb of the Viparts at Bordeaux.
[See note at end of volume.]

I KNOW not, Time and Space so intervene,
Whether, still waiting with a trust serene,
Thou bearest up thy fourscore years and ten,
Or, called at last, art now Heaven's citizen ;
But, here or there, a pleasant thought of
    thee,
Like an old friend, all day has been with me.
The shy, still boy, for whom thy kindly hand
Smoothed his hard pathway to the wonder-
    land
Of thought and fancy, in gray manhood yet
Keeps green the memory of his early debt.
To-day, when truth and falsehood speak
    their words
Through hot-lipped cannon and the teeth
    of swords,
Listening with quickened heart and ear in-
    tent
To each sharp clause of that stern argu-
    ment,
I still can hear at times a softer note
Of the old pastoral music round me float,
While through the hot gleam of our civil
    strife

Looms the green mirage of a simpler life.
As, at his alien post, the sentinel
Drops the old bucket in the homestead well,
And hears old voices in the winds that toss
Above his head the live-oak's beard of moss,
So, in our trial-time, and under skies
Shadowed by swords like Islam's paradise,
I wait and watch, and let my fancy stray
To milder scenes and youth's Arcadian day;
And howsoe'er the pencil dipped in dreams
Shades the brown woods or tints the sun-
      set streams,
The country doctor in the foreground seems,
Whose ancient sulky down the village lanes
Dragged, like a war-car, captive ills and
      pains.
I could not paint the scenery of my song,
Mindless of one who looked thereon so
      long ;
Who, night and day, on duty's lonely round,
Made friends o' the woods and rocks, and
      knew the sound
Of each small brook, and what the hillside
      trees
Said to the winds that touched their leafy
      keys ;
Who saw so keenly and so well could paint
The village-folk, with all their humors
      quaint, —
The parson ambling on his wall-eyed roan,
Grave and erect, with white hair backward
      blown;
The tough old boatman, half amphibious
      grown ;
The muttering witch-wife of the gossip's
      tale,
And the loud straggler levying his black-
      mail, —
Old customs, habits, superstitions, fears,
All that lies buried under fifty years.
To thee, as is most fit, I bring my lay,
And, grateful, own the debt I cannot pay.

Over the wooded northern ridge,
      Between its houses brown,
To the dark tunnel of the bridge
      The street comes straggling down.

You catch a glimpse, through birch and
      pine,
      Of gable, roof, and porch,
The tavern with its swinging sign,
      The sharp horn of the church.

The river's steel-blue crescent curves
      To meet, in ebb and flow,
The single broken wharf that serves
      For sloop and gundelow.

With salt sea-scents along its shores
      The heavy hay-boats crawl,
The long antennæ of their oars
      In lazy rise and fall.

Along the gray abutment's wall
      The idle shad-net dries ;
The toll-man in his cobbler's stall
      Sits smoking with closed eyes.

You hear the pier's low undertone
      Of waves that chafe and gnaw ;
You start, — a skipper's horn is blown
      To raise the creaking draw.

At times a blacksmith's anvil sounds
      With slow and sluggard beat,
Or stage-coach on its dusty rounds
      Wakes up the staring street.

A place for idle eyes and ears,
      A cobwebbed nook of dreams ;
Left by the stream whose waves are
      years
      The stranded village seems.

And there, like other moss and rust,
      The native dweller clings,
And keeps, in uninquiring trust,
      The old, dull round of things.

The fisher drops his patient lines,
      The farmer sows his grain,
Content to hear the murmuring pines
      Instead of railroad train.

Go where, along the tangled steep
      That slopes against the west,
The hamlet's buried idlers sleep
      In still profounder rest.

Throw back the locust's flowery plume,
      The birch's pale-green scarf,
And break the web of brier and bloom
      From name and epitaph.

A simple muster-roll of death,
      Of pomp and romance shorn,
The dry, old names that common breath
      Has cheapened and outworn.

Yet pause by one low mound, and part
  The wild vines o'er it laced,
And read the words by rustic art
  Upon its headstone traced.

Haply yon white-haired villager
  Of fourscore years can say
What means the noble name of her
  Who sleeps with common clay.

An exile from the Gascon land
  Found refuge here and rest,
And loved, of all the village band,
  Its fairest and its best.

He knelt with her on Sabbath morns,
  He worshipped through her eyes,
And on the pride that doubts and scorns
  Stole in her faith's surprise.

Her simple daily life he saw
  By homeliest duties tried,
In all things by an untaught law
  Of fitness justified.

For her his rank aside he laid ;
  He took the hue and tone
Of lowly life and toil, and made
  Her simple ways his own.

Yet still, in gay and careless ease,
  To harvest-field or dance
He brought the gentle courtesies,
  The nameless grace of France.

And she who taught him love not less
  From him she loved in turn
Caught in her sweet unconsciousness
  What love is quick to learn.

Each grew to each in pleased accord,
  Nor knew the gazing town
If she looked upward to her lord
  Or he to her looked down.

How sweet, when summer's day was
    o'er,
  His violin's mirth and wail,
The walk on pleasant Newbury's shore,
  The river's moonlit sail !

Ah ! life is brief, though love be long ;
  The altar and the bier,
The burial hymn and bridal song,
  Were both in one short year !

Her rest is quiet on the hill,
  Beneath the locust's bloom ;
Far off her lover sleeps as still
  Within his scutcheoned tomb.

The Gascon lord, the village maid,
  In death still clasp their hands ;
The love that levels rank and grade
  Unites their severed lands.

What matter whose the hillside grave,
  Or whose the blazoned stone ?
Forever to her western wave
  Shall whisper blue Garonne !

O Love ! — so hallowing every soil
  That gives thy sweet flower room,
Wherever, nursed by ease or toil,
  The human heart takes bloom ! —

Plant of lost Eden, from the sod
  Of sinful earth unriven,
White blossom of the trees of God
  Dropped down to us from heaven ! —

This tangled waste of mound and stone
  Is holy for thy sake ;
A sweetness which is all thy own
  Breathes out from fern and brake.

And while ancestral pride shall twine
  The Gascon's tomb with flowers,
Fall sweetly here, O song of mine,
  With summer's bloom and showers !

And let the lines that severed seem
  Unite again in thee,
As western wave and Gallic stream
  Are mingled in one sea !

AMONG THE HILLS

This poem, when originally published, was dedicated to Annie Fields, wife of the distinguished publisher, James T. Fields, of Boston, in grateful acknowledgment of the strength and inspiration I have found in her friendship and sympathy.

The poem in its first form was entitled *The Wife: an Idyl of Bearcamp Water*, and appeared in *The Atlantic Monthly* for January, 1868. When I published the volume *Among the Hills*, in December of the same year, I expanded the Prelude and filled out also the outlines of the story.

PRELUDE

ALONG the roadside, like the flowers of
    gold
That tawny Incas for their gardens wrought,
Heavy with sunshine droops the golden-rod,
And the red pennons of the cardinal-flowers
Hang motionless upon their upright staves.
The sky is hot and hazy, and the wind,
Wing-weary with its long flight from the
    south,
Unfelt ; yet, closely scanned, yon maple
    leaf
With faintest motion, as one stirs in dreams,
Confesses it.   The locust by the wall
Stabs the noon-silence with his sharp alarm.
A single hay-cart down the dusty road
Creaks slowly, with its driver fast asleep
On the load's top.   Against the neighbor-
    ing hill,
Huddled along the stone wall's shady side,
The sheep show white, as if a snowdrift
    still
Defied the dog-star.   Through the open
    door
A drowsy smell of flowers — gray helio-
    trope,
And white sweet clover, and shy mignon-
    ette —
Comes faintly in, and silent chorus lends
To the pervading symphony of peace.

No time is this for hands long over-worn
To task their strength : and (unto Him be
    praise
Who giveth quietness !) the stress and
    strain
Of years that did the work of centuries
Have ceased, and we can draw our breath
    once more
Freely and full.   So, as yon harvesters
Make glad their nooning underneath the
    elms
With tale and riddle and old snatch of song,
I lay aside grave themes, and idly turn
The leaves of memory's sketch-book, dream-
    ing o'er
Old summer pictures of the quiet hills,
And human life, as quiet, at their feet.

And yet not idly all.   A farmer's son,
Proud of field-lore and harvest craft, and
    feeling
All their fine possibilities, how rich
And restful even poverty and toil

Become when beauty, harmony, and love
Sit at their humble hearth as angels sat
At evening in the patriarch's tent, when man
Makes labor noble, and his farmer's frock
The symbol of a Christian chivalry
Tender and just and generous to her
Who clothes with grace all duty ; still, I
    know
Too well the picture has another side, —
How wearily the grind of toil goes on
Where love is wanting, how the eye and
    ear
And heart are starved amidst the plenitude
Of nature, and how hard and colorless
Is life without an atmosphere.   I look
Across the lapse of half a century,
And call to mind old homesteads, where no
    flower
Told that the spring had come, but evil
    weeds,
Nightshade and rough-leaved burdock in
    the place
Of the sweet doorway greeting of the rose
And honeysuckle, where the house walls
    seemed
Blistering in sun, without a tree or vine
To cast the tremulous shadow of its leaves
Across the curtainless windows, from whose
    panes
Fluttered the signal rags of shiftlessness.
Within, the cluttered kitchen floor, un-
    washed
(Broom-clean I think they called it); the
    best room
Stifling with cellar-damp, shut from the air
In hot midsummer bookless, pictureless
Save the inevitable sampler hung
Over the fireplace, or a mourning piece,
A green-haired woman, peony-cheeked, be-
    neath
Impossible willows ;   the wide - throated
    hearth
Bristling with faded pine-boughs half con-
    cealing
The piled - up rubbish at the chimney's
    back ;
And, in sad keeping with all things about
    them,
Shrill, querulous women, sour and sullen
    men,
Untidy, loveless, old before their time,
With scarce a human interest save their own
Monotonous round of small economies,
Or the poor scandal of the neighborhood ;
Blind to the beauty everywhere revealed,

Treading the May-flowers with regardless
    feet ;
For them the song-sparrow and the bobolink
Sang not, nor winds made music in the
    leaves ;
For them in vain October's holocaust
Burned, gold and crimson, over all the hills,
The sacramental mystery of the woods.
Church-goers, fearful of the unseen Powers,
But grumbling over pulpit-tax and pew-
    rent,
Saving, as shrewd economists, their souls
And winter pork with the least possible
    outlay
Of salt and sanctity ; in daily life
Showing as little actual comprehension
Of Christian charity and love and duty,
As if the Sermon on the Mount had been
Outdated like a last year's almanac :
Rich in broad woodlands and in half-tilled
    fields,
And yet so pinched and bare and comfort-
    less,
The veriest straggler limping on his rounds,
The sun and air his sole inheritance,
Laughed at a poverty that paid its taxes,
And hugged his rags in self-complacency !

Not such should be the homesteads of a
    land
Where whoso wisely wills and acts may
    dwell
As king and lawgiver, in broad-acred state,
With beauty, art, taste, culture, books, to
    make
His hour of leisure richer than a life
Of fourscore to the barons of old time,
Our yeoman should be equal to his home
Set in the fair, green valleys, purple walled,
A man to match his mountains, not to creep
Dwarfed and abased below them.   I would
    fain
In this light way (of which I needs must
    own
With the knife-grinder of whom Canning
    sings,
"Stcry, God bless you ! I have none to tell
    you ! ")
Invite the eye to see and heart to feel
The beauty and the joy within their reach, —
Home, and home loves, and the beatitudes
Of nature free to all.   Haply in years
That wait to take the places of our own,
Heard where some breezy balcony looks
    down

On happy homes, or where the lake in the
    moon
Sleeps dreaming of the mountains, fair as
    Ruth,
In the old Hebrew pastoral, at the feet
Of Boaz, even this simple lay of mine
May seem the burden of a prophecy,
Finding its late fulfilment in a change
Slow as the oak's growth, lifting manhood up
Through broader culture, finer manners,
    love,
And reverence, to the level of the hills.

O Golden Age, whose light is of the dawn,
And not of sunset, forward, not behind,
Flood the new heavens and earth, and with
    thee bring
All the old virtues, whatsoever things
Are pure and honest and of good repute,
But add thereto whatever bard has sung
Or seer has told of when in trance and dream
They saw the Happy Isles of prophecy !
Let Justice hold her scale, and Truth divide
Between the right and wrong ; but give the
    heart
The freedom of its fair inheritance ;
Let the poor prisoner, cramped and starved
    so long,
At Nature's table feast his ear and eye
With joy and wonder ; let all harmonies
Of sound, form, color, motion, wait upon
The princely guest, whether in soft attire
Of leisure clad, or the coarse frock of
    toil,
And, lending life to the dead form of faith,
Give human nature reverence for the sake
Of One who bore it, making it divine
With the ineffable tenderness of God ;
Let common need, the brotherhood of
    prayer,
The heirship of an unknown destiny,
The unsolved mystery round about us, make
A man more precious than the gold of Ophir.
Sacred, inviolate, unto whom all things
Should minister, as outward types and signs
Of the eternal beauty which fulfils
The one great purpose of creation, Love,
The sole necessity of Earth and Heaven !

For weeks the clouds had raked the hills
    And vexed the vales with raining,
And all the woods were sad with mist,
    And all the brooks complaining.

At last, a sudden night-storm tore
  The mountain veils asunder,
And swept the valleys clean before
  The besom of the thunder.

Through Sandwich notch the west-wind
    sang
Good morrow to the cotter ;
And once again Chocorua's horn
  Of shadow pierced the water.

Above his broad lake Ossipee,
  Once more the sunshine wearing,
Stooped, tracing on that silver shield
  His grim armorial bearing.

Clear drawn against the hard blue sky,
  The peaks had winter's keenness ;
And, close on autumn's frost, the vales
  Had more than June's fresh greenness.

Again the sodden forest floors
  With golden lights were checkered,
Once more rejoicing leaves in wind
  And sunshine danced and flickered.

It was as if the summer's late
  Atoning for its sadness
Had borrowed every season's charm
  To end its days in gladness.

I call to mind those banded vales
  Of shadow and of shining,
Through which, my hostess at my side,
  I drove in day's declining.

We held our sideling way above
  The river's whitening shallows,
By homesteads old, with wide-flung barns
  Swept through and through by swallows ;

By maple orchards, belts of pine
  And larches climbing darkly
The mountain slopes, and, over all,
  The great peaks rising starkly.

You should have seen that long hill-range
  With gaps of brightness riven, —
How through each pass and hollow streamed
  The purpling lights of heaven, —

Rivers of gold-mist flowing down
  From far celestial fountains, —
The great sun flaming through the rifts
  Beyond the wall of mountains !

We paused at last where home-bound cows
  Brought down the pasture's treasure,
And in the barn the rhythmic flails
  Beat out a harvest measure.

We heard the night-hawk's sullen plunge,
  The crow his tree-mates calling :
The shadows lengthening down the slopes
  About our feet were falling.

And through them smote the level sun
  In broken lines of splendor,
Touched the gray rocks and made the
    green
  Of the shorn grass more tender.

The maples bending o'er the gate,
  Their arch of leaves just tinted
With yellow warmth, the golden glow
  Of coming autumn hinted.

Keen white between the farm-house showed,
  And smiled on porch and trellis,
The fair democracy of flowers
  That equals cot and palace.

And weaving garlands for her dog,
  'Twixt chidings and caresses,
A human flower of childhood shook
  The sunshine from her tresses.

On either hand we saw the signs
  Of fancy and of shrewdness,
Where taste had wound its arms of vines
  Round thrift's uncomely rudeness.

The sun-brown farmer in his frock
  Shook hands, and called to Mary :
Bare-armed, as Juno might, she came,
  White-aproned from her dairy.

Her air, her smile, her motions, told
  Of womanly completeness ;
A music as of household songs
  Was in her voice of sweetness.

Not fair alone in curve and line,
  But something more and better,
The secret charm eluding art,
  Its spirit, not its letter ; —

An inborn grace that nothing lacked
  Of culture or appliance, —
The warmth of genial courtesy,
  The calm of self-reliance.

Before her queenly womanhood
  How dared our hostess utter
The paltry errand of her need
  To buy her fresh-churned butter ?

She led the way with housewife pride,
  Her goodly store disclosing,
Full tenderly the golden balls
  With practised hands disposing.

Then, while along the western hills
  We watched the changeful glory
Of sunset, on our homeward way,
  I heard her simple story.

The early crickets sang ; the stream
  Plashed through my friend's narration :
Her rustic patois of the hills
  Lost in my free translation.

"More wise," she said, "than those who
    swarm
  Our hills in middle summer,
She came, when June's first roses blow,
  To greet the early comer.

"From school and ball and rout she came,
  The city's fair, pale daughter,
To drink the wine of mountain air
  Beside the Bearcamp Water.

"Her step grew firmer on the hills
  That watch our homesteads over ;
On cheek and lip, from summer fields,
  She caught the bloom of clover.

"For health comes sparkling in the streams
  From cool Chocorua stealing :
There's iron in our Northern winds ;
  Our pines are trees of healing.

"She sat beneath the broad-armed elms
  That skirt the mowing meadow,
And watched the gentle west-wind weave
  The grass with shine and shadow.

"Beside her, from the summer heat
  To share her grateful screening,
With forehead bared, the farmer stood,
  Upon his pitchfork leaning.

"Framed in its damp, dark locks, his face
  Had nothing mean or common, —
Strong, manly, true, the tenderness
  And pride beloved of woman.

"She looked up, glowing with the health
  The country air had brought her,
And, laughing, said : 'You lack a wife,
  Your mother lacks a daughter.

"'To mend your frock and bake your
    bread
  You do not need a lady :
Be sure among these brown old homes
  Is some one waiting ready, —

"'Some fair, sweet girl with skilful hand
  And cheerful heart for treasure,
Who never played with ivory keys,
  Or danced the polka's measure.'

"He bent his black brows to a frown,
  He set his white teeth tightly.
''T is well,' he said, 'for one like you
  To choose for me so lightly.

"'You think because my life is rude
  I take no note of sweetness :
I tell you love has naught to do
  With meetness or unmeetness.

"'Itself its best excuse, it asks
  No leave of pride or fashion
When silken zone or homespun frock
  It stirs with throbs of passion.

"'You think me deaf and blind : you bring
  Your winning graces hither
As free as if from cradle-time
  We two had played together.

"'You tempt me with your laughing eyes,
  Your cheek of sundown's blushes,
A motion as of waving grain,
  A music as of thrushes.

"'The plaything of your summer sport,
  The spells you weave around me
You cannot at your will undo,
  Nor leave me as you found me.

"'You go as lightly as you came,
  Your life is well without me ;
What care you that these hills will close
  Like prison-walls about me ?

"'No mood is mine to seek a wife,
  Or daughter for my mother :
Who loves you loses in that love
  All power to love another !

" ' I dare your pity or your scorn,
  With pride your own exceeding ;
I fling my heart into your lap
  Without a word of pleading.'

" She looked up in his face of pain
  So archly, yet so tender :
' And if I lend you mine,' she said,
  ' Will you forgive the lender ?

" ' Nor frock nor tan can hide the man ;
  And see you not, my farmer,
How weak and fond a woman waits
  Behind the silken armor ?

" ' I love you : on that love alone,
  And not my worth, presuming,
Will you not trust for summer fruit
  The tree in May-day blooming ? '

" Alone the hangbird overhead,
  His hair-swung cradle straining,
Looked down to see love's miracle, —
  The giving that is gaining.

" And so the farmer found a wife,
  His mother found a daughter :
There looks no happier home than hers
  On pleasant Bearcamp Water.

" Flowers spring to blossom where she
    walks
  The careful ways of duty ;
Our hard, stiff lines of life with her
  Are flowing curves of beauty.

" Our homes are cheerier for her sake,
  Our door-yards brighter blooming,
And all about the social air
  Is sweeter for her coming.

" Unspoken homilies of peace
  Her daily life is preaching ;
The still refreshment of the dew
  Is her unconscious teaching.

" And never tenderer hand than hers
  Unknits the brow of ailing ;
Her garments to the sick man's ear
  Have music in their trailing.

" And when, in pleasant harvest moons,
  The youthful huskers gather,
Or sleigh-drives on the mountain ways
  Defy the winter weather, —

" In sugar-camps, when south and warm
  The winds of March are blowing,
And sweetly from its thawing veins
  The maple's blood is flowing, —

" In summer, where some lilied pond
  Its virgin zone is baring,
Or where the ruddy autumn fire
  Lights up the apple-paring, —

" The coarseness of a ruder time
  Her finer mirth displaces,
A subtler sense of pleasure fills
  Each rustic sport she graces.

" Her presence lends its warmth and
    health
  To all who come before it.
If woman lost us Eden, such
  As she alone restore it.

" For larger life and wiser aims
  The farmer is her debtor ;
Who holds to his another's heart
  Must needs be worse or better.

" Through her his civic service shows
  A purer-toned ambition ;
No double consciousness divides
  The man and politician.

" In party's doubtful ways he trusts
  Her instincts to determine ;
At the loud polls, the thought of her
  Recalls Christ's Mountain Sermon.

" He owns her logic of the heart,
  And wisdom of unreason,
Supplying, while he doubts and weighs,
  The needed word in season.

" He sees with pride her richer thought,
  Her fancy's freer ranges ;
And love thus deepened to respect
  Is proof against all changes.

" And if she walks at ease in ways
  His feet are slow to travel,
And if she reads with cultured eyes
  What his may scarce unravel,

" Still clearer, for her keener sight
  Of beauty and of wonder,
He learns the meaning of the hills
  He dwelt from childhood under.

" And higher, warmed with summer lights,
  Or winter-crowned and hoary,
The ridged horizon lifts for him
  Its inner veils of glory.

" He has his own free, bookless lore,
  The lessons nature taught him,
The wisdom which the woods and hills
  And toiling men have brought him :

" The steady force of will whereby
  Her flexile grace seems sweeter ;
The sturdy counterpoise which makes
  Her woman's life completer ;

" A latent fire of soul which lacks
  No breath of love to fan it ;
And wit, that, like his native brooks,
  Plays over solid granite.

" How dwarfed against his manliness
  She sees the poor pretension,
The wants, the aims, the follies, born
  Of fashion and convention !

" How life behind its accidents
  Stands strong and self-sustaining,
The human fact transcending all
  The losing and the gaining.

" And so in grateful interchange
  Of teacher and of hearer,
Their lives their true distinctness keep
  While daily drawing nearer.

" And if the husband or the wife
  In home's strong light discovers
Such slight defaults as failed to meet
  The blinded eyes of lovers,

" Why need we care to ask ? — who
    dreams
  Without their thorns of roses,
Or wonders that the truest steel
  The readiest spark discloses ?

" For still in mutual sufferance lies
  The secret of true living ;
Love scarce is love that never knows
  The sweetness of forgiving.

" We send the Squire to General Court,
  He takes his young wife thither ;
No prouder man election day
  Rides through the sweet June weather.

" He sees with eyes of manly trust
  All hearts to her inclining ;
Not less for him his household light
  That others share its shining."

Thus, while my hostess spake, there grew
  Before me, warmer tinted
And outlined with a tenderer grace,
  The picture that she hinted.

The sunset smouldered as we drove
  Beneath the deep hill-shadows.
Below us wreaths of white fog walked
  Like ghosts the haunted meadows.

Sounding the summer night, the stars
  Dropped down their golden plummets ;
The pale arc of the Northern lights
  Rose o'er the mountain summits,

Until, at last, beneath its bridge,
  We heard the Bearcamp flowing,
And saw across the mapled lawn
  The welcome home-lights glowing.

And, musing on the tale I heard,
  'T were well, thought I, if often
To rugged farm-life came the gift
  To harmonize and soften ;

If more and more we found the troth
  Of fact and fancy plighted,
And culture's charm and labor's strength
  In rural homes united, —

The simple life, the homely hearth,
  With beauty's sphere surrounding,
And blessing toil where toil abounds
  With graces more abounding.

THE DOLE OF JARL THORKELL

THE land was pale with famine
  And racked with fever-pain ;
The frozen fiords were fishless,
  The earth withheld her grain.

Men saw the boding Fylgja
  Before them come and go,
And, through their dreams, the Urdarmoon
  From west to east sailed slow !

Jarl Thorkell of Thevera
  At Yule-time made his vow ;

On Rykdal's holy Doom-stone
  He slew to Frey his cow.

To bounteous Frey he slew her ;
  To Skuld, the younger Norn,
Who watches over birth and death,
  He gave her calf unborn.

And his little gold-haired daughter
  Took up the sprinkling-rod,
And smeared with blood the temple
  And the wide lips of the god.

Hoarse below, the winter water
  Ground its ice blocks o'er and o'er ;
Jets of foam, like ghosts of dead waves,
  Rose and fell along the shore.

The red torch of the Jokul,
  Aloft in icy space,
Shone down on the bloody Horg-stones
  And the statue's carven face.

And closer round and grimmer
  Beneath its baleful light
The Jotun shapes of mountains
  Came crowding through the night.

The gray-haired Hersir trembled
  As a flame by wind is blown ;
A weird power moved his white lips,
  And their voice was not his own !

" The Æsir thirst ! " he muttered ;
  " The gods must have more blood
Before the tun shall blossom
  Or fish shall fill the flood.

" The Æsir thirst and hunger,
  And hence our blight and ban ;
The mouths of the strong gods water
  For the flesh and blood of man !

" Whom shall we give the strong ones ?
  Not warriors, sword on thigh ;
But let the nursling infant
  And bedrid old man die."

" So be it ! " cried the young men,
  " There needs nor doubt nor parle."
But, knitting hard his red brows,
  In silence stood the Jarl.

A sound of woman's weeping
  At the temple door was heard,

But the old men bowed their white heads,
  And answered not a word.

Then the Dream-wife of Thingvalla,
  A Vala young and fair,
Sang softly, stirring with her breath
  The veil of her loose hair.

She sang : " The winds from Alfheim
  Bring never sound of strife ;
The gifts for Frey the meetest
  Are not of death, but life.

" He loves the grass-green meadows,
  The grazing kine's sweet breath ;
He loathes your bloody Horg-stones,
  Your gifts that smell of death.

" No wrong by wrong is righted,
  No pain is cured by pain ;
The blood that smokes from Doom-rings
  Falls back in redder rain.

" The gods are what you make them,
  As earth shall Asgard prove ;
And hate will come of hating,
  And love will come of love.

" Make dole of skyr and black bread
  That old and young may live ;
And look to Frey for favor
  When first like Frey you give.

" Even now o'er Njord's sea-meadows
  The summer dawn begins :
The tun shall have its harvest,
  The fiord its glancing fins."

Then up and swore Jarl Thorkell :
  " By Gimli and by Hel,
O Vala of Thingvalla,
  Thou singest wise and well !

" Too dear the Æsir's favors
  Bought with our children's lives ;
Better die than shame in living
  Our mothers and our wives.

" The full shall give his portion
  To him who hath most need ;
Of curdled skyr and black bread,
  Be daily dole decreed."

He broke from off his neck-chain
  Three links of beaten gold ;

And each man, at his bidding,
  Brought gifts for young and old.

Then mothers nursed their children,
  And daughters fed their sires,
And Health sat down with Plenty
  Before the next Yule fires.

The Horg-stones stand in Rykdal;
  The Doom-ring still remains;
But the snows of a thousand winters
  Have washed away the stains.

Christ ruleth now; the Æsir
  Have found their twilight dim;
And, wiser than she dreamed, of old
  The Vala sang of Him!

THE TWO RABBINS

THE Rabbi Nathan twoscore years and ten
Walked blameless through the evil world,
    and then,
Just as the almond blossomed in his hair,
Met a temptation all too strong to bear,
And miserably sinned. So, adding not
Falsehood to guilt, he left his seat, and
    taught
No more among the elders, but went out
From the great congregation girt about
With sackcloth, and with ashes on his head,
Making his gray locks grayer. Long he
    prayed,
Smiting his breast; then, as the Book he
    laid
Open before him for the Bath-Col's choice,
Pausing to hear that Daughter of a Voice,
Behold the royal preacher's words: "A
    friend
Loveth at all times, yea, unto the end;
And for the evil day thy brother lives."
Marvelling, he said: "It is the Lord who
    gives
Counsel in need. At Ecbatana dwells
Rabbi Ben Isaac, who all men excels
In righteousness and wisdom, as the trees
Of Lebanon the small weeds that the bees
Bow with their weight. I will arise, and
    lay
My sins before him."

                And he went his way
Barefooted, fasting long, with many prayers;
But even as one who, followed unawares,

Suddenly in the darkness feels a·hand
Thrill with its touch his own, and his cheek
    fanned
By odors subtly sweet, and whispers near
Of words he loathes, yet cannot choose but
    hear,
So, while the Rabbi journeyed, chanting low
The wail of David's penitential woe,
Before him still the old temptation came,
And mocked him with the motion and the
    shame
Of such desires that, shuddering, he ab-
    horred
Himself; and, crying mightily to the Lord
To free his soul and cast the demon out,
Smote with his staff the blankness round
    about.

At length, in the low light of a spent day,
The towers of Ecbatana far away
Rose on the desert's rim; and Nathan, faint
And footsore, pausing where for some dead
    saint
The faith of Islam reared a domëd tomb,
Saw some one kneeling in the shadow, whom
He greeted kindly: "May the Holy One
Answer thy prayers, O stranger!" Where-
    upon
The shape stood up with a loud cry, and
    then,
Clasped in each other's arms, the two gray
    men
Wept, praising Him whose gracious provi-
    dence
Made their paths one. But straightway, as
    the sense
Of his transgression smote him, Nathan tore
Himself away: "O friend beloved, no
    more
Worthy am I to touch thee, for I came,
Foul from my sins, to tell thee all my shame.
Haply thy prayers, since naught availeth
    mine,
May purge my soul, and make it white like
    thine.
Pity me, O Ben Isaac, I have sinned!"

Awestruck Ben Isaac stood. The desert
    wind
Blew his long mantle backward, laying bare
The mournful secret of his shirt of hair.
"I too, O friend, if not in act," he said,
"In thought have verily sinned. Hast
    thou not read,
'Better the eye should see than that desire

Should wander ? ' Burning with a hidden
fire
That tears and prayers quench not, I come
to thee
For pity and for help, as thou to me.
Pray for me, O my friend !" But Nathan
cried,
" Pray thou for me, Ben Isaac !"

Side by side
In the low sunshine by the turban stone
They knelt ; each made his brother's woe
his own,
Forgetting, in the agony and stress
Of pitying love, his claim of selfishness ;
Peace, for his friend besought, his own be-
came ;
His prayers were answered in another's
name ;
And, when at last they rose up to embrace,
Each saw God's pardon in his brother's face !

Long after, when his headstone gathered
moss,
Traced on the targum-marge of Onkelos
In Rabbi Nathan's hand these words were
read :
" *Hope not the cure of sin till Self is dead ;*
Forget it in love's service, and the debt
Thou canst not pay the angels shall forget ;
Heaven's gate is shut to him who comes alone ;
Save thou a soul, and it shall save thy own !"

NOREMBEGA

Norembega, or Norimbegue, is the name
given by early French fishermen and explorers
to a fabulous country south of Cape Breton,
first discovered by Verrazzani in 1524. It was
supposed to have a magnificent city of the
same name on a great river, probably the Pe-
nobscot. The site of this barbaric city is laid
down on a map published at Antwerp in 1570.
In 1604 Champlain sailed in search of the
Northern Eldorado, twenty-two leagues up the
Penobscot from the Isle Haute. He supposed
the river to be that of Norembega, but wisely
came to the conclusion that those travellers
who told of the great city had never seen it.
He saw no evidences of anything like civiliza-
tion, but mentions the finding of a cross, very
old and mossy, in the woods.

THE winding way the serpent takes
The mystic water took,

From where, to count its beaded lakes,
The forest sped its brook.

A narrow space 'twixt shore and shore,
For sun or stars to fall,
While evermore, behind, before,
Closed in the forest wall.

The dim wood hiding underneath
Wan flowers without a name ;
Life tangled with decay and death,
League after league the same.

Unbroken over swamp and hill
The rounding shadow lay,
Save where the river cut at will
A pathway to the day.

Beside that track of air and light,
Weak as a child unweaned,
At shut of day a Christian knight
Upon his henchman leaned.

The embers of the sunset's fires
Along the clouds burned down ;
" I see," he said, " the domes and spires
Of Norembega town."

" Alack ! the domes, O master mine,
Are golden clouds on high ;
Yon spire is but the branchless pine
That cuts the evening sky."

" Oh, hush and hark ! What sounds are these
But chants and holy hymns ? "
" Thou hear'st the breeze that stirs the trees
Through all their leafy limbs."

" Is it a chapel bell that fills
The air with its low tone ? "
" Thou hear'st the tinkle of the rills,
The insect's vesper drone."

" The Christ be praised ! — He sets for me
A blessed cross in sight ! "
" Now, nay, 't is but yon blasted tree
With two gaunt arms outright ! "

" Be it wind so sad or tree so stark,
It mattereth not, my knave ;
Methinks to funeral hymns I hark,
The cross is for my grave !

" My life is sped ; I shall not see
My home-set sails again ;

The sweetest eyes of Normandie
  Shall watch for me in vain.

" Yet onward still to ear and eye
  The baffling marvel calls ;
I fain would look before I die
  On Norembega's walls.

" So, haply, it shall be thy part
  At Christian feet to lay
The mystery of the desert's heart
  My dead hand plucked away.

" Leave me an hour of rest ; go thou
  And look from yonder heights ;
Perchance the valley even now
  Is starred with city lights."

The henchman climbed the nearest hill,
  He saw nor tower nor town,
But, through the drear woods, lone and still,
  The river rolling down.

He heard the stealthy feet of things
  Whose shapes he could not see,
A flutter as of evil wings,
  The fall of a dead tree.

The pines stood black against the moon,
  A sword of fire beyond ;
He heard the wolf howl, and the loon
  Laugh from his reedy pond.

He turned him back : " O master dear,
  We are but men misled ;
And thou hast sought a city here
  To find a grave instead."

" As God shall will ! what matters where
  A true man's cross may stand,
So Heaven be o'er it here as there
  In pleasant Norman land ?

" These woods, perchance, no secret hide
  Of lordly tower and hall ;
Yon river in its wanderings wide
  Has washed no city wall ;

" Yet mirrored in the sullen stream
  The holy stars are given :
Is Norembega, then, a dream
  Whose waking is in Heaven ?

" No builded wonder of these lands
  My weary eyes shall see ;

A city never made with hands
  Alone awaiteth me —

" ' *Urbs Syon mystica ;* ' I see
  Its mansions passing fair,
' *Condita cœlo ;* ' let me be,
  Dear Lord, a dweller there ! "

Above the dying exile hung
  The vision of the bard,
As faltered on his failing tongue
  The song of good Bernard.

The henchman dug at dawn a grave
  Beneath the hemlocks brown,
And to the desert's keeping gave
  The lord of fief and town.

Years after, when the Sieur Champlain
  Sailed up the unknown stream,
And Norembega proved again
  A shadow and a dream,

He found the Norman's nameless grave
  Within the hemlock's shade,
And, stretching wide its arms to save,
  The sign that God had made,

The cross-boughed tree that marked the
    spot
  And made it holy ground :
He needs the earthly city not
  Who hath the heavenly found.

MIRIAM

TO FREDERICK A. P. BARNARD

[When Whittier was an editor in Hartford,
Mr. Barnard, afterward President of Columbia
College, was a teacher in the Asylum for the
Deaf and Dumb in that place. Both men were
at the time especially interested in Eastern his-
tory and romance.]

THE years are many since, in youth and
    hope,
Under the Charter Oak, our horoscope
We drew thick-studded with all favoring
    stars.
Now, with gray beards, and faces seamed
    with scars
From life's hard battle, meeting once again,
We smile, half sadly, over dreams so vain ;

Knowing, at last, that it is not in man
Who walketh to direct his steps, or plan
His permanent house of life. Alike we
    loved
The muses' haunts, and all our fancies
    moved
To measures of old song. How since that
    day
Our feet have parted from the path that
    lay
So fair before us ! Rich, from lifelong
    search
Of truth, within thy Academic porch
Thou sittest now, lord of a realm of fact,
Thy servitors the sciences exact ;
Still listening with thy hand on Nature's
    keys,
To hear the Samian's spheral harmonies
And rhythm of law. I, called from dream
    and song,
Thank God ! so early to a strife so long,
That, ere it closed, the black, abundant
    hair
Of boyhood rested silver-sown and spare
On manhood's temples, now at sunset-chime
Tread with fond feet the path of morning
    time.
And if perchance too late I linger where
The flowers have ceased to blow, and trees
    are bare,
Thou, wiser in thy choice, wilt scarcely
    blame
The friend who shields his folly with thy
    name.

One Sabbath day my friend and I,
After the meeting, quietly
Passed from the crowded village lanes,
White with dry dust for lack of rains,
And climbed the neighboring slope, with
    feet
Slackened and heavy from the heat,
Although the day was wellnigh done,
And the low angle of the sun
Along the naked hillside cast
Our shadows as of giants vast.
We reached, at length, the topmost swell,
Whence, either way, the green turf fell
In terraces of nature down
To fruit-hung orchards, and the town
With white, pretenceless houses, tall
Church-steeples, and, o'ershadowing all,
Huge mills whose windows had the look
Of eager eyes that ill could brook

The Sabbath rest. We traced the track
Of the sea-seeking river back,
Glistening for miles above its mouth,
Through the long valley to the south,
And, looking eastward, cool to view,
Stretched the illimitable blue
Of ocean, from its curved coast-line ;
Sombred and still the warm sunshine
Filled with pale gold-dust all the reach
Of slumberous woods from hill to beach, —
Slanted on walls of thronged retreats
From city toil and dusty streets,
On grassy bluff, and dune of sand,
And rocky islands miles from land ;
Touched the far-glancing sails, and showed
White lines of foam where long waves
    flowed
Dumb in the distance. In the north,
Dim through their misty hair, looked forth
The space-dwarfed mountains to the sea,
From mystery to mystery !

So, sitting on that green hill-slope,
We talked of human life, its hope
And fear, and unsolved doubts, and what
It might have been, and yet was not.
And, when at last the evening air
Grew sweeter for the bells of prayer
Ringing in steeples far below,
We watched the people churchward go,
Each to his place, as if thereon
The true shekinah only shone ;
And my friend queried how it came
To pass that they who owned the same
Great Master still could not agree
To worship Him in company.
Then, broadening in his thought, he ran
Over the whole vast field of man, —
The varying forms of faith and creed
That somehow served the holders' need ;
In which, unquestioned, undenied,
Uncounted millions lived and died ;
The bibles of the ancient folk,
Through which the heart of nations spoke ;
The old moralities which lent
To home its sweetness and content,
And rendered possible to bear
The life of peoples everywhere :
And asked if we, who boast of light,
Claim not a too exclusive right
To truths which must for all be meant,
Like rain and sunshine freely sent.
In bondage to the letter still,
We give it power to cramp and kill, —
To tax God's fulness with a scheme

Narrower than Peter's house-top dream,
His wisdom and his love with plans
Poor and inadequate as man's.
It must be that He witnesses
Somehow to all men that He is :
That something of His saving grace
Reaches the lowest of the race,
Who, through strange creed and rite, may
    draw
The hints of a diviner law.
We walk in clearer light ; — but then,
Is He not God ? — are they not men ?
Are His responsibilities
For us alone and not for these ?

And I made answer : " Truth is one ;
And, in all lands beneath the sun,
Whoso hath eyes to see may see
The tokens of its unity.
No scroll of creed its fulness wraps,
We trace it not by school-boy maps,
Free as the sun and air it is
Of latitudes and boundaries.
In Vedic verse, in dull Korán,
Are messages of good to man ;
The angels to our Aryan sires
Talked by the earliest household fires ;
The prophets of the elder day,
The slant-eyed sages of Cathay,
Read not the riddle all amiss
Of higher life evolved from this.

" Nor doth it lessen what He taught,
Or make the gospel Jesus brought
Less precious, that His lips retold
Some portion of that truth of old ;
Denying not the proven seers,
The tested wisdom of the years ;
Confirming with His own impress
The common law of righteousness.
We search the world for truth ; we
    cull
The good, the pure, the beautiful,
From graven stone and written scroll,
From all old flower-fields of the soul ;
And, weary seekers of the best,
We come back laden from our quest,
To find that all the sages said
Is in the Book our mothers read,
And all our treasure of old thought
In His harmonious fulness wrought
Who gathers in one sheaf complete
The scattered blades of God's sown wheat,
The common growth that maketh good
His all-embracing Fatherhood.

" Wherever through the ages rise
The altars of self-sacrifice,
Where love its arms has opened wide,
Or man for man has calmly died,
I see the same white wings outspread
That hovered o'er the Master's head !
Up from undated time they come,
The martyr souls of heathendom,
And to His cross and passion bring
Their fellowship of suffering.
I trace His presence in the blind
Pathetic gropings of my kind, —
In prayers from sin and sorrow wrung,
In cradle-hymns of life they sung,
Each, in its measure, but a part
Of the unmeasured Over-heart ;
And with a stronger faith confess
The greater that it owns the less.
Good cause it is for thankfulness
That the world-blessing of His life
With the long past is not at strife ;
That the great marvel of His death
To the one order witnesseth,
No doubt of changeless goodness wakes,
No link of cause and sequence breaks,
But, one with nature, rooted is
In the eternal verities ;
Whereby, while differing in degree
As finite from infinity,
The pain and loss for others borne,
Love's crown of suffering meekly worn,
The life man giveth for his friend
Becomes vicarious in the end ;
Their healing place in nature take,
And make life sweeter for their sake.

" So welcome I from every source
The tokens of that primal Force,
Older than heaven itself, yet new
As the young heart it reaches to,
Beneath whose steady impulse rolls
The tidal wave of human souls ;
Guide, comforter, and inward word,
The eternal spirit of the Lord !
Nor fear I aught that science brings
From searching through material things ;
Content to let its glasses prove,
Not by the letter's oldness move,
The myriad worlds on worlds that course
The spaces of the universe ;
Since everywhere the Spirit walks
The garden of the heart, and talks
With man, as under Eden's trees,
In all his varied languages.
Why mourn above some hopeless flaw

In the stone tables of the law,
When scripture every day afresh
Is traced on tablets of the flesh ?
By inward sense, by outward signs,
God's presence still the heart divines ;
Through deepest joy of Him we learn,
In sorest grief to Him we turn,
And reason stoops its pride to share
The child-like instinct of a prayer."

And then, as is my wont, I told
A story of the days of old,
Not found in printed books, — in sooth,
A fancy, with slight hint of truth,
Showing how differing faiths agree
In one sweet law of charity.
Meanwhile the sky had golden grown,
Our faces in its glory shone ;
But shadows down the valley swept,
And gray below the ocean slept,
As time and space I wandered o'er
To tread the Mogul's marble floor,
And see a fairer sunset fall
On Jumna's wave and Agra's wall.

The good Shah Akbar (peace be his alway !)
Came forth from the Divan at close of day
Bowed with the burden of his many cares,
Worn with the hearing of unnumbered
     prayers, —
Wild cries for justice, the importunate
Appeals of greed and jealousy and hate,
And all the strife of sect and creed and rite,
Santon and Gouroo waging holy fight :
For the wise monarch, claiming not to be
Allah's avenger, left his people free,
With a faint hope, his Book scarce justified,
That all the paths of faith, though severed
     wide,
O'er which the feet of prayerful reverence
     passed,
Met at the gate of Paradise at last.

He sought an alcove of his cool hareem,
Where, far beneath, he heard the Jumna's
     stream
Lapse soft and low along his palace wall,
And all about the cool sound of the fall
Of fountains, and of water circling free
Through marble ducts along the balcony ;
The voice of women in the distance sweet,
And, sweeter still, of one who, at his feet,
Soothed his tired ear with songs of a far
     land
Where Tagus shatters on the salt sea-sand

The mirror of its cork-grown hills of drouth
And vales of vine, at Lisbon's harbor-
     mouth.

The date-palms rustled not ;   the peepul
     laid
Its topmost boughs against the balustrade,
Motionless as the mimic leaves and vines
That, light and graceful as the shawl-
     designs
Of Delhi or Umritsir, twined in stone ;
And the tired monarch, who aside had
     thrown
The day's hard burden, sat from care apart,
And let the quiet steal into his heart
From the still hour.   Below him Agra slept
By the long light of sunset overswept :
The river flowing through a level land,
By mango-groves and banks of yellow sand,
Skirted with lime and orange, gay kiosks,
Fountains at play, tall minarets of mosques,
Fair pleasure-gardens, with their flowering
     trees
Relieved against the mournful cypresses ;
And, air-poised lightly as the blown sea-
     foam,
The marble wonder of some holy dome
Hung a white moonrise over the still wood,
Glassing its beauty in a stiller flood.

Silent the monarch gazed, until the night
Swift-falling hid the city from his sight ;
Then to the woman at his feet he said :
" Tell me, O Miriam, something thou hast
     read
In childhood of the Master of thy faith,
Whom Islam also owns. Our Prophet saith :
' He was a true apostle, yea, a Word
And Spirit sent before me from the Lord.'
Thus the Book witnesseth ; and well I know
By what thou art, O dearest, it is so.
As the lute's tone the maker's hand be-
     trays,
The sweet disciple speaks her Master's
     praise."

Then Miriam, glad of heart, (for in some
     sort
She cherished in the Moslem's liberal court
The sweet traditions of a Christian child ;
And, through her life of sense, the un-
     defiled
And chaste ideal of the sinless One
Gazed on her with an eye she might not
     shun,

The sad, reproachful look of pity, born
Of love that hath no part in wrath or scorn,)
Began, with low voice and moist eyes, to tell
Of the all-loving Christ, and what befell
When the fierce zealots, thirsting for her
blood,
Dragged to his feet a shame of womanhood.
How, when his searching answer pierced
within
Each heart, and touched the secret of its sin,
And her accusers fled his face before,
He bade the poor one go and sin no more.
And Akbar said, after a moment's thought,
"Wise is the lesson by thy prophet taught;
Woe unto him who judges and forgets
What hidden evil his own heart besets !
Something of this large charity I find
In all the sects that sever humankind ;
I would to Allah that their lives agreed
More nearly with the lesson of their creed !
Those yellow Lamas who at Meerut pray
By wind and water power, and love to say :
'He who forgiveth not shall, unforgiven,
Fail of the rest of Buddha,' and who even
Spare the black gnat that stings them, vex
my ears
With the poor hates and jealousies and fears
Nursed in their human hives. That lean,
fierce priest
Of thy own people, (be his heart increased
By Allah's love !) his black robes smelling
yet
Of Goa's roasted Jews, have I not met
Meek-faced, barefooted, crying in the street
The saying of his prophet true and sweet, —
'He who is merciful shall mercy meet ! '"

But, next day, so it chanced, as night be-
gan
To fall, a murmur through the hareem ran
That one, recalling in her dusky face
The full-lipped, mild-eyed beauty of a race
Known as the blameless Ethiops of Greek
song,
Plotting to do her royal master wrong,
Watching, reproachful of the lingering
light,
The evening shadows deepen for her flight,
Love-guided, to her home in a far land,
Now waited death at the great Shah's com-
mand.

Shapely as that dark princess for whose
smile
A world was bartered, daughter of the Nile

Herself, and veiling in her large, soft eyes
The passion and the languor of her skies,
The Abyssinian knelt low at the feet
Of her stern lord : "O king, if it be meet,
And for thy honor's sake," she said, "that I,
Who am the humblest of thy slaves, should
die,
I will not tax thy mercy to forgive.
Easier it is to die than to outlive
All that life gave me, — him whose wrong
of thee
Was but the outcome of his love for me,
Cherished from childhood, when, beneath
the shade
Of templed Axum, side by side we played.
Stolen from his arms, my lover followed me
Through weary seasons over land and sea ;
And two days since, sitting disconsolate
Within the shadow of the hareem gate,
Suddenly, as if dropping from the sky,
Down from the lattice of the balcony
Fell the sweet song by Tigre's cowherds
sung
In the old music of his native tongue.
He knew my voice, for love is quick of ear,
Answering in song.
         This night he waited near
To fly with me. The fault was mine alone ;
He knew thee not, he did but seek his own ;
Who, in the very shadow of thy throne,
Sharing thy bounty, knowing all thou art,
Greatest and best of men, and in her heart
Grateful to tears for favor undeserved,
Turned ever homeward, nor one moment
swerved
From her young love. He looked into my
eyes,
He heard my voice, and could not otherwise
Than he hath done ; yet, save one wild em-
brace
When first we stood together face to face,
And all that fate had done since last we met
Seemed but a dream and left us children
yet,
He hath not wronged thee nor thy royal bed :
Spare him, O king ! and slay me in his
stead !"

But over Akbar's brows the frown hung
black,
And, turning to the eunuch at his back,
"Take them," he said, "and let the Jumna's
waves
Hide both my shame and these accursed
slaves !"

His loathly length the unsexed bondman
     bowed :
" On my head be it ! "
                    Straightway from a cloud
Of dainty shawls and veils of woven mist
The Christian Miriam rose, and, stooping,
     kissed
The monarch's hand.   Loose down her
     shoulders bare
Swept all the rippled darkness of her hair,
Veiling the bosom that, with high, quick
     swell
Of fear and pity, through it rose and fell.

" Alas ! " she cried, " hast thou forgotten
     quite
The words of Him we spake of yesternight ?
Or thy own prophet's, ' Whoso doth endure
And pardon, of eternal life is sure ' ?
O great and good ! be thy revenge alone
Felt in thy mercy to the erring shown ;
Let thwarted love and youth their pardon
     plead,
Who sinned but in intent, and not in deed ! "

One moment the strong frame of Akbar
     shook
With the great storm of passion.   Then his
     look
Softened to her uplifted face, that still
Pleaded more strongly than all words, until
Its pride and anger seemed like overblown,
Spent clouds of thunder left to tell alone
Of strife and overcoming.   With bowed
     head,
And smiting on his bosom : " God," he said,
" Alone is great, and let His holy name
Be honored, even to His servant's shame !
Well spake thy prophet, Miriam, — he alone
Who hath not sinned is meet to cast a stone
At such as these, who here their doom
     await,
Held like myself in the strong grasp of
     fate.
They sinned through love, as I through love
     forgive ;
Take them beyond my realm, but let them
     live ! "

And, like a chorus to the words of grace,
The ancient Fakir, sitting in his place,
Motionless as an idol and as grim,
In the pavilion Akbar built for him
Under the court-yard trees, (for he was
     wise,

Knew Menu's laws, and through his close-
     shut eyes
Saw things far off, and as an open book
Into the thoughts of other men could look,)
Began, half chant, half howling, to rehearse
The fragment of a holy Vedic verse ;
And thus it ran : " He who all things for-
     gives
Conquers himself and all things else, and
     lives
Above the reach of wrong or hate or fear,
Calm as the gods, to whom he is most dear."

Two leagues from Agra still the traveller
     sees
The tomb of Akbar through its cypress-
     trees ;
And, near at hand, the marble walls that
     hide
The Christian Begum sleeping at his side.
And o'er her vault of burial (who shall tell
If it be chance alone or miracle ?)
The Mission press with tireless hand unrolls
The words of Jesus on its lettered scrolls, —
Tells, in all tongues, the tale of mercy o'er,
And bids the guilty, " Go and sin no more ! "

———

It now was dew-fall ; very still
The night lay on the lonely hill,
Down which our homeward steps we bent,
And, silent, through great silence went,
Save that the tireless crickets played
Their long, monotonous serenade.
A young moon, at its narrowest,
Curved sharp against the darkening west ;
And, momently, the beacon's star,
Slow wheeling o'er its rock afar,
From out the level darkness shot
One instant and again was not.
And then my friend spake quietly
The thought of both : " Yon crescent see!
Like Islam's symbol-moon it gives
Hints of the light whereby it lives :
Somewhat of goodness, something true
From sun and spirit shining through
All faiths, all worlds, as through the dark
Of ocean shines the lighthouse spark,
Attests the presence everywhere
Of love and providential care.
The faith the old Norse heart confessed
In one dear name, — the hopefulest
And tenderest heard from mortal lips
In pangs of birth or death, from ships

Ice-bitten in the winter sea,
Or lisped beside a mother's knee, —
The wiser world hath not outgrown,
And the All-Father is our own ! "

NAUHAUGHT, THE DEACON

NAUHAUGHT, the Indian deacon, who of old
Dwelt, poor but blameless, where his nar-
    rowing Cape
Stretches its shrunk arm out to all the winds
And the relentless smiting of the waves,
Awoke one morning from a pleasant dream
Of a good angel dropping in his hand
A fair, broad gold-piece, in the name of God.

He rose and went forth with the early day
Far inland, where the voices of the waves
Mellowed and mingled with the whispering
    leaves,
As, through the tangle of the low, thick
    woods,
He searched his traps. Therein nor beast
    nor bird
He found ; though meanwhile in the reedy
    pools
The otter plashed, and underneath the pines
The partridge drummed : and as his
    thoughts went back
To the sick wife and little child at home,
What marvel that the poor man felt his faith
Too weak to bear its burden, — like a rope
That, strand by strand uncoiling, breaks
    above
The hand that grasps it. "Even now, O
    Lord !
Send me," he prayed, " the angel of my
    dream !
Nauhaught is very poor ; he cannot wait."

Even as he spake he heard at his bare feet
A low, metallic clink, and, looking down,
He saw a dainty purse with disks of gold
Crowding its silken net. Awhile he held
The treasure up before his eyes, alone
With his great need, feeling the wondrous
    coins
Slide through his eager fingers, one by one.
So then the dream was true. The angel
    brought
One broad piece only ; should he take all
    these ?
Who would be wiser, in the blind, dumb
    woods ?

The loser, doubtless rich, would scarcely
    miss
This dropped crumb from a table always
    full.
Still, while he mused, he seemed to hear
    the cry
Of a starved child ; the sick face of his wife
Tempted him. Heart and flesh in fierce
    revolt
Urged the wild license of his savage youth
Against his later scruples. Bitter toil,
Prayer, fasting, dread of blame, and pitiless
    eyes
To watch his halting, — had he lost for
    these
The freedom of the woods ; — the hunting-
    grounds
Of happy spirits for a walled-in heaven
Of everlasting psalms ? One healed the sick
Very far off thousands of moons ago :
Had he not prayed him night and day to
    come
And cure his bed-bound wife ? Was there
    a hell ?
Were all his fathers' people writhing
    there —
Like the poor shell-fish set to boil alive —
Forever, dying never ? If he kept
This gold, so needed, would the dreadful
    God
Torment him like a Mohawk's captive
    stuck
With slow-consuming splinters ? Would
    the saints
And the white angels dance and laugh to
    see him
Burn like a pitch-pine torch ? His Chris-
    tian garb
Seemed falling from him ; with the fear
    and shame
Of Adam naked at the cool of day,
He gazed around. A black snake lay in coil
On the hot sand, a crow with sidelong eye
Watched from a dead bough. All his In-
    dian lore
Of evil blending with a convert's faith
In the supernal terrors of the Book,
He saw the Tempter in the coiling snake
And ominous, black-winged bird ; and all
    the while
The low rebuking of the distant waves
Stole in upon him like the voice of God
Among the trees of Eden. Girding up
His soul's loins with a resolute hand, he
    thrust

The base thought from him : " Nauhaught,
    be a man !
Starve, if need be ; but, while you live, look
    out
From honest eyes on all men, unashamed.
God help me ! I am deacon of the church,
A baptized, praying Indian ! Should I do
This secret meanness, even the barken
    knots
Of the old trees would turn to eyes to see
    it,
The birds would tell of it, and all the leaves
Whisper above me : ' Nauhaught is a
    thief !'
The sun would know it, and the stars that
    hide
Behind his light would watch me, and at
    night
Follow me with their sharp, accusing eyes.
Yea, thou, God, seest me !" Then Nau-
    haught drew
Closer his belt of leather, dulling thus
The pain of hunger, and walked bravely
    back
To the brown fishing-hamlet by the sea ;
And, pausing at the inn - door, cheerily
    asked :
" Who hath lost aught to-day ? "
                " I," said a voice ;
" Ten golden pieces, in a silken purse,
My daughter's handiwork." He looked,
    and lo !
One stood before him in a coat of frieze,
And the glazed hat of a seafaring man,
Shrewd-faced, broad-shouldered, with no
    trace of wings.
Marvelling, he dropped within the stran-
    ger's hand
The silken web, and turned to go his way.
But the man said : " A tithe at least is
    yours ;
Take it in God's name as an honest man."
And as the deacon's dusky fingers closed
Over the golden gift, " Yea, in God's name
I take it, with a poor man's thanks," he
    said.
So down the street that, like a river of
    sand,
Ran, white in sunshine, to the summer sea,
He sought his home, singing and praising
    God ;
And when his neighbors in their careless
    way
Spoke of the owner of the silken purse —
A Wellfleet skipper, known in every port

That the Cape opens in its sandy wall —
He answered, with a wise smile, to him-
    self :
" I saw the angel where they see a man."

THE SISTERS

ANNIE and Rhoda, sisters twain,
Woke in the night to the sound of rain,

The rush of wind, the ramp and roar
Of great waves climbing a rocky shore.

Annie rose up in her bed-gown white,
And looked out into the storm and night.

" Hush, and hearken ! " she cried in fear,
" Hearest thou nothing, sister dear ? "

" I hear the sea, and the plash of rain,
And roar of the northeast hurricane.

" Get thee back to the bed so warm,
No good comes of watching a storm.

" What is it to thee, I fain would know,
That waves are roaring and wild winds
    blow ?

" No lover of thine 's afloat to miss
The harbor-lights on a night like this."

" But I heard a voice cry out my name,
Up from the sea on the wind it came !

" Twice and thrice have I heard it call,
And the voice is the voice of Estwick
    Hall ! "

On her pillow the sister tossed her head.
" Hall of the Heron is safe," she said.

" In the tautest schooner that ever swam
He rides at anchor in Annisquam.

" And, if in peril from swamping sea
Or lee shore rocks, would he call on thee ? "

But the girl heard only the wind and tide,
And wringing her small white hands she
    cried :

" O sister Rhoda, there 's something wrong ;
I hear it again, so loud and long.

" ' Annie ! Annie ! ' I hear it call,
And the voice is the voice of Estwick
Hall ! "

Up sprang the elder, with eyes aflame,
" Thou liest ! He never would call thy
name !

" If he did, I would pray the wind and
sea
To keep him forever from thee and me ! "

Then out of the sea blew a dreadful
blast ;
Like the cry of a dying man it passed.

The young girl hushed on her lips a groan,
But through her tears a strange light
shone, —

The solemn joy of her heart's release
To own and cherish its love in peace.

" Dearest ! " she whispered, under breath,
" Life was a lie, but true is death.

" The love I hid from myself away
Shall crown me now in the light of day.

" My ears shall never to wooer list,
Never by lover my lips be kissed.

" Sacred to thee am I henceforth,
Thou in heaven and I on earth ! "

She came and stood by her sister's bed :
" Hall of the Heron is dead ! " she said.

" The wind and the waves their work have
done,
We shall see him no more beneath the
sun.

" Little will reck that heart of thine ;
It loved him not with a love like mine.

" I, for his sake, were he but here,
Could hem and 'broider thy bridal gear,

" Though hands should tremble and eyes
be wet,
And stitch for stitch in my heart be set.

" But now my soul with his soul I wed ;
Thine the living, and mine the dead ! "

MARGUERITE

MASSACHUSETTS BAY, 1760

Upwards of one thousand of the Acadian
peasants forcibly taken from their homes on
the Gaspereau and Basin of Minas were as-
signed to the several towns of the Massachu-
setts colony, the children being bound by the
authorities to service or labor.

THE robins sang in the orchard, the buds
into blossoms grew ;
Little of human sorrow the buds and the
robins knew !

Sick, in an alien household, the poor French
neutral lay ;
Into her lonesome garret fell the light of
the April day,

Through the dusty window, curtained by
the spider's warp and woof,
On the loose-laid floor of hemlock, on
oaken ribs of roof,

The bedquilt's faded patchwork, the tea-
cups on the stand,
The wheel with flaxen tangle, as it dropped
from her sick hand !

What to her was the song of the robin, or
warm morning light,
As she lay in the trance of the dying, heed-
less of sound or sight ?

Done was the work of her hands, she had
eaten her bitter bread ;
The world of the alien people lay behind
her dim and dead.

But her soul went back to its child-time ;
she saw the sun o'erflow
With gold the Basin of Minas, and set over
Gaspereau ;

The low, bare flats at ebb-tide, the rush of
the sea at flood,
Through inlet and creek and river, from
dike to upland wood ;

The gulls in the red of morning, the fish-
hawk's rise and fall,
The drift of the fog in moonshine, over the
dark coast-wall.

She saw the face of her mother, she heard
    the song she sang ;
And far off, faintly, slowly, the bell for
    vespers rang !

By her bed the hard-faced mistress sat,
    smoothing the wrinkled sheet,
Peering into the face, so helpless, and feel-
    ing the ice-cold feet.

With a vague remorse atoning for her greed
    and long abuse,
By care no longer heeded and pity too late
    for use.

Up the stairs of the garret softly the son of
    the mistress stepped,
Leaned over the head-board, covering his
    face with his hands, and wept.

Outspake the mother, who watched him
    sharply, with brow a-frown :
" What ! love you the Papist, the beggar,
    the charge of the town ? "

" Be she Papist or beggar who lies here, I
    know and God knows
I love her, and fain would go with her
    wherever she goes !

" O mother ! that sweet face came pleading,
    for love so athirst.
You saw but the town-charge ; I knew her
    God's angel at first."

Shaking her gray head, the mistress hushed
    down a bitter cry ;
And awed by the silence and shadow of
    death drawing nigh,

She murmured a psalm of the Bible ; but
    closer the young girl pressed,
With the last of her life in her fingers, the
    cross to her breast.

" My son, come away," cried the mother,
    her voice cruel grown.
" She is joined to her idols, like Ephraim ;
    let her alone ! "

But he knelt with his hand on her forehead,
    his lips to her ear,
And he called back the soul that was
    passing : " Marguerite, do you
    hear ? "

She paused on the threshold of heaven ;
    love, pity, surprise,
Wistful, tender, lit up for an instant the
    cloud of her eyes.

With his heart on his lips he kissed her,
    but never her cheek grew red,
And the words the living long for he spake
    in the ear of the dead.

And the robins sang in the orchard, where
    buds to blossoms grew ;
Of the folded hands and the still face never
    the robins knew !

THE ROBIN

MY old Welsh neighbor over the way
    Crept slowly out in the sun of spring,
Pushed from her ears the locks of gray,
    And listened to hear the robins sing.

Her grandson, playing at marbles, stopped,
    And, cruel in sport as boys will be,
Tossed a stone at the bird, who hopped
    From bough to bough in the apple-tree.

" Nay ! " said the grandmother ; " have you
    not heard,
My poor, bad boy ! of the fiery pit,
And how, drop by drop, this merciful bird
    Carries the water that quenches it ?

" He brings cool dew in his little bill,
    And lets it fall on the souls of sin :
You can see the mark on his red breast still
    Of fires that scorch as he drops it in.

" My poor Bron rhuddyn ! my breast-
    burned bird,
Singing so sweetly from limb to limb,
Very dear to the heart of Our Lord
    Is he who pities the lost like Him ! "

" Amen ! " I said to the beautiful myth ;
    " Sing, bird of God, in my heart as well :
Each good thought is a drop wherewith
    To cool and lessen the fires of hell.

" Prayers of love like rain-drops fall,
    Tears of pity are cooling dew,
And dear to the heart of Our Lord are all
    Who suffer like Him in the good they
    do ! "

THE PENNSYLVANIA PILGRIM

[For the preface which introduced this poem when first published, see the notes at the end of this volume. The verses which precede the prelude are from the Latin of FRANCIS DANIEL PASTORIUS in the *Germantown Records*, 1688.]

HAIL to posterity !
Hail, future men of Germanopolis !
  Let the young generations yet to be
  Look kindly upon this.
Think how your fathers left their native
      land, —
  Dear German-land ! O sacred hearths
      and homes ! —
  And, where the wild beast roams,
    In patience planned
New forest-homes beyond the mighty sea,
  There undisturbed and free
To live as brothers of one family.
  What pains and cares befell,
    What trials and what fears,
Remember, and wherein we have done well
  Follow our footsteps, men of coming
      years !
    Where we have failed to do
      Aright, or wisely live,
Be warned by us, the better way pursue,
And, knowing we were human, even as you,
    Pity us and forgive !
    Farewell, Posterity !
    Farewell, dear Germany!
    Forevermore farewell !

PRELUDE

I SING the Pilgrim of a softer clime
  And milder speech than those brave men's
      who brought
To the ice and iron of our winter time
  A will as firm, a creed as stern, and
      wrought
  With one mailed hand, and with the other
      fought.
Simply, as fits my theme, in homely rhyme
  I sing the blue-eyed German Spener
      taught,
Through whose veiled, mystic faith the In-
      ward Light,
  Steady and still, an easy brightness,
      shone,
Transfiguring all things in its radiance
      white.

The garland which his meekness never
      sought
  I bring him ; over fields of harvest sown
With seeds of blessing, now to ripeness
      grown,
I bid the sower pass before the reapers'
      sight.

Never in tenderer quiet lapsed the day
From Pennsylvania's vales of spring away,
Where, forest-walled, the scattered hamlets
      lay

Along the wedded rivers. One long bar
Of purple cloud, on which the evening
      star
Shone like a jewel on a scimitar,

Held the sky's golden gateway. Through
      the deep
Hush of the woods a murmur seemed to
      creep,
The Schuylkill whispering in a voice of
      sleep.

All else was still. The oxen from their
      ploughs
Rested at last, and from their long day's
      browse
Came the dun files of Krisheim's home-
      bound cows.

And the young city, round whose virgin
      zone
The rivers like two mighty arms were
      thrown,
Marked by the smoke of evening fires
      alone,

Lay in the distance, lovely even then
With its fair women and its stately men
Gracing the forest court of William Penn,

Urban yet sylvan ; in its rough - hewn
      frames
Of oak and pine the dryads held their
      claims,
And lent its streets their pleasant woodland
      names.

Anna Pastorius down the leafy lane
Looked city-ward, then stooped to prune
      again
Her vines and simples, with a sigh of pain.

For fast the streaks of ruddy sunset paled
In the oak clearing, and, as daylight failed,
Slow, overhead, the dusky night-birds
   sailed.

Again she looked : between green walls of
   shade,
With low-bent head as if with sorrow
   weighed,
Daniel Pastorius slowly came and said,

"God's peace be with thee, Anna !" Then
   he stood
Silent before her, wrestling with the mood
Of one who sees the evil and not good.

"What is it, my Pastorius ? " As she spoke,
A slow, faint smile across his features broke,
Sadder than tears. "Dear heart," he said,
   " our folk

"Are even as others. Yea, our goodliest
   Friends
Are frail ; our elders have their selfish ends,
And few dare trust the Lord to make
   amends

"For duty's loss. So even our feeble word
For the dumb slaves the startled meeting
   heard
As if a stone its quiet waters stirred ;

"And, as the clerk ceased reading, there
   began
A ripple of dissent which downward ran
In widening circles, as from man to man.

"Somewhat was said of running before
   sent,
Of tender fear that some their guide out-
   went,
Troublers of Israel. I was scarce intent

"On hearing, for behind the reverend row
Of gallery Friends, in dumb and piteous
   show,
I saw, methought, dark faces full of woe.

"And, in the spirit, I was taken where
They toiled and suffered ; I was made aware
Of shame and wrath and anguish and de-
   spair !

"And while the meeting smothered our
   poor plea

With cautious phrase, a Voice there seemed
   to be,
'As ye have done to these ye do to me !'

"So it all passed ; and the old tithe went on
Of anise, mint, and cumin, till the sun
Set, leaving still the weightier work un-
   done.

"Help, for the good man faileth ! Who is
   strong,
If these be weak ? Who shall rebuke the
   wrong,
If these consent ? How long, O Lord !
   how long ! "

He ceased ; and, bound in spirit with the
   bound,
With folded arms, and eyes that sought the
   ground,
Walked musingly his little garden round.

About him, beaded with the falling dew,
Rare plants of power and herbs of healing
   grew,
Such as Van Helmont and Agrippa knew.

For, by the lore of Gorlitz' gentle sage,
With the mild mystics of his dreamy age
He read the herbal signs of nature's page,

As once he heard in sweet Von Merlau's
   bowers
Fair as herself, in boyhood's happy hours,
The pious Spener read his creed in flowers.

"The dear Lord give us patience !" said
   his wife,
Touching with finger-tip an aloe, rife
With leaves sharp-pointed like an Aztec
   knife

Or Carib spear, a gift to William Penn
From the rare gardens of John Evelyn,
Brought from the Spanish Main by mer-
   chantmen.

"See this strange plant its steady purpose
   hold,
And, year by year, its patient leaves unfold,
Till the young eyes that watched it first are
   old.

"But some time, thou hast told me, there
   shall come

A sudden beauty, brightness, and perfume ;
The century-moulded bud shall burst in
    bloom.

"So may the seed which hath been sown
    to-day
Grow with the years, and, after long delay,
Break into bloom, and God's eternal Yea

"Answer at last the patient prayers of them
Who now, by faith alone, behold its stem
Crowned with the flowers of Freedom's
    diadem.

"Meanwhile, to feel and suffer, work and
    wait,
Remains for us. The wrong indeed is
    great,
But love and patience conquer soon or late."

"Well hast thou said, my Anna!" Ten-
    derer
Than youth's caress upon the head of her
Pastorius laid his hand. "Shall we demur

"Because the vision tarrieth? In an hour
We dream not of, the slow-grown bud may
    flower,
And what was sown in weakness rise in
    power!"

Then through the vine-draped door whose
    legend read,
"Procul este profani!" Anna led
To where their child upon his little bed

Looked up and smiled. "Dear heart," she
    said, "if we
Must bearers of a heavy burden be,
Our boy, God willing, yet the day shall see

"When from the gallery to the farthest seat,
Slave and slave-owner shall no longer meet,
But all sit equal at the Master's feet."

On the stone hearth the blazing walnut block
Set the low walls a-glimmer, showed the
    cock
Rebuking Peter on the Van Wyck clock,

Shone on old tomes of law and physic, side
By side with Fox and Behmen, played at
    hide
And seek with Anna, midst her household
    pride

Of flaxen webs, and on the table, bare
Of costly cloth or silver cup, but where,
Tasting the fat shads of the Delaware,

The courtly Penn had praised the good-
    wife's cheer,
And quoted Horace o'er her home-brewed
    beer,
Till even grave Pastorius smiled to hear.

In such a home, beside the Schuylkill's
    wave,
He dwelt in peace with God and man, and
    gave
Food to the poor and shelter to the slave.

For all too soon the New World's scandal
    shamed
The righteous code by Penn and Sidney
    framed,
And men withheld the human rights they
    claimed.

And slowly wealth and station sanction lent,
And hardened avarice, on its gains intent,
Stifled the inward whisper of dissent.

Yet all the while the burden rested sore
On tender hearts. At last Pastorius bore
Their warning message to the Church's
    door

In God's name ; and the leaven of the word
Wrought ever after in the souls who heard,
And a dead conscience in its grave-clothes
    stirred

To troubled life, and urged the vain excuse
Of Hebrew custom, patriarchal use,
Good in itself if evil in abuse.

Gravely Pastorius listened, not the less
Discerning through the decent fig-leaf dress
Of the poor plea its shame of selfishness.

One Scripture rule, at least, was unforgot,
He hid the outcast, and bewrayed him not :
And, when his prey the human hunter
    sought,

He scrupled not, while Anna's wise delay
And proffered cheer prolonged the master's
    stay,
To speed the black guest safely on his
    way.

Yet who shall guess his bitter grief who
    lends
His life to some great cause, and finds his
    friends
Shame or betray it for their private ends?

How felt the Master when his chosen strove
In childish folly for their seats above;
And that fond mother, blinded by her love,

Besought him that her sons, beside his
    throne,
Might sit on either hand?   Amidst his own
A stranger oft, companionless and lone,

God's priest and prophet stands.   The
    martyr's pain
Is not alone from scourge and cell and
    chain;
Sharper the pang when, shouting in his
    train,

His weak disciples by their lives deny
The loud hosannas of their daily cry,
And make their echo of his truth a lie.

His forest home no hermit's cell he found,
Guests, motley-minded, drew his hearth
    around,
And held armed truce upon its neutral
    ground.

There Indian chiefs with battle-bows un-
    strung,
Strong, hero-limbed, like those whom Ho-
    mer sung,
Pastorius fancied, when the world was
    young,

Came with their tawny women, lithe and
    tall,
Like bronzes in his friend Von Rodeck's
    hall,
Comely, if black, and not unpleasing all.

There hungry folk in homespun drab and
    gray
Drew round his board on Monthly Meeting
    day,
Genial, half merry in their friendly way.

Or, haply, pilgrims from the Fatherland,
Weak, timid, homesick, slow to understand
The New World's promise, sought his help-
    ing hand.

Or painful Kelpius from his hermit den
By Wissahickon, maddest of good men,
Dreamed o'er the Chiliast dreams of Peter-
    sen.

Deep in the woods, where the small river
    slid
Snake-like in shade, the Helmstadt Mystic
    hid,
Weird as a wizard, over arts forbid,

Reading the books of Daniel and of John,
And Behmen's Morning-Redness, through
    the Stone
Of Wisdom, vouchsafed to his eyes alone,

Whereby he read what man ne'er read be-
    fore,
And saw the visions man shall see no more,
Till the great angel, striding sea and shore,

Shall bid all flesh await, on land or ships,
The warning trump of the Apocalypse,
Shattering the heavens before the dread
    eclipse.

Or meek-eyed Mennonist his bearded chin
Leaned o'er the gate;   or Ranter, pure
    within,
Aired his perfection in a world of sin.

Or, talking of old home scenes, Op der
    Graaf
Teased the low back-log with his shodden
    staff,
Till the red embers broke into a laugh

And dance of flame, as if they fain would
    cheer
The rugged face, half tender, half austere,
Touched with the pathos of a homesick
    tear!

Or Sluyter, saintly familist, whose word
As law the Brethren of the Manor heard,
Announced the speedy terrors of the Lord,

And turned, like Lot at Sodom, from his
    race,
Above a wrecked world with complacent
    face
Riding secure upon his plank of grace!

Haply, from Finland's birchen groves ex-
    iled,

Manly in thought, in simple ways a child,
His white hair floating round his visage
      mild,

The Swedish pastor sought the Quaker's
      door,
Pleased from his neighbor's lips to hear
      once more
His long-disused and half-forgotten lore.

For both could baffle Babel's lingual curse,
And speak in Bion's Doric, and rehearse
Cleanthes' hymn or Virgil's sounding verse.

And oft Pastorius and the meek old man
Argued as Quaker and as Lutheran,
Ending in Christian love, as they began.

With lettered Lloyd on pleasant morns he
      strayed
Where Sommerhausen over vales of shade
Looked miles away, by every flower de-
      layed,

Or song of bird, happy and free with one
Who loved, like him, to let his memory run
Over old fields of learning, and to sun

Himself in Plato's wise philosophies,
And dream with Philo over mysteries
Whereof the dreamer never finds the keys ;

To touch all themes of thought, nor weakly
      stop
For doubt of truth, but let the buckets drop
Deep down and bring the hidden waters
      up.

For there was freedom in that wakening
      time
Of tender souls ; to differ was not crime ;
The varying bells made up the perfect
      chime.

On lips unlike was laid the altar's coal,
The white, clear light, tradition-colored,
      stole
Through the stained oriel of each human
      soul.

Gathered from many sects, the Quaker
      brought
His old beliefs, adjusting to the thought
That moved his soul the creed his fathers
      taught.

One faith alone, so broad that all mankind
Within themselves its secret witness find,
The soul's communion with the Eternal
      Mind,

The Spirit's law, the Inward Rule and
      Guide,
Scholar and peasant, lord and serf, allied,
The polished Penn and Cromwell's Ironside.

As still in Hemskerck's Quaker Meeting,
      face
By face in Flemish detail, we may trace
How loose-mouthed boor and fine ancestral
      grace

Sat in close contrast, — the clipt-headed
      churl,
Broad market-dame, and simple serving-
      girl
By skirt of silk and periwig in curl !

For soul touched soul ; the spiritual treas-
      ure-trove
Made all men equal, none could rise above
Nor sink below that level of God's love.

So, with his rustic neighbors sitting down,
The homespun frock beside the scholar's
      gown,
Pastorius to the manners of the town

Added the freedom of the woods, and
      sought
The bookless wisdom by experience taught,
And learned to love his new-found home,
      while not

Forgetful of the old ; the seasons went
Their rounds, and somewhat to his spirit
      lent
Of their own calm and measureless content.

Glad even to tears, he heard the robin sing
His song of welcome to the Western spring,
And bluebird borrowing from the sky his
      wing.

And when the miracle of autumn came,
And all the woods with many-colored flame
Of splendor, making summer's greenness
      tame,

Burned, unconsumed, a voice without a
      sound

Spake to him from each kindled bush
    around,
And made the strange, new landscape holy
    ground !

And when the bitter north-wind, keen and
    swift,
Swept the white street and piled the door-
    yard drift,
He exercised, as Friends might say, his gift

Of verse, Dutch, English, Latin, like the
    hash
Of corn and beans in Indian succotash ;
Dull, doubtless, but with here and there a
    flash

Of wit and fine conceit, — the good man's
    play
Of quiet fancies, meet to while away
The slow hours measuring off an idle day.

At evening, while his wife put on her look
Of love's endurance, from its niche he
    took
The written pages of his ponderous book.

And read, in half the languages of man,
His " Rusca Apium," which with bees be-
    gan,
And through the gamut of creation ran.

Or, now and then, the missive of some friend
In gray Altorf or storied Nürnberg penned
Dropped in upon him like a guest to spend

The night beneath his roof-tree.   Mystical
The fair Von Merlau spake as waters fall
And voices sound in dreams, and yet withal

Human and sweet, as if each far, low tone,
Over the roses of her gardens blown
Brought the warm sense of beauty all her
    own.

Wise Spener questioned what his friend
    could trace
Of spiritual influx or of saving grace
In the wild natures of the Indian race.

And learned Schurmberg, fain, at times, to
    look
From Talmud, Koran, Veds, and Penta-
    teuch,
Sought out his pupil in his far-off nook,

To query with him of climatic change,
Of bird, beast, reptile, in his forest range,
Of flowers and fruits and simples new and
    strange.

And thus the Old and New World reached
    their hands
Across the water, and the friendly lands
Talked with each other from their severed
    strands.

Pastorius answered all : while seed and root
Sent from his new home grew to flower and
    fruit
Along the Rhine and at the Spessart's foot ;

And, in return, the flowers his boyhood knew
Smiled at his door, the same in form and
    hue,
And on his vines the Rhenish clusters grew.

No idler he ; whoever else might shirk,
He set his hand to every honest work, —
Farmer and teacher, court and meeting
    clerk.

Still on the town seal his device is found,
Grapes, flax, and thread-spool on a trefoil
    ground,
With " Vinum, Linum et Textrinum "
    wound.

One house sufficed for gospel and for law,
Where Paul and Grotius, Scripture text and
    saw,
Assured the good, and held the rest in awe.

Whatever legal maze he wandered through,
He kept the Sermon on the Mount in view,
And justice always into mercy grew.

No whipping-post he needed, stocks, nor
    jail,
Nor ducking-stool ; the orchard-thief grew
    pale
At his rebuke, the vixen ceased to rail,

The usurer's grasp released the forfeit land ;
The slanderer faltered at the witness-stand,
And all men took his counsel for command.

Was it caressing air, the brooding love
Of tenderer skies than German land knew
    of,
Green calm below, blue quietness above,

Still flow of water, deep repose of wood
That, with a sense of loving Fatherhood
And childlike trust in the Eternal Good,

Softened all hearts, and dulled the edge of
hate,
Hushed strife, and taught impatient zeal to
wait
The slow assurance of the better state ?

Who knows what goadings in their sterner
way
O'er jagged ice, relieved by granite gray,
Blew round the men of Massachusetts Bay ?

What hate of heresy the east-wind woke ?
What hints of pitiless power and terror
spoke
In waves that on their iron coast-line broke ?

Be it as it may : within the Land of Penn
The sectary yielded to the citizen,
And peaceful dwelt the many-creeded men.

Peace brooded over all.   No trumpet stung
The air to madness, and no steeple flung
Alarums down from bells at midnight rung.

The land slept well.   The Indian from his
face
Washed all his war-paint off, and in the
place
Of battle-marches sped the peaceful chase,

Or wrought for wages at the white man's
side, —
Giving to kindness what his native pride
And lazy freedom to all else denied.

And well the curious scholar loved the
old
Traditions that his swarthy neighbors
told
By wigwam-fires when nights were growing
cold,

Discerned the fact round which their fancy
drew
Its dreams, and held their childish faith
more true
To God and man than half the creeds he
knew.

The desert blossomed round him ; wheat-
fields rolled

Beneath the warm wind waves of green
and gold ;
The planted ear returned its hundred-fold.

Great clusters ripened in a warmer sun
Than that which by the Rhine stream shines
upon
The purpling hillsides with low vines o'er-
run.

About each rustic porch the humming-bird
Tried with light bill, that scarce a petal
stirred,
The Old World flowers to virgin soil trans-
ferred ;

And the first - fruits of pear and apple,
bending
The young boughs down, their gold and
russet blending,
Made glad his heart, familiar odors lend-
ing

To the fresh fragrance of the birch and
pine,
Life-everlasting, bay, and eglantine,
And all the subtle scents the woods combine.

Fair First-Day mornings, steeped in sum-
mer calm,
Warm, tender, restful, sweet with woodland
balm,
Came to him, like some mother-hallowed
psalm

To the tired grinder at the noisy wheel
Of labor, winding off from memory's reel
A golden thread of music.   With no peal

Of bells to call them to the house of
praise,
The scattered settlers through green forest-
ways
Walked meeting-ward.   In reverent amaze

The Indian trapper saw them, from the
dim
Shade of the alders on the rivulet's rim,
Seek the Great Spirit's house to talk with
Him.

There, through the gathered stillness mul-
tiplied
And made intense by sympathy, outside
The sparrows sang, and the gold-robin cried,

A-swing upon his elm. A faint perfume
Breathed through the open windows of the
    room
From locust-trees, heavy with clustered
    bloom.

Thither, perchance, sore-tried confessors
    came,
Whose fervor jail nor pillory could tame,
Proud of the cropped ears meant to be their
    shame,

Men who had eaten slavery's bitter bread
In Indian isles ; pale women who had bled
Under the hangman's lash, and bravely
    said

God's message through their prison's iron
    bars ;
And gray old soldier-converts, seamed with
    scars
From every stricken field of England's wars.

Lowly before the Unseen Presence knelt
Each waiting heart, till haply some one felt
On his moved lips the seal of silence melt.

Or, without spoken words, low breathings
    stole
Of a diviner life from soul to soul,
Baptizing in one tender thought the whole.

When shaken hands announced the meeting
    o'er,
The friendly group still lingered at the door,
Greeting, inquiring, sharing all the store

Of weekly tidings. Meanwhile youth and
    maid
Down the green vistas of the woodland
    strayed,
Whispered and smiled and oft their feet de-
    layed.

Did the boy's whistle answer back the
    thrushes ?
Did light girl laughter ripple through the
    bushes,
As brooks make merry over roots and
    rushes ?

Unvexed the sweet air seemed. Without a
    wound
The ear of silence heard, and every sound
Its place in nature's fine accordance found.

And solemn meeting, summer sky and wood,
Old kindly faces, youth and maidenhood
Seemed, like God's new creation, very good !

And, greeting all with quiet smile and word,
Pastorius went his way. The unscared bird
Sang at his side ; scarcely the squirrel
    stirred

At his hushed footstep on the mossy sod ;
And, wheresoe'er the good man looked or
    trod,
He felt the peace of nature and of God.

His social life wore no ascetic form,
He loved all beauty, without fear of harm,
And in his veins his Teuton blood ran warm.

Strict to himself, of other men no spy,
He made his own no circuit-judge to try
The freer conscience of his neighbors by.

With love rebuking, by his life alone,
Gracious and sweet, the better way was
    shown,
The joy of one, who, seeking not his own,

And faithful to all scruples, finds at last
The thorns and shards of duty overpast,
And daily life, beyond his hope's forecast,

Pleasant and beautiful with sight and sound
And flowers upspringing in its narrow
    round,
And all his days with quiet gladness
    crowned.

He sang not ; but if sometimes tempted
    strong,
He hummed what seemed like Altorf's
    Burschen-song,
His good wife smiled and did not count it
    wrong.

For well he loved his boyhood's brother
    band ;
His Memory, while he trod the New World's
    strand,
A double-ganger walked the Fatherland !

If, when on frosty Christmas eves the light
Shone on his quiet hearth, he missed the
    sight
Of Yule-log, Tree, and Christ-child all in
    white ;

And closed his eyes, and listened to the sweet
Old wait-songs sounding down his native street,
And watched again the dancers' mingling feet ;

Yet not the less, when once the vision passed,
He held the plain and sober maxims fast
Of the dear Friends with whom his lot was cast.

Still all attuned to nature's melodies
He loved the bird's song in his door-yard trees,
And the low hum of home-returning bees ;

The blossomed flax, the tulip-trees in bloom
Down the long street, the beauty and perfume
Of apple-boughs, the mingling light and gloom

Of Sommerhausen's woodlands, woven through
With sun-threads ; and the music the wind drew,
Mournful and sweet, from leaves it overblew.

And evermore, beneath this outward sense,
And through the common sequence of events,
He felt the guiding hand of Providence

Reach out of space. A Voice spake in his ear,
And lo ! all other voices far and near
Died at that whisper, full of meanings clear.

The Light of Life shone round him ; one by one
The wandering lights, that all-misleading run,
Went out like candles paling in the sun.

That Light he followed, step by step, where'er
It led, as in the vision of the seer
The wheels moved as the spirit in the clear

And terrible crystal moved, with all their eyes
Watching the living splendor sink or rise,
Its will their will, knowing no otherwise.

Within himself he found the law of right,
He walked by faith and not the letter's sight,
And read his Bible by the Inward Light.

And if sometimes the slaves of form and rule,
Frozen in their creeds like fish in winter's pool,
Tried the large tolerance of his liberal school,

His door was free to men of every name,
He welcomed all the seeking souls who came,
And no man's faith he made a cause of blame.

But best he loved in leisure hours to see
His own dear Friends sit by him knee to knee,
In social converse, genial, frank, and free.

There sometimes silence (it were hard to tell
Who owned it first) upon the circle fell,
Hushed Anna's busy wheel, and laid its spell

On the black boy who grimaced by the hearth,
To solemnize his shining face of mirth ;
Only the old clock ticked amidst the dearth

Of sound ; nor eye was raised nor hand was stirred
In that soul-sabbath, till at last some word
Of tender counsel or low prayer was heard.

Then guests, who lingered but farewell to say
And take love's message, went their homeward way ;
So passed in peace the guileless Quaker's day.

His was the Christian's unsung Age of Gold,
A truer idyl than the bards have told
Of Arno's banks or Arcady of old.

Where still the Friends their place of burial keep,
And century-rooted mosses o'er it creep,
The Nürnberg scholar and his helpmeet sleep.

And Anna's aloe ?   If it flowered at last
In Bartram's garden, did John Woolman
　　cast
A glance upon it as he meekly passed ?

And did a secret sympathy possess
That tender soul, and for the slave's redress
Lend hope. strength, patience ?   It were
　　vain to guess.

Nay, were the plant itself but mythical,
Set in the fresco of tradition's wall
Like Jotham's bramble, mattereth not at
　　all.

Enough to know that, through tne winter's
　　frost
And summer's heat, no seed of truth is lost,
And every duty pays at last its cost.

For, ere Pastorius left the sun and air,
God sent the answer to his life-long prayer ;
The child was born beside the Delaware,

Who, in the power a holy purpose lends,
Guided his people unto nobler ends,
And left them worthier of the name of
　　Friends.

And lo ! the fulness of the time has come,
And over all the exile's Western home,
From sea to sea the flowers of freedom
　　bloom !

And joy-bells ring, and silver trumpets
　　blow ;
But not for thee, Pastorius !   Even so
The world forgets, but the wise angels
　　know.

KING VOLMER AND ELSIE

AFTER THE DANISH OF CHRISTIAN WINTER

[A Danish gentleman, Mr. P. Taft, sent the
poet an unrhymed outline in English of Win-
ter's ballad.]

WHERE, over heathen doom-rings and gray
　　stones of the Horg,
In its little Christian city stands the church
　　of Vordingborg,

In merry mood King Volmer sat, forgetful
　　of his power,
As idle as the Goose of Gold that brooded
　　on his tower.

Out spake the King to Henrik, his young
　　and faithful squire :
" Dar'st trust thy little Elsie, the maid of
　　thy desire ? "
" Of all the men in Denmark she loveth
　　only me :
As true to me is Elsie as thy Lily is to
　　thee."

Loud laughed the king : " To-morrow shall
　　bring another day,
When I myself will test her ; she will not
　　say me nay."
Thereat the lords and gallants, that round
　　about him stood,
Wagged all their heads in concert and
　　smiled as courtiers should.

The gray lark sings o'er Vordingborg, and
　　on the ancient town
From the tall tower of Valdemar the
　　Golden Goose looks down ;
The yellow grain is waving in the pleasant
　　wind of morn,
The wood resounds with cry of hounds and
　　blare of hunter's horn.

In the garden of her father little Elsie sits
　　and spins,
And, singing with the early birds, her daily
　　task begins.
Gay tulips bloom and sweet mint curls
　　around her garden-bower,
But she is sweeter than the mint and fairer
　　than the flower.

About her form her kirtle blue clings lov-
　　ingly, and, white
As snow, her loose sleeves only leave her
　　small, round wrists in sight ;
Below, the modest petticoat can only half
　　conceal
The motion of the lightest foot that ever
　　turned a wheel.

The cat sits purring at her side, bees hum
　　in sunshine warm ;
But, look ! she starts, she lifts her face.
　　she shades it with her arm.

And, hark ! a train of horsemen, with sound
    of dog and horn,
Come leaping o'er the ditches, come tramp-
    ling down the corn !

Merrily rang the bridle-reins, and scarf and
    plume streamed gay,
As fast beside her father's gate the riders
    held their way ;
And one was brave in scarlet cloak, with
    golden spur on heel,
And, as he checked his foaming steed, the
    maiden checked her wheel.

" All hail among thy roses, the fairest rose
    to me !
For weary months in secret my heart has
    longed for thee ! "
What noble knight was this ? What words
    for modest maiden's ear ?
She dropped a lowly courtesy of bashful-
    ness and fear.

She lifted up her spinning-wheel ; she fain
    would seek the door,
Trembling in every limb, her cheek with
    blushes crimsoned o'er.
" Nay. fear me not," the rider said, " I
    offer heart and hand,
Bear witness these good Danish knights
    who round about me stand.

" I grant you time to think of this, to an-
    swer as you may,
For to - morrow, little Elsie, shall bring
    another day."
He spake the old phrase slyly, as glancing
    round his train,
He saw his merry followers seek to hide
    their smiles in vain.

" The snow of pearls I 'll scatter in your
    curls of golden hair,
I 'll line with furs the velvet of the kirtle
    that you wear ;
All precious gems shall twine your neck ;
    and in a chariot gay
You shall ride, my little Elsie, behind four
    steeds of gray.

" And harps shall sound, and flutes shall
    play, and brazen lamps shall glow ;
On marble floors your feet shall weave the
    dances to and fro.

At frosty eventide for us the blazing hearth
    shall shine,
While at our ease we play at draughts, and
    drink the blood-red wine."

Then Elsie raised her head and met her
    wooer face to face ;
A roguish smile shone in her eye and on
    her lip found place.
Back from her low white forehead the
    curls of gold she threw,
And lifted up her eyes to his, steady and
    clear and blue.

" I am a lowly peasant, and you a gallant
    knight ;
I will not trust a love that soon may cool
    and turn to slight.
If you would wed me henceforth be a
    peasant, not a lord ;
I bid you hang upon the wall your tried
    and trusty sword."

" To please you, Elsie, I will lay keen Dy-
    nadel away,
And in its place will swing the scythe and
    mow your father's hay."
" Nay, but your gallant scarlet cloak my
    eyes can never bear ;
A Vadmal coat, so plain and gray, is all
    that you must wear."

" Well, Vadmal will I wear for you," the
    rider gayly spoke,
" And on the Lord's high altar I 'll lay my
    scarlet cloak."
" But mark," she said, " no stately horse
    my peasant love must ride,
A yoke of steers before the plough is all
    that he must guide."

The knight looked down upon his steed :
    " Well, let him wander free :
No other man must ride the horse that has
    been backed by me.
Henceforth I 'll tread the furrow and to
    my oxen talk,
If only little Elsie beside my plough will
    walk."

" You must take from out your cellar cask
    of wine and flask and can ;
The homely mead I brew you may serve a
    peasant-man."

"Most willingly, fair Elsie, I'll drink that
    mead of thine,
And leave my minstrel's thirsty throat to
    drain my generous wine."

"Now break your shield asunder, and
    shatter sign and boss,
Unmeet for peasant - wedded arms, your
    knightly knee across.
And pull me down your castle from top to
    basement wall,
And let your plough trace furrows in the
    ruins of your hall!"

Then smiled he with a lofty pride; right
    well at last he knew
The maiden of the spinning-wheel was to
    her troth-plight true.
"Ah, roguish little Elsie! you act your part
    full well:
You know that I must bear my shield and
    in my castle dwell!

"The lions ramping on that shield between
    the hearts aflame
Keep watch o'er Denmark's honor, and
    guard her ancient name.
For know that I am Volmer; I dwell in
    yonder towers,
Who ploughs them ploughs up Denmark,
    this goodly home of ours!

"I tempt no more, fair Elsie! your heart
    I know is true;
Would God that all our maidens were good
    and pure as you!
Well have you pleased your monarch, and
    he shall well repay;
God's peace! Farewell! To-morrow will
    bring another day!"

He lifted up his bridle hand, he spurred his
    good steed then,
And like a whirl-blast swept away with all
    his gallant men.
The steel hoofs beat the rocky path; again
    on winds of morn
The wood resounds with cry of hounds and
    blare of hunter's horn.

"Thou true and ever faithful!" the listen-
    ing Henrik cried;
And, leaping o'er the green hedge, he stood
    by Elsie's side.

None saw the fond embracing, save, shin-
    ing from afar,
The Golden Goose that watched them from
    the tower of Valdemar.

O darling girls of Denmark! of all the
    flowers that throng
Her vales of spring the fairest, I sing for
    you my song.
No praise as yours so bravely rewards the
    singer's skill;
Thank God! of maids like Elsie the land
    has plenty still!

THE THREE BELLS

BENEATH the low-hung night cloud
    That raked her splintering mast
The good ship settled slowly,
    The cruel leak gained fast.

Over the awful ocean
    Her signal guns pealed out.
Dear God! was that Thy answer
    From the horror round about?

A voice came down the wild wind,
    "Ho! ship ahoy!" its cry:
"Our stout Three Bells of Glasgow
    Shall lay till daylight by!"

Hour after hour crept slowly,
    Yet on the heaving swells
Tossed up and down the ship-lights,
    The lights of the Three Bells!

And ship to ship made signals,
    Man answered back to man,
While oft, to cheer and hearten,
    The Three Bells nearer ran;

And the captain from her taffrail
    Sent down his hopeful cry:
"Take heart! Hold on!" he shouted
    "The Three Bells shall lay by!"

All night across the waters
    The tossing lights shone clear;
All night from reeling taffrail
    The Three Bells sent her cheer.

And when the dreary watches
    Of storm and darkness passed,

Just as the wreck lurched under,
All souls were saved at last.

Sail on, Three Bells, forever,
In grateful memory sail !
Ring on, Three Bells of rescue,
Above the wave and gale !

Type of the Love eternal,
Repeat the Master's cry,
As tossing through our darkness
The lights of God draw nigh !

JOHN UNDERHILL

A SCORE of years had come and gone
Since the Pilgrims landed on Plymouth
stone,
When Captain Underhill, bearing scars
From Indian ambush and Flemish wars,
Left three - hilled Boston and wandered
down,
East by north, to Cocheco town.

With Vane the younger, in council sweet,
He had sat at Anna Hutchinson's feet,
And, when the bolt of banishment fell
On the head of his saintly oracle,
He had shared her ill as her good report,
And braved the wrath of the General
Court.

He shook from his feet as he rode away
The dust of the Massachusetts Bay.
The world might bless and the world might
ban,
What did it matter the perfect man.
To whom the freedom of earth was given,
Proof against sin, and sure of heaven ?

He cheered his heart as he rode along
With screed of Scripture and holy song,
Or thought how he rode with his lances
free
By the Lower Rhine and the Zuyder-Zee,
Till his wood - path grew to a trodden
road,
And Hilton Point in the distance showed.

He saw the church with the block-house
nigh,
The two fair rivers, the flakes thereby,
And, tacking to windward, low and crank,
The little shallop from Strawberry Bank ;

And he rose in his stirrups and looked
abroad
Over land and water, and praised the Lord.

Goodly and stately and grave to see,
Into the clearing's space rode he,
With the sun on the hilt of his sword in
sheath,
And his silver buckles and spurs beneath,
And the settlers welcomed him, one and all,
From swift Quampeagan to Gonic Fall.

And he said to the elders : "Lo, I come
As the way seemed open to seek a home.
Somewhat the Lord hath wrought by my
hands
In the Narragansett and Netherlands,
And if here ye have work for a Christian
man,
I will tarry, and serve ye as best I can.

"I boast not of gifts, but fain would own
The wonderful favor God hath shown,
The special mercy vouchsafed one day
On the shore of Narragansett Bay,
As I sat, with my pipe, from the camp aside,
And mused like Isaac at eventide.

"A sudden sweetness of peace I found,
A garment of gladness wrapped me round ;
I felt from the law of works released,
The strife of the flesh and spirit ceased,
My faith to a full assurance grew,
And all I had hoped for myself I knew.

"Now, as God appointeth, I keep my
way,
I shall not stumble, I shall not stray ;
He hath taken away my fig-leaf dress,
I wear the robe of His righteousness ;
And the shafts of Satan no more avail
Than Pequot arrows on Christian mail."

"Tarry with us," the settlers cried,
"Thou man of God, as our ruler and guide."
And Captain Underhill bowed his head.
"The will of the Lord be done !" he said.
And the morrow beheld him sitting down
In the ruler's seat in Cocheco town.

And he judged therein as a just man should ;
His words were wise and his rule was good ;
He coveted not his neighbor's land,
From the holding of bribes he shook his
hand ;

And through the camps of the heathen ran
A wholesome fear of the valiant man.

But the heart is deceitful, the good Book saith,
And life hath ever a savor of death.
Through hymns of triumph the tempter calls,
And whoso thinketh he standeth falls.
Alas! ere their round the seasons ran,
There was grief in the soul of the saintly man.

The tempter's arrows that rarely fail
Had found the joints of his spiritual mail;
And men took note of his gloomy air,
The shame in his eye, the halt in his prayer,
The signs of a battle lost within,
The pain of a soul in the coils of sin.

Then a whisper of scandal linked his name
With broken vows and a life of blame;
And the people looked askance on him
As he walked among them sullen and grim,
Ill at ease, and bitter of word,
And prompt of quarrel with hand or sword.

None knew how, with prayer and fasting still,
He strove in the bonds of his evil will;
But he shook himself like Samson at length,
And girded anew his loins of strength,
And bade the crier go up and down
And call together the wondering town.

Jeer and murmur and shaking of head
Ceased as he rose in his place and said:
" Men, brethren, and fathers, well ye know
How I came among you a year ago,
Strong in the faith that my soul was freed
From sin of feeling, or thought, or deed.

"I have sinned, I own it with grief and shame,
But not with a lie on my lips I came.
In my blindness I verily thought my heart
Swept and garnished in every part.
He chargeth His angels with folly; He sees
The heavens unclean. Was I more than these?

" I urge no plea. At your feet I lay
The trust you gave me, and go my way.

Hate me or pity me, as you will,
The Lord will have mercy on sinners still;
And I, who am chiefest, say to all,
Watch and pray, lest ye also fall."

No voice made answer : a sob so low
That only his quickened ear could know
Smote his heart with a bitter pain,
As into the forest he rode again,
And the veil of its oaken leaves shut down
On his latest glimpse of Cocheco town.

Crystal-clear on the man of sin
The streams flashed up, and the sky shone in;
On his cheek of fever the cool wind blew,
The leaves dropped on him their tears of dew,
And angels of God, in the pure, sweet guise
Of flowers, looked on him with sad surprise.

Was his ear at fault that brook and breeze
Sang in their saddest of minor keys?
What was it the mournful wood-thrush said?
What whispered the pine-trees overhead?
Did he hear the Voice on his lonely way
That Adam heard in the cool of day?

Into the desert alone rode he,
Alone with the Infinite Purity;
And, bowing his soul to its tender rebuke,
As Peter did to the Master's look,
He measured his path with prayers of pain
For peace with God and nature again.

And in after years to Cocheco came
The bruit of a once familiar name;
How among the Dutch of New Netherlands,
From wild Danskamer to Haarlem sands,
A penitent soldier preached the Word,
And smote the heathen with Gideon's sword!

And the heart of Boston was glad to hear
How he harried the foe on the long frontier,
And heaped on the land against him barred
The coals of his generous watch and ward.
Frailest and bravest! the Bay State still
Counts with her worthies John Underhill.

CONDUCTOR BRADLEY

A railway conductor who lost his life in an accident on a Connecticut railway, May 9, 1873.

CONDUCTOR BRADLEY, (always may his
    name
Be said with reverence !) as the swift doom
    came,
Smitten to death, a crushed and mangled
    frame,

Sank, with the brake he grasped just where
    he stood
To do the utmost that a brave man could,
And die, if needful, as a true man should.

Men stooped above him ; women dropped
    their tears
On that poor wreck beyond all hopes or
    fears,
Lost in the strength and glory of his years.

What heard they ? Lo ! the ghastly lips
    of pain,
Dead to all thought save duty's, moved
    again :
"Put out the signals for the other train !"

No nobler utterance since the world began
From lips of saint or martyr ever ran,
Electric, through the sympathies of man.

Ah me ! how poor and noteless seem to this
The sick-bed dramas of self-consciousness,
Our sensual fears of pain and hopes of
    bliss !

Oh, grand, supreme endeavor ! Not in
    vain
That last brave act of failing tongue and
    brain !
Freighted with life the downward rushing
    train,

Following the wrecked one, as wave follows
    wave,
Obeyed the warning which the dead lips
    gave.
Others he saved, himself he could not save.

Nay, the lost life *was* saved. He is not dead
Who in his record still the earth shall tread
With God's clear aureole shining round his
    head.

We bow as in the dust, with all our pride
Of virtue dwarfed the noble deed be-
    side.
God give us grace to live as Bradley died !

THE WITCH OF WENHAM

The house is still standing in Danvers, Mass., where, it is said, a suspected witch was confined overnight in the attic, which was bolted fast. In the morning, when the constable came to take her to Salem for trial, she was missing, although the door was still bolted. Her escape was doubtless aided by her friends, but at the time it was attributed to Satanic interference.

I

ALONG Crane River's sunny slopes
    Blew warm the winds of May,
And over Naumkeag's ancient oaks
    The green outgrew the gray.

The grass was green on Rial-side,
    The early birds at will
Waked up the violet in its dell,
    The wind-flower on its hill.

"Where go you, in your Sunday coat,
    Son Andrew, tell me, pray."
"For stripëd perch in Wenham Lake
    I go to fish to-day."

"Unharmed of thee in Wenham Lake
    The mottled perch shall be :
A blue-eyed witch sits on the bank
    And weaves her net for thee.

"She weaves her golden hair ; she sings
    Her spell-song low and faint ;
The wickedest witch in Salem jail
    Is to that girl a saint."

"Nay, mother, hold thy cruel tongue ;
    God knows," the young man cried,
"He never made a whiter soul
    Than hers by Wenham side.

"She tends her mother sick and blind,
    And every want supplies ;
To her above the blessed Book
    She lends her soft blue eyes.

"Her voice is glad with holy songs,
    Her lips are sweet with prayer ;

Go where you will, in ten miles round
Is none more good and fair."

" Son Andrew, for the love of God
And of thy mother, stay ! "
She clasped her hands, she wept aloud,
But Andrew rode away.

" O reverend sir, my Andrew's soul
The Wenham witch has caught ;
She holds him with the curlèd gold
Whereof her snare is wrought.

" She charms him with her great blue eyes,
She binds him with her hair ;
Oh, break the spell with holy words,
Unbind him with a prayer ! "

" Take heart," the painful preacher said,
" This mischief shall not be ;
The witch shall perish in her sins
And Andrew shall go free.

" Our poor Ann Putnam testifies
She saw her weave a spell,
Bare-armed, loose-haired, at full of moon,
Around a dried-up well.

" ' Spring up, O well ! ' she softly sang
The Hebrew's old refrain
(For Satan uses Bible words),
Till water flowed amain.

" And many a goodwife heard her speak
By Wenham water words
That made the buttercups take wings
And turn to yellow birds.

" They say that swarming wild bees seek
The hive at her command ;
And fishes swim to take their food
From out her dainty hand.

" Meek as she sits in meeting-time,
The godly minister
Notes well the spell that doth compel
The young men's eyes to her.

" The mole upon her dimpled chin
Is Satan's seal and sign ;
Her lips are red with evil bread
And stain of unblest wine.

" For Tituba, my Indian, saith
At Quasycung she took

The Black Man's godless sacrament
And signed his dreadful book.

" Last night my sore-afflicted child
Against the young witch cried.
To take her Marshal Herrick rides
Even now to Wenham side."

The marshal in his saddle sat,
His daughter at his knee ;
" I go to fetch that arrant witch,
Thy fair playmate," quoth he.

" Her spectre walks the parsonage,
And haunts both hall and stair ;
They know her by the great blue eyes
And floating gold of hair."

" They lie, they lie, my father dear !
No foul old witch is she,
But sweet and good and crystal-pure
As Wenham waters be."

" I tell thee, child, the Lord hath set
Before us good and ill,
And woe to all whose carnal loves
Oppose His righteous will.

" Between Him and the powers of hell
Choose thou, my child, to-day :
No sparing hand, no pitying eye,
When God commands to slay ! "

He went his way ; the old wives shook
With fear as he drew nigh ;
The children in the dooryards held
Their breath as he passed by.

Too well they knew the gaunt gray
horse
The grim witch-hunter rode,
The pale Apocalyptic beast
By grisly Death bestrode.

II

Oh, fair the face of Wenham Lake
Upon the young girl's shone,
Her tender mouth, her dreaming eyes,
Her yellow hair outblown.

By happy youth and love attuned
To natural harmonies,
The singing birds, the whispering wind,
She sat beneath the trees.

Sat shaping for her bridal dress
　Her mother's wedding gown,
When lo ! the marshal, writ in hand,
　From Alford hill rode down.

His face was hard with cruel fear,
　He grasped the maiden's hands :
"Come with me unto Salem town,
　For so the law commands ! "

"Oh, let me to my mother say
　Farewell before I go ! "
He closer tied her little hands
　Unto his saddle bow.

"Unhand me," cried she piteously,
　"For thy sweet daughter's sake."
"I 'll keep my daughter safe," he said,
　"From the witch of Wenham Lake."

"Oh, leave me for my mother's sake,
　She needs my eyes to see."
"Those eyes, young witch, the crows shall
　　peck
From off the gallows-tree."

He bore her to a farm-house old
　And up its stairway long,
And closed on her the garret-door
　With iron bolted strong.

The day died out, the night came down :
　Her evening prayer she said,
While, through the dark, strange faces
　　seemed
To mock her as she prayed.

The present horror deepened all
　The fears her childhood knew ;
The awe wherewith the air was filled
　With every breath she drew.

And could it be, she trembling asked,
　Some secret thought or sin
Had shut good angels from her heart
　And let the bad ones in ?

Had she in some forgotten dream
　Let go her hold on Heaven,
And sold herself unwittingly
　To spirits unforgiven ?

Oh, weird and still the dark hours
　　passed ;
　No human sound she heard,

But up and down the chimney stack
　The swallows moaned and stirred.

And o'er her, with a dread surmise
　Of evil sight and sound,
The blind bats on their leathern wings
　Went wheeling round and round.

Low hanging in the midnight sky
　Looked in a half-faced moon.
Was it a dream, or did she hear
　Her lover's whistled tune ?

She forced the oaken scuttle back ;
　A whisper reached her ear :
"Slide down the roof to me," it said,
　"So softly none may hear."

She slid along the sloping roof
　Till from its eaves she hung,
And felt the loosened shingles yield
　To which her fingers clung.

Below, her lover stretched his hands
　And touched her feet so small ;
"Drop down to me, dear heart," he said,
　"My arms shall break the fall."

He set her on his pillion soft,
　Her arms about him twined ;
And, noiseless as if velvet-shod,
　They left the house behind.

But when they reached the open way,
　Full free the rein he cast ;
Oh, never through the mirk midnight
　Rode man and maid more fast.

Along the wild wood-paths they sped,
　The bridgeless streams they swam ;
At set of moon they passed the Bass,
　At sunrise Agawam.

At high noon on the Merrimac
　The ancient ferryman
Forgot, at times, his idle oars,
　So fair a freight to scan.

And when from off his grounded boat
　He saw them mount and ride,
"God keep her from the evil eye,
　And harm of witch ! " he cried.

The maiden laughed, as youth will laugh
　At all its fears gone by ;

"He does not know," she whispered
 low,
" A little witch am I."

All day he urged his weary horse,
 And, in the red sundown,
Drew rein before a friendly door
 In distant Berwick town.

A fellow-feeling for the wronged
 The Quaker people felt ;
And safe beside their kindly hearths
 The hunted maiden dwelt,

Until from off its breast the land
 The haunting horror threw,
And hatred, born of ghastly dreams,
 To shame and pity grew.

Sad were the year's spring morns, and
 sad
 Its golden summer day,
But blithe and glad its withered fields,
 And skies of ashen gray ;

For spell and charm had power no more,
 The spectres ceased to roam,
And scattered households knelt again
 Around the hearths of home.

And when once more by Beaver Dam
 The meadow-lark outsang,
And once again on all the hills
 The early violets sprang,

And all the windy pasture slopes
 Lay green within the arms
Of creeks that bore the salted sea
 To pleasant inland farms,

The smith filed off the chains he forged,
 The jail-bolts backward fell ;
And youth and hoary age came forth
 Like souls escaped from hell.

KING SOLOMON AND THE ANTS

Out from Jerusalem
 The king rode with his great
 War chiefs and lords of state,
And Sheba's queen with them ;

Comely, but black withal,
 To whom, perchance, belongs

That wondrous Song of songs,
Sensuous and mystical,

Whereto devout souls turn
 In fond, ecstatic dream,
 And through its earth-born theme
The Love of loves discern.

Proud in the Syrian sun,
 In gold and purple sheen,
 The dusky Ethiop queen
Smiled on King Solomon.

Wisest of men, he knew
 The languages of all
 The creatures great or small
That trod the earth or flew.

Across an ant-hill led
 The king's path, and he heard
 Its small folk, and their word
He thus interpreted :

" Here comes the king men greet
 As wise and good and just,
 To crush us in the dust
Under his heedless feet."

The great king bowed his head,
 And saw the wide surprise
 Of the Queen of Sheba's eyes
As he told her what they said.

"O king !" she whispered sweet,
 " Too happy fate have they
 Who perish in thy way
Beneath thy gracious feet !

" Thou of the God-lent crown,
 Shall these vile creatures dare
 Murmur against thee where
The knees of kings kneel down ? "

"Nay," Solomon replied,
 " The wise and strong should seek
 The welfare of the weak,"
And turned his horse aside.

His train, with quick alarm,
 Curved with their leader round
 The ant-hill's peopled mound,
And left it free from harm.

The jewelled head bent low ;
 "O king !" she said, " henceforth

The secret of thy worth
And wisdom well I know.

" Happy must be the State
Whose ruler heedeth more
The murmurs of the poor
Than flatteries of the great."

IN THE "OLD SOUTH"

On the 8th of July, 1677, Margaret Brewster with four other Friends went into the South Church in time of meeting, "in sackcloth, with ashes upon her head, barefoot, and her face blackened," and delivered "a warning from the great God of Heaven and Earth to the Rulers and Magistrates of Boston." For the offence she was sentenced to be "whipped at a cart's tail up and down the Town, with twenty lashes."

SHE came and stood in the Old South Church,
A wonder and a sign,
With a look the old-time sibyls wore,
Half-crazed and half-divine.

Save the mournful sackcloth about her wound,
Unclothed as the primal mother,
With limbs that trembled and eyes that blazed
With a fire she dare not smother.

Loose on her shoulders fell her hair,
With sprinkled ashes gray ;
She stood in the broad aisle strange and weird
As a soul at the judgment day.

And the minister paused in his sermon's midst,
And the people held their breath,
For these were the words the maiden spoke
Through lips as the lips of death :

" Thus saith the Lord, with equal feet
All men my courts shall tread,
And priest and ruler no more shall eat
My people up like bread !

" Repent ! repent ! ere the Lord shall speak
In thunder and breaking seals !

Let all souls worship Him in the way
His light within reveals."

She shook the dust from her naked feet,
And her sackcloth closer drew,
And into the porch of the awe - hushed church
She passed like a ghost from view.

They whipped her away at the tail o' the cart
Through half the streets of the town,
But the words she uttered that day nor fire
Could burn nor water drown.

And now the aisles of the ancient church
By equal feet are trod,
And the bell that swings in its belfry rings
Freedom to worship God !

And now whenever a wrong is done
It thrills the conscious walls ;
The stone from the basement cries aloud
And the beam from the timber calls.

There are steeple-houses on every hand,
And pulpits that bless and ban,
And the Lord will not grudge the single church
That is set apart for man.

For in two commandments are all the law
And the prophets under the sun,
And the first is last and the last is first,
And the twain are verily one.

So long as Boston shall Boston be,
And her bay-tides rise and fall,
Shall freedom stand in the Old South Church
And plead for the rights of all !

THE HENCHMAN

[Written at the request of a young lady, who said to the poet : " Mr. Whittier, you never wrote a love song. I do not believe you can write one. I wish you would try to write one for me to sing." In sending the poem afterward to the editor of *The Independent*, Whittier wrote : " I send, in compliance with the wish of Mr. Bowen and thyself, a ballad upon which, though not long, I have bestowed a good deal of labor. It is not exactly a

Quakerly piece, nor is it didactic, and it has
no moral that I know of. But it is, I think,
natural, simple, and not unpoetical."]

My lady walks her morning round,
My lady's page her fleet greyhound,
My lady's hair the fond winds stir,
And all the birds make songs for her.

Her thrushes sing in Rathburn bowers,
And Rathburn side is gay with flowers ;
But ne'er like hers, in flower or bird,
Was beauty seen or music heard.

The distance of the stars is hers ;
The least of all her worshippers,
The dust beneath her dainty heel,
She knows not that I see or feel.

Oh, proud and calm ! — she cannot know
Where'er she goes with her I go ;
Oh, cold and fair ! — she cannot guess
I kneel to share her hound's caress !

Gay knights beside her hunt and hawk,
I rob their ears of her sweet talk ;
Her suitors come from east and west,
I steal her smiles from every guest.

Unheard of her, in loving words,
I greet her with the song of birds ;
I reach her with her green - armed bow-
    ers,
I kiss her with the lips of flowers.

The hound and I are on her trail,
The wind and I uplift her veil ;
As if the calm, cold moon she were,
And I the tide, I follow her.

As unrebuked as they, I share
The license of the sun and air,
And in a common homage hide
My worship from her scorn and pride.

World-wide apart, and yet so near,
I breathe her charmèd atmosphere,
Wherein to her my service brings
The reverence due to holy things.

Her maiden pride, her haughty name,
My dumb devotion shall not shame ;
The love that no return doth crave
To knightly levels lifts the slave.

No lance have I, in joust or fight,
To splinter in my lady's sight ;
But, at her feet, how blest were I
For any need of hers to die !

THE DEAD FEAST OF THE KOL-FOLK

E. B. Tylor in his *Primitive Culture*, chapter
xii., gives an account of the reverence paid the
dead by the Kol tribes of Chota Nagpur, Assam.
" When a Ho or Munda," he says, " has been
burned on the funeral pile, collected morsels
of his bones are carried in procession with a
solemn, ghostly, sliding step, keeping time to
the deep-sounding drum, and when the old
woman who carries the bones on her bamboo
tray lowers it from time to time, then girls
who carry pitchers and brass vessels mournfully
reverse them to show that they are empty ; thus
the remains are taken to visit every house in the
village, and every dwelling of a friend or rela-
tive for miles, and the inmates come out to
mourn and praise the goodness of the departed ;
the bones are carried to all the dead man's
favorite haunts, to the fields he cultivated, to
the grove he planted, to the threshing-floor
where he worked, to the village dance-room
where he made merry. At last they are taken
to the grave, and buried in an earthen vase
upon a store of food, covered with one of those
huge stone slabs which European visitors won-
der at in the districts of the aborigines of
India." In the *Journal of the Asiatic Society,
Bengal*, vol. ix. p. 795, is a Ho dirge.

WE have opened the door,
    Once, twice, thrice !
We have swept the floor,
    We have boiled the rice.
Come hither, come hither !
Come from the far lands,
Come from the star lands,
    Come as before !
We lived long together,
We loved one another ;
    Come back to our life.
Come father, come mother,
Come sister and brother,
    Child, husband, and wife,
For you we are sighing.
Come take your old places,
Come look in our faces,
The dead on the dying,
    Come home !

We have opened the door,
  Once, twice, thrice !
We have kindled the coals,
  And we boil the rice
For the feast of souls.
  Come hither, come hither !
Think not we fear you,
Whose hearts are so near you.
Come tenderly thought on,
Come all unforgotten,
Come from the shadow-lands,
From the dim meadow-lands
Where the pale grasses bend
Low to our sighing.
Come father, come mother,
Come sister and brother,
Come husband and friend,
  The dead to the dying,
    Come home !

We have opened the door
  You entered so oft ;
For the feast of souls
We have kindled the coals,
  And we boil the rice soft.
Come you who are dearest
To us who are nearest,
Come hither, come hither,
From out the wild weather ;
The storm clouds are flying,
The peepul is sighing ;
  Come in from the rain.
Come father, come mother,
Come sister and brother,
Come husband and lover,
Beneath our roof-cover.
  Look on us again,
The dead on the dying,
    Come home !

We have opened the door !
For the feast of souls
We have kindled the coals
We may kindle no more !
Snake, fever, and famine,
The curse of the Brahmin,
  The sun and the dew,
They burn us, they bite us,
They waste us and smite us ;
  Our days are but few !
In strange lands far yonder
To wonder and wander
  We hasten to you.
List then to our sighing,
  While yet we are here :

Nor seeing nor hearing,
We wait without fearing
  To feel you draw near.
O dead, to the dying
  Come home !

THE KHAN'S DEVIL

THE Khan came from Bokhara town
To Hamza, santon of renown.

" My head is sick, my hands are weak ;
Thy help, O holy man, I seek."

In silence marking for a space
The Khan's red eyes and purple face,

Thick voice, and loose, uncertain tread,
" Thou hast a devil ! " Hamza said.

" Allah forbid ! " exclaimed the Khan.
" Rid me of him at once, O man ! "

" Nay," Hamza said, " no spell of mine
Can slay that cursed thing of thine.

" Leave feast and wine, go forth and drink
Water of healing on the brink

" Where clear and cold from mountain
    snows,
The Nahr el Zeben downward flows.

" Six moons remain, then come to me ;
May Allah's pity go with thee ! "

Awestruck, from feast and wine the Khan
Went forth where Nahr el Zeben ran.

Roots were his food, the desert dust
His bed, the water quenched his thirst ;

And when the sixth moon's scimitar
Curved sharp above the evening star,

He sought again the santon's door,
Not weak and trembling as before,

But strong of limb and clear of brain ;
" Behold," he said, " the fiend is slain."

" Nay," Hamza answered, "starved and
    drowned,
The curst one lies in death-like swound.

"But evil breaks the strongest gyves,
And jins like him have charmëd lives.

"One beaker of the juice of grape
May call him up in living shape.

"When the red wine of Badakshan
Sparkles for thee, beware, O Khan!

"With water quench the fire within,
And drown each day thy devilkin!"

Thenceforth the great Khan shunned the cup
As Shitan's own, though offered up,

With laughing eyes and jewelled hands,
By Yarkand's maids and Samarcand's.

And, in the lofty vestibule
Of the medress of Kaush Kodul,

The students of the holy law
A golden-lettered tablet saw,

With these words, by a cunning hand,
Graved on it at the Khan's command:

"In Allah's name, to him who hath
A devil, Khan el Hamed saith,

"Wisely our Prophet cursed the vine:
The fiend that loves the breath of wine

"No prayer can slay, no marabout
Nor Meccan dervis can drive out.

"I, Khan el Hamed, know the charm
That robs him of his power to harm.

"Drown him, O Islam's child! the spell
To save thee lies in tank and well!"

THE KING'S MISSIVE

1661

This ballad, originally written for *The Memorial History of Boston*, describes, with pardonable poetic license, a memorable incident in the annals of the city. The interview between Shattuck and the Governor took place, I have since learned, in the residence of the latter, and not in the Council Chamber. The publication of the ballad led to some discussion as to the historical truthfulness of the picture, but I have seen no reason to rub out any of the figures or alter the lines and colors.

UNDER the great hill sloping bare
To cove and meadow and Common lot,
In his council chamber and oaken chair,
Sat the worshipful Governor Endicott.
A grave, strong man, who knew no peer
In the pilgrim land, where he ruled in fear
Of God, not man, and for good or ill
Held his trust with an iron will.

He had shorn with his sword the cross from
out
The flag, and cloven the May-pole down,
Harried the heathen round about,
And whipped the Quakers from town to
town.
Earnest and honest, a man at need
To burn like a torch for his own harsh creed,
He kept with the flaming brand of his zeal
The gate of the holy common weal.

His brow was clouded, his eye was stern,
With a look of mingled sorrow and
wrath;
"Woe 's me!" he murmured: "at every
turn
The pestilent Quakers are in my path!
Some we have scourged, and banished some,
Some hanged, more doomed, and still they
come,
Fast as the tide of yon bay sets in,
Sowing their heresy's seed of sin.

"Did we count on this? Did we leave be-
hind
The graves of our kin, the comfort and
ease
Of our English hearths and homes, to find
Troublers of Israel such as these?
Shall I spare? Shall I pity them? God
forbid!
I will do as the prophet to Agag did:
They come to poison the wells of the Word,
I will hew them in pieces before the Lord!"

The door swung open, and Rawson the clerk
Entered, and whispered under breath,
"There waits below for the hangman's work
A fellow banished on pain of death —
Shattuck, of Salem, unhealed of the whip,
Brought over in Master Goldsmith's ship
At anchor here in a Christian port,
With freight of the devil and all his sort!"

Twice and thrice on the chamber floor
Striding fiercely from wall to wall,

"The Lord do so to me and more,"
  The Governor cried, "if I hang not all!
Bring hither the Quaker." Calm, sedate,
With the look of a man at ease with fate,
Into that presence grim and dread
Came Samuel Shattuck, with hat on head.

"Off with the knave's hat!" An angry
    hand
  Smote down the offence; but the wearer
    said,
With a quiet smile, "By the king's com-
    mand
I bear his message and stand in his stead."
In the Governor's hand a missive he laid
With the royal arms on its seal displayed,
And the proud man spake as he gazed
    thereat,
Uncovering, "Give Mr. Shattuck his hat."

He turned to the Quaker, bowing low, —
  "The king commandeth your friends'
    release;
Doubt not he shall be obeyed, although
  To his subjects' sorrow and sin's increase.
What he here enjoineth, John Endicott,
His loyal servant, questioneth not.
You are free! God grant the spirit you
    own
May take you from us to parts unknown."

So the door of the jail was open cast,
  And, like Daniel, out of the lion's den
Tender youth and girlhood passed,
  With age-bowed women and gray-locked
    men.
And the voice of one appointed to die
Was lifted in praise and thanks on high,
And the little maid from New Netherlands
Kissed, in her joy, the doomed man's hands.

And one, whose call was to minister
  To the souls in prison, beside him went,
An ancient woman, bearing with her
  The linen shroud for his burial meant.
For she, not counting her own life dear,
In the strength of a love that cast out fear,
Had watched and served where her brethren
    died,
Like those who waited the cross beside.

One moment they paused on their way to
    look
  On the martyr graves by the Common
    side,

And much scourged Wharton of Salem took
  His burden of prophecy up and cried:
"Rest, souls of the valiant! Not in vain
Have ye borne the Master's cross of pain;
Ye have fought the fight, ye are victors
    crowned,
With a fourfold chain ye have Satan
    bound!"

The autumn haze lay soft and still
  On wood and meadow and upland farms;
On the brow of Snow Hill the great wind-
    mill
  Slowly and lazily swung its arms;
Broad in the sunshine stretched away,
With its capes and islands, the turquoise
    bay;
And over water and dusk of pines
Blue hills lifted their faint outlines.

The topaz leaves of the walnut glowed,
  The sumach added its crimson fleck,
And double in air and water showed
  The tinted maples along the Neck;
Through frost flower clusters of pale star-
    mist,
And gentian fringes of amethyst,
And royal plumes of golden-rod,
The grazing cattle on Centry trod.

But as they who see not, the Quakers saw
  The world about them; they only thought
With deep thanksgiving and pious awe
  On the great deliverance God had
    wrought.
Through lane and alley the gazing town
Noisily followed them up and down;
Some with scoffing and brutal jeer,
Some with pity and words of cheer.

One brave voice rose above the din.
  Upsall, gray with his length of days,
Cried from the door of his Red Lion Inn:
  "Men of Boston, give God the praise!
No more shall innocent blood call down
The bolts of wrath on your guilty town.
The freedom of worship, dear to you,
Is dear to all, and to all is due.

"I see the vision of days to come,
  When your beautiful City of the Bay
Shall be Christian liberty's chosen home,
  And none shall his neighbor's rights
    gainsay.
The varying notes of worship shall blend

And as one great prayer to God ascend,
And hands of mutual charity raise
Walls of salvation and gates of praise."

So passed the Quakers through Boston town,
    Whose painful ministers sighed to see
The walls of their sheep-fold falling down,
    And wolves of heresy prowling free.
But the years went on, and brought no wrong ;
With milder counsels the State grew strong,
As outward Letter and inward Light
Kept the balance of truth aright.

The Puritan spirit perishing not,
    To Concord's yeomen the signal sent,
And spake in the voice of the cannon-shot
    That severed the chains of a continent.
With its gentler mission of peace and good-will
The thought of the Quaker is living still,
And the freedom of soul he prophesied
Is gospel and law where the martyrs died.

VALUATION

THE old Squire said, as he stood by his gate,
    And his neighbor, the Deacon, went by,
" In spite of my bank stock and real estate,
    You are better off, Deacon, than I.

" We 're both growing old, and the end 's drawing near,
    You have less of this world to resign,
But in Heaven's appraisal your assets, I fear,
    Will reckon up greater than mine.

" They say I am rich, but I 'm feeling so poor,
    I wish I could swap with you even :
The pounds I have lived for and laid up in store
    For the shillings and pence you have given."

" Well, Squire," said the Deacon, with shrewd common sense,
    While his eye had a twinkle of fun,
" Let your pounds take the way of my shillings and pence,
    And the thing can be easily done ! "

RABBI ISHMAEL

" Rabbi Ishmael Ben Elisha said, Once I entered into the Holy of Holies [as High Priest] to burn incense, when I saw Aktriel [the Divine Crown] Jah, Lord of Hosts, sitting upon a throne, high and lifted up, who said unto me, ' Ishmael, my son, bless me.' I answered, *'May it please Thee to make Thy compassion prevail over Thine anger ; may it be revealed above Thy other attributes ; mayest Thou deal with Thy children according to it, and not according to the strict measure of judgment.'* It seemed to me that He bowed His head, as though to answer Amen to my blessing." —*Talmud* (Berachô'h, i. f. 6 b.).

THE Rabbi Ishmael, with the woe and sin
Of the world heavy upon him, entering in
The Holy of Holies, saw an awful Face
With terrible splendor filling all the place.
" O Ishmael Ben Elisha ! " said a voice,
" What seekest thou ?   What blessing is thy choice ? "
And, knowing that he stood before the Lord,
Within the shadow of the cherubim,
Wide-winged between the blinding light and him,
He bowed himself, and uttered not a word,
But in the silence of his soul was prayer :
" O Thou Eternal !   I am one of all,
And nothing ask that others may not share.
Thou art almighty ; we are weak and small,
And yet Thy children : let Thy mercy spare ! "
Trembling, he raised his eyes, and in the place
Of the insufferable glory, lo ! a face
Of more than mortal tenderness, that bent
Graciously down in token of assent,
And, smiling, vanished !   With strange joy elate,
The wondering Rabbi sought the temple's gate.
Radiant as Moses from the Mount, he stood
And cried aloud unto the multitude :
" O Israel, hear !   The Lord our God is good !
Mine eyes have seen His glory and His grace ;
Beyond His judgments shall His love endure ;
The mercy of the All Merciful is sure ! "

THE ROCK-TOMB OF BRADORE

H. Y. Hind, in *Explorations in the Interior of the Labrador Peninsula* (ii. 166), mentions the finding of a rock tomb near the little fishing port of Bradore, with the inscription upon it which is given in the poem.

A DREAR and desolate shore !
Where no tree unfolds its leaves,
And never the spring wind weaves
Green grass for the hunter's tread ;
A land forsaken and dead,
Where the ghostly icebergs go
And come with the ebb and flow
Of the waters of Bradore !

A wanderer, from a land
By summer breezes fanned,
Looked round him, awed, subdued,
By the dreadful solitude,
Hearing alone the cry
Of sea-birds clanging by,
The crash and grind of the floe,
Wail of wind and wash of tide.
" O wretched land ! " he cried,
" Land of all lands the worst,
God forsaken and curst !
Thy gates of rock should show
The words the Tuscan seer
Read in the Realm of Woe :
Hope entereth not here ! "

Lo ! at his feet there stood
A block of smooth larch wood,
Waif of some wandering wave,
Beside a rock-closed cave
By Nature fashioned for a grave ;
Safe from the ravening bear
And fierce fowl of the air,
Wherein to rest was laid
A twenty summers' maid,
Whose blood had equal share
Of the lands of vine and snow,
Half French, half Eskimo.
In letters uneffaced,
Upon the block were traced
The grief and hope of man,
And thus the legend ran :
    " *We loved her !*
Words cannot tell how well !
    We loved her !
    God loved her !
And called her home to peace and rest.
    We love her ! "

The stranger paused and read.
" O winter land ! " he said,
" Thy right to be I own ;
God leaves thee not alone.
And if thy fierce winds blow
Over drear wastes of rock and snow,
And at thy iron gates
The ghostly iceberg waits,
    Thy homes and hearts are dear.
Thy sorrow o'er thy sacred dust
Is sanctified by hope and trust ;
    God's love and man's are here.
And love where'er it goes
Makes its own atmosphere ;
Its flowers of Paradise
Take root in the eternal ice,
    And bloom through Polar snows ! "

THE BAY OF SEVEN ISLANDS

The volume in which *The Bay of Seven Islands* was published was dedicated to the late Edwin Percy Whipple, to whom more than to any other person I was indebted for public recognition as one worthy of a place in American literature, at a time when it required a great degree of courage to urge such a claim for a proscribed abolitionist. Although younger than I, he had gained the reputation of a brilliant essayist, and was regarded as the highest American authority in criticism. His wit and wisdom enlivened a small literary circle of young men, including Thomas Starr King, the eloquent preacher, and Daniel N. Haskell, of the *Daily Transcript*, who gathered about our common friend James T. Fields at the Old Corner Bookstore. The poem which gave title to the volume I inscribed to my friend and neighbor, Harriet Prescott Spofford, whose poems have lent a new interest to our beautiful river-valley.

FROM the green Amesbury hill which bears
    the name
Of that half mythic ancestor of mine
Who trod its slopes two hundred years ago,
Down the long valley of the Merrimac,
Midway between me and the river's mouth,
I see thy home, set like an eagle's nest
Among Deer Island's immemorial pines,
Crowning the crag on which the sunset
    breaks
Its last red arrow. Many a tale and song,
Which thou hast told or sung, I call to
    mind,
Softening with silvery mist the woods and
    hills,

The out-thrust headlands and inreaching
    bays
Of our northeastern coast-line, trending
    where
The Gulf, midsummer, feels the chill block-
    ade
Of icebergs stranded at its northern gate.

To thee the echoes of the Island Sound
Answer not vainly, nor in vain the moan
Of the South Breaker prophesying storm.
And thou hast listened, like myself, to men
Sea-periled oft where Anticosti lies
Like a fell spider in its web of fog,
Or where the Grand Bank shallows with
    the wrecks
Of sunken fishers, and to whom strange
    isles
And frost-rimmed bays and trading stations
    seem
Familiar as Great Neck and Kettle Cove,
Nubble and Boon, the common names of
    home.
So let me offer thee this lay of mine,
Simple and homely, lacking much thy play
Of color and of fancy. If its theme
And treatment seem to thee befitting youth
Rather than age, let this be my excuse :
It has beguiled some heavy hours and called
Some pleasant memories up ; and, better
    still,
Occasion lent me for a kindly word
To one who is my neighbor and my friend.

The skipper sailed out of the harbor mouth,
Leaving the apple-bloom of the South
    For the ice of the Eastern seas,
    In his fishing schooner Breeze.

Handsome and brave and young was he,
And the maids of Newbury sighed to see
    His lessening white sail fall
    Under the sea's blue wall.

Through the Northern Gulf and the misty
    screen
Of the isles of Mingan and Madeleine,
    St. Paul's and Blanc Sablon,
    The little Breeze sailed on,

Backward and forward, along the shore
Of lorn and desolate Labrador,
    And found at last her way
    To the Seven Islands Bay.

The little hamlet, nestling below
Great hills white with lingering snow
    With its tin-roofed chapel stood
    Half hid in the dwarf spruce wood ;

Green-turfed, flower-sown, the last outpost
Of summer upon the dreary coast,
    With its gardens small and spare,
    Sad in the frosty air.

Hard by where the skipper's schooner lay,
A fisherman's cottage looked away
    Over isle and bay, and behind
    On mountains dim-defined.

And there twin sisters, fair and young,
Laughed with their stranger guest, and
    sung
    In their native tongue the lays
    Of the old Provençal days.

Alike were they, save the faint outline
Of a scar on Suzette's forehead fine ;
    And both, it so befell,
    Loved the heretic stranger well.

Both were pleasant to look upon,
But the heart of the skipper clave to one ;
    Though less by his eye than heart
    He knew the twain apart.

Despite of alien race and creed,
Well did his wooing of Marguerite speed ;
    And the mother's wrath was vain
    As the sister's jealous pain.

The shrill-tongued mistress her house for-
    bade,
And solemn warning was sternly said
    By the black-robed priest, whose word
    As law the hamlet heard.

But half by voice and half by signs
The skipper said, " A warm sun shines
    On the green-banked Merrimac ;
    Wait, watch, till I come back.

" And when you see, from my mast head,
The signal fly of a kerchief red,
    My boat on the shore shall wait;
    Come, when the night is late."

Ah ! weighed with childhood's haunts and
    friends,
And all that the home sky overbends,

Did ever young love fail
To turn the trembling scale ?

Under the night, on the wet sea sands,
Slowly unclasped their plighted hands :
    One to the cottage hearth,
    And one to his sailor's berth.

What was it the parting lovers heard ?
Nor leaf, nor ripple, nor wing of bird,
    But a listener's stealthy tread
    On the rock-moss, crisp and dead.

He weighed his anchor, and fished once
    more
By the black coast-line of Labrador ;
    And by love and the north wind driven,
    Sailed back to the Islands Seven.

In the sunset's glow the sisters twain
Saw the Breeze come sailing in again ;
    Said Suzette, "Mother dear,
    The heretic's sail is here."

"Go, Marguerite, to your room, and hide ;
Your door shall be bolted !" the mother
    cried :
    While Suzette, ill at ease,
    Watched the red sign of the Breeze.

At midnight, down to the waiting skiff
She stole in the shadow of the cliff ;
    And out of the Bay's mouth ran
    The schooner with maid and man.

And all night long, on a restless bed,
Her prayers to the Virgin Marguerite said :
    And thought of her lover's pain
    Waiting for her in vain.

Did he pace the sands ? Did he pause to
    hear
The sound of her light step drawing near ?
    And, as the slow hours passed,
    Would he doubt her faith at last ?

But when she saw through the misty pane,
The morning break on a sea of rain,
    Could even her love avail
    To follow his vanished sail ?

Meantime the Breeze, with favoring wind,
Left the rugged Moisic hills behind,
    And heard from an unseen shore
    The falls of Manitou roar.

On the morrow's morn in the thick, gray
    weather
They sat on the reeling deck together,
    Lover and counterfeit
    Of hapless Marguerite.

With a lover's hand, from her forehead fair
He smoothed away her jet-black hair,
    What was it his fond eyes met ?
    The scar of the false Suzette !

Fiercely he shouted : "Bear away
East by north for the Seven Isles Bay !"
    The maiden wept and prayed,
    But the ship her helm obeyed.

Once more the Bay of the Isles they found :
They heard the bell of the chapel sound,
    And the chant of the dying sung
    In the harsh, wild Indian tongue.

A feeling of mystery, change, and awe
Was in all they heard and all they saw :
    Spell-bound the hamlet lay
    In the hush of its lonely bay.

And when they came to the cottage door,
The mother rose up from her weeping sore,
    And with angry gestures met
    The scared look of Suzette.

"Here is your daughter," the skipper said ;
"Give me the one I love instead."
    But the woman sternly spake ;
    "Go, see if the dead will wake !"

He looked. Her sweet face still and white
And strange in the noonday taper light,
    She lay on her little bed,
    With the cross at her feet and head.

In a passion of grief the strong man bent
Down to her face, and, kissing it, went
    Back to the waiting Breeze,
    Back to the mournful seas.

Never again to the Merrimac
And Newbury's homes that bark came back
    Whether her fate she met
    On the shores of Carraquette,

Miscou, or Tracadie, who can say ?
But even yet at Seven Isles Bay
    Is told the ghostly tale
    Of a weird, unspoken sail,

In the pale, sad light of the Northern
    day
Seen by the blanketed Montagnais,
    Or squaw, in her small kyack,
    Crossing the spectre's track.

On the deck a maiden wrings her hands ;
Her likeness kneels on the gray coast
    sands ;
    One in her wild despair,
    And one in the trance of prayer.

She flits before no earthly blast,
The red sign fluttering from her mast,
    Over the solemn seas,
    The ghost of the schooner Breeze !

THE WISHING BRIDGE

Among the legends sung or said
    Along our rocky shore,
The Wishing Bridge of Marblehead
    May well be sung once more.

An hundred years ago (so ran
    The old-time story) all
Good wishes said above its span
    Would, soon or late, befall.

If pure and earnest, never failed
    The prayers of man or maid
For him who on the deep sea sailed,
    For her at home who stayed.

Once thither came two girls from school,
    And wished in childish glee :
And one would be a queen and rule,
    And one the world would see.

Time passed ; with change of hopes and
    fears,
    And in the self-same place,
Two women, gray with middle years,
    Stood, wondering, face to face.

With wakened memories, as they met,
    They queried what had been :
" A poor man's wife am I, and yet,"
    Said one, " I am a queen.

" My realm a little homestead is,
    Where, lacking crown and throne,
I rule by loving services
    And patient toil alone."

The other said : " The great world lies
    Beyond me as it lay ;
O'er love's and duty's boundaries
    My feet may never stray.

" I see but common sights of home,
    Its common sounds I hear,
My widowed mother's sick-bed room
    Sufficeth for my sphere.

" I read to her some pleasant page
    Of travel far and wide,
And in a dreamy pilgrimage
    We wander side by side.

" And when at last she falls asleep,
    My book becomes to me
A magic glass : my watch I keep,
    But all the world I see.

" A farm-wife queen your place you fill,
    While fancy's privilege
Is mine to walk the earth at will,
    Thanks to the Wishing Bridge."

" Nay, leave the legend for the truth,"
    The other cried, " and say
God gives the wishes of our youth,
    But in His own best way !"

HOW THE WOMEN WENT FROM DOVER

The following is a copy of the warrant is-
sued by Major Waldron, of Dover, in 1662.
The Quakers, as was their wont, prophesied
against him, and saw, as they supposed, the
fulfilment of their prophecy when, many years
after, he was killed by the Indians.

*To the constables of Dover, Hampton, Salisbury,
Newbury, Rowley, Ipswich, Wenham, Lynn,
Boston, Roxbury, Dedham, and until these vaga-
bond Quakers are carried out of this jurisdiction.*

You, and every one of you, are required, in
the King's Majesty's name, to take these vag-
abond Quakers, Anne Colman, Mary Tomkins,
and Alice Ambrose, and make them fast to the
cart's tail, and driving the cart through your
several towns, to whip them upon their naked
backs not exceeding ten stripes apiece on each
of them, in each town ; and so to convey them
from constable to constable till they are out of
this jurisdiction, as you will answer it at your
peril ; and this shall be your warrant.
                       RICHARD WALDRON.
Dated at Dover, December 22, 1662.

This warrant was executed only in Dover and Hampton. At Salisbury the constable refused to obey it. He was sustained by the town's people, who were under the influence of Major Robert Pike, the leading man in the lower valley of the Merrimac, who stood far in advance of his time, as an advocate of religious freedom and an opponent of ecclesiastical authority. He had the moral courage to address an able and manly letter to the court at Salem, remonstrating against the witchcraft trials.

THE tossing spray of Cocheco's fall
Hardened to ice on its rocky wall,
As through Dover town in the chill, gray
    dawn,
Three women passed, at the cart - tail
    drawn !

Bared to the waist, for the north wind's grip
And keener sting of the constable's whip,
The blood that followed each hissing blow
Froze as it sprinkled the winter snow.

Priest and ruler, boy and maid
Followed the dismal cavalcade ;
And from door and window, open thrown,
Looked and wondered gaffer and crone.

" God is our witness," the victims cried,
" We suffer for Him who for all men died ;
The wrong ye do has been done before,
We bear the stripes that the Master bore !

" And thou, O Richard Waldron, for whom
We hear the feet of a coming doom,
On thy cruel heart and thy hand of wrong
Vengeance is sure, though it tarry long.

" In the light of the Lord, a flame we see
Climb and kindle a proud roof-tree ;
And beneath it an old man lying dead,
With stains of blood on his hoary head."

" Smite, Goodman Hate - Evil ! — harder
    still ! "
The magistrate cried, " lay on with a will !
Drive out of their bodies the Father of
    Lies,
Who through them preaches and prophe-
    sies ! "

So into the forest they held their way,
By winding river and frost-rimmed bay,
Over wind-swept hills that felt the beat
Of the winter sea at their icy feet.

The Indian hunter, searching his traps,
Peered stealthily through the forest gaps ;
And the outlying settler shook his head, —
" They 're witches going to jail," he said.

At last a meeting-house came in view ;
A blast on his horn the constable blew ;
And the boys of Hampton cried up and down
" The Quakers have come ! " to the won-
    dering town.

From barn and woodpile the goodman came;
The goodwife quitted her quilting frame,
With her child at her breast ; and, hobbling
    slow,
The grandam followed to see the show.

Once more the torturing whip was swung,
Once more keen lashes the bare flesh stung.
" Oh, spare ! they are bleeding ! " a little
    maid cried,
And covered her face the sight to hide.

A murmur ran round the crowd : " Good
    folks,"
Quoth the constable, busy counting the
    strokes,
" No pity to wretches like these is due,
They have beaten the gospel black and
    blue ! "

Then a pallid woman, in wild-eyed fear,
With her wooden noggin of milk drew near.
" Drink, poor hearts ! " a rude hand smote
Her draught away from a parching throat.

" Take heed," one whispered, " they 'll take
    your cow
For fines, as they took your horse and
    plough,
And the bed from under you." " Even so,"
She said ; " they are cruel as death, I know."

Then on they passed, in the waning day,
Through Seabrook woods, a weariful way ;
By great salt meadows and sand-hills bare,
And glimpses of blue sea here and there.

By the meeting-house in Salisbury town,
The sufferers stood, in the red sundown
Bare for the lash ! O pitying Night,
Drop swift thy curtain and hide the sight !

With shame in his eye and wrath on his lip
The Salisbury constable dropped his whip.

" This warrant means murder foul and red ;
Cursed is he who serves it," he said.

"Show me the order, and meanwhile strike
A blow at your peril !" said Justice Pike.
Of all the rulers the land possessed,
Wisest and boldest was he and best.

He scoffed at witchcraft ; the priest he met
As man meets man ; his feet he set
Beyond his dark age, standing upright,
Soul-free, with his face to the morning light.

He read the warrant : " *These convey*
From our precincts ; at every town on the way
Give each ten lashes." "God judge the
    brute !
I tread his order under my foot !

"Cut loose these poor ones and let them
    go ;
Come what will of it, all men shall know
No warrant is good, though backed by the
    Crown,
For whipping women in Salisbury town !"

The hearts of the villagers, half released
From creed of terror and rule of priest,
By a primal instinct owned the right
Of human pity in law's despite.

For ruth and chivalry only slept,
His Saxon manhood the yeoman kept ;
Quicker or slower, the same blood ran
In the Cavalier and the Puritan.

The Quakers sank on their knees in praise
And thanks. A last, low sunset blaze
Flashed out from under a cloud, and shed
A golden glory on each bowed head.

The tale is one of an evil time,
When souls were fettered and thought was
    crime,
And heresy's whisper above its breath
Meant shameful scourging and bonds and
    death !

What marvel, that hunted and sorely tried,
Even woman rebuked and prophesied,
And soft words rarely answered back
The grim persuasion of whip and rack !

If her cry from the whipping-post and jail
Pierced sharp as the Kenite's driven nail,

O woman, at ease in these happier days,
Forbear to judge of thy sister's ways !

How much thy beautiful life may owe
To her faith and courage thou canst not
    know,
Nor how from the paths of thy calm re-
    treat
She smoothed the thorns with her bleeding
    feet.

SAINT GREGORY'S GUEST

A TALE for Roman guides to tell
    To careless, sight-worn travellers still,
Who pause beside the narrow cell
    Of Gregory on the Cælian Hill.

One day before the monk's door came
    A beggar, stretching empty palms,
Fainting and fast-sick, in the name
    Of the Most Holy asking alms.

And the monk answered, " All I have
    In this poor cell of mine I give,
The silver cup my mother gave ;
    In Christ's name take thou it, and
    live."

Years passed ; and, called at last to bear
    The pastoral crook and keys of Rome,
The poor monk, in Saint Peter's chair,
    Sat the crowned lord of Christendom.

" Prepare a feast," Saint Gregory cried,
    " And let twelve beggars sit thereat."
The beggars came, and one beside,
    An unknown stranger, with them sat.

" I asked thee not," the Pontiff spake,
    " O stranger ; but if need be thine,
I bid thee welcome, for the sake
    Of Him who is thy Lord and mine."

A grave, calm face the stranger raised,
    Like His who on Gennesaret trod,
Or His on whom the Chaldeans gazed,
    Whose form was as the Son of God.

" Know'st thou," he said, " thy gift of
    old ?"
    And in the hand he lifted up
The Pontiff marvelled to behold
    Once more his mother's silver cup.

"Thy prayers and alms have risen, and bloom
  Sweetly among the flowers of heaven.
I am The Wonderful, through whom
  Whate'er thou askest shall be given."

He spake and vanished. Gregory fell
  With his twelve guests in mute accord
Prone on their faces, knowing well
  Their eyes of flesh had seen the Lord.

The old-time legend is not vain ;
  Nor vain thy art, Verona's Paul,
Telling it o'er and o'er again
  On gray Vicenza's frescoed wall.

Still wheresoever pity shares
  Its bread with sorrow, want, and sin,
And love the beggar's feast prepares,
  The uninvited Guest comes in.

Unheard, because our ears are dull,
  Unseen, because our eyes are dim,
He walks our earth, The Wonderful,
  And all good deeds are done to Him.

BIRCHBROOK MILL

A NOTELESS stream, the Birchbrook runs
  Beneath its leaning trees ;
That low, soft ripple is its own,
  That dull roar is the sea's.

Of human signs it sees alone
  The distant church spire's tip,
And, ghost-like, on a blank of gray,
  The white sail of a ship.

No more a toiler at the wheel,
  It wanders at its will ;
Nor dam nor pond is left to tell
  Where once was Birchbrook mill.

The timbers of that mill have fed
  Long since a farmer's fires ;
His doorsteps are the stones that ground
  The harvest of his sires.

Man trespassed here ; but Nature lost
  No right of her domain ;
She waited, and she brought the old
  Wild beauty back again.

By day the sunlight through the leaves
  Falls on its moist, green sod,
And wakes the violet bloom of spring
  And autumn's golden-rod.

Its birches whisper to the wind,
  The swallow dips her wings
In the cool spray, and on its banks
  The gray song-sparrow sings.

But from it, when the dark night falls,
  The school-girl shrinks with dread ;
The farmer, home-bound from his fields,
  Goes by with quickened tread.

They dare not pause to hear the grind
  Of shadowy stone on stone ;
The plashing of a water-wheel
  Where wheel there now is none.

Has not a cry of pain been heard
  Above the clattering mill ?
The pawing of an unseen horse,
  Who waits his mistress still ?

Yet never to the listener's eye
  Has sight confirmed the sound ;
A wavering birch line marks alone
  The vacant pasture ground.

No ghostly arms fling up to heaven
  The agony of prayer ;
No spectral steed impatient shakes
  His white mane on the air.

The meaning of that common dread
  No tongue has fitly told ;
The secret of the dark surmise
  The brook and birches hold.

What nameless horror of the past
  Broods here forevermore ?
What ghost his unforgiven sin
  Is grinding o'er and o'er ?

Does, then, immortal memory play
  The actor's tragic part,
Rehearsals of a mortal life
  And unveiled human heart ?

God's pity spare a guilty soul
  That drama of its ill,
And let the scenic curtain fall
  On Birchbrook's haunted mill !

THE TWO ELIZABETHS

Read at the unveiling of the bust of Elizabeth
Fry at the Friends' School, Providence, R. I.

A. D. 1207

AMIDST Thuringia's wooded hills she dwelt,
  A high-born princess, servant of the poor,
Sweetening with gracious words the food
    she dealt
  To starving throngs at Wartburg's bla-
    zoned door.

A blinded zealot held her soul in chains,
  Cramped the sweet nature that he could
    not kill,
Scarred her fair body with his penance-
    pains,
  And gauged her conscience by his narrow
    will.

God gave her gifts of beauty and of grace,
  With fast and vigil she denied them all ;
Unquestioning, with sad, pathetic face,
  She followed meekly at her stern guide's
    call.

So drooped and died her home-blown rose
    of bliss
  In the chill rigor of a discipline
That turned her fond lips from her chil-
    dren's kiss,
  And made her joy of motherhood a sin.

To their sad level by compassion led,
  One with the low and vile herself she
    made,
While thankless misery mocked the hand
    that fed,
  And laughed to scorn her piteous mas-
    querade.

But still, with patience that outwearied
    hate,
  She gave her all while yet she had to
    give ;
And then her empty hands, importunate,
  In prayer she lifted that the poor might
    live.

Sore pressed by grief, and wrongs more
    hard to bear,
  And dwarfed and stifled by a harsh con-
    trol,

She kept life fragrant with good deeds and
    prayer,
  And fresh and pure the white flower of
    her soul.

Death found her busy at her task : one
    word
  Alone she uttered as she paused to die,
"Silence !" — then listened even as one
    who heard
  With song and wing the angels drawing
    nigh !

Now Fra Angelico's roses fill her hands,
  And, on Murillo's canvas, Want and
    Pain
Kneel at her feet. Her marble image
    stands
  Worshipped and crowned in Marburg's
    holy fane.

Yea, wheresoe'er her Church its cross up-
    rears,
  Wide as the world her story still is told ;
In manhood's reverence, woman's prayers
    and tears,
  She lives again whose grave is centuries
    old.

And still, despite the weakness or the blame
  Of blind submission to the blind, she
    hath
A tender place in hearts of every name,
  And more than Rome owns Saint Eliza-
    beth !

A. D. 1780

Slow ages passed : and lo ! another came,
  An English matron, in whose simple faith
Nor priestly rule nor ritual had claim,
  A plain, uncanonized Elizabeth.

No sackcloth robe, nor ashen - sprinkled
    hair,
  Nor wasting fast, nor scourge, nor vigil
    long,
Marred her calm presence. God had made
    her fair,
  And she could do His goodly work no
    wrong.

Their yoke is easy and their burden light
  Whose sole confessor is the Christ of
    God ;

Her quiet trust and faith transcending
    sight
Smoothed to her feet the difficult paths
    she trod.

And there she walked, as duty bade her
    go,
Safe and unsullied as a cloistered nun,
Shamed with her plainness Fashion's gaudy
    show,
    And overcame the world she did not
    shun.

In Earlham's bowers, in Plashet's liberal
    hall,
    In the great city's restless crowd and
    din,
Her ear was open to the Master's call,
    And knew the summons of His voice
    within.

Tender as mother, beautiful as wife,
    Amidst the throngs of prisoned crime
    she stood
In modest raiment faultless as her life,
    The type of England's worthiest woman-
    hood !

To melt the hearts that harshness turned to
    stone
    The sweet persuasion of her lips sufficed,
And guilt, which only hate and fear had
    known,
    Saw in her own the pitying love of Christ.

So wheresoe'er the guiding Spirit went
    She followed, finding every prison cell
It opened for her sacred as a tent
    Pitched by Gennesaret or by Jacob's well.

And Pride and Fashion felt her strong ap-
    peal,
    And priest and ruler marvelled as they
    saw
How hand in hand went wisdom with her
    zeal,
    And woman's pity kept the bounds of
    law.

She rests in God's peace ; but her memory
    stirs
    The air of earth as with an angel's wings,
And warms and moves the hearts of men
    like hers,
    The sainted daughter of Hungarian kings.

United now, the Briton and the Hun,
    Each, in her own time, faithful unto
    death,
Live sister souls ! in name and spirit one,
    Thuringia's saint and our Elizabeth !

REQUITAL

As Islam's Prophet, when his last day drew
    Nigh to its close, besought all men to
    say
    Whom he had wronged, to whom he then
    should pay
A debt forgotten, or for pardon sue,
And, through the silence of his weeping
    friends,
    A strange voice cried : " Thou owest me
    a debt,"
    " Allah be praised ! " he answered.
    " Even yet
He gives me power to make to thee amends.
O friend ! I thank thee for thy timely
    word."
    So runs the tale. Its lesson all may
    heed,
    For all have sinned in thought, or word,
    or deed,
Or, like the Prophet, through neglect have
    erred.
All need forgiveness, all have debts to pay
Ere the night cometh, while it still is day.

THE HOMESTEAD

AGAINST the wooded hills it stands,
    Ghost of a dead home, staring through
Its broken lights on wasted lands
    Where old-time harvests grew.

Unploughed, unsown, by scythe unshorn,
    The poor, forsaken farm-fields lie,
Once rich and rife with golden corn
    And pale green breadths of rye.

Of healthful herb and flower bereft,
    The garden plot no housewife keeps ;
Through weeds and tangle only left,
    The snake, its tenant, creeps.

A lilac spray, still blossom-clad,
    Sways slow before the empty rooms ;
Beside the roofless porch a sad
    Pathetic red rose blooms.

His track, in mould and dust of drouth,
  On floor and hearth the squirrel leaves,
And in the fireless chimney's mouth
  His web the spider weaves.

The leaning barn, about to fall,
  Resounds no more on husking eves ;
No cattle low in yard or stall,
  No thresher beats his sheaves.

So sad, so drear ! It seems almost
  Some haunting Presence makes its sign ;
That down yon shadowy lane some ghost
  Might drive his spectral kine !

O home so desolate and lorn !
  Did all thy memories die with thee ?
Were any wed, were any born,
  Beneath this low roof-tree ?

Whose axe the wall of forest broke,
  And let the waiting sunshine through ?
What goodwife sent the earliest smoke
  Up the great chimney flue ?

Did rustic lovers hither come ?
  Did maidens, swaying back and forth
In rhythmic grace, at wheel and loom,
  Make light their toil with mirth ?

Did child feet patter on the stair ?
  Did boyhood frolic in the snow ?
Did gray age, in her elbow chair,
  Knit, rocking to and fro ?

The murmuring brook, the sighing breeze,
  The pine's slow whisper, cannot tell ;
Low mounds beneath the hemlock-trees
  Keep the home secrets well.

Cease, mother-land, to fondly boast
  Of sons far off who strive and thrive,
Forgetful that each swarming host
  Must leave an emptier hive !

O wanderers from ancestral soil,
  Leave noisome mill and chaffering store :
Gird up your loins for sturdier toil,
  And build the home once more !

Come back to bayberry-scented slopes,
  And fragrant fern, and ground-nut vine ;
Breathe airs blown over holt and copse
  Sweet with black birch and pine.

What matter if the gains are small
  That life's essential wants supply ?
Your homestead's title gives you all
  That idle wealth can buy.

All that the many-dollared crave,
  The brick-walled slaves of 'Change and
    mart,
Lawns, trees, fresh air, and flowers, you
    have,
  More dear for lack of art.

Your own sole masters, freedom-willed,
  With none to bid you go or stay,
Till the old fields your fathers tilled,
  As manly men as they !

With skill that spares your toiling hands,
  And chemic aid that science brings,
Reclaim the waste and outworn lands,
  And reign thereon as kings !

HOW THE ROBIN CAME

AN ALGONQUIN LEGEND

HAPPY young friends, sit by me,
Under May's blown apple-tree,
While these home-birds in and out
Through the blossoms flit about.
Hear a story, strange and old,
By the wild red Indians told,
How the robin came to be :
Once a great chief left his son, —
Well-beloved, his only one, —
When the boy was well-nigh grown,
In the trial-lodge alone.
Left for tortures long and slow
Youths like him must undergo,
Who their pride of manhood test,
Lacking water, food, and rest.

Seven days the fast he kept,
Seven nights he never slept.
Then the young boy, wrung with pain,
Weak from nature's overstrain,
Faltering, moaned a low complaint :
" Spare me, father, for I faint ! "
But the chieftain, haughty-eyed,
Hid his pity in his pride.
" You shall be a hunter good,
Knowing never lack of food :

You shall be a warrior great,
Wise as fox and strong as bear ;
Many scalps your belt shall wear,
If with patient heart you wait
Bravely till your task is done.
Better you should starving die
Than that boy and squaw should cry
Shame upon your father's son ! "

When next morn the sun's first rays
Glistened on the hemlock sprays,
Straight that lodge the old chief sought,
And boiled samp and moose meat
    brought.
" Rise and eat, my son ! " he said.
Lo, he found the poor boy dead !
As with grief his grave they made,
And his bow beside him laid,
Pipe, and knife, and wampum-braid,
On the lodge-top overhead,
Preening smooth its breast of red
And the brown coat that it wore,
Sat a bird, unknown before.
And as if with human tongue,
"Mourn me not," it said, or sung ;
" I, a bird, am still your son,
Happier than if hunter fleet,
Or a brave, before your feet
Laying scalps in battle won.
Friend of man, my song shall cheer
Lodge and corn-land ; hovering near,
To each wigwam I shall bring
Tidings of the coming spring ;
Every child my voice shall know
In the moon of melting snow,
When the maple's red bud swells,
And the wind-flower lifts its bells.
As their fond companion
Men shall henceforth own your son,
And my song shall testify
That of human kin am I."

Thus the Indian legend saith
How, at first, the robin came
With a sweeter life than death,
Bird for boy, and still the same.
If my young friends doubt that this
Is the robin's genesis,
Not in vain is still the myth
If a truth be found therewith :
Unto gentleness belong
Gifts unknown to pride and wrong ;
Happier far than hate is praise, —
He who sings than he who slays.

BANISHED FROM MASSACHU-
SETTS

1660

On a painting by E. A. Abbey. The Gen-
eral Court of Massachusetts enacted Oct. 19,
1658, that " any person or persons of the cursed
sect of Quakers " should, on conviction of the
same, be banished, on pain of death, from the
jurisdiction of the commonwealth.

OVER the threshold of his pleasant home
    Set in green clearings passed the exiled
      Friend,
  In simple trust, misdoubting not the end.
" Dear heart of mine ! " he said, " the time
    has come
To trust the Lord for shelter." One long
    gaze
    The goodwife turned on each familiar
      thing, —
  The lowing kine, the orchard blossoming,
The open door that showed the hearth-fire's
    blaze, —
And calmly answered, "Yes, He will pro-
    vide."
    Silent and slow they crossed the home-
      stead's bound,
  Lingering the longest by their child's
      grave-mound.
" Move on, or stay and hang ! " the sheriff
    cried.
They left behind them more than home or
    land,
And set sad faces to an alien strand.

Safer with winds and waves than human
    wrath,
    With ravening wolves than those whose
      zeal for God
  Was cruelty to man, the exiles trod
Drear leagues of forest without guide or
    path,
Or launching frail boats on the uncharted
    sea,
    Round storm-vexed capes, whose teeth of
      granite ground
  The waves to foam, their perilous way
    they wound,
Enduring all things so their souls were free.
Oh, true confessors, shaming them who did
    Anew the wrong their Pilgrim Fathers
    bore !

For you the Mayflower spread her sail
    once more,
Freighted with souls, to all that duty bid
Faithful as they who sought an unknown
    land,
O'er wintry seas, from Holland's Hook of
    Sand !

So from his lost home to the darkening main,
    Bodeful of storm, stout Macy held his
        way,
    And, when the green shore blended with
        the gray,
His poor wife moaned : " Let us turn back
    again."
" Nay, woman, weak of faith, kneel down,"
    said he,
    " And say thy prayers : the Lord himself
        will steer ;
    And led by Him, nor man nor devils I
        fear ! "
So the gray Southwicks, from a rainy sea,
Saw, far and faint, the loom of land, and
        gave
    With feeble voices thanks for friendly
        ground
    Whereon to rest their weary feet, and
        found
A peaceful death-bed and a quiet grave
Where, ocean-walled, and wiser than his
        age,
The lord of Shelter scorned the bigot's
    rage.

Aquidneck's isle, Nantucket's lonely shores,
    And Indian-haunted Narragansett saw
    The way-worn travellers round their
        camp-fire draw,
Or heard the plashing of their weary oars.
And every place whereon they rested grew
    Happier for pure and gracious woman-
        hood,
    And men whose names for stainless honor
        stood,
Founders of States and rulers wise and true.
The Muse of history yet shall make amends
    To those who freedom, peace, and justice
        taught,
    Beyond their dark age led the van of
        thought,
And left unforfeited the name of Friends.
O mother State, how foiled was thy de-
    sign !
The gain was theirs, the loss alone was
    thine.

THE BROWN DWARF OF RÜGEN

The hint of this ballad is found in Arndt's
Märchen, Berlin, 1816. The ballad appeared
first in *St. Nicholas*, whose young readers were
advised, while smiling at the absurd supersti-
tion, to remember that bad companionship and
evil habits, desires, and passions are more to
be dreaded now than the Elves and Trolls who
frightened the children of past ages.

THE pleasant isle of Rügen looks the Baltic
        water o'er,
To the silver-sanded beaches of the Pom-
    eranian shore ;

And in the town of Rambin a little boy and
        maid
Plucked the meadow-flowers together and
    in the sea-surf played.

Alike were they in beauty if not in their
        degree :
He was the Amptman's first-born, the mil-
    ler's child was she.

Now of old the isle of Rügen was full of
        Dwarfs and Trolls,
The brown-faced little Earth-men, the
    people without souls ;

And for every man and woman in Rügen's
        island found
Walking in air and sunshine, a Troll was
    underground.

It chanced the little maiden, one morning,
        strolled away
Among the haunted Nine Hills, where the
    elves and goblins play.

That day, in barley fields below, the har-
        vesters had known
Of evil voices in the air, and heard the
    small horns blown.

She came not back ; the search for her in
        field and wood was vain :
They cried her east, they cried her west,
    but she came not again.

" She's down among the Brown Dwarfs,"
        said the dream-wives wise and old,
And prayers were made, and masses said,
    and Rambin's church bell tolled.

Five years her father mourned her ; and
    then John Deitrich said :
" I will find my little playmate, be she
    alive or dead."

He watched among the Nine Hills, he
    heard the Brown Dwarfs sing,
And saw them dance by moonlight merrily
    in a ring.

And when their gay-robed leader tossed up
    his cap of red,
Young Deitrich caught it as it fell, and
    thrust it on his head.

The Troll came crouching at his feet and
    wept for lack of it.
" Oh, give me back my magic cap, for your
    great head unfit ! "

" Nay," Deitrich said ; " the Dwarf who
    throws his charmëd cap away,
Must serve its finder at his will, and for
    his folly pay.

" You stole my pretty Lisbeth, and hid her
    in the earth ;
And you shall ope the door of glass and let
    me lead her forth."

" She will not come ; she 's one of us ; she 's
    mine ! " the Brown Dwarf said ;
" The day is set, the cake is baked, to-mor-
    row we shall wed."

" The fell fiend fetch thee ! " Deitrich cried,
    " and keep thy foul tongue still.
Quick ! open, to thy evil world, the glass
    door of the hill ! "

The Dwarf obeyed ; and youth and Troll
    down the long stairway passed,
And saw in dim and sunless light a country
    strange and vast.

Weird, rich, and wonderful, he saw the
    elfin under-land, —
Its palaces of precious stones, its streets of
    golden sand.

He came unto a banquet-hall with tables
    richly spread,
Where a young maiden served to him the
    red wine and the bread.

How fair she seemed among the Trolls so
    ugly and so wild !
Yet pale and very sorrowful, like one who
    never smiled !

Her low, sweet voice, her gold-brown hair,
    her tender blue eyes seemed
Like something he had seen elsewhere or
    something he had dreamed.

He looked ; he clasped her in his arms ; he
    knew the long-lost one ;
" O Lisbeth ! See thy playmate — I am the
    Amptman's son ! "

She leaned her fair head on his breast, and
    through her sobs she spoke :
" Oh, take me from this evil place, and
    from the elfin folk !

" And let me tread the grass-green fields
    and smell the flowers again,
And feel the soft wind on my cheek and
    hear the dropping rain !

" And oh, to hear the singing bird, the
    rustling of the tree,
The lowing cows, the bleat of sheep, the
    voices of the sea ;

" And oh, upon my father's knee to sit be-
    side the door,
And hear the bell of vespers ring in Ram-
    bin church once more ! "

He kissed her cheek, he kissed her lips ;
    the Brown Dwarf groaned to see,
And tore his tangled hair and ground his
    long teeth angrily.

But Deitrich said : " For five long years
    this tender Christian maid
Has served you in your evil world, and well
    must she be paid !

" Haste ! — hither bring me precious gems,
    the richest in your store ;
Then when we pass the gate of glass, you 'll
    take your cap once more."

No choice was left the baffled Troll, and,
    murmuring, he obeyed,
And filled the pockets of the youth and
    apron of the maid.

They left the dreadful under-land and
    passed the gate of glass ;
They felt the sunshine's warm caress, they
    trod the soft, green grass.

And when, beneath, they saw the Dwarf
    stretch up to them his brown
And crooked claw-like fingers, they tossed
    his red cap down.

Oh, never shone so bright a sun, was never
    sky so blue,
As hand in hand they homeward walked
    the pleasant meadows through !

And never sang the birds so sweet in Ram-
    bin's woods before,
And never washed the waves so soft along
    the Baltic shore ;

And when beneath his door-yard trees the
    father met his child,
The bells rung out their merriest peal, the
    folks with joy ran wild.

And soon from Rambin's holy church the
    twain came forth as one,
The Amptman kissed a daughter, the mil-
    ler blest a son.

John Deitrich's fame went far and wide,
    and nurse and maid crooned o'er
Their cradle song : " Sleep on, sleep well,
    the Trolls shall come no more ! "

For in the haunted Nine Hills he set a
    cross of stone ;
And Elf and Brown Dwarf sought in vain
    a door where door was none.

The tower he built in Rambin, fair Rügen's
    pride and boast,
Looked o'er the Baltic water to the Pome-
    ranian coast ;

And, for his worth ennobled, and rich be-
    yond compare,
Count Deitrich and his lovely bride dwelt
    long and happy there.

POEMS OF NATURE

THE FROST SPIRIT

HE comes, — he comes, — the Frost Spirit
    comes !   You may trace his foot-
    steps now
On the naked woods and the blasted fields
    and the brown hill's withered brow.
He has smitten the leaves of the gray old
    trees where their pleasant green
    came forth,
And the winds, which follow wherever he
    goes, have shaken them down to
    earth.

He comes, — he comes, — the Frost Spirit
    comes ! from the frozen Labrador,
From the icy bridge of the Northern seas,
    which the white bear wanders o'er,
Where the fisherman's sail is stiff with ice,
    and the luckless forms below
In the sunless cold of the lingering night
    into marble statues grow !

He comes, — he comes, — the Frost Spirit
    comes ! on the rushing Northern
    blast,
And the dark Norwegian pines have bowed
    as his fearful breath went past.
With an unscorched wing he has hurried on,
    where the fires of Hecla glow
On the darkly beautiful sky above and the
    ancient ice below.

He comes, — he comes, — the Frost Spirit
    comes ! and the quiet lake shall feel
The torpid touch of his glazing breath, and
    ring to the skater's heel ;
And the streams which danced on the
    broken rocks, or sang to the leaning
    grass,
Shall bow again to their winter chain, and
    in mournful silence pass.

He comes, — he comes, — the Frost Spirit
    comes ! Let us meet him as we may,
And turn with the light of the parlor-fire
    his evil power away ;
And gather closer the circle round, when
    that firelight dances high,
And laugh at the shriek of the baffled Fiend
    as his sounding wing goes by !

THE MERRIMAC

" The Indians speak of a beautiful river, far
to the south, which they call Merrimac." —
SIEUR DE MONTS, 1604.

STREAM of my fathers ! sweetly still
The sunset rays thy valley fill ;
Poured slantwise down the long defile,
Wave, wood, and spire beneath them smile.
I see the winding Powow fold
The green hill in its belt of gold,
And following down its wavy line,
Its sparkling waters blend with thine.
There 's not a tree upon thy side,
Nor rock, which thy returning tide
As yet hath left abrupt and stark
Above thy evening water-mark ;
No calm cove with its rocky hem,
No isle whose emerald swells begem
Thy broad, smooth current ; not a sail
Bowed to the freshening ocean gale ;
No small boat with its busy oars,
Nor gray wall sloping to thy shores ;
Nor farm-house with its maple shade,
Or rigid poplar colonnade,
But lies distinct and full in sight,
Beneath this gush of sunset light.
Centuries ago, that harbor-bar,
Stretching its length of foam afar,
And Salisbury's beach of shining sand,
And yonder island's wave-smoothed strand,
Saw the adventurer's tiny sail,
Flit, stooping from the eastern gale ;
And o'er these woods and waters broke
The cheer from Britain's hearts of oak,
As brightly on the voyager's eye,

Weary of forest, sea, and sky,
Breaking the dull continuous wood,
The Merrimac rolled down his flood ;
Mingling that clear pellucid brook,
Which channels vast Agioochook
When spring-time's sun and shower unlock
The frozen fountains of the rock,
And more abundant waters given
From that pure lake, "The Smile of
    Heaven,"
Tributes from vale and mountain-side, —
With ocean's dark, eternal tide !

On yonder rocky cape, which braves
The stormy challenge of the waves,
Midst tangled vine and dwarfish wood,
The hardy Anglo-Saxon stood,
Planting upon the topmost crag
The staff of England's battle-flag ;
And, while from out its heavy fold
Saint George's crimson cross unrolled,
Midst roll of drum and trumpet blare,
And weapons brandishing in air,
He gave to that lone promontory
The sweetest name in all his story ;
Of her, the flower of Islam's daughters,
Whose harems look on Stamboul's wa-
    ters, —
Who, when the chance of war had bound
The Moslem chain his limbs around,
Wreathed o'er with silk that iron chain,
Soothed with her smiles his hours of pain,
And fondly to her youthful slave
A dearer gift than freedom gave.

But look ! the yellow light no more
Streams down on wave and verdant shore ;
And clearly on the calm air swells
The twilight voice of distant bells.
From Ocean's bosom, white and thin,
The mists come slowly rolling in ;
Hills, woods, the river's rocky rim,
Amidst the sea-like vapor swim,
While yonder lonely coast-light, set
Within its wave-washed minaret,
Half quenched, a beamless star and pale,
Shines dimly through its cloudy veil !

Home of my fathers ! — I have stood
Where Hudson rolled his lordly flood :
Seen sunrise rest and sunset fade
Along his frowning Palisade ;
Looked down the Appalachian peak
On Juniata's silver streak ;
Have seen along his valley gleam

The Mohawk's softly winding stream ;
The level light of sunset shine
Through broad Potomac's hem of pine ;
And autumn's rainbow-tinted banner
Hang lightly o'er the Susquehanna ;
Yet wheresoe'er his step might be,
Thy wandering child looked back to thee !
Heard in his dreams thy river's sound
Of murmuring on its pebbly bound,
The unforgotten swell and roar
Of waves on thy familiar shore ;
And saw, amidst the curtained gloom
And quiet of his lonely room,
Thy sunset scenes before him pass ;
As, in Agrippa's magic glass,
The loved and lost arose to view,
Remembered groves in greenness grew,
Bathed still in childhood's morning dew,
Along whose bowers of beauty swept
Whatever Memory's mourners wept,
Sweet faces, which the charnel kept,
Young, gentle eyes, which long had slept ;
And while the gazer leaned to trace,
More near, some dear familiar face,
He wept to find the vision flown, —
A phantom and a dream alone !

HAMPTON BEACH

THE sunlight glitters keen and bright,
    Where, miles away,
Lies stretching to my dazzled sight
A luminous belt, a misty light,
Beyond the dark pine bluffs and wastes of
    sandy gray.

The tremulous shadow of the Sea !
    Against its ground
Of silvery light, rock, hill, and tree,
Still as a picture, clear and free,
With varying outline mark the coast for
    miles around.

On — on — we tread with loose-flung rein
    Our seaward way,
Through dark-green fields and blossom-
    ing grain,
Where the wild brier-rose skirts the lane,
And bends above our heads the flowering
    locust spray.

Ha ! like a kind hand on my brow
    Comes this fresh breeze,
Cooling its dull and feverish glow,

While through my being seems to flow
The breath of a new life, the healing of
    the seas !

Now rest we, where this grassy mound
    His feet hath set
In the great waters, which have bound
His granite ankles greenly round
With long and tangled moss, and weeds
    with cool spray wet.

Good-by to Pain and Care ! I take
    Mine ease to-day :
Here where these sunny waters break,
And ripples this keen breeze, I shake
All burdens from the heart, all weary
    thoughts away.

I draw a freer breath, I seem
    Like all I see —
Waves in the sun, the white-winged
    gleam
Of sea-birds in the slanting beam,
And far-off sails which flit before the south-
    wind free.

So when Time's veil shall fall asunder,
    The soul may know
No fearful change, nor sudden wonder,
Nor sink the weight of mystery under,
But with the upward rise, and with the
    vastness grow.

And all we shrink from now may
    seem
    No new revealing ;
Familiar as our childhood's stream,
Or pleasant memory of a dream
The loved and cherished Past upon the
    new life stealing.

Serene and mild the untried light
    May have its dawning ;
And, as in summer's northern night
The evening and the dawn unite,
The sunset hues of Time blend with the
    soul's new morning.

I sit alone ; in foam and spray
    Wave after wave
Breaks on the rocks which, stern and
    gray,
Shoulder the broken tide away,
Or murmurs hoarse and strong through
    mossy cleft and cave.

What heed I of the dusty land
    And noisy town ?
I see the mighty deep expand
From its white line of glimmering sand
To where the blue of heaven on bluer
    waves shuts down !

In listless quietude of mind,
    I yield to all
The change of cloud and wave and wind;
And passive on the flood reclined,
I wander with the waves, and with them
    rise and fall.

But look, thou dreamer ! wave and shore
    In shadow lie ;
The night-wind warns me back once more
To where, my native hill-tops o'er,
Bends like an arch of fire the glowing sun-
    set sky.

So then, beach, bluff, and wave, farewell !
    I bear with me
No token stone nor glittering shell,
But long and oft shall Memory tell
Of this brief thoughtful hour of musing by
    the Sea.

A DREAM OF SUMMER

BLAND as the morning breath of June
    The southwest breezes play ;
And, through its haze, the winter noon
    Seems warm as summer's day.
The snow-plumed Angel of the North
    Has dropped his icy spear ;
Again the mossy earth looks forth,
    Again the streams gush clear.

The fox his hillside cell forsakes,
    The muskrat leaves his nook,
The bluebird in the meadow brakes
    Is singing with the brook.
" Bear up, O Mother Nature ! " cry
    Bird, breeze, and streamlet free ;
" Our winter voices prophesy
    Of summer days to thee ! "

So, in those winters of the soul,
    By bitter blasts and drear
O'erswept from Memory's frozen pole,
    Will sunny days appear.
Reviving Hope and Faith, they show
    The soul its living powers,

And how beneath the winter's snow
   Lie germs of summer flowers !

The Night is mother of the Day,
   The Winter of the Spring,
And ever upon old Decay
   The greenest mosses cling.
Behind the cloud the starlight lurks,
   Through showers the sunbeams fall ;
For God, who loveth all His works,
   Has left His hope with all !

THE LAKESIDE

THE shadows round the inland sea
   Are deepening into night ;
Slow up the slopes of Ossipee
   They chase the lessening light.
Tired of the long day's blinding heat,
   I rest my languid eye,
Lake of the Hills ! where, cool and sweet,
   Thy sunset waters lie !

Along the sky, in wavy lines,
   O'er isle and reach and bay,
Green-belted with eternal pines,
   The mountains stretch away.
Below, the maple masses sleep
   Where shore with water blends,
While midway on the tranquil deep
   The evening light descends.

So seemed it when yon hill's red crown,
   Of old, the Indian trod,
And, through the sunset air, looked down
   Upon the Smile of God.
To him of light and shade the laws
   No forest skeptic taught ;
Their living and eternal Cause
   His truer instinct sought.

He saw these mountains in the light
   Which now across them shines ;
This lake, in summer sunset bright,
   Walled round with sombering pines.
God near him seemed ; from earth and
     skies
   His loving voice he heard,
As, face to face, in Paradise,
   Man stood before the Lord.

Thanks, O our Father ! that, like him,
   Thy tender love I see,
In radiant hill and woodland dim,

And tinted sunset sea.
For not in mockery dost Thou fill
   Our earth with light and grace ;
Thou hid'st no dark and cruel will
   Behind Thy smiling face !

AUTUMN THOUGHTS

GONE hath the Spring, with all its flowers,
   And gone the Summer's pomp and
     show,
And Autumn, in his leafless bowers,
   Is waiting for the Winter's snow.

I said to Earth, so cold and gray,
   "An emblem of myself thou art."
"Not so," the Earth did seem to say,
   "For Spring shall warm my frozen
     heart."

I soothe my wintry sleep with dreams
   Of warmer sun and softer rain,
And wait to hear the sound of streams
   And songs of merry birds again.

But thou, from whom the Spring hath
     gone,
   For whom the flowers no longer blow,
Who standest blighted and forlorn,
   Like Autumn waiting for the snow ;

No hope is thine of sunnier hours,
   Thy Winter shall no more depart ;
No Spring revive thy wasted flowers,
   Nor Summer warm thy frozen heart.

ON RECEIVING AN EAGLE'S QUILL FROM LAKE SUPERIOR

ALL day the darkness and the cold
   Upon my heart have lain,
Like shadows on the winter sky,
   Like frost upon the pane ;

But now my torpid fancy wakes,
   And, on thy Eagle's plume,
Rides forth, like Sindbad on his bird,
   Or witch upon her broom !

Below me roar the rocking pines,
   Before me spreads the lake
Whose long and solemn-sounding waves
   Against the sunset break.

I hear the wild Rice-Eater thresh
  The grain he has not sown ;
I see, with flashing scythe of fire,
  The prairie harvest mown !

I hear the far-off voyager's horn ;
  I see the Yankee's trail, —
His foot on every mountain-pass,
  On every stream his sail.

By forest, lake, and waterfall,
  I see his pedler show ;
The mighty mingling with the mean,
  The lofty with the low.

He 's whittling by St. Mary's Falls,
  Upon his loaded wain ;
He 's measuring o'er the Pictured Rocks,
  With eager eyes of gain.

I hear the mattock in the mine,
  The axe-stroke in the dell,
The clamor from the Indian lodge,
  The Jesuit chapel bell !

I see the swarthy trappers come
  From Mississippi's springs ;
And war-chiefs with their painted brows,
  And crests of eagle wings.

Behind the scared squaw's birch canoe,
  The steamer smokes and raves ;
And city lots are staked for sale
  Above old Indian graves.

I hear the tread of pioneers
  Of nations yet to be ;
The first low wash of waves, where soon
  Shall roll a human sea.

The rudiments of empire here
  Are plastic yet and warm ;
The chaos of a mighty world
  Is rounding into form !

Each rude and jostling fragment soon
  Its fitting place shall find, —
The raw material of a State,
  Its muscle and its mind !

And, westering still, the star which leads
  The New World in its train
Has tipped with fire the icy spears
  Of many a mountain chain.

The snowy cones of Oregon
  Are kindling on its way ;
And California's golden sands
  Gleam brighter in its ray !

Then blessings on thy eagle quill,
  As, wandering far and wide,
I thank thee for this twilight dream
  And Fancy's airy ride !

Yet, welcomer than regal plumes,
  Which Western trappers find,
Thy free and pleasant thoughts, chance
    sown,
  Like feathers on the wind.

Thy symbol be the mountain-bird,
  Whose glistening quill I hold ;
Thy home the ample air of hope,
  And memory's sunset gold !

In thee, let joy with duty join,
  And strength unite with love,
The eagle's pinions folding round
  The warm heart of the dove !

So, when in darkness sleeps the vale
  Where still the blind bird clings,
The sunshine of the upper sky
  Shall glitter on thy wings !

APRIL

"The spring comes slowly up this way."
                              Christabel.

'T IS the noon of the spring-time, yet never
    a bird
In the wind-shaken elm or the maple is
    heard ;
For green meadow-grasses wide levels of
    snow,
And blowing of drifts where the crocus
    should blow ;
Where wind-flower and violet, amber and
    white,
On south-sloping brooksides should smile
    in the light,
O'er the cold winter-beds of their late-
    waking roots
The frosty flake eddies, the ice-crystal
    shoots ;
And, longing for light, under wind-driven
    heaps,

Round the boles of the pine-wood the
  ground-laurel creeps,
Unkissed of the sunshine, unbaptized of
  showers,
With buds scarcely swelled, which should
  burst into flowers!
We wait for thy coming, sweet wind of the
  south!
For the touch of thy light wings, the kiss
  of thy mouth;
For the yearly evangel thou bearest from
  God,
Resurrection and life to the graves of the
  sod!
Up our long river-valley, for days, have not
  ceased
The wail and the shriek of the bitter north-
  east,
Raw and chill, as if winnowed through ices
  and snow,
All the way from the land of the wild Es-
  quimau,
Until all our dreams of the land of the blest,
Like that red hunter's, turn to the sunny
  southwest.
O soul of the spring-time, its light and its
  breath,
Bring warmth to this coldness, bring life to
  this death;
Renew the great miracle; let us behold
The stone from the mouth of the sepulchre
  rolled,
And Nature, like Lazarus, rise, as of old!
Let our faith, which in darkness and cold-
  ness has lain,
Revive with the warmth and the brightness
  again,
And in blooming of flower and budding of
  tree
The symbols and types of our destiny see;
The life of the spring-time, the life of the
  whole,
And, as sun to the sleeping earth, love to
  the soul!

PICTURES

I

LIGHT, warmth, and sprouting greenness,
  and o'er all
  Blue, stainless, steel-bright ether, raining
  down
  Tranquillity upon the deep-hushed town,
  The freshening meadows, and the hill-
  sides brown;

Voice of the west-wind from the hills
  of pine,
And the brimmed river from its distant fall,
  Low hum of bees, and joyous interlude
  Of bird-songs in the streamlet-skirting
  wood, —
  Heralds and prophecies of sound and
  sight,
  Blessed forerunners of the warmth and
  light,
Attendant angels to the house of prayer,
  With reverent footsteps keeping pace
  with mine, —
Once more, through God's great love, with
  you I share
A morn of resurrection sweet and fair
  As that which saw, of old, in Palestine,
  Immortal Love uprising in fresh bloom
  From the dark night and winter of the
  tomb!

II

White with its sun-bleached dust, the path-
  way winds
  Before me; dust is on the shrunken grass,
  And on the trees beneath whose boughs
  I pass;
  Frail screen against the Hunter of the
  sky,
  Who, glaring on me with his lidless eye,
  While mounting with his dog-star high
  and higher
Ambushed in light intolerable, unbinds
  The burnished quiver of his shafts of
  fire.
  Between me and the hot fields of his
  South
  A tremulous glow, as from a furnace-
  mouth,
  Glimmers and swims before my dazzled
  sight,
  As if the burning arrows of his ire
  Broke as they fell, and shattered into
  light;
Yet on my cheek I feel the western wind,
  And hear it telling to the orchard trees,
  And to the faint and flower-forsaken bees,
  Tales of fair meadows, green with con-
  stant streams,
And mountains rising blue and cool behind,
  Where in moist dells the purple orchis
  gleams,
And starred with white the virgin's bower
  is twined.
So the o'erwearied pilgrim, as he fares

Along life's summer waste, at times is
    fanned,
Even at noontide, by the cool, sweet airs
    Of a serener and a holier land,
    Fresh as the morn, and as the dewfall
        bland.
Breath of the blessed Heaven for which
    we pray,
Blow from the eternal hills ! make glad
    our earthly way !

SUMMER BY THE LAKESIDE

LAKE WINNIPESAUKEE

I. NOON

WHITE clouds, whose shadows haunt the
        deep,
Light mists, whose soft embraces keep
The sunshine on the hills asleep !

O isles of calm ! O dark, still wood !
And stiller skies that overbrood
Your rest with deeper quietude !

O shapes and hues, dim beckoning, through
Yon mountain gaps, my longing view
Beyond the purple and the blue,

To stiller sea and greener land,
And softer lights and airs more bland,
And skies, — the hollow of God's hand !

Transfused through you, O mountain
    friends !
With mine your solemn spirit blends,
And life no more hath separate ends.

I read each misty mountain sign,
I know the voice of wave and pine,
And I am yours, and ye are mine.

Life's burdens fall, its discords cease,
I lapse into the glad release
Of Nature's own exceeding peace.

O welcome calm of heart and mind !
As falls yon fir-tree's loosened rind
To leave a tenderer growth behind,

So fall the weary years away ;
A child again, my head I lay
Upon the lap of this sweet day.

This western wind hath Lethean powers,
Yon noonday cloud nepenthe showers,
The lake is white with lotus-flowers !

Even Duty's voice is faint and low,
And slumberous Conscience, waking slow,
Forgets her blotted scroll to show.

The Shadow which pursues us all,
Whose ever-nearing steps appall,
Whose voice we hear behind us call, —

That Shadow blends with mountain gray,
It speaks but what the light waves say, —
Death walks apart from Fear to-day !

Rocked on her breast, these pines and I
Alike on Nature's love rely ;
And equal seems to live or die.

Assured that He whose presence fills
With light the spaces of these hills
No evil to His creatures wills,

The simple faith remains, that He
Will do, whatever that may be,
The best alike for man and tree.

What mosses over one shall grow,
What light and life the other know,
Unanxious, leaving Him to show.

II. EVENING

Yon mountain's side is black with night,
    While, broad-orbed, o'er its gleaming
        crown
The moon, slow-rounding into sight,
    On the hushed inland sea looks down.

How start to light the clustering isles,
    Each silver - hemmed ! How sharply
        show
The shadows of their rocky piles,
    And tree-tops in the wave below !

How far and strange the mountains seem,
    Dim-looming through the pale, still light !
The vague, vast grouping of a dream,
    They stretch into the solemn night.

Beneath, lake, wood, and peopled vale,
    Hushed by that presence grand and grave,
Are silent, save the cricket's wail,
    And low response of leaf and wave.

Fair scenes ! whereto the Day and Night
  Make rival love, I leave ye soon,
What time before the eastern light
  The pale ghost of the setting moon

Shall hide behind yon rocky spines,
  And the young archer, Morn, shall break
His arrows on the mountain pines,
  And, golden-sandalled, walk the lake !

Farewell ! around this smiling bay
  Gay-hearted Health, and Life in bloom,
With lighter steps than mine, may stray
  In radiant summers yet to come.

But none shall more regretful leave
  These waters and these hills than I :
Or, distant, fonder dream how eve
  Or dawn is painting wave and sky ;

How rising moons shine sad and mild
  On wooded isle and silvering bay ;
Or setting suns beyond the piled
  And purple mountains lead the day ;

Nor laughing girl, nor bearding boy,
  Nor full-pulsed manhood, lingering here,
Shall add, to life's abounding joy,
  The charmed repose to suffering dear.

Still waits kind Nature to impart
  Her choicest gifts to such as gain
An entrance to her loving heart
  Through the sharp discipline of pain.

Forever from the Hand that takes
  One blessing from us others fall ;
And, soon or late, our Father makes
  His perfect recompense to all !

Oh, watched by Silence and the Night,
  And folded in the strong embrace
Of the great mountains, with the light
  Of the sweet heavens upon thy face,

Lake of the Northland ! keep thy dower
  Of beauty still, and while above
Thy solemn mountains speak of power,
  Be thou the mirror of God's love.

THE FRUIT-GIFT

Last night, just as the tints of autumn's sky
  Of sunset faded from our hills and
    streams,

I sat, vague listening, lapped in twilight
    dreams,
To the leaf's rustle, and the cricket's cry.
Then, like that basket, flush with summer
    fruit,
Dropped by the angels at the Prophet's
    foot,
Came, unannounced, a gift of clustered
    sweetness,
  Full-orbed, and glowing with the prisoned
    beams
Of summery suns, and rounded to com-
    pleteness
By kisses of the south-wind and the dew.
Thrilled with a glad surprise, methought I
    knew
The pleasure of the homeward-turning
    Jew,
When Eshcol's clusters on his shoulders
    lay,
Dropping their sweetness on his desert way.

I said, " This fruit beseems no world of
    sin.
  Its parent vine, rooted in Paradise,
  O'ercrept the wall, and never paid the
    price
  Of the great mischief, — an ambrosial
    tree,
Eden's exotic, somehow smuggled in,
  To keep the thorns and thistles company."
Perchance our frail, sad mother plucked in
    haste
  A single vine-slip as she passed the gate,
Where the dread sword alternate paled
    and burned,
  And the stern angel, pitying her fate,
Forgave the lovely trespasser, and turned
Aside his face of fire ; and thus the waste
And fallen world hath yet its annual taste
Of primal good, to prove of sin the cost,
And show by one gleaned ear the mighty
    harvest lost.

FLOWERS IN WINTER

PAINTED UPON A PORTE LIVRE

How strange to greet, this frosty morn,
  In graceful counterfeit of flowers,
These children of the meadows, born
  Of sunshine and of showers !

How well the conscious wood retains
  The pictures of its flower-sown home,

The lights and shades, the purple stains,
  And golden hues of bloom !

It was a happy thought to bring
  To the dark season's frost and rime
This painted memory of spring,
  This dream of summer-time.

Our hearts are lighter for its sake,
  Our fancy's age renews its youth,
And dim-remembered fictions take
  The guise of present truth.

A wizard of the Merrimac, —
  So old ancestral legends say, —
Could call green leaf and blossom back
  To frosted stem and spray.

The dry logs of the cottage wall,
  Beneath his touch, put out their leaves ;
The clay-bound swallow, at his call,
  Played round the icy eaves.

The settler saw his oaken flail
  Take bud, and bloom before his eyes ;
From frozen pools he saw the pale,
  Sweet summer lilies rise.

To their old homes, by man profaned,
  Came the sad dryads, exiled long,
And through their leafy tongues complained
  Of household use and wrong.

The beechen platter sprouted wild,
  The pipkin wore its old-time green,
The cradle o'er the sleeping child
  Became a leafy screen.

Haply our gentle friend hath met,
  While wandering in her sylvan quest,
Haunting his native woodlands yet,
  That Druid of the West ;

And, while the dew on leaf and flower
  Glistened in moonlight clear and still,
Learned the dusk wizard's spell of power,
  And caught his trick of skill.

But welcome, be it new or old,
  The gift which makes the day more bright,
And paints, upon the ground of cold
  And darkness, warmth and light !

Without is neither gold nor green ;
  Within, for birds, the birch-logs sing ;

Yet, summer-like, we sit between
  The autumn and the spring.

The one, with bridal blush of rose,
  And sweetest breath of woodland balm,
And one whose matron lips unclose
  In smiles of saintly calm.

Fill soft and deep, O winter snow !
  The sweet azalea's oaken dells,
And hide the bank where roses blow,
  And swing the azure bells !

O'erlay the amber violet's leaves,
  The purple aster's brookside home,
Guard all the flowers her pencil gives
  A life beyond their bloom.

And she, when spring comes round again,
  By greening slope and singing flood
Shall wander, seeking, not in vain,
  Her darlings of the wood.

THE MAYFLOWERS

The trailing arbutus, or mayflower, grows abundantly in the vicinity of Plymouth, and was the first flower that greeted the Pilgrims after their fearful winter. The name *mayflower* was familiar in England, as the application of it to the historic vessel shows, but it was applied by the English, and still is, to the hawthorn. Its use in New England in connection with *Epigœa repens* dates from a very early day, some claiming that the first Pilgrims so used it, in affectionate memory of the vessel and its English flower association.

SAD Mayflower ! watched by winter stars,
  And nursed by winter gales,
With petals of the sleeted spars,
  And leaves of frozen sails !

What had she in those dreary hours,
  Within her ice-rimmed bay,
In common with the wild-wood flowers,
  The first sweet smiles of May ?

Yet, "God be praised !" the Pilgrim said,
  Who saw the blossoms peer
Above the brown leaves, dry and dead,
  "Behold our Mayflower here !"

"God wills it : here our rest shall be,
  Our years of wandering o'er ;

For us the Mayflower of the sea
  Shall spread her sails no more."

O sacred flowers of faith and hope,
  As sweetly now as then
Ye bloom on many a birchen slope,
  In many a pine-dark glen.

Behind the sea-wall's rugged length,
  Unchanged, your leaves unfold,
Like love behind the manly strength
  Of the brave hearts of old.

So live the fathers in their sons,
  Their sturdy faith be ours,
And ours the love that overruns
  Its rocky strength with flowers.

The Pilgrim's wild and wintry day
  Its shadow round us draws;
The Mayflower of his stormy bay,
  Our Freedom's struggling cause.

But warmer suns erelong shall bring
  To life the frozen sod;
And through dead leaves of hope shall
    spring
  Afresh the flowers of God!

THE LAST WALK IN AUTUMN

I

O'ER the bare woods, whose outstretched
    hands
  Plead with the leaden heavens in vain,
I see, beyond the valley lands,
  The sea's long level dim with rain.
Around me all things, stark and dumb,
Seem praying for the snows to come,
And, for the summer bloom and greenness
    gone,
With winter's sunset lights and dazzling
    morn atone.

II

Along the river's summer walk,
  The withered tufts of asters nod;
And trembles on its arid stalk
  The hoar plume of the golden-rod.
And on a ground of sombre fir,
And azure-studded juniper,
The silver birch its buds of purple shows,
And scarlet berries tell where bloomed the
    sweet wild-rose!

III

With mingled sound of horns and bells,
  A far-heard clang, the wild geese fly,
Storm-sent, from Arctic moors and fells,
  Like a great arrow through the sky,
Two dusky lines converged in one,
Chasing the southward-flying sun;
While the brave snow-bird and the hardy
    jay
Call to them from the pines, as if to bid
    them stay.

IV

I passed this way a year ago:
  The wind blew south; the noon of day
Was warm as June's; and save that snow
  Flecked the low mountains far away,
And that the vernal-seeming breeze
Mocked faded grass and leafless trees,
I might have dreamed of summer as I lay,
Watching the fallen leaves with the soft
    wind at play.

V

Since then, the winter blasts have piled
  The white pagodas of the snow
On these rough slopes, and, strong and
    wild,
  Yon river, in its overflow
Of spring-time rain and sun, set free,
Crashed with its ices to the sea;
And over these gray fields, then green and
    gold,
The summer corn has waved, the thunder's
    organ rolled.

VI

Rich gift of God! A year of time!
  What pomp of rise and shut of day,
What hues wherewith our Northern clime
  Makes autumn's dropping woodlands
    gay,
What airs outblown from ferny dells,
And clover-bloom and sweetbrier smells,
What songs of brooks and birds, what fruits
    and flowers,
Green woods and moonlit snows, have in
    its round been ours!

VII

I know not how, in other lands,
  The changing seasons come and go;
What splendors fall on Syrian sands,
  What purple lights on Alpine snow!

Nor how the pomp of sunrise waits
On Venice at her watery gates ;
A dream alone to me is Arno's vale,
And the Alhambra's halls are but a travel-
ler's tale.

VIII

Yet, on life's current, he who drifts
Is one with him who rows or sails ;
And he who wanders widest lifts
No more of beauty's jealous veils
Than he who from his doorway sees
The miracle of flowers and trees,
Feels the warm Orient in the noonday air,
And from cloud minarets hears the sunset
call to prayer !

IX

The eye may well be glad that looks
Where Pharpar's fountains rise and
fall ;
But he who sees his native brooks
Laugh in the sun, has seen them all.
The marble palaces of Ind
Rise round him in the snow and wind ;
From his lone sweetbrier Persian Hafiz
smiles,
And Rome's cathedral awe is in his wood-
land aisles.

X

And thus it is my fancy blends
The near at hand and far and rare ;
And while the same horizon bends
Above the silver-sprinkled hair
Which flashed the light of morning skies
On childhood's wonder-lifted eyes,
Within its round of sea and sky and field,
Earth wheels with all her zones, the Kosmos
stands revealed.

XI

And thus the sick man on his bed,
The toiler to his task-work bound,
Behold their prison-walls outspread,
Their clipped horizon widen round !
While freedom-giving fancy waits,
Like Peter's angel at the gates,
The power is theirs to baffle care and pain,
To bring the lost world back, and make it
theirs again !

XII

What lack of goodly company,
When masters of the ancient lyre

Obey my call, and trace for me
Their words of mingled tears and fire !
I talk with Bacon, grave and wise,
I read the world with Pascal's eyes ;
And priest and sage, with solemn brows
austere,
And poets, garland-bound, the Lords of
Thought, draw near.

XIII

Methinks, O friend, I hear thee say,
" In vain the human heart we mock ;
Bring living guests who love the day,
Not ghosts who fly at crow of cock !
The herbs we share with flesh and blood
Are better than ambrosial food
With laurelled shades."   I grant it, nothing
loath,
But doubly blest is he who can partake of
both.

XIV

He who might Plato's banquet grace,
Have I not seen before me sit,
And watched his puritanic face,
With more than Eastern wisdom lit ?
Shrewd mystic ! who, upon the back
Of his Poor Richard's Almanac
Writing the Sufi's song, the Gentoo's dream,
Links Manu's age of thought to Fulton's
age of steam !

XV

Here too, of answering love secure,
Have I not welcomed to my hearth
The gentle pilgrim troubadour,
Whose songs have girdled half the
earth ;
Whose pages, like the magic mat
Whereon the Eastern lover sat,
Have borne me over Rhine-land's purple
vines,
And Nubia's tawny sands, and Phrygia's
mountain pines !

XVI

And he, who to the lettered wealth
Of ages adds the lore unpriced,
The wisdom and the moral health,
The ethics of the school of Christ ;
The statesman to his holy trust,
As the Athenian archon, just,
Struck down, exiled like him for truth alone,
Has he not graced my home with beauty
all his own ?

XVII

What greetings smile, what farewells
    wave,
    What loved ones enter and depart !
The good, the beautiful, the brave,
    The Heaven-lent treasures of the
      heart !
How conscious seems the frozen sod
And beechen slope whereon they trod !
The oak-leaves rustle, and the dry grass
    bends
Beneath the shadowy feet of lost or absent
    friends.

XVIII

Then ask not why to these bleak hills
    I cling, as clings the tufted moss,
To bear the winter's lingering chills,
    The mocking spring's perpetual loss.
I dream of lands where summer smiles,
And soft winds blow from spicy isles,
But scarce would Ceylon's breath of flow-
    ers be sweet,
Could I not feel thy soil, New England, at
    my feet !

XIX

At times I long for gentler skies,
    And bathe in dreams of softer air,
But homesick tears would fill the eyes
    That saw the Cross without the Bear.
The pine must whisper to the palm,
The north-wind break the tropic calm ;
And with the dreamy languor of the Line,
The North's keen virtue blend, and strength
    to beauty join.

XX

Better to stem with heart and hand
    The roaring tide of life, than lie,
Unmindful, on its flowery strand,
    Of God's occasions drifting by !
Better with naked nerve to bear
The needles of this goading air,
Than, in the lap of sensual ease, forego
The godlike power to do, the godlike aim
    to know.

XXI

Home of my heart ! to me more fair
    Than gay Versailles or Windsor's halls,
The painted, shingly town-house where
    The freeman's vote for Freedom falls !

The simple roof where prayer is made,
    Than Gothic groin and colonnade ;
The living temple of the heart of man,
    Than Rome's sky-mocking vault, or many-
      spired Milan !

XXII

More dear thy equal village schools,
    Where rich and poor the Bible read,
Than classic halls where Priestcraft rules,
    And Learning wears the chains of
      Creed ;
Thy glad Thanksgiving, gathering in
The scattered sheaves of home and kin,
Than the mad license ushering Lenten
    pains,
Or holidays of slaves who laugh and dance
    in chains.

XXIII

And sweet homes nestle in these dales,
    And perch along these wooded swells ;
And, blest beyond Arcadian vales,
    They hear the sound of Sabbath bells !
Here dwells no perfect man sublime,
Nor woman winged before her time,
But with the faults and follies of the race,
Old home-bred virtues hold their not un-
    honored place.

XXIV

Here manhood struggles for the sake
    Of mother, sister, daughter, wife,
The graces and the loves which make
    The music of the march of life ;
And woman, in her daily round
Of duty, walks on holy ground.
No unpaid menial tills the soil, nor here
Is the bad lesson learned at human rights
    to sneer.

XXV

Then let the icy north-wind blow
    The trumpets of the coming storm,
To arrowy sleet and blinding snow
    Yon slanting lines of rain transform.
Young hearts shall hail the drifted cold,
As gayly as I did of old ;
And I, who watch them through the frosty
    pane,
Unenvious, live in them my boyhood o'er
    again.

XXVI

And I will trust that He who heeds
  The life that hides in mead and wold,
Who hangs yon alder's crimson beads,
  And stains these mosses green and gold,
Will still, as He hath done, incline
His gracious care to me and mine ;
Grant what we ask aright, from wrong debar,
And, as the earth grows dark, make brighter
    every star !

XXVII

I have not seen, I may not see,
  My hopes for man take form in fact,
But God will give the victory
  In due time ; in that faith I act.
And he who sees the future sure,
The baffling present may endure,
And bless, meanwhile, the unseen Hand
    that leads
The heart's desires beyond the halting step
    of deeds.

XXVIII

And thou, my song, I send thee forth,
  Where harsher songs of mine have
    flown ;
Go, find a place at home and hearth
  Where'er thy singer's name is known ;
Revive for him the kindly thought
Of friends ; and they who love him
    not,
Touched by some strain of thine, perchance
    may take
The hand he proffers all, and thank him for
    thy sake.

THE FIRST FLOWERS

For ages, on our river borders,
  These tassels in their tawny bloom,
And willowy studs of downy silver,
  Have prophesied of Spring to come.

For ages have the unbound waters
  Smiled on them from their pebbly hem,
And the clear carol of the robin
  And song of bluebird welcomed them.

But never yet from smiling river,
  Or song of early bird, have they
Been greeted with a gladder welcome
  Than whispers from my heart to-day.

They break the spell of cold and darkness,
  The weary watch of sleepless pain ;
And from my heart, as from the river,
  The ice of winter melts again.

Thanks, Mary ! for this wild-wood token
  Of Freya's footsteps drawing near ;
Almost, as in the rune of Asgard,
  The growing of the grass I hear.

It is as if the pine-trees called me
  From ceilëd room and silent books,
To see the dance of woodland shadows,
  And hear the song of April brooks !

As in the old Teutonic ballad
  Of Odenwald live bird and tree,
Together live in bloom and music,
  I blend in song thy flowers and thee.

Earth's rocky tablets bear forever
  The dint of rain and small bird's track :
Who knows but that my idle verses
  May leave some trace by Merrimac !

The bird that trod the mellow layers
  Of the young earth is sought in vain ;
The cloud is gone that wove the sandstone,
  From God's design, with threads of rain !

So, when this fluid age we live in
  Shall stiffen round my careless rhyme,
Who made the vagrant tracks may puzzle
  The savants of the coming time ;

And, following out their dim suggestions,
  Some idly-curious hand may draw
My doubtful portraiture, as Cuvier
  Drew fish and bird from fin and claw.

And maidens in the far-off twilights,
  Singing my words to breeze and stream,
Shall wonder if the old-time Mary
  Were real, or the rhymer's dream !

THE OLD BURYING-GROUND

Our vales are sweet with fern and rose,
  Our hills are maple-crowned ;
But not from them our fathers chose
  The village burying-ground.

The dreariest spot in all the land
  To Death they set apart ;

With scanty grace from Nature's hand,
  And none from that of art.

A winding wall of mossy stone,
  Frost-flung and broken, lines
A lonesome acre thinly grown
  With grass and wandering vines.

Without the wall a birch-tree shows
  Its drooped and tasselled head ;
Within, a stag-horn sumach grows,
  Fern-leafed, with spikes of red.

There, sheep that graze the neighboring
    plain
  Like white ghosts come and go,
The farm-horse drags his fetlock chain,
  The cow-bell tinkles slow.

Low moans the river from its bed,
  The distant pines reply ;
Like mourners shrinking from the dead,
  They stand apart and sigh.

Unshaded smites the summer sun,
  Unchecked the winter blast ;
The school-girl learns the place to shun,
  With glances backward cast.

For thus our fathers testified,
  That he might read who ran,
The emptiness of human pride,
  The nothingness of man.

They dared not plant the grave with flow-
    ers,
  Nor dress the funeral sod,
Where, with a love as deep as ours,
  They left their dead with God.

The hard and thorny path they kept
  From beauty turned aside ;
Nor missed they over those who slept
  The grace to life denied.

Yet still the wilding flowers would blow,
  The golden leaves would fall,
The seasons come, the seasons go,
  And God be good to all.

Above the graves the blackberry hung
  In bloom and green its wreath,

And harebells swung as if they rung
  The chimes of peace beneath.

The beauty Nature loves to share,
  The gifts she hath for all,
The common light, the common air,
  O'ercrept the graveyard's wall.

It knew the glow of eventide,
  The sunrise and the noon,
And glorified and sanctified
  It slept beneath the moon.

With flowers or snow-flakes for its sod,
  Around the seasons ran,
And evermore the love of God
  Rebuked the fear of man.

We dwell with fears on either hand
  Within a daily strife,
And spectral problems waiting stand
  Before the gates of life.

The doubts we vainly seek to solve,
  The truths we know, are one ;
The known and nameless stars revolve
  Around the Central Sun.

And if we reap as we have sown,
  And take the dole we deal,
The law of pain is love alone,
  The wounding is to heal.

Unharmed from change to change we glide
  We fall as in our dreams ;
The far-off terror at our side
  A smiling angel seems.

Secure on God's all-tender heart
  Alike rest great and small ;
Why fear to lose our little part,
  When He is pledged for all ?

O fearful heart and troubled brain !
  Take hope and strength from this, —
That Nature never hints in vain,
  Nor prophesies amiss.

Her wild birds sing the same sweet stave,
  Her lights and airs are given
Alike to playground and the grave ;
  And over both is Heaven.

THE PALM-TREE

Is it the palm, the cocoa-palm,
On the Indian Sea, by the isles of balm?
Or is it a ship in the breezeless calm?

A ship whose keel is of palm beneath,
Whose ribs of palm have a palm-bark
   sheath,
And a rudder of palm it steereth with.

Branches of palm are its spars and rails,
Fibres of palm are its woven sails,
And the rope is of palm that idly trails!

What does the good ship bear so well?
The cocoa-nut with its stony shell,
And the milky sap of its inner cell.

What are its jars, so smooth and fine,
But hollowed nuts, filled with oil and
   wine,
And the cabbage that ripens under the
   Line?

Who smokes his nargileh, cool and calm?
The master, whose cunning and skill could
   charm
Cargo and ship from the bounteous palm.

In the cabin he sits on a palm-mat soft,
From a beaker of palm his drink is quaffed,
And a palm-thatch shields from the sun
   aloft!

His dress is woven of palmy strands,
And he holds a palm-leaf scroll in his
   hands,
Traced with the Prophet's wise commands!

The turban folded about his head
Was daintily wrought of the palm-leaf
   braid,
And the fan that cools him of palm was
   made.

Of threads of palm was the carpet spun
Whereon he kneels when the day is done,
And the foreheads of Islam are bowed as
   one!

To him the palm is a gift divine,
Wherein all uses of man combine, —
House, and raiment, and food, and wine!

And, in the hour of his great release,
His need of the palm shall only cease
With the shroud wherein he lieth in peace.

"Allah il Allah!" he sings his psalm,
On the Indian Sea, by the isles of balm;
"Thanks to Allah who gives the palm!"

THE RIVER PATH

No bird-song floated down the hill,
The tangled bank below was still;

No rustle from the birchen stem,
No ripple from the water's hem.

The dusk of twilight round us grew,
We felt the falling of the dew;

For, from us, ere the day was done,
The wooded hills shut out the sun.

But on the river's farther side
We saw the hill-tops glorified, —

A tender glow, exceeding fair,
A dream of day without its glare.

With us the damp, the chill, the gloom:
With them the sunset's rosy bloom;

While dark, through willowy vistas seen,
The river rolled in shade between.

From out the darkness where we trod,
We gazed upon those hills of God,

Whose light seemed not of moon or sun.
We spake not, but our thought was one.

We paused, as if from that bright shore
Beckoned our dear ones gone before;

And stilled our beating hearts to hear
The voices lost to mortal ear!

Sudden our pathway turned from night;
The hills swung open to the light;

Through their green gates the sunshine
   showed,
A long, slant splendor downward flowed.

Down glade and glen and bank it rolled;
It bridged the shaded stream with gold;

And, borne on piers of mist, allied
The shadowy with the sunlit side !

"So," prayed we, "when our feet draw
    near
The river dark, with mortal fear,

"And the night cometh chill with dew,
O Father ! let Thy light break through !

"So let the hills of doubt divide,
So bridge with faith the sunless tide !

"So let the eyes that fail on earth
On Thy eternal hills look forth ;

"And in Thy beckoning angels know
The dear ones whom we loved below !"

MOUNTAIN PICTURES

I. FRANCONIA FROM THE PEMIGEWASSET

ONCE more, O Mountains of the North, un-
    veil
    Your brows, and lay your cloudy mantles
        by !
And once more, ere the eyes that seek ye
        fail,
    Uplift against the blue walls of the sky
Your mighty shapes, and let the sunshine
    weave
    Its golden net-work in your belting woods,
    Smile down in rainbows from your fall-
        ing floods,
And on your kingly brows at morn and eve
    Set crowns of fire ! So shall my soul
        receive
Haply the secret of your calm and strength,
    Your unforgotten beauty interfuse
    My common life, your glorious shapes and
        hues
    And sun-dropped splendors at my bidding
        come,
    Loom vast through dreams, and stretch
        in billowy length
From the sea-level of my lowland home !

They rise before me ! Last night's thun-
        der-gust
Roared not in vain : for where its light-
        nings thrust
Their tongues of fire, the great peaks seem
        so near,

Burned clean of mist, so starkly bold and
        clear,
I almost pause the wind in the pines to hear,
The loose rock's fall, the steps of browsing
        deer.
The clouds that shattered on yon slide-worn
        walls
    And splintered on the rocks their spears
        of rain
Have set in play a thousand waterfalls,
Making the dusk and silence of the woods
Glad with the laughter of the chasing floods,
And luminous with blown spray and silver
        gleams,
While, in the vales below, the dry-lipped
        streams
    Sing to the freshened meadow-lands
        again.
So, let me hope, the battle-storm that beats
    The land with hail and fire may pass away
    With its spent thunders at the break of
        day,
Like last night's clouds, and leave, as it
        retreats,
    A greener earth and fairer sky behind,
    Blown crystal-clear by Freedom's North-
        ern wind !

II. MONADNOCK FROM WACHUSET

I would I were a painter, for the sake
    Of a sweet picture, and of her who led,
    A fitting guide, with reverential tread,
Into that mountain mystery. First a lake
    Tinted with sunset ; next the wavy lines
        Of far receding hills ; and yet more
        far,
    Monadnock lifting from his night of pines
        His rosy forehead to the evening star.
Beside us, purple-zoned, Wachuset laid
His head against the West, whose warm
        light made
    His aureole ; and o'er him, sharp and
        clear,
Like a shaft of lightning in mid-launching
        stayed,
    A single level cloud-line, shone upon
    By the fierce glances of the sunken sun,
        Menaced the darkness with its golden
        spear !

So twilight deepened round us. Still and
        black
The great woods climbed the mountain at
        our back ;

And on their skirts, where yet the lingering
    day
On the shorn greenness of the clearing lay,
  The brown old farm-house like a bird's-
    nest hung.
With home-life sounds the desert air was
    stirred :
The bleat of sheep along the hill we
    heard,
The bucket plashing in the cool, sweet
    well,
The pasture - bars that clattered as they
    fell ;
Dogs barked, fowls fluttered, cattle lowed ;
    the gate
Of the barn-yard creaked beneath the mer-
    ry weight
  Of sun-brown children, listening, while
    they swung,
    The welcome sound of supper-call to
    hear ;
    And down the shadowy lane, in tink-
    lings clear,
The pastoral curfew of the cow-bell rung.
Thus soothed and pleased, our backward
    path we took,
  Praising the farmer's home. He only
    spake,
Looking into the sunset o'er the lake,
  Like one to whom the far-off is most
    near :
" Yes, most folks think it has a pleasant
    look ;
  I love it for my good old mother's sake,
  Who lived and died here in the peace
    of God ! "
  The lesson of his words we pondered
    o'er,
As silently we turned the eastern flank
Of the mountain, where its shadow deepest
    sank,
Doubling the night along our rugged road :
We felt that man was more than his
    abode, —
  The inward life than Nature's raiment
    more ;
And the warm sky, the sundown-tinted hill,
  The forest and the lake, seemed dwarfed
    and dim
Before the saintly soul, whose human will
  Meekly in the Eternal footsteps trod,
Making her homely toil and household ways
An earthly echo of the song of praise
  Swelling from angel lips and harps of
    seraphim.

THE VANISHERS

SWEETEST of all childlike dreams
  In the simple Indian lore
Still to me the legend seems
  Of the shapes who flit before.

Flitting, passing, seen and gone,
  Never reached nor found at rest,
Baffling search, but beckoning on
  To the Sunset of the Blest.

From the clefts of mountain rocks,
  Through the dark of lowland firs,
Flash the eyes and flow the locks
  Of the mystic Vanishers !

And the fisher in his skiff,
  And the hunter on the moss,
Hear their call from cape and cliff,
  See their hands the birch-leaves toss.

Wistful, longing, through the green
  Twilight of the clustered pines,
In their faces rarely seen
  Beauty more than mortal shines.

Fringed with gold their mantles flow
  On the slopes of westering knolls ;
In the wind they whisper low
  Of the Sunset Land of Souls.

Doubt who may, O friend of mine !
  Thou and I have seen them too ;
On before with beck and sign
  Still they glide, and we pursue.

More than clouds of purple trail
  In the gold of setting day ;
More than gleams of wing or sail
  Beckon from the sea-mist gray.

Glimpses of immortal youth,
  Gleams and glories seen and flown,
Far-heard voices sweet with truth,
  Airs from viewless Eden blown ;

Beauty that eludes our grasp,
  Sweetness that transcends our taste,
Loving hands we may not clasp,
  Shining feet that mock our haste ;

Gentle eyes we closed below,
  Tender voices heard once more,

Smile and call us, as they go
  On and onward, still before.

Guided thus, O friend of mine !
  Let us walk our little way,
Knowing by each beckoning sign
  That we are not quite astray.

Chase we still, with baffled feet,
  Smiling eye and waving hand,
Sought and seeker soon shall meet,
  Lost and found, in Sunset Land !

THE PAGEANT

A SOUND as if from bells of silver,
  Or elfin cymbals smitten clear,
  Through the frost-pictured panes I
    hear.

A brightness which outshines the morning,
  A splendor brooking no delay,
  Beckons and tempts my feet away.

I leave the trodden village highway
  For virgin snow-paths glimmering
    through
  A jewelled elm-tree avenue ;

Where, keen against the walls of sap-
    phire,
  The gleaming tree-bolls, ice-embossed,
  Hold up their chandeliers of frost.

I tread in Orient halls enchanted,
  I dream the Saga's dream of caves
  Gem-lit beneath the North Sea waves !

I walk the land of Eldorado,
  I touch its mimic garden bowers,
  Its silver leaves and diamond flowers !

The flora of the mystic mine-world
  Around me lifts on crystal stems
  The petals of its clustered gems !

What miracle of weird transforming
  In this wild work of frost and light,
  This glimpse of glory infinite !

This foregleam of the Holy City
  Like that to him of Patmos given,
  The white bride coming down from
    heaven !

How flash the ranked and mail-clad alders,
  Through what sharp-glancing spears of
    reeds
  The brook its muffled water leads !

Yon maple, like the bush of Horeb,
  Burns unconsumed : a white, cold fire
  Rays out from every grassy spire.

Each slender rush and spike of mullein,
  Low laurel shrub and drooping fern,
  Transfigured, blaze where'er I turn.

How yonder Ethiopian hemlock
  Crowned with his glistening circlet
    stands !
  What jewels light his swarthy hands !

Here, where the forest opens southward,
  Between its hospitable pines,
  As through a door, the warm sun shines,

The jewels loosen on the branches,
  And lightly, as the soft winds blow,
  Fall, tinkling, on the ice below.

And through the clashing of their cymbals
  I hear the old familiar fall
  Of water down the rocky wall,

Where, from its wintry prison breaking,
  In dark and silence hidden long,
  The brook repeats its summer song.

One instant flashing in the sunshine,
  Keen as a sabre from its sheath,
  Then lost again the ice beneath.

I hear the rabbit lightly leaping,
  The foolish screaming of the jay,
  The chopper's axe-stroke far away ;

The clamor of some neighboring barn-
    yard,
  The lazy cock's belated crow,
  Or cattle-tramp in crispy snow.

And, as in some enchanted forest
  The lost knight hears his comrades
    sing,
  And, near at hand, their bridles ring, —

So welcome I these sounds and voices,
  These airs from far-off summer blown,
  This life that leaves me not alone.

For the white glory overawes me ;
   The crystal terror of the seer
   Of Chebar's vision blinds me here.

Rebuke me not, O sapphire heaven !
   Thou stainless earth, lay not on me
   Thy keen reproach of purity,

If, in this august presence-chamber,
   I sigh for summer's leaf-green gloom
   And warm airs thick with odorous
      bloom !

Let the strange frost-work sink and crumble,
   And let the loosened tree-boughs swing,
   Till all their bells of silver ring.

Shine warmly down, thou sun of noontime,
   On this chill pageant, melt and move
   The winter's frozen heart with love.

And, soft and low, thou wind south-blowing,
   Breathe through a veil of tenderest
      haze
   Thy prophecy of summer days.

Come with thy green relief of promise,
   And to this dead, cold splendor bring
   The living jewels of the spring !

THE PRESSED GENTIAN

THE time of gifts has come again,
And, on my northern window-pane,
Outlined against the day's brief light,
A Christmas token hangs in sight.
The wayside travellers, as they pass,
Mark the gray disk of clouded glass ;
And the dull blankness seems, perchance,
Folly to their wise ignorance.

They cannot from their outlook see
The perfect grace it hath for me ;
For there the flower, whose fringes through
The frosty breath of autumn blew,
Turns from without its face of bloom
To the warm tropic of my room,
As fair as when beside its brook
The hue of bending skies it took.

So from the trodden ways of earth,
Seem some sweet souls who veil their worth,
And offer to the careless glance
The clouding gray of circumstance.

They blossom best where hearth-fires burn,
To loving eyes alone they turn
The flowers of inward grace, that hide
Their beauty from the world outside.

But deeper meanings come to me,
My half-immortal flower, from thee !
Man judges from a partial view,
None ever yet his brother knew ;
The Eternal Eye that sees the whole
May better read the darkened soul,
And find, to outward sense denied,
The flower upon its inmost side !

A MYSTERY

THE river hemmed with leaning trees
   Wound through its meadows green ;
A low, blue line of mountains showed
   The open pines between.

One sharp, tall peak above them all
   Clear into sunlight sprang :
I saw the river of my dreams,
   The mountains that I sang !

No clue of memory led me on,
   But well the ways I knew ;
A feeling of familiar things
   With every footstep grew.

Not otherwise above its crag
   Could lean the blasted pine ;
Not otherwise the maple hold
   Aloft its red ensign.

So up the long and shorn foot-hills
   The mountain road should creep ;
So, green and low, the meadow fold
   Its red-haired kine asleep.

The river wound as it should wind ;
   Their place the mountains took ;
The white torn fringes of their clouds
   Wore no unwonted look.

Yet ne'er before that river's rim
   Was pressed by feet of mine,
Never before mine eyes had crossed
   That broken mountain line.

A presence, strange at once and known,
   Walked with me as my guide ;
The skirts of some forgotten life
   Trailed noiseless at my side.

Was it a dim-remembered dream ?
  Or glimpse through æons old ?
The secret which the mountains kept
  The river never told.

But from the vision ere it passed
  A tender hope I drew,
And, pleasant as a dawn of spring,
  The thought within me grew,

That love would temper every change,
  And soften all surprise,
And, misty with the dreams of earth,
  The hills of Heaven arise.

A SEA DREAM

WE saw the slow tides go and come,
  The curving surf-lines lightly drawn,
The gray rocks touched with tender bloom
Beneath the fresh-blown rose of dawn.

We saw in richer sunsets lost
  The sombre pomp of showery noons ;
And signalled spectral sails that crossed
  The weird, low light of rising moons.

On stormy eves from cliff and head
  We saw the white spray tossed and
    spurned ;
While over all, in gold and red,
  Its face of fire the lighthouse turned.

The rail-car brought its daily crowds,
  Half curious, half indifferent,
Like passing sails or floating clouds,
  We saw them as they came and went.

But, one calm morning, as we lay
  And watched the mirage-lifted wall
Of coast, across the dreamy bay,
  And heard afar the curlew call,

And nearer voices, wild or tame,
  Of airy flock and childish throng,
Up from the water's edge there came
  Faint snatches of familiar song.

Careless we heard the singer's choice
  Of old and common airs ; at last
The tender pathos of his voice
  In one low chanson held us fast.

A song that mingled joy and pain,
  And memories old and sadly sweet ;

While, timing to its minor strain,
  The waves in lapsing cadence beat.

———

The waves are glad in breeze and sun ;
  The rocks are fringed with foam ;
I walk once more a haunted shore,
  A stranger, yet at home,
  A land of dreams I roam.

Is this the wind, the soft sea-wind
  That stirred thy locks of brown ?
Are these the rocks whose mosses knew
  The trail of thy light gown,
  Where boy and girl sat down ?

I see the gray fort's broken wall,
  The boats that rock below ;
And, out at sea, the passing sails
  We saw so long ago
  Rose-red in morning's glow.

The freshness of the early time
  On every breeze is blown ;
As glad the sea, as blue the sky, —
  The change is ours alone ;
  The saddest is my own.

A stranger now, a world-worn man,
  Is he who bears my name ;
But thou, methinks, whose mortal life
  Immortal youth became,
  Art evermore the same.

Thou art not here, thou art not there,
  Thy place I cannot see ;
I only know that where thou art
  The blessed angels be,
  And heaven is glad for thee.

Forgive me if the evil years
  Have left on me their sign ;
Wash out, O soul so beautiful,
  The many stains of mine
  In tears of love divine !

I could not look on thee and live,
  If thou wert by my side ;
The vision of a shining one,
  The white and heavenly bride,
  Is well to me denied.

But turn to me thy dear girl-face
  Without the angel's crown,

The wedded roses of thy lips,
  Thy loose hair rippling down
  In waves of golden brown.

Look forth once more through space and time,
  And let thy sweet shade fall
In tenderest grace of soul and form
  On memory's frescoed wall,
  A shadow, and yet all !

Draw near, more near, forever dear !
  Where'er I rest or roam,
Or in the city's crowded streets,
  Or by the blown sea foam,
  The thought of thee is home !

At breakfast hour the singer read
  The city news, with comment wise,
Like one who felt the pulse of trade
  Beneath his finger fall and rise.

His look, his air, his curt speech, told
  The man of action, not of books,
To whom the corners made in gold
  And stocks were more than seaside nooks.

Of life beneath the life confessed
  His song had hinted unawares ;
Of flowers in traffic's ledgers pressed,
  Of human hearts in bulls and bears.

But eyes in vain were turned to watch
  That face so hard and shrewd and strong ;
And ears in vain grew sharp to catch
  The meaning of that morning song.

In vain some sweet-voiced querist sought
  To sound him, leaving as she came ;
Her baited album only caught
  A common, unromantic name.

No word betrayed the mystery fine,
  That trembled on the singer's tongue ;
He came and went, and left no sign
  Behind him save the song he sung.

HAZEL BLOSSOMS

THE summer warmth has left the sky,
  The summer songs have died away ;
And, withered, in the footpaths lie
  The fallen leaves, but yesterday
  With ruby and with topaz gay.

The grass is browning on the hills ;
  No pale, belated flowers recall
The astral fringes of the rills,
  And drearily the dead vines fall,
  Frost-blackened, from the roadside wall

Yet through the gray and sombre wood,
  Against the dusk of fir and pine,
Last of their floral sisterhood,
  The hazel's yellow blossoms shine,
  The tawny gold of Afric's mine !

Small beauty hath my unsung flower,
  For spring to own or summer hail ;
But, in the season's saddest hour,
  To skies that weep and winds that wail
  Its glad surprisals never fail.

O days grown cold ! O life grown old !
  No rose of June may bloom again ;
But, like the hazel's twisted gold,
  Through early frost and latter rain
  Shall hints of summer-time remain.

And as within the hazel's bough
  A gift of mystic virtue dwells,
That points to golden ores below,
  And in dry desert places tells
  Where flow unseen the cool, sweet wells, —

So, in the wise Diviner's hand,
  Be mine the hazel's grateful part
To feel, beneath a thirsty land,
  The living waters thrill and start,
  The beating of the rivulet's heart !

Sufficeth me the gift to light
  With latest bloom the dark, cold days ;
To call some hidden spring to sight
  That, in these dry and dusty ways,
  Shall sing its pleasant song of praise.

O Love ! the hazel-wand may fail,
  But thou canst lend the surer spell,
That, passing over Baca's vale,
  Repeats the old-time miracle,
  And makes the desert-land a well.

SUNSET ON THE BEARCAMP

A GOLD fringe on the purpling hem
  Of hills the river runs,
As down its long, green valley falls

The last of summer's suns.
Along its tawny gravel-bed
　Broad-flowing, swift, and still,
As if its meadow levels felt
　The hurry of the hill,
Noiseless between its banks of green
　From curve to curve it slips ;
The drowsy maple-shadows rest
　Like fingers on its lips.

A waif from Carroll's wildest hills,
　Unstoried and unknown ;
The ursine legend of its name
　Prowls on its banks alone.
Yet flowers as fair its slopes adorn
　As ever Yarrow knew,
Or, under rainy Irish skies,
　By Spenser's Mulla grew ;
And through the gaps of leaning trees
　Its mountain cradle shows :
The gold against the amethyst,
　The green against the rose.

Touched by a light that hath no name,
　A glory never sung,
Aloft on sky and mountain wall
　Are God's great pictures hung.
How changed the summits vast and old !
　No longer granite-browed,
They melt in rosy mist ; the rock
　Is softer than the cloud ;
The valley holds its breath ; no leaf
　Of all its elms is twirled :
The silence of eternity
　Seems falling on the world.

The pause before the breaking seals
　Of mystery is this ;
Yon miracle-play of night and day
　Makes dumb its witnesses.
What unseen altar crowns the hills
　That reach up stair on stair ?
What eyes look through, what white wings
　fan
　These purple veils of air ?
What Presence from the heavenly heights
　To those of earth stoops down ?
Not vainly Hellas dreamed of gods
　On Ida's snowy crown !

Slow fades the vision of the sky,
　The golden water pales,
And over all the valley-land
　A gray-winged vapor sails.
I go the common way of all ;

The sunset fires will burn,
The flowers will blow, the river flow,
　When I no more return.
No whisper from the mountain pine
　Nor lapsing stream shall tell
The stranger, treading where I tread,
　Of him who loved them well.

But beauty seen is never lost,
　God's colors all are fast ;
The glory of this sunset heaven
　Into my soul has passed,
A sense of gladness unconfined
　To mortal date or clime ;
As the soul liveth, it shall live
　Beyond the years of time.
Beside the mystic asphodels
　Shall bloom the home-born flowers,
And new horizons flush and glow
　With sunset hues of ours.

Farewell ! these smiling hills must wear
　Too soon their wintry frown,
And snow-cold winds from off them shake
　The maple's red leaves down.
But I shall see a summer sun
　Still setting broad and low ;
The mountain slopes shall blush and bloom,
　The golden water flow.
A lover's claim is mine on all
　I see to have and hold, —
The rose-light of perpetual hills,
　And sunsets never cold !

THE SEEKING OF THE WATER-FALL

THEY left their home of summer ease
Beneath the lowland's sheltering trees,
To seek, by ways unknown to all,
The promise of the waterfall.

Some vague, faint rumor to the vale
Had crept — perchance a hunter's tale —
Of its wild mirth of waters lost
On the dark woods through which it tossed

Somewhere it laughed and sang ; some
　where
Whirled in mad dance its misty hair ;
But who had raised its veil, or seen
The rainbow skirts of that Undine ?

They sought it where the mountain brook
Its swift way to the valley took ;

Along the rugged slope they clomb,
Their guide a thread of sound and foam.

Height after height they slowly won ;
The fiery javelins of the sun
Smote the bare ledge ; the tangled shade
With rock and vine their steps delayed.

But, through leaf-openings, now and then
They saw the cheerful homes of men,
And the great mountains with their wall
Of misty purple girdling all.

The leaves through which the glad winds
    blew
Shared the wild dance the waters knew ;
And where the shadows deepest fell
The wood-thrush rang his silver bell.

Fringing the stream, at every turn
Swung low the waving fronds of fern ;
From stony cleft and mossy sod
Pale asters sprang, and golden-rod.

And still the water sang the sweet,
Glad song that stirred its gliding feet,
And found in rock and root the keys
Of its beguiling melodies.

Beyond, above, its signals flew
Of tossing foam the birch-trees through ;
Now seen, now lost, but baffling still
The weary seekers' slackening will.

Each called to each : "Lo here ! Lo
    there !
Its white scarf flutters in the air !"
They climbed anew ; the vision fled,
To beckon higher overhead.

So toiled they up the mountain-slope
With faint and ever fainter hope ;
With faint and fainter voice the brook
Still bade them listen, pause, and look.

Meanwhile below the day was done ;
Above the tall peaks saw the sun
Sink, beam-shorn, to its misty set
Behind the hills of violet.

"Here ends our quest !" the seekers
    cried,
"The brook and rumor both have lied !
The phantom of a waterfall
Has led us at its beck and call."

But one, with years grown wiser, said :
"So, always baffled, not misled,
We follow where before us runs
The vision of the shining ones.

"Not where they seem their signals fly,
Their voices while we listen die ;
We cannot keep, however fleet,
The quick time of their wingèd feet.

"From youth to age unresting stray
These kindly mockers in our way ;
Yet lead they not, the baffling elves,
To something better than themselves ?

"Here, though unreached the goal we
    sought,
Its own reward our toil has brought :
The winding water's sounding rush,
The long note of the hermit thrush,

"The turquoise lakes, the glimpse of pond
And river track, and, vast, beyond
Broad meadows belted round with pines,
The grand uplift of mountain lines !

"What matter though we seek with pain
The garden of the gods in vain,
If lured thereby we climb to greet
Some wayside blossom Eden-sweet ?

"To seek is better than to gain,
The fond hope dies as we attain ;
Life's fairest things are those which seem,
The best is that of which we dream.

"Then let us trust our waterfall
Still flashes down its rocky wall,
With rainbow crescent curved across
Its sunlit spray from moss to moss.

"And we, forgetful of our pain,
In thought shall seek it oft again ;
Shall see this aster-blossomed sod,
This sunshine of the golden-rod,

"And haply gain, through parting boughs,
Grand glimpses of great mountain brows
Cloud-turbaned, and the sharp steel sheen
Of lakes deep set in valleys green.

"So failure wins ; the consequence
Of loss becomes its recompense ;
And evermore the end shall tell
The unreached ideal guided well.

" Our sweet illusions only die
Fulfilling love's sure prophecy ;
And every wish for better things
An undreamed beauty nearer brings.

" For fate is servitor of love ;
Desire and hope and longing prove
The secret of immortal youth,
And Nature cheats us into truth.

" O kind allurers, wisely sent,
Beguiling with benign intent,
Still move us, through divine unrest,
To seek the loveliest and the best !

" Go with us when our souls go free,
And, in the clear, white light to be,
Add unto Heaven's beatitude
The old delight of seeking good ! "

THE TRAILING ARBUTUS

I WANDERED lonely where the pine-trees
    made
Against the bitter East their barricade,
    And, guided by its sweet
Perfume, I found, within a narrow dell,
The trailing spring flower tinted like a
    shell
    Amid dry leaves and mosses at my
    feet.

From under dead boughs, for whose loss
    the pines
Moaned ceaseless overhead, the blossoming
    vines
    Lifted their glad surprise,
While yet the bluebird smoothed in leafless
    trees
His feathers ruffled by the chill sea-breeze,
    And snow-drifts lingered under April
    skies.

As, pausing, o'er the lonely flower I bent,
I thought of lives thus lowly, clogged and
    pent,
    Which yet find room,
Through care and cumber, coldness and
    decay,
To lend a sweetness to the ungenial day,
    And make the sad earth happier for their
    bloom.

ST. MARTIN'S SUMMER

This name in some parts of Europe is given
to the season we call Indian Summer, in honor
of the good St. Martin. The title of the poem
was suggested by the fact that the day it refers
to was the exact date of that set apart to the
Saint, the 11th of November.

THOUGH flowers have perished at the touch
    Of Frost, the early comer,
I hail the season loved so much,
    The good St. Martin's summer.

O gracious morn, with rose-red dawn,
    And thin moon curving o'er it !
The old year's darling, latest born,
    More loved than all before it !

How flamed the sunrise through the pines !
    How stretched the birchen shadows,
Braiding in long, wind-wavered lines
    The westward sloping meadows !

The sweet day, opening as a flower
    Unfolds its petals tender,
Renews for us at noontide's hour
    The summer's tempered splendor.

The birds are hushed ; alone the wind,
    That through the woodland searches,
The red-oak's lingering leaves can find,
    And yellow plumes of larches.

But still the balsam-breathing pine
    Invites no thought of sorrow,
No hint of loss from air like wine
    The earth's content can borrow.

The summer and the winter here
    Midway a truce are holding,
A soft, consenting atmosphere
    Their tents of peace enfolding.

The silent woods, the lonely hills,
    Rise solemn in their gladness ;
The quiet that the valley fills
    Is scarcely joy or sadness.

How strange ! The autumn yesterday
    In winter's grasp seemed dying ;
On whirling winds from skies of gray
    The early snow was flying.

And now, while over Nature's mood
   There steals a soft relenting,
I will not mar the present good,
   Forecasting or lamenting.

My autumn time and Nature's hold
   A dreamy tryst together,
And, both grown old, about us fold
   The golden-tissued weather.

I lean my heart against the day
   To feel its bland caressing ;
I will not let it pass away
   Before it leaves its blessing.

God's angels come not as of old
   The Syrian shepherds knew them ;
In reddening dawns, in sunset gold,
   And warm noon lights I view them.

Nor need there is, in times like this
   When heaven to earth draws nearer,
Of wing or song as witnesses
   To make their presence clearer.

O stream of life, whose swifter flow
   Is of the end forewarning,
Methinks thy sundown afterglow
   Seems less of night than morning !

Old cares grow light ; aside I lay
   The doubts and fears that troubled ;
The quiet of the happy day
   Within my soul is doubled.

That clouds must veil this fair sunshine
   Not less a joy I find it ;
Nor less yon warm horizon line
   That winter lurks behind it.

The mystery of the untried days
   I close my eyes from reading ;
His will be done whose darkest ways
   To light and life are leading !

Less drear the winter night shall be,
   If memory cheer and hearten
Its heavy hours with thoughts of thee,
   Sweet summer of St. Martin !

STORM ON LAKE ASQUAM

A cloud, like that the old-time Hebrew saw
   On Carmel prophesying rain, began

To lift itself o'er wooded Cardigan,
Growing and blackening. Suddenly, a flaw
Of chill wind menaced ; then a strong blast
    beat
   Down the long valley's murmuring pines,
    and woke
The noon-dream of the sleeping lake, and
    broke
Its smooth steel mirror at the mountains'
    feet.

Thunderous and vast, a fire-veined darkness
    swept
   Over the rough pine-bearded Asquam
    range ;
   A wraith of tempest, wonderful and
    strange,
From peak to peak the cloudy giant stepped.

One moment, as if challenging the storm,
   Chocorua's tall, defiant sentinel
   Looked from his watch-tower ; then the
    shadow fell,
And the wild rain-drift blotted out his form.

And over all the still unhidden sun,
   Weaving its light through slant-blown
    veils of rain,
   Smiled on the trouble, as hope smiles on
    pain ;
And, when the tumult and the strife were
    done,

With one foot on the lake, and one on land,
   Framing within his crescent's tinted streak
   A far-off picture of the Melvin peak,
Spent broken clouds the rainbow's angel
    spanned.

A SUMMER PILGRIMAGE

To kneel before some saintly shrine,
To breathe the health of airs divine,
Or bathe where sacred rivers flow,
The cowled and turbaned pilgrims go.
I too, a palmer, take, as they
With staff and scallop-shell, my way
To feel, from burdening cares and ills,
The strong uplifting of the hills.

The years are many since, at first,
For dreamed-of wonders all athirst,
I saw on Winnipesaukee fall

The shadow of the mountain wall.
Ah! where are they who sailed with me
The beautiful island-studded sea?
And am I he whose keen surprise
Flashed out from such unclouded eyes?

Still, when the sun of summer burns,
My longing for the hills returns;
And northward, leaving at my back
The warm vale of the Merrimac,
I go to meet the winds of morn,
Blown down the hill-gaps, mountain-born,
Breathe scent of pines, and satisfy
The hunger of a lowland eye.

Again I see the day decline
Along a ridged horizon line;
Touching the hill-tops, as a nun
Her beaded rosary, sinks the sun.
One lake lies golden, which shall soon
Be silver in the rising moon;
And one, the crimson of the skies
And mountain purple multiplies.

With the untroubled quiet blends
The distance-softened voice of friends;
The girl's light laugh no discord brings
To the low song the pine-tree sings;
And, not unwelcome, comes the hail
Of boyhood from his nearing sail.
The human presence breaks no spell,
And sunset still is miracle!

Calm as the hour, methinks I feel
A sense of worship o'er me steal;
Not that of satyr-charming Pan,
No cult of Nature shaming man,
Not Beauty's self, but that which lives
And shines through all the veils it weaves, —
Soul of the mountain, lake, and wood,
Their witness to the Eternal Good!

And if, by fond illusion, here
The earth to heaven seems drawing near,
And yon outlying range invites
To other and serener heights,
Scarce hid behind its topmost swell,
The shining Mounts Delectable!
A dream may hint of truth no less
Than the sharp light of wakefulness.

As through her veil of incense smoke
Of old the spell-rapt priestess spoke,
More than her heathen oracle,
May not this trance of sunset tell

That Nature's forms of loveliness
Their heavenly archetypes confess,
Fashioned like Israel's ark alone
From patterns in the Mount made known?

A holier beauty overbroods
These fair and faint similitudes;
Yet not unblest is he who sees
Shadows of God's realities,
And knows beyond this masquerade
Of shape and color, light and shade,
And dawn and set, and wax and wane,
Eternal verities remain.

O gems of sapphire, granite set!
O hills that charmed horizons fret!
I know how fair your morns can break,
In rosy light on isle and lake;
How over wooded slopes can run
The noonday play of cloud and sun,
And evening droop her oriflamme
Of gold and red in still Asquam.

The summer moons may round again,
And careless feet these hills profane;
These sunsets waste on vacant eyes
The lavish splendor of the skies;
Fashion and folly, misplaced here,
Sigh for their natural atmosphere,
And travelled pride the outlook scorn
Of lesser heights than Matterhorn:

But let me dream that hill and sky
Of unseen beauty prophesy;
And in these tinted lakes behold
The trailing of the raiment fold
Of that which, still eluding gaze,
Allures to upward-tending ways,
Whose footprints make, wherever found,
Our common earth a holy ground.

SWEET FERN

THE subtle power in perfume found
　　Nor priest nor sibyl vainly learned;
On Grecian shrine or Aztec mound
　　No censer idly burned.

That power the old-time worships knew,
　　The Corybantes' frenzied dance,
The Pythian priestess swooning through
　　The wonderland of trance.

And Nature holds, in wood and field,
　　Her thousand sunlit censers still;

To spells of flower and shrub we yield
  Against or with our will.

I climbed a hill path strange and new
  With slow feet, pausing at each turn ;
A sudden waft of west wind blew
  The breath of the sweet fern.

That fragrance from my vision swept
  The alien landscape ; in its stead,
Up fairer hills of youth I stepped,
  As light of heart as tread.

I saw my boyhood's lakelet shine
  Once more through rifts of woodland
    shade ;
I knew my river's winding line
  By morning mist betrayed.

With me June's freshness, lapsing brook,
  Murmurs of leaf and bee, the call
Of birds, and one in voice and look
  In keeping with them all.

A fern beside the way we went
  She plucked, and, smiling, held it up,
While from her hand the wild, sweet
    scent
  I drank as from a cup.

O potent witchery of smell !
  The dust-dry leaves to life return,
And she who plucked them owns the spell
  And lifts her ghostly fern.

Or sense or spirit ? Who shall say
  What touch the chord of memory thrills ?
It passed, and left the August day
  Ablaze on lonely hills.

THE WOOD GIANT

[Written at Sturtevant's Farm, about a mile
from Centre Harbor, N. H.]

FROM Alton Bay to Sandwich Dome,
  From Mad to Saco river,
For patriarchs of the primal wood
  We sought with vain endeavor.

And then we said : "The giants old
  Are lost beyond retrieval ;
This pygmy growth the axe has spared
  Is not the wood primeval.

"Look where we will o'er vale and hill,
  How idle are our searches
For broad-girthed maples, wide-limbed
    oaks,
  Centennial pines and birches !

"Their tortured limbs the axe and saw
  Have changed to beams and trestles ;
They rest in walls, they float on seas,
  They rot in sunken vessels.

"This shorn and wasted mountain land
  Of underbrush and boulder, —
Who thinks to see its full-grown tree
  Must live a century older."

At last to us a woodland path,
  To open sunset leading,
Revealed the Anakim of pines
  Our wildest wish exceeding.

Alone, the level sun before ;
  Below, the lake's green islands ;
Beyond, in misty distance dim,
  The rugged Northern Highlands.

Dark Titan on his Sunset Hill
  Of time and change defiant !
How dwarfed the common woodland
    seemed,
  Before the old-time giant !

What marvel that, in simpler days
  Of the world's early childhood,
Men crowned with garlands, gifts, and
    praise
  Such monarchs of the wild-wood ?

That Tyrian maids with flower and song
  Danced through the hill grove's spaces,
And hoary-bearded Druids found
  In woods their holy places ?

With somewhat of that Pagan awe
  With Christian reverence blending,
We saw our pine-tree's mighty arms
  Above our heads extending.

We heard his needles' mystic rune,
  Now rising, and now dying,
As erst Dodona's priestess heard
  The oak leaves prophesying.

Was it the half-unconscious moan
  Of one apart and mateless,

The weariness of unshared power,
  The loneliness of greatness ?

O dawns and sunsets, lend to him
  Your beauty and your wonder !
Blithe sparrow, sing thy summer song
  His solemn shadow under !

Play lightly on his slender keys,
  O wind of summer, waking
For hills like these the sound of seas
  On far-off beaches breaking !

And let the eagle and the crow
  Find shelter in his branches,
When winds shake down his winter snow
  In silver avalanches.

The brave are braver for their cheer,
  The strongest need assurance,
The sigh of longing makes not less
  The lesson of endurance.

A DAY

TALK not of sad November, when a day
  Of warm, glad sunshine fills the sky of
    noon,
  And a wind, borrowed from some morn
    of June,
Stirs the brown grasses and the leafless
  spray.

On the unfrosted pool the pillared pines
  Lay their long shafts of shadow : the
    small rill,

Singing a pleasant song of summer still,
A line of silver, down the hill-slope shines.

Hushed the bird - voices and the hum of
    bees,
  In the thin grass the crickets pipe no
    more ;
  But still the squirrel hoards his winter
    store,
And drops his nut-shells from the shag-
    bark trees.

Softly the dark green hemlocks whisper :
    high
  Above, the spires of yellowing larches
    show,
  Where the woodpecker and home-loving
    crow
And jay and nut - hatch winter's threat
    defy.

O gracious beauty, ever new and old !
  O sights and sounds of nature, doubly
    dear
  When the low sunshine warns the closing
    year
Of snow-blown fields and waves of Arctic
    cold !

Close to my heart I fold each lovely
    thing
  The sweet day yields ; and, not disconso-
    late,
  With the calm patience of the woods I
    wait
For leaf and blossom when God gives us
    Spring !

A LAMENT

*"The parted spirit,
Knoweth it not our sorrow ?   Answereth not
Its blessing to our tears ? "*

THE circle is broken, one seat is forsaken,
One bud from the tree of our friendship is
    shaken ;
One heart from among us no longer shall
    thrill
With joy in our gladness, or grief in our
    ill.

Weep ! lonely and lowly are slumbering
    now
The light of her glances, the pride of her
    brow ;
Weep ! sadly and long shall we listen in
    vain
To hear the soft tones of her welcome again.

Give our tears to the dead ! For human-
    ity's claim
From its silence and darkness is ever the
    same ;
The hope of that world whose existence is
    bliss
May not stifle the tears of the mourners of
    this.

For, oh ! if one glance the freed spirit can
    throw
On the scene of its troubled probation be-
    low,
Than the pride of the marble, the pomp of
    the dead,
To that glance will be dearer the tears which
    we shed.

Oh, who can forget the mild light of her
    smile,
Over lips moved with music and feeling the
    while,
The eye's deep enchantment, dark, dream-
    like, and clear,
In the glow of its gladness, the shade of its
    tear.

And the charm of her features, while over
    the whole
Played the hues of the heart and the sun-
    shine of soul ;
And the tones of her voice, like the music
    which seems
Murmured low in our ears by the Angel of
    dreams !

But holier and dearer our memories hold
Those treasures of feeling, more precious
    than gold,
The love and the kindness and pity which
    gave
Fresh flowers for the bridal, green wreaths
    for the grave !

The heart ever open to Charity's claim,
Unmoved from its purpose by censure and
    blame,
While vainly alike on her eye and her ear
Fell the scorn of the heartless, the jesting
    and jeer.

How true to our hearts was that beautiful
    sleeper !
With smiles for the joyful, with tears for
    the weeper !
Yet, evermore prompt, whether mournful
    or gay,
With warnings in love to the passing astray.

For, though spotless herself, she could sor-
    row for them
Who sullied with evil the spirit's pure gem ;
And a sigh or a tear could the erring reprove,
And the sting of reproof was still tempered
    by love.

As a cloud of the sunset, slow melting in
    heaven,
As a star that is lost when the daylight is
    given,
As a glad dream of slumber, which wakens
    in bliss,
She hath passed to the world of the holy
    from this.

TO THE MEMORY OF CHARLES B. STORRS

Late President of Western Reserve College, who died at his post of duty, overworn by his strenuous labors with tongue and pen in the cause of Human Freedom.

THOU hast fallen in thine armor,
　Thou martyr of the Lord!
With thy last breath crying "Onward!"
　And thy hand upon the sword.
The haughty heart derideth,
　And the sinful lip reviles,
But the blessing of the perishing
　Around thy pillow smiles!

When to our cup of trembling
　The added drop is given,
And the long-suspended thunder
　Falls terribly from Heaven,—
When a new and fearful freedom
　Is proffered of the Lord
To the slow-consuming Famine,
　The Pestilence and Sword!

When the refuges of Falsehood
　Shall be swept away in wrath,
And the temple shall be shaken,
　With its idol, to the earth,
Shall not thy words of warning
　Be all remembered then?
And thy now unheeded message
　Burn in the hearts of men?

Oppression's hand may scatter
　Its nettles on thy tomb,
And even Christian bosoms
　Deny thy memory room;
For lying lips shall torture
　Thy mercy into crime,
And the slanderer shall flourish
　As the bay-tree for a time.

But where the south-wind lingers
　On Carolina's pines,
Or falls the careless sunbeam
　Down Georgia's golden mines;
Where now beneath his burthen
　The toiling slave is driven;
Where now a tyrant's mockery
　Is offered unto Heaven;

Where Mammon hath its altars
　Wet o'er with human blood,
And pride and lust debases
　The workmanship of God,—
There shall thy praise be spoken,
　Redeemed from Falsehood's ban,
When the fetters shall be broken,
　And the slave shall be a man!

Joy to thy spirit, brother!
　A thousand hearts are warm,
A thousand kindred bosoms
　Are baring to the storm.
What though red-handed Violence
　With secret Fraud combine?
The wall of fire is round us,
　Our Present Help was thine.

Lo, the waking up of nations,
　From Slavery's fatal sleep;
The murmur of a Universe,
　Deep calling unto Deep!
Joy to thy spirit, brother!
　On every wind of heaven
The onward cheer and summons
　Of Freedom's voice is given!

Glory to God forever!
　Beyond the despot's will
The soul of Freedom liveth
　Imperishable still.
The words which thou hast uttered
　Are of that soul a part,
And the good seed thou hast scattered
　Is springing from the heart.

In the evil days before us,
　And the trials yet to come,
In the shadow of the prison,
　Or the cruel martyrdom,—
We will think of thee, O brother!
　And thy sainted name shall be
In the blessing of the captive,
　And the anthem of the free.

LINES

ON THE DEATH OF S. OLIVER TORREY, SECRETARY OF THE BOSTON YOUNG MEN'S ANTI–SLAVERY SOCIETY

GONE before us, O our brother,
　To the spirit-land!
Vainly look we for another
　In thy place to stand.
Who shall offer youth and beauty

On the wasting shrine
Of a stern and lofty duty,
With a faith like thine ?

Oh, thy gentle smile of greeting
Who again shall see ?
Who amidst the solemn meeting
Gaze again on thee ?
Who, when peril gathers o'er us,
Wear so calm a brow ?
Who, with evil men before us,
So serene as thou ?

Early hath the spoiler found thee,
Brother of our love !
Autumn's faded earth around thee,
And its storms above !
Evermore that turf lie lightly,
And, with future showers,
O'er thy slumbers fresh and brightly
Blow the summer flowers !

In the locks thy forehead gracing,
Not a silvery streak ;
Nor a line of sorrow's tracing
On thy fair young cheek ;
Eyes of light and lips of roses,
Such as Hylas wore, —
Over all that curtain closes,
Which shall rise no more !

Will the vigil Love is keeping
Round that grave of thine,
Mournfully, like Jazer weeping
Over Sibmah's vine ;
Will the pleasant memories, swelling
Gentle hearts, of thee,
In the spirit's distant dwelling
All unheeded be ?

If the spirit ever gazes,
From its journeyings, back ;
If the immortal ever traces
O'er its mortal track ;
Wilt thou not, O brother, meet us
Sometimes on our way,
And, in hours of sadness, greet us
As a spirit may ?

Peace be with thee, O our brother,
In the spirit-land !
Vainly look we for another
In thy place to stand.
Unto Truth and Freedom giving
All thy early powers,

Be thy virtues with the living,
And thy spirit ours !

TO ———

WITH A COPY OF WOOLMAN'S JOURNAL

"Get the writings of John Woolman by
heart." — *Essays of Elia.*

MAIDEN ! with the fair brown tresses
Shading o'er thy dreamy eye,
Floating on thy thoughtful forehead
Cloud wreaths of its sky.

Youthful years and maiden beauty,
Joy with them should still abide, —
Instinct take the place of Duty,
Love, not Reason, guide.

Ever in the New rejoicing,
Kindly beckoning back the Old,
Turning, with the gift of Midas,
All things into gold.

And the passing shades of sadness
Wearing even a welcome guise,
As, when some bright lake lies open
To the sunny skies,

Every wing of bird above it,
Every light cloud floating on,
Glitters like that flashing mirror
In the self-same sun.

But upon thy youthful forehead
Something like a shadow lies ;
And a serious soul is looking
From thy earnest eyes.

With an early introversion,
Through the forms of outward things,
Seeking for the subtle essence,
And the hidden springs.

Deeper than the gilded surface
Hath thy wakeful vision seen,
Farther than the narrow present
Have thy journeyings been.

Thou hast midst Life's empty noises
Heard the solemn steps of Time,
And the low mysterious voices
Of another clime.

All the mystery of Being
　Hath upon thy spirit pressed, —
Thoughts which, like the Deluge wanderer,
　Find no place of rest :

That which mystic Plato pondered,
　That which Zeno heard with awe,
And the star-rapt Zoroaster
　In his night watch saw.

From the doubt and darkness springing
　Of the dim, uncertain Past,
Moving to the dark still shadows
　O'er the Future cast,

Early hath Life's mighty question
　Thrilled within thy heart of youth,
With a deep and strong beseeching :
　What and where is Truth ?

Hollow creed and ceremonial,
　Whence the ancient life hath fled,
Idle faith unknown to action,
　Dull and cold and dead.

Oracles, whose wire-worked meanings
　Only wake a quiet scorn, —
Not from these thy seeking spirit
　Hath its answer drawn.

But, like some tired child at even,
　On thy mother Nature's breast,
Thou, methinks, art vainly seeking
　Truth, and peace, and rest.

O'er that mother's rugged features
　Thou art throwing Fancy's veil,
Light and soft as woven moonbeams,
　Beautiful and frail !

O'er the rough chart of Existence,
　Rocks of sin and wastes of woe,
Soft airs breathe, and green leaves tremble,
　And cool fountains flow.

And to thee an answer cometh
　From the earth and from the sky,
And to thee the hills and waters
　And the stars reply.

But a soul-sufficing answer
　Hath no outward origin ;
More than Nature's many voices
　May be heard within.

Even as the great Augustine
　Questioned earth and sea and sky,
And the dusty tomes of learning
　And old poesy.

But his earnest spirit needed
　More than outward Nature taught ;
More than blest the poet's vision
　Or the sage's thought.

Only in the gathered silence
　Of a calm and waiting frame,
Light and wisdom as from Heaven
　To the seeker came.

Not to ease and aimless quiet
　Doth that inward answer tend,
But to works of love and duty
　As our being's end ;

Not to idle dreams and trances,
　Length of face, and solemn tone,
But to Faith, in daily striving
　And performance shown.

Earnest toil and strong endeavor
　Of a spirit which within
Wrestles with familiar evil
　And besetting sin ;

And without, with tireless vigor,
　Steady heart, and weapon strong,
In the power of truth assailing
　Every form of wrong.

Guided thus, how passing lovely
　Is the track of Woolman's feet !
And his brief and simple record
　How serenely sweet !

O'er life's humblest duties throwing
　Light the earthling never knew,
Freshening all its dark waste places
　As with Hermon's dew.

All which glows in Pascal's pages,
　All which sainted Guion sought,
Or the blue-eyed German Rahel
　Half-unconscious taught :

Beauty, such as Goethe pictured,
　Such as Shelley dreamed of, shed
Living warmth and starry brightness
　Round that poor man's head.

Not a vain and cold ideal,
  Not a poet's dream alone,
But a presence warm and real,
  Seen and felt and known.

When the red right-hand of slaughter
  Moulders with the steel it swung,
When the name of seer and poet
  Dies on Memory's tongue,

All bright thoughts and pure shall gather
  Round that meek and suffering one, —
Glorious, like the seer-seen angel
  Standing in the sun !

Take the good man's book and ponder
  What its pages say to thee ;
Blessed as the hand of healing
  May its lesson be.

If it only serves to strengthen
  Yearnings for a higher good,
For the fount of living waters
  And diviner food ;

If the pride of human reason
  Feels its meek and still rebuke,
Quailing like the eye of Peter
  From the Just One's look !

If with readier ear thou heedest
  What the Inward Teacher saith,
Listening with a willing spirit
  And a childlike faith, —

Thou mayst live to bless the giver,
  Who, himself but frail and weak,
Would at least the highest welfare
  Of another seek ;

And his gift, though poor and lowly
  It may seem to other eyes,
Yet may prove an angel holy
  In a pilgrim's guise.

LEGGETT'S MONUMENT

William Leggett, who died in 1839 at the age of thirty-seven, was the intrepid editor of the *New York Evening Post* and afterwards of *The Plain Dealer*. His vigorous assault upon the system of slavery brought down upon him the enmity of political defenders of the system.

" Ye build the tombs of the prophets." — *Holy Writ.*

YES, pile the marble o'er him ! It is well
  That ye who mocked him in his long
    stern strife,
And planted in the pathway of his life
The ploughshares of your hatred hot from
    hell,
  Who clamored down the bold reformer
    when
He pleaded for his captive fellow-men,
Who spurned him in the market-place, and
    sought
  Within thy walls, St. Tammany, to bind
In party chains the free and honest thought,
  The angel utterance of an upright mind,
Well is it now that o'er his grave ye raise
The stony tribute of your tardy praise,
For not alone that pile shall tell to Fame
Of the brave heart beneath, but of the
    builders' shame !

TO A FRIEND

ON HER RETURN FROM EUROPE

How smiled the land of France
Under thy blue eye's glance,
    Light-hearted rover !
Old walls of chateaux gray,
Towers of an early day,
Which the Three Colors play
    Flauntingly over.

Now midst the brilliant train
Thronging the banks of Seine :
    Now midst the splendor
Of the wild Alpine range,
Waking with change on change
Thoughts in thy young heart strange,
    Lovely, and tender.

Vales, soft Elysian,
Like those in the vision
    Of Mirza, when, dreaming,
He saw the long hollow dell,
Touched by the prophet's spell,
Into an ocean swell
    With its isles teeming.

Cliffs wrapped in snows of years,
Splintering with icy spears
    Autumn's blue heaven :
Loose rock and frozen slide,
Hung on the mountain-side,

Waiting their hour to glide
　　Downward, storm-driven !

Rhine-stream, by castle old,
Baron's and robber's hold,
　　Peacefully flowing ;
Sweeping through vineyards green,
Or where the cliffs are seen
O'er the broad wave between
　　Grim shadows throwing.

Or, where St. Peter's dome
Swells o'er eternal Rome,
　　Vast, dim, and solemn ;
Hymns ever chanting low,
Censers swung to and fro,
Sable stoles sweeping slow,
　　Cornice and column !

Oh, as from each and all
Will there not voices call
　　Evermore back again ?
In the mind's gallery
Wilt thou not always see
Dim phantoms beckon thee
　　O'er that old track again ?

New forms thy presence haunt,
New voices softly chant,
　　New faces greet thee !
Pilgrims from many a shrine
Hallowed by poet's line,
At memory's magic sign,
　　Rising to meet thee.

And when such visions come
Unto thy olden home,
　　Will they not waken
Deep thoughts of Him whose hand
Led thee o'er sea and land
Back to the household band
　　Whence thou wast taken ?

While, at the sunset time,
Swells the cathedral's chime,
　　Yet, in thy dreaming,
While to thy spirit's eye
Yet the vast mountains lie
Piled in the Switzer's sky,
　　Icy and gleaming :

Prompter of silent prayer,
Be the wild picture there
　　In the mind's chamber,
And, through each coming day

Him who, as staff and stay,
Watched o'er thy wandering way,
　　Freshly remember.

So, when the call shall be
Soon or late unto thee,
　　As to all given,
Still may that picture live,
All its fair forms survive,
And to thy spirit give
　　Gladness in Heaven !

LUCY HOOPER

Lucy Hooper died at Brooklyn, L.I., on the 1st of 8th mo., 1841, aged twenty-four years.

THEY tell me, Lucy, thou art dead,
　　That all of thee we loved and cherished
　　Has with thy summer roses perished ;
And left, as its young beauty fled,
An ashen memory in its stead,
The twilight of a parted day
　　Whose fading light is cold and vain,
　　The heart's faint echo of a strain
Of low, sweet music passed away.
That true and loving heart, that gift
　　Of a mind, earnest, clear, profound,
Bestowing, with a glad unthrift,
　　Its sunny light on all around,
Affinities which only could
Cleave to the pure, the true, and good ;
　　And sympathies which found no rest,
　　Save with the loveliest and best.
Of them — of thee — remains there naught
　　But sorrow in the mourner's breast ?
A shadow in the land of thought ?
No !　Even my weak and trembling faith
　　Can lift for thee the veil which doubt
　　And human fear have drawn about
The all-awaiting scene of death.

Even as thou wast I see thee still ;
And, save the absence of all ill
And pain and weariness, which here
Summoned the sigh or wrung the tear,
The same as when, two summers back,
Beside our childhood's Merrimac,
I saw thy dark eye wander o'er
Stream, sunny upland, rocky shore,
And heard thy low, soft voice alone
Midst lapse of waters, and the tone
Of pine-leaves by the west-wind blown,
There 's not a charm of soul or brow,
　　Of all we knew and loved in thee,

But lives in holier beauty now,
  Baptized in immortality !
Not mine the sad and freezing dream
  Of souls that, with their earthly mould,
  Cast off the loves and joys of old,
Unbodied, like a pale moonbeam,
  As pure, as passionless, and cold;
Nor mine the hope of Indra's son,
  Of slumbering in oblivion's rest,
Life's myriads blending into one,
  In blank annihilation blest ;
Dust-atoms of the infinite,
Sparks scattered from the central light,
And winning back through mortal pain
Their old unconsciousness again.
No ! I have friends in Spirit Land,
Not shadows in a shadowy band,
  Not others, but themselves are they.
And still I think of them the same
As when the Master's summons came ;
Their change, — the holy morn-light break-
    ing
Upon the dream-worn sleeper, waking, —
  A change from twilight into day.

They 've laid thee midst the household
    graves,
  Where father, brother, sister lie ;
Below thee sweep the dark blue waves,
  Above thee bends the summer sky.
Thy own loved church in sadness read
Her solemn ritual o'er thy head,
And blessed and hallowed with her prayer
The turf laid lightly o'er thee there.
That church, whose rites and liturgy,
Sublime and old, were truth to thee,
Undoubted to thy bosom taken,
As symbols of a faith unshaken.
Even I, of simpler views, could feel
The beauty of thy trust and zeal ;
And, owning not thy creed, could see
How deep a truth it seemed to thee,
And how thy fervent heart had thrown
O'er all, a coloring of its own,
And kindled up, intense and warm,
A life in every rite and form,
As, when on Chebar's banks of old,
The Hebrew's gorgeous vision rolled,
A spirit filled the vast machine,
A life " within the wheels " was seen.

Farewell ! A little time, and we
  Who knew thee well, and loved thee here,
One after one shall follow thee
  As pilgrims through the gate of fear,

Which opens on eternity.
Yet shall we cherish not the less
  All that is left our hearts meanwhile ;
The memory of thy loveliness
  Shall round our weary pathway smile,
Like moonlight when the sun has set,
A sweet and tender radiance yet.
Thoughts of thy clear-eyed sense of duty,
  Thy generous scorn of all things wrong,
The truth, the strength, the graceful beauty
  Which blended in thy song.
All lovely things, by thee beloved,
  Shall whisper to our hearts of thee ;
These green hills, where thy childhood
    roved,
  Yon river winding to the sea,
The sunset light of autumn eves
Reflecting on the deep, still floods,
Cloud, crimson sky, and trembling leaves
Of rainbow-tinted woods,
These, in our view, shall henceforth take
A tenderer meaning for thy sake ;
And all thou lovedst of earth and sky
Seem sacred to thy memory.

FOLLEN

ON READING HIS ESSAY ON THE "FUTURE STATE"

Charles Follen, one of the noblest contribu-
tions of Germany to American citizenship, was
at an early age driven from his professorship
in the University of Jena, and compelled to seek
shelter from official prosecution in Switzerland,
on account of his liberal political opinions. He
became Professor of Civil Law in the Univer-
sity of Basle. The governments of Prussia,
Austria, and Russia united in demanding his
delivery as a political offender ; and, in conse-
quence, he left Switzerland, and came to the
United States. At the time of the formation
of the American Anti-Slavery Society he was
a Professor in Harvard University, honored for
his genius, learning, and estimable character.
His love of liberty and hatred of oppression led
him to seek an interview with Garrison and ex-
press his sympathy with him. Soon after, he
attended a meeting of the New England Anti-
Slavery Society. An able speech was made by
Rev. A. A. Phelps, and a letter of mine ad-
dressed to the Secretary of the Society was
read. Whereupon he rose and stated that his
views were in unison with those of the Society,
and that after hearing the speech and the let-
ter, he was ready to join it, and abide the
probable consequences of such an unpopular
act. He lost by so doing his professorship.

He was an able member of the Executive
Committee of the American Anti-Slavery Soci-
ety. He perished in the ill-fated steamer Lex-
ington, which was burned on its passage from
New York, January 13, 1840. The few writings
left behind him show him to have been a
profound thinker of rare spiritual insight.

FRIEND of my soul! as with moist eye
  I look up from this page of thine,
Is it a dream that thou art nigh,
  Thy mild face gazing into mine?

That presence seems before me now,
  A placid heaven of sweet moonrise,
When, dew-like, on the earth below
  Descends the quiet of the skies.

The calm brow through the parted hair,
  The gentle lips which knew no guile,
Softening the blue eye's thoughtful care
  With the bland beauty of their smile.

Ah me! at times that last dread scene
  Of Frost and Fire and moaning Sea
Will cast its shade of doubt between
  The failing eyes of Faith and thee.

Yet, lingering o'er thy charmëd page,
  Where through the twilight air of earth,
Alike enthusiast and sage,
  Prophet and bard, thou gazest forth,

Lifting the Future's solemn veil;
  The reaching of a mortal hand
To put aside the cold and pale
  Cloud-curtains of the Unseen Land;

In thoughts which answer to my own,
  In words which reach my inward ear,
Like whispers from the void Unknown,
  I feel thy living presence here.

The waves which lull thy body's rest,
  The dust thy pilgrim footsteps trod,
Unwasted, through each change, attest
  The fixed economy of God.

Shall these poor elements outlive
  The mind whose kingly will they
      wrought?
Their gross unconsciousness survive
  Thy godlike energy of thought?

Thou livest, Follen! not in vain
  Hath thy fine spirit meekly borne

The burthen of Life's cross of pain,
  And the thorned crown of suffering worn.

Oh, while Life's solemn mystery glooms
  Around us like a dungeon's wall,
Silent earth's pale and crowded tombs,
  Silent the heaven which bends o'er
      all!

While day by day our loved ones glide
  In spectral silence, hushed and lone,
To the cold shadows which divide
  The living from the dread Unknown;

While even on the closing eye,
  And on the lip which moves in vain,
The seals of that stern mystery
  Their undiscovered trust retain;

And only midst the gloom of death,
  Its mournful doubts and haunting fears,
Two pale, sweet angels, Hope and Faith,
  Smile dimly on us through their tears;

'T is something to a heart like mine
  To think of thee as living yet;
To feel that such a light as thine
  Could not in utter darkness set.

Less dreary seems the untried way
  Since thou hast left thy footprints there,
And beams of mournful beauty play
  Round the sad Angel's sable hair.

Oh! at this hour when half the sky
  Is glorious with its evening light,
And fair broad fields of summer lie
  Hung o'er with greenness in my sight;

While through these elm-boughs wet with
      rain
  The sunset's golden walls are seen,
With clover-bloom and yellow grain
  And wood-draped hill and stream be-
      tween;

I long to know if scenes like this
  Are hidden from an angel's eyes;
If earth's familiar loveliness
  Haunts not thy heaven's serener skies.

For sweetly here upon thee grew
  The lesson which that beauty gave,
The ideal of the pure and true
  In earth and sky and gliding wave.

And it may be that all which lends
  The soul an upward impulse here,
With a diviner beauty blends,
  And greets us in a holier sphere.

Through groves where blighting never fell
  The humbler flowers of earth may twine ;
And simple draughts from childhood's well
  Blend with the angel-tasted wine.

But be the prying vision veiled,
  And let the seeking lips be dumb,
Where even seraph eyes have failed
  Shall mortal blindness seek to come ?

We only know that thou hast gone,
  And that the same returnless tide
Which bore thee from us still glides on,
  And we who mourn thee with it glide.

On all thou lookest we shall look,
  And to our gaze erelong shall turn
That page of God's mysterious book
  We so much wish yet dread to learn.

With Him, before whose awful power
  Thy spirit bent its trembling knee ;
Who, in the silent greeting flower,
  And forest leaf, looked out on thee,

We leave thee, with a trust serene,
  Which Time, nor Change, nor Death can
      move,
While with thy childlike faith we lean
  On Him whose dearest name is Love !

TO J. P.

John Pierpont, the eloquent preacher and
poet of Boston.

NOT as a poor requital of the joy
  With which my childhood heard that lay
      of thine,
Which, like an echo of the song divine
At Bethlehem breathed above the Holy
      Boy,
  Bore to my ear the Airs of Palestine, —
Not to the poet, but the man I bring
In friendship's fearless trust my offering :
How much it lacks I feel, and thou wilt see,
Yet well I know that thou hast deemed with
      me
Life all too earnest, and its time too short

For dreamy ease and Fancy's graceful
      sport ;
  And girded for thy constant strife with
      wrong,
Like Nehemiah fighting while he wrought
  The broken walls of Zion, even thy song
Hath a rude martial tone, a blow in every
      thought !

CHALKLEY HALL

Chalkley Hall, near Frankford, Pa., was the
residence of Thomas Chalkley, an eminent min-
ister of the Friends' denomination. He was one
of the early settlers of the Colony, and his *Jour-
nal*, which was published in 1749, presents a
quaint but beautiful picture of a life of unosten-
tatious and simple goodness. He was the mas-
ter of a merchant vessel, and, in his visits to
the West Indies and Great Britain, omitted no
opportunity to labor for the highest interests of
his fellow-men. During a temporary residence
in Philadelphia, in the summer of 1838, the
quiet and beautiful scenery around the ancient
village of Frankford frequently attracted me
from the heat and bustle of the city. I have
referred to my youthful acquaintance with his
writings in *Snow-Bound*.

How bland and sweet the greeting of this
      breeze
    To him who flies
From crowded street and red wall's weary
      gleam,
Till far behind him like a hideous dream
    The close dark city lies !

Here, while the market murmurs, while men
      throng
    The marble floor
Of Mammon's altar, from the crush and din
Of the world's madness let me gather in
    My better thoughts once more.

Oh, once again revive, while on my ear
    The cry of Gain
And low hoarse hum of Traffic die away,
Ye blessed memories of my early day
    Like sere grass wet with rain !

Once more let God's green earth and sunset
      air
    Old feelings waken ;
Through weary years of toil and strife and
      ill,

Oh, let me feel that my good angel still
Hath not his trust forsaken.

And well do time and place befit my mood :
Beneath the arms
Of this embracing wood, a good man made
His home, like Abraham resting in the shade
Of Mamre's lonely palms.

Here, rich with autumn gifts of countless
years,
The virgin soil
Turned from the share he guided, and in
rain
And summer sunshine throve the fruits and
grain
Which blessed his honest toil.

Here, from his voyages on the stormy seas,
Weary and worn,
He came to meet his children and to bless
The Giver of all good in thankfulness
And praise for his return.

And here his neighbors gathered in to greet
Their friend again,
Safe from the wave and the destroying gales,
Which reap untimely green Bermuda's
vales,
And vex the Carib main.

To hear the good man tell of simple truth,
Sown in an hour
Of weakness in some far-off Indian isle,
From the parched bosom of a barren soil,
Raised up in life and power :

How at those gatherings in Barbadian vales,
A tendering love
Came o'er him, like the gentle rain from
heaven,
And words of fitness to his lips were given,
And strength as from above :

How the sad captive listened to the Word,
Until his chain
Grew lighter, and his wounded spirit felt
The healing balm of consolation melt
Upon its life-long pain :

How the armed warrior sat him down to hear
Of Peace and Truth,
And the proud ruler and his Creole dame,
Jewelled and gorgeous in her beauty came,
And fair and bright-eyed youth.

Oh, far away beneath New England's sky,
Even when a boy,
Following my plough by Merrimac's green
shore,
His simple record I have pondered o'er
With deep and quiet joy.

And hence this scene, in sunset glory
warm, —
Its woods around,
Its still stream winding on in light and
shade,
Its soft, green meadows and its upland
glade, —
To me is holy ground.

And dearer far than haunts where Genius
keeps
His vigils still ;
Than that where Avon's son of song is laid,
Or Vaucluse hallowed by its Petrarch's
shade,
Or Virgil's laurelled hill.

To the gray walls of fallen Paraclete,
To Juliet's urn,
Fair Arno and Sorrento's orange-grove,
Where Tasso sang, let young Romance and
Love
Like brother pilgrims turn.

But here a deeper and serener charm
To all is given ;
And blessed memories of the faithful dead
O'er wood and vale and meadow-stream
have shed
The holy hues of Heaven !

GONE

ANOTHER hand is beckoning us,
Another call is given ;
And glows once more with Angel-steps
The path which reaches Heaven.

Our young and gentle friend, whose smile
Made brighter summer hours,
Amid the frosts of autumn time
Has left us with the flowers.

No paling of the cheek of bloom
Forewarned us of decay ;
No shadow from the Silent Land
Fell round our sister's way.

The light of her young life went down,
As sinks behind the hill
The glory of a setting star,
Clear, suddenly, and still.

As pure and sweet, her fair brow seemed
Eternal as the sky ;
And like the brook's low song, her voice, —
A sound which could not die.

And half we deemed she needed not
The changing of her sphere,
To give to Heaven a Shining One,
Who walked an Angel here.

The blessing of her quiet life
Fell on us like the dew ;
And good thoughts where her footsteps
pressed
Like fairy blossoms grew.

Sweet promptings unto kindest deeds
Were in her very look ;
We read her face, as one who reads
A true and holy book :

The measure of a blessed hymn,
To which our hearts could move ;
The breathing of an inward psalm,
A canticle of love.

We miss her in the place of prayer,
And by the hearth-fire's light ;
We pause beside her door to hear
Once more her sweet "Good-night !"

There seems a shadow on the day,
Her smile no longer cheers ;
A dimness on the stars of night,
Like eyes that look through tears.

Alone unto our Father's will
One thought hath reconciled ;
That He whose love exceedeth ours
Hath taken home His child.

Fold her, O Father ! in Thine arms,
And let her henceforth be
A messenger of love between
Our human hearts and Thee.

Still let her mild rebuking stand
Between us and the wrong,
And her dear memory serve to make
Our faith in Goodness strong.

And grant that she who, trembling, here
Distrusted all her powers,
May welcome to her holier home
The well-beloved of ours.

TO RONGE

This was written after reading the powerful and manly protest of Johannes Ronge against the "pious fraud" of the Bishop of Treves. The bold movement of the young Catholic priest of Prussian Silesia seemed to me full of promise to the cause of political as well as religious liberty in Europe. That it failed was due partly to the faults of the reformer, but mainly to the disagreement of the Liberals of Germany upon a matter of dogma, which prevented them from unity of action. Ronge was born in Silesia in 1813 and died in October, 1887. His autobiography was translated into English and published in London in 1846.

STRIKE home, strong-hearted man ! Down
to the root
Of old oppression sink the Saxon steel.
Thy work is to hew down. In God's name
then
Put nerve into thy task. Let other men
Plant, as they may, that better tree whose
fruit
The wounded bosom of the Church shall
heal.
Be thou the image-breaker. Let thy blows
Fall heavy as the Suabian's iron hand,
On crown or crosier, which shall interpose
Between thee and the weal of Fatherland.
Leave creeds to closet idlers. First of all,
Shake thou all German dream-land with
the fall
Of that accursed tree, whose evil trunk
Was spared of old by Erfurt's stalwart
monk.
Fight not with ghosts and shadows. Let
us hear
The snap of chain-links. Let our gladdened
ear
Catch the pale prisoner's welcome, as the
light
Follows thy axe-stroke, through his cell of
night.
Be faithful to both worlds ; nor think to
feed
Earth's starving millions with the husks of
creed.
Servant of Him whose mission high and holy

Was to the wronged, the sorrowing, and the
    lowly,
Thrust not his Eden promise from our
    sphere,
Distant and dim beyond the blue sky's
    span ;
Like him of Patmos, see it, now and here,
The New Jerusalem comes down to man !
Be warned by Luther's error. Nor like
    him,
When the roused Teuton dashes from his
    limb
The rusted chain of ages, help to bind
His hands for whom thou claim'st the free-
    dom of the mind !

CHANNING

The last time I saw Dr. Channing was in the
summer of 1841, when, in company with my
English friend, Joseph Sturge, so well known
for his philanthropic labors and liberal political
opinions, I visited him in his summer residence
in Rhode Island. In recalling the impressions
of that visit, it can scarcely be necessary to say,
that I have no reference to the peculiar reli-
gious opinions of a man whose life, beautifully
and truly manifested above the atmosphere of
sect, is now the world's common legacy.

Not vainly did old poets tell,
  Nor vainly did old genius paint
God's great and crowning miracle,
  The hero and the saint !

For even in a faithless day
  Can we our sainted ones discern ;
And feel, while with them on the way,
  Our hearts within us burn.

And thus the common tongue and pen
  Which, world - wide, echo Channing's
    fame,
As one of Heaven's anointed men,
  Have sanctified his name.

In vain shall Rome her portals bar,
  And shut from him her saintly prize,
Whom, in the world's great calendar,
  All men shall canonize.

By Narragansett's sunny bay,
  Beneath his green embowering wood,
To me it seems but yesterday
  Since at his side I stood.

The slopes lay green with summer rains,
  The western wind blew fresh and free,
And glimmered down the orchard lanes
  The white surf of the sea.

With us was one, who, calm and true,
  Life's highest purpose understood,
And, like his blessed Master, knew
  The joy of doing good.

Unlearned, unknown to lettered fame,
  Yet on the lips of England's poor
And toiling millions dwelt his name,
  With blessings evermore.

Unknown to power or place, yet where
  The sun looks o'er the Carib sea,
It blended with the freeman's prayer
  And song of jubilee.

He told of England's sin and wrong,
  The ills her suffering children know,
The squalor of the city's throng,
  The green field's want and woe.

O'er Channing's face the tenderness
  Of sympathetic sorrow stole,
Like a still shadow, passionless,
  The sorrow of the soul.

But when the generous Briton told
  How hearts were answering to his own,
And Freedom's rising murmur rolled
  Up to the dull-eared throne,

I saw, methought, a glad surprise
  Thrill through that frail and pain-worn
    frame,
And, kindling in those deep, calm eyes,
  A still and earnest flame.

His few, brief words were such as move
  The human heart, — the Faith-sown seeds
Which ripen in the soil of love
  To high heroic deeds.

No bars of sect or clime were felt,
  The Babel strife of tongues had ceased,
And at one common altar knelt
  The Quaker and the priest.

And not in vain : with strength renewed,
  And zeal refreshed, and hope less dim,
For that brief meeting, each pursued
  The path allotted him.

How echoes yet each Western hill
    And vale with Channing's dying word !
How are the hearts of freemen still
    By that great warning stirred !

The stranger treads his native soil,
    And pleads, with zeal unfelt before,
The honest right of British toil,
    The claim of England's poor.

Before him time-wrought barriers fall,
    Old fears subside, old hatreds melt,
And, stretching o'er the sea's blue wall,
    The Saxon greets the Celt.

The yeoman on the Scottish lines,
    The Sheffield grinder, worn and grim,
The delver in the Cornwall mines,
    Look up with hope to him.

Swart smiters of the glowing steel,
    Dark feeders of the forge's flame,
Pale watchers at the loom and wheel,
    Repeat his honored name.

And thus the influence of that hour
    Of converse on Rhode Island's strand
Lives in the calm, resistless power
    Which moves our fatherland.

God blesses still the generous thought,
    And still the fitting word He speeds,
And Truth, at His requiring taught,
    He quickens into deeds.

Where is the victory of the grave ?
    What dust upon the spirit lies ?
God keeps the sacred life he gave, —
    The prophet never dies !

TO MY FRIEND ON THE DEATH
OF HIS SISTER

Sophia Sturge, sister of Joseph Sturge, of
Birmingham, the President of the British Com-
plete Suffrage Association, died in the 6th
month, 1845. She was the colleague, counsel-
lor, and ever-ready helpmate of her brother
in all his vast designs of beneficence. The
Birmingham Pilot says of her: "Never, per-
haps, were the active and passive virtues of
the human character more harmoniously and
beautifully blended than in this excellent wo-
man."

THINE is a grief, the depth of which an-
        other
    May never know ;
Yet, o'er the waters, O my stricken brother !
    To thee I go.

I lean my heart unto thee, sadly folding
    Thy hand in mine ;
With even the weakness of my soul uphold-
        ing
    The strength of thine.

I never knew, like thee, the dear departed;
    I stood not by
When, in calm trust, the pure and tranquil-
        hearted
    Lay down to die.

And on thy ears my words of weak condol-
        ing
    Must vainly fall :
The funeral bell which in thy heart is toll-
        ing,
    Sounds over all !

I will not mock thee with the poor world's
        common
    And heartless phrase,
Nor wrong the memory of a sainted woman
    With idle praise.

With silence only as their benediction,
    God's angels come
Where, in the shadow of a great affliction,
    The soul sits dumb !

Yet, would I say what thy own heart ap-
        proveth :
    Our Father's will,
Calling to Him the dear one whom He lov-
        eth,
    Is mercy still.

Not upon thee or thine the solemn angel
    Hath evil wrought :
Her funeral anthem is a glad evangel, —
    The good die not !

God calls our loved ones, but we lose not
        wholly
    What He hath given ;
They live on earth, in thought and deed, as
        truly
    As in His heaven.

And she is with thee ; in thy path of trial
　　She walketh yet ;
Still with the baptism of thy self-denial
　　Her locks are wet.

Up, then, my brother ! Lo, the fields of
　　harvest
Lie white in view !
She lives and loves thee, and the God thou
　　servest
　　To both is true.

Thrust in thy sickle ! England's toilworn
　　peasants
　　Thy call abide ;
And she thou mourn'st, a pure and holy
　　presence,
　　Shall glean beside !

DANIEL WHEELER

Daniel Wheeler, a minister of the Society of
Friends, who had labored in the cause of his
Divine Master in Great Britain, Russia, and
the islands of the Pacific, died in New York in
the spring of 1840, while on a religious visit to
this country.

O DEARLY loved !
And worthy of our love ! No more
Thy aged form shall rise before
The hushed and waiting worshipper,
In meek obedience utterance giving
To words of truth, so fresh and living,
That, even to the inward sense,
They bore unquestioned evidence
Of an anointed Messenger !
Or, bowing down thy silver hair
In reverent awfulness of prayer,
　　The world, its time and sense, shut out,
The brightness of Faith's holy trance
Gathered upon thy countenance,
　　As if each lingering cloud of doubt,
The cold, dark shadows resting here
In Time's unluminous atmosphere,
　　Were lifted by an angel's hand,
And through them on thy spiritual eye
Shone down the blessedness on high,
　　The glory of the Better Land !

　　The oak has fallen !
While, meet for no good work, the vine
May yet its worthless branches twine,
Who knoweth not that with thee fell
A great man in our Israel ?

Fallen, while thy loins were girded still,
Thy feet with Zion's dews still wet,
And in thy hand retaining yet
The pilgrim's staff and scallop-shell !
Unharmed and safe, where, wild and free,
　　Across the Neva's cold morass
The breezes from the Frozen Sea
　　With winter's arrowy keenness pass ;
Or where the unwarning tropic gale
Smote to the waves thy tattered sail,
Or where the noon-hour's fervid heat
Against Tahiti's mountains beat ;
　　The same mysterious Hand which gave
　　Deliverance upon land and wave,
Tempered for thee the blasts which blew
　　Ladaga's frozen surface o'er,
And blessed for thee the baleful dew
　　Of evening upon Eimeo's shore,
Beneath this sunny heaven of ours,
Midst our soft airs and opening flowers
　　Hath given thee a grave !

　　His will be done,
Who seeth not as man, whose way
　　Is not as ours ! 'T is well with thee !
Nor anxious doubt nor dark dismay
Disquieted thy closing day,
But, evermore, thy soul could say,
　"My Father careth still for me !"
Called from thy hearth and home, — from
　　her,
　　The last bud on thy household tree,
The last dear one to minister
　　In duty and in love to thee,
From all which nature holdeth dear,
　　Feeble with years and worn with pain,
　　To seek our distant land again,
Bound in the spirit, yet unknowing
　　The things which should befall thee here,
　　Whether for labor or for death,
In childlike trust serenely going
　　To that last trial of thy faith !

　　Oh, far away,
Where never shines our Northern star
On that dark waste which Balboa saw
From Darien's mountains stretching far,
So strange, heaven-broad, and lone, that
　　there,
With forehead to its damp wind bare,
　　He bent his mailèd knee in awe ;
In many an isle whose coral feet
The surges of that ocean beat,
In thy palm shadows, Oahu,
　　And Honolulu's silver bay,

Amidst Owyhee's hills of blue,
  And taro-plains of Tooboonai,
Are gentle hearts, which long shall be
Sad as our own at thought of thee,
Worn sowers of Truth's holy seed,
Whose souls in weariness and need
    Were strengthened and refreshed by
        thine.
For blessëd by our Father's hand
  Was thy deep love and tender care,
  Thy ministry and fervent prayer, —
Grateful as Eshcol's clustered vine
To Israel in a weary land !

          And they who drew
By thousands round thee, in the hour
  Of prayerful waiting, hushed and deep,
  That He who bade the islands keep
Silence before Him, might renew
    Their strength with His unslumbering
        power,
They too shall mourn that thou art gone,
  That nevermore thy aged lip
Shall soothe the weak, the erring warn,
Of those who first, rejoicing, heard
Through thee the Gospel's glorious word, —
  Seals of thy true apostleship.
And, if the brightest diadem,
  Whose gems of glory purely burn
  Around the ransomed ones in bliss,
Be evermore reserved for them
    Who here, through toil and sorrow,
        turn
    Many to righteousness,
May we not think of thee as wearing
That star-like crown of light, and bear-
        ing,
Amidst Heaven's white and blissful band,
Th' unfading palm-branch in thy hand ;
And joining with a seraph's tongue
In that new song the elders sung,
Ascribing to its blessed Giver
Thanksgiving, love, and praise forever !

          Farewell !
And though the ways of Zion mourn
When her strong ones are called away,
Who like thyself have calmly borne
The heat and burden of the day,
Yet He who slumbereth not nor sleepeth
His ancient watch around us keepeth ;
Still, sent from His creating hand,
New witnesses for Truth shall stand,
New instruments to sound abroad
The Gospel of a risen Lord ;

To gather to the fold once more
The desolate and gone astray,
The scattered of a cloudy day,
  And Zion's broken walls restore ;
And, through the travail and the toil
  Of true obedience, minister
Beauty for ashes, and the oil
  Of joy for mourning, unto her !
So shall her holy bounds increase
With walls of praise and gates of peace :
So shall the Vine, which martyr tears
And blood sustained in other years,
  With fresher life be clothed upon ;
And to the world in beauty show
Like the rose-plant of Jericho,
  And glorious as Lebanon !

TO FREDRIKA BREMER

It is proper to say that these lines are the
joint impromptus of my sister and myself. They
are inserted here as an expression of our admira-
tion of the gifted stranger whom we have since
learned to love as a friend.

SEERESS of the misty Norland,
  Daughter of the Vikings bold,
Welcome to the sunny Vineland,
  Which thy fathers sought of old !

Soft as flow of Silja's waters,
  When the moon of summer shines,
Strong as Winter from his mountains
  Roaring through the sleeted pines.

Heart and ear, we long have listened
  To thy saga, rune, and song ;
As a household joy and presence
  We have known and loved thee long.

By the mansion's marble mantel,
  Round the log-walled cabin's hearth,
Thy sweet thoughts and northern fancies
  Meet and mingle with our mirth.

And o'er weary spirits keeping
  Sorrow's night-watch, long and chill,
Shine they like thy sun of summer
  Over midnight vale and hill.

We alone to thee are strangers,
  Thou our friend and teacher art ;
Come, and know us as we know thee ;
  Let us meet thee heart to heart !

To our homes and household altars
 We, in turn, thy steps would lead,
As thy loving hand has led us
 O'er the threshold of the Swede.

TO AVIS KEENE

ON RECEIVING A BASKET OF SEA-MOSSES

THANKS for thy gift
 Of ocean flowers,
Born where the golden drift
 Of the slant sunshine falls
Down the green, tremulous walls
Of water, to the cool, still coral bowers,
Where, under rainbows of perpetual
 showers,
 God's gardens of the deep
 His patient angels keep ;
Gladdening the dim, strange solitude
 With fairest forms and hues, and thus
 Forever teaching us
The lesson which the many-colored skies,
The flowers, and leaves, and painted butter-
 flies,
The deer's branched antlers, the gay bird
 that flings
The tropic sunshine from its golden wings,
The brightness of the human countenance,
Its play of smiles, the magic of a glance,
 Forevermore repeat,
 In varied tones and sweet,
That beauty, in and of itself, is good.

O kind and generous friend, o'er whom
 The sunset hues of Time are cast,
 Painting, upon the overpast
 And scattered clouds of noonday sorrow
 The promise of a fairer morrow,
An earnest of the better life to come ;
 The binding of the spirit broken,
 The warning to the erring spoken,
 The comfort of the sad,
 The eye to see, the hand to cull
 Of common things the beautiful,
 The absent heart made glad
By simple gift or graceful token
Of love it needs as daily food,
All own one Source, and all are good !
Hence, tracking sunny cove and reach,
Where spent waves glimmer up the
 beach,
And toss their gifts of weed and shell
From foamy curve and combing swell,

No unbefitting task was thine
 To weave these flowers so soft and
 fair
In unison with His design
 Who loveth beauty everywhere ;
And makes in every zone and clime,
 In ocean and in upper air,
" All things beautiful in their time."

For not alone in tones of awe and power
 He speaks to man ;
The cloudy horror of the thunder-shower
 His rainbows span ;
 And where the caravan
Winds o'er the desert, leaving, as in air
The crane-flock leaves, no trace of passage
 there,
 He gives the weary eye
The palm-leaf shadow for the hot noon
 hours,
 And on its branches dry
Calls out the acacia's flowers ;
And where the dark shaft pierces down
 Beneath the mountain roots,
Seen by the miner's lamp alone,
 The star-like crystal shoots ;
 So, where, the winds and waves below,
 The coral-branchèd gardens grow,
 His climbing weeds and mosses show,
 Like foliage, on each stony bough,
 Of varied hues more strangely gay
 Than forest leaves in autumn's day ; —
 Thus evermore,
 On sky, and wave, and shore,
 An all-pervading beauty seems to say :
 God's love and power are one ; and
 they,
 Who, like the thunder of a sultry day,
 Smite to restore,
And they, who, like the gentle wind, uplift
The petals of the dew-wet flowers, and drift
 Their perfume on the air,
Alike may serve Him, each, with their own
 gift,
 Making their lives a prayer !

THE HILL-TOP

THE burly driver at my side,
 We slowly climbed the hill,
Whose summit, in the hot noontide,
 Seemed rising, rising still.
At last, our short noon-shadows hid
 The top-stone, bare and brown,

From whence, like Gizeh's pyramid,
  The rough mass slanted down.

I felt the cool breath of the North ;
  Between me and the sun,
O'er deep, still lake, and ridgy earth,
  I saw the cloud-shades run.
Before me, stretched for glistening miles,
  Lay mountain-girdled Squam ;
Like green-winged birds, the leafy isles
  Upon its bosom swam.

And, glimmering through the sun-haze
      warm,
  Far as the eye could roam,
Dark billows of an earthquake storm
  Beflecked with clouds like foam,
Their vales in misty shadow deep,
  Their rugged peaks in shine,
I saw the mountain ranges sweep
  The horizon's northern line.

There towered Chocorua's peak ; and west,
  Moosehillock's woods were seen,
With many a nameless slide-scarred crest
  And pine-dark gorge between.
Beyond them, like a sun-rimmed cloud,
  The great Notch mountains shone,
Watched over by the solemn-browed
  And awful face of stone !

" A good look-off ! " the driver spake :
  " About this time last year,
I drove a party to the Lake,
  And stopped, at evening, here.
'T was duskish down below ; but all
  These hills stood in the sun,
Till, dipped behind yon purple wall,
  He left them, one by one.

" A lady, who, from Thornton hill,
  Had held her place outside,
And, as a pleasant woman will,
  Had cheered the long, dull ride,
Besought me, with so sweet a smile,
  That — though I hate delays —
I could not choose but rest awhile, —
  (These women have such ways !)

" On yonder mossy ledge she sat,
  Her sketch upon her knees,
A stray brown lock beneath her hat
  Unrolling in the breeze ;
Her sweet face, in the sunset light

Upraised and glorified, —
I never saw a prettier sight
  In all my mountain ride.

" As good as fair ; it seemed her joy
  To comfort and to give ;
My poor, sick wife, and cripple boy,
  Will bless her while they live ! "
The tremor in the driver's tone
  His manhood did not shame :
" I dare say, sir, you may have known " —
  He named a well-known name.

Then sank the pyramidal mounds,
  The blue lake fled away ;
For mountain-scope a parlor's bounds,
  A lighted hearth for day !
From lonely years and weary miles
  The shadows fell apart ;
Kind voices cheered, sweet human smiles
  Shone warm into my heart.

We journeyed on ; but earth and sky
  Had power to charm no more ;
Still dreamed my inward-turning eye
  The dream of memory o'er.
Ah ! human kindness, human love, —
  To few who seek denied ;
Too late we learn to prize above
  The whole round world beside !

ELLIOTT

Ebenezer Elliott was to the artisans of Eng-
land what Burns was to the peasantry of Scot-
land. His *Corn-law Rhymes* contributed not a
little to that overwhelming tide of popular
opinion and feeling which resulted in the repeal
of the tax on bread. Well has the eloquent
author of *The Reforms and Reformers of Great
Britain* said of him, " Not corn-law repealers
alone, but all Britons who moisten their scanty
bread with the sweat of the brow, are largely
indebted to his inspiring lay, for the mighty
bound which the laboring mind of England
has taken in our day."

HANDS off ! thou tithe-fat plunderer ! play
  No trick of priestcraft here !
Back, puny lordling ! darest thou lay
  A hand on Elliott's bier ?
Alive, your rank and pomp, as dust,
  Beneath his feet he trod :
He knew the locust swarm that cursed
  The harvest-fields of God.

On these pale lips, the smothered thought
  Which England's millions feel.
A fierce and fearful splendor caught,
  As from his forge the steel.
Strong-armed as Thor, a shower of fire
  His smitten anvil flung ;
God's curse, Earth's wrong, dumb Hunger's
    ire,
  He gave them all a tongue !

Then let the poor man's horny hands
  Bear up the mighty dead,
And labor's swart and stalwart bands
  Behind as mourners tread.
Leave cant and craft their baptized bounds,
  Leave rank its minster floor ;
Give England's green and daisied grounds
  The poet of the poor !

Lay down upon his Sheaf's green verge
  That brave old heart of oak,
With fitting dirge from sounding forge,
  And pall of furnace smoke !
Where whirls the stone its dizzy rounds,
  And axe and sledge are swung,
And, timing to their stormy sounds,
  His stormy lays are sung.

There let the peasant's step be heard,
  The grinder chant his rhyme ;
Nor patron's praise nor dainty word
  Befits the man or time.
No soft lament nor dreamer's sigh
  For him whose words were bread ;
The Runic rhyme and spell whereby
  The foodless poor were fed !

Pile up the tombs of rank and pride,
  O England, as thou wilt !
With pomp to nameless worth denied,
  Emblazon titled guilt !
No part or lot in these we claim ;
  But, o'er the sounding wave,
A common right to Elliott's name,
  A freehold in his grave !

ICHABOD

This poem was the outcome of the surprise
and grief and forecast of evil consequences
which I felt on reading the seventh of March
speech of Daniel Webster in support of the
"compromise," and the Fugitive Slave Law.
No partisan or personal enmity dictated it.
On the contrary my admiration of the splendid
personality and intellectual power of the great
Senator was never stronger than when I laid
down his speech, and, in one of the saddest
moments of my life, penned my protest. I
saw, as I wrote, with painful clearness its sure
results, — the Slave Power arrogant and defi-
ant, strengthened and encouraged to carry out
its scheme for the extension of its baleful sys-
tem, or the dissolution of the Union, the guar-
anties of personal liberty in the free States
broken down, and the whole country made the
hunting-ground of slave-catchers. In the hor-
ror of such a vision, so soon fearfully fulfilled,
if one spoke at all, he could only speak in tones
of stern and sorrowful rebuke.

But death softens all resentments, and the
consciousness of a common inheritance of frail-
ty and weakness modifies the severity of
judgment. Years after, in *The Lost Occasion*,
I gave utterance to an almost universal regret
that the great statesman did not live to see the
flag which he loved trampled under the feet of
Slavery, and, in view of this desecration, make
his last days glorious in defence of " Liberty
and Union, one and inseparable."

So fallen ! so lost ! the light withdrawn
  Which once he wore !
The glory from his gray hairs gone
  Forevermore !

Revile him not, the Tempter hath
  A snare for all ;
And pitying tears, not scorn and wrath,
  Befit his fall !

Oh, dumb be passion's stormy rage,
  When he who might
Have lighted up and led his age,
  Falls back in night.

Scorn ! would the angels laugh, to mark
  A bright soul driven,
Fiend-goaded, down the endless dark,
  From hope and heaven !

Let not the land once proud of him
  Insult him now,
Nor brand with deeper shame his dim,
  Dishonored brow.

But let its humbled sons, instead,
  From sea to lake,
A long lament, as for the dead,
  In sadness make.

Of all we loved and honored, naught
  Save power remains ;

A fallen angel's pride of thought,
  Still strong in chains.

All else is gone ; from those great eyes
  The soul has fled :
When faith is lost, when honor dies,
  The man is dead !

Then, pay the reverence of old days
  To his dead fame ;
Walk backward, with averted gaze,
  And hide the shame !

THE LOST OCCASION

Some die too late and some too soon,
At early morning, heat of noon,
Or the chill evening twilight. Thou,
Whom the rich heavens did so endow
With eyes of power and Jove's own
    brow,
With all the massive strength that fills
Thy home-horizon's granite hills,
With rarest gifts of heart and head
From manliest stock inherited,
New England's stateliest type of man,
In port and speech Olympian ;
Whom no one met, at first, but took
A second awed and wondering look
(As turned, perchance, the eyes of Greece
On Phidias' unveiled masterpiece) ;
Whose words in simplest homespun clad,
The Saxon strength of Cædmon's had,
With power reserved at need to reach
The Roman forum's loftiest speech,
Sweet with persuasion, eloquent
In passion, cool in argument,
Or, ponderous, falling on thy foes
As fell the Norse god's hammer blows,
Crushing as if with Talus' flail
Through Error's logic-woven mail,
And failing only when they tried
The adamant of the righteous side, —
Thou, foiled in aim and hope, bereaved
Of old friends, by the new deceived,
Too soon for us, too soon for thee,
Beside thy lonely Northern sea,
Where long and low the marsh-lands spread,
Laid wearily down thy august head.

Thou shouldst have lived to feel below
Thy feet Disunion's fierce upthrow ;

The late-sprung mine that underlaid
Thy sad concessions vainly made.
Thou shouldst have seen from Sumter's
    wall
The star-flag of the Union fall,
And armed rebellion pressing on
The broken lines of Washington !
No stronger voice than thine had then
Called out the utmost might of men,
To make the Union's charter free
And strengthen law by liberty.
How had that stern arbitrament
To thy gray age youth's vigor lent,
Shaming ambition's paltry prize
Before thy disillusioned eyes ;
Breaking the spell about thee wound
Like the green withes that Samson
    bound ;
Redeeming in one effort grand,
Thyself and thy imperilled land !
Ah, cruel fate, that closed to thee,
O sleeper by the Northern sea,
The gates of opportunity !
God fills the gaps of human need,
Each crisis brings its word and deed.
Wise men and strong we did not lack ;
But still, with memory turning back,
In the dark hours we thought of thee,
And thy lone grave beside the sea.

Above that grave the east winds blow,
And from the marsh-lands drifting slow
The sea-fog comes, with evermore
The wave-wash of a lonely shore,
And sea-bird's melancholy cry,
As Nature fain would typify
The sadness of a closing scene,
The loss of that which should have been.
But, where thy native mountains bare
Their foreheads to diviner air,
Fit emblem of enduring fame,
One lofty summit keeps thy name.
For thee the cosmic forces did
The rearing of that pyramid,
The prescient ages shaping with
Fire, flood, and frost thy monolith.
Sunrise and sunset lay thereon
With hands of light their benison,
The stars of midnight pause to set
Their jewels in its coronet.
And evermore that mountain mass
Seems climbing from the shadowy pass
To light, as if to manifest
Thy nobler self, thy life at best !

WORDSWORTH

WRITTEN ON A BLANK LEAF OF HIS
MEMOIRS

DEAR friends, who read the world aright,
   And in its common forms discern
A beauty and a harmony
   The many never learn !

Kindred in soul of him who found
   In simple flower and leaf and stone
The impulse of the sweetest lays
   Our Saxon tongue has known, —

Accept this record of a life
   As sweet and pure, as calm and good.
As a long day of blandest June
   In green field and in wood.

How welcome to our ears, long pained
   By strife of sect and party noise,
The brook-like murmur of his song
   Of nature's simple joys !

The violet by its mossy stone,
   The primrose by the river's brim,
And chance-sown daffodil, have found
   Immortal life through him.

The sunrise on his breezy lake,
   The rosy tints his sunset brought,
World-seen, are gladdening all the vales
   And mountain-peaks of thought.

Art builds on sand ; the works of pride
   And human passion change and fall ;
But that which shares the life of God
   With Him surviveth all.

TO ——

LINES WRITTEN AFTER A SUMMER DAY'S
EXCURSION

FAIR Nature's priestesses ! to whom,
In hieroglyph of bud and bloom,
   Her mysteries are told ;
Who, wise in lore of wood and mead,
The seasons' pictured scrolls can read,
   In lessons manifold !

Thanks for the courtesy, and gay
Good-humor, which on Washing Day
   Our ill-timed visit bore ;

Thanks for your graceful oars, which broke
The morning dreams of Artichoke,
   Along his wooded shore !

Varied as varying Nature's ways,
Sprites of the river, woodland fays,
   Or mountain nymphs, ye seem ;
Free-limbed Dianas on the green,
Loch Katrine's Ellen, or Undine,
   Upon your favorite stream.

The forms of which the poets told,
The fair benignities of old,
   Were doubtless such as you ;
What more than Artichoke the rill
Of Helicon ?   Than Pipe-stave hill
   Arcadia's mountain-view ?

No sweeter bowers the bee delayed,
In wild Hymettus' scented shade,
   Than those you dwell among ;
Snow-flowered azaleas, intertwined
With roses, over banks inclined
   With trembling harebells hung !

A charmèd life unknown to death,
Immortal freshness Nature hath ;
   Her fabled fount and glen
Are now and here : Dodona's shrine
Still murmurs in the wind-swept pine, —
   All is that e'er hath been.

The Beauty which old Greece or Rome
Sung, painted, wrought, lies close at home ;
   We need but eye and ear
In all our daily walks to trace
The outlines of incarnate grace,
   The hymns of gods to hear !

IN PEACE

A TRACK of moonlight on a quiet lake,
   Whose small waves on a silver-sanded
      shore
Whisper of peace, and with the low winds
      make
Such harmonies as keep the woods awake,
And listening all night long for their sweet
      sake ;
   A green-waved slope of meadow, hovered
      o'er
By angel-troops of lilies, swaying light
On viewless stems, with folded wings of
      white ;

A slumberous stretch of mountain-land, far
    seen
Where the low westering day, with gold
    and green,
Purple and amber, softly blended, fills
The wooded vales, and melts among the
    hills ;
A vine-fringed river, winding to its rest
  On the calm bosom of a stormless sea,
Bearing alike upon its placid breast,
With earthly flowers and heavenly stars im-
    pressed,
  The hues of time and of eternity :
Such are the pictures which the thought of
    thee,
O friend, awakeneth, — charming the keen
    pain
Of thy departure, and our sense of loss
Requiting with the fullness of thy gain.
  Lo ! on the quiet grave thy life-borne
    cross,
Dropped only at its side, methinks doth
    shine,
Of thy beatitude the radiant sign !
  No sob of grief, no wild lament be there,
  To break the Sabbath of the holy air ;
But, in their stead, the silent-breathing
    prayer
Of hearts still waiting for a rest like thine.
O spirit redeemed ! Forgive us, if hence-
    forth,
With sweet and pure similitudes of earth,
  We keep thy pleasant memory freshly
    green,
Of love's inheritance a priceless part,
  Which Fancy's self, in reverent awe, is
    seen
To paint, forgetful of the tricks of art,
  With pencil dipped alone in colors of the
    heart.

BENEDICITE

God's love and peace be with thee, where
Soe'er this soft autumnal air
Lifts the dark tresses of thy hair !

Whether through city casements comes
Its kiss to thee, in crowded rooms,
Or, out among the woodland blooms,

It freshens o'er thy thoughtful face,
Imparting, in its glad embrace,
Beauty to beauty, grace to grace !

Fair Nature's book together read,
The old wood-paths that knew our tread,
The maple shadows overhead, —

The hills we climbed, the river seen
By gleams along its deep ravine, —
All keep thy memory fresh and green.

Where'er I look, where'er I stray,
Thy thought goes with me on my way,
And hence the prayer I breathe to-day ;

O'er lapse of time and change of scene,
The weary waste which lies between
Thyself and me, my heart I lean.

Thou lack'st not Friendship's spell-word,
    nor
The half-unconscious power to draw
All hearts to thine by Love's sweet law.

With these good gifts of God is cast
Thy lot, and many a charm thou hast
To hold the blessed angels fast.

If, then, a fervent wish for thee
The gracious heavens will heed from me,
What should, dear heart, its burden be ?

The sighing of a shaken reed, —
What can I more than meekly plead
The greatness of our common need ?

God's love, — unchanging, pure, and true, —
The Paraclete white-shining through
His peace, — the fall of Hermon's dew !

With such a prayer, on this sweet day,
As thou mayst hear and I may say,
I greet thee, dearest, far away !

KOSSUTH

It can scarcely be necessary to say that there
are elements in the character and passages in
the history of the great Hungarian statesman
and orator, which necessarily command the ad-
miration of those, even, who believe that no
political revolution was ever worth the price of
human blood.

Type of two mighty continents ! — com-
    bining
  The strength of Europe with the warmth
    and glow

Of Asian song and prophecy, — the shining
Of Orient splendors over Northern snow !
Who shall receive him ?　Who, unblush-
　　ing, speak
Welcome to him, who, while he strove to
　　break
The Austrian yoke from Magyar necks,
　　smote off
At the same blow the fetters of the serf,
Rearing the altar of his Fatherland
　　On the firm base of freedom, and thereby
Lifting to Heaven a patriot's stainless hand,
　　Mocked not the God of Justice with a
　　lie !
Who shall be Freedom's mouthpiece ?　Who
　　shall give
Her welcoming cheer to the great fugitive ?
Not he who, all her sacred trusts betray-
　　ing,
　　Is scourging back to slavery's hell of pain
The swarthy Kossuths of our land again !
Not he whose utterance now from lips de-
　　signed
The bugle-march of Liberty to wind,
And call her hosts beneath the breaking
　　light,
The keen reveille of her morn of fight,
　　Is but the hoarse note of the blood-
　　hound's baying,
The wolf's long howl behind the bondman's
　　flight !
Oh for the tongue of him who lies at rest
　　In Quincy's shade of patrimonial trees,
Last of the Puritan tribunes and the best,
　　To lend a voice to Freedom's sympa-
　　thies,
And hail the coming of the noblest guest
The Old World's wrong has given the New
　　World of the West !

TO MY OLD SCHOOLMASTER

AN EPISTLE NOT AFTER THE MANNER OF HORACE

These lines were addressed to my worthy
friend Joshua Coffin, teacher, historian, and an-
tiquarian. He was one of the twelve persons
who with William Lloyd Garrison formed the
first anti-slavery society in New England.

OLD friend, kind friend ! lightly down
Drop time's snow-flakes on thy crown !
Never be thy shadow less,

Never fail thy cheerfulness ;
Care, that kills the cat, may plough
Wrinkles in the miser's brow,
Deepen envy's spiteful frown,
Draw the mouths of bigots down,
Plague ambition's dream, and sit
Heavy on the hypocrite,
Haunt the rich man's door, and ride
In the gilded coach of pride ; —
Let the fiend pass ! — what can he
Find to do with such as thee ?
Seldom comes that evil guest
Where the conscience lies at rest,
And brown health and quiet wit
Smiling on the threshold sit.

I, the urchin unto whom,
In that smoked and dingy room,
Where the district gave thee rule
O'er its ragged winter school,
Thou didst teach the mysteries
Of those weary A B C's, —
Where, to fill the every pause
Of thy wise and learned saws,
Through the cracked and crazy wall
Came the cradle-rock and squall,
And the goodman's voice, at strife
With his shrill and tipsy wife, —
Luring us by stories old,
With a comic unction told,
More than by the eloquence
Of terse birchen arguments
(Doubtful gain, I fear), to look
With complacence on a book ! —
Where the genial pedagogue
Half forgot his rogues to flog,
Citing tale or apologue,
Wise and merry in its drift
As was Phædrus' twofold gift,
Had the little rebels known it,
Risum et prudentiam monet !
I, — the man of middle years,
In whose sable locks appears
Many a warning fleck of gray, —
Looking back to that far day,
And thy primal lessons, feel
Grateful smiles my lips unseal,
As, remembering thee, I blend
Olden teacher, present friend,
Wise with antiquarian search,
In the scrolls of State and Church :
Named on history's title-page,
Parish-clerk and justice sage ;
For the ferule's wholesome awe
Wielding now the sword of law.

Threshing Time's neglected sheaves,
Gathering up the scattered leaves
Which the wrinkled sibyl cast
Careless from her as she passed, —
Twofold citizen art thou,
Freeman of the past and now.
He who bore thy name of old
Midway in the heavens did hold
Over Gibeon moon and sun ;
Thou hast bidden them backward run ;
Of to-day the present ray
Flinging over yesterday !

Let the busy ones deride
What I deem of right thy pride :
Let the fools their treadmills grind,
Look not forward nor behind,
Shuffle in and wriggle out,
Veer with every breeze about,
Turning like a windmill sail,
Or a dog that seeks his tail ;
Let them laugh to see thee fast
Tabernacled in the Past,
Working out with eye and lip
Riddles of old penmanship,
Patient as Belzoni there
Sorting out, with loving care,
Mummies of dead questions stripped
From their sevenfold manuscript !

Dabbling, in their noisy way,
In the puddles of to-day,
Little know they of that vast
Solemn ocean of the past,
On whose margin, wreck-bespread,
Thou art walking with the dead,
Questioning the stranded years,
Waking smiles by turns, and tears,
As thou callest up again
Shapes the dust has long o'erlain, —
Fair-haired woman, bearded man,
Cavalier and Puritan ;
In an age whose eager view
Seeks but present things, and new,
Mad for party, sect and gold,
Teaching reverence for the old.

On that shore, with fowler's tact,
Coolly bagging fact on fact,
Naught amiss to thee can float,
Tale, or song, or anecdote ;
Village gossip, centuries old,
Scandals by our grandams told,
What the pilgrim's table spread,
Where he lived, and whom he wed,

Long-drawn bill of wine and beer
For his ordination cheer,
Or the flip that wellnigh made
Glad his funeral cavalcade ;
Weary prose, and poet's lines,
Flavored by their age, like wines,
Eulogistic of some quaint,
Doubtful, Puritanic saint ;
Lays that quickened husking jigs,
Jests that shook grave periwigs,
When the parson had his jokes
And his glass, like other folks ;
Sermons that, for mortal hours,
Taxed our fathers' vital powers,
As the long nineteenthlies poured
Downward from the sounding-board,
And, for fire of Pentecost,
Touched their beards December's frost.

Time is hastening on, and we
What our fathers are shall be, —
Shadow-shapes of memory !
Joined to that vast multitude
Where the great are but the good,
And the mind of strength shall prove
Weaker than the heart of love ;
Pride of graybeard wisdom less
Than the infant's guilelessness,
And his song of sorrow more
Than the crown the Psalmist wore !
Who shall then, with pious zeal,
At our moss-grown thresholds kneel,
From a stained and stony page
Reading to a careless age,
With a patient eye like thine,
Prosing tale and limping line,
Names and words the hoary rime
Of the Past has made sublime ?
Who shall work for us as well
The antiquarian's miracle ?
Who to seeming life recall
Teacher grave and pupil small ?
Who shall give to thee and me
Freeholds in futurity ?

Well, whatever lot be mine,
Long and happy days be thine,
Ere thy full and honored age
Dates of time its latest page !
Squire for master, State for school,
Wisely lenient, live and rule ;
Over grown-up knave and rogue
Play the watchful pedagogue ;
Or, while pleasure smiles on duty,
At the call of youth and beauty,

Speak for them the spell of law
Which shall bar and bolt withdraw,
And the flaming sword remove
From the Paradise of Love.
Still, with undimmed eyesight, pore
Ancient tome and record o'er ;
Still thy week-day lyrics croon,
Pitch in church the Sunday tune,
Showing something, in thy part,
Of the old Puritanic art,
Singer after Sternhold's heart !
In thy pew, for many a year,
Homilies from Oldbug hear,
Who to wit like that of South,
And the Syrian's golden mouth,
Doth the homely pathos add
Which the pilgrim preachers had ;
Breaking, like a child at play,
Gilded idols of the day,
Cant of knave and pomp of fool
Tossing with his ridicule,
Yet, in earnest or in jest,
Ever keeping truth abreast.
And, when thou art called, at last,
To thy townsmen of the past,
Not as stranger shalt thou come ;
Thou shalt find thyself at home
With the little and the big,
Woollen cap and periwig,
Madam in her high-laced ruff,
Goody in her home-made stuff, —
Wise and simple, rich and poor,
Thou hast known them all before !

THE CROSS

Richard Dillingham, a young member of the
Society of Friends, died in the Nashville peni-
tentiary, where he was confined for the act of
aiding the escape of fugitive slaves.

"The cross, if rightly borne, shall be
No burden, but support to thee ; "
So, moved of old time for our sake,
The holy monk of Kempen spake.

Thou brave and true one ! upon whom
Was laid the cross of martyrdom,
How didst thou, in thy generous youth,
Bear witness to this blessed truth !

Thy cross of suffering and of shame
A staff within thy hands became,

In paths where faith alone could see
The Master's steps supporting thee.

Thine was the seed-time ; God alone
Beholds the end of what is sown ;
Beyond our vision, weak and dim,
The harvest-time is hid with Him.

Yet, unforgotten where it lies,
That seed of generous sacrifice,
Though seeming on the desert cast,
Shall rise with bloom and fruit at last.

THE HERO

The hero of the incident related in this poem
was Dr. Samuel Gridley Howe, the well-known
philanthropist, who when a young man volun-
teered his aid in the Greek struggle for inde-
pendence.

"Oh for a knight like Bayard,
    Without reproach or fear ;
My light glove on his casque of steel,
    My love-knot on his spear !

"Oh for the white plume floating
    Sad Zutphen's field above, —
The lion heart in battle,
    The woman's heart in love !

"Oh that man once more were manly,
    Woman's pride, and not her scorn :
That once more the pale young mother
    Dared to boast 'a man is born' !

"But now life's slumberous current
    No sun-bowed cascade wakes ;
No tall, heroic manhood
    The level dulness breaks.

"Oh for a knight like Bayard,
    Without reproach or fear !
My light glove on his casque of steel,
    My love-knot on his spear ! "

Then I said, my own heart throbbing
    To the time her proud pulse beat,
"Life hath its regal natures yet,
    True, tender, brave, and sweet !

"Smile not, fair unbeliever !
    One man, at least, I know,
Who might wear the crest of Bayard
    Or Sidney's plume of snow.

"Once, when over purple mountains
Died away the Grecian sun,
And the far Cyllenian ranges
Paled and darkened, one by one, —

"Fell the Turk, a bolt of thunder,
Cleaving all the quiet sky,
And against his sharp steel lightnings
Stood the Suliote but to die.

"Woe for the weak and halting !
The crescent blazed behind
A curving line of sabres,
Like fire before the wind !

"Last to fly, and first to rally,
Rode he of whom I speak,
When, groaning in his bridle-path,
Sank down a wounded Greek.

"With the rich Albanian costume
Wet with many a ghastly stain,
Gazing on earth and sky as one
Who might not gaze again !

"He looked forward to the mountains,
Back on foes that never spare,
Then flung him from his saddle,
And placed the stranger there.

"'Allah ! hu !' Through flashing sabres,
Through a stormy hail of lead,
The good Thessalian charger
Up the slopes of olives sped.

"Hot spurred the turbaned riders ;
He almost felt their breath,
Where a mountain stream rolled darkly
    down
Between the hills and death.

"One brave and manful struggle, —
He gained the solid land,
And the cover of the mountains,
And the carbines of his band ! "

"It was very great and noble,"
Said the moist-eyed listener then,
"But one brave deed makes no hero ;
Tell me what he since hath been ! "

"Still a brave and generous manhood,
Still an honor without stain,
In the prison of the Kaiser,
By the barricades of Seine.

"But dream not helm and harness
The sign of valor true ;
Peace hath higher tests of manhood
Than battle ever knew.

"Wouldst know him now ?   Behold him,
The Cadmus of the blind,
Giving the dumb lip language,
The idiot-clay a mind.

"Walking his round of duty
Serenely day by day,
With the strong man's hand of labor
And childhood's heart of play.

"True as the knights of story,
Sir Lancelot and his peers,
Brave in his calm endurance
As they in tilt of spears.

"As waves in stillest waters,
As stars in noonday skies,
All that wakes to noble action
In his noon of calmness lies.

"Wherever outraged Nature
Asks word or action brave,
Wherever struggles labor,
Wherever groans a slave, —

"Wherever rise the peoples,
Wherever sinks a throne,
The throbbing heart of Freedom finds
An answer in his own.

"Knight of a better era,
Without reproach or fear !
Said I not well that Bayards
And Sidneys still are here ? "

RANTOUL

No more fitting inscription could be placed
on the tombstone of Robert Rantoul than this :
" He died at his post in Congress, and his last
words were a protest in the name of Democracy
against the Fugitive-Slave Law."

ONE day, along the electric wire
His manly word for Freedom sped ;
We came next morn : that tongue of fire
Said only, " He who spake is dead ! "

Dead ! while his voice was living yet,
In echoes round the pillared dome !

Dead ! while his blotted page lay wet
  With themes of state and loves of home !

Dead ! in that crowning grace of time,
  That triumph of life's zenith hour !
Dead ! while we watched his manhood's
    prime
  Break from the slow bud into flower !

Dead ! he so great, and strong, and wise,
  While the mean thousands yet drew
    breath ;
How deepened, through that dread surprise,
  The mystery and the awe of death !

From the high place whereon our votes
  Had borne him, clear, calm, earnest, fell
His first words, like the prelude notes
  Of some great anthem yet to swell.

We seemed to see our flag unfurled,
  Our champion waiting in his place
For the last battle of the world,
  The Armageddon of the race.

Through him we hoped to speak the word
  Which wins the freedom of a land ;
And lift, for human right, the sword
  Which dropped from Hampden's dying
    hand.

For he had sat at Sidney's feet,
  And walked with Pym and Vane apart ;
And, through the centuries, felt the beat
  Of Freedom's march in Cromwell's
    heart.

He knew the paths the worthies held,
  Where England's best and wisest trod ;
And, lingering, drank the springs that
    welled
  Beneath the touch of Milton's rod.

No wild enthusiast of the right,
  Self-poised and clear, he showed alway
The coolness of his northern night,
  The ripe repose of autumn's day.

His steps were slow, yet forward still
  He pressed where others paused or failed ;
The calm star clomb with constant will,
  The restless meteor flashed and paled !

Skilled in its subtlest wile, he knew
  And owned the higher ends of Law ;

Still rose majestic on his view
  The awful Shape the schoolman saw.

Her home the heart of God ; her voice
  The choral harmonies whereby
The stars, through all their spheres, rejoice
  The rhythmic rule of earth and sky !

We saw his great powers misapplied
  To poor ambitions ; yet, through all,
We saw him take the weaker side,
  And right the wronged, and free the
    thrall.

Now, looking o'er the frozen North,
  For one like him in word and act,
To call her old, free spirit forth,
  And give her faith the life of fact, —

To break her party bonds of shame,
  And labor with the zeal of him
To make the Democratic name
  Of Liberty the synonyme, —

We sweep the land from hill to strand,
  We seek the strong, the wise, the brave,
And, sad of heart, return to stand
  In silence by a new-made grave !

There, where his breezy hills of home
  Look out upon his sail-white seas,
The sounds of winds and waters come,
  And shape themselves to words like
    these:

" Why, murmuring, mourn that he, whose
    power
  Was lent to Party over-long,
Heard the still whisper at the hour
  He set his foot on Party wrong ?

" The human life that closed so well
  No lapse of folly now can stain :
The lips whence Freedom's protest fell
  No meaner thought can now profane.

" Mightier than living voice his grave
  That lofty protest utters o'er ;
Through roaring wind and smiting wave
  It speaks his hate of wrong once more.

" Men of the North ! your weak regret
  Is wasted here ; arise and pay
To freedom and to him your debt,
  By following where he led the way ! "

WILLIAM FORSTER

William Forster, of Norwich, England, died
in East Tennessee, in the 1st month, 1854, while
engaged in presenting to the governors of the
States of this Union the address of his religious
society on the evils of slavery. He was the
relative and coadjutor of the Buxtons, Gurneys,
and Frys; and his whole life, extending almost
to threescore and ten years, was a pure and
beautiful example of Christian benevolence.
He had travelled over Europe, and visited most
of its sovereigns, to plead against the slave-
trade and slavery; and had twice before made
visits to this country, under impressions of re-
ligious duty. He was the father of the Right
Hon. William Edward Forster. He visited my
father's house in Haverhill during his first tour
in the United States.

THE years are many since his hand
  Was laid upon my head,
Too weak and young to understand
  The serious words he said.

Yet often now the good man's look
  Before me seems to swim,
As if some inward feeling took
  The outward guise of him.

As if, in passion's heated war,
  Or near temptation's charm,
Through him the low-voiced monitor
  Forewarned me of the harm.

Stranger and pilgrim! from that day
  Of meeting, first and last,
Wherever Duty's pathway lay,
  His reverent steps have passed.

The poor to feed, the lost to seek,
  To proffer life to death,
Hope to the erring, — to the weak
  The strength of his own faith.

To plead the captive's right; remove
  The sting of hate from Law;
And soften in the fire of love
  The hardened steel of War.

He walked the dark world, in the mild,
  Still guidance of the Light;
In tearful tenderness a child,
  A strong man in the right.

From what great perils, on his way,
  He found, in prayer, release;
Through what abysmal shadows lay
  His pathway unto peace,

God knoweth: we could only see
  The tranquil strength he gained;
The bondage lost in liberty,
  The fear in love unfeigned.

And I, — my youthful fancies grown
  The habit of the man,
Whose field of life by angels sown
  The wilding vines o'erran, —

Low bowed in silent gratitude,
  My manhood's heart enjoys
That reverence for the pure and good
  Which blessed the dreaming boy's.

Still shines the light of holy lives
  Like star-beams over doubt;
Each sainted memory, Christlike, drives
  Some dark possession out.

O friend! O brother! not in vain
  Thy life so calm and true,
The silver dropping of the rain,
  The fall of summer dew!

How many burdened hearts have prayed
  Their lives like thine might be!
But more shall pray henceforth for aid
  To lay them down like thee.

With weary hand, yet steadfast will,
  In old age as in youth,
Thy Master found thee sowing still
  The good seed of His truth.

As on thy task-field closed the day
  In golden-skied decline,
His angel met thee on the way,
  And lent his arm to thine.

Thy latest care for man, — thy last
  Of earthly thought a prayer, —
Oh, who thy mantle, backward cast,
  Is worthy now to wear?

Methinks the mound which marks thy bed
  Might bless our land and save,
As rose, of old, to life the dead
  Who touched the prophet's grave!

TO CHARLES SUMNER

IF I have seemed more prompt to censure
 wrong
  Than praise the right ; if seldom to thine
  ear
  My voice hath mingled with the exultant
  cheer
Borne upon all our Northern winds along ;
If I have failed to join the fickle throng
In wide-eyed wonder, that thou standest
 strong
In victory, surprised in thee to find
Brougham's scathing power with Canning's
 grace combined ;
That he, for whom the ninefold Muses
 sang,
From their twined arms a giant athlete
 sprang,
Barbing the arrows of his native tongue
With the spent shafts Latona's archer
 flung,
To smite the Python of our land and
 time,
Fell as the monster born of Crissa's slime,
Like the blind bard who in Castalian
 springs
Tempered the steel that clove the crest of
 kings,
And on the shrine of England's freedom
 laid
The gifts of Cumæ and of Delphi's shade, —
Small need hast thou of words of praise
 from me.
  Thou knowest my heart, dear friend, and
  well canst guess
  That, even though silent, I have not the
  less
Rejoiced to see thy actual life agree
With the large future which I shaped for
 thee,
When, years ago, beside the summer sea,
White in the moon, we saw the long waves
 fall
Baffled and broken from the rocky wall,
That, to the menace of the brawling flood,
Opposed alone its massive quietude,
Calm as a fate ; with not a leaf nor vine
Nor birch-spray trembling in the still
 moonshine,
Crowning it like God's peace. I sometimes
 think
  That night - scene by the sea prophet-
  ical

(For Nature speaks in symbols and in signs,
And through her pictures human fate
 divines),
That rock, wherefrom we saw the billows
 sink
  In murmuring rout, uprising clear and
  tall
In the white light of heaven, the type of
 one
Who, momently by Error's host assailed,
Stands strong as Truth, in greaves of
 granite mailed ;
And, tranquil-fronted, listening over all
The tumult, hears the angels say, Well
 done !

BURNS

ON RECEIVING A SPRIG OF HEATHER IN BLOSSOM

No more these simple flowers belong
 To Scottish maid and lover ;
Sown in the common soil of song,
 They bloom the wide world over.

In smiles and tears, in sun and showers,
 The minstrel and the heather,
The deathless singer and the flowers
 He sang of live together.

Wild heather-bells and Robert Burns !
 The moorland flower and peasant !
How, at their mention, memory turns
 Her pages old and pleasant !

The gray sky wears again its gold
 And purple of adorning,
And manhood's noonday shadows hold
 The dews of boyhood's morning.

The dews that washed the dust and soil
 From off the wings of pleasure,
The sky, that flecked the ground of toil
 With golden threads of leisure.

I call to mind the summer day,
 The early harvest mowing,
The sky with sun and clouds at play,
 And flowers with breezes blowing.

I hear the blackbird in the corn,
 The locust in the haying ;
And, like the fabled hunter's horn,
 Old tunes my heart is playing.

How oft that day, with fond delay,
　I sought the maple's shadow,
And sang with Burns the hours away,
　Forgetful of the meadow !

Bees hummed, birds twittered, overhead
　I heard the squirrels leaping,
The good dog listened while I read,
　And wagged his tail in keeping.

I watched him while in sportive mood
　I read " *The Twa Dogs'* " story,
And half believed he understood
　The poet's allegory.

Sweet day, sweet songs !　The golden hours
　Grew brighter for that singing,
From brook and bird and meadow flowers
　A dearer welcome bringing.

New light on home-seen Nature beamed,
　New glory over Woman ;
And daily life and duty seemed
　No longer poor and common.

I woke to find the simple truth
　Of fact and feeling better
Than all the dreams that held my youth
　A still repining debtor :

That Nature gives her handmaid, Art,
　The themes of sweet discoursing ;
The tender idyls of the heart
　In every tongue rehearsing.

Why dream of lands of gold and pearl,
　Of loving knight and lady,
When farmer boy and barefoot girl
　Were wandering there already ?

I saw through all familiar things
　The romance underlying ;
The joys and griefs that plume the wings
　Of Fancy skyward flying.

I saw the same blithe day return,
　The same sweet fall of even,
That rose on wooded Craigie-burn,
　And sank on crystal Devon.

I matched with Scotland's heathery hills
　The sweetbrier and the clover ;
With Ayr and Doon, my native rills,
　Their wood hymns chanting over.

O'er rank and pomp, as he had seen,
　I saw the Man uprising ;
No longer common or unclean,
　The child of God's baptizing !

With clearer eyes I saw the worth
　Of life among the lowly ;
The Bible at his Cotter's hearth
　Had made my own more holy.

And if at times an evil strain,
　To lawless love appealing,
Broke in upon the sweet refrain
　Of pure and healthful feeling,

It died upon the eye and ear,
　No inward answer gaining ;
No heart had I to see or hear
　The discord and the staining.

Let those who never erred forget
　His worth, in vain bewailings ;
Sweet Soul of Song !　I own my debt
　Uncancelled by his failings !

Lament who will the ribald line
　Which tells his lapse from duty,
How kissed the maddening lips of wine
　Or wanton ones of beauty ;

But think, while falls that shade between
　The erring one and Heaven,
That he who loved like Magdalen,
　Like her may be forgiven.

Not his the song whose thunderous chime
　Eternal echoes render ;
The mournful Tuscan's haunted rhyme,
　And Milton's starry splendor !

But who his human heart has laid
　To Nature's bosom nearer ?
Who sweetened toil like him, or paid
　To love a tribute dearer ?

Through all his tuneful art, how strong
　The human feeling gushes !
The very moonlight of his song
　Is warm with smiles and blushes !

Give lettered pomp to teeth of Time,
　So " Bonnie Doon " but tarry ;
Blot out the Epic's stately rhyme,
　But spare his Highland Mary !

TO GEORGE B. CHEEVER

So spake Esaias : so, in words of flame,
Tekoa's prophet-herdsman smote with
    blame
The traffickers in men, and put to shame,
    All earth and heaven before,
The sacerdotal robbers of the poor.

All the dread Scripture lives for thee again,
To smite like lightning on the hands profane
Lifted to bless the slave-whip and the chain.
    Once more the old Hebrew tongue
Bends with the shafts of God a bow new-
    strung !

Take up the mantle which the prophets
    wore ;
Warn with their warnings, show the Christ
    once more
Bound, scourged, and crucified in His
    blameless poor ;
    And shake above our land
The unquenched bolts 'hat blazed in Hosea's
    hand !

Not vainly shalt thou cast upon our years
The solemn burdens of the Orient seers,
And smite with truth a guilty nation's ears.
    Mightier was Luther's word
Than Seckingen's mailed arm or Hutton's
    sword !

TO JAMES T. FIELDS

ON A BLANK LEAF OF " POEMS PRINTED,
NOT PUBLISHED "

WELL thought ! who would not rather hear
    The songs to Love and Friendship sung
    Than those which move the stranger's
      tongue,
And feed his unselected ear ?

Our social joys are more than fame ;
    Life withers in the public look.
    Why mount the pillory of a book,
Or barter comfort for a name ?

Who in a house of glass would dwell,
    With curious eyes at every pane ?
    To ring him in and out again,
Who wants the public crier's bell ?

To see the angel in one's way,
    Who wants to play the ass's part, —
    Bear on his back the wizard Art,
And in his service speak or bray ?

And who his manly locks would shave,
    And quench the eyes of common sense,
    To share the noisy recompense
That mocked the shorn and blinded slave?

The heart has needs beyond the head,
    And, starving in the plenitude
    Of strange gifts, craves its common
      food, —
Our human nature's daily bread.

We are but men : no gods are we,
    To sit in mid-heaven, cold and bleak,
    Each separate, on his painful peak,
Thin-cloaked in self-complacency !

Better his lot whose axe is swung
    In Wartburg's woods, or that poor girl's
    Who by the Ilm her spindle whirls
And sings the songs that Luther sung,

Than his who, old, and cold, and vain,
    At Weimar sat, a demigod,
    And bowed with Jove's imperial nod
His votaries in and out again !

Ply, Vanity, thy wingèd feet !
    Ambition, hew thy rocky stair !
    Who envies him who feeds on air
The icy splendor of his seat ?

I see your Alps, above me, cut
    The dark, cold sky ; and dim and lone
    I see ye sitting, — stone on stone, —
With human senses dulled and shut.

I could not reach you, if I would,
    Nor sit among your cloudy shapes ;
    And (spare the fable of the grapes
And fox) I would not if I could.

Keep to your lofty pedestals !
    The safer plain below I choose :
    Who never wins can rarely lose,
Who never climbs as rarely falls.

Let such as love the eagle's scream
    Divide with him his home of ice :
    For me shall gentler notes suffice, —
The valley-song of bird and stream ;

The pastoral bleat, the drone of bees,
  The flail-beat chiming far away,
  The cattle-low, at shut of day,
The voice of God in leaf and breeze !

Then lend thy hand, my wiser friend,
  And help me to the vales below,
  (In truth, I have not far to go,)
Where sweet with flowers the fields extend.

THE MEMORY OF BURNS

Read at the Boston celebration of the hun-
dredth anniversary of the birth of Robert
Burns, 25th 1st mo., 1859. In my absence
these lines were read by Ralph Waldo Emerson.

How sweetly come the holy psalms
  From saints and martyrs down,
The waving of triumphal palms
  Above the thorny crown !
The choral praise, the chanted prayers
  From harps by angels strung,
The hunted Cameron's mountain airs,
  The hymns that Luther sung !

Yet, jarring not the heavenly notes,
  The sounds of earth are heard,
As through the open minster floats
  The song of breeze and bird !
Not less the wonder of the sky
  That daisies bloom below ;
The brook sings on, though loud and high
  The cloudy organs blow !

And, if the tender ear be jarred
  That, haply, hears by turns
The saintly harp of Olney's bard,
  The pastoral pipe of Burns,
No discord mars His perfect plan
  Who gave them both a tongue ;
For he who sings the love of man
  The love of God hath sung !

To-day be every fault forgiven
  Of him in whom we joy !
We take, with thanks, the gold of Heaven
  And leave the earth's alloy.
Be ours his music as of spring,
  His sweetness as of flowers,
The songs the bard himself might sing
  In holier ears than ours.

Sweet airs of love and home, the hum
  Of household melodies,
Come singing, as the robins come
  To sing in door-yard trees.
And, heart to heart, two nations lean,
  No rival wreaths to twine,
But blending in eternal green
  The holly and the pine !

IN REMEMBRANCE OF JOSEPH STURGE

In the fair land o'erwatched by Ischia's
      mountains,
    Across the charmèd bay
Whose blue waves keep with Capri's silver
      fountains
    Perpetual holiday,

A king lies dead, his wafer duly eaten,
    His gold-bought masses given ;
And Rome's great altar smokes with gums
      to sweeten
    Her foulest gift to Heaven.

And while all Naples thrills with mute
      thanksgiving,
    The court of England's queen
For the dead monster so abhorred while
      living
    In mourning garb is seen.

With a true sorrow God rebukes that feign-
      ing ;
    By lone Edgbaston's side
Stands a great city in the sky's sad raining,
    Bareheaded and wet-eyed !

Silent for once the restless hive of labor,
    Save the low funeral tread,
Or voice of craftsman whispering to his
      neighbor
    The good deeds of the dead.

For him no minster's chant of the immor-
      tals
    Rose from the lips of sin ;
No mitred priest swung back the heavenly
      portals
    To let the white soul in.

But Age and Sickness framed their tearful
      faces
    In the low hovel's door,
And prayers went up from all the dark by-
      places
    And Ghettos of the poor.

The pallid toiler and the negro chattel,
     The vagrant of the street,
The human dice wherewith in games of
          battle
     The lords of earth compete,

Touched with a grief that needs no outward
          draping,
     All swelled the long lament,
Of grateful hearts, instead of marble,
          shaping
     His viewless monument !

For never yet, with ritual pomp and splen-
          dor,
     In the long heretofore,
A heart more loyal, warm, and true, and
          tender,
     Has England's turf closed o'er.

And if there fell from out her grand old
          steeples
     No crash of brazen wail,
The murmurous woe of kindreds, tongues,
          and peoples
     Swept in on every gale.

It came from Holstein's birchen-belted
          meadows,
     And from the tropic calms
Of Indian islands in the sun-smit shadows
     Of Occidental palms ;

From the locked roadsteads of the Bothnian
          peasants,
     And harbors of the Finn,
Where war's worn victims saw his gentle
          presence
     Come sailing, Christ-like, in,

To seek the lost, to build the old waste
          places,
     To link the hostile shores
Of severing seas, and sow with England's
          daisies
     The moss of Finland's moors.

Thanks for the good man's beautiful ex-
          ample,
     Who in the vilest saw
Some sacred crypt or altar of a temple
     Still vocal with God's law ;

And heard with tender ear the spirit sighing
     As from its prison cell,

Praying for pity, like the mournful cry-
          ing
     Of Jonah out of hell.

Not his the golden pen's or lip's persua-
          sion,
     But a fine sense of right,
And Truth's directness, meeting each occa-
          sion
     Straight as a line of light.

His faith and works, like streams that in-
          termingle,
     In the same channel ran :
The crystal clearness of an eye kept sin-
          gle
     Shamed all the frauds of man.

The very gentlest of all human natures
     He joined to courage strong,
And love outreaching unto all God's crea-
          tures
     With sturdy hate of wrong.

Tender as woman, manliness and meek-
          ness
     In him were so allied
That they who judged him by his strength
          or weakness
     Saw but a single side.

Men failed, betrayed him, but his zeal
          seemed nourished
     By failure and by fall ;
Still a large faith in human-kind he cher-
          ished,
     And in God's love for all.

And now he rests : his greatness and his
          sweetness
     No more shall seem at strife,
And death has moulded into calm complete-
          ness
     The statue of his life.

Where the dews glisten and the songbirds
          warble,
     His dust to dust is laid,
In Nature's keeping, with no pomp of
          marble
     To shame his modest shade.

The forges glow, the hammers all are ring-
          ing ;
     Beneath its smoky veil,

Hard by, the city of his love is swinging
    Its clamorous iron flail.

But round his grave are quietude and beauty,
    And the sweet heaven above, —
The fitting symbols of a life of duty
    Transfigured into love !

BROWN OF OSSAWATOMIE

JOHN BROWN of Ossawatomie spake on his
    dying day :
" I will not have to shrive my soul a priest
    in Slavery's pay.
But let some poor slave-mother whom I
    have striven to free,
With her children, from the gallows-stair
    put up a prayer for me ! "

John Brown of Ossawatomie, they led him
    out to die ;
And lo ! a poor slave-mother with her little
    child pressed nigh.
Then the bold, blue eye grew tender, and
    the old harsh face grew mild,
As he stooped between the jeering ranks and
    kissed the negro's child !

The shadows of his stormy life that moment
    fell apart ;
And they who blamed the bloody hand for-
    gave the loving heart.
That kiss from all its guilty means re-
    deemed the good intent,
And round the grisly fighter's hair the mar-
    tyr's aureole bent !

Perish with him the folly that seeks through
    evil good !
Long live the generous purpose unstained
    with human blood !
Not the raid of midnight terror, but the
    thought which underlies ;
Not the borderer's pride of daring, but the
    Christian's sacrifice.

Nevermore may yon Blue Ridges the North-
    ern rifle hear,
Nor see the light of blazing homes flash on
    the negro's spear.
But let the free-winged angel Truth their
    guarded passes scale,
To teach that right is more than might, and
    justice more than mail !

So vainly shall Virginia set her battle in
    array ;
In vain her trampling squadrons knead the
    winter snow with clay.
She may strike the pouncing eagle, but she
    dares not harm the dove ;
And every gate she bars to Hate shall open
    wide to Love !

NAPLES

INSCRIBED TO ROBERT C. WATERSTON,
OF BOSTON

    Helen Waterston died at Naples in her
eighteenth year, and lies buried in the Prot-
estant cemetery there. The stone over her
grave bears the lines,

> Fold her, O Father, in Thine arms,
>   And let her henceforth be
> A messenger of love between
>   Our human hearts and Thee.

I GIVE thee joy ! — I know to thee
  The dearest spot on earth must be
Where sleeps thy loved one by the summer
    sea ;

  Where, near her sweetest poet's tomb,
  The land of Virgil gave thee room
To lay thy flower with her perpetual bloom.

  I know that when the sky shut down
  Behind thee on the gleaming town,
On Baiæ's baths and Posilippo's crown ;

  And, through thy tears, the mocking
    day
Burned Ischia's mountain lines away,
And Capri melted in its sunny bay ;

  Through thy great farewell sorrow shot
  The sharp pang of a bitter thought
That slaves must tread around that holy
    spot.

  Thou knewest not the land was blest
  In giving thy beloved rest,
Holding the fond hope closer to her breast

  That every sweet and saintly grave
  Was freedom's prophecy, and gave
The pledge of Heaven to sanctify and
    save.

That pledge is answered. To thy ear
The unchained city sends its cheer,
And, tuned to joy, the muffled bells of fear

Ring Victor in. The land sits free
And happy by the summer sea,
And Bourbon Naples now is Italy !

She smiles above her broken chain
The languid smile that follows pain,
Stretching her cramped limbs to the sun
    again.

Oh, joy for all, who hear her call
From gray Camaldoli's convent-wall
And Elmo's towers to freedom's carnival !

A new life breathes among her vines
And olives, like the breath of pines
Blown downward from the breezy Apen-
    nines.

Lean, O my friend, to meet that breath,
Rejoice as one who witnesseth
Beauty from ashes rise, and life from death!

Thy sorrow shall no more be pain,
    Its tears shall fall in sunlit rain,
Writing the grave with flowers : " Arisen
    again ! "

A MEMORIAL

Moses Austin Cartland, a dear friend and re-
lation, who led a faithful life as a teacher, and
died in the summer of 1863.

OH, thicker, deeper, darker growing,
    The solemn vista to the tomb
Must know henceforth another shadow,
    And give another cypress room.

In love surpassing that of brothers,
    We walked, O friend, from childhood's
        day;
And, looking back o'er fifty summers,
    Our footprints track a common way.

One in our faith, and one our longing
    To make the world within our reach
Somewhat the better for our living,
    And gladder for our human speech.

Thou heard'st with me the far-off voices,
    The old beguiling song of fame,

But life to thee was warm and present,
    And love was better than a name.

To homely joys and loves and friendships
    Thy genial nature fondly clung ;
And so the shadow on the dial
    Ran back and left thee always young.

And who could blame the generous weak-
        ness
    Which, only to thyself unjust,
So overprized the worth of others,
    And dwarfed thy own with self-distrust ?

All hearts grew warmer in the presence
    Of one who, seeking not his own,
Gave freely for the love of giving,
    Nor reaped for self the harvest sown.

Thy greeting smile was pledge and prelude
    Of generous deeds and kindly words ;
In thy large heart were fair guest-chambers,
    Open to sunrise and the birds !

The task was thine to mould and fashion
    Life's plastic newness into grace :
To make the boyish heart heroic,
    And light with thought the maiden's
        face.

O'er all the land, in town and prairie,
    With bended heads of mourning, stand
The living forms that owe their beauty
    And fitness to thy shaping hand.

Thy call has come in ripened manhood,
    The noonday calm of heart and mind,
While I, who dreamed of thy remaining
    To mourn me, linger still behind :

Live on, to own, with self-upbraiding,
    A debt of love still due from me, —
The vain remembrance of occasions,
    Forever lost, of serving thee.

It was not mine among thy kindred
    To join the silent funeral prayers,
But all that long sad day of summer
    My tears of mourning dropped with
        theirs.

All day the sea-waves sobbed with sorrow,
    The birds forgot their merry trills :
All day I heard the pines lamenting
    With thine upon thy homestead hills.

Green be those hillside pines forever,
  And green the meadowy lowlands be,
And green the old memorial beeches,
  Name-carven in the woods of Lee !

Still let them greet thy life companions
  Who thither turn their pilgrim feet,
In every mossy line recalling
  A tender memory sadly sweet.

O friend ! if thought and sense avail not
  To know thee henceforth as thou art,
That all is well with thee forever
  I trust the instincts of my heart.

Thine be the quiet habitations,
  Thine the green pastures, blossom-sown,
And smiles of saintly recognition,
  As sweet and tender as thy own.

Thou com'st not from the hush and shadow
  To meet us, but to thee we come,
With thee we never can be strangers,
  And where thou art must still be home.

BRYANT ON HIS BIRTHDAY

Mr. Bryant's seventieth birthday, November
3, 1864, was celebrated by a festival to which
these verses were sent.

WE praise not now the poet's art,
  The rounded beauty of his song ;
Who weighs him from his life apart
  Must do his nobler nature wrong.

Not for the eye, familiar grown
  With charms to common sight denied, —
The marvellous gift he shares alone
  With him who walked on Rydal-side ;

Not for rapt hymn nor woodland lay,
  Too grave for smiles, too sweet for
    tears ;
We speak his praise who wears to-day
  The glory of his seventy years.

When Peace brings Freedom in her train,
  Let happy lips his songs rehearse ;
His life is now his noblest strain,
  His manhood better than his verse !

Thank God ! his hand on Nature's keys
  Its cunning keeps at life's full span ;

But, dimmed and dwarfed, in times like
    these,
  The poet seems beside the man !

So be it ! let the garlands die,
  The singer's wreath, the painter's meed,
Let our names perish, if thereby
  Our country may be saved and freed !

THOMAS STARR KING

Published originally as a prelude to the post-
humous volume of selections edited by Richard
Frothingham.

THE great work laid upon his twoscore years
Is done, and well done. If we drop our
    tears,
Who loved him as few men were ever loved,
We mourn no blighted hope nor broken plan
With him whose life stands rounded and
    approved
In the full growth and stature of a man.
Mingle, O bells, along the Western slope,
With your deep toll a sound of faith and
    hope !
Wave cheerily still, O banner, half-way
    down,
From thousand-masted bay and steepled
    town !
Let the strong organ with its loftiest swell
Lift the proud sorrow of the land, and tell
That the brave sower saw his ripened grain.
O East and West ! O morn and sunset
    twain
No more forever ! — has he lived in vain
Who, priest of Freedom, made ye one, and
    told
Your bridal service from his lips of gold ?

LINES ON A FLY-LEAF

[Suggested by the book *A New Atmosphere*,
by Gail Hamilton. The other friends referred
to in the lines are Lydia Maria Child, Grace
Greenwood, Anna E. Dickinson and Mrs.
Stowe.]

I NEED not ask thee, for my sake,
  To read a book which well may make
Its way by native force of wit
Without my manual sign to it.
Its piquant writer needs from me
No gravely masculine guaranty,

And well might laugh her merriest laugh
At broken spears in her behalf ;
Yet, spite of all the critics tell,
I frankly own I like her well.
It may be that she wields a pen
Too sharply nibbed for thin-skinned men,
That her keen arrows search and try
The armor joints of dignity,
And, though alone for error meant,
Sing through the air irreverent.
I blame her not, the young athlete
Who plants her woman's tiny feet,
And dares the chances of debate
Where bearded men might hesitate,
Who, deeply earnest, seeing well
The ludicrous and laughable,
Mingling in eloquent excess
Her anger and her tenderness,
And, chiding with a half-caress,
Strives, less for her own sex than ours,
With principalities and powers,
And points us upward to the clear
Sunned heights of her new atmosphere.

Heaven mend her faults ! — I will not pause
To weigh and doubt and peck at flaws,
Or waste my pity when some fool
Provokes her measureless ridicule.
Strong-minded is she ? Better so
Than dulness set for sale or show,
A household folly, capped and belled
In fashion's dance of puppets held,
Or poor pretence of womanhood,
Whose formal, flavorless platitude
Is warranted from all offence
Of robust meaning's violence.
Give me the wine of thought whose bead
Sparkles along the page I read, —
Electric words in which I find
The tonic of the northwest wind ;
The wisdom which itself allies
To sweet and pure humanities,
Where scorn of meanness, hate of wrong,
Are underlaid by love as strong ;
The genial play of mirth that lights
Grave themes of thought, as when, on nights
Of summer-time, the harmless blaze
Of thunderless heat-lightning plays,
And tree and hill-top resting dim
And doubtful on the sky's vague rim,
Touched by that soft and lambent gleam,
Start sharply outlined from their dream.

Talk not to me of woman's sphere,
Nor point with Scripture texts a sneer,
Nor wrong the manliest saint of all
By doubt, if he were here, that Paul
Would own the heroines who have lent
Grace to truth's stern arbitrament,
Foregone the praise to woman sweet,
And cast their crowns at Duty's feet ;
Like her, who by her strong Appeal
Made Fashion weep and Mammon feel,
Who, earliest summoned to withstand
The color-madness of the land,
Counted her life-long losses gain,
And made her own her sisters' pain ;
Or her who, in her greenwood shade,
Heard the sharp call that Freedom made,
And, answering, struck from Sappho's lyre
Of love the Tyrtæan carmen's fire :
Or that young girl, — Domrémy's maid
Revived a nobler cause to aid, —
Shaking from warning finger-tips
The doom of her apocalypse ;
Or her, who world-wide entrance gave
To the log-cabin of the slave,
Made all his want and sorrow known,
And all earth's languages his own.

GEORGE L. STEARNS

No man rendered greater service to the
cause of Freedom than Major Stearns in the
great struggle between invading slave-holders
and the free settlers of Kansas.

He has done the work of a true man, —
  Crown him, honor him, love him.
Weep over him, tears of woman,
  Stoop manliest brows above him !

O dusky mothers and daughters,
  Vigils of mourning keep for him !
Up in the mountains, and down by the
      waters,
  Lift up your voices and weep for him !

For the warmest of hearts is frozen,
  The freest of hands is still ;
And the gap in our picked and chosen
  The long years may not fill.

No duty could overtask him,
  No need his will outrun ;
Or ever our lips could ask him,
  His hands the work had done.

He forgot his own soul for others,
  Himself to his neighbor lending ;

He found the Lord in his suffering brothers,
And not in the clouds descending.

So the bed was sweet to die on,
Whence he saw the doors wide swung
Against whose bolted iron
The strength of his life was flung.

And he saw ere his eye was darkened
The sheaves of the harvest-bringing,
And knew while his ear yet hearkened
The voice of the reapers singing.

Ah, well ! The world is discreet ;
There are plenty to pause and wait ;
But here was a man who set his feet
Sometimes in advance of fate ;

Plucked off the old bark when the inner
Was slow to renew it,
And put to the Lord's work the sinner
When saints failed to do it.

Never rode to the wrong's redressing
A worthier paladin.
Shall he not hear the blessing,
"Good and faithful, enter in ! "

GARIBALDI

In trance and dream of old, God's prophet saw
The casting down of thrones. Thou, watching lone
The hot Sardinian coast-line, hazy-hilled,
Where, fringing round Caprera's rocky zone
With foam, the slow waves gather and withdraw,
Behold'st the vision of the seer fulfilled,
And hear'st the sea-winds burdened with a sound
Of falling chains, as, one by one, unbound,
The nations lift their right hands up and swear
Their oath of freedom. From the chalk-white wall
Of England, from the black Carpathian range,
Along the Danube and the Theiss, through all
The passes of the Spanish Pyrenees,
And from the Seine's thronged banks, a murmur strange
And glad floats to thee o'er thy summer seas
On the salt wind that stirs thy whitening hair, —
The song of freedom's bloodless victories !
Rejoice, O Garibaldi ! Though thy sword
Failed at Rome's gates, and blood seemed vainly poured
Where, in Christ's name, the crownëd infidel
Of France wrought murder with the arms of hell
On that sad mountain slope whose ghostly dead,
Unmindful of the gray exorcist's ban,
Walk, unappeased, the chambered Vatican,
And draw the curtains of Napoleon's bed !
God's providence is not blind, but, full of eyes,
It searches all the refuges of lies ;
And in His time and way, the accursed things
Before whose evil feet thy battle-gage
Has clashed defiance from hot youth to age
Shall perish. All men shall be priests and kings,
One royal brotherhood, one church made free
By love, which is the law of liberty !

TO LYDIA MARIA CHILD

ON READING HER POEM IN "THE STAN-
DARD"

Mrs. Child wrote her lines, beginning, "Again the trees are clothed in vernal green," May 24, 1859, on the first anniversary of Ellis Gray Loring's death, but did not publish them for some years afterward, when I first read them, or I could not have made the reference which I did to the extinction of slavery.

The sweet spring day is glad with music,
But through it sounds a sadder strain ;
The worthiest of our narrowing circle
Sings Loring's dirges o'er again.

O woman greatly loved ! I join thee
In tender memories of our friend ;
With thee across the awful spaces
The greeting of a soul I send !

What cheer hath he ?　　How is it with him ?
　Where lingers he this weary while ?
Over what pleasant fields of Heaven
　Dawns the sweet sunrise of his smile ?

Does he not know our feet are treading
　The earth hard down on Slavery's grave ?
That, in our crowning exultations,
　We miss the charm his presence gave ?

Why on this spring air comes no whisper
　From him to tell us all is well ?
Why to our flower-time comes no token
　Of lily and of asphodel ?

I feel the unutterable longing,
　Thy hunger of the heart is mine ;
I reach and grope for hands in darkness,
　My ear grows sharp for voice or sign.

Still on the lips of all we question
　The finger of God's silence lies ;
Will the lost hands in ours be folded ?
　Will the shut eyelids ever rise ?

O friend ! no proof beyond this yearning,
　This outreach of our hearts, we need ;
God will not mock the hope He giveth,
　No love He prompts shall vainly plead.

Then let us stretch our hands in darkness,
　And call our loved ones o'er and o'er ;
Some day their arms shall close about us,
　And the old voices speak once more.

No dreary splendors wait our coming
　Where rapt ghost sits from ghost apart ;
Homeward we go to Heaven's thanksgiving,
　The harvest-gathering of the heart.

THE SINGER

This poem was written on the death of Alice
Cary.　Her sister Phœbe, heart-broken by her
loss, followed soon after.　Noble and richly
gifted, lovely in person and character, they
left behind them only friends and admirers.

YEARS since (but names to me before),
Two sisters sought at eve my door ;
Two song-birds wandering from their nest,
A gray old farm-house in the West.

How fresh of life the younger one,
Half smiles, half tears, like rain in sun !

Her gravest mood could scarce displace
The dimples of her nut-brown face.

Wit sparkled on her lips not less
For quick and tremulous tenderness ;
And, following close her merriest glance,
Dreamed through her eyes the heart's ro-
　mance.

Timid and still, the elder had
Even then a smile too sweetly sad ;
The crown of pain that all must wear
Too early pressed her midnight hair.

Yet ere the summer eve grew long,
Her modest lips were sweet with song ;
A memory haunted all her words
Of clover-fields and singing birds.

Her dark, dilating eyes expressed
The broad horizons of the west ;
Her speech dropped prairie flowers ; the
　gold
Of harvest wheat about her rolled.

Fore-doomed to song she seemed to me :
I queried not with destiny :
I knew the trial and the need,
Yet, all the more, I said, God speed !

What could I other than I did ?
Could I a singing-bird forbid ?
Deny the wind-stirred leaf ?　Rebuke
The music of the forest brook ?

She went with morning from my door,
But left me richer than before ;
Thenceforth I knew her voice of cheer,
The welcome of her partial ear.

Years passed : through all the land her
　name
A pleasant household word became :
All felt behind the singer stood
A sweet and gracious womanhood.

Her life was earnest work, not play ;
Her tired feet climbed a weary way ;
And even through her lightest strain
We heard an undertone of pain.

Unseen of her her fair fame grew,
The good she did she rarely knew,
Unguessed of her in life the love
That rained its tears her grave above.

When last I saw her, full of peace,
She waited for her great release ;
And that old friend so sage and bland,
Our later Franklin, held her hand.

For all that patriot bosoms stirs
Had moved that woman's heart of hers,
And men who toiled in storm and sun
Found her their meet companion.

Our converse, from her suffering bed
To healthful themes of life she led :
The out-door world of bud and bloom
And light and sweetness filled her room.

Yet evermore an underthought
Of loss to come within us wrought,
And all the while we felt the strain
Of the strong will that conquered pain.

God giveth quietness at last !
The common way that all have passed
She went, with mortal yearnings fond,
To fuller life and love beyond.

Fold the rapt soul in your embrace,
My dear ones ! Give the singer place !
To you, to her, — I know not where, —
I lift the silence of a prayer.

For only thus our own we find ;
The gone before, the left behind,
All mortal voices die between ;
The unheard reaches the unseen.

Again the blackbirds sing ; the streams
Wake, laughing, from their winter dreams,
And tremble in the April showers
The tassels of the maple flowers.

But not for her has spring renewed
The sweet surprises of the wood ;
And bird and flower are lost to her
Who was their best interpreter !

What to shut eyes has God revealed ?
What hear the ears that death has
  sealed ?
What undreamed beauty passing show
Requites the loss of all we know ?

O silent land, to which we move,
Enough if there alone be love,

And mortal need can ne'er outgrow
What it is waiting to bestow !

O white soul ! from that far-off shore
Float some sweet song the waters o'er,
Our faith confirm, our fears dispel,
With the old voice we loved so well !

HOW MARY GREW

These lines were in answer to an invitation
to hear a lecture of Mary Grew, of Philadelphia,
before the Boston Radical Club. The reference
in the last stanza is to an essay on Sappho by
T. W. Higginson, read at the club the preceding
month.

WITH wisdom far beyond her years,
And graver than her wondering peers,
So strong, so mild, combining still
The tender heart and queenly will,
To conscience and to duty true,
So, up from childhood, Mary Grew !

Then in her gracious womanhood
She gave her days to doing good.
She dared the scornful laugh of men,
The hounding mob, the slanderer's pen.
She did the work she found to do, —
A Christian heroine, Mary Grew !

The freed slave thanks her ; blessing comes
To her from women's weary homes ;
The wronged and erring find in her
Their censor mild and comforter.
The world were safe if but a few
Could grow in grace as Mary Grew !

So, New Year's Eve, I sit and say,
By this low wood-fire, ashen gray ;
Just wishing, as the night shuts down,
That I could hear in Boston town,
In pleasant Chestnut Avenue,
From her own lips, how Mary Grew !

And hear her graceful hostess tell
The silver-voicëd oracle
Who lately through her parlors spoke,
As through Dodona's sacred oak,
A wiser truth than any told
By Sappho's lips of ruddy gold, —
The way to make the world anew
Is just to grow — as Mary Grew !

SUMNER

"I am not one who has disgraced beauty of sentiment by deformity of conduct, or the maxims of a freeman by the actions of a slave; but, by the grace of God, I have kept my life unsullied." — MILTON's *Defence of the People of England.*

O MOTHER STATE ! the winds of March
    Blew chill o'er Auburn's Field of God,
Where, slow, beneath a leaden arch
    Of sky, thy mourning children trod.

And now, with all thy woods in leaf,
    Thy fields in flower, beside thy dead
Thou sittest, in thy robes of grief,
    A Rachel yet uncomforted !

And once again the organ swells,
    Once more the flag is half-way hung,
And yet again the mournful bells
    In all thy steeple-towers are rung.

And I, obedient to thy will,
    Have come a simple wreath to lay,
Superfluous, on a grave that still
    Is sweet with all the flowers of May.

I take, with awe, the task assigned ;
    It may be that my friend might miss,
In his new sphere of heart and mind,
    Some token from my hand in this.

By many a tender memory moved,
    Along the past my thought I send ;
The record of the cause he loved
    Is the best record of its friend.

No trumpet sounded in his ear,
    He saw not Sinai's cloud and flame,
But never yet to Hebrew seer
    A clearer voice of duty came.

God said : "Break thou these yokes ; undo
These heavy burdens. I ordain
A work to last thy whole life through,
    A ministry of strife and pain.

"Forego thy dreams of lettered ease,
    Put thou the scholar's promise by,
The rights of man are more than these."
    He heard, and answered : "Here am I !"

He set his face against the blast,
    His feet against the flinty shard,
Till the hard service grew, at last,
    Its own exceeding great reward.

Lifted like Saul's above the crowd,
    Upon his kingly forehead fell
The first sharp bolt of Slavery's cloud,
    Launched at the truth he urged so well.

Ah ! never yet, at rack or stake,
    Was sorer loss made Freedom's gain,
Than his, who suffered for her sake
    The beak-torn Titan's lingering pain !

The fixed star of his faith, through all
    Loss, doubt, and peril, shone the same ;
As through a night of storm, some tall,
    Strong lighthouse lifts its steady flame.

Beyond the dust and smoke he saw
    The sheaves of Freedom's large increase,
The holy fanes of equal law,
    The New Jerusalem of peace.

The weak might fear, the worldling mock,
    The faint and blind of heart regret ;
All knew at last th' eternal rock
    On which his forward feet were set.

The subtlest scheme of compromise
    Was folly to his purpose bold ;
The strongest mesh of party lies
    Weak to the simplest truth he told.

One language held his heart and lip,
    Straight onward to his goal he trod,
And proved the highest statesmanship
    Obedience to the voice of God.

No wail was in his voice, — none heard,
    When treason's storm-cloud blackest grew,
The weakness of a doubtful word ;
    His duty, and the end, he knew.

The first to smite, the first to spare ;
    When once the hostile ensigns fell,
He stretched out hands of generous care
    To lift the foe he fought so well.

For there was nothing base or small
    Or craven in his soul's broad plan ;
Forgiving all things personal,
    He hated only wrong to man.

The old traditions of his State,
  The memories of her great and good,
Took from his life a fresher date,
  And in himself embodied stood.

How felt the greed of gold and place,
  The venal crew that schemed and planned,
The fine scorn of that haughty face,
  The spurning of that bribeless hand !

If than Rome's tribunes statelier
  He wore his senatorial robe,
His lofty port was all for her,
  The one dear spot on all the globe.

If to the master's plea he gave
  The vast contempt his manhood felt,
He saw a brother in the slave, —
  With man as equal man he dealt.

Proud was he ? If his presence kept
  Its grandeur wheresoe'er he trod,
As if from Plutarch's gallery stepped
  The hero and the demigod,

None failed, at least, to reach his ear,
  Nor want nor woe appealed in vain ;
The homesick soldier knew his cheer,
  And blessed him from his ward of pain.

Safely his dearest friends may own
  The slight defects he never hid,
The surface-blemish in the stone
  Of the tall, stately pyramid.

Suffice it that he never brought
  His conscience to the public mart ;
But lived himself the truth he taught,
  White - souled, clean - handed, pure of
    heart.

What if he felt the natural pride
  Of power in noble use, too true
With thin humilities to hide
  The work he did, the lore he knew ?

Was he not just ? Was any wronged
  By that assured self-estimate ?
He took but what to him belonged,
  Unenvious of another's state.

Well might he heed the words he spake,
  And scan with care the written page
Through which he still shall warm and wake
  The hearts of men from age to age.

Ah ! who shall blame him now because
  He solaced thus his hours of pain !
Should not the o'erworn thresher pause,
  And hold to light his golden grain ?

No sense of humor dropped its oil
  On the hard ways his purpose went ;
Small play of fancy lightened toil ;
  He spake alone the thing he meant.

He loved his books, the Art that hints
  A beauty veiled behind its own,
The graver's line, the pencil's tints,
  The chisel's shape evoked from stone.

He cherished, void of selfish ends,
  The social courtesies that bless
And sweeten life, and loved his friends
  With most unworldly tenderness.

But still his tired eyes rarely learned
  The glad relief by Nature brought ;
Her mountain ranges never turned
  His current of persistent thought.

The sea rolled chorus to his speech
  Three-banked like Latium's tall trireme,
With laboring oars ; the grove and beach
  Were Forum and the Academe.

The sensuous joy from all things fair
  His strenuous bent of soul repressed,
And left from youth to silvered hair
  Few hours for pleasure, none for rest.

For all his life was poor without,
  O Nature, make the last amends !
Train all thy flowers his grave about,
  And make thy singing-birds his friends !

Revive again, thou summer rain,
  The broken turf upon his bed !
Breathe, summer wind, thy tenderest
    strain
  Of low, sweet music overhead !

With calm and beauty symbolize
  The peace which follows long annoy,
And lend our earth-bent, mourning eyes,
  Some hint of his diviner joy.

For safe with right and truth he is,
  As God lives he must live alway ;
There is no end for souls like his,
  No night for children of the day !

Nor cant nor poor solicitudes
  Made weak his life's great argument ;
Small leisure his for frames and moods
  Who followed Duty where she went.

The broad, fair fields of God he saw
  Beyond the bigot's narrow bound ;
The truths he moulded into law
  In Christ's beatitudes he found.

His state-craft was the Golden Rule,
  His right of vote a sacred trust ;
Clear, over threat and ridicule,
  All heard his challenge : " Is it just ? "

And when the hour supreme had come,
  Not for himself a thought he gave ;
In that last pang of martyrdom,
  His care was for the half-freed slave.

Not vainly dusky hands upbore,
  In prayer, the passing soul to heaven
Whose mercy to His suffering poor
  Was service to the Master given.

Long shall the good State's annals tell,
  Her children's children long be taught,
How, praised or blamed, he guarded
    well
  The trust he neither shunned nor sought.

If for one moment turned thy face,
  O Mother, from thy son, not long
He waited calmly in his place
  The sure remorse which follows wrong.

Forgiven be the State he loved
  The one brief lapse, the single blot;
Forgotten be the stain removed,
  Her righted record shows it not !

The lifted sword above her shield
  With jealous care shall guard his fame ;
The pine-tree on her ancient field
  To all the winds shall speak his name.

The marble image of her son
  Her loving hands shall yearly crown,
And from her pictured Pantheon
  His grand, majestic face look down.

O State so passing rich before,
  Who now shall doubt thy highest claim ?
The world that counts thy jewels o'er
  Shall longest pause at Sumner's name !

THIERS

I

FATE summoned, in gray-bearded age, to
    act
A history stranger than his written fact,
  Him who portrayed the splendor and the
    gloom
Of that great hour when throne and altar
    fell
With long death-groan which still is audi-
    ble.
  He, when around the walls of Paris
    rung
  The Prussian bugle like the blast of doom,
And every ill which follows unblest war
Maddened all France from Finistère to
    Var,
  The weight of fourscore from his
    shoulders flung,
And guided Freedom in the path he saw
Lead out of chaos into light and law,
Peace, not imperial, but republican,
And order pledged to all the Rights of
  Man.

II

Death called him from a need as immi-
    nent
As that from which the Silent William
    went
When powers of evil, like the smiting
    seas
On Holland's dikes, assailed her liberties.
Sadly, while yet in doubtful balance hung
The weal and woe of France, the bells were
    rung
For her lost leader. Paralyzed of will,
Above his bier the hearts of men stood
    still.
Then, as if set to his dead lips, the horn
Of Roland wound once more to rouse and
    warn,
The old voice filled the air ! His last brave
    word
Not vainly France to all her boundaries
    stirred.
Strong as in life, he still for Freedom
    wrought,
As the dead Cid at red Toloso fought.

FITZ-GREENE HALLECK

AT THE UNVEILING OF HIS STATUE

AMONG their graven shapes to whom
 Thy civic wreaths belong,
O city of his love, make room
 For one whose gift was song.

Not his the soldier's sword to wield,
 Nor his the helm of state,
Nor glory of the stricken field,
 Nor triumph of debate.

In common ways, with common men,
 He served his race and time
As well as if his clerkly pen
 Had never danced to rhyme.

If, in the thronged and noisy mart,
 The Muses found their son,
Could any say his tuneful art
 A duty left undone ?

He toiled and sang ; and year by year
 Men found their homes more sweet,
And through a tenderer atmosphere
 Looked down the brick-walled street.

The Greek's wild onset Wall Street
 knew ;
 The Red King walked Broadway ;
And Alnwick Castle's roses blew
 From Palisades to Bay.

Fair City by the Sea ! upraise
 His veil with reverent hands ;
And mingle with thy own the praise
 And pride of other lands.

Let Greece his fiery lyric breathe
 Above her hero-urns ;
And Scotland, with her holly, wreathe
 The flower he culled for Burns.

Oh, stately stand thy palace walls,
 Thy tall ships ride the seas ;
To-day thy poet's name recalls
 A prouder thought than these.

Not less thy pulse of trade shall beat,
 Nor less thy tall fleets swim,
That shaded square and dusty street
 Are classic ground through him.

Alive, he loved, like all who sing,
 The echoes of his song ;
Too late the tardy meed we bring,
 The praise delayed so long.

Too late, alas ! Of all who knew
 The living man, to-day
Before his unveiled face, how few
 Make bare their locks of gray !

Our lips of praise must soon be dumb,
 Our grateful eyes be dim ;
O brothers of the days to come,
 Take tender charge of him !

New hands the wires of song may sweep,
 New voices challenge fame ;
But let no moss of years o'ercreep
 The lines of Halleck's name.

WILLIAM FRANCIS BARTLETT

OH, well may Essex sit forlorn
 Beside her sea-blown shore;
Her well beloved, her noblest born,
 Is hers in life no more !

No lapse of years can render less
 Her memory's sacred claim ;
No fountain of forgetfulness
 Can wet the lips of Fame.

A grief alike to wound and heal,
 A thought to soothe and pain,
The sad, sweet pride that mothers feel
 To her must still remain.

Good men and true she has not lacked,
 And brave men yet shall be ;
The perfect flower, the crowning fact,
 Of all her years was he !

As Galahad pure, as Merlin sage,
 What worthier knight was found
To grace in Arthur's golden age
 The fabled Table Round ?

A voice, the battle's trumpet-note,
 To welcome and restore ;
A hand, that all unwilling smote,
 To heal and build once more !

A soul of fire, a tender heart
 Too warm for hate, he knew

The generous victor's graceful part
  To sheathe the sword he drew.

When Earth, as if on evil dreams,
  Looks back upon her wars,
And the white light of Christ outstreams
  From the red disk of Mars,

His fame who led the stormy van
  Of battle well may cease,
But never that which crowns the man
  Whose victory was Peace.

Mourn, Essex, on thy sea-blown shore
  Thy beautiful and brave,
Whose failing hand the olive bore,
  Whose dying lips forgave !

Let age lament the youthful chief,
  And tender eyes be dim ;
The tears are more of joy than grief
  That fall for one like him !

BAYARD TAYLOR

I

" AND where now, Bayard, will thy foot-
    steps tend ? "
  My sister asked our guest one winter's
    day.
  Smiling he answered in the Friends' sweet
    way
Common to both : " Wherever thou shalt
    send !
What wouldst thou have me see for thee ? "
    She laughed,
  Her dark eyes dancing in the wood-fire's
    glow :
" Loffoden isles, the Kilpis, and the low,
Unsetting sun on Finmark's fishing-craft."
" All these and more I soon shall see for
    thee ! "
  He answered cheerily : and he kept his
    pledge
  On Lapland snows, the North Cape's
    windy wedge,
And Tromsö freezing in its winter sea.
  He went and came. But no man knows
    the track
  Of his last journey, and he comes not
    back !

II

He brought us wonders of the new and
    old ;
  We shared all climes with him. The
    Arab's tent
  To him its story-telling secret lent.
And, pleased, we listened to the tales he
    told.
His task, beguiled with songs that shall en-
    dure,
  In manly, honest thoroughness he
    wrought ;
  From humble home-lays to the heights
    of thought
Slowly he climbed, but every step was
    sure.
How, with the generous pride that friend-
    ship hath,
  We, who so loved him, saw at last the
    crown
  Of civic honor on his brows pressed down,
Rejoiced, and knew not that the gift was
    death.
  And now for him, whose praise in deaf-
    ened ears
  Two nations speak, we answer but with
    tears !

III

O Vale of Chester ! trod by him so oft,
  Green as thy June turf keep his memory.
    Let
  Nor wood, nor dell, nor storied stream
    forget,
Nor winds that blow round lonely Cedar-
    croft ;
Let the home voices greet him in the far,
  Strange land that holds him ; let the
    messages
  Of love pursue him o'er the chartless
    seas
And unmapped vastness of his unknown
    star !
Love's language, heard beyond the loud
    discourse
  Of perishable fame, in every sphere
  Itself interprets ; and its utterance here
Somewhere in God's unfolding universe
  Shall reach our traveller, softening the
    surprise
  Of his rapt gaze on unfamiliar skies !

OUR AUTOCRAT

Read at the breakfast given in honor of Dr.
Holmes by the publishers of the *Atlantic
Monthly*, December 3, 1879.

HIS laurels fresh from song and lay,
　Romance, art, science, rich in all,
And young of heart, how dare we say
　We keep his seventieth festival ?

No sense is here of loss or lack ;
　Before his sweetness and his light
The dial holds its shadow back,
　The charmëd hours delay their flight.

His still the keen analysis
　Of men and moods, electric wit,
Free play of mirth, and tenderness
　To heal the slightest wound from it.

And his the pathos touching all
　Life's sins and sorrows and regrets,
Its hopes and fears, its final call
　And rest beneath the violets.

His sparkling surface scarce betrays
　The thoughtful tide beneath it rolled,
The wisdom of the latter days,
　And tender memories of the old.

What shapes and fancies, grave or gay,
　Before us at his bidding come !
The Treadmill tramp, the One-Horse Shay,
　The dumb despair of Elsie's doom !

The tale of Avis and the Maid,
　The plea for lips that cannot speak,
The holy kiss that Iris laid
　On Little Boston's pallid cheek !

Long may he live to sing for us
　His sweetest songs at evening time,
And, like his Chambered Nautilus,
　To holier heights of beauty climb !

Though now unnumbered guests surround
　The table that he rules at will,
Its Autocrat, however crowned,
　Is but our friend and comrade still.

The world may keep his honored name,
　The wealth of all his varied powers ;
A stronger claim has love than fame,
　And he himself is only ours !

WITHIN THE GATE

L. M. C.

I have more fully expressed my admiration
and regard for Lydia Maria Child in the bio-
graphical introduction which I wrote for the
volume of *Letters*, published after her death.

WE sat together, last May-day, and talked
　Of the dear friends who walked
Beside us, sharers of the hopes and fears
　Of five and forty years,

Since first we met in Freedom's hope for-
　　lorn,
　And heard her battle-horn
Sound through the valleys of the sleeping
　　North,
　Calling her children forth,

And youth pressed forward with hope-
　　lighted eyes,
　And age, with forecast wise
Of the long strife before the triumph won,
　Girded his armor on.

Sadly, as name by name we called the roll,
　We heard the dead-bells toll
For the unanswering many, and we knew
　The living were the few.

And we, who waited our own call before
　The inevitable door,
Listened and looked, as all have done, to
　　win
　Some token from within.

No sign we saw, we heard no voices call ;
　The impenetrable wall
Cast down its shadow, like an awful doubt,
　On all who sat without.

Of many a hint of life beyond the veil,
　And many a ghostly tale
Wherewith the ages spanned the gulf be-
　　tween
　The seen and the unseen,

Seeking from omen, trance, and dream to
　　gain
　Solace to doubtful pain,
And touch, with groping hands, the gar-
　　ment hem
　Of truth sufficing them,

We talked ; and, turning from the sore
  unrest
Of an all-baffling quest,
We thought of holy lives that from us passed
  Hopeful unto the last,

As if they saw beyond the river of death,
  Like Him of Nazareth,
The many mansions of the Eternal days
  Lift up their gates of praise.

And, hushed to silence by a reverent awe,
  Methought, O friend, I saw
In thy true life of word, and work, and
  thought
  The proof of all we sought.

Did we not witness in the life of thee
  Immortal prophecy ?
And feel, when with thee, that thy footsteps
  trod
  An everlasting road ?

Not for brief days thy generous sympathies,
  Thy scorn of selfish ease ;
Not for the poor prize of an earthly goal
  Thy strong uplift of soul.

Than thine was never turned a fonder heart
  To nature and to art
In fair-formed Hellas in her golden prime,
  Thy Philothea's time.

Yet, loving beauty, thou couldst pass it by,
  And for the poor deny
Thyself, and see thy fresh, sweet flower of
  fame
  Wither in blight and blame.

Sharing His love who holds in His embrace
  The lowliest of our race,
Sure the Divine economy must be
  Conservative of thee !

For truth must live with truth, self-sacri-
  fice
  Seek out its great allies ;
Good must find good by gravitation sure,
  And love with love endure.

And so, since thou hast passed within the
  gate
  Whereby awhile I wait,
I give blind grief and blinder sense the lie :
  Thou hast not lived to die !

IN MEMORY

JAMES T. FIELDS

As a guest who may not stay
Long and sad farewells to say
Glides with smiling face away,

Of the sweetness and the zest
Of thy happy life possessed
Thou hast left us at thy best.

Warm of heart and clear of brain,
Of thy sun-bright spirit's wane
Thou hast spared us all the pain.

Now that thou hast gone away,
What is left of one to say
Who was open as the day ?

What is there to gloss or shun ?
Save with kindly voices none
Speak thy name beneath the sun.

Safe thou art on every side,
Friendship nothing finds to hide,
Love's demand is satisfied.

Over manly strength and worth,
At thy desk of toil, or hearth,
Played the lambent light of mirth, —

Mirth that lit, but never burned ;
All thy blame to pity turned ;
Hatred thou hadst never learned.

Every harsh and vexing thing
At thy home-fire lost its sting ;
Where thou wast was always spring.

And thy perfect trust in good,
Faith in man and womanhood,
Chance and change and time withstood

Small respect for cant and whine,
Bigot's zeal and hate malign,
Had that sunny soul of thine.

But to thee was duty's claim
Sacred, and thy lips became
Reverent with one holy Name.

Therefore, on thy unknown way,
Go in God's peace ! We who stay
But a little while delay.

Keep for us, O friend, where'er
Thou art waiting, all that here
Made thy earthly presence dear ;

Something of thy pleasant past
On a ground of wonder cast,
In the stiller waters glassed !

Keep the human heart of thee ;
Let the mortal only be
Clothed in immortality.

And when fall our feet as fell
Thine upon the asphodel,
Let thy old smile greet us well ;

Proving in a world of bliss
What we fondly dream in this, —
Love is one with holiness !

WILSON

Read at the Massachusetts Club on the seven-
tieth anniversary of the birthday of Vice-Pres-
ident Wilson, February 16, 1882.

THE lowliest born of all the land,
He wrung from Fate's reluctant hand
   The gifts which happier boyhood claims ;
And, tasting on a thankless soil
The bitter bread of unpaid toil,
   He fed his soul with noble aims.

And Nature, kindly provident,
To him the future's promise lent ;
   The powers that shape man's destinies,
Patience and faith and toil, he knew,
The close horizon round him grew
   Broad with great possibilities.

By the low hearth-fire's fitful blaze
He read of old heroic days,
   The sage's thought, the patriot's speech ;
Unhelped, alone, himself he taught,
His school the craft at which he wrought,
   His lore the book within his reach.

He felt his country's need ; he knew
The work her children had to do ;
   And when, at last, he heard the call
In her behalf to serve and dare,
Beside his senatorial chair
   He stood the unquestioned peer of
   all.

Beyond the accident of birth
He proved his simple manhood's worth ;
   Ancestral pride and classic grace
Confessed the large-brained artisan,
So clear of sight, so wise in plan
   And counsel, equal to his place.

With glance intuitive he saw
Through all disguise of form and law,
   And read men like an open book ;
Fearless and firm, he never quailed
Nor turned aside for threats, nor failed
   To do the thing he undertook.

How wise, how brave, he was, how well
He bore himself, let history tell
   While waves our flag o'er land and sea,
No black thread in its warp or weft ;
He found dissevered States, he left
   A grateful Nation, strong and free !

THE POET AND THE CHILDREN

LONGFELLOW

WITH a glory of winter sunshine
   Over his locks of gray,
In the old historic mansion
   He sat on his last birthday ;

With his books and his pleasant pictures,
   And his household and his kin,
While a sound as of myriads singing
   From far and near stole in.

It came from his own fair city,
   From the prairie's boundless plain,
From the Golden Gate of sunset,
   And the cedarn woods of Maine.

And his heart grew warm within him,
   And his moistening eyes grew dim,
For he knew that his country's children
   Were singing the songs of him :

The lays of his life's glad morning,
   The psalms of his evening time,
Whose echoes shall float forever
   On the winds of every clime.

All their beautiful consolations,
   Sent forth like birds of cheer,
Came flocking back to his windows,
   And sang in the Poet's ear.

Grateful, but solemn and tender,
  The music rose and fell
With a joy akin to sadness
  And a greeting like farewell.

With a sense of awe he listened
  To the voices sweet and young ;
The last of earth and the first of heaven
  Seemed in the songs they sung.

And waiting a little longer
  For the wonderful change to come,
He heard the Summoning Angel,
  Who calls God's children home !

And to him in a holier welcome
  Was the mystical meaning given
Of the words of the blessed Master :
  " Of such is the kingdom of heaven ! "

A WELCOME TO LOWELL

Take our hands, James Russell Lowell,
  Our hearts are all thy own ;
To-day we bid thee welcome
  Not for ourselves alone.

In the long years of thy absence
  Some of us have grown old,
And some have passed the portals
  Of the Mystery untold ;

For the hands that cannot clasp thee,
  For the voices that are dumb,
For each and all I bid thee
  A grateful welcome home !

For Cedarcroft's sweet singer
  To the nine-fold Muses dear ;
For the Seer the winding Concord
  Paused by his door to hear ;

For him, our guide and Nestor,
  Who the march of song began,
The white locks of his ninety years
  Bared to thy winds, Cape Ann !

For him who, to the music
  Her pines and hemlocks played,
Set the old and tender story
  Of the lorn Acadian maid ;

For him, whose voice for freedom
  Swayed friend and foe at will,
Hushed is the tongue of silver,
  The golden lips are still !

For her whose life of duty
  At scoff and menace smiled,
Brave as the wife of Roland,
  Yet gentle as a Child.

And for him the three-hilled city
  Shall hold in memory long,
Whose name is the hint and token
  Of the pleasant Fields of Song !

For the old friends unforgotten,
  For the young thou hast not known,
I speak their heart-warm greeting ;
  Come back and take thy own !

From England's royal farewells,
  And honors fitly paid,
Come back, dear Russell Lowell,
  To Elmwood's waiting shade !

Come home with all the garlands
  That crown of right thy head.
I speak for comrades living,
  I speak for comrades dead !

AN ARTIST OF THE BEAUTIFUL

GEORGE FULLER

Haunted of Beauty, like the marvellous
  youth
Who sang Saint Agnes' Eve ! How passing
  fair
Her shapes took color in thy homestead air !
How on thy canvas even her dreams were
  truth !
Magician ! who from commonest elements
Called up divine ideals, clothed upon
By mystic lights soft blending into one
Womanly grace and child-like innocence.
Teacher ! thy lesson was not given in vain,
Beauty is goodness ; ugliness is sin :
Art's place is sacred : nothing foul therein
May crawl or tread with bestial feet profane
If rightly choosing is the painter's test,
Thy choice, O master, ever was the best.

MULFORD

Author of The Nation *and* The Republic of God.

UNNOTED as the setting of a star
  He passed ; and sect and party scarcely
    knew
  When from their midst a sage and seer
    withdrew
To fitter audience, where the great dead are
  In God's republic of the heart and mind,
  Leaving no purer, nobler soul behind.

TO A CAPE ANN SCHOONER

LUCK to the craft that bears this name of
    mine,
Good fortune follow with her golden spoon
The glazëd hat and tarry pantaloon ;
And wheresoe'er her keel shall cut the brine,
Cod, hake and haddock quarrel for her line.
Shipped with her crew, whatever wind may
    blow,
Or tides delay, my wish with her shall go,
Fishing by proxy.   Would that it might
    show
At need her course, in lack of sun and star,
Where icebergs threaten, and the sharp
    reefs are ;
Lift the blind fog on Anticosti's lee
And Avalon's rock ; make populous the sea
Round Grand Manan with eager finny
    swarms,
Break the long calms, and charm away the
    storms.

SAMUEL J. TILDEN

GREYSTONE, AUGUST 4, 1886

ONCE more, O all-adjusting Death !
  The nation's Pantheon opens wide ;
Once more a common sorrow saith
  A strong, wise man has died.

Faults doubtless had he.   Had we not
  Our own, to question and asperse
The worth we doubted or forgot
  Until beside his hearse ?

Ambitious, cautious, yet the man
  To strike down fraud with resolute hand
A patriot, if a partisan,
  He loved his native land.

So let the mourning bells be rung,
  The banner droop its folds half way,
And while the public pen and tongue
  Their fitting tribute pay,

Shall we not vow above his bier
  To set our feet on party lies,
And wound no more a living ear
  With words that Death denies ?

OCCASIONAL POEMS

EVA

Suggested by Mrs. Stowe's tale of Uncle
Tom's Cabin, *and written when the characters
in the tale were realities by the fireside of
countless American homes.*

DRY the tears for holy Eva,
With the blessed angels leave her;
Of the form so soft and fair
Give to earth the tender care.

For the golden locks of Eva
Let the sunny south-land give her
Flowery pillow of repose,
Orange-bloom and budding rose.

In the better home of Eva
Let the shining ones receive her,
With the welcome-voicèd psalm,
Harp of gold and waving palm!

All is light and peace with Eva;
There the darkness cometh never;
Tears are wiped, and fetters fall,
And the Lord is all in all.

Weep no more for happy Eva,
Wrong and sin no more shall grieve her;
Care and pain and weariness
Lost in love so measureless.

Gentle Eva, loving Eva,
Child confessor, true believer,
Listener at the Master's knee,
"Suffer such to come to me."

Oh, for faith like thine, sweet Eva,
Lighting all the solemn river,
And the blessings of the poor
Wafting to the heavenly shore!

A LAY OF OLD TIME

*Written for the Essex County Agricultural
Fair, and sung at the banquet at Newburyport,
October 2, 1856.*

ONE morning of the first sad Fall,
  Poor Adam and his bride
Sat in the shade of Eden's wall —
  But on the outer side.

She, blushing in her fig-leaf suit
  For the chaste garb of old;
He, sighing o'er his bitter fruit
  For Eden's drupes of gold.

Behind them, smiling in the morn,
  Their forfeit garden lay,
Before them, wild with rock and thorn,
  The desert stretched away.

They heard the air above them fanned,
  A light step on the sward,
And lo! they saw before them stand
  The angel of the Lord!

"Arise," he said, "why look behind,
  When hope is all before,
And patient hand and willing mind
  Your loss may yet restore?

"I leave with you a spell whose power
  Can make the desert glad,
And call around you fruit and flower
  As fair as Eden had.

"I clothe your hands with power to lift
  The curse from off your soil;
Your very doom shall seem a gift,
  Your loss a gain through Toil.

"Go, cheerful as yon humming-bees,
  To labor as to play."
White glimmering over Eden's trees
  The angel passed away.

The pilgrims of the world went forth
  Obedient to the word,
And found where'er they tilled the earth
  A garden of the Lord!

The thorn-tree cast its evil fruit
  And blushed with plum and pear,

And seeded grass and trodden root
  Grew sweet beneath their care.

We share our primal parents' fate,
  And, in our turn and day,
Look back on Eden's sworded gate
  As sad and lost as they.

But still for us his native skies
  The pitying Angel leaves,
And leads through Toil to Paradise
  New Adams and new Eves !

A SONG OF HARVEST

For the Agricultural and Horticultural Exhibition at Amesbury and Salisbury, September 28, 1858.

THIS day, two hundred years ago,
  The wild grape by the river's side,
And tasteless groundnut trailing low,
  The table of the woods supplied.

Unknown the apple's red and gold,
  The blushing tint of peach and pear ;
The mirror of the Powow told
  No tale of orchards ripe and rare.

Wild as the fruits he scorned to till,
  These vales the idle Indian trod ;
Nor knew the glad, creative skill,
  The joy of him who toils with God.

O Painter of the fruits and flowers !
  We thank Thee for thy wise design
Whereby these human hands of ours
  In Nature's garden work with Thine.

And thanks that from our daily need
  The joy of simple faith is born ;
That he who smites the summer weed,
  May trust Thee for the autumn corn.

Give fools their gold, and knaves their
        power ;
  Let fortune's bubbles rise and fall ;
Who sows a field, or trains a flower,
  Or plants a tree, is more than all.

For he who blesses most is blest ;
  And God and man shall own his worth
Who toils to leave as his bequest
  An added beauty to the earth.

And, soon or late, to all that sow,
  The time of harvest shall be given ;
The flower shall bloom, the fruit shall grow,
  If not on earth, at last in heaven.

KENOZA LAKE

This beautiful lake in East Haverhill was the " Great Pond " of the writer's boyhood. In 1859 a movement was made for improving its shores as a public park. At the opening of the park, August 31, 1859, the poem which gave it the name of Kenoza (in the Indian language signifying Pickerel) was read.

As Adam did in Paradise,
  To-day the primal right we claim :
Fair mirror of the woods and skies,
  We give to thee a name.

Lake of the pickerel ! — let no more
  The echoes answer back, " Great Pond,"
But sweet Kenoza, from thy shore
  And watching hills beyond,

Let Indian ghosts, if such there be
  Who ply unseen their shadowy lines,
Call back the ancient name to thee,
  As with the voice of pines.

The shores we trod as barefoot boys,
  The nutted woods we wandered through,
To friendship, love, and social joys
  We consecrate anew.

Here shall the tender song be sung,
  And memory's dirges soft and low,
And wit shall sparkle on the tongue,
  And mirth shall overflow,

Harmless as summer lightning plays
  From a low, hidden cloud by night,
A light to set the hills ablaze,
  But not a bolt to smite.

In sunny South and prairied West
  Are exiled hearts remembering still,
As bees their hive, as birds their nest,
  The homes of Haverhill.

They join us in our rites to-day ;
  And, listening, we may hear, erelong,
From inland lake and ocean bay,
  The echoes of our song.

Kenoza ! o'er no sweeter lake
   Shall morning break or noon-cloud sail, —
No fairer face than thine shall take
   The sunset's golden veil.

Long be it ere the tide of trade
   Shall break with harsh-resounding din
The quiet of thy banks of shade,
   And hills that fold thee in.

Still let thy woodlands hide the hare,
   The shy loon sound his trumpet-note.
Wind-weary from his fields of air,
   The wild-goose on thee float.

Thy peace rebuke our feverish stir,
   Thy beauty our deforming strife ;
Thy woods and waters minister
   The healing of their life.

And sinless Mirth, from care released,
   Behold, unawed, thy mirrored sky,
Smiling as smiled on Cana's feast
   The Master's loving eye.

And when the summer day grows dim,
   And light mists walk thy mimic sea,
Revive in us the thought of Him
   Who walked on Galilee !

FOR AN AUTUMN FESTIVAL

THE Persian's flowery gifts, the shrine
   Of fruitful Ceres charm no more ;
The woven wreaths of oak and pine
   Are dust along the Isthmian shore.

But beauty hath its homage still,
   And nature holds us still in debt ;
And woman's grace and household skill,
   And manhood's toil, are honored yet.

And we, to-day, amidst our flowers
   And fruits, have come to own again
The blessings of the summer hours,
   The early and the latter rain ;

To see our Father's hand once more
   Reverse for us the plenteous horn
Of autumn, filled and running o'er
   With fruit, and flower, and golden corn !

Once more the liberal year laughs out
   O'er richer stores than gems or gold ;

Once more with harvest-song and shout
   Is Nature's bloodless triumph told.

Our common mother rests and sings,
   Like Ruth, among her garnered sheaves ;
Her lap is full of goodly things,
   Her brow is bright with autumn leaves.

Oh, favors every year made new !
   Oh, gifts with rain and sunshine sent !
The bounty overruns our due,
   The fulness shames our discontent.

We shut our eyes, the flowers bloom on ;
   We murmur, but the corn-ears fill,
We choose the shadow, but the sun
   That casts it shines behind us still.

God gives us with our rugged soil
   The power to make it Eden-fair,
And richer fruits to crown our toil
   Than summer-wedded islands bear.

Who murmurs at his lot to-day ?
   Who scorns his native fruit and bloom ?
Or sighs for dainties far away,
   Beside the bounteous board of home ?

Thank Heaven, instead, that Freedom's arm
   Can change a rocky soil to gold, —
That brave and generous lives can warm
   A clime with northern ices cold.

And let these altars, wreathed with flowers
   And piled with fruits, awake again
Thanksgivings for the golden hours,
   The early and the latter rain !

THE QUAKER ALUMNI

Read at the Friends' School Anniversary,
Providence, R. I., 6th mo., 1860.

FROM the well-springs of Hudson, the sea-
     cliffs of Maine,
Grave men, sober matrons, you gather
     again ;
And, with hearts warmer grown as your
     heads grow more cool,
Play over the old game of going to school.

All your strifes and vexations, your whims
     and complaints,
(You were not saints yourselves, if the
     children of saints !)

All your petty self-seekings and rivalries
    done,
Round the dear Alma Mater your hearts
    beat as one !

How widely soe'er you have strayed from
    the fold,
Though your "thee" has grown "you," and
    your drab blue and gold,
To the old friendly speech and the garb's
    sober form,
Like the heart of Argyle to the tartan, you
    warm.

But, the first greetings over, you glance
    round the hall ;
Your hearts call the roll, but they answer
    not all :
Through the turf green above them the dead
    cannot hear ;
Name by name, in the silence, falls sad as
    a tear !

In love, let us trust, they were summoned
    so soon
From the morning of life, while we toil
    through its noon ;
They were frail like ourselves, they had
    needs like our own,
And they rest as we rest in God's mercy
    alone.

Unchanged by our changes of spirit and
    frame,
Past, now, and henceforward the Lord is
    the same ;
Though we sink in the darkness, His arms
    break our fall,
And in death as in life, He is Father of
    all !

We are older : our footsteps, so light in
    the play
Of the far-away school-time, move slower
    to-day ; —
Here a beard touched with frost, there a
    bald, shining crown,
And beneath the cap's border gray mingles
    with brown.

But faith should be cheerful, and trust
    should be glad,
And our follies and sins, not our years, make
    us sad.

Should the heart closer shut as the bonnet
    grows prim,
And the face grow in length as the hat grows
    in brim ?

Life is brief, duty grave ; but, with rain-
    folded wings,
Of yesterday's sunshine the grateful heart
    sings ;
And we, of all others, have reason to pay
The tribute of thanks, and rejoice on our
    way ;

For the counsels that turned from the follies
    of youth ;
For the beauty of patience, the whiteness of
    truth ;
For the wounds of rebuke, when love tem-
    pered its edge ;
For the household's restraint, and the disci-
    pline's hedge ;

For the lessons of kindness vouchsafed to
    the least
Of the creatures of God, whether human
    or beast,
Bringing hope to the poor, lending strength
    to the frail,
In the lanes of the city, the slave-hut, and
    jail ;

For a womanhood higher and holier, by all
Her knowledge of good, than was Eve ere
    her fall, —
Whose task-work of duty moves lightly as
    play,
Serene as the moonlight and warm as the
    day ;

And, yet more, for the faith which embraces
    the whole,
Of the creeds of the ages the life and the
    soul,
Wherein letter and spirit the same channel
    run,
And man has not severed what God has
    made one !

For a sense of the Goodness revealed every-
    where,
As sunshine impartial, and free as the air ;
For a trust in humanity, Heathen or Jew,
And a hope for all darkness the Light
    shineth through.

Who scoffs at our birthright ? — the words
    of the seers,
And the songs of the bards in the twilight
    of years,
All the foregleams of wisdom in santon and
    sage,
In prophet and priest, are our true heritage.

The Word which the reason of Plato dis-
    cerned ;
The truth, as whose symbol the Mithra-fire
    burned ;
The soul of the world which the Stoic but
    guessed,
In the Light Universal the Quaker con-
    fessed !

No honors of war to our worthies be-
    long ;
Their plain stem of life never flowered into
    song ;
But the fountains they opened still gush by
    the way,
And the world for their healing is better to-
    day.

He who lies where the minster's groined
    arches curve down
To the tomb-crowded transept of England's
    renown,
The glorious essayist, by genius enthroned,
Whose pen as a sceptre the Muses all
    owned, —

Who through the world's pantheon walked
    in his pride,
Setting new statues up, thrusting old ones
    aside,
And in fiction the pencils of history dipped,
To gild o'er or blacken each saint in his
    crypt, —

How vainly he labored to sully with
    blame
The white bust of Penn, in the niche of his
    fame !
Self - will is self - wounding, perversity
    blind :
On himself fell the stain for the Quaker
    designed !

For the sake of his true-hearted father be-
    fore him ;
For the sake of the dear Quaker mother
    that bore him ;

For the sake of his gifts, and the works that
    outlive him,
And his brave words for freedom, we freely
    forgive him !

There are those who take note that our
    numbers are small, —
New Gibbons who write our decline and our
    fall ;
But the Lord of the seed-field takes care of
    His own,
And the world shall yet reap what our sow-
    ers have sown.

The last of the sect to his fathers may go,
Leaving only his coat for some Barnum to
    show ;
But the truth will outlive him, and broaden
    with years,
Till the false dies away, and the wrong dis-
    appears.

Nothing fails of its end. Out of sight
    sinks the stone,
In the deep sea of time, but the circles
    sweep on,
Till the low-rippled murmurs along the
    shores run,
And the dark and dead waters leap glad in
    the sun.

Meanwhile shall we learn, in our ease, to
    forget
To the martyrs of Truth and of Freedom
    our debt ? —
Hide their words out of sight, like the garb
    that they wore,
And for Barclay's Apology offer one more ?

Shall we fawn round the priestcraft that
    glutted the shears,
And festooned the stocks with our grand-
    fathers' ears ?
Talk of Woolman's unsoundness ? count
    Penn heterodox ?
And take Cotton Mather in place of George
    Fox ?

Make our preachers war-chaplains ? quote
    Scripture to take
The hunted slave back, for Onesimus' sake ?
Go to burning church-candles, and chanting
    in choir,
And on the old meeting-house stick up a
    spire ?

No ! the old paths we 'll keep until better
are shown,
Credit good where we find it, abroad or our
own ;
And while " Lo here " and " Lo there " the
multitude call,
Be true to ourselves, and do justice to all.

The good round about us we need not refuse,
Nor talk of our Zion as if we were Jews;
But why shirk the badge which our fathers
have worn,
Or beg the world's pardon for having been
born ?

We need not pray over the Pharisee's prayer,
Nor claim that our wisdom is Benjamin's
share ;
Truth to us and to others is equal and one :
Shall we bottle the free air, or hoard up the
sun ?

Well know we our birthright may serve
but to show
How the meanest of weeds in the richest
soil grow ;
But we need not disparage the good which
we hold ;
Though the vessels be earthen, the treasure
is gold !

Enough and too much of the sect and the
name.
What matters our label, so truth be our
aim ?
The creed may be wrong, but the life may
be true,
And hearts beat the same under drab coats
or blue.

So the man be a man, let him worship, at
will,
In Jerusalem's courts, or on Gerizim's hill.
When she makes up her jewels, what cares
yon good town
For the Baptist of Wayland, the Quaker of
Brown ?

And this green, favored island, so fresh and
sea-blown,
When she counts up the worthies her annals
have known,
Never waits for the pitiful gaugers of sect
To measure her love, and mete out her re-
spect.

Three shades at this moment seem walking
her strand,
Each with head halo-crowned, and with
palms in his hand, —
Wise Berkeley, grave Hopkins, and, smiling
serene
On prelate and puritan, Channing is seen.

One holy name bearing, no longer they
need
Credentials of party, and pass-words of
creed:
The new song they sing hath a threefold
accord,
And they own one baptism, one faith, and
one Lord !

But the golden sands run out : occasions
like these
Glide swift into shadow, like sails on the
seas :
While we sport with the mosses and pebbles
ashore,
They lessen and fade, and we see them no
more.

Forgive me, dear friends, if my vagrant
thoughts seem
Like a school-boy's who idles and plays with
his theme.
Forgive the light measure whose changes
display
The sunshine and rain of our brief April
day.

There are moments in life when the lip and
the eye
Try the question of whether to smile or to
cry ;
And scenes and reunions that prompt like
our own
The tender in feeling, the playful in tone.

I, who never sat down with the boys and the
girls
At the feet of your Slocums, and Cartlands,
and Earles, —
By courtesy only permitted to lay
On your festival's altar my poor gift, to-
day, —

I would joy in your joy : let me have a
friend's part
In the warmth of your welcome of hand
and of heart, —

On your play-ground of boyhood unbend
   the brow's care,
And shift the old burdens our shoulders
   must bear.

Long live the good School ! giving out year
   by year
Recruits to true manhood and womanhood
   dear :
Brave boys, modest maidens, in beauty sent
   forth,
The living epistles and proof of its worth !

In and out let the young life as steadily
   flow
As in broad Narragansett the tides come
   and go ;
And its sons and its daughters in prairie
   and town
Remember its honor, and guard its renown.

Not vainly the gift of its founder was
   made ;
Not prayerless the stones of its corner were
   laid :
The blessing of Him whom in secret they
   sought
Has owned the good work which the fathers
   have wrought.

To Him be the glory forever ! We bear
To the Lord of the Harvest our wheat with
   the tare.
What we lack in our work may He find in
   our will,
And winnow in mercy our good from the
   ill !

OUR RIVER

FOR A SUMMER FESTIVAL AT "THE LAURELS" ON THE MERRIMAC

Jean Pierre Brissot, the famous leader of the
Girondist party in the French Revolution, when
a young man travelled extensively in the United
States. He visited the valley of the Merrimac,
and speaks in terms of admiration of the view
from Moulton's hill opposite Amesbury. The
"Laurel Party," so called, was composed of
ladies and gentlemen in the lower valley of the
Merrimac, and invited friends and guests in
other sections of the country. Its thoroughly
enjoyable annual festivals were held in the early
summer on the pine-shaded, laurel-blossomed
slopes of the Newbury side of the river opposite
Pleasant Valley in Amesbury. The several
poems called out by these gatherings are here
printed in sequence.

ONCE more on yonder laurelled height
   The summer flowers have budded ;
Once more with summer's golden light
   The vales of home are flooded ;
And once more, by the grace of Him
   Of every good the Giver,
We sing upon its wooded rim
   The praises of our river :

Its pines above, its waves below,
   The west-wind down it blowing,
As fair as when the young Brissot
   Beheld it seaward flowing, —
And bore its memory o'er the deep,
   To soothe the martyr's sadness,
And fresco, in his troubled sleep,
   His prison-walls with gladness.

We know the world is rich with streams
   Renowned in song and story,
Whose music murmurs through our dreams
   Of human love and glory :
We know that Arno's banks are fair,
   And Rhine has castled shadows,
And, poet-tuned, the Doon and Ayr
   Go singing down their meadows.

But while, unpictured and unsung
   By painter or by poet,
Our river waits the tuneful tongue
   And cunning hand to show it, —
We only know the fond skies lean
   Above it, warm with blessing,
And the sweet soul of our Undine
   Awakes to our caressing.

No fickle sun-god holds the flocks
   That graze its shores in keeping ;
No icy kiss of Dian mocks
   The youth beside it sleeping :
Our Christian river loveth most
   The beautiful and human ;
The heathen streams of Naiads boast,
   But ours of man and woman.

The miner in his cabin hears
   The ripple we are hearing ;
It whispers soft to homesick ears
   Around the settler's clearing :
In Sacramento's vales of corn,

Or Santee's bloom of cotton,
Our river by its valley-born
  Was never yet forgotten.

The drum rolls loud, the bugle fills
  The summer air with clangor ;
The war-storm shakes the solid hills
  Beneath its tread of anger ;
Young eyes that last year smiled in ours
  Now point the rifle's barrel,
And hands then stained with fruits and
    flowers
  Bear redder stains of quarrel.

But blue skies smile, and flowers bloom on,
  And rivers still keep flowing,
The dear God still his rain and sun
  On good and ill bestowing.
His pine-trees whisper, "Trust and wait !"
  His flowers are prophesying
That all we dread of change or fate
  His love is underlying.

And thou, O Mountain-born ! — no more
  We ask the wise Allotter
Than for the firmness of thy shore,
  The calmness of thy water,
The cheerful lights that overlay
  Thy rugged slopes with beauty,
To match our spirits to our day
  And make a joy of duty.

REVISITED

Read at "The Laurels," on the Merrimac,
6th month, 1865.

THE roll of drums and the bugle's wailing
  Vex the air of our vales no more ;
The spear is beaten to hooks of pruning,
  The share is the sword the soldier wore !

Sing soft, sing low, our lowland river,
  Under thy banks of laurel bloom ;
Softly and sweet, as the hour beseemeth,
  Sing us the songs of peace and home.

Let all the tenderer voices of nature
  Temper the triumph and chasten mirth,
Full of the infinite love and pity
  For fallen martyr and darkened hearth.

But to Him who gives us beauty for ashes,
  And the oil of joy for mourning long,

Let thy hills give thanks, and all thy waters
  Break into jubilant waves of song !

Bring us the airs of hills and forests,
  The sweet aroma of birch and pine,
Give us a waft of the north-wind laden
  With sweetbrier odors and breath of kine !

Bring us the purple of mountain sunsets,
  Shadows of clouds that rake the hills,
The green repose of thy Plymouth meadows,
  The gleam and ripple of Campton rills.

Lead us away in shadow and sunshine,
  Slaves of fancy, through all thy miles,
The winding ways of Pemigewasset,
  And Winnipesaukee's hundred isles.

Shatter in sunshine over thy ledges,
  Laugh in thy plunges from fall to fall ;
Play with thy fringes of elms, and darken
  Under the shade of the mountain wall.

The cradle-song of thy hillside fountains
  Here in thy glory and strength repeat ;
Give us a taste of thy upland music,
  Show us the dance of thy silver feet.

Into thy dutiful life of uses
  Pour the music and weave the flowers :
With the song of birds and bloom of mead-
      ows
  Lighten and gladden thy heart and ours.

Sing on ! bring down, O lowland river,
  The joy of the hills to the waiting sea ;
The wealth of the vales, the pomp of moun-
      tains,
  The breath of the woodlands, bear with
      thee.

Here, in the calm of thy seaward valley,
  Mirth and labor shall hold their truce ;
Dance of water and mill of grinding,
  Both are beauty and both are use.

Type of the Northland's strength and glory,
  Pride and hope of our home and race, —
Freedom lending to rugged labor
  Tints of beauty and lines of grace.

Once again, O beautiful river,
  Hear our greetings and take our thanks ;
Hither we come, as Eastern pilgrims
  Throng to the Jordan's sacred banks.

For though by the Master's feet untrod-
den,
   Though never His word has stilled thy
waves,
Well for us may thy shores be holy,
   With Christian altars and saintly graves.

And well may we own thy hint and token
   Of fairer valleys and streams than these,
Where the rivers of God are full of water,
   And full of sap are His healing trees !

"THE LAURELS"

At the twentieth and last anniversary.

FROM these wild rocks I look to-day
   O'er leagues of dancing waves, and see
The far, low coast-line stretch away
   To where our river meets the sea.

The light wind blowing off the land
   Is burdened with old voices ; through
Shut eyes I see how lip and hand
   The greeting of old days renew.

O friends whose hearts still keep their
prime,
   Whose bright example warms and cheers,
Ye teach us how to smile at Time,
   And set to music all his years !

I thank you for sweet summer days,
   For pleasant memories lingering long,
For joyful meetings, fond delays,
   And ties of friendship woven strong.

As for the last time, side by side,
   You tread the paths familiar grown,
I reach across the severing tide,
   And blend my farewells with your own.

Make room, O river of our home !
   For other feet in place of ours,
And in the summers yet to come,
   Make glad another Feast of Flowers !

Hold in thy mirror, calm and deep,
   The pleasant pictures thou hast seen ;
Forget thy lovers not, but keep
   Our memory like thy laurels green.

JUNE ON THE MERRIMAC

O DWELLERS in the stately towns,
   What come ye out to see ?
This common earth, this common sky,
   This water flowing free ?

As gayly as these kalmia flowers
   Your door-yard blossoms spring ;
As sweetly as these wild-wood birds
   Your cagèd minstrels sing.

You find but common bloom and green
   The rippling river's rune,
The beauty which is everywhere
   Beneath the skies of June ;

The Hawkswood oaks, the storm - torn
plumes
   Of old pine-forest kings,
Beneath whose century-woven shade
   Deer Island's mistress sings.

And here are pictured Artichoke,
   And Curson's bowery mill ;
And Pleasant Valley smiles between
   The river and the hill.

You know full well these banks of bloom,
   The upland's wavy line,
And how the sunshine tips with fire
   The needles of the pine.

Yet, like some old remembered psalm,
   Or sweet, familiar face,
Not less because of commonness
   You love the day and place.

And not in vain in this soft air
   Shall hard-strung nerves relax,
Not all in vain the o'erworn brain
   Forego its daily tax.

The lust of power, the greed of gain
   Have all the year their own ;
The haunting demons well may let
   Our one bright day alone.

Unheeded let the newsboy call,
   Aside the ledger lay :
The world will keep its treadmill step
   Though we fall out to-day.

The truants of life's weary school,
  Without excuse from thrift
We change for once the gains of toil
  For God's unpurchased gift.

From ceilëd rooms, from silent books,
  From crowded car and town,
Dear Mother Earth, upon thy lap
  We lay our tired heads down.

Cool, summer wind, our heated brows ;
  Blue river, through the green
Of clustering pines, refresh the eyes
  Which all too much have seen.

For us these pleasant woodland ways
  Are thronged with memories old,
Have felt the grasp of friendly hands
  And heard love's story told.

A sacred presence overbroods
  The earth whereon we meet ;
These winding forest-paths are trod
  By more than mortal feet.

Old friends called from us by the voice
  Which they alone could hear,
From mystery to mystery,
  From life to life, draw near.

More closely for the sake of them
  Each other's hands we press ;
Our voices take from them a tone
  Of deeper tenderness.

Our joy is theirs, their trust is ours,
  Alike below, above,
Or here or there, about us fold
  The arms of one great love !

We ask to-day no countersign,
  No party names we own ;
Unlabelled, individual,
  We bring ourselves alone.

What cares the unconventioned wood
  For pass-words of the town ?
The sound of fashion's shibboleth
  The laughing waters drown.

Here cant forgets his dreary tone,
  And care his face forlorn ;
The liberal air and sunshine laugh
  The bigot's zeal to scorn.

From manhood's weary shoulder falls
  His load of selfish cares ;
And woman takes her rights as flowers
  And brooks and birds take theirs.

The license of the happy woods,
  The brook's release are ours ;
The freedom of the unshamed wind
  Among the glad-eyed flowers.

Yet here no evil thought finds place,
  Nor foot profane comes in ;
Our grove, like that of Samothrace,
  Is set apart from sin.

We walk on holy ground ; above
  A sky more holy smiles ;
The chant of the beatitudes
  Swells down these leafy aisles.

Thanks to the gracious Providence
  That brings us here once more ;
For memories of the good behind
  And hopes of good before !

And if, unknown to us, sweet days
  Of June like this must come,
Unseen of us these laurels clothe
  The river-banks with bloom ;

And these green paths must soon be trod
  By other feet than ours,
Full long may annual pilgrims come
  To keep the Feast of Flowers ;

The matron be a girl once more,
  The bearded man a boy,
And we, in heaven's eternal June,
  Be glad for earthly joy !

HYMN

FOR THE OPENING OF THOMAS STARR KING'S HOUSE OF WORSHIP, 1864

The poetic and patriotic preacher, who had
won fame in the East, went to California in
1860 and became a power on the Pacific coast.
It was not long after the opening of the house
of worship built for him that he died.

AMIDST these glorious works of Thine,
The solemn minarets of the pine,
And awful Shasta's icy shrine, —

Where swell Thy hymns from wave and
      gale,
And organ-thunders never fail,
Behind the cataract's silver veil, —

Our puny walls to Thee we raise,
Our poor reed-music sounds Thy praise :
Forgive, O Lord, our childish ways !

For, kneeling on these altar-stairs,
We urge Thee not with selfish prayers,
Nor murmur at our daily cares.

Before Thee, in an evil day,
Our country's bleeding heart we lay,
And dare not ask Thy hand to stay ;

But, through the war-cloud, pray to Thee
For union, but a union free,
With peace that comes of purity !

That Thou wilt bare Thy arm to save
And, smiting through this Red Sea wave,
Make broad a pathway for the slave !

For us, confessing all our need,
We trust nor rite nor word nor deed,
Nor yet the broken staff of creed.

Assured alone that Thou art good
To each, as to the multitude,
Eternal Love and Fatherhood, —

Weak, sinful, blind, to Thee we kneel,
Stretch dumbly forth our hands, and
      feel
Our weakness is our strong appeal.

So, by these Western gates of Even
We wait to see with Thy forgiven
The opening Golden Gate of Heaven !

Suffice it now.   In time to be
Shall holier altars rise to Thee, —
Thy Church our broad humanity !

White flowers of love its walls shall
      climb,
Soft bells of peace shall ring its chime,
Its days shall all be holy time.

A sweeter song shall then be heard, —
The music of the world's accord
Confessing Christ, the Inward Word !

That song shall swell from shore to shore,
One hope, one faith, one love, restore
The seamless robe that Jesus wore.

HYMN

FOR THE HOUSE OF WORSHIP AT GEORGE-
TOWN, ERECTED IN MEMORY OF A
MOTHER

The giver of the house was the late George
Peabody, of London.

THOU dwellest not, O Lord of all !
    In temples which thy children raise ;
Our work to Thine is mean and small,
    And brief to Thy eternal days.

Forgive the weakness and the pride,
    If marred thereby our gift may be,
For love, at least, has sanctified
    The altar that we rear to thee.

The heart and not the hand has wrought
    From sunken base to tower above
The image of a tender thought,
    The memory of a deathless love !

And though should never sound of speech
    Or organ echo from its wall,
Its stones would pious lessons teach,
    Its shade in benedictions fall.

Here should the dove of peace be found,
    And blessings and not curses given ;
Nor strife profane, nor hatred wound
    The mingled loves of earth and heaven.

Thou, who didst soothe with dying breath
    The dear one watching by Thy cross,
Forgetful of the pains of death
    In sorrow for her mighty loss,

In memory of that tender claim,
    O Mother-born, the offering take,
And make it worthy of Thy name,
    And bless it for a mother's sake !

A SPIRITUAL MANIFESTATION

Read at the President's Levee, Brown Uni-
versity, 29th 6th month, 1870.

To-DAY the plant by Williams set
  Its summer bloom discloses ;
The wilding sweetbrier of his prayers
  Is crowned with cultured roses.

Once more the Island State repeats
  The lesson that he taught her,
And binds his pearl of charity
  Upon her brown-locked daughter.

Is 't fancy that he watches still
  His Providence plantations ?
That still the careful Founder takes
  A part on these occasions ?

Methinks I see that reverend form,
  Which all of us so well know :
He rises up to speak ; he jogs
  The presidential elbow.

" Good friends," he says, " you reap a field
  I sowed in self-denial,
For toleration had its griefs
  And charity its trial.

" Great grace, as saith Sir Thomas More,
  To him must needs be given
Who heareth heresy and leaves
  The heretic to Heaven !

" I hear again the snuffled tones,
  I see in dreary vision
Dyspeptic dreamers, spiritual bores,
  And prophets with a mission.

" Each zealot thrust before my eyes
  His Scripture-garbled label ;
All creeds were shouted in my ears
  As with the tongues of Babel.

" Scourged at one cart-tail, each denied
  The hope of every other ;
Each martyr shook his branded fist
  At the conscience of his brother !

" How cleft the dreary drone of man
  The shriller pipe of woman,
As Gorton led his saints elect,
  Who held all things in common !

" Their gay robes trailed in ditch and
    swamp,
  And torn by thorn and thicket,
The dancing-girls of Merry Mount
  Came dragging to my wicket.

" Shrill Anabaptists, shorn of ears ;
  Gray witch-wives, hobbling slowly ;
And Antinomians, free of law,
  Whose very sins were holy.

" Hoarse ranters, crazed Fifth Monarch-
    ists
Of stripes and bondage braggarts,
Pale Churchmen, with singed rubrics
    snatched
  From Puritanic fagots.

" And last, not least, the Quakers came,
  With tongues still sore from burning,
The Bay State's dust from off their feet
  Before my threshold spurning ;

" A motley host, the Lord's *débris*,
  Faith's odds and ends together ;
Well might I shrink from guests with
    lungs
  Tough as their breeches leather :

" If, when the hangman at their heels
  Came, rope in hand to catch them,
I took the hunted outcasts in,
  I never sent to fetch them.

" I fed, but spared them not a whit ;
  I gave to all who walked in,
Not clams and succotash alone,
  But stronger meat of doctrine.

" I proved the prophets false, I pricked
  The bubble of perfection,
And clapped upon their inner light
  The snuffers of election.

" And looking backward on my times,
  This credit I am taking ;
I kept each sectary's dish apart,
  No spiritual chowder making.

" Where now the blending signs of sect
  Would puzzle their assorter,
The dry-shod Quaker kept the land,
  The Baptist held the water.

" A common coat now serves for both,
  The hat 's no more a fixture ;
And which was wet and which was dry,
  Who knows in such a mixture ?

" Well ! He who fashioned Peter's dream
  To bless them all is able ;

And bird and beast and creeping thing
  Make clean upon His table !

" I walked by my own light ; but when
  The ways of faith divided,
Was I to force unwilling feet
  To tread the path that I did ?

" I touched the garment-hem of truth,
  Yet saw not all its splendor ;
I knew enough of doubt to feel
  For every conscience tender.

" God left men free of choice, as when
  His Eden-trees were planted ;
Because they chose amiss, should I
  Deny the gift He granted ?

" So, with a common sense of need,
  Our common weakness feeling,
I left them with myself to God
  And His all-gracious dealing !

" I kept His plan whose rain and sun
  To tare and wheat are given ;
And if the ways to hell were free,
  I left them free to heaven ! "

Take heart with us, O man of old,
  Soul-freedom's brave confessor,
So love of God and man wax strong,
  Let sect and creed be lesser.

The jarring discords of thy day
  In ours one hymn are swelling ;
The wandering feet, the severed paths,
  All seek our Father's dwelling.

And slowly learns the world the truth
  That makes us all thy debtor, —
That holy life is more than rite,
  And spirit more than letter ;

That they who differ pole-wide serve
  Perchance the common Master,
And other sheep He hath than they
  Who graze one narrow pasture !

For truth's worst foe is he who claims
  To act as God's avenger,
And deems, beyond his sentry-beat,
  The crystal walls in danger !

Who sets for heresy his traps
  Of verbal quirk and quibble,

And weeds the garden of the Lord
  With Satan's borrowed dibble.

To-day our hearts like organ keys
  One Master's touch are feeling ;
The branches of a common Vine
  Have only leaves of healing.

Co-workers, yet from varied fields,
  We share this restful nooning ;
The Quaker with the Baptist here
  Believes in close communing.

Forgive, dear saint, the playful tone,
  Too light for thy deserving ;
Thanks for thy generous faith in man,
  Thy trust in God unswerving.

Still echo in the hearts of men
  The words that thou hast spoken
No forge of hell can weld again
  The fetters thou hast broken.

The pilgrim needs a pass no more
  From Roman or Genevan ;
Thought-free, no ghostly tollman keeps
  Henceforth the road to Heaven !

CHICAGO

    The great fire at Chicago was on 8–10 October, 1871.

MEN said at vespers : " All is well ! "
In one wild night the city fell ;
Fell shrines of prayer and marts of gain
Before the fiery hurricane.

On threescore spires had sunset shone,
Where ghastly sunrise looked on none.
Men clasped each other's hands, and said :
" The City of the West is dead ! "

Brave hearts who fought, in slow retreat,
The fiends of fire from street to street,
Turned, powerless, to the blinding glare,
The dumb defiance of despair.

A sudden impulse thrilled each wire
That signalled round that sea of fire ;
Swift words of cheer, warm heart - throbs
    came ;
In tears of pity died the flame !

From East, from West, from South and
    North,
The messages of hope shot forth,
And, underneath the severing wave,
The world, full-handed, reached to save.

Fair seemed the old ; but fairer still
The new, the dreary void shall fill
With dearer homes than those o'erthrown,
For love shall lay each corner-stone.

Rise, stricken city ! from thee throw
The ashen sackcloth of thy woe ;
And build, as to Amphion's strain,
To songs of cheer thy walls again !

How shrivelled in thy hot distress
The primal sin of selfishness !
How instant rose, to take thy part,
The angel in the human heart !

Ah ! not in vain the flames that tossed
Above thy dreadful holocaust ;
The Christ again has preached through thee
The Gospel of Humanity !

Then lift once more thy towers on high,
And fret with spires the western sky,
To tell that God is yet with us,
And love is still miraculous !

KINSMAN

Died at the Island of Panay (Philippine
group), aged nineteen years.

WHERE ceaseless Spring her garland twines,
    As sweetly shall the loved one rest,
As if beneath the whispering pines
    And maple shadows of the West.

Ye mourn, O hearts of home ! for him,
    But, haply, mourn ye not alone ;
For him shall far-off eyes be dim,
    And pity speak in tongues unknown.

There needs no graven line to give
    The story of his blameless youth ;
All hearts shall throb intuitive,
    And nature guess the simple truth.

The very meaning of his name
    Shall many a tender tribute win ;
The stranger own his sacred claim,
    And all the world shall be his kin.

And there, as here, on main and isle,
    The dews of holy peace shall fall,
The same sweet heavens above him smile
And God's dear love be over all !

THE GOLDEN WEDDING OF LONGWOOD

Longwood, not far from Bayard Taylor's
birthplace in Kennett Square, Pennsylvania,
was the home of my esteemed friends John and
Hannah Cox, whose golden wedding was cele-
brated in 1874.

WITH fifty years between you and your
    well-kept wedding vow,
The Golden Age, old friends of mine, is not
    a fable now.

And, sweet as has life's vintage been through
    all your pleasant past,
Still, as at Cana's marriage-feast, the best
    wine is the last !

Again before me, with your names, fair
    Chester's landscape comes,
Its meadows, woods, and ample barns, and
    quaint, stone-builded homes.

The smooth-shorn vales, the wheaten slopes,
    the boscage green and soft,
Of which their poet sings so well from
    towered Cedarcroft.

And lo ! from all the country-side come
    neighbors, kith and kin ;
From city, hamlet, farm-house old, the
    wedding guests come in.

And they who, without scrip or purse, mob-
    hunted, travel-worn,
In Freedom's age of martyrs came, as
    victors now return.

Older and slower, yet the same, files in the
    long array,
And hearts are light and eyes are glad,
    though heads are badger-gray.

The fire-tried men of Thirty-eight who saw
    with me the fall,
Midst roaring flames and shouting mob, of
    Pennsylvania Hall ;

And they of Lancaster who turned the
    cheeks of tyrants pale,
Singing of freedom through the grates of
    Moyamensing jail !

And haply with them, all unseen, old com-
    rades, gone before,
Pass, silently as shadows pass, within your
    open door, —

The eagle face of Lindley Coates, brave
    Garrett's daring zeal,
The Christian grace of Pennock, the stead-
    fast heart of Neal.

Ah me ! beyond all power to name, the
    worthies tried and true,
Grave men, fair women, youth and maid,
    pass by in hushed review.

Of varying faiths, a common cause fused
    all their hearts in one.
God give them now, whate'er their names,
    the peace of duty done !

How gladly would I tread again the old-
    remembered places,
Sit down beside your hearth once more and
    look in the dear old faces !

And thank you for the lessons your fifty
    years are teaching,
For honest lives that louder speak than
    half our noisy preaching ;

For your steady faith and courage in that
    dark and evil time,
When the Golden Rule was treason, and to
    feed the hungry crime ;

For the poor slave's house of refuge when
    the hounds were on his track,
And saint and sinner, church and state,
    joined hands to send him back.

Blessings upon you ! — What you did for
    each sad, suffering one,
So homeless, faint, and naked, unto our
    Lord was done !

Fair fall on Kennett's pleasant vales and
    Longwood's bowery ways
The mellow sunset of your lives, friends of
    my early days.

May many more of quiet years be added to
    your sum,
And, late at last, in tenderest love, the
    beckoning angel come.

Dear hearts are here, dear hearts are there,
    alike below, above ;
Our friends are now in either world, and
    love is sure of love.

HYMN

FOR THE OPENING OF PLYMOUTH CHURCH,
ST. PAUL, MINNESOTA

ALL things are Thine : no gift have we,
Lord of all gifts, to offer Thee ;
And hence with grateful hearts to-day,
Thy own before Thy feet we lay.

Thy will was in the builders' thought ;
Thy hand unseen amidst us wrought ;
Through mortal motive, scheme and plan,
Thy wise eternal purpose ran.

No lack Thy perfect fulness knew ;
For human needs and longings grew
This house of prayer, this home of rest,
In the fair garden of the West.

In weakness and in want we call
On Thee for whom the heavens are small;
Thy glory is Thy children's good,
Thy joy Thy tender Fatherhood.

O Father ! deign these walls to bless,
Fill with Thy love their emptiness,
And let their door a gateway be
To lead us from ourselves to Thee !

LEXINGTON

1775

No Berserk thirst of blood had they,
    No battle-joy was theirs, who set
    Against the alien bayonet
Their homespun breasts in that old day.

Their feet had trodden peaceful ways ;
    They loved not strife, they dreaded
    pain ;

They saw not, what to us is plain,
That God would make man's wrath His
 praise.

No seers were they, but simple men ;
 Its vast results the future hid :
 The meaning of the work they did
Was strange and dark and doubtful then.

Swift as their summons came they left
 The plough mid - furrow standing
  still,
 The half - ground corn grist in the
  mill
The spade in earth, the axe in cleft.

They went where duty seemed to call,
 They scarcely asked the reason why ;
 They only knew they could but die,
And death was not the worst of all !

Of man for man the sacrifice,
 All that was theirs to give, they
  gave.
 The flowers that blossomed from their
  grave
Have sown themselves beneath all skies.

Their death-shot shook the feudal tower,
 And shattered slavery's chain as
  well ;
 On the sky's dome, as on a bell,
Its echo struck the world's great hour.

That fateful echo is not dumb :
 The nations listening to its sound
 Wait, from a century's vantage-ground,
The holier triumphs yet to come, —

The bridal time of Law and Love,
 The gladness of the world's release,
 When, war-sick, at the feet of Peace
The hawk shall nestle with the dove ! —

The golden age of brotherhood
 Unknown to other rivalries
 Than of the mild humanities,
And gracious interchange of good,

When closer strand shall lean to strand,
 Till meet, beneath saluting flags,
 The eagle of our mountain-crags,
The lion of our Motherland !

THE LIBRARY

Sung at the opening of the Haverhill Library,
November 11, 1875.

"Let there be light !" God spake of old,
And over chaos dark and cold,
And through the dead and formless frame
Of nature, life and order came.

Faint was the light at first that shone
On giant fern and mastodon,
On half-formed plant and beast of prey,
And man as rude and wild as they.

Age after age, like waves, o'erran
The earth, uplifting brute and man ;
And mind, at length, in symbols dark
Its meanings traced on stone and bark.

On leaf of palm, on sedge-wrought roll ;
On plastic clay and leathern scroll,
Man wrote his thoughts ; the ages passed,
And lo ! the Press was found at last !

Then dead souls woke; the thoughts of men
Whose bones were dust revived again ;
The cloister's silence found a tongue,
Old prophets spake, old poets sung.

And here, to-day, the dead look down,
The kings of mind again we crown ;
We hear the voices lost so long,
The sage's word, the sibyl's song.

Here Greek and Roman find themselves
Alive along these crowded shelves ;
And Shakespeare treads again his stage,
And Chaucer paints anew his age.

As if some Pantheon's marbles broke
Their stony trance, and lived and spoke,
Life thrills along the alcoved hall,
The lords of thought await our call !

"I WAS A STRANGER AND YE TOOK ME IN"

An incident in St. Augustine, Florida.

'Neath skies that winter never knew
 The air was full of light and balm,

And warm and soft the Gulf wind blew
  Through orange bloom and groves of
    palm.

A stranger from the frozen North,
  Who sought the fount of health in vain,
Sank homeless on the alien earth,
  And breathed the languid air with pain.

God's angel came ! The tender shade
  Of pity made her blue eye dim;
Against her woman's breast she laid
  The drooping, fainting head of him.

She bore him to a pleasant room,
  Flower-sweet and cool with salt sea air,
And watched beside his bed, for whom
  His far-off sisters might not care.

She fanned his feverish brow and smoothed
  Its lines of pain with tenderest touch.
With holy hymn and prayer she soothed
  The trembling soul that feared so much.

Through her the peace that passeth sight
  Came to him, as he lapsed away
As one whose troubled dreams of night
  Slide slowly into tranquil day.

The sweetness of the Land of Flowers
  Upon his lonely grave she laid :
The jasmine dropped its golden showers,
  The orange lent its bloom and shade.

And something whispered in her thought,
  More sweet than mortal voices be :
"The service thou for him hast wrought
  O daughter ! hath been done for me."

CENTENNIAL HYMN

Written for the opening of the International
Exhibition, Philadelphia, May 10, 1876. The
music for the hymn was written by John K.
Paine, and may be found in *The Atlantic
Monthly* for June, 1876.

I

Our fathers' God ! from out whose hand
The centuries fall like grains of sand,
We meet to-day, united, free,
And loyal to our land and Thee,
To thank Thee for the era done,
And trust Thee for the opening one.

II

Here, where of old, by Thy design,
The fathers spake that word of Thine
Whose echo is the glad refrain
Of rended bolt and falling chain,
To grace our festal time, from all
The zones of earth our guests we call.

III

Be with us while the New World greets
The Old World thronging all its streets,
Unveiling all the triumphs won
By art or toil beneath the sun ;
And unto common good ordain
This rivalship of hand and brain.

IV

Thou, who hast here in concord furled
The war flags of a gathered world,
Beneath our Western skies fulfil
The Orient's mission of good-will,
And, freighted with love's Golden Fleece,
Send back its Argonauts of peace.

V

For art and labor met in truce,
For beauty made the bride of use,
We thank Thee ; but, withal, we crave
The austere virtues strong to save,
The honor proof to place or gold,
The manhood never bought nor sold !

VI

Oh make Thou us, through centuries long,
In peace secure, in justice strong ;
Around our gift of freedom draw
The safeguards of thy righteous law :
And, cast in some diviner mould,
Let the new cycle shame the old !

AT SCHOOL-CLOSE

BOWDOIN STREET, BOSTON, 1877

The end has come, as come it must
  To all things ; in these sweet June
    days
The teacher and the scholar trust
  Their parting feet to separate ways.

They part : but in the years to be
  Shall pleasant memories cling to each,
As shells bear inland from the sea
  The murmur of the rhythmic beach.

One knew the joy the sculptor knows
  When, plastic to his lightest touch,
His clay-wrought model slowly grows
  To that fine grace desired so much.

So daily grew before her eyes
  The living shapes whereon she wrought,
Strong, tender, innocently wise,
  The child's heart with the woman's thought.

And one shall never quite forget
  The voice that called from dream and play,
The firm but kindly hand that set
  Her feet in learning's pleasant way, —

The joy of Undine soul-possessed,
  The wakening sense, the strange delight
That swelled the fabled statue's breast
  And filled its clouded eyes with sight !

O Youth and Beauty, loved of all !
  Ye pass from girlhood's gate of dreams ;
In broader ways your footsteps fall,
  Ye test the truth of all that seems.

Her little realm the teacher leaves,
  She breaks her wand of power apart,
While, for your love and trust, she gives
  The warm thanks of a grateful heart.

Hers is the sober summer noon
  Contrasted with your morn of spring,
The waning with the waxing moon,
  The folded with the outspread wing.

Across the distance of the years
  She sends her God-speed back to you ;
She has no thought of doubts or fears :
  Be but yourselves, be pure, be true,

And prompt in duty ; heed the deep,
  Low voice of conscience ; through the ill
And discord round about you, keep
  Your faith in human nature still.

Be gentle : unto griefs and needs,
  Be pitiful as woman should,
And, spite of all the lies of creeds,
  Hold fast the truth that God is good.

Give and receive ; go forth and bless
  The world that needs the hand and heart
Of Martha's helpful carefulness
  No less than Mary's better part.

So shall the stream of time flow by
  And leave each year a richer good,
And matron loveliness outvie
  The nameless charm of maidenhood.

And, when the world shall link your names
  With gracious lives and manners fine,
The teacher shall assert her claims,
  And proudly whisper, " These were mine ! "

HYMN OF THE CHILDREN

Sung at the anniversary of the Children's Mission, Boston, 1878.

THINE are all the gifts, O God !
  Thine the broken bread ;
Let the naked feet be shod,
  And the starving fed.

Let Thy children, by Thy grace,
  Give as they abound,
Till the poor have breathing-space,
  And the lost are found.

Wiser than the miser's hoards
  Is the giver's choice ;
Sweeter than the song of birds
  Is the thankful voice.

Welcome smiles on faces sad
  As the flowers of spring ;
Let the tender hearts be glad
  With the joy they bring.

Happier for their pity's sake
  Make their sports and plays,
And from lips of childhood take
  Thy perfected praise !

THE LANDMARKS

This poem was read at a meeting of citizens of Boston having for its object the preservation of the Old South Church, famous in Colonial and Revolutionary history.

I

THROUGH the streets of Marblehead
Fast the red-winged terror sped ;

Blasting, withering, on it came,
With its hundred tongues of flame,

Where St. Michael's on its way
Stood like chained Andromeda,

Waiting on the rock, like her,
Swift doom or deliverer !

Church that, after sea-moss grew
Over walls no longer new,

Counted generations five,
Four entombed and one alive ;

Heard the martial thousand tread
Battleward from Marblehead ;

Saw within the rock-walled bay
Treville's lilied pennons play,

And the fisher's dory met
By the barge of Lafayette,

Telling good news in advance
Of the coming fleet of France !

Church to reverend memories dear,
Quaint in desk and chandelier ;

Bell, whose century-rusted tongue
Burials tolled and bridals rung ;

Loft, whose tiny organ kept
Keys that Snetzler's hand had swept ;

Altar, o'er whose tablet old
Sinai's law its thunders rolled !

Suddenly the sharp cry came :
"Look ! St. Michael's is aflame !"

Round the low tower wall the fire
Snake-like wound its coil of ire.

Sacred in its gray respect
From the jealousies of sect,

"Save it," seemed the thought of all,
"Save it, though our roof-trees fall ! "

Up the tower the young men sprung ;
One, the bravest, outward swung

By the rope, whose kindling strands
Smoked beneath the holder's hands,

Smiting down with strokes of power
Burning fragments from the tower.

Then the gazing crowd beneath
Broke the painful pause of breath ;

Brave men cheered from street to street,
With home's ashes at their feet ;

Houseless women kerchiefs waved :
"Thank the Lord ! St. Michael's saved !"

II

In the heart of Boston town
Stands the church of old renown,

From whose walls the impulse went
Which set free a continent ;

From whose pulpit's oracle
Prophecies of freedom fell ;

And whose steeple-rocking din
Rang the nation's birth-day in !

Standing at this very hour
Perilled like St. Michael's tower,

Held not in the clasp of flame,
But by mammon's grasping claim.

Shall it be of Boston said
She is shamed by Marblehead ?

City of our pride ! as there,
Hast thou none to do and dare ?

Life was risked for Michael's shrine ;
Shall not wealth be staked for thine ?

Woe to thee, when men shall search
Vainly for the Old South Church ;

When from Neck to Boston Stone,
All thy pride of place is gone ;

When from Bay and railroad car,
Stretched before them wide and far,

Men shall only see a great
Wilderness of brick and slate,

Every holy spot o'erlaid
By the commonplace of trade !

City of our love ! to thee
Duty is but destiny.

True to all thy record saith,
Keep with thy traditions faith ;

Ere occasion's overpast,
Hold its flowing forelock fast ;

Honor still the precedents
Of a grand munificence ;

In thy old historic way
Give, as thou didst yesterday

At the South-land's call, or on
Need's demand from fired St. John.

Set thy Church's muffled bell
Free the generous deed to tell.

Let thy loyal hearts rejoice
In the glad, sonorous voice,

Ringing from the brazen mouth
Of the bell of the Old South, —

Ringing clearly, with a will,
" What she was is Boston still ! "

GARDEN

A hymn for the American Horticultural So-
ciety, 1882. [Originally written to be sung at
an agricultural and horticultural fair in Ames-
bury in 1853. It was translated into Portu-
guese by Dom Pedro, Emperor of Brazil, and
read at a harvest festival. It has been trans-
lated into Italian also and sung by peasants at
the gathering of the vintage.]

O PAINTER of the fruits and flowers,
We own Thy wise design,
Whereby these human hands of ours
May share the work of Thine !

Apart from Thee we plant in vain
The root and sow the seed ;
Thy early and Thy later rain,
Thy sun and dew we need.

Our toil is sweet with thankfulness,
Our burden is our boon ;
The curse of Earth's gray morning is
The blessing of its noon.

Why search the wide world everywhere
For Eden's unknown ground ?
That garden of the primal pair
May nevermore be found.

But, blest by Thee, our patient toil
May right the ancient wrong,
And give to every clime and soil
The beauty lost so long.

Our homestead flowers and fruited trees
May Eden's orchard shame ;
We taste the tempting sweets of these
Like Eve, without her blame.

And, North and South and East and West,
The pride of every zone,
The fairest, rarest, and the best
May all be made our own.

Its earliest shrines the young world sought
In hill-groves and in bowers,
The fittest offerings thither brought
Were Thy own fruits and flowers.

And still with reverent hands we cull
Thy gifts each year renewed ;
The good is always beautiful,
The beautiful is good.

A GREETING

Read at Harriet Beecher Stowe's seventieth
anniversary, June 14, 1882, at a garden party
at ex-Governor Claflin's in Newtonville, Mass.

THRICE welcome from the Land of Flowers
And golden-fruited orange bowers
To this sweet, green-turfed June of ours !

To her who, in our evil time,
Dragged into light the nation's crime
With strength beyond the strength of men,
And, mightier than their swords, her pen !
To her who world-wide entrance gave
To the log-cabin of the slave ;
Made all his wrongs and sorrows known,
And all earth's languages his own, —
North, South, and East and West, made all
The common air electrical,
Until the o'ercharged bolts of heaven
Blazed down, and every chain was riven !

Welcome from each and all to her
Whose Wooing of the Minister
Revealed the warm heart of the man
Beneath the creed-bound Puritan,
And taught the kinship of the love
Of man below and God above ;
To her whose vigorous pencil-strokes
Sketched into life her Oldtown Folks ;
Whose fireside stories, grave or gay,
In quaint Sam Lawson's vagrant way,
With old New England's flavor rife,
Waifs from her rude idyllic life,
Are racy as the legends old
By Chaucer or Boccaccio told ;
To her who keeps, through change of place
And time, her native strength and grace,
Alike where warm Sorrento smiles,
Or where, by birchen-shaded isles,
Whose summer winds have shivered o'er
The icy drift of Labrador,
She lifts to light the priceless Pearl
Of Harpswell's angel-beckoned girl !
To her at threescore years and ten
Be tributes of the tongue and pen ;
Be honor, praise, and heart-thanks given,
The loves of earth, the hopes of heaven !

Ah, dearer than the praise that stirs
The air to-day, our love is hers !
She needs no guaranty of fame
Whose own is linked with Freedom's name.
Long ages after ours shall keep
Her memory living while we sleep ;
The waves that wash our gray coast lines,
The winds that rock the Southern pines,
Shall sing of her ; the unending years
Shall tell her tale in unborn ears.
And when, with sins and follies past,
Are numbered color-hate and caste,
White, black, and red shall own as one
The noblest work by woman done.

GODSPEED

Written on the occasion of a voyage made by my friends Annie Fields and Sarah Orne Jewett.

OUTBOUND, your bark awaits you. Were I one
  Whose prayer availeth much, my wish should be
  Your favoring trade-wind and consenting sea.
By sail or steed was never love outrun,
And, here or there, love follows her in whom
  All graces and sweet charities unite,
  The old Greek beauty set in holier light ;
And her for whom New England's byways bloom,
Who walks among us welcome as the Spring,
  Calling up blossoms where her light feet stray.
God keep you both, make beautiful your way,
Comfort, console, and bless ; and safely bring,
Ere yet I make upon a vaster sea
The unreturning voyage, my friends to me.

WINTER ROSES

In reply to a flower gift from Mrs. Putnam's school at Jamaica Plain.

My garden roses long ago
  Have perished from the leaf - strewn walks ;
Their pale, fair sisters smile no more
  Upon the sweet-brier stalks.

Gone with the flower-time of my life,
  Spring's violets, summer's blooming pride,
And Nature's winter and my own
  Stand, flowerless, side by side.

So might I yesterday have sung ;
  To-day, in bleak December's noon,
Come sweetest fragrance, shapes, and hues,
  The rosy wealth of June !

Bless the young hands that culled the gift,
  And bless the hearts that prompted it ;
If undeserved it comes, at least
  It seems not all unfit.

Of old my Quaker ancestors
  Had gifts of forty stripes save one ;
To-day as many roses crown
  The gray head of their son.

And with them, to my fancy's eye,
  The fresh-faced givers smiling come,
And nine and thirty happy girls
  Make glad a lonely room.

They bring the atmosphere of youth ;
  The light and warmth of long ago
Are in my heart, and on my cheek
  The airs of morning blow.

O buds of girlhood, yet unblown,
  And fairer than the gift ye chose,
For you may years like leaves unfold
  The heart of Sharon's rose !

THE REUNION

Read September 10, 1885, to the surviving
students of Haverhill Academy in 1827–1830.

THE gulf of seven and fifty years
  We stretch our welcoming hands across ;
  The distance but a pebble's toss
Between us and our youth appears.

For in life's school we linger on
  The remnant of a once full list ;
  Conning our lessons, undismissed,
With faces to the setting sun.

And some have gone the unknown way,
  And some await the call to rest ;
  Who knoweth whether it is best
For those who went or those who stay ?

And yet despite of loss and ill,
  If faith and love and hope remain,
  Our length of days is not in vain,
And life is well worth living still.

Still to a gracious Providence
  The thanks of grateful hearts are due,
  For blessings when our lives were new,
For all the good vouchsafed us since.

The pain that spared us sorer hurt,
  The wish denied, the purpose crossed,
  And pleasure's fond occasions lost,
Were mercies to our small desert.

'T is something that we wander back,
  Gray pilgrims, to our ancient ways,
  And tender memories of old days
Walk with us by the Merrimac ;

That even in life's afternoon
  A sense of youth comes back again,
  As through this cool September rain
The still green woodlands dream of June.

The eyes grown dim to present things
  Have keener sight for bygone years,
  And sweet and clear, in deafening ears,
The bird that sang at morning sings.

Dear comrades, scattered wide and far,
  Send from their homes their kindly word,
  And dearer ones, unseen, unheard,
Smile on us from some heavenly star.

For life and death with God are one,
  Unchanged by seeming change His care
  And love are round us here and there ;
He breaks no thread His hand has spun.

Soul touches soul, the muster roll
  Of life eternal has no gaps ;
  And after half a century's lapse
Our school-day ranks are closed and whole.

Hail and farewell ! We go our way ;
  Where shadows end, we trust in light ;
  The star that ushers in the night
Is herald also of the day !

NORUMBEGA HALL

Norumbega Hall at Wellesley College,
named in honor of Eben Norton Horsford, who
was one of the most munificent patrons of
that noble institution, and who had just pub-
lished an essay claiming the discovery of the
site of the somewhat mythical city of Norum-
bega, was opened with appropriate ceremonies,
in April, 1886. The following sonnet was writ-
ten for the occasion, and was read by President
Alice E. Freeman, to whom it was addressed.

NOT on Penobscot's wooded bank the spires
Of the sought City rose, nor yet beside

The winding Charles, nor where the daily
    tide
Of Naumkeag's haven rises and retires,
The vision tarried ; but somewhere we knew
The beautiful gates must open to our
    quest,
Somewhere that marvellous City of the
    West
Would lift its towers and palace domes in
    view,
And, lo ! at last its mystery is made
    known —
Its only dwellers maidens fair and young,
Its Princess such as England's Laureate
    sung ;
And safe from capture, save by love alone,
It lends its beauty to the lake's green
    shore,
And Norumbega is a myth no more.

THE BARTHOLDI STATUE

1886

THE land, that, from the rule of kings,
    In freeing us, itself made free,
Our Old World Sister, to us brings
    Her sculptured Dream of Liberty :

Unlike the shapes on Egypt's sands
    Uplifted by the toil-worn slave,
On Freedom's soil with freemen's hands
    We rear the symbol free hands gave.

O France, the beautiful ! to thee
    Once more a debt of love we owe :
In peace beneath thy Colors Three,
    We hail a later Rochambeau !

Rise, stately Symbol ! holding forth
    Thy light and hope to all who sit
In chains and darkness ! Belt the earth
    With watch-fires from thy torch up-
    lit !

Reveal the primal mandate still
    Which Chaos heard and ceased to be,
Trace on mid-air th' Eternal Will
    In signs of fire : " Let man be free ! "

Shine far, shine free, a guiding light
    To Reason's ways and Virtue's aim,
A lightning-flash the wretch to smite
    Who shields his license with thy name !

ONE OF THE SIGNERS

Written for the unveiling of the statue of
Josiah Bartlett at Amesbury, Mass., July 4,
1888. Governor Bartlett, who was a native
of the town, was a signer of the Declaration
of Independence. Amesbury or Ambresbury,
so called from the "anointed stones" of the
great Druidical temple near it, was the seat of
one of the earliest religious houses in Britain.
The tradition that the guilty wife of King Ar-
thur fled thither for protection forms one of
the finest passages in Tennyson's *Idylls of the
King.*

O STORIED vale of Merrimac,
    Rejoice through all thy shade and
      shine,
And from his century's sleep call back
    A brave and honored son of thine.

Unveil his effigy between
    The living and the dead to-day ;
The fathers of the Old Thirteen
    Shall witness bear as spirits may.

Unseen, unheard, his gray compeers,
    The shades of Lee and Jefferson,
Wise Franklin reverend with his years,
    And Carroll, lord of Carrollton !

Be thine henceforth a pride of place
    Beyond thy namesake's over-sea,
Where scarce a stone is left to trace
    The Holy House of Amesbury.

A prouder memory lingers round
    The birthplace of thy true man here
Than that which haunts the refuge found
    By Arthur's mythic Guinevere.

The plain deal table where he sat
    And signed a nation's title-deed
Is dearer now to fame than that
    Which bore the scroll of Runnymede.

Long as, on Freedom's natal morn,
    Shall ring the Independence bells,
Give to thy dwellers yet unborn
    The lesson which his image tells.

For in that hour of Destiny,
    Which tried the men of bravest stock,
He knew the end alone must be
    A free land or a traitor's block.

Among those picked and chosen men
  Than his, who here first drew his breath,
No firmer fingers held the pen
  Which wrote for liberty or death.

Not for their hearths and homes alone,
  But for the world their work was done ;
On all the winds their thought has flown
  Through all the circuit of the sun.

We trace its flight by broken chains,
  By songs of grateful Labor still ;

To-day, in all her holy fanes,
  It rings the bells of freed Brazil.

O hills that watched his boyhood's home,
  O earth and air that nursed him, give,
In this memorial semblance, room
  To him who shall its bronze outlive !

And thou, O Land he loved, rejoice
  That in the countless years to come,
Whenever Freedom needs a voice,
  These sculptured lips shall not be dumb !

THE TENT ON THE BEACH

It can scarcely be necessary to name as the two companions whom I reckoned with myself in this poetical picnic, Fields the lettered magnate, and Taylor the free cosmopolite. The long line of sandy beach which defines almost the whole of the New Hampshire sea-coast is especially marked near its southern extremity, by the salt-meadows of Hampton. The Hampton River winds through these meadows, and the reader may, if he choose, imagine my tent pitched near its mouth, where also was the scene of the *Wreck of Rivermouth.* The green bluff to the northward is Great Boar's Head; southward is the Merrimac, with Newburyport lifting its steeples above brown roofs and green trees on its banks. [Mr. Whittier originally designed following the Decameron method and feigning that each person read his own poem, but abandoned it as too hackneyed.]

I WOULD not sin, in this half-playful strain, —
  Too light perhaps for serious years, though born
Of the enforced leisure of slow pain, —
  Against the pure ideal which has drawn
My feet to follow its far-shining gleam.
A simple plot is mine : legends and runes
Of credulous days, old fancies that have lain
Silent from boyhood taking voice again,
Warmed into life once more, even as the tunes
That, frozen in the fabled hunting-horn,
Thawed into sound : — a winter fireside dream
Of dawns and sunsets by the summer sea,
Whose sands are traversed by a silent throng
Of voyagers from that vaster mystery
Of which it is an emblem ; — and the dear
Memory of one who might have tuned my song
To sweeter music by her delicate ear.

When heats as of a tropic clime
  Burned all our inland valleys through,

Three friends, the guests of summer time,
  Pitched their white tent where sea-winds blew.
Behind them, marshes, seamed and crossed
With narrow creeks, and flower-embossed,
Stretched to the dark oak wood, whose leafy arms
Screened from the stormy East the pleasant inland farms.

At full of tide their bolder shore
  Of sun-bleached sand the waters beat ;
At ebb, a smooth and glistening floor
  They touched with light, receding feet.
Northward a green bluff broke the chain
Of sand-hills ; southward stretched a plain
Of salt grass, with a river winding down,
Sail-whitened, and beyond the steeples of the town, —

Whence sometimes, when the wind was light
  And dull the thunder of the beach,
They heard the bells of morn and night
  Swing, miles away, their silver speech.
Above low scarp and turf-grown wall
They saw the fort-flag rise and fall ;
And, the first star to signal twilight's hour,
The lamp-fire glimmer down from the tall light-house tower.

They rested there, escaped awhile
  From cares that wear the life away,
To eat the lotus of the Nile
  And drink the poppies of Cathay, —
To fling their loads of custom down,
Like drift-weed, on the sand-slopes brown,
And in the sea-waves drown the restless pack
Of duties, claims, and needs that barked upon their track.

One, with his beard scarce silvered, bore
    A ready credence in his looks,
A lettered magnate, lording o'er
    An ever-widening realm of books.
In him brain-currents, near and far,
Converged as in a Leyden jar ;
The old, dead authors thronged him round
    about,
And Elzevir's gray ghosts from leathern
    graves looked out.

He knew each living pundit well,
    Could weigh the gifts of him or her,
And well the market value tell
    Of poet and philosopher.
But if he lost, the scenes behind,
Somewhat of reverence vague and blind,
Finding the actors human at the best,
No readier lips than his the good he saw
    confessed.

His boyhood fancies not outgrown,
    He loved himself the singer's art ;
Tenderly, gently, by his own
    He knew and judged an author's heart.
No Rhadamanthine brow of doom
Bowed the dazed pedant from his room ;
And bards, whose name is legion, if denied,
Bore off alike intact their verses and their
    pride.

Pleasant it was to roam about
    The lettered world as he had done,
And see the lords of song without
    Their singing robes and garlands on.
With Wordsworth paddle Rydal mere,
Taste rugged Elliott's home-brewed beer,
And with the ears of Rogers, at fourscore,
Hear Garrick's buskined tread and Wal-
    pole's wit once more.

And one there was, a dreamer born,
    Who, with a mission to fulfil,
Had left the Muses' haunts to turn
    The crank of an opinion-mill,
Making his rustic reed of song
A weapon in the war with wrong,
Yoking his fancy to the breaking-plough
That beam-deep turned the soil for truth to
    spring and grow.

Too quiet seemed the man to ride
    The wingèd Hippogriff Reform ;
Was his a voice from side to side
    To pierce the tumult of the storm ?

A silent, shy, peace-loving man,
    He seemed no fiery partisan
To hold his way against the public frown,
    The ban of Church and State, the fierce
    mob's hounding down.

For while he wrought with strenuous will
    The work his hands had found to do,
He heard the fitful music still
    Of winds that out of dream-land blew.
The din about him could not drown
What the strange voices whispered down ;
Along his task-field weird processions swept,
The visionary pomp of stately phantoms
    stepped.

The common air was thick with dreams,—
    He told them to the toiling crowd ;
Such music as the woods and streams
    Sang in his ear he sang aloud ;
In still, shut bays, on windy capes,
He heard the call of beckoning shapes,
And, as the gray old shadows prompted
    him,
To homely moulds of rhyme he shaped
    their legends grim.

He rested now his weary hands,
    And lightly moralized and laughed,
As, tracing on the shifting sands
    A burlesque of his paper-craft,
He saw the careless waves o'errun
His words, as time before had done,
Each day's tide-water washing clean away,
Like letters from the sand, the work of
    yesterday.

And one, whose Arab face was tanned
    By tropic sun and boreal frost,
So travelled there was scarce a land
    Or people left him to exhaust,
In idling mood had from him hurled
The poor squeezed orange of the world,
And in the tent - shade, sat beneath a
    palm,
Smoked, cross-legged like a Turk, in Ori-
    ental calm.

The very waves that washed the sand
    Below him, he had seen before
Whitening the Scandinavian strand
    And sultry Mauritanian shore.
From ice-rimmed isles, from summer
    seas
Palm-fringed, they bore him messages ;

He heard the plaintive Nubian songs again,
And mule-bells tinkling down the mountain-
paths of Spain.

His memory round the ransacked earth
On Puck's long girdle slid at ease ;
And, instant, to the valley's girth
Of mountains, spice isles of the seas,
Faith flowered in minster stones, Art's
guess
At truth and beauty, found access ;
Yet loved the while, that free cosmopolite,
Old friends, old ways, and kept his boy-
hood's dreams in sight.

Untouched as yet by wealth and pride,
That virgin innocence of beach :
No shingly monster, hundred-eyed,
Stared its gray sand-birds out of reach ;
Unhoused, save where, at intervals,
The white tents showed their canvas
walls,
Where brief sojourners, in the cool, soft
air,
Forgot their inland heats, hard toil, and
year-long care.

Sometimes along the wheel-deep sand
A one-horse wagon slowly crawled,
Deep laden with a youthful band,
Whose look some homestead old re-
called ;
Brother perchance, and sisters twain,
And one whose blue eyes told, more
plain
Than the free language of her rosy lip,
Of the still dearer claim of love's relation-
ship.

With cheeks of russet-orchard tint,
The light laugh of their native rills,
The perfume of their garden's mint,
The breezy freedom of the hills,
They bore, in unrestrained delight,
The motto of the Garter's knight,
Careless as if from every gazing thing
Hid by their innocence, as Gyges by his
ring.

The clanging sea-fowl came and went,
The hunter's gun in the marshes rang ;
At nightfall from a neighboring tent
A flute-voiced woman sweetly sang.
Loose-haired, barefooted, hand-in-hand,
Young girls went tripping down the sand ;

And youths and maidens, sitting in the
moon,
Dreamed o'er the old fond dream from
which we wake too soon.

At times their fishing-lines they plied,
With an old Triton at the oar,
Salt as the sea-wind, tough and dried
As a lean cusk from Labrador.
Strange tales he told of wreck and
storm, —
Had seen the sea-snake's awful form,
And heard the ghosts on Haley's Isle com-
plain,
Speak him off shore, and beg a passage to
old Spain !

And there, on breezy morns, they saw
The fishing-schooners outward run,
Their low-bent sails in tack and flaw
Turned white or dark to shade and
sun.
Sometimes, in calms of closing day,
They watched the spectral mirage play,
Saw low, far islands looming tall and nigh,
And ships, with upturned keels, sail like a
sea the sky.

Sometimes a cloud, with thunder black,
Stooped low upon the darkening main,
Piercing the waves along its track
With the slant javelins of rain.
And when west-wind and sunshine warm
Chased out to sea its wrecks of storm,
They saw the prismy hues in thin spray
showers
Where the green buds of waves burst into
white froth flowers.

And when along the line of shore
The mists crept upward chill and
damp,
Stretched, careless, on their sandy floor
Beneath the flaring lantern lamp,
They talked of all things old and new,
Read, slept, and dreamed as idlers do ;
And in the unquestioned freedom of the
tent,
Body and o'er-taxed mind to healthful ease
unbent.

Once, when the sunset splendors died,
And, trampling up the sloping sand,
In lines outreaching far and wide,
The white-maned billows swept to land,

Dim seen across the gathering shade,
A vast and ghostly cavalcade,
They sat around their lighted kerosene,
Hearing the deep bass roar their every
    pause between.

Then, urged thereto, the Editor
    Within his full portfolio dipped,
Feigning excuse while searching for
    (With secret pride) his manuscript.
His pale face flushed from eye to beard,
With nervous cough his throat he cleared,
And, in a voice so tremulous it betrayed
The anxious fondness of an author's heart,
    he read :

THE WRECK OF RIVERMOUTH

The Goody Cole who figures in this poem and
The Changeling was Eunice Cole, who for a
quarter of a century or more was feared, per-
secuted, and hated as the witch of Hampton.
She lived alone in a hovel a little distant from
the spot where the Hampton Academy now
stands, and there she died, unattended. When
her death was discovered, she was hastily cov-
ered up in the earth near by, and a stake
driven through her body, to exorcise the evil
spirit. Rev. Stephen Bachiler or Batchelder
was one of the ablest of the early New Eng-
land preachers. His marriage late in life to a
woman regarded by his church as disreputable
induced him to return to England, where he
enjoyed the esteem and favor of Oliver Crom-
well during the Protectorate.

RIVERMOUTH Rocks are fair to see,
    By dawn or sunset shone across,
When the ebb of the sea has left them
    free
    To dry their fringes of gold-green moss :
For there the river comes winding down,
From salt sea-meadows and uplands brown,
And waves on the outer rocks afoam
Shout to its waters, " Welcome home ! "

And fair are the sunny isles in view
    East of the grisly Head of the Boar,
And Agamenticus lifts its blue
    Disk of a cloud the woodlands o'er ;
And southerly, when the tide is down,
'Twixt white sea-waves and sand-hills
    brown,
The beach-birds dance and the gray gulls
    wheel
Over a floor of burnished steel.

Once, in the old Colonial days,
    Two hundred years ago and more,
A boat sailed down through the winding
    ways
Of Hampton River to that low shore,
Full of a goodly company
Sailing out on the summer sea,
Veering to catch the land-breeze light,
With the Boar to left and the Rocks to
    right.

In Hampton meadows, where mowers laid
    Their scythes to the swaths of salted
    grass,
" Ah, well-a-day ! our hay must be made ! "
    A young man sighed, who saw them
    pass.
Loud laughed his fellows to see him stand
Whetting his scythe with a listless hand,
Hearing a voice in a far-off song,
Watching a white hand beckoning long.

" Fie on the witch ! " cried a merry girl,
    As they rounded the point where Goody
    Cole
Sat by her door with her wheel atwirl,
    A bent and blear-eyed poor old soul.
" Oho ! " she muttered, " ye 're brave to-
    day !
But I hear the little waves laugh and say,
' The broth will be cold that waits at home ;
For it 's one to go, but another to come ! ' "

" She 's cursed," said the skipper ; " speak
    her fair :
I 'm scary always to see her shake
Her wicked head, with its wild gray hair,
    And nose like a hawk, and eyes like a
    snake."
But merrily still, with laugh and shout,
From Hampton River the boat sailed out,
Till the huts and the flakes on Star seemed
    nigh,
And they lost the scent of the pines of Rye.

They dropped their lines in the lazy tide,
    Drawing up haddock and mottled cod ;
They saw not the Shadow that walked be-
    side,
They heard not the feet with silence shod.
But thicker and thicker a hot mist grew,
Shot by the lightnings through and through;
And muffled growls, like the growl of a
    beast,
Ran along the sky from west to east.

Then the skipper looked from the darken-
ing sea
Up to the dimmed and wading sun ;
But he spake like a brave man cheerily,
"Yet there is time for our homeward
run."
Veering and tacking, they backward wore ;
And just as a breath from the woods ashore
Blew out to whisper of danger past,
The wrath of the storm came down at
last !

The skipper hauled at the heavy sail :
"God be our help !" he only cried,
As the roaring gale, like the stroke of a
flail,
Smote the boat on its starboard side.
The Shoalsmen looked, but saw alone
Dark films of rain-cloud slantwise blown,
Wild rocks lit up by the lightning's glare,
The strife and torment of sea and air.

Goody Cole looked out from her door :
The Isles of Shoals were drowned and
gone,
Scarcely she saw the Head of the Boar
Toss the foam from tusks of stone.
She clasped her hands with a grip of pain,
The tear on her cheek was not of rain :
"They are lost," she muttered, "boat and
crew !
Lord, forgive me ! my words were true !"

Suddenly seaward swept the squall ;
The low sun smote through cloudy rack ;
The Shoals stood clear in the light, and all
The trend of the coast lay hard and
black.
But far and wide as eye could reach,
No life was seen upon wave or beach ;
The boat that went out at morning never
Sailed back again into Hampton River.

O mower, lean on thy bended snath,
Look from the meadows green and low :
The wind of the sea is a waft of death,
The waves are singing a song of woe !
By silent river, by moaning sea,
Long and vain shall thy watching be :
Never again shall the sweet voice call,
Never the white hand rise and fall !

O Rivermouth Rocks, how sad a sight
Ye saw in the light of breaking day !
Dead faces looking up cold and white

From sand and seaweed where they lay
The mad old witch-wife wailed and wept,
And cursed the tide as it backward crept :
"Crawl back, crawl back, blue water-snake!
Leave your dead for the hearts that break!"

Solemn it was in that old day
In Hampton town and its log-built
church,
Where side by side the coffins lay
And the mourners stood in aisle and
porch.
In the singing-seats young eyes were dim,
The voices faltered that raised the hymn,
And Father Dalton, grave and stern,
Sobbed through his prayer and wept in turn.

But his ancient colleague did not pray ;
Under the weight of his fourscore years
He stood apart with the iron-gray
Of his strong brows knitted to hide his
tears ;
And a fair-faced woman of doubtful fame,
Linking her own with his honored name,
Subtle as sin, at his side withstood
The felt reproach of her neighborhood.

Apart with them, like them forbid,
Old Goody Cole looked drearily round,
As, two by two, with their faces hid,
The mourners walked to the burying-
ground.
She let the staff from her clasped hands
fall :
"Lord, forgive us ! we 're sinners all !"
And the voice of the old man answered her :
"Amen !" said Father Bachiler.

So, as I sat upon Appledore
In the calm of a closing summer day,
And the broken lines of Hampton shore
In purple mist of cloudland lay,
The Rivermouth Rocks their story told ;
And waves aglow with sunset gold,
Rising and breaking in steady chime,
Beat the rhythm and kept the time.

And the sunset paled, and warmed once
more
With a softer, tenderer after-glow ;
In the east was moon-rise, with boats off-
shore
And sails in the distance drifting slow.
The beacon glimmered from Portsmouth
bar,

The White Isle kindled its great red star ;
And life and death in my old-time lay
Mingled in peace like the night and day !

" Well ! " said the Man of Books, " your
    story
  Is really not ill told in verse.
As the Celt said of purgatory,
  One might go farther and fare worse."
The Reader smiled ; and once again
With steadier voice took up his strain,
While the fair singer from the neighboring
    tent
Drew near, and at his side a graceful lis-
    tener bent.

THE GRAVE BY THE LAKE

At the mouth of the Melvin River, which
empties into Moultonboro Bay in Lake Winni-
pesaukee, is a great mound. The Ossipee In-
dians had their home in the neighborhood of
the bay, which is plentifully stocked with fish,
and many relics of their occupation have been
found.

WHERE the Great Lake's sunny smiles
Dimple round its hundred isles,
And the mountain's granite ledge
Cleaves the water like a wedge,
Ringed about with smooth, gray stones,
Rest the giant's mighty bones.

Close beside, in shade and gleam,
Laughs and ripples Melvin stream;
Melvin water, mountain-born,
All fair flowers its banks adorn ;
All the woodland voices meet,
Mingling with its murmurs sweet.

Over lowlands forest-grown,
Over waters island-strown,
Over silver-sanded beach,
Leaf-locked bay and misty reach,
Melvin stream and burial-heap,
Watch and ward the mountains keep.

Who that Titan cromlech fills ?
Forest-kaiser, lord o' the hills ?
Knight who on the birchen tree
Carved his savage heraldry ?
Priest o' the pine-wood temples dim,
Prophet, sage, or wizard grim ?

Rugged type of primal man,
Grim utilitarian,
Loving woods for hunt and prowl,
Lake and hill for fish and fowl,
As the brown bear blind and dull
To the grand and beautiful :

Not for him the lesson drawn
From the mountains smit with dawn.
Star-rise, moon-rise, flowers of May,
Sunset's purple bloom of day, —
Took his life no hue from thence,
Poor amid such affluence ?

Haply unto hill and tree
All too near akin was he :
Unto him who stands afar
Nature's marvels greatest are ;
Who the mountain purple seeks
Must not climb the higher peaks.

Yet who knows, in winter tramp,
Or the midnight of the camp,
What revealings faint and far,
Stealing down from moon and star,
Kindled in that human clod
Thought of destiny and God ?

Stateliest forest patriarch,
Grand in robes of skin and bark,
What sepulchral mysteries,
What weird funeral-rites, were his ?
What sharp wail, what drear lament,
Back scared wolf and eagle sent ?

Now, whate'er he may have been,
Low he lies as other men ;
On his mound the partridge drums,
There the noisy blue-jay comes ;
Rank nor name nor pomp has he
In the grave's democracy.

Part thy blue lips, Northern lake !
Moss-grown rocks, your silence break !
Tell the tale, thou ancient tree !
Thou, too, slide-worn Ossipee !
Speak, and tell us how and when
Lived and died this king of men !

Wordless moans the ancient pine ;
Lake and mountain give no sign ;
Vain to trace this ring of stones ;
Vain the search of crumbling bones :
Deepest of all mysteries,
And the saddest, silence is.

Nameless, noteless, clay with clay
Mingles slowly day by day ;
But somewhere, for good or ill,
That dark soul is living still ;
Somewhere yet that atom's force
Moves the light-poised universe.

Strange that on his burial-sod
Harebells bloom, and golden-rod,
While the soul's dark horoscope
Holds no starry sign of hope !
Is the Unseen with sight at odds ?
Nature's pity more than God's ?

Thus I mused by Melvin's side,
While the summer eventide
Made the woods and inland sea
And the mountains mystery ;
And the hush of earth and air
Seemed the pause before a prayer, —

Prayer for him, for all who rest,
Mother Earth, upon thy breast, —
Lapped on Christian turf, or hid
In rock-cave or pyramid :
All who sleep, as all who live,
Well may need the prayer, " Forgive ! "

Desert-smothered caravan,
Knee-deep dust that once was man,
Battle-trenches ghastly piled,
Ocean-floors with white bones tiled,
Crowded tomb and mounded sod,
Dumbly crave that prayer to God.

Oh, the generations old
Over whom no church-bells tolled,
Christless, lifting up blind eyes
To the silence of the skies !
For the innumerable dead
Is my soul disquieted.

Where be now these silent hosts ?
Where the camping-ground of ghosts ?
Where the spectral conscripts led
To the white tents of the dead ?
What strange shore or chartless sea
Holds the awful mystery ?

Then the warm sky stooped to make
Double sunset in the lake ;
While above I saw with it,
Range on range, the mountains lit ;
And the calm and splendor stole
Like an answer to my soul.

Hear'st thou, O of little faith,
What to thee the mountain saith,
What is whispered by the trees ? —
" Cast on God thy care for these ;
Trust Him, if thy sight be dim :
Doubt for them is doubt of Him.

" Blind must be their close-shut eyes
Where like night the sunshine lies,
Fiery-linked the self-forged chain
Binding ever sin to pain,
Strong their prison-house of will,
But without He waiteth still.

" Not with hatred's undertow
Doth the Love Eternal flow ;
Every chain that spirits wear
Crumbles in the breath of prayer ;
And the penitent's desire
Opens every gate of fire.

" Still Thy love, O Christ arisen,
Yearns to reach these souls in prison !
Through all depths of sin and loss
Drops the plummet of Thy cross !
Never yet abyss was found
Deeper than that cross could sound ! "

Therefore well may Nature keep
Equal faith with all who sleep,
Set her watch of hills around
Christian grave and heathen mound,
And to cairn and kirkyard send
Summer's flowery dividend.

Keep, O pleasant Melvin stream,
Thy sweet laugh in shade and gleam !
On the Indian's grassy tomb
Swing, O flowers, your bells of bloom !
Deep below, as high above,
Sweeps the circle of God's love.

————

He paused and questioned with his eye
The hearers' verdict on his song.
A low voice asked : " Is 't well to pry
Into the secrets which belong
Only to God ? — The life to be
Is still the unguessed mystery :
Unscaled, unpierced the cloudy walls re-
main,
We beat with dream and wish the soundless
doors in vain.

" But faith beyond our sight may go."
He said : " The gracious Fatherhood
Can only know above, below,
  Eternal purposes of good.
From our free heritage of will,
The bitter springs of pain and ill
Flow only in all worlds. The perfect day
Of God is shadowless, and love is love
    alway."

" I know," she said, " the letter kills ;
  That on our arid fields of strife
And heat of clashing texts distils
  The dew of spirit and of life.
But, searching still the written Word,
I fain would find, Thus saith the Lord,
A voucher for the hope I also feel
That sin can give no wound beyond love's
    power to heal."

"Pray," said the Man of Books, "give o'er
  A theme too vast for time and place.
Go on, Sir Poet, ride once more
  Your hobby at his old free pace.
But let him keep, with step discreet,
The solid earth beneath his feet.
In the great mystery which around us lies,
The wisest is a fool, the fool Heaven-helped
    is wise."

The Traveller said : " If songs have
    creeds,
  Their choice of them let singers make ;
But Art no other sanction needs
  Than beauty for its own fair sake.
It grinds not in the mill of use,
Nor asks for leave, nor begs excuse ;
It makes the flexile laws it deigns to own,
And gives its atmosphere its color and its
    tone.

" Confess, old friend, your austere school
  Has left your fancy little chance ;
You square to reason's rigid rule
  The flowing outlines of romance.
With conscience keen from exercise,
And chronic fear of compromise,
You check the free play of your rhymes,
    to clap
A moral underneath, and spring it like a
    trap."

The sweet voice answered : " Better so
  Than bolder flights that know no
    check ;

Better to use the bit, than throw
  The reins all loose on fancy's neck.
The liberal range of Art should be
The breadth of Christian liberty,
Restrained alone by challenge and alarm
Where its charmed footsteps tread the bor-
    der land of harm.

" Beyond the poet's sweet dream lives
  The eternal epic of the man.
He wisest is who only gives,
  True to himself, the best he can ;
Who, drifting in the winds of praise,
The inward monitor obeys ;
And, with the boldness that confesses fear,
Takes in the crowded sail, and lets his con-
    science steer.

" Thanks for the fitting word he speaks,
  Nor less for doubtful word unspoken,
For the false model that he breaks,
  As for the moulded grace unbroken ;
For what is missed and what remains,
For losses which are truest gains,
For reverence conscious of the Eternal eye,
And truth too fair to need the garnish of a
    lie."

Laughing, the Critic bowed. " I yield
  The point without another word ;
Who ever yet a case appealed
  Where beauty's judgment had been
    heard ?
And you, my good friend, owe to me
Your warmest thanks for such a plea,
As true withal as sweet. For my offence
Of cavil, let her words be ample recom-
    pense."

Across the sea one lighthouse star,
  With crimson ray that came and went,
Revolving on its tower afar,
  Looked through the doorway of the
    tent.
While outward, over sand-slopes wet,
The lamp flashed down its yellow jet
On the long wash of waves, with red and
    green
Tangles of weltering weed through the
    white foam-wreaths seen.

" ' Sing while we may, — another day
  May bring enough of sorrow ; ' — thus
Our Traveller in his own sweet lay,
  His Crimean camp-song, hints to us,"

The lady said. " So let it be ;
Sing us a song," exclaimed all three.
She smiled : " I can but marvel at your
    choice
To hear our poet's words through my poor
    borrowed voice."

Her window opens to the bay,
On glistening light or misty gray,
And there at dawn and set of day
    In prayer she kneels.
" Dear Lord ! " she saith, " to many a home
From wind and wave the wanderers come ;
I only see the tossing foam
    Of stranger keels.

" Blown out and in by summer gales,
The stately ships, with crowded sails,
And sailors leaning o'er their rails,
    Before me glide ;
They come, they go, but nevermore,
Spice-laden from the Indian shore,
I see his swift-winged Isidore
    The waves divide.

" O Thou ! with whom the night is day
And one the near and far away,
Look out on yon gray waste, and say
    Where lingers he.
Alive, perchance, on some lone beach
Or thirsty isle beyond the reach
Of man, he hears the mocking speech
    Of wind and sea.

" O dread and cruel deep, reveal
The secret which thy waves conceal,
And, ye wild sea-birds, hither wheel
    And tell your tale.
Let winds that tossed his raven hair
A message from my lost one bear, —
Some thought of me, a last fond prayer
    Or dying wail !

" Come, with your dreariest truth shut out
The fears that haunt me round about ;
O God ! I cannot bear this doubt
    That stifles breath.
The worst is better than the dread ;
Give me but leave to mourn my dead
Asleep in trust and hope, instead
    Of life in death ! "

It might have been the evening breeze
That whispered in the garden trees,

It might have been the sound of seas
    That rose and fell ;
But, with her heart, if not her ear,
The old loved voice she seemed to hear :
" I wait to meet thee : be of cheer,
    For all is well ! "

_____

The sweet voice into silence went,
    A silence which was almost pain
As through it rolled the long lament,
    The cadence of the mournful main.
Glancing his written pages o'er,
The Reader tried his part once more ;
Leaving the land of hackmatack and pine
For Tuscan valleys glad with olive and with
    vine.

THE BROTHER OF MERCY

[Suggested by reading C. E. Norton's account.]

PIERO LUCA, known of all the town
As the gray porter by the Pitti wall
Where the noon shadows of the gardens
    fall,
Sick and in dolor, waited to lay down
His last sad burden, and beside his mat
The barefoot monk of La Certosa sat.

Unseen, in square and blossoming garden
    drifted,
Soft sunset lights through green Val d'
    Arno sifted ;
Unheard, below the living shuttles shifted
Backward and forth, and wove, in love or
    strife,
In mirth or pain, the mottled web of life :
But when at last came upward from the
    street
Tinkle of bell and tread of measured feet,
The sick man started, strove to rise in
    vain,
Sinking back heavily with a moan of pain.
And the monk said, " 'T is but the Brother-
    hood
Of Mercy going on some errand good :
Their black masks by the palace-wall I see."
Piero answered faintly, " Woe is me !
This day for the first time in forty years
In vain the bell hath sounded in my ears,
Calling me with my brethren of the mask,
Beggar and prince alike, to some new task

Of love or pity, — haply from the street
To bear a wretch plague-stricken, or, with
    feet
Hushed to the quickened ear and feverish
    brain,
To tread the crowded lazaretto's floors,
Down the long twilight of the corridors,
Midst tossing arms and faces full of pain.
I loved the work : it was its own reward.
I never counted on it to offset
My sins, which are many, or make less my
    debt
To the free grace and mercy of our Lord ;
But somehow, father, it has come to be
In these long years so much a part of me,
I should not know myself, if lacking it,
But with the work the worker too would die,
And in my place some other self would sit
Joyful or sad, — what matters, if not I ?
And now all 's over.   Woe is me ! " — " My
    son,"
The monk said soothingly, " thy work is
    done ;
And no more as a servant, but the guest
Of God thou enterest thy eternal rest.
No toil, no tears, no sorrow for the lost,
Shall mar thy perfect bliss.   Thou shalt sit
    down
Clad in white robes, and wear a golden
    crown
Forever and forever." — Piero tossed
On his sick-pillow : " Miserable me !
I am too poor for such grand company ;
The crown would be too heavy for this gray
Old head ; and God forgive me if I say
It would be hard to sit there night and day,
Like an image in the Tribune, doing naught
With these hard hands, that all my life have
    wrought,
Not for bread only, but for pity's sake.
I 'm dull at prayers : I could not keep
    awake,
Counting my beads.   Mine 's but a crazy
    head,
Scarce worth the saving, if all else be dead.
And if one goes to heaven without a heart,
God knows he leaves behind his better part.
I love my fellow-men : the worst I know
I would do good to.   Will death change
    me so
That I shall sit among the lazy saints,
Turning a deaf ear to the sore complaints
Of souls that suffer ?   Why, I never yet
Left a poor dog in the *strada* hard beset,
Or ass o'erladen !   Must I rate man less

Than dog or ass, in holy selfishness ?
Methinks (Lord, pardon, if the thought be
    sin !)
The world of pain were better, if therein
One's heart might still be human, and de-
    sires
Of natural pity drop upon its fires
Some cooling tears."
            Thereat the pale monk crossed
His brow, and muttering, " Madman ! thou
    art lost ! "
Took up his pyx and fled ; and, left alone,
The sick man closed his eyes with a great
    groan
That sank into a prayer, " Thy will be
    done ! "

Then was he made aware, by soul or ear,
Of somewhat pure and holy bending o'er
    him,
And of a voice like that of her who bore
    him,
Tender and most compassionate : " Never
    fear !
For heaven is love, as God himself is love ;
Thy work below shall be thy work above."
And when he looked, lo ! in the stern
    monk's place
He saw the shining of an angel's face !

————

The Traveller broke the pause.   " I 've seen
    The Brothers down the long street steal,
Black, silent, masked, the crowd between,
    And felt to doff my hat and kneel
With heart, if not with knee, in prayer,
For blessings on their pious care."
The Reader wiped his glasses : " Friends
    of mine,
We 'll try our home-brewed next, instead
    of foreign wine."

THE CHANGELING

For the fairest maid in Hampton
    They needed not to search,
Who saw young Anna Favor
    Come walking into church, —

Or bringing from the meadows,
    At set of harvest-day,
The frolic of the blackbirds,
    The sweetness of the hay.

Now the weariest of all mothers,
  The saddest two years' bride,
She scowls in the face of her husband,
  And spurns her child aside.

"Rake out the red coals, goodman, —
  For there the child shall lie,
Till the black witch comes to fetch her
  And both up chimney fly.

"It's never my own little daughter,
  It's never my own," she said ;
"The witches have stolen my Anna,
  And left me an imp instead.

"Oh, fair and sweet was my baby,
  Blue eyes, and hair of gold ;
But this is ugly and wrinkled,
  Cross, and cunning, and old.

"I hate the touch of her fingers,
  I hate the feel of her skin ;
It's not the milk from my bosom,
  But my blood, that she sucks in.

"My face grows sharp with the torment ;
  Look ! my arms are skin and bone !
Rake open the red coals, goodman,
  And the witch shall have her own.

"She'll come when she hears it crying,
  In the shape of an owl or bat,
And she'll bring us our darling Annà
  In place of her screeching brat."

Then the goodman, Ezra Dalton,
  Laid his hand upon her head :
"Thy sorrow is great, O woman !
  I sorrow with thee," he said.

"The paths to trouble are many,
  And never but one sure way
Leads out to the light beyond it :
  My poor wife, let us pray."

Then he said to the great All-Father,
  "Thy daughter is weak and blind ;
Let her sight come back, and clothe her
  Once more in her right mind.

"Lead her out of this evil shadow,
  Out of these fancies wild ;
Let the holy love of the mother
  Turn again to her child.

"Make her lips like the lips of Mary
  Kissing her blessed Son ;
Let her hands, like the hands of Jesus,
  Rest on her little one.

"Comfort the soul of thy handmaid,
  Open her prison-door,
And thine shall be all the glory
  And praise forevermore."

Then into the face of its mother
  The baby looked up and smiled ;
And the cloud of her soul was lifted,
  And she knew her little child.

A beam of the slant west sunshine
  Made the wan face almost fair,
Lit the blue eyes' patient wonder
  And the rings of pale gold hair.

She kissed it on lip and forehead,
  She kissed it on cheek and chin,
And she bared her snow-white bosom
  To the lips so pale and thin.

Oh, fair on her bridal morning
  Was the maid who blushed and smiled,
But fairer to Ezra Dalton
  Looked the mother of his child.

With more than a lover's fondness
  He stooped to her worn young face,
And the nursing child and the mother
  He folded in one embrace.

"Blessed be God !" he murmured.
  "Blessed be God !" she said ;
"For I see, who once was blinded, —
  I live, who once was dead.

"Now mount and ride, my goodman,
  As thou lovest thy own soul !
Woe's me, if my wicked fancies
  Be the death of Goody Cole !"

His horse he saddled and bridled,
  And into the night rode he,
Now through the great black woodland,
  Now by the white-beached sea.

He rode through the silent clearings,
  He came to the ferry wide,
And thrice he called to the boatman
  Asleep on the other side.

He set his horse to the river,
He swam to Newbury town,
And he called up Justice Sewall
In his nightcap and his gown.

And the grave and worshipful justice
(Upon whose soul be peace !)
Set his name to the jailer's warrant
For Goodwife Cole's release.

Then through the night the hoof-beats
Went sounding like a flail ;
And Goody Cole at cockcrow
Came forth from Ipswich jail.

"Here is a rhyme : I hardly dare
To venture on its theme worn out ;
What seems so sweet by Doon and Ayr
Sounds simply silly hereabout ;
And pipes by lips Arcadian blown
Are only tin horns at our own.
Yet still the muse of pastoral walks with
us,
While Hosea Biglow sings, our new Theoc-
ritus."

THE MAIDS OF ATTITASH

Attitash, an Indian word signifying "huckle-
berry." is the name of a large and beautiful
lake in the northern part of Amesbury. [In a
letter to Mr. Fields, Whittier wrote : "I should
like to show thee Attitash, as it is as pretty
as St. Mary's Lake which Wordsworth sings,
in fact a great deal prettier. The glimpse of
the Pawtuckaway range of mountains in Not-
tingham seen across it is very fine, and it has
noble groves of pines and maples and ash
trees."]

In sky and wave the white clouds swam,
And the blue hills of Nottingham
Through gaps of leafy green
Across the lake were seen,

When, in the shadow of the ash
That dreams its dream in Attitash,
In the warm summer weather,
Two maidens sat together.

They sat and watched in idle mood
The gleam and shade of lake and wood ;
The beach the keen light smote,
The white sail of a boat ;

Swan flocks of lilies shoreward lying,
In sweetness, not in music, dying ;
Hardhack, and virgin's-bower,
And white-spiked clethra-flower.

With careless ears they heard the plash
And breezy wash of Attitash,
The wood-bird's plaintive cry,
The locust's sharp reply.

And teased the while, with playful hand,
The shaggy dog of Newfoundland,
Whose uncouth frolic spilled
Their baskets berry-filled.

Then one, the beauty of whose eyes
Was evermore a great surprise,
Tossed back her queenly head,
And lightly laughing, said :

"No bridegroom's hand be mine to hold
That is not lined with yellow gold ;
I tread no cottage-floor ;
I own no lover poor.

"My love must come on silken wings,
With bridal lights of diamond rings,
Not foul with kitchen smirch,
With tallow-dip for torch."

The other, on whose modest head
Was lesser dower of beauty shed,
With look for home-hearths meet,
And voice exceeding sweet,

Answered, "We will not rivals be ;
Take thou the gold, leave love to me ;
Mine be the cottage small,
And thine the rich man's hall.

"I know, indeed, that wealth is good ;
But lowly roof and simple food,
With love that hath no doubt,
Are more than gold without."

Hard by a farmer hale and young
His cradle in the rye-field swung,
Tracking the yellow plain
With windrows of ripe grain.

And still, whene'er he paused to whet
His scythe, the sidelong glance he met
Of large dark eyes, where strove
False pride and secret love.

Be strong, young mower of the grain ;
That love shall overmatch disdain,
  Its instincts soon or late
  The heart shall vindicate.

In blouse of gray, with fishing-rod,
Half screened by leaves, a stranger trod
  The margin of the pond,
  Watching the group beyond.

The supreme hours unnoted come ;
Unfelt the turning tides of doom ;
  And so the maids laughed on,
  Nor dreamed what Fate had done, —

Nor knew the step was Destiny's
That rustled in the birchen trees,
  As, with their lives forecast,
  Fisher and mower passed.

Erelong by lake and rivulet side
The summer roses paled and died,
  And Autumn's fingers shed
  The maple's leaves of red.

Through the long gold-hazed afternoon,
Alone, but for the diving loon,
  The partridge in the brake,
  The black duck on the lake,

Beneath the shadow of the ash
Sat man and maid by Attitash ;
  And earth and air made room
  For human hearts to bloom.

Soft spread the carpets of the sod,
And scarlet-oak and golden-rod
  With blushes and with smiles
  Lit up the forest aisles.

The mellow light the lake aslant,
The pebbled margin's ripple-chant
  Attempered and low-toned,
  The tender mystery owned.

And through the dream the lovers dreamed
Sweet sounds stole in and soft lights
      streamed ;
  The sunshine seemed to bless,
  The air was a caress.

Not she who lightly laughed is there,
With scornful toss of midnight hair,
  Her dark, disdainful eyes,
  And proud lip worldly-wise.

Her haughty vow is still unsaid,
But all she dreamed and coveted
  Wears, half to her surprise,
  The youthful farmer's guise !

With more than all her old-time pride
She walks the rye-field at his side,
  Careless of cot or hall,
  Since love transfigures all.

Rich beyond dreams, the vantage-ground
Of life is gained ; her hands have found
  The talisman of old
  That changes all to gold.

While she who could for love dispense
With all its glittering accidents,
  And trust her heart alone,
  Finds love and gold her own.

What wealth can buy or art can build
Awaits her ; but her cup is filled
  Even now unto the brim ;
  Her world is love and him !

The while he heard, the Book-man drew
  A length of make-believing face,
With   smothered   mischief   laughing
        through :
  " Why, you shall sit in Ramsay's place.
And, with his Gentle Shepherd, keep
On Yankee hills immortal sheep,
While love-lorn swains and maids the seas
        beyond
Hold dreamy tryst around your huckle-
        berry-pond."

The Traveller laughed : " Sir Galahad
  Singing of love the Trouvere's lay !
How should he know the blindfold lad
  From one of Vulcan's forge-boys ? " —
  " Nay,
He better sees who stands outside
Than they who in procession ride,"
The Reader answered : " selectmen and
        squire
Miss, while they make, the show that way-
        side folks admire.

" Here is a wild tale of the North,
  Our travelled friend will own as one
Fit for a Norland Christmas hearth
  And lips of Christian Andersen.

They tell it in the valleys green
Of the fair island he has seen,
Low lying off the pleasant Swedish shore,
Washed by the Baltic Sea, and watched by
Elsinore."

KALLUNDBORG CHURCH

" Tie stille, barn min !
Imorgen kommer Fin,
Fa'er din,
Og gi'er dig Esbern Snares öine og hjerte at lege med ! "
Zealand Rhyme.

" BUILD at Kallundborg by the sea
A church as stately as church may be,
And there shalt thou wed my daughter
fair,"
Said the Lord of Nesvek to Esbern Snare.

And the Baron laughed. But Esbern said,
" Though I lose my soul, I will Helva wed ! "
And off he strode, in his pride of will,
To the Troll who dwelt in Ulshoi hill.

" Build, O Troll, a church for me
At Kallundborg by the mighty sea ;
Build it stately, and build it fair,
Build it quickly," said Esbern Snare.

But the sly Dwarf said, " No work is
wrought
By Trolls of the Hills, O man, for naught.
What wilt thou give for thy church so fair ? "
" Set thy own price," quoth Esbern Snare.

" When Kallundborg church is builded well,
Thou must the name of its builder tell,
Or thy heart and thy eyes must be my
boon."
" Build," said Esbern, " and build it soon."

By night and by day the Troll wrought
on ;
He hewed the timbers, he piled the stone ;
But day by day, as the walls rose fair,
Darker and sadder grew Esbern Snare.

He listened by night, he watched by day,
He sought and thought, but he dared not
pray ;
In vain he called on the Elle-maids shy,
And the Neck and the Nis gave no reply.

Of his evil bargain far and wide
A rumor ran through the country-side ;

And Helva of Nesvek, young and fair,
Prayed for the soul of Esbern Snare.

And now the church was wellnigh done ;
One pillar it lacked, and one alone ;
And the grim Troll muttered, " Fool thou
art !
To-morrow gives me thy eyes and heart ! "

By Kallundborg in black despair,
Through wood and meadow, walked Esbern
Snare,
Till, worn and weary, the strong man
sank
Under the birches on Ulshoi bank.

At his last day's work he heard the Troll
Hammer and delve in the quarry's hole ;
Before him the church stood large and
fair :
" I have builded my tomb," said Esbern
Snare.

And he closed his eyes the sight to hide,
When he heard a light step at his side :
" O Esbern Snare ! " a sweet voice said,
" Would I might die now in thy stead ! "

With a grasp by love and by fear made
strong,
He held her fast, and he held her long :
With the beating heart of a bird afeard,
She hid her face in his flame-red beard.

" O love ! " he cried, " let me look to-day
In thine eyes ere mine are plucked away ;
Let me hold thee close, let me feel thy
heart
Ere mine by the Troll is torn apart !

" I sinned, O Helva, for love of thee !
Pray that the Lord Christ pardon me ! "
But fast as she prayed, and faster still,
Hammered the Troll in Ulshoi hill.

He knew, as he wrought, that a loving
heart
Was somehow baffling his evil art ;
For more than spell of Elf or Troll
Is a maiden's prayer for her lover's soul.

And Esbern listened, and caught the sound
Of a Troll-wife singing underground :
" To-morrow comes Fine, father thine :
Lie still and hush thee, baby mine !

"Lie still, my darling! next sunrise
Thou 'lt play with Esbern Snare's heart and
　　eyes !"
"Ho! ho!" quoth Esbern, "is that your
　　game?
Thanks to the Troll-wife, I know his
　　name!"

The Troll he heard him, and hurried on
To Kallundborg church with the lacking
　　stone.
"Too late, Gaffer Fine!" cried Esbern
　　Snare;
And Troll and pillar vanished in air!

That night the harvesters heard the sound
Of a woman sobbing underground,
And the voice of the Hill-Troll loud with
　　blame
Of the careless singer who told his name.

Of the Troll of the Church they sing the
　　rune
By the Northern Sea in the harvest moon;
And the fishers of Zealand hear him still
Scolding his wife in Ulshoi hill.

And seaward over its groves of birch
Still looks the tower of Kallundborg church,
Where, first at its altar, a wedded pair,
Stood Helva of Nesvek and Esbern Snare!

"What," asked the Traveller, "would
　　our sires,
　　The old Norse story-tellers, say
Of sun-graved pictures, ocean wires,
　　And smoking steamboats of to-day?
And this, O lady, by your leave,
Recalls your song of yester eve:
Pray, let us have that Cable-hymn once
　　more."
"Hear, hear!" the Book-man cried, "the
　　lady has the floor.

"These noisy waves below perhaps
　　To such a strain will lend their ear,
With softer voice and lighter lapse
　　Come stealing up the sands to hear,
And what they once refused to do
For old King Knut accord to you.
Nay, even the fishes shall your listeners be,
As once, the legend runs, they heard St.
　　Anthony."

THE CABLE HYMN

O LONELY bay of Trinity,
　　O dreary shores, give ear!
Lean down unto the white-lipped sea
　　The voice of God to hear!

From world to world His couriers fly,
　　Thought-winged and shod with fire;
The angel of His stormy sky
　　Rides down the sunken wire.

What saith the herald of the Lord?
　　"The world's long strife is done;
Close wedded by that mystic cord,
　　Its continents are one.

"And one in heart, as one in blood,
　　Shall all her peoples be;
The hands of human brotherhood
　　Are clasped beneath the sea.

"Through Orient seas, o'er Afric's plain
　　And Asian mountains borne,
The vigor of the Northern brain
　　Shall nerve the world outworn.

"From clime to clime, from shore to shore,
　　Shall thrill the magic thread;
The new Prometheus steals once more
　　The fire that wakes the dead."

Throb on, strong pulse of thunder! beat
　　From answering beach to beach;
Fuse nations in thy kindly heat,
　　And melt the chains of each!

Wild terror of the sky above,
　　Glide tamed and dumb below!
Bear gently, Ocean's carrier-dove,
　　Thy errands to and fro.

Weave on, swift shuttle of the Lord,
　　Beneath the deep so far,
The bridal robe of earth's accord,
　　The funeral shroud of war!

For lo! the fall of Ocean's wall
　　Space mocked and time outrun;
And round the world the thought of all
　　Is as the thought of one!

The poles unite, the zones agree,
　　The tongues of striving cease;

As on the Sea of Galilee
　The Christ is whispering, Peace !

" Glad prophecy ! to this at last,"
　The Reader said, " shall all things
　　come.
Forgotten be the bugle's blast,
　And battle-music of the drum.
A little while the world may run
Its old mad way, with needle-gun
And ironclad, but truth, at last, shall reign :
The cradle-song of Christ was never sung
　　in vain ! "

Shifting his scattered papers, " Here,"
　He said, as died the faint applause,
" Is something that I found last year
　Down on the island known as Orr's.
I had it from a fair-haired girl
Who, oddly, bore the name of Pearl,
(As if by some droll freak of circumstance,)
Classic, or wellnigh so, in Harriet Stowe's
　　romance."

THE DEAD SHIP OF HARPSWELL

WHAT flecks the outer gray beyond
　The sundown's golden trail ?
The white flash of a sea-bird's wing,
　Or gleam of slanting sail ?
Let young eyes watch from Neck and Point,
　And sea-worn elders pray,—
The ghost of what was once a ship
　Is sailing up the bay !

From gray sea-fog, from icy drift,
　From peril and from pain,
The home-bound fisher greets thy lights,
　O hundred-harbored Maine !
But many a keel shall seaward turn,
　And many a sail outstand,
When, tall and white, the Dead Ship looms
　Against the dusk of land.

She rounds the headland's bristling pines ;
　She threads the isle-set bay ;
No spur of breeze can speed her on,
　Nor ebb of tide delay.
Old men still walk the Isle of Orr
　Who tell her date and name,
Old shipwrights sit in Freeport yards
　Who hewed her oaken frame.

What weary doom of baffled quest,
　Thou sad sea-ghost, is thine ?
What makes thee in the haunts of home
　A wonder and a sign ?
No foot is on thy silent deck,
　Upon thy helm no hand ;
No ripple hath the soundless wind
　That smites thee from the land !

For never comes the ship to port,
　Howe'er the breeze may be ;
Just when she nears the waiting shore
　She drifts again to sea.
No tack of sail, nor turn of helm,
　Nor sheer of veering side ;
Stern-fore she drives to sea and night,
　Against the wind and tide.

In vain o'er Harpswell Neck the star
　Of evening guides her in ;
In vain for her the lamps are lit
　Within thy tower, Seguin !
In vain the harbor-boat shall hail,
　In vain the pilot call ;
No hand shall reef her spectral sail,
　Or let her anchor fall.

Shake, brown old wives, with dreary joy,
　Your gray-head hints of ill ;
And, over sick-beds whispering low,
　Your prophecies fulfil.
Some home amid yon birchen trees
　Shall drape its door with woe ;
And slowly where the Dead Ship sails,
　The burial boat shall row !

From Wolf Neck and from Flying Point,
　From island and from main,
From sheltered cove and tided creek,
　Shall glide the funeral train.
The dead-boat with the bearers four,
　The mourners at her stern, —
And one shall go the silent way
　Who shall no more return !

And men shall sigh, and women weep,
　Whose dear ones pale and pine,
And sadly over sunset seas
　Await the ghostly sign.
They know not that its sails are filled
　By pity's tender breath,
Nor see the Angel at the helm
　Who steers the Ship of Death !

"Chill as a down-east breeze should be,"
The Book-man said. "A ghostly touch
The legend has. I'm glad to see
Your flying Yankee beat the Dutch."
"Well, here is something of the sort
Which one midsummer day I caught
In Narragansett Bay, for lack of fish."
"We wait," the Traveller said; "serve
hot or cold your dish."

THE PALATINE

Block Island in Long Island Sound, called
by the Indians Manisees, the isle of the little
god, was the scene of a tragic incident a hun-
dred years or more ago, when *The Palatine*, an
emigrant ship bound for Philadelphia, driven
off its course, came upon the coast at this point.
A mutiny on board, followed by an inhuman
desertion on the part of the crew, had brought
the unhappy passengers to the verge of starva-
tion and madness. Tradition says that wreck-
ers on shore, after rescuing all but one of the
survivors, set fire to the vessel, which was driven
out to sea before a gale which had sprung up.
Every twelvemonth, according to the same tradi-
tion, the spectacle of a ship on fire is visible to
the inhabitants of the island.

LEAGUES north, as fly the gull and auk,
Point Judith watches with eye of hawk;
Leagues south, thy beacon flames, Mon-
tauk!

Lonely and wind-shorn, wood-forsaken,
With never a tree for Spring to waken,
For tryst of lovers or farewells taken,

Circled by waters that never freeze,
Beaten by billow and swept by breeze,
Lieth the island of Manisees,

Set at the mouth of the Sound to hold
The coast lights up on its turret old,
Yellow with moss and sea-fog mould.

Dreary the land when gust and sleet
At its doors and windows howl and beat,
And Winter laughs at its fires of peat!

But in summer time, when pool and
pond,
Held in the laps of valleys fond,
Are blue as the glimpses of sea beyond;

When the hills are sweet with the brier-
rose,
And, hid in the warm, soft dells, unclose
Flowers the mainland rarely knows;

When boats to their morning fishing go,
And, held to the wind and slanting low,
Whitening and darkening the small sails
show, —

Then is that lonely island fair;
And the pale health-seeker findeth there
The wine of life in its pleasant air.

No greener valleys the sun invite,
On smoother beaches no sea-birds light,
No blue waves shatter to foam more
white!

There, circling ever their narrow range,
Quaint tradition and legend strange
Live on unchallenged, and know no change.

Old wives spinning their webs of tow,
Or rocking weirdly to and fro
In and out of the peat's dull glow,

And old men mending their nets of twine,
Talk together of dream and sign,
Talk of the lost ship Palatine, —

The ship that, a hundred years before,
Freighted deep with its goodly store,
In the gales of the equinox went ashore.

The eager islanders one by one
Counted the shots of her signal gun,
And heard the crash when she drove right
on!

Into the teeth of death she sped:
(May God forgive the hands that fed
The false lights over the rocky Head!)

O men and brothers! what sights were
there!
White upturned faces, hands stretched in
prayer!
Where waves had pity, could ye not spare?

Down swooped the wreckers, like birds of
prey
Tearing the heart of the ship away,
And the dead had never a word to say.

And then, with ghastly shimmer and
  shine
Over the rocks and the seething brine,
They burned the wreck of the Palatine.

In their cruel hearts, as they homeward
  sped,
"The sea and the rocks are dumb," they
  said:
"There 'll be no reckoning with the dead."

But the year went round, and when once
  more
Along their foam-white curves of shore
They heard the line-storm rave and roar,

Behold! again, with shimmer and shine,
Over the rocks and the seething brine,
The flaming wreck of the Palatine!

So, haply in fitter words than these,
Mending their nets on their patient knees,
They tell the legend of Manisees.

Nor looks nor tones a doubt betray;
"It is known to us all," they quietly
  say;
"We too have seen it in our day."

Is there, then, no death for a word once
  spoken?
Was never a deed but left its token
Written on tables never broken?

Do the elements subtle reflections give?
Do pictures of all the ages live
On Nature's infinite negative,

Which, half in sport, in malice half,
She shows at times, with shudder or
  laugh,
Phantom and shadow in photograph?

For still, on many a moonless night,
From Kingston Head and from Montauk
  light
The spectre kindles and burns in sight.

Now low and dim, now clear and higher,
Leaps up the terrible Ghost of Fire,
Then, slowly sinking, the flames expire.

And the wise Sound skippers, though skies
  be fine,

Reef their sails when they see the sign
Of the blazing wreck of the Palatine!

"A fitter tale to scream than sing,"
  The Book-man said. "Well, fancy,
  then,"
The Reader answered, "on the wing
  The sea-birds shriek it, not for men,
But in the ear of wave and breeze!"
The Traveller mused: "Your Manisees
Is fairy-land: off Narragansett shore
Who ever saw the isle or heard its name
  before?

"'T is some strange land of Flyaway,
  Whose dreamy shore the ship beguiles,
St. Brandan's in its sea-mist gray,
  Or sunset loom of Fortunate Isles!"
"No ghost, but solid turf and rock
Is the good island known as Block,"
The Reader said. "For beauty and for
  ease
I chose its Indian name, soft-flowing Mani-
  sees!

"But let it pass; here is a bit
  Of unrhymed story, with a hint
Of the old preaching mood in it,
  The sort of sidelong moral squint
Our friend objects to, which has grown,
I fear, a habit of my own.
'T was written when the Asian plague drew
  near,
And the land held its breath and paled
  with sudden fear."

ABRAHAM DAVENPORT

The famous Dark Day of New England, May
19, 1780, was a physical puzzle for many years
to our ancestors, but its occurrence brought
something more than philosophical speculation
into the minds of those who passed through it.
The incident of Colonel Abraham Davenport's
sturdy protest is a matter of history.

In the old days (a custom laid aside
With breeches and cocked hats) the people
  sent
Their wisest men to make the public laws.
And so, from a brown homestead, where the
  Sound

Drinks the small tribute of the Mianas,
Waved over by the woods of Rippowams,
And hallowed by pure lives and tranquil
      deaths,
Stamford sent up to the councils of the State
Wisdom and grace in Abraham Davenport.

'T was on a May-day of the far old year
Seventeen hundred eighty, that there fell
Over the bloom and sweet life of the Spring,
Over the fresh earth and the heaven of noon,
A horror of great darkness, like the night
In day of which the Norland sagas tell, —
The Twilight of the Gods. The low-hung
      sky
Was black with ominous clouds, save where
      its rim
Was fringed with a dull glow, like that
      which climbs
The crater's sides from the red hell below.
Birds ceased to sing, and all the barn-yard
      fowls
Roosted ; the cattle at the pasture bars
Lowed, and looked homeward ; bats on
      leathern wings
Flitted abroad ; the sounds of labor died ;
Men prayed, and women wept ; all ears
      grew sharp
To hear the doom - blast of the trumpet
      shatter
The black sky, that the dreadful face of
      Christ
Might look from the rent clouds, not as
      he looked
A loving guest at Bethany, but stern
As Justice and inexorable Law.

Meanwhile in the old State House, dim
      as ghosts,
Sat the lawgivers of Connecticut,
Trembling beneath their legislative robes.
"It is the Lord's Great Day ! Let us ad-
      journ,"
Some said ; and then, as if with one accord,
All eyes were turned to Abraham Daven-
      port.
He rose, slow cleaving with his steady voice
The intolerable hush. "This well may be
The Day of Judgment which the world
      awaits ;
But be it so or not, I only know
My present duty, and my Lord's command
To occupy till He come. So at the post
Where He hath set me in His providence,

I choose, for one, to meet Him face to
      face, —
No faithless servant frightened from my
      task,
But ready when the Lord of the harvest
      calls ;
And therefore, with all reverence, I would
      say,
Let God do His work, we will see to
      ours.
Bring in the candles." And they brought
      them in.

Then by the flaring lights the Speaker
      read,
Albeit with husky voice and shaking hands,
An act to amend an act to regulate
The shad and alewive fisheries. Where-
      upon
Wisely and well spake Abraham Davenport,
Straight to the question, with no figures of
      speech
Save the ten Arab signs, yet not without
The shrewd dry humor natural to the man :
His awe-struck colleagues listening all the
      while,
Between the pauses of his argument,
To hear the thunder of the wrath of God
Break from the hollow trumpet of the cloud.

And there he stands in memory to this
      day,
Erect, self-poised, a rugged face, half seen
Against the background of unnatural dark,
A witness to the ages as they pass,
That simple duty hath no place for fear.

———

He ceased : just then the ocean seemed
      To lift a half-faced moon in sight ;
And, shore - ward, o'er the waters
      gleamed,
      From crest to crest, a line of light,
Such as of old, with solemn awe,
      The fishers by Gennesaret saw,
When dry-shod o'er it walked the Son of
      God,
Tracking the waves with light where'er his
      sandals trod.

Silently for a space each eye
      Upon that sudden glory turned :
Cool from the land the breeze blew by,

The tent-ropes flapped, the long beach
  churned
Its waves to foam ; on either hand
Stretched, far as sight, the hills of sand ;
With bays of marsh, and capes of bush
  and tree,
The wood's black shore-line loomed beyond
  the meadowy sea.

The lady rose to leave. " One song,
  Or hymn," they urged, " before we
    part."
And she, with lips to which belong
  Sweet intuitions of all art,
Gave to the winds of night a strain
Which they who heard would hear again ;
And to her voice the solemn ocean lent,
Touching its harp of sand, a deep accom-
  paniment.

THE WORSHIP OF NATURE

The harp at Nature's advent strung
  Has never ceased to play ;
The song the stars of morning sung
  Has never died away.

And prayer is made, and praise is given,
  By all things near and far ;
The ocean looketh up to heaven,
  And mirrors every star.

Its waves are kneeling on the strand,
  As kneels the human knee,
Their white locks bowing to the sand,
  The priesthood of the sea !

They pour their glittering treasures forth,
  Their gifts of pearl they bring,
And all the listening hills of earth
  Take up the song they sing.

The green earth sends her incense up
  From many a mountain shrine ;
From folded leaf and dewy cup
  She pours her sacred wine.

The mists above the morning rills
  Rise white as wings of prayer ;
The altar-curtains of the hills
  Are sunset's purple air.

The winds with hymns of praise are loud,
  Or low with sobs of pain, —
The thunder-organ of the cloud,
  The dropping tears of rain.

With drooping head and branches crossed
  The twilight forest grieves,
Or speaks with tongues of Pentecost
  From all its sunlit leaves.

The blue sky is the temple's arch,
  Its transept earth and air,
The music of its starry march
  The chorus of a prayer.

So Nature keeps the reverent frame
  With which her years began,
And all her signs and voices shame
  The prayerless heart of man.

The singer ceased. The moon's white rays
  Fell on the rapt, still face of her.
" Allah il Allah ! He hath praise
  From all things," said the Traveller.
" Oft from the desert's silent nights,
  And mountain hymns of sunset lights,
My heart has felt rebuke, as in his tent
The Moslem's prayer has shamed my
  Christian knee unbent."

He paused, and lo ! far, faint, and slow
  The bells in Newbury's steeples tolled
The twelve dead hours ; the lamp burned
  low ;
  The singer sought her canvas fold.
One sadly said, " At break of day
We strike our tent and go our way."
But one made answer cheerily, " Never fear,
We 'll pitch this tent of ours in type an-
  other year."

ANTI-SLAVERY POEMS

TO WILLIAM LLOYD GARRISON

[Read at the Convention which formed the American Anti-Slavery Society, in Philadelphia, December, 1833.]

CHAMPION of those who groan beneath
  Oppression's iron hand :
In view of penury, hate, and death,
  I see thee fearless stand.
Still bearing up thy lofty brow,
  In the steadfast strength of truth,
In manhood sealing well the vow
  And promise of thy youth.

Go on, for thou hast chosen well ;
  On in the strength of God !
Long as one human heart shall swell
  Beneath the tyrant's rod.
Speak in a slumbering nation's ear,
  As thou hast ever spoken,
Until the dead in sin shall hear,
  The fetter's link be broken !

I love thee with a brother's love,
  I feel my pulses thrill,
To mark thy spirit soar above
  The cloud of human ill.
My heart hath leaped to answer thine,
  And echo back thy words,
As leaps the warrior's at the shine
  And flash of kindred swords !

They tell me thou art rash and vain,
  A searcher after fame ;
That thou art striving but to gain
  A long-enduring name ;
That thou hast nerved the Afric's hand
  And steeled the Afric's heart,
To shake aloft his vengeful brand,
  And rend his chain apart.

Have I not known thee well, and read
  Thy mighty purpose long ?
And watched the trials which have made
  Thy human spirit strong ?

And shall the slanderer's demon breath
  Avail with one like me,
To dim the sunshine of my faith
  And earnest trust in thee ?

Go on, the dagger's point may glare
  Amid thy pathway's gloom ;
The fate which sternly threatens there
  Is glorious martyrdom !
Then onward with a martyr's zeal ;
  And wait thy sure reward
When man to man no more shall kneel,
  And God alone be Lord !

TOUSSAINT L'OUVERTURE

Toussaint L'Ouverture, the black chieftain of Hayti, was a slave on the plantation "de Libertas," belonging to M. Bayou. When the rising of the negroes took place, in 1791, Toussaint refused to join them until he had aided M. Bayou and his family to escape to Baltimore. The white man had discovered in Toussaint many noble qualities, and had instructed him in some of the first branches of education ; and the preservation of his life was owing to the negro's gratitude for this kindness.

In 1797, Toussaint L'Ouverture was appointed, by the French government, General-in-Chief of the armies of St. Domingo, and, as such, signed the Convention with General Maitland for the evacuation of the island by the British. From this period until 1801 the island, under the government of Toussaint, was happy, tranquil, and prosperous. The miserable attempt of Napoleon to reëstablish slavery in St. Domingo, although it failed of its intended object, proved fatal to the negro chieftain. Treacherously seized by Leclerc, he was hurried on board a vessel by night, and conveyed to France, where he was confined in a cold subterranean dungeon, at Besançon, where, in April, 1803, he died. The treatment of Toussaint finds a parallel only in the murder of the Duke D'Enghien. It was the remark of Godwin, in his Lectures, that the West India Islands, since their first discovery

by Columbus, could not boast of a single name
which deserves comparison with that of Tous-
saint L'Ouverture.

'TWAS night.   The tranquil moonlight
      smile
  With which Heaven dreams of Earth,
      shed down
Its beauty on the Indian isle, —
  On broad green field and white-walled
      town ;
And inland waste of rock and wood,
In searching sunshine, wild and rude,
Rose, mellowed through the silver gleam,
Soft as the landscape of a dream.
All motionless and dewy wet,
Tree, vine, and flower in shadow met :
The myrtle with its snowy bloom,
Crossing the nightshade's solemn gloom, —
The white cecropia's silver rind
Relieved by deeper green behind,
The orange with its fruit of gold,
The lithe paullinia's verdant fold,
The passion-flower with symbol holy,
Twining its tendrils long and lowly,
The rhexias dark, and cassia tall,
And proudly rising over all,
The kingly palm's imperial stem,
Crowned with its leafy diadem,
Star-like, beneath whose sombre shade,
The fiery-winged cucullo played !

How lovely was thine aspect, then,
  Fair island of the Western Sea !
Lavish of beauty, even when
Thy brutes were happier than thy men,
  For they, at least, were free !
Regardless of thy glorious clime,
  Unmindful of thy soil of flowers,
The toiling negro sighed, that Time
  No faster sped his hours.
For, by the dewy moonlight still,
He fed the weary-turning mill,
Or bent him in the chill morass,
To pluck the long and tangled grass,
And hear above his scar-worn back
The heavy slave-whip's frequent crack :
While in his heart one evil thought
In solitary madness wrought,
One baleful fire surviving still
  The quenching of the immortal mind,
  One sterner passion of his kind,
Which even fetters could not kill,
The savage hope, to deal, erelong,
A vengeance bitterer than his wrong !

Hark to that cry ! long, loud, and shrill,
From field and forest, rock and hill,
Thrilling and horrible it rang,
  Around, beneath, above ;
The wild beast from his cavern sprang,
  The wild bird from her grove !
Nor fear, nor joy, nor agony
Were mingled in that midnight cry ;
But like the lion's growl of wrath,
When falls that hunter in his path
Whose barbèd arrow, deeply set,
Is rankling in his bosom yet,
It told of hate, full, deep, and strong,
Of vengeance kindling out of wrong ;
It was as if the crimes of years —
The unrequited toil, the tears,
The shame and hate, which liken well
Earth's garden to the nether hell —
Had found in nature's self a tongue,
On which the gathered horror hung ;
As if from cliff, and stream, and glen
Burst on the startled ears of men
That voice which rises unto God,
Solemn and stern, — the cry of blood !
It ceased, and all was still once more,
Save ocean chafing on his shore,
The sighing of the wind between
The broad banana's leaves of green,
Or bough by restless plumage shook,
Or murmuring voice of mountain brook.

Brief was the silence.   Once again
  Pealed to the skies that frantic yell,
Glowed on the heavens a fiery stain,
  And flashes rose and fell ;
And painted on the blood-red sky,
Dark, naked arms were tossed on high ;
And, round the white man's lordly hall,
  Trod, fierce and free, the brute he made ;
And those who crept along the wall,
And answered to his lightest call
  With more than spaniel dread,
The creatures of his lawless beck,
Were trampling on his very neck !
And on the night-air, wild and clear,
Rose woman's shriek of more than fear ;
For bloodied arms were round her thrown,
And dark cheeks pressed against her own !

Then, injured Afric ! for the shame
Of thy own daughters, vengeance came
Full on the scornful hearts of those,
Who mocked thee in thy nameless woes,
And to thy hapless children gave
One choice, — pollution or the grave !

Where then was he whose fiery zeal
Had taught the trampled heart to feel,
Until despair itself grew strong,
And vengeance fed its torch from wrong?
Now, when the thunderbolt is speeding ;
Now, when oppression's heart is bleed-
    ing ;
Now, when the latent curse of Time
    Is raining down in fire and blood,
That curse which, through long years of
        crime,
    Has gathered, drop by drop, its flood, —
Why strikes he not, the foremost one,
Where murder's sternest deeds are done ?

He stood the aged palms beneath,
    That shadowed o'er his humble door,
Listening, with half-suspended breath,
To the wild sounds of fear and death,
    Toussaint L'Ouverture !
What marvel that his heart beat high !
    The blow for freedom had been given,
And blood had answered to the cry
    Which Earth sent up to Heaven !
What marvel that a fierce delight
Smiled grimly o'er his brow of night,
As groan and shout and bursting flame
Told where the midnight tempest came,
With blood and fire along its van,
And death behind ! he was a Man !

Yes, dark-souled chieftain ! if the light
    Of mild Religion's heavenly ray
Unveiled not to thy mental sight
    The lowlier and the purer way,
In which the Holy Sufferer trod,
    Meekly amidst the sons of crime ;
That calm reliance upon God
    For justice in His own good time ;
That gentleness to which belongs
Forgiveness for its many wrongs,
Even as the primal martyr, kneeling
For mercy on the evil-dealing ;
Let not the favored white man name
Thy stern appeal, with words of blame.
Has he not, with the light of heaven
    Broadly around him, made the same ?
Yea, on his thousand war-fields striven,
    And gloried in his ghastly shame ?
Kneeling amidst his brother's blood,
To offer mockery unto God,
As if the High and Holy One
Could smile on deeds of murder done !
As if a human sacrifice
Were purer in His holy eyes,

Though offered up by Christian hands,
Than the foul rites of Pagan lands !

.   .   .   .

Sternly, amidst his household band,
His carbine grasped within his hand,
    The white man stood, prepared and still,
Waiting the shock of maddened men,
Unchained, and fierce as tigers, when
    The horn winds through their caverned
        hill.
And one was weeping in his sight,
    The sweetest flower of all the isle,
The bride who seemed but yesternight
    Love's fair embodied smile.
And, clinging to her trembling knee,
Looked up the form of infancy,
With tearful glance in either face
The secret of its fear to trace.

" Ha ! stand or die ! " The white man's eye
    His steady musket gleamed along,
As a tall Negro hastened nigh,
    With fearless step and strong.
" What ho, Toussaint ! "   A moment more,
His shadow crossed the lighted floor.
" Away ! " he shouted ; " fly with me,
The white man's bark is on the sea ;
Her sails must catch the seaward wind,
For sudden vengeance sweeps behind.
Our brethren from their graves have spoken,
The yoke is spurned, the chain is broken ;
On all the hills our fires are glowing,
Through all the vales red blood is flowing !
No more the mocking White shall rest
His foot upon the Negro's breast ;
No more, at morn or eve, shall drip
The warm blood from the driver's whip :
Yet, though Toussaint has vengeance sworn
For all the wrongs his race have borne,
Though for each drop of Negro blood
The white man's veins shall pour a flood ;
Not all alone the sense of ill
Around his heart is lingering still,
Nor deeper can the white man feel
The generous warmth of grateful zeal.
Friends of the Negro ! fly with me,
The path is open to the sea :
Away, for life ! "   He spoke, and pressed
The young child to his manly breast,
As, headlong, through the cracking cane,
Down swept the dark insurgent train,
Drunken and grim, with shout and yell
Howled through the dark, like sounds from
    hell.

Far out, in peace, the white man's sail
Swayed free before the sunrise gale.
Cloud-like that island hung afar,
  Along the bright horizon's verge,
O'er which the curse of servile war
  Rolled its red torrent, surge on surge ;
And he, the Negro champion, where
  In the fierce tumult struggled he ?
Go trace him by the fiery glare
Of dwellings in the midnight air,
The yells of triumph and despair,
  The streams that crimson to the sea !

Sleep calmly in thy dungeon-tomb,
  Beneath Besançon's alien sky,
Dark Haytien ! for the time shall come,
  Yea, even now is nigh,
When, everywhere, thy name shall be
Redeemed from color's infamy ;
And men shall learn to speak of thee
As one of earth's great spirits, born
In servitude, and nursed in scorn,
Casting aside the weary weight
And fetters of its low estate,
In that strong majesty of soul
  Which knows no color, tongue, or clime,
Which still hath spurned the base control
  Of tyrants through all time !
Far other hands than mine may wreathe
The laurel round thy brow of death,
And speak thy praise, as one whose word
A thousand fiery spirits stirred,
Who crushed his foeman as a worm,
Whose step on human hearts fell firm :
Be mine the better task to find
A tribute for thy lofty mind,
Amidst whose gloomy vengeance shone
Some milder virtues all thine own,
Some gleams of feeling pure and warm,
Like sunshine on a sky of storm,
Proofs that the Negro's heart retains
Some nobleness amid its chains, —
That kindness to the wronged is never
  Without its excellent reward,
Holy to human-kind and ever
  Acceptable to God.

THE SLAVE-SHIPS

"That fatal, that perfidious bark,
Built i' the eclipse, and rigged with curses dark."
MILTON'S *Lycidas.*

"The French ship Le Rodeur, with a crew
of twenty-two men, and with one hundred and
sixty negro slaves, sailed from Bonny, in Africa,
April, 1819. On approaching the line, a terrible
malady broke out, — an obstinate disease of the
eyes, — contagious, and altogether beyond the
resources of medicine. It was aggravated by
the scarcity of water among the slaves (only
half a wine-glass per day being allowed to an
individual), and by the extreme impurity of
the air in which they breathed. By the advice
of the physician, they were brought upon deck
occasionally ; but some of the poor wretches,
locking themselves in each other's arms, leaped
overboard, in the hope, which so universally
prevails among them, of being swiftly trans-
ported to their own homes in Africa. To
check this, the captain ordered several, who
were stopped in the attempt, to be shot, or
hanged, before their companions. The disease
extended to the crew ; and one after another
were smitten with it, until only *one* remained
unaffected. Yet even this dreadful condition
did not preclude calculation : to save the ex-
pense of supporting slaves rendered unsalable,
and to obtain grounds for a claim against the
underwriters, *thirty-six of the negroes, having
become blind, were thrown into the sea and
drowned !*" — *Speech of M. Benjamin Constant,
in the French Chamber of Deputies,* June 17,
1820.

In the midst of their dreadful fears lest the
solitary individual whose sight remained un-
affected should also be seized with the malady,
a sail was discovered. It was the Spanish sla-
ver, Leon. The same disease had been there ;
and, horrible to tell, all the crew had become
blind ! Unable to assist each other, the ves-
sels parted. The Spanish ship has never since
been heard of. The Rodeur reached Guada-
loupe on the 21st of June ; the only man who
had escaped the disease, and had thus been
enabled to steer the slaver into port, caught it
in three days after its arrival. — *Bibliothèque
Ophthalmologique* for November, 1819.

" ALL ready ? " cried the captain ;
  " Ay, ay ! " the seamen said ;
" Heave up the worthless lubbers, —
  The dying and the dead."
Up from the slave-ship's prison
  Fierce, bearded heads were thrust !
" Now let the sharks look to it, —
  Toss up the dead ones first ! "

Corpse after corpse came up, —
  Death had been busy there ;
Where every blow is mercy,
  Why should the spoiler spare ?
Corpse after corpse they cast
  Sullenly from the ship,

Yet bloody with the traces
  Of fetter-link and whip.

Gloomily stood the captain,
  With his arms upon his breast,
With his cold brow sternly knotted
  And his iron lip compressed.
"Are all the dead dogs over?"
  Growled through that matted lip;
"The blind ones are no better,
  Let's lighten the good ship."

Hark! from the ship's dark bosom,
  The very sounds of hell!
The ringing clank of iron,
  The maniac's short, sharp yell!
The hoarse, low curse, throat-stifled;
  The starving infant's moan,
The horror of a breaking heart
  Poured through a mother's groan.

Up from that loathsome prison
  The stricken blind ones came;
Below, had all been darkness,
  Above, was still the same.
Yet the holy breath of heaven
  Was sweetly breathing there,
And the heated brow of fever
  Cooled in the soft sea air.

"Overboard with them, shipmates!"
  Cutlass and dirk were plied;
Fettered and blind, one after one,
  Plunged down the vessel's side.
The sabre smote above,
  Beneath, the lean shark lay,
Waiting with wide and bloody jaw
  His quick and human prey.

God of the earth! what cries
  Rang upward unto thee?
Voices of agony and blood,
  From ship-deck and from sea.
The last dull plunge was heard,
  The last wave caught its stain,
And the unsated shark looked up
  For human hearts in vain.

. . . .

Red glowed the western waters,
  The setting sun was there,
Scattering alike on wave and cloud
  His fiery mesh of hair.
Amidst a group in blindness,
  A solitary eye

Gazed, from the burdened slaver's deck,
  Into that burning sky.

"A storm," spoke out the gazer,
  "Is gathering and at hand;
Curse on 't, I'd give my other eye
  For one firm rood of land."
And then he laughed, but only
  His echoed laugh replied,
For the blinded and the suffering
  Alone were at his side.

Night settled on the waters,
  And on a stormy heaven,
While fiercely on that lone ship's track
  The thunder-gust was driven.
"A sail! — thank God, a sail!"
  And as the helmsman spoke,
Up through the stormy murmur
  A shout of gladness broke.

Down came the stranger vessel,
  Unheeding on her way,
So near that on the slaver's deck
  Fell off her driven spray.
"Ho! for the love of mercy,
  We're perishing and blind!"
A wail of utter agony
  Came back upon the wind:

"Help us! for we are stricken
  With blindness every one;
Ten days we've floated fearfully,
  Unnoting star or sun.
Our ship's the slaver Leon, —
  We've but a score on board;
Our slaves are all gone over, —
  Help, for the love of God!"

On livid brows of agony
  The broad red lightning shone;
But the roar of wind and thunder
  Stifled the answering groan;
Wailed from the broken waters
  A last despairing cry,
As, kindling in the stormy light,
  The stranger ship went by.

. . . .

In the sunny Guadaloupe
  A dark-hulled vessel lay,
With a crew who noted never
  The nightfall or the day.
The blossom of the orange
  Was white by every stream,

And tropic leaf, and flower, and bird
  Were in the warm sunbeam.

And the sky was bright as ever,
  And the moonlight slept as well,
On the palm-trees by the hillside,
  And the streamlet of the dell :
And the glances of the Creole
  Were still as archly deep,
And her smiles as full as ever
  Of passion and of sleep.

But vain were bird and blossom,
  The green earth and the sky,
And the smile of human faces,
  To the slaver's darkened eye ;
At the breaking of the morning,
  At the star-lit evening time,
O'er a world of light and beauty
  Fell the blackness of his crime.

EXPOSTULATION

[Originally termed *Stanzas*, then *Follen*.]
Dr. Charles Follen, a German patriot, who
had come to America for the freedom which was
denied him in his native land, allied himself
with the abolitionists, and at a convention of
delegates from all the anti-slavery organiza-
tions in New England, held at Boston in May,
1834, was chairman of a committee to prepare
an address to the people of New England.
Toward the close of the address occurred the
passage which suggested these lines.
"The despotism which our fathers could
not bear in their native country is expiring,
and the sword of justice in her reformed hands
has applied its exterminating edge to slavery.
Shall the United States — the free United
States, which could not bear the bonds of a
king — cradle the bondage which a king is
abolishing ?   Shall a Republic be less free than
a Monarchy ?   Shall we, in the vigor and buoy-
ancy of our manhood, be less energetic in right-
eousness than a kingdom in its age ? " — *Dr.
Follen's Address.*
"Genius of America ! — Spirit of our free
institution ! — where art thou ?   How art thou
fallen, O Lucifer ! son of the morning, — how
art thou fallen from Heaven !   Hell from be-
neath is moved for thee, to meet thee at thy
coming !   The kings of the earth cry out to
thee, Aha ! Aha ! Art thou become like unto
us ? " — *Speech of Samuel J. May.*

OUR fellow-countrymen in chains !
  Slaves, in a land of light and law !

Slaves, crouching on the very plains
  Where rolled the storm of Freedom's
        war !
A groan from Eutaw's haunted wood,
  A wail where Camden's martyrs fell,
By every shrine of patriot blood,
  From Moultrie's wall and Jasper's well !

By storied hill and hallowed grot,
  By mossy wood and marshy glen,
Whence rang of old the rifle-shot,
  And hurrying shout of Marion's men !
The groan of breaking hearts is there,
  The falling lash, the fetter's clank !
Slaves, slaves are breathing in that air
  Which old De Kalb and Sumter drank !

What ho ! our countrymen in chains !
  The whip on woman's shrinking flesh !
Our soil yet reddening with the stains
  Caught from her scourging, warm and
        fresh !
What ! mothers from their children riven !
  What ! God's own image bought and
        sold !
Americans to market driven,
  And bartered as the brute for gold !

Speak ! shall their agony of prayer
  Come thrilling to our hearts in vain ?
To us whose fathers scorned to bear
  The paltry menace of a chain ;
To us, whose boast is loud and long
  Of holy Liberty and Light ;
Say, shall these writhing slaves of Wrong
  Plead vainly for their plundered Right ?

What ! shall we send, with lavish breath,
  Our sympathies across the wave,
Where Manhood, on the field of death,
  Strikes for his freedom or a grave ?
Shall prayers go up, and hymns be sung
  For Greece, the Moslem fetter spurning,
And millions hail with pen and tongue
  Our light on all her altars burning ?

Shall Belgium feel, and gallant France,
  By Vendome's pile and Schoenbrun's
        wall,
And Poland, gasping on her lance,
  The impulse of our cheering call ?
And shall the slave, beneath our eye,
  Clank o'er our fields his hateful chain ?
And toss his fettered arms on high,
  And groan for Freedom's gift, in vain ?

Oh, say, shall Prussia's banner be
  A refuge for the stricken slave ?
And shall the Russian serf go free
  By Baikal's lake and Neva's wave ?
And shall the wintry-bosomed Dane
  Relax the iron hand of pride,
And bid his bondmen cast the chain
  From fettered soul and limb aside ?

Shall every flap of England's flag
  Proclaim that all around are free,
From farthest Ind to each blue crag
  That beetles o'er the Western Sea ?
And shall we scoff at Europe's kings,
When Freedom's fire is dim with us,
And round our country's altar clings
  The damning shade of Slavery's curse ?

Go, let us ask of Constantine
  To loose his grasp on Poland's throat ;
And beg the lord of Mahmoud's line
  To spare the struggling Suliote ;
Will not the scorching answer come
  From turbaned Turk, and scornful Russ :
"Go, loose your fettered slaves at home,
  Then turn and ask the like of us ! "

Just God ! and shall we calmly rest,
  The Christian's scorn, the heathen's
    mirth,
Content to live the lingering jest
  And by-word of a mocking Earth ?
Shall our own glorious land retain
  That curse which Europe scorns to
    bear ?
Shall our own brethren drag the chain
  Which not even Russia's menials wear ?

Up, then, in Freedom's manly part,
  From graybeard eld to fiery youth,
And on the nation's naked heart
  Scatter the living coals of Truth !
Up ! while ye slumber, deeper yet
  The shadow of our fame is growing !
Up ! while ye pause, our sun may set
  In blood around our altars flowing !

Oh ! rouse ye, ere the storm comes forth,
  The gathered wrath of God and man,
Like that which wasted Egypt's earth,
  When hail and fire above it ran.
Hear ye no warnings in the air ?
  Feel ye no earthquake underneath ?
Up, up ! why will ye slumber where
  The sleeper only wakes in death ?

Rise now for Freedom ! not in strife
  Like that your sterner fathers saw,
The awful waste of human life,
  The glory and the guilt of war :
But break the chain, the yoke remove,
  And smite to earth Oppression's rod,
With those mild arms of Truth and Love,
  Made mighty through the living God !

Down let the shrine of Moloch sink,
  And leave no traces where it stood ;
Nor longer let its idol drink
  His daily cup of human blood ;
But rear another altar there,
  To Truth and Love and Mercy given,
And Freedom's gift, and Freedom's prayer,
  Shall call an answer down from Heaven!

HYMN

Written for the meeting of the Anti-Slavery
Society, at Chatham Street Chapel, New York,
held on the 4th of the seventh month, 1834.
[Originally entitled *Lines*.]

O Thou, whose presence went before
  Our fathers in their weary way,
As with Thy chosen moved of yore
  The fire by night, the cloud by day !

When from each temple of the free,
  A nation's song ascends to Heaven,
Most Holy Father ! unto Thee
  May not our humble prayer be given ?

Thy children all, though hue and form
  Are varied in Thine own good will,
With Thy own holy breathings warm,
  And fashioned in Thine image still.

We thank Thee, Father ! hill and plain
  Around us wave their fruits once more,
And clustered vine and blossomed grain
  Are bending round each cottage door.

And peace is here ; and hope and love
  Are round us as a mantle thrown,
And unto Thee, supreme above,
  The knee of prayer is bowed alone.

But oh, for those this day can bring,
  As unto us, no joyful thrill ;
For those who, under Freedom's wing,
  Are bound in Slavery's fetters still :

For those to whom Thy written word
  Of light and love is never given ;
For those whose ears have never heard
  The promise and the hope of heaven !

For broken heart, and clouded mind,
  Whereon no human mercies fall ;
Oh, be Thy gracious love inclined,
  Who, as a Father, pitiest all !

And grant, O Father ! that the time
  Of Earth's deliverance may be near,
When every land and tongue and clime
  The message of Thy love shall hear ;

When, smitten as with fire from heaven,
  The captive's chain shall sink in dust,
And to his fettered soul be given
  The glorious freedom of the just !

THE YANKEE GIRL

SHE sings by her wheel at that low cot-
    tage-door,
Which the long evening shadow is stretch-
    ing before,
With a music as sweet as the music which
    seems
Breathed softly and faint in the ear of our
    dreams !

How brilliant and mirthful the light of her
    eye,
Like a star glancing out from the blue of
    the sky !
And lightly and freely her dark tresses
    play
O'er a brow and a bosom as lovely as they !

Who comes in his pride to that low cot-
    tage-door,
The haughty and rich to the humble and
    poor ?
'T is the great Southern planter, the mas-
    ter who waves
His whip of dominion o'er hundreds of
    slaves.

" Nay, Ellen, for shame ! Let those Yan-
    kee fools spin,
Who would pass for our slaves with a
    change of their skin ;

Let them toil as they will at the loom or
    the wheel,
Too stupid for shame, and too vulgar to
    feel !

" But thou art too lovely and precious a
    gem
To be bound to their burdens and sullied
    by them ;
For shame, Ellen, shame, cast thy bondage
    aside,
And away to the South, as my blessing and
    pride.

" Oh, come where no winter thy footsteps
    can wrong,
But where flowers are blossoming all the
    year long,
Where the shade of the palm-tree is over
    my home,
And the lemon and orange are white in
    their bloom !

" Oh, come to my home, where my servants
    shall all
Depart at thy bidding and come at thy call ;
They shall heed thee as mistress with
    trembling and awe,
And each wish of thy heart shall be felt as
    a law."

Oh, could ye have seen her — that pride of
    our girls —
Arise and cast back the dark wealth of her
    curls,
With a scorn in her eye which the gazer
    could feel,
And a glance like the sunshine that flashes
    on steel !

" Go back, haughty Southron ! thy treas-
    ures of gold
Are dim with the blood of the hearts thou
    hast sold ;
Thy home may be lovely, but round it I
    hear
The crack of the whip and the footsteps of
    fear !

" And the sky of thy South may be brighter
    than ours,
And greener thy landscapes, and fairer thy
    flowers ;

But dearer the blast round our mountains
　　which raves,
Than the sweet summer zephyr which
　　breathes over slaves !

" Full low at thy bidding thy negroes may
　　kneel,
With the iron of bondage on spirit and
　　heel ;
Yet know that the Yankee girl sooner
　　would be
In fetters with them, than in freedom with
　　thee ! "

THE HUNTERS OF MEN

These lines were written when the orators of
the American Colonization Society were de-
manding that the free blacks should be sent to
Africa, and opposing Emancipation unless ex-
patriation followed. See the report of the pro-
ceedings of the society at its annual meeting
in 1834.

HAVE ye heard of our hunting, o'er moun-
　　tain and glen,
Through cane-brake and forest, — the hunt-
　　ing of men ?
The lords of our land to this hunting have
　　gone,
As the fox-hunter follows the sound of the
　　horn ;
Hark ! the cheer and the hallo ! the crack
　　of the whip,
And the yell of the hound as he fastens his
　　grip !
All blithe are our hunters, and noble their
　　match,
Though hundreds are caught, there are mil-
　　lions to catch.
So speed to their hunting, o'er mountain
　　and glen,
Through cane-brake and forest, — the hunt-
　　ing of men !

Gay luck to our hunters ! how nobly they
　　ride
In the glow of their zeal, and the strength
　　of their pride !
The priest with his cassock flung back on
　　the wind,
Just screening the politic statesman behind ;
The saint and the sinner, with cursing and
　　prayer,

The drunk and the sober, ride merrily there.
And woman, kind woman, wife, widow, and
　　maid,
For the good of the hunted, is lending her
　　aid :
Her foot 's in the stirrup, her hand on the
　　rein,
How blithely she rides to the hunting of
　　men !

Oh, goodly and grand is our hunting to see,
In this " land of the brave and this home of
　　the free."
Priest, warrior, and statesman, from Geor-
　　gia to Maine,
All mounting the saddle, all grasping the
　　rein ;
Right merrily hunting the black man, whose
　　sin
Is the curl of his hair and the hue of his
　　skin !
Woe, now, to the hunted who turns him at
　　bay !
Will our hunters be turned from their pur-
　　pose and prey ?
Will their hearts fail within them ? their
　　nerves tremble, when
All roughly they ride to the hunting of men?

Ho ! alms for our hunters ! all weary and
　　faint,
Wax the curse of the sinner and prayer of
　　the saint.
The horn is wound faintly, the echoes are
　　still,
Over cane-brake and river, and forest and
　　hill.
Haste, alms for our hunters ! the hunted
　　once more
Have turned from their flight with their
　　backs to the shore :
What right have they here in the home of
　　the white,
Shadowed o'er by our banner of Freedom
　　and Right ?
Ho ! alms for the hunters ! or never again
Will they ride in their pomp to the hunting
　　of men !

Alms, alms for our hunters ! why will ye de-
　　lay,
When their pride and their glory are melt-
　　ing away ?
The parson has turned ; for, on charge of
　　his own,

Who goeth a warfare, or hunting, alone ?
The politic statesman looks back with a
    sigh,
There is doubt in his heart, there is fear in
    his eye.
Oh, haste, lest that doubting and fear shall
    prevail,
And the head of his steed take the place of
    the tail.
Oh, haste, ere he leave us ! for who will
    ride then,
For pleasure or gain, to the hunting of
    men ?

STANZAS FOR THE TIMES

The " Times " referred to were those evil
times of the pro-slavery meeting in Faneuil
Hall, August 21, 1835, in which a demand was
made for the suppression of free speech, lest it
should endanger the foundation of commercial
society.

Is this the land our fathers loved,
    The freedom which they toiled to win ?
Is this the soil whereon they moved ?
    Are these the graves they slumber in ?
Are we the sons by whom are borne
The mantles which the dead have worn ?

And shall we crouch above these graves,
    With craven soul and fettered lip ?
Yoke in with marked and branded slaves,
    And tremble at the driver's whip ?
Bend to the earth our pliant knees,
And speak but as our masters please ?

Shall outraged Nature cease to feel ?
    Shall Mercy's tears no longer flow ?
Shall ruffian threats of cord and steel,
    The dungeon's gloom, the assassin's blow,
Turn back the spirit roused to save
The Truth, our Country, and the slave ?

Of human skulls that shrine was made,
    Round which the priests of Mexico
Before their loathsome idol prayed ;
    Is Freedom's altar fashioned so ?
And must we yield to Freedom's God,
As offering meet, the negro's blood ?

Shall tongue be mute, when deeds are
    wrought
    Which well might shame extremest hell ?

Shall freemen lock the indignant thought ?
    Shall Pity's bosom cease to swell ?
Shall Honor bleed ? — shall Truth suc-
    cumb ?
Shall pen, and press, and soul be dumb ?

No ; by each spot of haunted ground,
    Where Freedom weeps her children's
    fall ;
By Plymouth's rock, and Bunker's mound ;
    By Griswold's stained and shattered
    wall ;
By Warren's ghost, by Langdon's shade ;
By all the memories of our dead !

By their enlarging souls, which burst
    The bands and fetters round them set ;
By the free Pilgrim spirit nursed
    Within our inmost bosoms, yet,
By all above, around, below,
Be ours the indignant answer, — No !

No ; guided by our country's laws,
    For truth, and right, and suffering man,
Be ours to strive in Freedom's cause,
    As Christians may, as freemen can !
Still pouring on unwilling ears
That truth oppression only fears.

What ! shall we guard our neighbor still,
    While woman shrieks beneath his rod,
And while he tramples down at will
    The image of a common God ?
Shall watch and ward be round him set,
Of Northern nerve and bayonet ?

And shall we know and share with him
    The danger and the growing shame ?
And see our Freedom's light grow dim,
    Which should have filled the world with
    flame ?
And, writhing, feel, where'er we turn,
A world's reproach around us burn ?

Is 't not enough that this is borne ?
    And asks our haughty neighbor more ?
Must fetters which his slaves have worn
    Clank round the Yankee farmer's door ?
Must he be told, beside his plough,
What he must speak, and when, and how ?

Must he be told his freedom stands
    On Slavery's dark foundations strong ;
On breaking hearts and fettered hands,
    On robbery, and crime, and wrong ?

That all his fathers taught is vain, —
That Freedom's emblem is the chain?

Its life, its soul, from slavery drawn!
  False, foul, profane! Go, teach as well
Of holy Truth from Falsehood born!
  Of Heaven refreshed by airs from Hell!
Of Virtue in the arms of Vice!
Of Demons planting Paradise!

Rail on, then, brethren of the South,
  Ye shall not hear the truth the less;
No seal is on the Yankee's mouth,
  No fetter on the Yankee's press!
From our Green Mountains to the sea,
One voice shall thunder, We are free!

CLERICAL OPPRESSORS

In the report of the celebrated pro-slavery meeting in Charleston, S. C., on the 4th of the ninth month, 1835, published in the *Courier* of that city, it is stated: "The clergy of all denominations attended in a body, lending their sanction to the proceedings, and adding by their presence to the impressive character of the scene!"

Just God! and these are they
Who minister at thine altar, God of Right!
Men who their hands with prayer and bless-
    ing lay
  On Israel's Ark of light!

What! preach, and kidnap men?
Give thanks, and rob thy own afflicted
    poor?
Talk of thy glorious liberty, and then
  Bolt hard the captive's door?

What! servants of thy own
Merciful Son, who came to seek and save
The homeless and the outcast, fettering
    down
  The tasked and plundered slave!

Pilate and Herod, friends!
Chief priests and rulers, as of old, com-
    bine!
Just God and holy! is that church, which
    lends
  Strength to the spoiler, thine?

Paid hypocrites, who turn
Judgment aside, and rob the Holy Book

Of those high words of truth which search
    and burn
  In warning and rebuke;

Feed fat, ye locusts, feed!
And, in your tasselled pulpits, thank the
    Lord
That, from the toiling bondman's utter need,
  Ye pile your own full board.

How long, O Lord! how long
Shall such a priesthood barter truth away,
And in Thy name, for robbery and wrong
  At Thy own altars pray?

Is not Thy hand stretched forth
Visibly in the heavens, to awe and smite?
Shall not the living God of all the earth,
  And heaven above, do right?

Woe, then, to all who grind
Their brethren of a common Father down!
To all who plunder from the immortal
    mind
  Its bright and glorious crown!

Woe to the priesthood! woe
To those whose hire is with the price of
    blood;
Perverting, darkening, changing, as they
    go,
  The searching truths of God!

Their glory and their might
Shall perish; and their very names shall
    be
Vile before all the people, in the light
  Of a world's liberty.

Oh, speed the moment on
When Wrong shall cease, and Liberty and
    Love
And Truth and Right throughout the earth
    be known
  As in their home above.

A SUMMONS

Written on the adoption of Pinckney's Resolutions in the House of Representatives, and the passage of Calhoun's "Bill for excluding Papers written or printed, touching the subject of Slavery, from the U. S. Post-office," in the Senate of the United States.

Mr. Pinckney's resolutions were in brief that Congress had no authority to interfere in any way with slavery in the States; that it ought not to interfere with it in the District of Columbia, and that all resolutions to that end should be laid on the table without printing. Mr. Calhoun's bill made it a penal offence for postmasters in any State, District, or Territory " knowingly to deliver, to any person whatever, any pamphlet, newspaper, handbill, or other printed paper or pictorial representation, touching the subject of slavery, where, by the laws of the said State, District, or Territory, their circulation was prohibited." [Originally entitled *Lines*.]

MEN of the North-land! where's the manly
    spirit
Of the true-hearted and the unshackled
    gone?
Sons of old freemen, do we but inherit
    Their names alone?

Is the old Pilgrim spirit quenched within us,
    Stoops the strong manhood of our souls
    so low,
That Mammon's lure or Party's wile can
    win us
    To silence now?

Now, when our land to ruin's brink is
    verging,
    In God's name, let us speak while there
    is time!
Now, when the padlocks for our lips are
    forging,
    Silence is crime!

What! shall we henceforth humbly ask
    as favors
Rights all our own? In madness shall
    we barter,
For treacherous peace, the freedom Nature
    gave us,
    God and our charter?

Here shall the statesman forge his human
    fetters,
Here the false jurist human rights deny,
And in the church, their proud and skilled
    abettors
    Make truth a lie?

Torture the pages of the hallowed Bible,
    To sanction crime, and robbery, and
    blood?

And, in Oppression's hateful service, libel
    Both man and God?

Shall our New England stand erect no
    longer,
    But stoop in chains upon her downward
    way,
Thicker to gather on her limbs and stronger
    Day after day?

Oh no; methinks from all her wild, green
    mountains;
    From valleys where her slumbering
    fathers lie;
From her blue rivers and her welling
    fountains,
    And clear, cold sky;

From her rough coast, and isles, which
    hungry Ocean
    Gnaws with his surges; from the fisher's skiff,
With white sail swaying to the billow's motion
    Round rock and cliff;

From the free fireside of her unbought
    farmer;
    From her free laborer at his loom and
    wheel;
From the brown smith-shop, where, beneath the hammer,
    Rings the red steel;

From each and all, if God hath not forsaken
Our land, and left us to an evil choice,
Loud as the summer thunderbolt shall
    waken
    A People's voice.

Startling and stern! the Northern winds
    shall bear it
Over Potomac's to St. Mary's wave;
And buried Freedom shall awake to hear it
    Within her grave.

Oh, let that voice go forth! The bondman sighing
    By Santee's wave, in Mississippi's cane,
Shall feel the hope, within his bosom dying,
    Revive again.

Let it go forth! The millions who are
    gazing
    Sadly upon us from afar shall smile,

And unto God devout thanksgiving raising,
　　Bless us the while.

Oh for your ancient freedom, pure and
　　holy,
　For the deliverance of a groaning earth,
For the wronged captive, bleeding, crushed,
　　and lowly,
　　　Let it go forth !

Sons of the best of fathers ! will ye fal-
　　ter
　With all they left ye perilled and at
　　stake ?
Ho ! once again on Freedom's holy altar
　　　The fire awake !

Prayer-strengthened for the trial, come to-
　　gether,
　Put on the harness for the moral fight,
And, with the blessing of your Heavenly
　　Father,
　　　Maintain the right !

TO THE MEMORY OF THOMAS SHIPLEY

　Thomas Shipley of Philadelphia was a life-
long Christian philanthropist, and advocate
of emancipation.　At his funeral thousands of
colored people came to take their last look at
their friend and protector.　He died Septem-
ber 17, 1836.

GONE to thy Heavenly Father's rest !
　The flowers of Eden round thee blow-
　　ing,
And on thine ear the murmurs blest
　Of Siloa's waters softly flowing !
Beneath that Tree of Life which gives
To all the earth its healing leaves
In the white robe of angels clad,
　And wandering by that sacred river,
Whose streams of holiness make glad
　The city of our God forever !

Gentlest of spirits ! not for thee
　Our tears are shed, our sighs are given ;
Why mourn to know thou art a free
　Partaker of the joys of heaven ?
Finished thy work, and kept thy faith
In Christian firmness unto death ;
And beautiful as sky and earth,

When autumn's sun is downward going,
The blessed memory of thy worth
　Around thy place of slumber glowing !

But woe for us ! who linger still
　With feebler strength and hearts less
　　lowly,
And minds less steadfast to the will
　Of Him whose every work is holy.
For not like thine, is crucified
The spirit of our human pride :
And at the bondman's tale of woe,
　And for the outcast and forsaken,
Not warm like thine, but cold and slow,
　Our weaker sympathies awaken.

Darkly upon our struggling way
　The storm of human hate is sweeping ;
Hunted and branded, and a prey,
　Our watch amidst the darkness keeping.
Oh, for that hidden strength which can
Nerve unto death the inner man !
Oh, for thy spirit, tried and true,
　And constant in the hour of trial,
Prepared to suffer, or to do,
　In meekness and in self-denial.

Oh, for that spirit, meek and mild,
　Derided, spurned, yet uncomplaining ;
By man deserted and reviled,
　Yet faithful to its trust remaining.
Still prompt and resolute to save
From scourge and chain the hunted slave ;
Unwavering in the Truth's defence,
　Even where the fires of Hate were burn-
　　ing,
The unquailing eye of innocence
　Alone upon the oppressor turning !

O loved of thousands ! to thy grave,
　Sorrowing of heart, thy brethren bore
　　thee.
The poor man and the rescued slave
　Wept as the broken earth closed o'er
　　thee ;
And grateful tears, like summer rain,
Quickened its dying grass again !
And there, as to some pilgrim-shrine,
　Shall come the outcast and the lowly,
Of gentle deeds and words of thine
　Recalling memories sweet and holy !

Oh, for the death the righteous die !
　An end, like autumn's day declining,

On human hearts, as on the sky,
  With holier, tenderer beauty shining ;
As to the parting soul were given
The radiance of an opening heaven !
As if that pure and blessed light,
  From off the Eternal altar flowing,
Were bathing, in its upward flight,
  The spirit to its worship going !

THE MORAL WARFARE

When Freedom, on her natal day,
Within her war-rocked cradle lay,
An iron race around her stood,
Baptized her infant brow in blood ;
And, through the storm which round her
    swept,
Their constant ward and watching kept.

Then, where our quiet herds repose,
The roar of baleful battle rose,
And brethren of a common tongue
To mortal strife as tigers sprung,
And every gift on Freedom's shrine
Was man for beast, and blood for wine !

Our fathers to their graves have gone ;
Their strife is past, their triumph won ;
But sterner trials wait the race
Which rises in their honored place ;
A moral warfare with the crime
And folly of an evil time.

So let it be. In God's own might
We gird us for the coming fight,
And, strong in Him whose cause is ours
In conflict with unholy powers,
We grasp the weapons He has given,—
The Light, and Truth, and Love of Heaven.

RITNER

Written on reading the Message of Governor
Ritner, of Pennsylvania, 1836. The fact re-
dounds to the credit and serves to perpetuate
the memory of the independent farmer and
high-souled statesman, that he alone of all the
Governors of the Union in 1836 met the insulting
demands and menaces of the South in a manner
becoming a freeman and hater of Slavery, in
his message to the Legislature of Pennsylvania.
[Originally entitled *Lines*.]

Thank God for the token ! one lip is still
    free,
One spirit untrammelled, unbending one
    knee !
Like the oak of the mountain, deep-rooted
    and firm,
Erect, when the multitude bends to the
    storm ;
When traitors to Freedom, and Honor,
    and God,
Are bowed at an Idol polluted with blood ;
When the recreant North has forgotten her
    trust,
And the lip of her honor is low in the dust,—
Thank God, that one arm from the shackle
    has broken !
Thank God, that one man as a freeman has
    spoken !

O'er thy crags, Alleghany, a blast has been
    blown !
Down thy tide, Susquehanna, the murmur
    has gone !
To the land of the South, of the charter and
    chain,
Of Liberty sweetened with Slavery's pain ;
Where the cant of Democracy dwells on the
    lips
Of the forgers of fetters, and wielders of
    whips !
Where " chivalric " honor means really no
    more
Than scourging of women, and robbing the
    poor !
Where the Moloch of Slavery sitteth on
    high,
And the words which he utters, are —Wor-
    ship, or die !

Right onward, oh, speed it !   Wherever the
    blood
Of the wronged and the guiltless is crying
    to God ;
Wherever a slave in his fetters is pining ;
Wherever the lash of the driver is twining ;
Wherever from kindred, torn rudely apart,
Comes the sorrowful wail of the broken of
    heart ;
Wherever the shackles of tyranny bind,
In silence and darkness, the God - given
    mind ;
There, God speed it onward ! its truth will
    be felt,
The bonds shall be loosened, the iron shall
    melt !

And oh, will the land where the free soul
    of Penn
Still lingers and breathes over mountain and
    glen ;
Will the land where a Benezet's spirit
    went forth
To the peeled and the meted, and outcast
    of Earth ;
Where the words of the Charter of Liberty
    first
From the soul of the sage and the patriot
    burst ;
Where first for the wronged and the weak
    of their kind,
The Christian and statesman their efforts
    combined ;
Will that land of the free and the good
    wear a chain ?
Will the call to the rescue of Freedom be
    vain ?

No, Ritner ! her "Friends" at thy warn-
    ing shall stand
Erect for the truth, like their ancestral
    band ;
Forgetting the feuds and the strife of past
    time,
Counting coldness injustice, and silence a
    crime ;
Turning back from the cavil of creeds, to
    unite
Once again for the poor in defence of the
    Right ;
Breasting calmly, but firmly, the full tide
    of Wrong,
Overwhelmed, but not borne on its surges
    along ;
Unappalled by the danger, the shame, and
    the pain,
And counting each trial for Truth as their
    gain !

And that bold-hearted yeomanry, honest
    and true,
Who, haters of fraud, give to labor its due ;
Whose fathers, of old, sang in concert
    with thine,
On the banks of Swetara, the songs of the
    Rhine, --
The German-born pilgrims, who first dared
    to brave
The scorn of the proud in the cause of the
    slave ;
Will the sons of such men yield the lords
    of the South

One brow for the brand, for the padlock
    one mouth ?
They cater to tyrants ? They rivet the
    chain,
Which their fathers smote off, on the negro
    again ?

No, never ! one voice, like the sound in the
    cloud,
When the roar of the storm waxes loud
    and more loud,
Wherever the foot of the freeman hath
    pressed
From the Delaware's marge to the Lake
    of the West,
On the South-going breezes shall deepen
    and grow
Till the land it sweeps over shall tremble
    below !
The voice of a people, uprisen, awake,
Pennsylvania's watchword, with Freedom
    at stake,
Thrilling up from each valley, flung down
    from each height,
"Our Country and Liberty ! God for the
    Right !"

THE PASTORAL LETTER

The General Association of Congregational
ministers in Massachusetts met at Brookfield,
June 27, 1837, and issued a Pastoral Letter to
the churches under its care. The immediate
occasion of it was the profound sensation pro-
duced by the recent public lecture in Massa-
chusetts by Angelina and Sarah Grimké, two
noble women from South Carolina, who bore
their testimony against slavery. The Letter
demanded that "the perplexed and agitating
subjects which are now common amongst us
. . . should not be forced upon any church
as matters for debate, at the hazard of aliena-
tion and division," and called attention to the
dangers now seeming " to threaten the female
character with widespread and permanent in-
jury."

So, this is all, — the utmost reach
    Of priestly power the mind to fetter !
When laymen think, when women preach,
    A war of words, a "Pastoral Letter !"
Now, shame upon ye, parish Popes !
    Was it thus with those, your predecessors,
Who sealed with racks, and fire, and ropes
    Their loving-kindness to transgressors ?

A " Pastoral Letter," grave and dull ;
　Alas ! in hoof and horns and features,
How different is your Brookfield bull
　From him who bellows from St. Peter's !
Your pastoral rights and powers from harm,
　Think ye, can words alone preserve them?
Your wiser fathers taught the arm
　And sword of temporal power to serve
　　them.

Oh, glorious days, when Church and State
　Were wedded by your spiritual fathers !
And on submissive shoulders sat
　Your Wilsons and your Cotton Mathers.
No vile " itinerant " then could mar
　The beauty of your tranquil Zion,
But at his peril of the scar
　Of hangman's whip and branding-iron.

Then, wholesome laws relieved the Church
　Of heretic and mischief-maker,
And priest and bailiff joined in search,
　By turns, of Papist, witch, and Quaker !
The stocks were at each church's door,
　The gallows stood on Boston Common,
A Papist's ears the pillory bore, —
　The gallows-rope, a Quaker woman !

Your fathers dealt not as ye deal
　With " non-professing " frantic teachers ;
They bored the tongue with red-hot steel,
　And flayed the backs of " female preach-
　　ers."
Old Hampton, had her fields a tongue,
　And Salem's streets could tell their story,
Of fainting woman dragged along,
　Gashed by the whip accursed and gory !

And will ye ask me, why this taunt
　Of memories sacred from the scorner ?
And why with reckless hand I plant
　A nettle on the graves ye honor ?
Not to reproach New England's dead
　This record from the past I summon,
Of manhood to the scaffold led,
　And suffering and heroic woman.

No, for yourselves alone, I turn
　The pages of intolerance over,
That, in their spirit, dark and stern,
　Ye haply may your own discover !
For, if ye claim the " pastoral right "
　To silence Freedom's voice of warning,
And from your precincts shut the light
　Of Freedom's day around ye dawning ;

If when an earthquake voice of power
　And signs in earth and heaven are show-
　　ing
That forth, in its appointed hour,
　The Spirit of the Lord is going !
And, with that Spirit, Freedom's light
　On kindred, tongue, and people break-
　　ing,
Whose slumbering millions, at the sight,
　In glory and in strength are waking !

When for the sighing of the poor,
　And for the needy, God hath risen,
And chains are breaking, and a door
　Is opening for the souls in prison !
If then ye would, with puny hands,
　Arrest the very work of Heaven,
And bind anew the evil bands
　Which God's right arm of power hath
　　riven ;

What marvel that, in many a mind,
　Those darker deeds of bigot madness
Are closely with your own combined,
　Yet " less in anger than in sadness " ?
What marvel, if the people learn
　To claim the right of free opinion ?
What marvel, if at times they spurn
　The ancient yoke of your dominion ?

A glorious remnant linger yet,
　Whose lips are wet at Freedom's foun-
　　tains,
The coming of whose welcome feet
　Is beautiful upon our mountains !
Men, who the gospel tidings bring
　Of Liberty and Love forever,
Whose joy is an abiding spring,
　Whose peace is as a gentle river !

But ye, who scorn the thrilling tale
　Of Carolina's high-souled daughters,
Which echoes here the mournful wail
　Of sorrow from Edisto's waters,
Close while ye may the public ear,
　With malice vex, with slander wound
　　them,
The pure and good shall throng to hear,
　And tried and manly hearts surround
　　them.

Oh, ever may the power which led
　Their way to such a fiery trial,
And strengthened womanhood to tread
　The wine-press of such self-denial,

Be round them in an evil land,
  With wisdom and with strength from
      Heaven,
With Miriam's voice, and Judith's hand,
  And Deborah's song, for triumph given !

And what are ye who strive with God
  Against the ark of His salvation,
Moved by the breath of prayer abroad,
  With blessings for a dying nation ?
What, but the stubble and the hay
  To perish, even as flax consuming,
With all that bars His glorious way,
  Before the brightness of His coming ?

And thou, sad Angel, who so long
  Hast waited for the glorious token,
That Earth from all her bonds of wrong
  To liberty and light has broken, —
Angel of Freedom ! soon to thee
  The sounding trumpet shall be given,
And over Earth's full jubilee
  Shall deeper joy be felt in Heaven !

                HYMN

  Written for the celebration of the third an-
niversary of British emancipation, at the Broad-
way Tabernacle, New York, first of August,
1837. [Originally entitled *Lines*.]

O HOLY FATHER ! just and true
  Are all Thy works and words and ways,
And unto Thee alone are due
  Thanksgiving and eternal praise !
As children of Thy gracious care,
  We veil the eye, we bend the knee,
With broken words of praise and prayer,
  Father and God, we come to Thee.

For Thou hast heard, O God of Right,
  The sighing of the island slave ;
And stretched for him the arm of might,
  Not shortened that it could not save.
The laborer sits beneath his vine,
  The shackled soul and hand are free ;
Thanksgiving ! for the work is Thine !
  Praise ! for the blessing is of Thee !

And oh, we feel Thy presence here,
  Thy awful arm in judgment bare !
Thine eye hath seen the bondman's tear ;
  Thine ear hath heard the bondman's
      prayer.

Praise ! for the pride of man is low,
  The counsels of the wise are naught,
The fountains of repentance flow ;
  What hath our God in mercy wrought ?

Speed on Thy work, Lord God of Hosts !
  And when the bondman's chain is riven,
And swells from all our guilty coasts
  The anthem of the free to Heaven,
Oh, not to those whom Thou hast led,
  As with Thy cloud and fire before,
But unto Thee, in fear and dread,
  Be praise and glory evermore.

              THE FAREWELL

OF A VIRGINIA SLAVE MOTHER TO HER
DAUGHTERS SOLD INTO SOUTHERN
BONDAGE

    GONE, gone, — sold and gone,
      To the rice-swamp dank and lone.
  Where the slave-whip ceaseless swings,
  Where the noisome insect stings,
  Where the fever demon strews
  Poison with the falling dews,
  Where the sickly sunbeams glare
  Through the hot and misty air ;
    Gone, gone, — sold and gone,
      To the rice-swamp dank and lone,
      From Virginia's hills and waters ;
    Woe is me, my stolen daughters .

    Gone, gone, — sold and gone,
      To the rice-swamp dank and lone.
  There no mother's eye is near them,
  There no mother's ear can hear them ;
  Never, when the torturing lash
  Seams their back with many a gash,
  Shall a mother's kindness bless them,
  Or a mother's arms caress them.
    Gone, gone, — sold and gone,
      To the rice-swamp dank and lone,
      From Virginia's hills and waters ;
    Woe is me, my stolen daughters !

    Gone, gone, — sold and gone,
      To the rice-swamp dank and lone.
  Oh, when weary, sad, and slow,
  From the fields at night they go,
  Faint with toil, and racked with pain,
  To their cheerless homes again,
  There no brother's voice shall greet them;
  There no father's welcome meet them.

Gone, gone, — sold and gone,
To the rice-swamp dank and lone,
From Virginia's hills and waters ;
Woe is me, my stolen daughters !

Gone, gone, — sold and gone,
To the rice-swamp dank and lone.
From the tree whose shadow lay
On their childhood's place of play ;
From the cool spring where they drank ;
Rock, and hill, and rivulet bank ;
From the solemn house of prayer,
And the holy counsels there ;
Gone, gone, — sold and gone,
To the rice-swamp dank and lone,
From Virginia's hills and waters ;
Woe is me, my stolen daughters !

Gone, gone, — sold and gone,
To the rice-swamp dank and lone ;
Toiling through the weary day,
And at night the spoiler's prey.
Oh, that they had earlier died,
Sleeping calmly, side by side,
Where the tyrant's power is o'er,
And the fetter galls no more !
Gone, gone, — sold and gone,
To the rice-swamp dank and lone,
From Virginia's hills and waters ;
Woe is me, my stolen daughters !

Gone, gone, — sold and gone,
To the rice-swamp dank and lone.
By the holy love He beareth ;
By the bruisëd reed He spareth ;
Oh, may He, to whom alone
All their cruel wrongs are known,
Still their hope and refuge prove,
With a more than mother's love.
Gone, gone, — sold and gone,
To the rice-swamp dank and lone,
From Virginia's hills and waters ;
Woe is me, my stolen daughters !

PENNSYLVANIA HALL

Read at the dedication of Pennsylvania Hall,
Philadelphia, May 15, 1838. The building was
erected by an association of gentlemen, irre-
spective of sect or party. " that the citizens of
Philadelphia should possess a room wherein
the principles of Liberty, and Equality of Civil
Rights, could be freely discussed, and the evils
of slavery fearlessly portrayed." On the even-
ing of the 17th it was burned by a mob, de-
stroying the office of the *Pennsylvania Free-
man*, of which I was editor, and with it my
books and papers.

NOT with the splendors of the days of old,
The spoil of nations, and barbaric gold ;
No weapons wrested from the fields of
blood,
Where dark and stern the unyielding Ro-
man stood,
And the proud eagles of his cohorts saw
A world, war-wasted, crouching to his law ;
Nor blazoned car, nor banners floating gay,
Like those which swept along the Appian
Way,
When, to the welcome of imperial Rome,
The victor warrior came in triumph home,
And trumpet peal, and shoutings wild and
high,
Stirred the blue quiet of the Italian sky ;
But calm and grateful, prayerful and sin-
cere,
As Christian freemen only, gathering here,
We dedicate our fair and lofty Hall,
Pillar and arch, entablature and wall,
As Virtue's shrine, as Liberty's abode,
Sacred to Freedom, and to Freedom's God !
Far statelier Halls, 'neath brighter skies
than these,
Stood darkly mirrored in the Ægean seas,
Pillar and shrine, and life-like statues seen,
Graceful and pure, the marble shafts be-
tween,
Where glorious Athens from her rocky hill
Saw Art and Beauty subject to her will ;
And the chaste temple, and the classic
grove,
The hall of sages, and the bowers of love,
Arch, fane, and column, graced the shores,
and gave
Their shadows to the blue Saronic wave ;
And statelier rose on Tiber's winding side,
The Pantheon's dome, the Coliseum's pride,
The Capitol, whose arches backward flung
The deep, clear cadence of the Roman
tongue,
Whence stern decrees, like words of fate,
went forth
To the awed nations of a conquered earth,
Where the proud Cæsars in their glory
came,
And Brutus lightened from his lips of
flame !
Yet in the porches of Athena's halls,
And in the shadow of her stately walls,

Lurked the sad bondman, and his tears of
    woe
Wet the cold marble with unheeded flow ;
And fetters clanked beneath the silver
    dome
Of the proud Pantheon of imperious Rome.
Oh, not for him, the chained and stricken
    slave,
By Tiber's shore, or blue Ægina's wave,
In the thronged forum, or the sages' seat,
The bold lip pleaded, and the warm heart
    beat ;
No soul of sorrow melted at his pain,
No tear of pity rusted on his chain !

But this fair Hall to Truth and Freedom
    given,
Pledged to the Right before all Earth and
    Heaven,
A free arena for the strife of mind,
To caste, or sect, or color unconfined,
Shall thrill with echoes such as ne'er of
    old
From Roman hall or Grecian temple rolled ;
Thoughts shall find utterance such as never
    yet
The Propylea or the Forum met.
Beneath its roof no gladiator's strife
Shall win applauses with the waste of life ;
No lordly lictor urge the barbarous game,
No wanton Lais glory in her shame.
But here the tear of sympathy shall flow,
As the ear listens to the tale of woe ;
Here in stern judgment of the oppressor's
    wrong
Shall strong rebukings thrill on Freedom's
    tongue,
No partial justice hold th' unequal scale,
No pride of caste a brother's rights assail,
No tyrant's mandates echo from this wall,
Holy to Freedom and the Rights of All !
But a fair field, where mind may close with
    mind,
Free as the sunshine and the chainless wind ;
Where the high trust is fixed on Truth
    alone,
And bonds and fetters from the soul are
    thrown ;
Where wealth, and rank, and worldly pomp,
    and might,
Yield to the presence of the True and Right.

And fitting is it that this Hall should stand
Where Pennsylvania's Founder led his band,
From thy blue waters, Delaware ! — to press

The virgin verdure of the wilderness.
Here, where all Europe with amazement
    saw
The soul's high freedom trammelled by nc
    law ;
Here, where the fierce and warlike forest-
    men
Gathered, in peace, around the home of
    Penn,
Awed by the weapons Love alone had given
Drawn from the holy armory of Heaven ;
Where Nature's voice against the bondman's
    wrong
First found an earnest and indignant
    tongue ;
Where Lay's bold message to the proud
    was borne ;
And Keith's rebuke, and Franklin's manly
    scorn !
Fitting it is that here, where Freedom first
From her fair feet shook off the Old World's
    dust,
Spread her white pinions to our Western
    blast,
And her free tresses to our sunshine cast,
One Hall should rise redeemed from Sla-
    very's ban,
One Temple sacred to the Rights of Man !

Oh ! if the spirits of the parted come,
Visiting angels, to their olden home ;
If the dead fathers of the land look forth
From their fair dwellings, to the things of
    earth,
Is it a dream, that with their eyes of love,
They gaze now on us from the bowers above?
Lay's ardent soul, and Benezet the mild,
Steadfast in faith, yet gentle as a child,
Meek-hearted Woolman, and that brother-
    band,
The sorrowing exiles from their " Father-
    land,"
Leaving their homes in Krieshiem's bowers
    of vine,
And the blue beauty of their glorious Rhine,
To seek amidst our solemn depths of wood
Freedom from man, and holy peace with
    God ;
Who first of all their testimonial gave
Against the oppressor, for the outcast slave,
Is it a dream that such as these look down,
And with their blessing our rejoicings
    crown ?
Let us rejoice, that while the pulpit's door
Is barred against the pleaders for the poor ;

While the Church, wrangling upon points
of faith,
Forgets her bondmen suffering unto death ;
While crafty Traffic and the lust of Gain
Unite to forge Oppression's triple chain,
One door is open, and one Temple free,
As a resting-place for hunted Liberty !
Where men may speak, unshackled and
unawed,
High words of Truth, for Freedom and for
God.
And when that truth its perfect work hath
done,
And rich with blessings o'er our land hath
gone ;
When not a slave beneath his yoke shall
pine,
From broad Potomac to the far Sabine :
When unto angel lips at last is given
The silver trump of Jubilee in Heaven :
And from Virginia's plains, Kentucky's
shades,
And through the dim Floridian everglades,
Rises, to meet that angel-trumpet's sound,
The voice of millions from their chains un-
bound ;
Then, though this Hall be crumbling in de-
cay,
Its strong walls blending with the common
clay,
Yet round the ruins of its strength shall
stand
The best and noblest of a ransomed land —
Pilgrims, like these who throng around the
shrine
Of Mecca, or of holy Palestine !
A prouder glory shall that ruin own
Than that which lingers round the Parthe-
non.
Here shall the child of after years be taught
The works of Freedom which his fathers
wrought ;
Told of the trials of the present hour,
Our weary strife with prejudice and power ;
How the high errand quickened woman's
soul,
And touched her lip as with a living coal ;
How Freedom's martyrs kept their lofty
faith
True and unwavering, unto bonds and death;
The pencil's art shall sketch the ruined
Hall,
The Muses' garland crown its aged wall,
And History's pen for after times record
Its consecration unto Freedom's God !

THE NEW YEAR

Addressed to the Patrons of the *Pennsylvania
Freeman.*

THE wave is breaking on the shore,
  The echo fading from the chime ;
Again the shadow moveth o'er
  The dial-plate of time !

O seer-seen Angel ! waiting now
  With weary feet on sea and shore,
Impatient for the last dread vow
  That time shall be no more !

Once more across thy sleepless eye
  The semblance of a smile has passed :
The year departing leaves more nigh
  Time's fearfullest and last.

Oh, in that dying year hath been
  The sum of all since time began ;
The birth and death, the joy and pain,
  Of Nature and of Man.

Spring, with her change of sun and shower,
  And streams released from Winter's
    chain,
And bursting bud, and opening flower,
  And greenly growing grain ;

And Summer's shade, and sunshine warm,
  And rainbows o'er her hill-tops bowed,
And voices in her rising storm ;
  God speaking from His cloud !

And Autumn's fruits and clustering sheaves,
  And soft, warm days of golden light,
The glory of her forest leaves,
  And harvest-moon at night ;

And Winter with her leafless grove,
  And prisoned stream, and drifting snow,
The brilliance of her heaven above
  And of her earth below :

And man, in whom an angel's mind
  With earth's low instincts finds abode,
The highest of the links which bind
  Brute nature to her God ;

His infant eye hath seen the light,
  His childhood's merriest laughter rung,
And active sports to manlier might
  The nerves of boyhood strung !

And quiet love, and passion's fires,
  Have soothed or burned in manhood's
    breast,
And lofty aims and low desires
  By turns disturbed his rest.

The wailing of the newly-born
  Has mingled with the funeral knell ;
And o'er the dying's ear has gone
  The merry marriage-bell.

And Wealth has filled his halls with mirth,
  While Want, in many a humble shed,
Toiled, shivering by her cheerless hearth,
  The live-long night for bread.

And worse than all, the human slave,
  The sport of lust, and pride, and scorn !
Plucked off the crown his Maker gave,
  His regal manhood gone !

Oh, still, my country ! o'er thy plains,
  Blackened with slavery's blight and ban,
That human chattel drags his chains,
  An uncreated man !

And still, where'er to sun and breeze,
  My country, is thy flag unrolled,
With scorn, the gazing stranger sees
  A stain on every fold.

Oh, tear the gorgeous emblem down !
  It gathers scorn from every eye,
And despots smile and good men frown
  Whene'er it passes by.

Shame ! shame ! its starry splendors glow
  Above the slaver's loathsome jail ;
Its folds are ruffling even now
  His crimson flag of sale.

Still round our country's proudest hall
  The trade in human flesh is driven,
And at each careless hammer-fall
  A human heart is riven.

And this, too, sanctioned by the men
  Vested with power to shield the right,
And throw each vile and robber den
  Wide open to the light.

Yet, shame upon them ! there they sit,
  Men of the North, subdued and still ;
Meek, pliant poltroons, only fit
  To work a master's will.

Sold, bargained off for Southern votes,
  A passive herd of Northern mules,
Just braying through their purchased
    throats
  Whate'er their owner rules.

And he, the basest of the base,
  The vilest of the vile, whose name,
Embalmed in infinite disgrace,
  Is deathless in its shame !

A tool, to bolt the people's door
  Against the people clamoring there,
An ass, to trample on their floor
  A people's right of prayer !

Nailed to his self-made gibbet fast,
  Self-pilloried to the public view,
A mark for every passing blast
  Of scorn to whistle through ;

There let him hang, and hear the boast
  Of Southrons o'er their pliant tool, —
A new Stylites on his post,
  "Sacred to ridicule ! "

Look we at home ! our noble hall,
  To Freedom's holy purpose given,
Now rears its black and ruined wall,
  Beneath the wintry heaven,

Telling the story of its doom,
  The fiendish mob, the prostrate law,
The fiery jet through midnight's gloom,
  Our gazing thousands saw.

Look to our State ! the poor man's right
  Torn from him : and the sons of those
Whose blood in Freedom's sternest fight
  Sprinkled the Jersey snows,

Outlawed within the land of Penn,
  That Slavery's guilty fears might cease,
And those whom God created men
  Toil on as brutes in peace.

Yet o'er the blackness of the storm
  A bow of promise bends on high,
And gleams of sunshine, soft and warm,
  Break through our clouded sky.

East, West, and North, the shout is heard
  Of freemen rising for the right :
Each valley hath its rallying word,
  Each hill its signal light.

O'er Massachusetts' rocks of gray
  The strengthening light of freedom
    shines,
Rhode Island's Narragansett Bay,
  And Vermont's snow-hung pines !

From Hudson's frowning palisades
  To Alleghany's laurelled crest,
O'er lakes and prairies, streams and glades,
  It shines upon the West.

Speed on the light to those who dwell
  In Slavery's land of woe and sin,
And through the blackness of that Hell
  Let Heaven's own light break in.

So shall the Southern conscience quake
  Before that light poured full and strong,
So shall the Southern heart awake
  To all the bondman's wrong.

And from that rich and sunny land
  The song of grateful millions rise,
Like that of Israel's ransomed band
  Beneath Arabia's skies :

And all who now are bound beneath
  Our banner's shade, our eagle's wing,
From Slavery's night of moral death
  To light and life shall spring.

Broken the bondman's chain, and gone
  The master's guilt, and hate, and fear,
And unto both alike shall dawn
  A New and Happy Year.

THE RELIC

Written on receiving a cane wrought from a
fragment of the wood-work of Pennsylvania
Hall which the fire had spared.

TOKEN of friendship true and tried,
  From one whose fiery heart of youth
With mine has beaten, side by side,
  For Liberty and Truth ;
With honest pride the gift I take,
And prize it for the giver's sake.

But not alone because it tells
  Of generous hand and heart sincere ;
Around that gift of friendship dwells
  A memory doubly dear ;
Earth's noblest aim, man's holiest thought,
With that memorial frail inwrought !

Pure thoughts and sweet like flowers unfold,
  And precious memories round it cling,
Even as the Prophet's rod of old
  In beauty blossoming :
And buds of feeling, pure and good,
Spring from its cold unconscious wood.

Relic of Freedom's shrine ! a brand
  Plucked from its burning ! let it be
Dear as a jewel from the hand
  Of a lost friend to me !
Flower of a perished garland left,
Of life and beauty unbereft !

Oh, if the young enthusiast bears,
  O'er weary waste and sea, the stone
Which crumbled from the Forum's stairs,
  Or round the Parthenon ;
Or olive-bough from some wild tree
Hung over old Thermopylæ :

If leaflets from some hero's tomb,
  Or moss-wreath torn from ruins hoary ;
Or faded flowers whose sisters bloom
  On fields renowned in story ;
Or fragment from the Alhambra's crest,
Or the gray rock by Druids blessed ;

Sad Erin's shamrock greenly growing
  Where Freedom led her stalwart kern,
Or Scotia's " rough bur thistle " blowing
  On Bruce's Bannockburn ;
Or Runnymede's wild English rose,
Or lichen plucked from Sempach's snows !

If it be true that things like these
  To heart and eye bright visions bring,
Shall not far holier memories
  To this memorial cling ?
Which needs no mellowing mist of time
To hide the crimson stains of crime !

Wreck of a temple, unprofaned ;
  Of courts where Peace with Freedom trod,
Lifting on high, with hands unstained,
  Thanksgiving unto God ;
Where Mercy's voice of love was pleading
For human hearts in bondage bleeding !

Where, midst the sound of rushing feet
  And curses on the night-air flung,
That pleading voice rose calm and sweet
  From woman's earnest tongue ;
And Riot turned his scowling glance,
Awed, from her tranquil countenance !

That temple now in ruin lies !
  The fire-stain on its shattered wall,
And open to the changing skies
  Its black and roofless hall,
It stands before a nation's sight,
A gravestone over buried Right !

But from that ruin, as of old,
  The fire-scorched stones themselves are
    crying,
And from their ashes white and cold
  Its timbers are replying !
A voice which slavery cannot kill
Speaks from the crumbling arches still !

And even this relic from thy shrine,
  O holy Freedom ! hath to me
A potent power, a voice and sign
  To testify of thee ;
And, grasping it, methinks I feel
A deeper faith, a stronger zeal.

And not unlike that mystic rod,
  Of old stretched o'er the Egyptian wave,
Which opened, in the strength of God,
  A pathway for the slave,
It yet may point the bondman's way,
And turn the spoiler from his prey.

THE WORLD'S CONVENTION

OF THE FRIENDS OF EMANCIPATION, HELD IN LONDON IN 1840

Joseph Sturge, the founder of the British and Foreign Anti-Slavery Society, proposed the calling of a world's anti-slavery convention, and the proposal was promptly seconded by the American Anti-Slavery Society. The call was adressed to "friends of the slave of every nation and of every clime."

Yes, let them gather ! Summon forth
The pledged philanthropy of Earth.
From every land, whose hills have heard
The bugle blast of Freedom waking ;
Or shrieking of her symbol-bird
From out his cloudy eyrie breaking :
Where Justice hath one worshipper,
Or truth one altar built to her ;
Where'er a human eye is weeping
  O'er wrongs which Earth's sad children
    know ;
Where'er a single heart is keeping
  Its prayerful watch with human woe :

Thence let them come, and greet each
    other,
And know in each a friend and brother !

Yes, let them come ! from each green vale
  Where England's old baronial halls
Still bear upon their storied walls
The grim crusader's rusted mail,
Battered by Paynim spear and brand
On Malta's rock or Syria's sand !
And mouldering pennon-staves once set
  Within the soil of Palestine,
By Jordan and Gennesaret ;
Or, borne with England's battle line,
O'er Acre's shattered turrets stooping,
Or, midst the camp their banners drooping,
  With dews from hallowed Hermon wet,
A holier summons now is given
Than that gray hermit's voice of old,
Which unto all the winds of heaven
  The banners of the Cross unrolled !
Not for the long-deserted shrine ;
  Not for the dull unconscious sod,
Which tells not by one lingering sign
  That there the hope of Israel trod ;
But for that truth, for which alone
  In pilgrim eyes are sanctified
The garden moss, the mountain stone,
Whereon His holy sandals pressed, —
The fountain which His lip hath blessed, —
Whate'er hath touched His garment's hem
  At Bethany or Bethlehem,
  Or Jordan's river-side.
For Freedom in the name of Him
Who came to raise Earth's drooping poor,
To break the chain from every limb,
The bolt from every prison door !
For these, o'er all the earth hath passed
An ever-deepening trumpet blast,
As if an angel's breath had lent
Its vigor to the instrument.

And Wales, from Snowden's mountain wall,
Shall startle at that thrilling call,
  As if she heard her bards again ;
And Erin's "harp on Tara's wall"
  Give out its ancient strain,
Mirthful and sweet, yet sad withal, —
  The melody which Erin loves,
When o'er that harp, 'mid bursts of gladness
And slogan cries and lyke-wake sadness,
  The hand of her O'Connell moves !
Scotland, from lake and tarn and rill,
And mountain hold, and heathery hill,

Shall catch and echo back the note,
As if she heard upon the air
Once more her Cameronian's prayer
  And song of Freedom float.
And cheering echoes shall reply
From each remote dependency,
Where Britain's mighty sway is known,
In tropic sea or frozen zone ;
Where'er her sunset flag is furling,
Or morning gun-fire's smoke is curling ;
From Indian Bengal's groves of palm
And rosy fields and gales of balm,
Where Eastern pomp and power are rolled
Through regal Ava's gates of gold ;
And from the lakes and ancient woods
And dim Canadian solitudes,
Whence, sternly from her rocky throne,
Queen of the North, Quebec looks down ;
And from those bright and ransomed Isles
Where all unwonted Freedom smiles,
And the dark laborer still retains
The scar of slavery's broken chains !

From the hoar Alps, which sentinel
The gateways of the land of Tell,
Where morning's keen and earliest glance
  On Jura's rocky wall is thrown,
And from the olive bowers of France
  And vine groves garlanding the Rhone, —
"Friends of the Blacks," as true and tried
As those who stood by Oge's side,
And heard the Haytien's tale of wrong,
Shall gather at that summons strong ;
Broglie, Passy, and he whose song
Breathed over Syria's holy sod,
And in the paths which Jesus trod,
And murmured midst the hills which hem
Crownless and sad Jerusalem,
Hath echoes wheresoe'er the tone
Of Israel's prophet-lyre is known.

Still let them come ; from Quito's walls,
  And from the Orinoco's tide,
From Lima's Inca-haunted halls,
From Santa Fé and Yucatan, —
  Men who by swart Guerrero's side
Proclaimed the deathless rights of man,
  Broke every bond and fetter off,
  And hailed in every sable serf
A free and brother Mexican !
Chiefs who across the Andes' chain
  Have followed Freedom's flowing pennon,
And seen on Junin's fearful plain,
Glare o'er the broken ranks of Spain
  The fire-burst of Bolivar's cannon !

And Hayti, from her mountain land,
  Shall send the sons of those who hurled
Defiance from her blazing strand,
The war-gage from her Petion's hand,
  Alone against a hostile world.

Nor all unmindful, thou, the while,
Land of the dark and mystic Nile !
  Thy Moslem mercy yet may shame
  All tyrants of a Christian name,
When in the shade of Gizeh's pile,
Or, where, from Abyssinian hills
El Gerek's upper fountain fills,
Or where from Mountains of the Moon
El Abiad bears his watery boon,
Where'er thy lotus blossoms swim
  Within their ancient hallowed waters ;
Where'er is heard the Coptic hymn,
  Or song of Nubia's sable daughters ;
The curse of slavery and the crime,
Thy bequest from remotest time,
At thy dark Mehemet's decree
Forevermore shall pass from thee ;
  And chains forsake each captive's limb
Of all those tribes, whose hills around
Have echoed back the cymbal sound
  And victor horn of Ibrahim.

And thou whose glory and whose crime
To earth's remotest bound and clime,
In mingled tones of awe and scorn,
The echoes of a world have borne,
My country ! glorious at thy birth,
A day-star flashing brightly forth,
  The herald-sign of Freedom's dawn !
Oh, who could dream that saw thee then,
  And watched thy rising from afar,
That vapors from oppression's fen
  Would cloud the upward tending star ?
Or, that earth's tyrant powers, which heard,
  Awe-struck, the shout which hailed thy
    dawning,
Would rise so soon, prince, peer, and king,
To mock thee with their welcoming,
Like Hades when her thrones were stirred
  To greet the down-cast Star of Morning !
"Aha ! and art thou fallen thus ?
Art thou become as one of us ? "

Land of my fathers ! there will stand,
Amidst that world-assembled band,
Those owning thy maternal claim
Unweakened by thy crime and shame ;
The sad reprovers of thy wrong ;
The children thou hast spurned so long.

Still with affection's fondest yearning
To their unnatural mother turning.
No traitors they ! but tried and leal,
Whose own is but thy general weal,
Still blending with the patriot's zeal
The Christian's love for human kind,
To caste and climate unconfined.

A holy gathering ! peaceful all :
No threat of war, no savage call
     For vengeance on an erring brother !
But in their stead the godlike plan
To teach the brotherhood of man
     To love and reverence one another,
As sharers of a common blood,
The children of a common God !
Yet, even at its lightest word,
Shall Slavery's darkest depths be stirred :
Spain, watching from her Moro's keep
Her slave-ships traversing the deep,
And Rio, in her strength and pride,
Lifting, along her mountain-side,
Her snowy battlements and towers,
Her lemon-groves and tropic bowers,
With bitter hate and sullen fear
Its freedom-giving voice shall hear ;
And where my country's flag is flowing,
On breezes from Mount Vernon blowing,
     Above the Nation's council halls,
Where Freedom's praise is loud and long,
     While close beneath the outward walls
The driver plies his reeking thong ;
     The hammer of the man-thief falls,
O'er hypocritic cheek and brow
The crimson flush of shame shall glow :
And all who for their native land
Are pledging life and heart and hand,
Worn watchers o'er her changing weal,
Who for her tarnished honor feel,
Through cottage door and council-hall
Shall thunder an awakening call.
The pen along its page shall burn
With all intolerable scorn ;
An eloquent rebuke shall go
On all the winds that Southward blow ;
From priestly lips, now sealed and dumb,
Warning and dread appeal shall come,
Like those which Israel heard from him,
The Prophet of the Cherubim ;
Or those which sad Esaias hurled
Against a sin-accursed world !
Its wizard leaves the Press shall fling
Unceasing from its iron wing,
With characters inscribed thereon,
     As fearful in the despot's hall

As to the pomp of Babylon
     The fire-sign on the palace wall !

And, from her dark iniquities,
Methinks I see my country rise :
Not challenging the nations round
     To note her tardy justice done ;
Her captives from their chains unbound,
     Her prisons opening to the sun :
But tearfully her arms extending
Over the poor and unoffending ;
     Her regal emblem now no longer
A bird of prey, with talons reeking,
Above the dying captive shrieking,
But, spreading out her ample wing,
     A broad, impartial covering,
The weaker sheltered by the stronger !
Oh, then to Faith's anointed eyes
     The promised token shall be given ;
And on a nation's sacrifice,
Atoning for the sin of years,
And wet with penitential tears,
     The fire shall fall from Heaven !

MASSACHUSETTS TO VIRGINIA

Written on reading an account of the proceedings of the citizens of Norfolk, Va., in reference to George Latimer, the alleged fugitive slave, who was seized in Boston without warrant at the request of James B. Grey, of Norfolk, claiming to be his master. The case caused great excitement North and South, and led to the presentation of a petition to Congress, signed by more than fifty thousand citizens of Massachusetts, calling for such laws and proposed amendments to the Constitution as should relieve the Commonwealth from all further participation in the crime of oppression. George Latimer himself was finally given free papers for the sum of four hundred dollars.

THE blast from Freedom's Northern hills,
     upon its Southern way,
Bears greeting to Virginia from Massachusetts Bay :
No word of haughty challenging, nor battle
     bugle's peal,
Nor steady tread of marching files, nor
     clang of horsemen's steel.

No trains of deep-mouthed cannon along
     our highways go ;
Around our silent arsenals untrodden lies
     the snow ;

And to the land-breeze of our ports, upon
their errands far,
A thousand sails of commerce swell, but
none are spread for war.

We hear thy threats, Virginia ! thy stormy
words and high
Swell harshly on the Southern winds which
melt along our sky ;
Yet, not one brown, hard hand foregoes its
honest labor here,
No hewer of our mountain oaks suspends
his axe in fear.

Wild are the waves which lash the reefs
along St. George's bank ;
Cold on the shores of Labrador the fog
lies white and dank ;
Through storm, and wave, and blinding
mist, stout are the hearts which man
The fishing-smacks of Marblehead, the sea-
boats of Cape Ann.

The cold north light and wintry sun glare
on their icy forms,
Bent grimly o'er their straining lines or
wrestling with the storms ;
Free as the winds they drive before, rough
as the waves they roam,
They laugh to scorn the slaver's threat
against their rocky home.

What means the Old Dominion ? Hath
she forgot the day
When o'er her conquered valleys swept
the Briton's steel array ?
How side by side, with sons of hers, the
Massachusetts men
Encountered Tarleton's charge of fire, and
stout Cornwallis, then ?

Forgets she how the Bay State, in answer
to the call
Of her old House of Burgesses, spoke out
from Faneuil Hall ?
When, echoing back her Henry's cry,
came pulsing on each breath
Of Northern winds the thrilling sounds of
" Liberty or Death ! "

What asks the Old Dominion ? If now
her sons have proved
False to their fathers' memory, false to the
faith they loved ;

If she can scoff at Freedom, and its great
charter spurn,
Must we of Massachusetts from truth and
duty turn ?

We hunt your bondmen, flying from Sla-
very's hateful hell ;
Our voices, at your bidding, take up the
bloodhound's yell ;
We gather, at your summons, above our
fathers' graves,
From Freedom's holy altar-horns to tear
your wretched slaves !

Thank God ! not yet so vilely can Massa-
chusetts bow ;
The spirit of her early time is with her even
now ;
Dream not because her Pilgrim blood moves
slow and calm and cool,
She thus can stoop her chainless neck, a sis-
ter's slave and tool !

All that a sister State should do, all that a
free State may,
Heart, hand, and purse we proffer, as in our
early day ;
But that one dark loathsome burden ye must
stagger with alone,
And reap the bitter harvest which ye your-
selves have sown !

Hold, while ye may, your struggling slaves,
and burden God's free air
With woman's shriek beneath the lash, and
manhood's wild despair ;
Cling closer to the " cleaving curse " that
writes upon your plains
The blasting of Almighty wrath against a
land of chains.

Still shame your gallant ancestry, the cava-
liers of old,
By watching round the shambles where hu-
man flesh is sold ;
Gloat o'er the new-born child, and count
his market value, when
The maddened mother's cry of woe shall
pierce the slaver's den !

Lower than plummet soundeth, sink the
Virginia name ;
Plant, if ye will, your fathers' graves with
rankest weeds of shame ;

Be, if ye will, the scandal of God's fair uni-
verse ;
We wash our hands forever of your sin and
shame and curse.

A voice from lips whereon the coal from
Freedom's shrine hath been,
Thrilled, as but yesterday, the hearts of
Berkshire's mountain men :
The echoes of that solemn voice are sadly
lingering still
In all our sunny valleys, on every wind-
swept hill.

And when the prowling man-thief came
hunting for his prey
Beneath the very shadow of Bunker's shaft
of gray,
How, through the free lips of the son, the
father's warning spoke ;
How, from its bonds of trade and sect, the
Pilgrim city broke !

A hundred thousand right arms were lifted
up on high,
A hundred thousand voices sent back their
loud reply ;
Through the thronged towns of Essex the
startling summons rang,
And up from bench and loom and wheel her
young mechanics sprang !

The voice of free, broad Middlesex, of thou-
sands as of one,
The shaft of Bunker calling to that of Lex-
ington ;
From Norfolk's ancient villages, from Ply-
mouth's rocky bound
To where Nantucket feels the arms of ocean
close her round ;

From rich and rural Worcester, where
through the calm repose
Of cultured vales and fringing woods the
gentle Nashua flows,
To where Wachuset's wintry blasts the
mountain larches stir,
Swelled up to Heaven the thrilling cry of
" God save Latimer ! "

And sandy Barnstable rose up, wet with the
salt sea spray ;
And Bristol sent her answering shout down
Narragansett Bay !

Along the broad Connecticut old Hampden
felt the thrill,
And the cheer of Hampshire's woodmen
swept down from Holyoke Hill.

The voice of Massachusetts ! Of her free
sons and daughters,
Deep calling unto deep aloud, the sound of
many waters !
Against the burden of that voice what ty-
rant power shall stand ?
No fetters in the Bay State ! No slave
upon her land !

Look to it well, Virginians ! In calmness
we have borne,
In answer to our faith and trust, your insult
and your scorn ;
You 've spurned our kindest counsels ;
you 've hunted for our lives ;
And shaken round our hearths and homes
your manacles and gyves !

We wage no war, we lift no arm, we fling
no torch within
The fire-damps of the quaking mine beneath
your soil of sin ;
We leave ye with your bondmen, to wrestle,
while ye can,
With the strong upward tendencies and
godlike soul of man !

But for us and for our children, the vow
which we have given
For freedom and humanity is registered in
heaven ;
No slave-hunt in our borders, — no pirate
on our strand !
No fetters in the Bay State, — no slave
upon our land !

THE CHRISTIAN SLAVE

In a publication of L. F. Tasistro — *Random
Shots and Southern Breezes* — is a description of
a slave auction at New Orleans, at which the
auctioneer recommended the woman on the
stand as " A GOOD CHRISTIAN ! " It was not
uncommon to see advertisements of slaves for
sale, in which they were described as pious or
as members of the church. In one advertise-
ment a slave was noted as " a Baptist preacher."

A CHRISTIAN ! going, gone !
Who bids for God's own image ? for his
    grace,
Which that poor victim of the market-place,
    Hath in her suffering won ?

My God ! can such things be ?
Hast Thou not said that whatsoe'er is done
Unto Thy weakest and Thy humblest one
    Is even done to Thee ?

In that sad victim, then,
Child of Thy pitying love, I see Thee stand ;
Once more the jest-word of a mocking band,
    Bound, sold, and scourged again !

A Christian up for sale !
Wet with her blood your whips, o'ertask
    her frame,
Make her life loathsome with your wrong
    and shame,
    Her patience shall not fail !

A heathen hand might deal
Back on your heads the gathered wrong of
    years :
But her low, broken prayer and nightly
    tears,
    Ye neither heed nor feel.

Con well thy lesson o'er,
Thou prudent teacher, tell the toiling slave
No dangerous tale of Him who came to save
    The outcast and the poor.

But wisely shut the ray
Of God's free Gospel from her simple heart,
And to her darkened mind alone impart
    One stern command, Obey !

So shalt thou deftly raise
The market price of human flesh ; and while
On thee, their pampered guest, the planters
    smile,
    Thy church shall praise.

Grave, reverend men shall tell
From Northern pulpits how thy work was
    blest,
While in that vile South Sodom first and
    best,
    Thy poor disciples sell.

Oh, shame ! the Moslem thrall,
Who, with his master, to the Prophet kneels,

While turning to the sacred Kebla feels
    His fetters break and fall.

Cheers for the turbaned Bey
Of robber-peopled Tunis ! he hath torn
The dark slave-dungeons open, and hath
    borne
    Their inmates into day :

But our poor slave in vain
Turns to the Christian shrine his aching
    eyes ;
Its rites will only swell his market price,
    And rivet on his chain.

God of all right ! how long
Shall priestly robbers at Thine altar stand,
Lifting in prayer to Thee the bloody hand
    And haughty brow of wrong ?

Oh, from the fields of cane,
From the low rice-swamp, from the trader's
    cell ;
From the black slave-ship's foul and loath-
    some hell,
    And coffle's weary chain ;

Hoarse, horrible, and strong,
Rises to Heaven that agonizing cry,
Filling the arches of the hollow sky,
    How long, O God, how long ?

THE   SENTENCE   OF   JOHN   L. BROWN

John L. Brown, a young white man of South
Carolina, was in 1844 sentenced to death for
aiding a young slave woman, whom he loved
and had married, to escape from slavery.   In
pronouncing the sentence Judge O'Neale ad-
dressed to the prisoner words of appalling blas-
phemy [of which the following passages give
some notion] : —

You are to die ! . . . Of your past life I know no-
thing, except what your trial furnished.   That told me
that the crime for which you are to suffer was the con-
sequence of a want of attention on your part to the
duties of life.   The strange woman snared you.   She
flattered you with her words, and you became her vic-
tim.   The consequence was, that, led on by a desire to
serve her, you committed the offence of aiding a slave
to run away and depart from her master's service ; and
now, for it you are to die ! . . .
You are young ; quite too young to be where you
are.   If you had remembered your Creator in your past
days, you would not now be in a felon's place, to re-
ceive a felon's judgment.   Still, it is not too late to
remember your Creator.   He calls early, and He calls

late. He stretches out the arms of a Father's love to you — to the vilest sinner — and says : " Come unto me and be saved."

No event in the history of the anti-slavery struggle so stirred the two hemispheres as did this dreadful sentence. A cry of horror was heard from Europe. In the British House of Lords Brougham and Denman spoke of it with mingled pathos and indignation. Thirteen hundred clergymen and church officers in Great Britain addressed a memorial to the churches of South Carolina against the atrocity. Indeed, so strong was the pressure of the sentiment of abhorrence and disgust that South Carolina yielded to it, and the sentence was commuted to scourging and banishment.

Ho ! thou who seekest late and long
    A License from the Holy Book
For brutal lust and fiendish wrong,
    Man of the Pulpit, look !
Lift up those cold and atheist eyes,
    This ripe fruit of thy teaching see ;
And tell us how to heaven will rise
The incense of this sacrifice —
    This blossom of the gallows tree !

Search out for slavery's hour of need
    Some fitting text of sacred writ ;
Give heaven the credit of a deed
    Which shames the nether pit.
Kneel, smooth blasphemer, unto Him
    Whose truth is on thy lips a lie ;
Ask that His bright winged cherubim
May bend around that scaffold grim
    To guard and bless and sanctify.

O champion of the people's cause !
    Suspend thy loud and vain rebuke
Of foreign wrong and Old World's laws,
    Man of the Senate, look !
Was this the promise of the free,
    The great hope of our early time,
That slavery's poison vine should be
Upborne by Freedom's prayer-nursed tree
    O'erclustered with such fruits of crime ?

Send out the summons East and West,
    And South and North, let all be there
Where he who pitied the oppressed
    Swings out in sun and air.
Let not a Democratic hand
    The grisly hangman's task refuse ;
There let each loyal patriot stand,
Awaiting slavery's command,
    To twist the rope and draw the noose !

But vain is irony — unmeet
    Its cold rebuke for deeds which start
In fiery and indignant beat
    The pulses of the heart.
Leave studied wit and guarded phrase
    For those who think but do not feel ;
Let men speak out in words which raise
Where'er they fall, an answering blaze
    Like flints which strike the fire from steel.

Still let a mousing priesthood ply
    Their garbled text and gloss of sin,
And make the lettered scroll deny
    Its living soul within :
Still let the place-fed, titled knave
    Plead robbery's right with purchased lips,
And tell us that our fathers gave
For Freedom's pedestal, a slave,
    The frieze and moulding, chains and
        whips !

But ye who own that Higher Law
    Whose tablets in the heart are set,
Speak out in words of power and awe
    That God is living yet !
Breathe forth once more those tones sublime
    Which thrilled the burdened prophet's
        lyre,
And in a dark and evil time
Smote down on Israel's fast of crime
    And gift of blood, a rain of fire !

Oh, not for us the graceful lay
    To whose soft measures lightly move
The footsteps of the faun and fay,
    O'er-locked by mirth and love !
But such a stern and startling strain
    As Britain's hunted bards flung down
From Snowden to the conquered plain,
Where harshly clanked the Saxon chain
    On trampled field and smoking town.

By Liberty's dishonored name,
    By man's lost hope and failing trust,
By words and deeds which bow with shame
    Our foreheads to the dust,
By the exulting strangers' sneer,
    Borne to us from the Old World's
        thrones,
And by their victims' grief who hear,
In sunless mines and dungeons drear,
    How Freedom's land her faith disowns !

Speak out in acts. The time for words
    Has passed, and deeds suffice alone ;

In vain against the clang of swords
  The wailing pipe is blown !
Act, act in God's name, while ye may !
  Smite from the church her leprous limb !
Throw open to the light of day
The bondman's cell, and break away
  The chains the state has bound on him !

Ho ! every true and living soul,
  To Freedom's perilled altar bear
The Freeman's and the Christian's whole
  Tongue, pen, and vote, and prayer !
One last, great battle for the right —
  One short, sharp struggle to be free !
To do is to succeed — our fight
Is waged in Heaven's approving sight ;
  The smile of God is Victory.

TEXAS

VOICE OF NEW ENGLAND

The five poems immediately following indicate the intense feeling of the friends of freedom in view of the annexation of Texas, with its vast territory sufficient, as was boasted, for six new slave States. [The first poem seems to have been written at the earnest entreaty of Lowell, who called on Whittier "to cry aloud and spare not against the accursed Texas plot."]

Up the hillside, down the glen,
Rouse the sleeping citizen;
Summon out the might of men !

Like a lion growling low,
Like a night-storm rising slow,
Like the tread of unseen foe ;

It is coming, it is nigh !
Stand your homes and altars by;
On your own free thresholds die.

Clang the bells in all your spires ;
On the gray hills of your sires
Fling to heaven your signal-fires.

From Wachuset, lone and bleak,
Unto Berkshire's tallest peak,
Let the flame-tongued heralds speak.

Oh, for God and duty stand,
Heart to heart and hand to hand,
Round the old graves of the land.

Whoso shrinks or falters now,
Whoso to the yoke would bow,
Brand the craven on his brow !

Freedom's soil hath only place
For a free and fearless race,
None for traitors false and base.

Perish party, perish clan ;
Strike together while ye can,
Like the arm of one strong man.

Like that angel's voice sublime,
Heard above a world of crime,
Crying of the end of time ;

With one heart and with one mouth,
Let the North unto the South
Speak the word befitting both :

"What though Issachar be strong !
Ye may load his back with wrong
Overmuch and over long :

"Patience with her cup o'errun,
With her weary thread outspun,
Murmurs that her work is done.

"Make our Union-bond a chain,
Weak as tow in Freedom's strain
Link by link shall snap in twain.

"Vainly shall your sand-wrought rope
Bind the starry cluster up,
Shattered over heaven's blue cope !

"Give us bright though broken rays,
Rather than eternal haze,
Clouding o'er the full-orbed blaze.

"Take your land of sun and bloom ;
Only leave to Freedom room
For her plough, and forge, and loom ;

"Take your slavery-blackened vales ;
Leave us but our own free gales,
Blowing on our thousand sails.

"Boldly, or with treacherous art,
Strike the blood-wrought chain apart ;
Break the Union's mighty heart ;

"Work the ruin, if ye will ;
Pluck upon your heads an ill
Which shall grow and deepen still.

" With your bondman's right arm bare,
  With his heart of black despair,
  Stand alone, if stand ye dare !

" Onward with your fell design ;
  Dig the gulf and draw the line :
  Fire beneath your feet the mine :

" Deeply, when the wide abyss
  Yawns between your land and this,
  Shall ye feel your helplessness.

" By the hearth, and in the bed,
  Shaken by a look or tread,
  Ye shall own a guilty dread.

" And the curse of unpaid toil,
  Downward through your generous soil
  Like a fire shall burn and spoil.

" Our bleak hills shall bud and blow,
  Vines our rocks shall overgrow,
  Plenty in our valleys flow ; —

" And when vengeance clouds your skies,
  Hither shall ye turn your eyes,
  As the lost on Paradise !

" We but ask our rocky strand,
  Freedom's true and brother band,
  Freedom's strong and honest hand ;

" Valleys by the slave untrod,
  And the Pilgrim's mountain sod,
  Blessëd of our fathers' God ! "

TO FANEUIL HALL

Written in 1844, on reading a call by " a
Massachusetts Freeman " for a meeting in
Faneuil Hall of the citizens of Massachusetts,
without distinction of party, opposed to the an-
nexation of Texas and the aggressions of South
Carolina, and in favor of decisive action against
slavery.

MEN ! if manhood still ye claim,
  If the Northern pulse can thrill,
Roused by wrong or stung by shame,
  Freely, strongly still ;
Let the sounds of traffic die :
  Shut the mill-gate, leave the stall,
Fling the axe and hammer by ;
  Throng to Faneuil Hall !

Wrongs which freemen never brooked,
  Dangers grim and fierce as they,
Which, like couching lions, looked
  On your fathers' way ;
These your instant zeal demand,
  Shaking with their earthquake-call
Every rood of Pilgrim land,
  Ho, to Faneuil Hall !

From your capes and sandy bars,
  From your mountain-ridges cold,
Through whose pines the westering stars
  Stoop their crowns of gold ;
Come, and with your footsteps wake
  Echoes from that holy wall ;
Once again, for Freedom's sake,
  Rock your fathers' hall !

Up, and tread beneath your feet
  Every cord by party spun :
Let your hearts together beat
  As the heart of one.
Banks and tariffs, stocks and trade,
  Let them rise or let them fall :
Freedom asks your common aid, —
  Up, to Faneuil Hall !

Up, and let each voice that speaks
  Ring from thence to Southern plains,
Sharply as the blow which breaks
  Prison-bolts and chains !
Speak as well becomes the free :
  Dreaded more than steel or ball,
Shall your calmest utterance be,
  Heard from Faneuil Hall !

Have they wronged us ?   Let us then
  Render back nor threats nor prayers ;
Have they chained our free-born men ?
  Let us unchain theirs !
Up, your banner leads the van,
  Blazoned, " Liberty for all ! "
Finish what your sires began !
  Up, to Faneuil Hall !

TO MASSACHUSETTS

WHAT though around thee blazes
  No fiery rallying sign ?
From all thy own high places,
  Give heaven the light of thine !
What though unthrilled, unmoving,
  The statesman stand apart,

And comes no warm approving
From Mammon's crowded mart ?

Still let the land be shaken
By a summons of thine own !
By all save truth forsaken,
Stand fast with that alone !
Shrink not from strife unequal !
With the best is always hope ;
And ever in the sequel
God holds the right side up !

But when, with thine uniting,
Come voices long and loud,
And far-off hills are writing
Thy fire-words on the cloud ;
When from Penobscot's fountains
A deep response is heard,
And across the Western mountains
Rolls back thy rallying word ;

Shall thy line of battle falter,
With its allies just in view ?
Oh, by hearth and holy altar,
My fatherland, be true !
Fling abroad thy scrolls of Freedom !
Speed them onward far and fast !
Over hill and valley speed them,
Like the sibyl's on the blast !

Lo ! the Empire State is shaking
The shackles from her hand ;
With the rugged North is waking
The level sunset land !
On they come, the free battalions !
East and West and North they come,
And the heart-beat of the millions
Is the beat of Freedom's drum.

" To the tyrant's plot no favor !
No heed to place-fed knaves !
Bar and bolt the door forever
Against the land of slaves ! "
Hear it, mother Earth, and hear it,
The heavens above us spread !
The land is roused, — its spirit
Was sleeping, but not dead !

NEW HAMPSHIRE

GOD bless New Hampshire ! from her
granite peaks
Once more the voice of Stark and Langdon
speaks.

The long-bound vassal of the exulting
South
For very shame her self-forged chain
has broken ;
Torn the black seal of slavery from her
mouth,
And in the clear tones of her old time
spoken !
Oh, all undreamed - of, all unhoped - for
changes !
The tyrant's ally proves his sternest foe ;
To all his biddings, from her mountain
ranges,
New Hampshire thunders an indignant
No !
Who is it now despairs ? Oh, faint of
heart,
Look upward to those Northern moun-
tains cold,
Flouted by Freedom's victor - flag un-
rolled,
And gather strength to bear a manlier
part !
All is not lost. The angel of God's bless-
ing
Encamps with Freedom on the field of
fight ;
Still to her banner, day by day, are press-
ing
Unlooked - for allies, striking for the
right !
Courage, then, Northern hearts ! Be firm,
be true :
What one brave State hath done, can ye not
also do ?

THE PINE–TREE

Written on hearing that the Anti-Slavery Re-
solves of Stephen C. Phillips had been rejected
by the Whig Convention in Faneuil Hall, in
1846.

LIFT again the stately emblem on the Bay
State's rusted shield,
Give to Northern winds the Pine-Tree on
our banner's tattered field.
Sons of men who sat in council with their
Bibles round the board,
Answering England's royal missive with a
firm, " Thus saith the Lord ! "
Rise again for home and freedom ! set the
battle in array !
What the fathers did of old time we their
sons must do to-day.

Tell us not of banks and tariffs, cease your
    paltry pedler cries ;
Shall the good State sink her honor that
    your gambling stocks may rise ?
Would ye barter man for cotton ? That
    your gains may sum up higher,
Must we kiss the feet of Moloch, pass our
    children through the fire ?
Is the dollar only real ? God and truth
    and right a dream ?
Weighed against your lying ledgers must
    our manhood kick the beam ?

O my God ! for that free spirit, which of
    old in Boston town
Smote the Province House with terror,
    struck the crest of Andros down !
For another strong-voiced Adams in the
    city's streets to cry,
"Up for God and Massachusetts ! Set
    your feet on Mammon's lie !
Perish banks and perish traffic, spin your
    cotton's latest pound,
But in Heaven's name keep your honor,
    keep the heart o' the Bay State
    sound ! "

Where 's the man for Massachusetts ?
    Where 's the voice to speak her free ?
Where 's the hand to light up bonfires from
    her mountains to the sea ?
Beats her Pilgrim pulse no longer ? Sits
    she dumb in her despair ?
Has she none to break the silence ? Has
    she none to do and dare ?
O my God ! for one right worthy to lift up
    her rusted shield,
And to plant again the Pine-Tree in her
    banner's tattered field !

TO A SOUTHERN STATESMAN

John C. Calhoun, who had strongly urged
the extension of slave territory by the annexa-
tion of Texas, even if it should involve a war
with England, was unwilling to promote the
acquisition of Oregon, which would enlarge
the Northern domain of freedom, and pleaded
as an excuse the peril of foreign complications
which he had defied when the interests of sla-
very were involved.

Is this thy voice whose treble notes of fear
Wail in the wind ? And dost thou shake
    to hear,

Actæon-like, the bay of thine own hounds,
Spurning the leash, and leaping o'er their
    bounds ?
Sore - baffled statesman ! when thy eager
    hand,
With game afoot, unslipped the hungry
    pack,
To hunt down Freedom in her chosen land,
Hadst thou no fear, that, erelong, doubling
    back,
These dogs of thine might snuff on Sla-
    very's track ?
Where 's now the boast, which even thy
    guarded tongue,
Cold, calm, and proud, in the teeth o' the
    Senate flung,
O'er the fulfilment of thy baleful plan,
Like Satan's triumph at the fall of man ?
How stood'st thou then, thy feet on Free-
    dom planting,
And pointing to the lurid heaven afar,
Whence all could see, through the south
    windows slanting,
Crimson as blood, the beams of that Lone
    Star !
The Fates are just ; they give us but our
    own ;
Nemesis ripens what our hands have sown.
There is an Eastern story, not unknown,
Doubtless, to thee, of one whose magic
    skill
Called demons up his water-jars to fill ;
Deftly and silently, they did his will,
But, when the task was done, kept pouring
    still.
In vain with spell and charm the wizard
    wrought,
Faster and faster were the buckets brought,
Higher and higher rose the flood around,
Till the fiends clapped their hands above
    their master drowned !
So, Carolinian, it may prove with thee,
For God still overrules man's schemes, and
    takes
Craftiness in its self-set snare, and makes
The wrath of man to praise Him. It may
    be,
That the roused spirits of Democracy
May leave to freer States the same wide
    door
Through which thy slave-cursed Texas en-
    tered in,
From out the blood and fire, the wrong and
    sin,
Of the stormed city and the ghastly plain,

Beat by hot hail, and wet with bloody rain,
The myriad-handed pioneer may pour,
And the wild West with the roused North
    combine
And heave the engineer of evil with his
    mine.

AT WASHINGTON

Suggested by a visit to the city of Washington, in the 12th month of 1845. [Originally entitled *Lines.*]

WITH a cold and wintry noon-light
  On its roofs and steeples shed,
Shadows weaving with the sunlight
  From the gray sky overhead,
Broadly, vaguely, all around me, lies the
  half-built town outspread.

Through this broad street, restless ever,
  Ebbs and flows a human tide,
Wave on wave a living river ;
  Wealth and fashion side by side ;
Toiler, idler, slave and master, in the same
  quick current glide.

Underneath yon dome, whose coping
  Springs above them, vast and tall,
Grave men in the dust are groping
  For the largess, base and small,
Which the hand of Power is scattering,
  crumbs which from its table fall.

Base of heart ! They vilely barter
  Honor's wealth for party's place ;
Step by step on Freedom's charter
  Leaving footprints of disgrace ;
For to-day's poor pittance turning from the
  great hope of their race.

Yet, where festal lamps are throwing
  Glory round the dancer's hair,
Gold-tressed, like an angel's, flowing
  Backward on the sunset air ;
And the low quick pulse of music beats its
  measure sweet and rare :

There to-night shall woman's glances,
  Star-like, welcome give to them ;
Fawning fools with shy advances
  Seek to touch their garments' hem,
With the tongue of flattery glozing deeds
  which God and Truth condemn.

From this glittering lie my vision
  Takes a broader, sadder range,
Full before me have arisen
  Other pictures dark and strange ;
From the parlor to the prison must the
  scene and witness change.

Hark ! the heavy gate is swinging
  On its hinges, harsh and slow ;
One pale prison lamp is flinging
  On a fearful group below
Such a light as leaves to terror whatsoe'er
  it does not show.

Pitying God ! Is that a woman
  On whose wrist the shackles clash ?
Is that shriek she utters human,
  Underneath the stinging lash ?
Are they men whose eyes of madness from
  that sad procession flash ?

Still the dance goes gayly onward !
  What is it to Wealth and Pride
That without the stars are looking
  On a scene which earth should hide ?
That the slave-ship lies in waiting, rocking
  on Potomac's tide !

Vainly to that mean Ambition
  Which, upon a rival's fall,
Winds above its old condition,
  With a reptile's slimy crawl,
Shall the pleading voice of sorrow, shall the
  slave in anguish call.

Vainly to the child of Fashion,
  Giving to ideal woe
Graceful luxury of compassion,
  Shall the stricken mourner go ;
Hateful seems the earnest sorrow, beautiful
  the hollow show !

Nay, my words are all too sweeping :
  In this crowded human mart,
Feeling is not dead, but sleeping ;
  Man's strong will and woman's heart,
In the coming strife for Freedom, yet shall
  bear their generous part.

And from yonder sunny valleys,
  Southward in the distance lost,
Freedom yet shall summon allies
  Worthier than the North can boast,
With the Evil by their hearth-stones grappling at severer cost.

Now, the soul alone is willing :
  Faint the heart and weak the knee ;
And as yet no lip is thrilling
  With the mighty words, " Be Free ! "
Tarrieth long the land's Good Angel, but
    his advent is to be !

Meanwhile, turning from the revel
  To the prison-cell my sight,
For intenser hate of evil,
  For a keener sense of right,
Shaking off thy dust, I thank thee, City of
    the Slaves, to-night !

" To thy duty now and ever !
  Dream no more of rest or stay :
Give to Freedom's great endeavor
  All thou art and hast to-day : "
Thus, above the city's murmur, saith a
    Voice, or seems to say.

Ye with heart and vision gifted
  To discern and love the right,
Whose worn faces have been lifted
  To the slowly-growing light,
Where from Freedom's sunrise drifted
    slowly back the murk of night !

Ye who through long years of trial
  Still have held your purpose fast,
While a lengthening shade the dial
  From the westering sunshine cast,
And of hope each hour's denial seemed an
    echo of the last !

O my brothers ! O my sisters !
  Would to God that ye were near,
Gazing with me down the vistas
  Of a sorrow strange and drear ;
Would to God that ye were listeners to the
    Voice I seem to hear !

With the storm above us driving,
  With the false earth mined below,
Who shall marvel if thus striving
  We have counted friend as foe ;
Unto one another giving in the darkness
    blow for blow.

Well it may be that our natures
  Have grown sterner and more hard,
And the freshness of their features
  Somewhat harsh and battle-scarred,
And their harmonies of feeling overtasked
    and rudely jarred.

Be it so. It should not swerve us
  From a purpose true and brave ;
Dearer Freedom's rugged service
  Than the pastime of the slave ;
Better is the storm above it than the quiet
    of the grave.

Let us then, uniting, bury
  All our idle feuds in dust,
And to future conflicts carry
  Mutual faith and common trust ;
Always he who most forgiveth in his brother
    is most just.

From the eternal shadow rounding
  All our sun and starlight here,
Voices of our lost ones sounding
  Bid us be of heart and cheer,
Through the silence, down the spaces, fall-
    ing on the inward ear.

Know we not our dead are looking
  Downward with a sad surprise,
All our strife of words rebuking
  With their mild and loving eyes ?
Shall we grieve the holy angels ? Shall we
    cloud their blessed skies ?

Let us draw their mantles o'er us
  Which have fallen in our way ;
Let us do the work before us,
  Cheerly, bravely, while we may,
Ere the long night-silence cometh, and
    with us it is not day !

THE BRANDED HAND

Captain Jonathan Walker, of Harwich, Mass., was solicited by several fugitive slaves at Pensacola, Florida, to carry them in his vessel to the British West Indies. Although well aware of the great hazard of the enterprise he attempted to comply with the request, but was seized at sea by an American vessel, consigned to the authorities at Key West, and thence sent back to Pensacola, where, after a long and rigorous confinement in prison, he was tried and sentenced to be branded on his right hand with the letters " S. S." (slave-stealer) and amerced in a heavy fine.

WELCOME home again, brave seaman !
    with thy thoughtful brow and gray,
And the old heroic spirit of our earlier,
    better day ;

With that front of calm endurance, on
  whose steady nerve in vain
Pressed the iron of the prison, smote the
  fiery shafts of pain !

Is the tyrant's brand upon thee ? Did the
  brutal cravens aim
To make God's truth thy falsehood, His
  holiest work thy shame ?
When, all blood-quenched, from the tor-
  ture the iron was withdrawn,
How laughed their evil angel the baffled
  fools to scorn !

They change to wrong the duty which God
  hath written out
On the great heart of humanity, too legible
  for doubt !
They, the loathsome moral lepers, blotched
  from footsole up to crown,
Give to shame what God hath given unto
  honor and renown !

Why, that brand is highest honor ! than
  its traces never yet
Upon old armorial hatchments was a
  prouder blazon set ;
And thy unborn generations, as they tread
  our rocky strand,
Shall tell with pride the story of their
  father's branded hand !

As the Templar home was welcome, bear-
  ing back from Syrian wars
The scars of Arab lances and of Paynim
  scimitars,
The pallor of the prison, and the shackle's
  crimson span,
So we meet thee, so we greet thee, truest
  friend of God and man.

He suffered for the ransom of the dear
  Redeemer's grave,
Thou for His living presence in the bound
  and bleeding slave ;
He for a soil no longer by the feet of an-
  gels trod,
Thou for the true Shechinah, the present
  home of God !

For, while the jurist, sitting with the
  slave-whip o'er him swung,
From the tortured truths of freedom the
  lie of slavery wrung,

And the solemn priest to Moloch, on each
  God-deserted shrine,
Broke the bondman's heart for bread, poured
  the bondman's blood for wine ;

While the multitude in blindness to a far-
  off Saviour knelt,
And spurned, the while, the temple where
  a present Saviour dwelt ;
Thou beheld'st Him in the task-field, in the
  prison shadows dim,
And thy mercy to the bondman, it was
  mercy unto Him !

In thy lone and long night-watches, sky
  above and wave below,
Thou didst learn a higher wisdom than the
  babbling schoolmen know ;
God's stars and silence taught thee, as His
  angels only can,
That the one sole sacred thing beneath the
  cope of heaven is Man !

That he who treads profanely on the scrolls
  of law and creed,
In the depth of God's great goodness may
  find mercy in his need ;
But woe to him who crushes the soul with
  chain and rod,
And herds with lower natures the awful
  form of God !

Then lift that manly right-hand, bold
  ploughman of the wave !
Its branded palm shall prophesy, " Salvation
  to the Slave ! "
Hold up its fire-wrought language, that
  whoso reads may feel
His heart swell strong within him, his
  sinews change to steel.

Hold it up before our sunshine, up against
  our Northern air ;
Ho ! men of Massachusetts, for the love of
  God, look there !
Take it henceforth for your standard, like
  the Bruce's heart of yore,
In the dark strife closing round ye, let that
  hand be seen before !

And the masters of the slave-land shall
  tremble at that sign,
When it points its finger Southward along
  the Puritan line :

Can the craft of State avail them ! Can a
    Christless church withstand,
In the van of Freedom's onset, the coming
    of that hand ?

THE FREED ISLANDS

Written for the anniversary celebration of
the first of August, at Milton, 1846. [Origi-
nally entitled *Lines.*]

A FEW brief years have passed away
    Since Britain drove her million slaves
Beneath the tropic's fiery ray :
God willed their freedom ; and to-day
    Life blooms above those island graves !

He spoke ! across the Carib Sea,
    We heard the clash of breaking chains,
And felt the heart-throb of the free,
The first strong pulse of liberty
    Which thrilled along the bondman's veins.

Though long delayed, and far, and slow,
    The Briton's triumph shall be ours :
Wears slavery here a prouder brow
Than that which twelve short years ago
    Scowled darkly from her island bow-
      ers ?

Mighty alike for good or ill
    With Mother-land, we fully share
The Saxon strength, the nerve of steel,
The tireless energy of will,
    The power to do, the pride to dare.

What she has done can we not do ?
    Our hour and men are both at hand ;
The blast which Freedom's angel blew
O'er her green islands, echoes through
    Each valley of our forest land.

Hear it, old Europe ! we have sworn
    The death of slavery. When it falls,
Look to your vassals in their turn,
Your poor dumb millions, crushed and worn,
    Your prisons and your palace walls !

O kingly mockers ! scoffing show
    What deeds in Freedom's name we do ;
Yet know that every taunt ye throw
Across the waters, goads our slow
    Progression towards the right and true.

Not always shall your outraged poor,
    Appalled by democratic crime,
Grind as their fathers ground before ;
The hour which sees our prison door
    Swing wide shall be their triumph time.

On then, my brothers ! every blow
    Ye deal is felt the wide earth through ;
Whatever here uplifts the low
Or humbles Freedom's hateful foe,
    Blesses the Old World through the New.

Take heart ! The promised hour draws
    near ;
I hear the downward beat of wings,
And Freedom's trumpet sounding clear :
" Joy to the people ! woe and fear
    To new-world tyrants, old-world kings ! "

A LETTER

Supposed to be written by the chairman of
the " Central Clique " at Concord, N. H., to
the Hon. M. N., Jr., at Washington, giving the
result of the election.

The following verses were published in the
Boston Chronotype in 1846. They refer to the
contest in New Hampshire, which resulted in
the defeat of the pro-slavery Democracy, and
in the election of John P. Hale to the United
States Senate. Although their authorship was
not acknowledged, it was strongly suspected.
They furnish a specimen of the way, on the
whole rather good-natured, in which the lib-
erty-lovers of half a century ago answered the
social and political outlawry and mob violence
to which they were subjected.

'TIS over, Moses ! All is lost !
    I hear the bells a-ringing ;
Of Pharaoh and his Red Sea host
    I hear the Free-Wills singing.
We're routed, Moses, horse and foot,
    If there be truth in figures,
With Federal Whigs in hot pursuit,
    And Hale, and all the " niggers."

Alack ! alas ! this month or more
    We've felt a sad foreboding ;
Our very dreams the burden bore
    Of central cliques exploding ;
Before our eyes a furnace shone,
    Where heads of dough were roasting,
And one we took to be your own
    The traitor Hale was toasting !

Our Belknap brother heard with awe
　The Congo minstrels playing ;
At Pittsfield Reuben Leavitt saw
　The ghost of Storrs a-praying ;
And Carroll's woods were sad to see,
　With black-winged crows a-darting ;
And Black Snout looked on Ossipee,
　New-glossed with Day and Martin.

We thought the " Old Man of the Notch "
　His face seemed changing wholly —
His lips seemed thick ; his nose seemed flat ;
　His misty hair looked woolly ;
And Coös teamsters, shrieking, fled
　From the metamorphosed figure.
" Look there ! " they said, " the Old Stone
　　Head
　Himself is turning nigger ! "

The schoolhouse, out of Canaan hauled,
　Seemed turning on its track again,
And like a great swamp-turtle crawled
　To Canaan village back again,
Shook off the mud and settled flat
　Upon its underpinning ;
A nigger on its ridge-pole sat,
　From ear to ear a-grinning.

Gray H——d heard o' nights the sound
　Of rail-cars onward faring ;
Right over Democratic ground
　The iron horse came tearing.
A flag waved o'er that spectral train,
　As high as Pittsfield steeple ;
Its emblem was a broken chain,
　Its motto : " To the people ! "

I dreamed that Charley took his bed,
　With Hale for his physician ;
His daily dose an old " unread
　And unreferred " petition.
There Hayes and Tuck as nurses sat,
　As near as near could be, man ;
They leeched him with the " Democrat ; "
　They blistered with the " Freeman."

Ah ! grisly portents ! What avail
　Your terrors of forewarning ?
We wake to find the nightmare Hale
　Astride our breasts at morning !
From Portsmouth lights to Indian stream
　Our foes their throats are trying ;
The very factory-spindles seem
　To mock us while they 're flying.

The hills have bonfires ; in our streets
　Flags flout us in our faces ;
The newsboys, peddling off their sheets,
　Are hoarse with our disgraces.
In vain we turn, for gibing wit
　And shoutings follow after,
As if old Kearsarge had split
　His granite sides with laughter !

What boots it that we pelted out
　The anti-slavery women,
And bravely strewed their hall about
　With tattered lace and trimming ?
Was it for such a sad reverse
　Our mobs became peacemakers,
And kept their tar and wooden horse
　For Englishmen and Quakers ?

For this did shifty Atherton
　Make gag rules for the Great House ?
Wiped we for this our feet upon
　Petitions in our State House ?
Plied we for this our axe of doom,
　No stubborn traitor sparing,
Who scoffed at our opinion loom,
　And took to homespun wearing ?

Ah, Moses ! hard it is to scan
　These crooked providences,
Deducing from the wisest plan
　The saddest consequences !
Strange that, in trampling as was meet
　The nigger-men's petition,
We sprung a mine beneath our feet
　Which opened up perdition.

How goodly, Moses, was the game
　In which we 've long been actors,
Supplying freedom with the name
　And slavery with the practice !
Our　smooth　words　fed　the　people's
　　mouth,
　Their ears our party rattle ;
We kept them headed to the South,
　As drovers do their cattle.

But now our game of politics
　The world at large is learning ;
And men grown gray in all our tricks
　State's evidence are turning.
Votes and preambles subtly spun
　They cram with meanings louder,
And load the Democratic gun
　With abolition powder.

The ides of June ! Woe worth the day
  When, turning all things over,
The traitor Hale shall make his hay
  From Democratic clover !
Who then shall take him in the law,
  Who punish crime so flagrant ?
Whose hand shall serve, whose pen shall draw,
  A writ against that " vagrant " ?

Alas ! no hope is left us here,
  And one can only pine for
The envied place of overseer
  Of slaves in Carolina !
Pray, Moses, give Calhoun the wink,
  And see what pay he 's giving !
We 've practised long enough, we think,
  To know the art of driving.

And for the faithful rank and file,
  Who know their proper stations,
Perhaps it may be worth their while
  To try the rice plantations.
Let Hale exult, let Wilson scoff,
  To see us southward scamper ;
The slaves, we know, are " better off
  Than laborers in New Hampshire !"

LINES

FROM A LETTER TO A YOUNG CLERICAL
FRIEND

A STRENGTH Thy service cannot tire,
  A faith which doubt can never dim,
A heart of love, a lip of fire,
  O Freedom's God ! be Thou to him !

Speak through him words of power and fear,
  As through Thy prophet bards of old,
And let a scornful people hear
  Once more Thy Sinai-thunders rolled.

For lying lips Thy blessing seek,
  And hands of blood are raised to Thee,
And on Thy children, crushed and weak,
  The oppressor plants his kneeling knee.

Let then, O God ! Thy servant dare
  Thy truth in all its power to tell,
Unmask the priestly thieves, and tear
  The Bible from the grasp of hell !

From hollow rite and narrow span
  Of law and sect by Thee released,
Oh, teach him that the Christian man
  Is holier than the Jewish priest.

Chase back the shadows, gray and old,
  Of the dead ages from his way,
And let his hopeful eyes behold
  The dawn of Thy millennial day;

That day when fettered limb and mind
  Shall know the truth which maketh free,
And he alone who loves his kind
  Shall, childlike, claim the love of Thee !

DANIEL NEALL

Dr. Neall, a worthy disciple of that vener-
ated philanthropist, Warner Mifflin, whom the
Girondist statesman, Jean Pierre Brissot, pro-
nounced " an angel of mercy, the best man he
ever knew," was one of the noble band of
Pennsylvania abolitionists, whose bravery was
equalled only by their gentleness and tender-
ness.

I

FRIEND of the Slave, and yet the friend of all ;
  Lover of peace, yet ever foremost when
  The need of battling Freedom called for men
To plant the banner on the outer wall ;
Gentle and kindly, ever at distress
Melted to more than woman's tenderness,
Yet firm and steadfast, at his duty's post
Fronting the violence of a maddened host,
Like some gray rock from which the waves are tossed !
Knowing his deeds of love, men questioned not
  The faith of one whose walk and word were right ;
Who tranquilly in Life's great task-field wrought,
And, side by side with evil, scarcely caught
  A stain upon his pilgrim garb of white :
Prompt to redress another's wrong, his own
Leaving to Time and Truth and Penitence alone.

II

Such was our friend. Formed on the good old plan,
A true and brave and downright honest man !

He blew no trumpet in the market-place,
Nor in the church with hypocritic face
Supplied with cant the lack of Christian
    grace ;
Loathing pretence, he did with cheerful
    will
What others talked of while their hands
    were still ;
And, while " Lord, Lord ! " the pious tyrants
    cried,
Who, in the poor, their Master crucified,
His daily prayer, far better understood
In acts than words, was simply doing
    good.
So calm, so constant was his rectitude,
That by his loss alone we know its worth,
And feel how true a man has walked with
    us on earth.

SONG OF SLAVES IN THE DESERT

[Suggested by a passage in Richardson's *Journal in Africa.*]

WHERE are we going ? where are we going,
  Where are we going, Rubee ?
Lord of peoples, lord of lands,
Look across these shining sands,
Through the furnace of the noon,
Through the white light of the moon.
Strong the Ghiblee wind is blowing,
Strange and large the world is growing !
Speak and tell us where we are going,
  Where are we going, Rubee ?

Bornou land was rich and good,
Wells of water, fields of food,
Dourra fields, and bloom of bean,
And the palm-tree cool and green :
Bornou land we see no longer,
Here we thirst and here we hunger,
Here the Moor-man smites in anger :
  Where are we going, Rubee ?

When we went from Bornou land,
We were like the leaves and sand,
We were many, we are few ;
Life has one, and death has two :
Whitened bones our path are showing,
Thou All-seeing, thou All-knowing !
Hear us, tell us, where are we going,
  Where are we going, Rubee ?

Moons of marches from our eyes
Bornou land behind us lies ;
Stranger round us day by day
Bends the desert circle gray ;
Wild the waves of sand are flowing,
Hot the winds above them blowing, —
Lord of all things ! where are we going ?
  Where are we going, Rubee ?

We are weak, but Thou art strong ;
Short our lives, but Thine is long ;
We are blind, but Thou hast eyes ;
We are fools, but Thou art wise !
Thou, our morrow's pathway knowing
Through the strange world round us grow‑
    ing,
Hear us, tell us where are we going,
  Where are we going, Rubee ?

TO DELAWARE

Written during the discussion in the Legis-
lature of that State, in the winter of 1846–47,
of a bill for the abolition of slavery.

THRICE welcome to thy sisters of the East,
  To the strong tillers of a rugged home,
With spray-wet locks to Northern winds
    released,
  And hardy feet o'erswept by ocean's
    foam ;
And to the young nymphs of the golden
    West,
  Whose harvest mantles, fringed with
    prairie bloom,
Trail in the sunset, — O redeemed and
    blest,
  To the warm welcome of thy sisters
    come !
Broad Pennsylvania, down her sail-white
    bay
  Shall give thee joy, and Jersey from her
    plains,
And the great lakes, where echo, free alway,
  Moaned never shoreward with the clank
    of chains,
Shall weave new sun-bows in their tossing
    spray,
And all their waves keep grateful holiday.
And, smiling on thee through her mountain
    rains,
  Vermont shall bless thee ; and the gran‑
    ite peaks,

And vast Katahdin o'er his woods, shall
   wear
Their snow-crowns brighter in the cold,
   keen air ;
  And Massachusetts, with her rugged
   cheeks
O'errun with grateful tears, shall turn to
   thee,
  When, at thy bidding, the electric wire
  Shall tremble northward with its words
   of fire ;
Glory and praise to God ! another State is
   free !

YORKTOWN

Dr. Thacher, surgeon in Scammel's regiment, in his description of the siege of Yorktown, says: " The labor on the Virginia plantations is performed altogether by a species of the human race cruelly wrested from their native country, and doomed to perpetual bondage, while their masters are manfully contending for freedom and the natural rights of man. Such is the inconsistency of human nature." Eighteen hundred slaves were found at Yorktown, after its surrender, and restored to their masters. Well was it said by Dr. Barnes, in his late work on Slavery : " No slave was any nearer his freedom after the surrender of Yorktown than when Patrick Henry first taught the notes of liberty to echo among the hills and vales of Virginia."

From Yorktown's ruins, ranked and still,
Two lines stretch far o'er vale and hill :
Who curbs his steed at head of one ?
Hark ! the low murmur : Washington !
Who bends his keen, approving glance,
Where down the gorgeous line of France
Shine knightly star and plume of snow ?
Thou too art victor, Rochambeau !

The earth which bears this calm array
Shook with the war-charge yesterday,
Ploughed deep with hurrying hoof and
   wheel,
Shot-sown and bladed thick with steel ;
October's clear and noonday sun
Paled in the breath-smoke of the gun,
And down night's double blackness fell,
Like a dropped star, the blazing shell.

Now all is hushed : the gleaming lines
Stand moveless as the neighboring pines ;

While through them, sullen, grim, and
   slow,
The conquered hosts of England go :
O'Hara's brow belies his dress,
Gay Tarleton's troop rides bannerless :
Shout, from thy fired and wasted homes,
Thy scourge, Virginia, captive comes !

Nor thou alone : with one glad voice
Let all thy sister States rejoice ;
Let Freedom, in whatever clime
She waits with sleepless eye her time,
Shouting from cave and mountain wood
Make glad her desert solitude,
While they who hunt her quail with fear :
The New World's chain lies broken here !

But who are they, who, cowering, wait
Within the shattered fortress gate ?
Dark tillers of Virginia's soil,
Classed with the battle's common spoil,
With household stuffs, and fowl, and swine,
With Indian weed and planters' wine,
With stolen beeves, and foraged corn, —
Are they not men, Virginian born ?

Oh, veil your faces, young and brave !
Sleep, Scammel, in thy soldier grave !
Sons of the Northland, ye who set
Stout hearts against the bayonet,
And pressed with steady footfall near
The moated battery's blazing tier,
Turn your scarred faces from the sight,
Let shame do homage to the right !

Lo ! fourscore years have passed ; and
   where
The Gallic bugles stirred the air,
And, through breached batteries, side by
   side,
To victory stormed the hosts allied,
And brave foes grounded, pale with pain,
The arms they might not lift again,
As abject as in that old day
The slave still toils his life away.

Oh, fields still green and fresh in story,
Old days of pride, old names of glory,
Old marvels of the tongue and pen,
Old thoughts which stirred the hearts of
   men,
Ye spared the wrong ; and over all
Behold the avenging shadow fall !

Your world-wide honor stained with
        shame, —
Your freedom's self a hollow name !

Where 's now the flag of that old war ?
Where flows its stripe ? Where burns its
        star ?
Bear witness, Palo Alto's day,
Dark Vale of Palms, red Monterey,
Where Mexic Freedom, young and weak,
Fleshes the Northern eagle's beak ;
Symbol of terror and despair,
Of chains and slaves, go seek it there !

Laugh, Prussia, midst thy iron ranks !
Laugh, Russia, from thy Neva's banks !
Brave sport to see the fledgling born
Of Freedom by its parent torn !
Safe now is Speilberg's dungeon cell,
Safe drear Siberia's frozen hell :
With Slavery's flag o'er both unrolled,
What of the New World fears the Old ?

RANDOLPH OF ROANOKE

[Though not published until 1847, several
lines indicate that the poem was written not
long after Randolph's death in 1833. In a letter
published in July, 1833, Whittier says : " In the
last hour of his [Randolph's] existence, when
his soul was struggling from its broken tene-
ment, his latest effort was the confirmation of
this generous act of a former period [the manu-
mission of his slaves]. Light rest the turf upon
him, beneath his patrimonial oaks! The prayers
of many hearts made happy by his benevolence
shall linger over his grave and bless it."]

O MOTHER EARTH ! upon thy lap
    Thy weary ones receiving,
And o'er them, silent as a dream,
    Thy grassy mantle weaving,
Fold softly in thy long embrace
    That heart so worn and broken,
And cool its pulse of fire beneath
    Thy shadows old and oaken.

Shut out from him the bitter word
    And serpent hiss of scorning ;
Nor let the storms of yesterday
    Disturb his quiet morning.
Breathe over him forgetfulness
    Of all save deeds of kindness,
And, save to smiles of grateful eyes,
    Press down his lids in blindness.

There, where with living ear and eye
    He heard Potomac's flowing,
And, through his tall ancestral trees,
    Saw autumn's sunset glowing,
He sleeps, still looking to the west,
    Beneath the dark wood shadow,
As if he still would see the sun
    Sink down on wave and meadow.

Bard, Sage, and Tribune ! in himself
    All moods of mind contrasting, —
The tenderest wail of human woe,
    The scorn like lightning blasting ;
The pathos which from rival eyes
    Unwilling tears could summon,
The stinging taunt, the fiery burst
    Of hatred scarcely human !

Mirth, sparkling like a diamond shower,
    From lips of life-long sadness ;
Clear picturings of majestic thought
    Upon a ground of madness ;
And over all Romance and Song
    A classic beauty throwing,
And laurelled Clio at his side
    Her storied pages showing.

All parties feared him : each in turn
    Beheld its schemes disjointed,
As right or left his fatal glance
    And spectral finger pointed.
Sworn foe of Cant, he smote it down
    With trenchant wit unsparing,
And, mocking, rent with ruthless hand
    The robe Pretence was wearing.

Too honest or too proud to feign
    A love he never cherished,
Beyond Virginia's border line
    His patriotism perished.
While others hailed in distant skies
    Our eagle's dusky pinion,
He only saw the mountain bird
    Stoop o'er his Old Dominion !

Still through each change of fortune
        strange,
    Racked nerve, and brain all burning,
His loving faith in Mother-land
    Knew never shade of turning ;
By Britain's lakes, by Neva's tide,
    Whatever sky was o'er him,
He heard her rivers' rushing sound,
    Her blue peaks rose before him.

He held his slaves, yet made withal
  No false and vain pretences,
Nor paid a lying priest to seek
  For Scriptural defences.
His harshest words of proud rebuke,
  His bitterest taunt and scorning,
Fell fire-like on the Northern brow
  That bent to him in fawning.

He held his slaves ; yet kept the while
  His reverence for the Human ;
In the dark vassals of his will
  He saw but Man and Woman !
No hunter of God's outraged poor
  His Roanoke valley entered ;
No trader in the souls of men
  Across his threshold ventured.

And when the old and wearied man
  Lay down for his last sleeping,
And at his side, a slave no more,
  His brother-man stood weeping,
His latest thought, his latest breath,
  To Freedom's duty giving,
With failing tongue and trembling hand
  The dying blest the living.

Oh, never bore his ancient State
  A truer son or braver !
None trampling with a calmer scorn
  On foreign hate or favor.
He knew her faults, yet never stooped
  His proud and manly feeling
To poor excuses of the wrong
  Or meanness of concealing.

But none beheld with clearer eye
  The plague-spot o'er her spreading,
None heard more sure the steps of Doom
  Along her future treading.
For her as for himself he spake,
  When, his gaunt frame upbracing,
He traced with dying hand "Remorse !"
  And perished in the tracing.

As from the grave where Henry sleeps,
  From Vernon's weeping willow,
And from the grassy pall which hides
  The Sage of Monticello,
So from the leaf-strewn burial-stone
  Of Randolph's lowly dwelling,
Virginia ! o'er thy land of slaves
  A warning voice is swelling !

And hark ! from thy deserted fields
  Are sadder warnings spoken,
From quenched hearths, where thy exiled
    sons
  Their household gods have broken.
The curse is on thee, — wolves for men,
  And briers for corn-sheaves giving !
Oh, more than all thy dead renown
  Were now one hero living !

THE LOST STATESMAN

Written on hearing of the death of Silas
Wright of New York. [Originally entitled
Lines.]

As they who, tossing midst the storm at
    night,
  While turning shoreward, where a bea-
    con shone,
  Meet the walled blackness of the heaven
    alone,
So, on the turbulent waves of party tossed,
In gloom and tempest, men have seen thy
    light
  Quenched in the darkness. At thy hour
    of noon,
While life was pleasant to thy undimmed
    sight,
And, day by day, within thy spirit grew
A holier hope than young Ambition knew,
As through thy rural quiet, not in vain,
Pierced the sharp thrill of Freedom's cry
    of pain,
  Man of the millions, thou art lost too
    soon !
Portents at which the bravest stand
    aghast, —
The birth-throes of a Future, strange and
    vast,
  Alarm the land ; yet thou, so wise and
    strong,
Suddenly summoned to the burial bed,
  Lapped in its slumbers deep and ever
    long,
Hear'st not the tumult surging overhead.
Who now shall rally Freedom's scattering
    host ?
Who wear the mantle of the leader lost ?
Who stay the march of slavery ? He
  whose voice

Hath called thee from thy task-field
  shall not lack
Yet bolder champions, to beat bravely
  back
The wrong which, through his poor ones,
  reaches Him :
Yet firmer hands shall Freedom's torch-
  lights trim,
  And wave them high across the abysmal
  black,
Till bound, dumb millions there shall see
  them and rejoice.

THE SLAVES OF MARTINIQUE

Suggested by a daguerreotype taken from
a small French engraving of two negro figures,
sent to the writer by Oliver Johnson.

BEAMS of noon, like burning lances, through
  the tree-tops flash and glisten,
As she stands before her lover, with raised
  face to look and listen.

Dark, but comely, like the maiden in the
  ancient Jewish song :
Scarcely has the toil of task-fields done her
  graceful beauty wrong.

He, the strong one and the manly, with the
  vassal's garb and hue,
Holding still his spirit's birthright, to his
  higher nature true ;

Hiding deep the strengthening purpose of
  a freeman in his heart,
As the gregree holds his Fetich from the
  white man's gaze apart.

Ever foremost of his comrades; when the
  driver's morning horn
Calls away to stifling mill-house, to the
  fields of cane and corn :

Fall the keen and burning lashes never on
  his back or limb ;
Scarce with look or word of censure, turns
  the driver unto him.

Yet, his brow is always thoughtful, and his
  eye is hard and stern ;
Slavery's last and humblest lesson he has
  never deigned to learn.

And, at evening, when his comrades dance
  before their master's door,
Folding arms and knitting forehead, stands
  he silent evermore.

God be praised for every instinct which
  rebels against a lot
Where the brute survives the human, and
  man's upright form is not !

As the serpent-like bejuco winds his spiral
  fold on fold
Round the tall and stately ceiba, till it
  withers in his hold ;

Slow decays the forest monarch, closer
  girds the fell embrace,
Till the tree is seen no longer, and the vine
  is in its place ;

So a base and bestial nature round the vas-
  sal's manhood twines,
And the spirit wastes beneath it, like the
  ceiba choked with vines.

God is Love, saith the Evangel ; and our
  world of woe and sin
Is made light and happy only when a Love
  is shining in.

Ye whose lives are free as sunshine, finding,
  wheresoe'er ye roam,
Smiles of welcome, looks of kindness, mak-
  ing all the world like home ;

In the veins of whose affections kindred
  blood is but a part,
Of one kindly current throbbing from the
  universal heart ;

Can ye know the deeper meaning of a love
  in Slavery nursed,
Last flower of a lost Eden, blooming in that
  Soil accursed ?

Love of Home, and Love of Woman ! —
  dear to all, but doubly dear
To the heart whose pulses elsewhere meas-
  ure only hate and fear.

All around the desert circles, underneath a
  brazen sky,
Only one green spot remaining where the
  dew is never dry !

From the horror of that desert, from its
    atmosphere of hell,
Turns the fainting spirit thither, as the
    diver seeks his bell.

'T is the fervid tropic noontime ; faint and
    low the sea-waves beat ;
Hazy rise the inland mountains through the
    glimmer of the heat, —

Where, through mingled leaves and blos-
    soms, arrowy sunbeams flash and
    glisten,
Speaks her lover to the slave-girl, and she
    lifts her head to listen : —

" We shall live as slaves no longer ! Free-
    dom's hour is close at hand !
Rocks her bark upon the waters, rests the
    boat upon the strand !

" I have seen the Haytien Captain ; I have
    seen his swarthy crew,
Haters of the pallid faces, to their race and
    color true.

" They have sworn to wait our coming till
    the night has passed its noon,
And the gray and darkening waters roll
    above the sunken moon ! "

Oh, the blessed hope of freedom ! how with
    joy and glad surprise,
For an instant throbs her bosom, for an in-
    stant beam her eyes !

But she looks across the valley, where her
    mother's hut is seen,
Through the snowy bloom of coffee, and
    the lemon-leaves so green.

And she answers, sad and earnest : " It
    were wrong for thee to stay ;
God hath heard thy prayer for freedom,
    and His finger points the way.

" Well I know with what endurance, for the
    sake of me and mine,
Thou hast borne too long a burden never
    meant for souls like thine.

" Go ; and at the hour of midnight, when
    our last farewell is o'er,
Kneeling on our place of parting, I will
    bless thee from the shore.

" But for me, my mother, lying on her sick-
    bed all the day,
Lifts her weary head to watch me, coming
    through the twilight gray.

" Should I leave her sick and helpless, even
    freedom, shared with thee,
Would be sadder far than bondage, lonely
    toil, and stripes to me.

" For my heart would die within me, and
    my brain would soon be wild ;
I should hear my mother calling through
    the twilight for her child ! "

Blazing upward from the ocean, shines the
    sun of morning-time,
Through the coffee-trees in blossom, and
    green hedges of the lime.

Side by side, amidst the slave-gang, toil the
    lover and the maid ;
Wherefore looks he o'er the waters, leaning
    forward on his spade ?

Sadly looks he, deeply sighs he : 't is the
    Haytien's sail he sees,
Like a white cloud of the mountains, driven
    seaward by the breeze !

But his arm a light hand presses, and he
    hears a low voice call :
Hate of Slavery, hope of Freedom, Love is
    mightier than all.

THE CURSE OF THE CHARTER-BREAKERS

The rights and liberties affirmed by Magna
Charta were deemed of such importance, in the
thirteenth century, that the Bishops, twice a
year, with tapers burning and in their pontifi-
cal robes, pronounced, in the presence of the
king and the representatives of the estates of
England, the greater excommunication against
the infringer of that instrument. The impos-
ing ceremony took place in the great Hall of
Westminster.

In Westminster's royal halls,
Robed in their pontificals,
England's ancient prelates stood
For the people's right and good.

Closed around the waiting crowd,
Dark and still, like winter's cloud ;

King and council, lord and knight,
Squire and yeoman, stood in sight ;

Stood to hear the priest rehearse,
In God's name, the Church's curse,
By the tapers round them lit,
Slowly, sternly uttering it.

" Right of voice in framing laws,
Right of peers to try each cause ;
Peasant homestead, mean and small,
Sacred as the monarch's hall, —

" Whoso lays his hand on these,
England's ancient liberties ;
Whoso breaks, by word or deed,
England's vow at Runnymede;

" Be he Prince or belted knight,
Whatsoe'er his rank or might,
If the highest, then the worst,
Let him live and die accursed.

" Thou, who to Thy Church hast given
Keys alike of hell and heaven,
Make our word and witness sure,
Let the curse we speak endure ! "

Silent, while that curse was said,
Every bare and listening head
Bowed in reverent awe, and then
All the people said, Amen !

Seven times the bells have tolled,
For the centuries gray and old,
Since that stoled and mitred band
Cursed the tyrants of their land.

Since the priesthood, like a tower,
Stood between the poor and power ;
And the wronged and trodden down
Blessed the abbot's shaven crown.

Gone, thank God, their wizard spell,
Lost their keys of heaven and hell ;
Yet I sigh for men as bold
As those bearded priests of old.

Now too oft the priesthood wait
At the threshold of the state ;
Waiting for the beck and nod
Of its power as law and God.

Fraud exults, while solemn words
Sanctify his stolen hoards ;

Slavery laughs, while ghostly lips
Bless his manacles and whips.

Not on them the poor rely,
Not to them looks liberty,
Who with fawning falsehood cower
To the wrong, when clothed with power.

Oh, to see them meanly cling,
Round the master, round the king,
Sported with, and sold and bought, —
Pitifuller sight is not !

Tell me not that this must be :
God's true priest is always free ;
Free the needed truth to speak,
Right the wronged, and raise the weak.

Not to fawn on wealth and state,
Leaving Lazarus at the gate ;
Not to peddle creeds like wares ;
Not to mutter hireling prayers ;

Nor to paint the new life's bliss
On the sable ground of this ;
Golden streets for idle knave,
Sabbath rest for weary slave !

Not for words and works like these,
Priest of God, thy mission is ;
But to make earth's desert glad,
In its Eden greenness clad ;

And to level manhood bring
Lord and peasant, serf and king ;
And the Christ of God to find
In the humblest of thy kind !

Thine to work as well as pray,
Clearing thorny wrongs away ;
Plucking up the weeds of sin,
Letting heaven's warm sunshine in ;

Watching on the hills of Faith ;
Listening what the spirit saith,
Of the dim-seen light afar,
Growing like a nearing star.

God's interpreter art thou
To the waiting ones below ;
'Twixt them and its light midway
Heralding the better day ;

Catching gleams of temple spires,
Hearing notes of angel choirs,

Where, as yet unseen of them,
Comes the New Jerusalem !

Like the seer of Patmos gazing,
On the glory downward blazing ;
Till upon Earth's grateful sod
Rests the City of our God !

PÆAN

This poem indicates the exultation of the anti-slavery party, in view of the revolt of the friends of Martin Van Buren in New York from the Democratic Presidential nomination in 1848.

Now, joy and thanks forevermore !
The dreary night has wellnigh passed,
The slumbers of the North are o'er,
The Giant stands erect at last !

More than we hoped in that dark time
When, faint with watching, few and worn,
We saw no welcome day-star climb
The cold gray pathway of the morn !

O weary hours ! O night of years !
What storms our darkling pathway swept,
Where, beating back our thronging fears,
By Faith alone our march we kept.

How jeered the scoffing crowd behind,
How mocked before the tyrant train,
As, one by one, the true and kind
Fell fainting in our path of pain !

They died, their brave hearts breaking slow,
But, self-forgetful to the last,
In words of cheer and bugle blow
Their breath upon the darkness passed.

A mighty host, on either hand,
Stood waiting for the dawn of day
To crush like reeds our feeble band ;
The morn has come, and where are they ?

Troop after troop their line forsakes ;
With peace-white banners waving free,
And from our own the glad shout breaks,
Of Freedom and Fraternity !

Like mist before the growing light,
The hostile cohorts melt away ;
Our frowning foemen of the night
Are brothers at the dawn of day !

As unto these repentant ones
We open wide our toil-worn ranks,
Along our line a murmur runs
Of song, and praise, and grateful thanks.

Sound for the onset ! Blast on blast !
Till Slavery's minions cower and quail ;
One charge of fire shall drive them fast
Like chaff before our Northern gale !

O prisoners in your house of pain,
Dumb, toiling millions, bound and sold,
Look ! stretched o'er Southern vale and plain,
The Lord's delivering hand behold !

Above the tyrant's pride of power,
His iron gates and guarded wall,
The bolts which shattered Shinar's tower
Hang, smoking, for a fiercer fall.

Awake ! awake ! my Fatherland !
It is thy Northern light that shines ;
This stirring march of Freedom's band
The storm-song of thy mountain pines.

Wake, dwellers where the day expires !
And hear, in winds that sweep your lakes
And fan your prairies' roaring fires,
The signal-call that Freedom makes !

THE CRISIS

Written on learning the terms of the treaty with Mexico.

ACROSS the Stony Mountains, o'er the desert's drouth and sand,
The circles of our empire touch the western ocean's strand ;
From slumberous Timpanogos, to Gila, wild and free,
Flowing down from Nuevo-Leon to California's sea ;
And from the mountains of the east, to Santa Rosa's shore,
The eagles of Mexitli shall beat the air no more.

O Vale of Rio Bravo ! Let thy simple children weep ;
Close watch about their holy fire let maids of Pecos keep ;

Let Taos send her cry across Sierra Madre's
  pines,
And Santa Barbara toll her bells amidst
  her corn and vines ;
For lo ! the pale land-seekers come, with
  eager eyes of gain,
Wide scattering, like the bison herds on
  broad Salada's plain.

Let Sacramento's herdsmen heed what
  sound the winds bring down
Of footsteps on the crisping snow, from
  cold Nevada's crown !
Full hot and fast the Saxon rides, with
  rein of travel slack,
And, bending o'er his saddle, leaves the
  sunrise at his back ;
By many a lonely river, and gorge of fir
  and pine,
On many a wintry hill-top, his nightly
  camp-fires shine.

O countrymen and brothers ! that land of
  lake and plain,
Of salt wastes alternating with valleys fat
  with grain ;
Of mountains white with winter, looking
  downward, cold, serene,
On their feet with spring-vines tangled and
  lapped in softest green ;
Swift through whose black volcanic gates,
  o'er many a sunny vale,
Wind-like the Arapahoe sweeps the bison's
  dusty trail !

Great spaces yet untravelled, great lakes
  whose mystic shores
The Saxon rifle never heard, nor dip of
  Saxon oars ;
Great herds that wander all unwatched,
  wild steeds that none have tamed,
Strange fish in unknown streams, and birds
  the Saxon never named ;
Deep mines, dark mountain crucibles,
  where Nature's chemic powers
Work out the Great Designer's will ; all
  these ye say are ours !

Forever ours ! for good or ill, on us the
  burden lies :
God's balance, watched by angels, is hung
  across the skies.
Shall Justice, Truth, and Freedom turn
  the poised and trembling scale ?

Or shall the Evil triumph, and robber
  Wrong prevail ?
Shall the broad land o'er which our flag in
  starry splendor waves,
Forego through us its freedom, and bear
  the tread of slaves ?

The day is breaking in the East of which
  the prophets told,
And brightens up the sky of Time the
  Christian Age of Gold ;
Old Might to Right is yielding, battle
  blade to clerkly pen,
Earth's monarchs are her peoples, and her
  serfs stand up as men ;
The isles rejoice together, in a day are
  nations born,
And the slave walks free in Tunis, and by
  Stamboul's Golden Horn !

Is this, O countrymen of mine ! a day for
  us to sow
The soil of new-gained empire with sla-
  very's seeds of woe ?
To feed with our fresh life-blood the Old
  World's cast-off crime,
Dropped, like some monstrous early birth,
  from the tired lap of Time ?
To run anew the evil race the old lost na-
  tions ran,
And die like them of unbelief of God, and
  wrong of man ?

Great Heaven ! Is this our mission ? End
  in this the prayers and tears,
The toil, the strife, the watchings of our
  younger, better years ?
Still as the Old World rolls in light, shall
  ours in shadow turn,
A beamless Chaos, cursed of God, through
  outer darkness borne ?
Where the far nations looked for light, a
  blackness in the air ?
Where for words of hope they listened, the
  long wail of despair ?

The Crisis presses on us ; face to face with
  us it stands,
With solemn lips of question, like the
  Sphinx in Egypt's sands !
This day we fashion Destiny, our web of
  Fate we spin ;
This day for all hereafter choose we holi-
  ness or sin ;

Even now from starry Gerizim, or Ebal's
    cloudy crown,
We call the dews of blessing or the bolts
    of cursing down !

By all for which the martyrs bore their
    agony and shame ;
By all the warning words of truth with
    which the prophets came ;
By the Future which awaits us ; by all the
    hopes which cast
Their faint and trembling beams across
    the blackness of the Past ;
And by the blessed thought of Him who
    for Earth's freedom died,
O my people ! O my brothers ! let us
    choose the righteous side.

So shall the Northern pioneer go joyful on
    his way ;
To wed Penobscot's waters to San Fran-
    cisco's bay,
To make the rugged places smooth, and
    sow the vales with grain ;
And bear, with Liberty and Law, the Bible
    in his train :
The mighty West shall bless the East, and
    sea shall answer sea,
And mountain unto mountain call, Praise
    God, for we are free !

LINES ON THE PORTRAIT OF A CELEBRATED PUBLISHER

The lines following were addressed to a
magazine publisher, who, alarmed for his
Southern circulation, not only dropped the
name of Grace Greenwood from his list of con-
tributors, but made an offensive parade of his
action, with the view of strengthening his posi-
tion among slaveholders and conservatives.
By some coincidence his portrait was issued
about the same time.

A MOONY breadth of virgin face,
    By thought unviolated ;
A patient mouth, to take from scorn
    The hook with bank-notes baited !
Its self-complacent sleekness shows
    How thrift goes with the fawner ;
An unctuous unconcern of all
    Which nice folks call dishonor !

A pleasant print to peddle out
    In lands of rice and cotton ;
The model of that face in dough
    Would make the artist's fortune.
For Fame to thee has come unsought,
    While others vainly woo her,
In proof how mean a thing can make
    A great man of its doer.

To whom shall men thyself compare,
    Since common models fail 'em,
Save classic goose of ancient Rome,
    Or sacred ass of Balaam ?
The gabble of that wakeful goose
    Saved Rome from sack of Brennus ;
The braying of the prophet's ass
    Betrayed the angel's menace !

So when Guy Fawkes, in petticoats,
    And azure-tinted hose on,
Was twisting from thy love-lorn sheets
    The slow-match of explosion —
An earthquake blast that would have tossed
    The Union as a feather,
Thy instinct saved a perilled land
    And perilled purse together.

Just think of Carolina's sage
    Sent whirling like a Dervis,
Of Quattlebum in middle air
    Performing strange drill-service !
Doomed like Assyria's lord of old,
    Who fell before the Jewess,
Or sad Abimelech, to sigh,
    " Alas ! a woman slew us ! "

Thou saw'st beneath a fair disguise
    The danger darkly lurking,
And maiden bodice dreaded more
    Than warrior's steel-wrought jerkin.
How keen to scent the hidden plot !
    How prompt wert thou to balk it,
With patriot zeal and pedler thrift,
    For country and for pocket !

Thy likeness here is doubtless well,
    But higher honor 's due it ;
On auction-block and negro-jail
    Admiring eyes should view it.
Or, hung aloft, it well might grace
    The nation's senate-chamber —
A greedy Northern bottle-fly
    Preserved in Slavery's amber !

DERNE

The storming of the city of Derne, in 1805, by General Eaton, at the head of nine Americans, forty Greeks, and a motley array of Turks and Arabs, was one of those feats of hardihood and daring which have in all ages attracted the admiration of the multitude. The higher and holier heroism of Christian self-denial and sacrifice, in the humble walks of private duty, is seldom so well appreciated.

NIGHT on the city of the Moor !
On mosque and tomb, and white-walled
    shore,
On sea-waves, to whose ceaseless knock
The narrow harbor-gates unlock,
On corsair's galley, carack tall,
And plundered Christian caraval !
The sounds of Moslem life are still ;
No mule-bell tinkles down the hill,
Stretched in the broad court of the khan,
The dusty Bornou caravan
Lies heaped in slumber, beast and man ;
The Sheik is dreaming in his tent,
His noisy Arab tongue o'erspent ;
The kiosk's glimmering lights are gone,
The merchant with his wares withdrawn ;
Rough pillowed on some pirate breast,
The dancing-girl has sunk to rest ;
And, save where measured footsteps fall
Along the Bashaw's guarded wall,
Or where, like some bad dream, the Jew
Creeps stealthily his quarter through,
Or counts with fear his golden heaps,
The City of the Corsair sleeps !

But where yon prison long and low
Stands black against the pale star-glow,
Chafed by the ceaseless wash of waves,
There watch and pine the Christian slaves ;
Rough-bearded men, whose far-off wives
Wear out with grief their lonely lives ;
And youth, still flashing from his eyes
The clear blue of New England skies,
A treasured lock of whose soft hair
Now wakes some sorrowing mother's
    prayer ;
Or, worn upon some maiden breast,
Stirs with the loving heart's unrest !

A bitter cup each life must drain,
The groaning earth is cursed with pain,
And, like the scroll the angel bore
The shuddering Hebrew seer before,

O'erwrit alike, without, within,
With all the woes which follow sin ;
But, bitterest of the ills beneath
Whose load man totters down to death,
Is that which plucks the regal crown
Of Freedom from his forehead down,
And snatches from his powerless hand
The sceptred sign of self-command,
Effacing with the chain and rod
The image and the seal of God ;
Till from his nature, day by day,
The manly virtues fall away,
And leave him naked, blind and mute,
The godlike merging in the brute !

Why mourn the quiet ones who die
Beneath affection's tender eye,
Unto their household and their kin
Like ripened corn-sheaves gathered in ?
O weeper, from that tranquil sod,
That holy harvest-home of God,
Turn to the quick and suffering, shed
Thy tears upon the living dead !
Thank God above thy dear ones' graves,
They sleep with Him, they are not slaves.

What dark mass, down the mountain-sides
Swift-pouring, like a stream divides ?
A long, loose, straggling caravan,
Camel and horse and arméd man.
The moon's low crescent, glimmering o'er
Its grave of waters to the shore,
Lights up that mountain cavalcade,
And gleams from gun and spear and blade
Near and more near ! now o'er them falls
The shadow of the city walls.
Hark to the sentry's challenge, drowned
In the fierce trumpet's charging sound !
The rush of men, the musket's peal,
The short, sharp clang of meeting steel !

Vain, Moslem, vain thy lifeblood poured
So freely on thy foeman's sword !
Not to the swift nor to the strong
The battles of the right belong ;
For he who strikes for Freedom wears
The armor of the captive's prayers,
And Nature proffers to his cause
The strength of her eternal laws ;
While he whose arm essays to bind
And herd with common brutes his kind
Strives evermore at fearful odds
With Nature and the jealous gods,
And dares the dread recoil which late
Or soon their right shall vindicate.

'T is done, the hornëd crescent falls !
The star-flag flouts the broken walls !
Joy to the captive husband ! joy
To thy sick heart, O brown-locked boy !
In sullen wrath the conquered Moor
Wide open flings your dungeon-door,
And leaves ye free from cell and chain,
The owners of yourselves again.
Dark as his allies desert-born,
Soiled with the battle's stain, and worn
With the long marches of his band
Through hottest wastes of rock and sand,
Scorched by the sun and furnace-breath
Of the red desert's wind of death,
With welcome words and grasping hands,
The victor and deliverer stands !

The tale is one of distant skies ;
The dust of half a century lies
Upon it ; yet its hero's name
Still lingers on the lips of Fame.
Men speak the praise of him who gave
Deliverance to the Moorman's slave,
Yet dare to brand with shame and crime
The heroes of our land and time, —
The self-forgetful ones, who stake
Home, name, and life for Freedom's sake.
God mend his heart who cannot feel
The impulse of a holy zeal,
And sees not, with his sordid eyes,
The beauty of self-sacrifice !
Though in the sacred place he stands,
Uplifting consecrated hands,
Unworthy are his lips to tell
Of Jesus' martyr-miracle,
Or name aright that dread embrace
Of suffering for a fallen race !

A SABBATH SCENE

This poem finds its justification in the readiness with which, even in the North, clergymen urged the prompt execution of the Fugitive Slave Law as a Christian duty, and defended the system of slavery as a Bible institution.

SCARCE had the solemn Sabbath-bell
  Ceased quivering in the steeple,
Scarce had the parson to his desk
  Walked stately through his people,

When down the summer-shaded street
  A wasted female figure,
With dusky brow and naked feet,
  Came rushing wild and eager.

She saw the white spire through the trees,
  She heard the sweet hymn swelling :
O pitying Christ ! a refuge give
  That poor one in Thy dwelling !

Like a scared fawn before the hounds,
  Right up the aisle she glided,
While close behind her, whip in hand,
  A lank-haired hunter strided.

She raised a keen and bitter cry,
  To Heaven and Earth appealing ;
Were manhood's generous pulses dead ?
  Had woman's heart no feeling ?

A score of stout hands rose between
  The hunter and the flying :
Age clenched his staff, and maiden eyes
  Flashed tearful, yet defying.

" Who dares profane this house and day ? "
  Cried out the angry pastor.
" Why, bless your soul, the wench 's a slave,
  And I 'm her lord and master !

" I 've law and gospel on my side,
  And who shall dare refuse me ? "
Down came the parson, bowing low,
  " My good sir, pray excuse me !

" Of course I know your right divine
  To own and work and whip her ;
Quick, deacon, throw that Polyglott
  Before the wench, and trip her ! "

Plump dropped the holy tome, and o'er
  Its sacred pages stumbling,
Bound hand and foot, a slave once more,
  The hapless wretch lay trembling.

I saw the parson tie the knots,
  The while his flock addressing,
The Scriptural claims of slavery
  With text on text impressing.

" Although," said he, " on Sabbath day
  All secular occupations
Are deadly sins, we must fulfil
  Our moral obligations :

"And this commends itself as one
  To every conscience tender ;
As Paul sent back Onesimus,
  My Christian friends, we send her ! "

Shriek rose on shriek, — the Sabbath air
    Her wild cries tore asunder ;
I listened, with hushed breath, to hear
    God answering with his thunder !

All still ! the very altar's cloth
    Had smothered down her shrieking,
And, dumb, she turned from face to face,
    For human pity seeking !

I saw her dragged along the aisle,
    Her shackles harshly clanking ;
I heard the parson, over all,
    The Lord devoutly thanking !

My brain took fire : " Is this," I cried,
    " The end of prayer and preaching ?
Then down with pulpit, down with priest,
    And give us Nature's teaching !

" Foul shame and scorn be on ye all
    Who turn the good to evil,
And steal the Bible from the Lord,
    To give it to the Devil !

" Than garbled text or parchment law
    I own a statute higher ;
And God is true, though every book
    And every man 's a liar ! "

Just then I felt the deacon's hand
    In wrath my coat-tail seize on ;
I heard the priest cry, " Infidel ! "
    The lawyer mutter, " Treason ! "

I started up, — where now were church,
    Slave, master, priest, and people ?
I only heard the supper-bell,
    Instead of clanging steeple.

But, on the open window's sill,
    O'er which the white blooms drifted,
The pages of a good old Book
    The wind of summer lifted,

And flower and vine, like angel wings
    Around the Holy Mother,
Waved softly there, as if God's truth
    And Mercy kissed each other.

And freely from the cherry-bough
    Above the casement swinging,
With golden bosom to the sun,
    The oriole was singing.

As bird and flower made plain of old
    The lesson of the Teacher,
So now I heard the written Word
    Interpreted by Nature !

For to my ear methought the breeze
    Bore Freedom's blessed word on ;
Thus saith the Lord : Break every yoke,
    Undo the heavy burden !

IN THE EVIL DAYS

This and the four following poems have
special reference to that darkest hour in the
aggression of slavery which preceded the dawn
of a better day, when the conscience of the
people was roused to action.   [Originally en-
titled *Stanzas for the Times*, 1850.]

THE evil days have come, the poor
    Are made a prey ;
Bar up the hospitable door,
Put out the fire-lights, point no more
    The wanderer's way.

For Pity now is crime ; the chain
    Which binds our States
Is melted at her hearth in twain,
Is rusted by her tears' soft rain :
    Close up her gates.

Our Union, like a glacier stirred
    By voice below,
Or bell of kine, or wing of bird,
A beggar's crust, a kindly word
    May overthrow !

Poor, whispering tremblers ! yet we boast
    Our blood and name ;
Bursting its century-bolted frost,
Each gray cairn on the Northman's coast
    Cries out for shame !

Oh for the open firmament,
    The prairie free,
The desert hillside, cavern-rent,
The Pawnee's lodge, the Arab's tent,
    The Bushman's tree !

Than web of Persian loom most rare,
    Or soft divan,
Better the rough rock, bleak and bare,
Or hollow tree, which man may share
    With suffering man.

I hear a voice : "Thus saith the Law,
　　Let Love be dumb ;
Clasping her liberal hands in awe,
Let sweet-lipped Charity withdraw
　　From hearth and home."

I hear another voice : "The poor
　　Are thine to feed ;
Turn not the outcast from thy door,
Nor give to bonds and wrong once more
　　Whom God hath freed."

Dear Lord ! between that law and Thee
　　No choice remains ;
Yet not untrue to man's decree,
Though spurning its rewards, is he
　　Who bears its pains.

Not mine Sedition's trumpet-blast
　　And threatening word ;
I read the lesson of the Past,
That firm endurance wins at last
　　More than the sword.

O clear-eyed Faith, and Patience thou
　　So calm and strong !
Lend strength to weakness, teach us how
The sleepless eyes of God look through
　　This night of wrong !

MOLOCH IN STATE STREET

In a foot-note of the Report of the Senate of
Massachusetts on the case of the arrest and
return to bondage of the fugitive slave Thomas
Sims it is stated that—
"It would have been impossible for the
U. S. marshal thus successfully to have resisted
the law of the State, without the assistance
of the municipal authorities of Boston, and
the countenance and support of a numerous,
wealthy, and powerful body of citizens. It was
in evidence that 1500 of the most wealthy and
respectable citizens — merchants, bankers, and
others — volunteered their services to aid the
marshal on this occasion. . . . No watch was
kept upon the doings of the marshal, and while
the State officers slept, after the moon had
gone down, in the darkest hour before day-
break, the accused was taken out of our juris-
diction by the armed police of the city of
Boston."

THE moon has set : while yet the dawn
　　Breaks cold and gray,
Between the midnight and the morn
　　Bear off your prey !

On, swift and still ! the conscious street
　　Is panged and stirred ;
Tread light ! that fall of serried feet
　　The dead have heard !

The first drawn blood of Freedom's veins
　　Gushed where ye tread ;
Lo ! through the dusk the martyr-stains
　　Blush darkly red !

Beneath the slowly-waning stars
　　And whitening day,
What stern and awful presence bars
　　That sacred way ?

What faces frown upon ye, dark
　　With shame and pain ?
Come these from Plymouth's Pilgrim bark ?
　　Is that young Vane ?

Who, dimly beckoning, speed ye on
　　With mocking cheer ?
Lo ! spectral Andros, Hutchinson,
　　And Gage are here !

For ready mart or favoring blast
　　Through Moloch's fire,
Flesh of his flesh, unsparing, passed
　　The Tyrian sire.

Ye make that ancient sacrifice
　　Of Man to Gain,
Your traffic thrives, where Freedom dies,
　　Beneath the chain.

Ye sow to-day ; your harvest, scorn
　　And hate, is near ;
How think ye freemen, mountain-born,
　　The tale will hear ?

Thank God ! our mother State can yet
　　Her fame retrieve ;
To you and to your children let
　　The scandal cleave.

Chain Hall and Pulpit, Court and Press,
　　Make gods of gold ;
Let honor, truth, and manliness
　　Like wares be sold.

Your hoards are great, your walls are
　　strong,
　　But God is just ;
The gilded chambers built by wrong
　　Invite the rust.

What ! know ye not the gains of Crime
　Are dust and dross ;
Its ventures on the waves of time
　Foredoomed to loss !

And still the Pilgrim State remains
　What she hath been ;
Her inland hills, her seaward plains,
　Still nurture men !

Nor wholly lost the fallen mart ;
　Her olden blood
Through many a free and generous heart
　Still pours its flood.

That brave old blood, quick-flowing yet,
　Shall know no check,
Till a free people's foot is set
　On Slavery's neck.

Even now, the peal of bell and gun,
　And hills aflame,
Tell of the first great triumph won
　In Freedom's name.

The long night dies : the welcome gray
　Of dawn we see ;
Speed up the heavens thy perfect day,
　God of the free !

OFFICIAL PIETY

Suggested by reading a state paper, wherein the higher law is invoked to sustain the lower one. [Originally entitled *Lines.*]

A PIOUS magistrate ! sound his praise
　　throughout
The wondering churches. Who shall hence-
　forth doubt
　That the long-wished millennium draw-
　　eth nigh ?
Sin in high places has become devout,
　Tithes mint, goes painful - faced, and
　　prays its lie
Straight up to Heaven, and calls it piety !

The pirate, watching from his bloody deck
　The weltering galleon, heavy with the
　　gold
Of Acapulco, holding death in check
　While prayers are said, brows crossed,
　　and beads are told ;
The robber, kneeling where the wayside
　cross

On dark Abruzzo tells of life's dread loss
From his own carbine, glancing still abroad
For some new victim, offering thanks to
　　God !
　Rome, listening at her altars to the cry
Of midnight Murder, while her hounds of
　　hell
Scour France, from baptized cannon and
　　holy bell
　And thousand-throated priesthood, loud
　　and high,
　Pealing Te Deums to the shuddering sky,
　"Thanks to the Lord, who giveth vic-
　　tory ! "
What prove these, but that crime was ne'er
　　so black
As ghostly cheer and pious thanks to lack ?
Satan is modest.　At Heaven's door he
　　lays
His evil offspring, and, in Scriptural phrase
And saintly posture, gives to God the praise
And honor of the monstrous progeny.
What marvel, then, in our own time to
　　see
His old devices, smoothly acted o'er, —
Official piety, locking fast the door
Of Hope against three million souls of
　　men, —
Brothers, God's children, Christ's re-
　　deemed, — and then,
With uprolled eyeballs and on bended knee,
Whining a prayer for help to hide the key !

THE RENDITION

On the 2d of June, 1854, Anthony Burns, a fugitive slave from Virginia, after being under arrest for ten days in the Boston Court House, was remanded to slavery under the Fugitive Slave Act, and taken down State Street to a steamer chartered by the United States Government, under guard of United States troops and artillery, Massachusetts militia and Boston police.　Public excitement ran high, a futile attempt to rescue Burns having been made during his confinement, and the streets were crowded with tens of thousands of people, of whom many came from other towns and cities of the State to witness the humiliating spec-tacle.

I HEARD the train's shrill whistle call,
　I saw an earnest look beseech,
　And rather by that look than speech
My neighbor told me all.

And, as I thought of Liberty
　　Marched handcuffed down that sworded
　　　　street,
The solid earth beneath my feet
Reeled fluid as the sea.

I felt a sense of bitter loss, —
　　Shame, tearless grief, and stifling wrath,
　　And loathing fear, as if my path
A serpent stretched across.

All love of home, all pride of place,
　　All generous confidence and trust,
　　Sank smothering in that deep disgust
And anguish of disgrace.

Down on my native hills of June,
　　And home's green quiet, hiding all,
　　Fell sudden darkness like the fall
Of midnight upon noon !

And Law, an unloosed maniac, strong,
　　Blood - drunken, through the blackness
　　　　trod,
　　Hoarse-shouting in the ear of God
The blasphemy of wrong.

"O Mother, from thy memories proud,
　　Thy old renown, dear Commonwealth,
　　Lend this dead air a breeze of health,
And smite with stars this cloud.

"Mother of Freedom, wise and brave,
　　Rise awful in thy strength," I said ;
　　Ah me ! I spake but to the dead ;
I stood upon her grave !

ARISEN AT LAST

On the passage of the bill to protect the
rights and liberties of the people of the State
against the Fugitive Slave Act. [Originally
entitled simply *Lines*.]

I said I stood upon thy grave,
　　My Mother State, when last the moon
　　Of blossoms clomb the skies of June.

And, scattering ashes on my head,
　　I wore, undreaming of relief,
　　The sackcloth of thy shame and grief.

Again that moon of blossoms shines
　　On leaf and flower and folded wing,
　　And thou hast risen with the spring !

Once more thy strong maternal arms
　　Are round about thy children flung, —
　　A lioness that guards her young !

No threat is on thy closèd lips,
　　But in thine eye a power to smite
　　The mad wolf backward from its light.

Southward the baffled robber's track
　　Henceforth runs only ; hereaway,
　　The fell lycanthrope finds no prey.

Henceforth, within thy sacred gates,
　　His first low howl shall downward draw
　　The thunder of thy righteous law.

Not mindless of thy trade and gain,
　　But, acting on the wiser plan,
　　Thou 'rt grown conservative of man.

So shalt thou clothe with life the hope,
　　Dream-painted on the sightless eyes
　　Of him who sang of Paradise, —

The vision of a Christian man,
　　In virtue, as in stature great
　　Embodied in a Christian State.

And thou, amidst thy sisterhood
　　Forbearing long, yet standing fast,
　　Shalt win their grateful thanks at last ;

When North and South shall strive no
　　　　more,
　　And all their feuds and fears be lost
　　In Freedom's holy Pentecost.

THE HASCHISH

Of all that Orient lands can vaunt
　　Of marvels with our own competing,
The strangest is the Haschish plant,
　　And what will follow on its eating.

What pictures to the taster rise,
　　Of Dervish or of Almeh dances !
Of Eblis, or of Paradise,
　　Set all aglow with Houri glances !

The poppy visions of Cathay,
　　The heavy beer-trance of the Suabian ;
The wizard lights and demon play
　　Of nights Walpurgis and Arabian !

The Mollah and the Christian dog
  Change place in mad metempsychosis ;
The Muezzin climbs the synagogue,
  The Rabbi shakes his beard at Moses !

The Arab by his desert well
  Sits choosing from some Caliph's daughters,
And hears his single camel's bell
  Sound welcome to his regal quarters.

The Koran's reader makes complaint
  Of Shitan dancing on and off it ;
The robber offers alms, the saint
  Drinks Tokay and blasphemes the Prophet.

Such scenes that Eastern plant awakes ;
  But we have one ordained to beat it,
The Haschish of the West, which makes
  Or fools or knaves of all who eat it.

The preacher eats, and straight appears
  His Bible in a new translation ;
Its angels negro overseers,
  And Heaven itself a snug plantation !

The man of peace, about whose dreams
  The sweet millennial angels cluster,
Tastes the mad weed, and plots and schemes,
  A raving Cuban filibuster !

The noisiest Democrat, with ease,
  It turns to Slavery's parish beadle ;
The shrewdest statesman eats and sees
  Due southward point the polar needle.

The Judge partakes, and sits erelong
  Upon his bench a railing blackguard ;
Decides off-hand that right is wrong,
  And reads the ten commandments backward.

O potent plant ! so rare a taste
  Has never Turk or Gentoo gotten ;
The hempen Haschish of the East
  Is powerless to our Western Cotton !

THE KANSAS EMIGRANTS

This poem and the three following were called out by the popular movement of Free State men to occupy the territory of Kansas, and by the use of the great democratic weapon — an overpowering majority — to settle the conflict on that ground between Freedom and Slavery. The opponents of the movement used another kind of weapon. [This song was sent to the first company of emigrants by the poet. "It is one of those prophecies," says E. E. Hale, "for which poets are born, uttered before the event and not after. In absolute hard fact, the song was sung by parties of emigrants, sung when they started, sung as they rode, and sung in the new home."]

WE cross the prairie as of old
  The pilgrims crossed the sea,
To make the West, as they the East,
  The homestead of the free !

We go to rear a wall of men
  On Freedom's southern line,
And plant beside the cotton-tree
  The rugged Northern pine !

We 're flowing from our native hills
  As our free rivers flow :
The blessing of our Mother-land
  Is on us as we go.

We go to plant her common schools
  On distant prairie swells,
And give the Sabbaths of the wild
  The music of her bells.

Upbearing, like the Ark of old,
  The Bible in our van,
We go to test the truth of God
  Against the fraud of man.

No pause, nor rest, save where the streams
  That feed the Kansas run,
Save where our Pilgrim gonfalon
  Shall flout the setting sun !

We 'll tread the prairie as of old
  Our fathers sailed the sea,
And make the West, as they the East,
  The homestead of the free !

FOR RIGHTEOUSNESS' SAKE

Inscribed to friends under arrest for treason against the slave power. [Originally entitled *Lines.*]

THE age is dull and mean. Men creep,
  Not walk ; with blood too pale and tame
  To pay the debt they owe to shame ;
Buy cheap, sell dear ; eat, drink, and sleep

Down-pillowed, deaf to moaning want ;
Pay tithes for soul-insurance ; keep
Six days to Mammon, one to Cant.

In such a time, give thanks to God,
    That somewhat of the holy rage
    With which the prophets in their age
On all its decent seemings trod,
    Has set your feet upon the lie,
That man and ox and soul and clod
    Are market stock to sell and buy !

The hot words from your lips, my own,
    To caution trained, might not repeat ;
    But if some tares among the wheat
Of generous thought and deed were sown,
    No common wrong provoked your zeal ;
The silken gauntlet that is thrown
    In such a quarrel rings like steel.

The brave old strife the fathers saw
    For Freedom calls for men again
    Like those who battled not in vain
For England's Charter, Alfred's law ;
    And right of speech and trial just
Wage in your name their ancient war
    With venal courts and perjured trust.

God's ways seem dark, but, soon or late,
    They touch the shining hills of day ;
    The evil cannot brook delay,
The good can well afford to wait.
    Give ermined knaves their hour of crime ;
Ye have the future grand and great,
    The safe appeal of Truth to Time !

LETTER

FROM A MISSIONARY OF THE METHO-
DIST EPISCOPAL CHURCH SOUTH, IN
KANSAS, TO A DISTINGUISHED POLI-
TICIAN

DOUGLAS MISSION, *August*, 1854.

LAST week — the Lord be praised for
    all His mercies
To His unworthy servant ! — I arrived
Safe at the Mission, via Westport where
I tarried over night, to aid in forming
A Vigilance Committee, to send back,
In shirts of tar, and feather-doublets
    quilted
With forty stripes save one, all Yankee
    comers,

Uncircumcised and Gentile, aliens from
The Commonwealth of Israel, who despise
The prize of the high calling of the saints,
Who plant amidst this heathen wilderness
Pure gospel institutions, sanctified
By patriarchal use. The meeting opened
With prayer, as was most fitting. Half
    an hour,
Or thereaway, I groaned, and strove, and
    wrestled,
As Jacob did at Penuel, till the power
Fell on the people, and they cried
    " Amen ! "
" Glory to God ! " and stamped and
    clapped their hands ;
And the rough river boatmen wiped their
    eyes ;
" Go it, old hoss ! " they cried, and cursed
    the niggers —
Fulfilling thus the word of prophecy,
" Cursëd be Canaan." After prayer, the
    meeting
Chose a committee — good and pious
    men —
A Presbyterian Elder, Baptist deacon,
A local preacher, three or four class-leaders,
Anxious inquirers, and renewed back-
    sliders,
A score in all — to watch the river ferry,
(As they of old did watch the fords of
    Jordan,)
And cut off all whose Yankee tongues re-
    fuse
The Shibboleth of the Nebraska bill.
And then, in answer to repeated calls,
I gave a brief account of what I saw
In Washington ; and truly many hearts
Rejoiced to know the President, and you
And all the Cabinet regularly hear
The gospel message of a Sunday morning,
Drinking with thirsty souls of the sincere
Milk of the Word. Glory ! Amen, and
    Selah !

Here, at the Mission, all things have
    gone well :
The brother who, throughout my absence,
    acted
As overseer, assures me that the crops
Never were better. I have lost one negro,
A first-rate hand, but obstinate and sullen.
He ran away some time last spring, and
    hid
In the river timber. There my Indian
    converts

Found him, and treed and shot him. For
    the rest,
The heathens round about begin to feel
The influence of our pious ministrations
And works of love ; and some of them al-
    ready
Have purchased negroes, and are settling
    down
As sober Christians ! Bless the Lord for
    this !
I know it will rejoice you. You, I hear,
Are on the eve of visiting Chicago,
To fight with the wild beasts of Ephesus,
Long John, and Dutch Free-Soilers. May
    your arm
Be clothed with strength, and on your
    tongue be found
The sweet oil of persuasion. So desires
Your brother and co-laborer. Amen !

    P. S. All 's lost. Even while I write
    these lines,
The Yankee abolitionists are coming
Upon us like a flood — grim, stalwart men,
Each face set like a flint of Plymouth Rock
Against our institutions — staking out
Their farm lots on the wooded Wakarusa,
Or squatting by the mellow - bottomed
    Kansas ;
The pioneers of mightier multitudes,
The small rain - patter, ere the thunder
    shower
Drowns the dry prairies. Hope from man
    is not.
Oh, for a quiet berth at Washington,
Snug naval chaplaincy, or clerkship, where
These rumors of free labor and free soil
Might never meet me more.   Better to be
Door-keeper in the White House, than to
    dwell
Amidst these Yankee tents, that, whiten-
    ing, show
On the green prairie like a fleet becalmed.
Methinks I hear a voice come up the river
From those far bayous where the alligators
Mount guard around the camping filibus-
    ters :
" Shake off the dust of Kansas. Turn to
    Cuba —
(That golden orange just about to fall,
O'er-ripe, into the Democratic lap ;)
Keep pace with Providence, or, as we say,
Manifest destiny. Go forth and follow
The message of *our* gospel, thither borne
Upon the point of Quitman's bowie knife,

And the persuasive lips of Colt's revolvers.
There may'st thou, underneath thy vine
    and fig-tree,
Watch thy increase of sugar cane and ne-
    groes,
Calm as a patriarch in his eastern tent ! "
Amen : So mote it be. So prays your
    friend.

BURIAL OF BARBER

Thomas Barber was shot December 6, 1855,
near Lawrence, Kansas.

BEAR him, comrades, to his grave ;
Never over one more brave
    Shall the prairie grasses weep,
In the ages yet to come,
When the millions in our room,
    What we sow in tears, shall reap.

Bear him up the icy hill,
With the Kansas, frozen still
    As his noble heart, below,
And the land he came to till
With a freeman's thews and will,
    And his poor hut roofed with snow !

One more look of that dead face,
Of his murder's ghastly trace !
    One more kiss, O widowed one !
Lay your left hands on his brow,
Lift your right hands up, and vow
    That his work shall yet be done.

Patience, friends ! The eye of God
Every path by Murder trod
    Watches, lidless, day and night ;
And the dead man in his shroud,
And his widow weeping loud,
    And our hearts, are in His sight.

Every deadly threat that swells
With the roar of gambling hells,
    Every brutal jest and jeer,
Every wicked thought and plan
Of the cruel heart of man,
    Though but whispered, He can hear !

We in suffering, they in crime,
Wait the just award of time,
    Wait the vengeance that is due ;
Not in vain a heart shall break,
Not a tear for Freedom's sake
    Fall unheeded : God is true.

While the flag with stars bedecked
Threatens where it should protect,
  And the Law shakes hands with Crime,
What is left us but to wait,
Match our patience to our fate,
  And abide the better time ?

Patience, friends ! The human heart
Everywhere shall take our part,
  Everywhere for us shall pray ;
On our side are nature's laws,
And God's life is in the cause
  That we suffer for to-day.

Well to suffer is divine ;
Pass the watchword down the line,
  Pass the countersign : "Endure."
Not to him who rashly dares,
But to him who nobly bears,
  Is the victor's garland sure.

Frozen earth to frozen breast,
Lay our slain one down to rest ;
  Lay him down in hope and faith,
And above the broken sod,
Once again, to Freedom's God,
  Pledge ourselves for life or death,

That the State whose walls we lay,
In our blood and tears, to-day,
  Shall be free from bonds of shame,
And our goodly land untrod
By the feet of Slavery, shod
  With cursing as with flame !

Plant the Buckeye on his grave,
For the hunter of the slave
  In its shadow cannot rest ;
And let martyr mound and tree
Be our pledge and guaranty
  Of the freedom of the West !

TO PENNSYLVANIA

O STATE prayer-founded ! never hung
Such choice upon a people's tongue,
  Such power to bless or ban,
As that which makes thy whisper Fate,
For which on thee the centuries wait,
  And destinies of man !

Across thy Alleghanian chain,
With groanings from a land in pain,
  The west-wind finds its way :

Wild-wailing from Missouri's flood
The crying of thy children's blood
  Is in thy ears to-day !

And unto thee in Freedom's hour
Of sorest need God gives the power
  To ruin or to save ;
To wound or heal, to blight or bless
With fertile field or wilderness,
  A free home or a grave !

Then let thy virtue match the crime,
Rise to a level with the time ;
  And, if a son of thine
Betray or tempt thee, Brutus-like
For Fatherland and Freedom strike
  As Justice gives the sign.

Wake, sleeper, from thy dream of ease,
The great occasion's forelock seize ;
  And let the north-wind strong,
And golden leaves of autumn, be
Thy coronal of Victory
  And thy triumphal song.

LE MARAIS DU CYGNE

The massacre of unarmed and unoffending
men, in Southern Kansas, in May, 1858, took
place near the Marais du Cygne of the French
voyageurs.

A BLUSH as of roses
  Where rose never grew !
Great drops on the bunch-grass,
  But not of the dew !
A taint in the sweet air
  For wild bees to shun !
A stain that shall never
  Bleach out in the sun !

Back, steed of the prairies !
  Sweet song-bird, fly back !
Wheel hither, bald vulture !
  Gray wolf, call thy pack !
The foul human vultures
  Have feasted and fled ;
The wolves of the Border
  Have crept from the dead.

From the hearths of their cabins,
  The fields of their corn,
Unwarned and unweaponed,
  The victims were torn, —

By the whirlwind of murder
  Swooped up and swept on
To the low, reedy fen-lands,
  The Marsh of the Swan.

With a vain plea for mercy
  No stout knee was crooked ;
In the mouths of the rifles
  Right manly they looked.
How paled the May sunshine,
  O Marais du Cygne !
On death for the strong life,
  On red grass for green !

In the homes of their rearing,
  Yet warm with their lives,
Ye wait the dead only,
  Poor children and wives !
Put out the red forge-fire,
  The smith shall not come ;
Unyoke the brown oxen,
  The ploughman lies dumb.

Wind slow from the Swan's Marsh,
  O dreary death-train,
With pressed lips as bloodless
  As lips of the slain !
Kiss down the young eyelids,
  Smooth down the gray hairs ;
Let tears quench the curses
  That burn through your prayers.

Strong man of the prairies,
  Mourn bitter and wild !
Wail, desolate woman !
  Weep, fatherless child !
But the grain of God springs up
  From ashes beneath,
And the crown of his harvest
  Is life out of death.

Not in vain on the dial
  The shade moves along,
To point the great contrasts
  Of right and of wrong :
Free homes and free altars,
  Free prairie and flood, —
The reeds of the Swan's Marsh,
  Whose bloom is of blood !

On the lintels of Kansas
  That blood shall not dry ;
Henceforth the Bad Angel
  Shall harmless go by ;

Henceforth to the sunset,
  Unchecked on her way,
Shall Liberty follow
  The march of the day.

THE PASS OF THE SIERRA

ALL night above their rocky bed
  They saw the stars march slow ;
The wild Sierra overhead,
  The desert's death below.

The Indian from his lodge of bark,
  The gray bear from his den,
Beyond their camp-fire's wall of dark,
  Glared on the mountain men.

Still upward turned, with anxious strain,
  Their leader's sleepless eye,
Where splinters of the mountain chain
  Stood black against the sky.

The night waned slow : at last, a glow,
  A gleam of sudden fire,
Shot up behind the walls of snow,
  And tipped each icy spire.

"Up, men !" he cried, " yon rocky cone,
  To-day, please God, we'll pass,
And look from Winter's frozen throne
  On Summer's flowers and grass ! "

They set their faces to the blast,
  They trod the eternal snow,
And faint, worn, bleeding, hailed at last
  The promised land below.

Behind, they saw the snow-cloud tossed
  By many an icy horn ;
Before, warm valleys, wood-embossed,
  And green with vines and corn.

They left the Winter at their backs
  To flap his baffled wing,
And downward, with the cataracts,
  Leaped to the lap of Spring.

Strong leader of that mountain band,
  Another task remains,
To break from Slavery's desert land
  A path to Freedom's plains.

The winds are wild, the way is drear,
  Yet, flashing through the night,

Lo ! icy ridge and rocky spear
  Blaze out in morning light !

Rise up, Frémont, and go before ;
  The Hour must have its Man ;
Put on the hunting-shirt once more,
  And lead in Freedom's van !

A SONG FOR THE TIME

Written in the summer of 1856, during the
political campaign of the Free Soil party under
the candidacy of John C. Frémont.

Up, laggards of Freedom ! — our free flag
    is cast
To the blaze of the sun and the wings of
    the blast ;
Will ye turn from a struggle so bravely
    begun,
From a foe that is breaking, a field that's
    half won ?

Whoso loves not his kind, and who fears
    not the Lord,
Let him join that foe's service, accursed and
    abhorred !
Let him do his base will, as the slave only
    can, —
Let him put on the bloodhound, and put off
    the Man !

Let him go where the cold blood that creeps
    in his veins
Shall stiffen the slave-whip, and rust on his
    chains ;
Where the black slave shall laugh in his
    bonds, to behold
The White Slave beside him, self-fettered
    and sold !

But ye, who still boast of hearts beating
    and warm,
Rise, from lake shore and ocean's, like
    waves in a storm,
Come, throng round our banner in Liberty's
    name,
Like winds from your mountains, like prai-
    ries aflame !

Our foe, hidden long in his ambush of night,
Now, forced from his covert, stands black
    in the light.

Oh, the cruel to Man, and the hateful to
    God,
Smite him down to the earth, that is cursed
    where he trod !

For deeper than thunder of summer's loud
    shower,
On the dome of the sky God is striking the
    hour !
Shall we falter before what we've prayed
    for so long,
When the Wrong is so weak, and the Right
    is so strong ?

Come forth all together ! come old and come
    young,
Freedom's vote in each hand, and her song
    on each tongue ;
Truth naked is stronger than Falsehood in
    mail ;
The Wrong cannot prosper, the Right can-
    not fail !

Like leaves of the summer once numbered
    the foe,
But the hoar-frost is falling, the northern
    winds blow ;
Like leaves of November erelong shall they
    fall,
For earth wearies of them, and God's over
    all !

WHAT OF THE DAY?

Written during the stirring weeks when the
great political battle for Freedom under Fré-
mont's leadership was permitting strong hope
of success, — a hope overshadowed and solem-
nized by a sense of the magnitude of the bar-
baric evil, and a forecast of the unscrupulous
and desperate use of all its powers in the last
and decisive struggle.

A sound of tumult troubles all the air,
  Like the low thunders of a sultry sky
Far-rolling ere the downright lightnings
    glare ;
  The hills blaze red with warnings ; foes
    draw nigh,
  Treading the dark with challenge and
    reply.
Behold the burden of the prophet's vision ;
The gathering hosts, — the Valley of Deci-
    sion,

Dusk with the wings of eagles wheeling
o'er.
Day of the Lord, of darkness and not
light!
It breaks in thunder and the whirlwind's
roar!
Even so, Father! Let Thy will be done;
Turn and o'erturn, end what Thou hast be-
gun
In judgment or in mercy: as for me,
If but the least and frailest, let me be
Evermore numbered with the truly free
Who find Thy service perfect liberty!
I fain would thank Thee that my mortal
life
Has reached the hour (albeit through care
and pain)
When Good and Evil, as for final strife,
Close dim and vast on Armageddon's
plain;
And Michael and his angels once again
Drive howling back the Spirits of the
Night.
Oh for the faith to read the signs aright
And, from the angle of Thy perfect sight,
See Truth's white banner floating on be-
fore;
And the Good Cause, despite of venal
friends,
And base expedients, move to noble ends;
See Peace with Freedom make to Time
amends,
And, through its cloud of dust, the thresh-
ing-floor,
Flailed by the thunder, heaped with
chaffless grain!

A SONG

INSCRIBED TO THE FRÉMONT CLUBS

Written after the election in 1856, which
showed the immense gains of the Free Soil
party, and insured its success in 1860.

BENEATH thy skies, November!
Thy skies of cloud and rain,
Around our blazing camp-fires
We close our ranks again.
Then sound again the bugles,
Call the muster-roll anew;
If months have well-nigh won the field,
What may not four years do?

For God be praised! New England
Takes once more her ancient place;
Again the Pilgrim's banner
Leads the vanguard of the race.
Then sound again the bugles, etc.

Along the lordly Hudson,
A shout of triumph breaks;
The Empire State is speaking,
From the ocean to the lakes.
Then sound again the bugles, etc.

The Northern hills are blazing,
The Northern skies are bright;
And the fair young West is turning
Her forehead to the light!
Then sound again the bugles, etc.

Push every outpost nearer,
Press hard the hostile towers!
Another Balaklava,
And the Malakoff is ours!
Then sound again the bugles,
Call the muster-roll anew;
If months have well-nigh won the field,
What may not four years do?

THE PANORAMA

[Written with a view to political effect in
the Presidential campaign of 1856. It was
read by T. Starr King at the opening of a
course of lectures on slavery delivered in Bos-
ton at that time.]

"A! fredome is a nobill thing!
Fredome mayse man to haif liking.
Fredome all solace to man giffis;
He levys at ese that frely levys!
A nobil hart may haif nane ese
Na ellys nocht that may him plese
Gyff Fredome failythe."
ARCHDEACON BARBOUR.

THROUGH the long hall the shuttered
windows shed
A dubious light on every upturned head;
On locks like those of Absalom the fair,
On the bald apex ringed with scanty hair,
On blank indifference and on curious stare;
On the pale Showman reading from his
stage
The hieroglyphics of that facial page;
Half sad, half scornful, listening to the
bruit
Of restless cane-tap and impatient foot,

And the shrill call, across the general din,
"Roll up your curtain! Let the show begin!"

At length a murmur like the winds that
break
Into green waves the prairie's grassy lake,
Deepened and swelled to music clear and
loud,
And, as the west-wind lifts a summer cloud,
The curtain rose, disclosing wide and far
A green land stretching to the evening star,
Fair rivers, skirted by primeval trees
And flowers hummed over by the desert
bees,
Marked by tall bluffs whose slopes of green-
ness show
Fantastic outcrops of the rock below ;
The slow result of patient Nature's pains,
And plastic fingering of her sun and rains ;
Arch, tower, and gate, grotesquely win-
dowed hall,
And long escarpment of half - crumbled
wall,
Huger than those which, from steep hills
of vine,
Stare through their loopholes on the trav-
elled Rhine ;
Suggesting vaguely to the gazer's mind
A fancy, idle as the prairie wind,
Of the land's dwellers in an age unguessed ;
The unsung Jotuns of the mystic West.

Beyond, the prairie's sea-like swells sur-
pass
The Tartar's marvels of his Land of Grass,
Vast as the sky against whose sunset shores
Wave after wave the billowy greenness
pours ;
And, onward still, like islands in that
main
Loom the rough peaks of many a mountain
chain,
Whence east and west a thousand waters
run
From winter lingering under summer's sun.
And, still beyond, long lines of foam and
sand
Tell where Pacific rolls his waves a-land,
From many a wide-lapped port and land-
locked bay,
Opening with thunderous pomp the world's
highway
To Indian isles of spice, and marts of far
Cathay.

"Such," said the Showman, as the cur-
tain fell,
"Is the new Canaan of our Israel ;
The land of promise to the swarming North
Which, hive-like, sends its annual surplus
forth,
To the poor Southron on his worn-out soil,
Scathed by the curses of unnatural toil ;
To Europe's exiles seeking home and rest,
And the lank nomads of the wandering
West,
Who, asking neither, in their love of change
And the free bison's amplitude of range,
Rear the log-hut, for present shelter meant,
Not future comfort, like an Arab's tent."

Then spake a shrewd on-looker, "Sir,"
said he,
"I like your picture, but I fain would see
A sketch of what your promised land will
be
When, with electric nerve and fiery-brained,
With Nature's forces to its chariot chained,
The future grasping, by the past obeyed,
The twentieth century rounds a new de-
cade."

Then said the Showman, sadly : "He
who grieves
Over the scattering of the sibyl's leaves
Unwisely mourns. Suffice it, that we know
What needs must ripen from the seeds we
sow ;
That present time is but the mould wherein
We cast the shapes of holiness and sin.
A painful watcher of the passing hour,
Its lust of gold, its strife for place and
power ;
Its lack of manhood, honor, reverence,
truth,
Wise-thoughted age, and generous-hearted
youth ;
Nor yet unmindful of each better sign,
The low, far lights, which on th' horizon
shine,
Like those which sometimes tremble on the
rim
Of clouded skies when day is closing dim,
Flashing athwart the purple spears of rain
The hope of sunshine on the hills again :
I need no prophet's word, nor shapes that
pass
Like clouding shadows o'er a magic glass ;
For now, as ever, passionless and cold,
Doth the dread angel of the future hold

Evil and good before us, with no voice
Or warning look to guide us in our choice ;
With spectral hands outreaching through
the gloom
The shadowy contrasts of the coming doom.
Transferred from these, it now remains to
give
The sun and shade of Fate's alternative."

Then, with a burst of music, touching
all
The keys of thrifty life, — the mill-stream's
fall,
The engine's pant along its quivering rails,
The anvil's ring, the measured beat of flails,
The sweep of scythes, the reaper's whistled
tune,
Answering the summons of the bells of noon,
The woodman's hail along the river shores,
The steamboat's signal, and the dip of oars :
Slowly the curtain rose from off a land
Fair as God's garden. Broad on either hand
The golden wheat-fields glimmered in the
sun,
And the tall maize its yellow tassels spun.
Smooth highways set with hedge-rows liv-
ing green,
With steepled towns through shaded vistas
seen,
The school-house murmuring with its hive-
like swarm,
The brook-bank whitening in the grist-mill's
storm,
The painted farm-house shining through the
leaves
Of fruited orchards bending at its eaves,
Where live again, around the Western
hearth,
The homely old-time virtues of the North ;
Where the blithe housewife rises with the
day,
And well-paid labor counts his task a play.
And, grateful tokens of a Bible free,
And the free Gospel of Humanity,
Of diverse sects and differing names the
shrines,
One in their faith, whate'er their outward
signs,
Like varying strophes of the same sweet
hymn
From many a prairie's swell and river's
brim,
A thousand church-spires sanctify the air
Of the calm Sabbath, with their sign of
prayer.

Like sudden nightfall over bloom and
green
The curtain dropped : and, momently, be-
tween
The clank of fetter and the crack of thong,
Half sob, half laughter, music swept along ;
A strange refrain, whose idle words and low,
Like drunken mourners, kept the time of
woe ;
As if the revellers at a masquerade
Heard in the distance funeral marches
played.
Such music, dashing all his smiles with tears,
The thoughtful voyager on Pontchartrain
hears,
Where, through the noonday dusk of
wooded shores
The negro boatman, singing to his oars,
With a wild pathos borrowed of his wrong
Redeems the jargon of his senseless song.
"Look," said the Showman, sternly, as he
rolled
His curtain upward. "Fate's reverse be-
hold !"

A village straggling in loose disarray
Of vulgar newness, premature decay ;
A tavern, crazy with its whiskey brawls,
With "Slaves at Auction !" garnishing its
walls ;
Without, surrounded by a motley crowd,
The shrewd-eyed salesman, garrulous and
loud,
A squire or colonel in his pride of place,
Known at free fights, the caucus, and the
race,
Prompt to proclaim his honor without blot,
And silence doubters with a ten-pace shot,
Mingling the negro-driving bully's rant
With pious phrase and democratic cant,
Yet never scrupling, with a filthy jest,
To sell the infant from its mother's breast,
Break through all ties of wedlock, home,
and kin,
Yield shrinking girlhood up to graybeard
sin ;
Sell all the virtues with his human stock,
The Christian graces on his auction-block,
And coolly count on shrewdest bargains
driven
In hearts regenerate, and in souls forgiven !

Look once again ! The moving canvas
shows
A slave plantation's slovenly repose,

Where, in rude cabins rotting midst their
    weeds,
The human chattel eats, and sleeps, and
    breeds ;
And, held a brute, in practice, as in law,
Becomes in fact the thing he 's taken for.
There, early summoned to the hemp and
    corn,
The nursing mother leaves her child new-
    born ;
There haggard sickness, weak and deathly
    faint,
Crawls to his task, and fears to make com-
    plaint ;
And sad-eyed Rachels, childless in decay,
Weep for their lost ones sold and torn
    away !
Of ampler size the master's dwelling stands,
In shabby keeping with his half-tilled lands ;
The gates unhinged, the yard with weeds
    unclean,
The cracked veranda with a tipsy lean.
Without, loose-scattered like a wreck adrift,
Signs of misrule and tokens of unthrift ;
Within, profusion to discomfort joined,
The listless body and the vacant mind ;
The fear, the hate, the theft and falsehood,
    born
In menial hearts of toil, and stripes, and
    scorn !
There, all the vices, which, like birds ob-
    scene,
Batten on slavery loathsome and unclean,
From the foul kitchen to the parlor rise,
Pollute the nursery where the child-heir
    lies,
Taint infant lips beyond all after cure,
With the fell poison of a breast impure ;
Touch boyhood's passions with the breath of
    flame,
From girlhood's instincts steal the blush of
    shame.
So swells, from low to high, from weak to
    strong,
The tragic chorus of the baleful wrong ;
Guilty or guiltless, all within its range
Feel the blind justice of its sure revenge.

Still scenes like these the moving chart
    reveals.
Up the long western steppes the blighting
    steals ;
Down the Pacific slope the evil Fate
Glides like a shadow to the Golden Gate :
From sea to sea the drear eclipse is thrown,

From sea to sea the *Mauvaises Terres* have
    grown,
A belt of curses on the New World's zone !

The curtain fell. All drew a freer breath,
As men are wont to do when mournful death
Is covered from their sight. The Showman
    stood
With drooping brow in sorrow's attitude
One moment, then with sudden gesture
    shook
His loose hair back, and with the air and
    look
Of one who felt, beyond the narrow stage
And listening group, the presence of the
    age,
And heard the footsteps of the things to be,
Poured out his soul in earnest words and
    free.

" O friends ! " he said, " in this poor trick
    of paint
You see the semblance, incomplete and
    faint,
Of the two-fronted Future, which, to-day,
Stands dim and silent, waiting in your way.
To-day your servant, subject to your will ;
To-morrow, master, or for good or ill.
If the dark face of Slavery on you turns,
If the mad curse its paper barrier spurns,
If the world granary of the West is made
The last foul market of the slaver's trade,
Why rail at fate ?   The mischief is your
    own.
Why hate your neighbor ?   Blame your-
    selves alone !

" Men of the North !   The South you
    charge with wrong
Is weak and poor, while you are rich and
    strong.
If questions, — idle and absurd as those
The old-time monks and Paduan doctors
    chose, —
Mere ghosts of questions, tariffs, and dead
    banks,
And scarecrow pontiffs, never broke your
    ranks,
Your thews united could, at once, roll back
The jostled nation to its primal track.
Nay, were you simply steadfast, manly, just,
True to the faith your fathers left in trust,
If stainless honor outweighed in your scale
A codfish quintal or a factory bale,
Full many a noble heart, (and such remain

In all the South, like Lot in Siddim's plain,
Who watch and wait, and from the wrong's
    control
Keep white and pure their chastity of soul,)
Now sick to loathing of your weak com-
    plaints,
Your tricks as sinners, and your prayers as
    saints,
Would half-way meet the frankness of your
    tone,
And feel their pulses beating with your
    own.

"The North! the South! no geographic
    line
Can fix the boundary or the point define,
Since each with each so closely interblends,
Where Slavery rises, and where Freedom
    ends.
Beneath your rocks the roots, far-reaching,
    hide
Of the fell Upas on the Southern side;
The tree whose branches in your north winds
    wave
Dropped its young blossoms on Mount
    Vernon's grave;
The nursing growth of Monticello's crest,
Is now the glory of the free Northwest;
To the wise maxims of her olden school
Virginia listened from thy lips, Rantoul;
Seward's words of power, and Sumner's
    fresh renown,
Flow from the pen that Jefferson laid down!
And when, at length, her years of madness
    o'er,
Like the crowned grazer on Euphrates'
    shore,
From her long lapse to savagery, her mouth
Bitter with baneful herbage, turns the
    South,
Resumes her old attire, and seeks to smooth
Her unkempt tresses at the glass of truth,
Her early faith shall find a tongue again,
New Wythes and Pinckneys swell that old
    refrain,
Her sons with yours renew the ancient
    pact,
The myth of Union prove at last a fact!
Then, if one murmur mars the wide con-
    tent,
Some Northern lip will drawl the last dis-
    sent,
Some Union-saving patriot of your own
Lament to find his occupation gone.

"Grant that the North's insulted,
    scorned, betrayed,
O'erreached in bargains with her neighbor
    made,
When selfish thrift and party held the scales
For peddling dicker, not for honest sales, —
Whom shall we strike? Who most de-
    serves our blame?
The braggart Southron, open in his aim,
And bold as wicked, crashing straight
    through all
That bars his purpose, like a cannon-ball?
Or the mean traitor, breathing northern
    air,
With nasal speech and puritanic hair,
Whose cant the loss of principle survives,
As the mud-turtle e'en its head outlives;
Who, caught, chin-buried in some foul
    offence,
Puts on a look of injured innocence,
And consecrates his baseness to the cause
Of constitution, union, and the laws?

"Praise to the place-man who can hold
    aloof
His still unpurchased manhood, office-
    proof
Who on his round of duty walks erect,
And leaves it only rich in self-respect;
As More maintained his virtue's lofty port
In the Eighth Henry's base and bloody
    court.
But, if exceptions here and there are found,
Who tread thus safely on enchanted ground,
The normal type, the fitting symbol still
Of those who fatten at the public mill,
Is the chained dog beside his master's door,
Or Circe's victim, feeding on all four!

"Give me the heroes who, at tuck of
    drum,
Salute thy staff, immortal Quattlebum!
Or they who, doubly armed with vote and
    gun,
Following thy lead, illustrious Atchison,
Their drunken franchise shift from scene
    to scene,
As tile-beard Jourdan did his guillotine!
Rather than him who, born beneath our
    skies,
To Slavery's hand its supplest tool sup-
    plies;
The party felon whose unblushing face
Looks from the pillory of his bribe of place,

And coolly makes a merit of disgrace,
Points to the footmarks of indignant scorn,
Shows the deep scars of satire's tossing
    horn ;
And passes to his credit side the sum
Of all that makes a scoundrel's martyr-
    dom !

"Bane of the North, its canker and its
    moth !
These modern Esaus, bartering rights for
    broth !
Taxing our justice, with their double claim,
As fools for pity, and as knaves for blame ;
Who, urged by party, sect, or trade, within
The fell embrace of Slavery's sphere of
    sin,
Part at the outset with their moral sense,
The watchful angel set for Truth's defence ;
Confound all contrasts, good and ill ; re-
    verse
The poles of life, its blessing and its curse ;
And lose thenceforth from their perverted
    sight
The eternal difference 'twixt the wrong
    and right ;
To them the Law is but the iron span
That girds the ankles of imbruted man ;
To them the Gospel has no higher aim
Than simple sanction of the master's claim,
Dragged in the slime of Slavery's loath-
    some trail,
Like Chalier's Bible at his ass's tail !

"Such are the men who, with instinctive
    dread,
Whenever Freedom lifts her drooping head,
Make prophet-tripods of their office-stools,
And scare the nurseries and the village
    schools
With dire presage of ruin grim and great,
A broken Union and a foundered State !
Such are the patriots, self-bound to the
    stake
Of office, martyrs for their country's sake:
Who fill themselves the hungry jaws of
    Fate,
And by their loss of manhood save the
    State.
In the wide gulf themselves like Curtius
    throw,
And test the virtues of cohesive dough ;
As tropic monkeys, linking heads and tails,
Bridge o'er some torrent of Ecuador's
    vales !

"Such are the men who in your churches
    rave
To swearing-point, at mention of the slave !
When some poor parson, haply unawares,
Stammers of freedom in his timid prayers ;
Who, if some foot-sore negro through the
    town
Steals northward, volunteer to hunt him
    down.
Or, if some neighbor, flying from disease,
Courts the mild balsam of the Southern
    breeze,
With hue and cry pursue him on his track,
And write *Free-soiler* on the poor man's
    back.
Such are the men who leave the pedler's
    cart,
While faring South, to learn the driver's
    art,
Or, in white neckcloth, soothe with pious
    aim
The graceful sorrows of some languid
    dame,
Who, from the wreck of her bereavement,
    saves
The double charm of widowhood and
    slaves !
Pliant and apt, they lose no chance to show
To what base depths apostasy can go ;
Outdo the natives in their readiness
To roast a negro, or to mob a press ;
Poise a tarred schoolmate on the lyncher's
    rail,
Or make a bonfire of their birthplace mail !

"So some poor wretch, whose lips no
    longer bear
The sacred burden of his mother's prayer,
By fear impelled, or lust of gold enticed,
Turns to the Crescent from the Cross of
    Christ,
And, overacting in superfluous zeal,
Crawls prostrate where the faithful only
    kneel,
Out-howls the Dervish, hugs his rags to
    court
The squalid Santon's sanctity of dirt ;
And, when beneath the city gateway's span
Files slow and long the Meccan caravan,
And through its midst, pursued by Islam's
    prayers,
The prophet's Word some favored camel
    bears,
The marked apostate has his place assigned
The Koran-bearer's sacred rump behind,

With brush and pitcher following, grave
and mute,
In meek attendance on the holy brute !

"Men of the North ! beneath your very
eyes,
By hearth and home, your real danger lies.
Still day by day some hold of freedom falls
Through home-bred traitors fed within its
walls.
Men whom yourselves with vote and purse
sustain,
At posts of honor, influence, and gain ;
The right of Slavery to your sons to teach,
And 'South-side' Gospels in your pulpits
preach,
Transfix the Law to ancient freedom dear
On the sharp point of her subverted spear,
And imitate upon her cushion plump
The mad Missourian lynching from his
stump ;
Or, in your name, upon the Senate's floor
Yield up to Slavery all it asks, and more ;
And, ere your dull eyes open to the cheat,
Sell your old homestead underneath your
feet !
While such as these your loftiest outlooks
hold,
While truth and conscience with your wares
are sold,
While grave-browed merchants band them-
selves to aid
An annual man-hunt for their Southern
trade,
What moral power within your grasp re-
mains
To stay the mischief on Nebraska's plains ?
High as the tides of generous impulse flow,
As far rolls back the selfish undertow ;
And all your brave resolves, though aimed
as true
As the horse-pistol Balmawhapple drew,
To Slavery's bastions lend as slight a shock
As the poor trooper's shot to Stirling rock!

"Yet, while the need of Freedom's cause
demands
The earnest efforts of your hearts and hands,
Urged by all motives that can prompt the
heart
To prayer and toil and manhood's manliest
part ;
Though to the soul's deep tocsin Nature
joins
The warning whisper of her Orphic pines,

The north-wind's anger, and the south-
wind's sigh,
The midnight sword-dance of the northern
sky,
And, to the ear that bends above the sod
Of the green grave-mounds in the Fields of
God,
In low, deep murmurs of rebuke or cheer,
The land's dead fathers speak their hope or
fear,
Yet let not Passion wrest from Reason's
hand
The guiding rein and symbol of command.
Blame not the caution proffering to your
zeal
A well-meant drag upon its hurrying wheel ;
Nor chide the man whose honest doubt ex-
tends
To the means only, not the righteous ends ;
Nor fail to weigh the scruples and the fears
Of milder natures and serener years.
In the long strife with evil which began
With the first lapse of new-created man,
Wisely and well has Providence assigned
To each his part, — some forward, some be-
hind ;
And they, too, serve who temper and re-
strain
The o'erwarm heart that sets on fire the
brain.
True to yourselves, feed Freedom's altar-
flame
With what you have ; let others do the same.
Spare timid doubters ; set like flint your
face
Against the self-sold knaves of gain and
place :
Pity the weak ; but with unsparing hand
Cast out the traitors who infest the land ;
From bar, press, pulpit, cast them every-
where,
By dint of fasting, if you fail by prayer.
And in their place bring men of antique
mould,
Like the grave fathers of your Age of Gold ;
Statesmen like those who sought the primal
fount
Of righteous law, the Sermon on the
Mount ;
Lawyers who prize, like Quincy, (to our day
Still spared, Heaven bless him !) honor
more than pay,
And Christian jurists, starry-pure, like Jay ;
Preachers like Woolman, or like them who
bore

The faith of Wesley to our Western shore,
And held no convert genuine till he broke
Alike his servants' and the Devil's yoke ;
And priests like him who Newport's market trod,
And o'er its slave-ships shook the bolts of God !
So shall your power, with a wise prudence used,
Strong but forbearing, firm but not abused,
In kindly keeping with the good of all,
The nobler maxims of the past recall,
Her natural home-born right to Freedom give,
And leave her foe his robber-right, — to live.
Live, as the snake does in his noisome fen !
Live, as the wolf does in his bone-strewn den !
Live, clothed with cursing like a robe of flame,
The focal point of million-fingered shame !
Live, till the Southron, who, with all his faults,
Has manly instincts, in his pride revolts,
Dashes from off him, midst the glad world's cheers,
The hideous nightmare of his dream of years,
And lifts, self-prompted, with his own right hand,
The vile encumbrance from his glorious land !

" So, wheresoe'er our destiny sends forth
Its widening circles to the South or North,
Where'er our banner flaunts beneath the stars
Its mimic splendors and its cloudlike bars,
There shall Free Labor's hardy children stand
The equal sovereigns of a slaveless land.
And when at last the hunted bison tires,
And dies o'ertaken by the squatter's fires ;
And westward, wave on wave, the living flood
Breaks on the snow-line of majestic Hood ;
And lonely Shasta listening hears the tread
Of Europe's fair-haired children, Hesperled ;
And, gazing downward through his hoarlocks, sees
The tawny Asian climb his giant knees,
The Eastern sea shall hush his waves to hear
Pacific's surf-beat answer Freedom's cheer,

And one long rolling fire of triumph run
Between the sunrise and the sunset gun ! "

———

My task is done.   The Showman and his show,
Themselves but shadows, into shadows go ;
And, if no song of idlesse I have sung,
Nor tints of beauty on the canvas flung ;
If the harsh numbers grate on tender ears,
And the rough picture overwrought appears,
With deeper coloring, with a sterner blast,
Before my soul a voice and vision passed,
Such as might Milton's jarring trump require,
Or glooms of Dante fringed with lurid fire.
Oh, not of choice, for themes of public wrong
I leave the green and pleasant paths of song,
The mild, sweet words which soften and adorn,
For sharp rebuke and bitter laugh of scorn.
More dear to me some song of private worth,
Some homely idyl of my native North,
Some summer pastoral of her inland vales,
Or, grim and weird, her winter fireside tales
Haunted by ghosts of unreturning sails,
Lost barks at parting hung from stem to helm
With prayers of love like dreams on Virgil's elm.
Nor private grief nor malice holds my pen ;
I owe but kindness to my fellow-men ;
And, South or North, wherever hearts of prayer
Their woes and weakness to our Father bear,
Wherever fruits of Christian love are found
In holy lives, to me is holy ground.
But the time passes.   It were vain to crave
A late indulgence.   What I had I gave.
Forget the poet, but his warning heed,
And shame his poor word with your nobler deed.

ON A PRAYER-BOOK

WITH ITS FRONTISPIECE, ARY SCHEFFER'S " CHRISTUS CONSOLATOR," AMERICANIZED BY THE OMISSION OF THE BLACK MAN

It is hardly to be credited, yet is true, that in the anxiety of the Northern merchant to conciliate his Southern customer, a publisher was found ready thus to mutilate Scheffer's picture. He intended his edition for use in the Southern States undoubtedly, but copies fell into the hands of those who believed literally in a gospel which was to preach liberty to the captive.

O ARY SCHEFFER ! when beneath thine eye,
    Touched with the light that cometh from
      above,
    Grew the sweet picture of the dear Lord's
      love,
No dream hadst thou that Christian hands
    would tear
Therefrom the token of His equal care,
    And make thy symbol of His truth a lie !
The poor, dumb slave whose shackles fall
    away
    In His compassionate gaze, grubbed
      smoothly out,
    To mar no more the exercise devout
Of sleek oppression kneeling down to pray
Where the great oriel stains the Sabbath
    day !
Let whoso can before such praying-books
    Kneel on his velvet cushion; I, for one,
Would sooner bow, a Parsee, to the sun,
Or tend a prayer-wheel in Thibetan brooks,
Or beat a drum on Yedo's temple-floor.
No falser idol man has bowed before,
In Indian groves or islands of the sea,
    Than that which through the quaint-
      carved Gothic door
Looks forth, — a Church without human-
    ity !
    Patron of pride, and prejudice, and
      wrong, —
    The rich man's charm and fetich of the
      strong,
The Eternal Fulness meted, clipped, and
    shorn,
The seamless robe of equal mercy torn,
The dear Christ hidden from His kindred
    flesh,
And, in His poor ones, crucified afresh !
Better the simple Lama scattering wide,
    Where sweeps the storm Alechan's
      steppes along,
His paper horses for the lost to ride,
And wearying Buddha with his prayers to
    make
The figures living for the traveller's sake,
Than he who hopes with cheap praise to
    beguile
The ear of God, dishonoring man the while ;
Who dreams the pearl gate's hinges, rusty
    grown,

Are moved by flattery's oil of tongue
    alone ;
That in the scale Eternal Justice bears
The generous deed weighs less than selfish
    prayers,
And words intoned with graceful unction
    move
The Eternal Goodness more than lives of
    truth and love.
Alas, the Church ! The reverend head of
    Jay,
    Enhaloed with its saintly silvered hair,
    Adorns no more the places of her prayer ;
And brave young Tyng, too early called
    away,
    Troubles the Haman of her courts no
      more
    Like the just Hebrew at the Assyr-
      ian's door ;
And her sweet ritual, beautiful but dead
As the dry husk from which the grain is
    shed,
And holy hymns from which the life de-
    vout
Of saints and martyrs has wellnigh gone
    out,
Like candles dying in exhausted air,
For Sabbath use in measured grists are
    ground ;
And, ever while the spiritual mill goes
    round,
Between the upper and the nether stones,
Unseen, unheard, the wretched bondman
    groans,
And urges his vain plea, prayer-smothered,
    anthem-drowned !

O heart of mine, keep patience ! Looking
    forth,
    As from the Mount of Vision, I behold,
Pure, just, and free, the Church of Christ
    on earth ;
    The martyr's dream, the golden age fore-
      told !
And found, at last, the mystic Graal I see,
    Brimmed with His blessing, pass from
      lip to lip
In sacred pledge of human fellowship ;
And over all the songs of angels hear ;
Songs of the love that casteth out all fear ;
Songs of the Gospel of Humanity !
Lo ! in the midst, with the same look He
    wore,
    Healing and blessing on Gennesaret's
    shore,

Folding together, with the all - tender
    might
Of His great love, the dark hands and the
    white,
Stands the Consoler, soothing every pain,
Making all burdens light, and breaking
    every chain.

THE SUMMONS

[After publishing this poem Whittier wrote
to Lucy Larcom: "I do not quite like the tone
of *The Summons* now that it is published.   It
was, however, an expression of a state of mind
which thee would regard as pardonable if thee
knew all the circumstances.   It is *too complain-
ing*, and I hope I shall not be left to do such a
thing again."]

My ear is full of summer sounds,
    Of summer sights my languid eye ;
Beyond the dusty village bounds
I loiter in my daily rounds,
    And in the noon-time shadows lie.

I hear the wild bee wind his horn,
    The bird swings on the ripened wheat,
The long green lances of the corn
Are tilting in the winds of morn,
    The locust shrills his song of heat.

Another sound my spirit hears,
    A deeper sound that drowns them all ;
A voice of pleading choked with tears,
The call of human hopes and fears,
    The Macedonian cry to Paul !

The storm-bell rings, the trumpet blows ;
    I know the word and countersign ;
Wherever Freedom's vanguard goes,
Where stand or fall her friends or foes,
    I know the place that should be mine.

Shamed be the hands that idly fold,
    And lips that woo the reed's accord,
When laggard Time the hour has tolled
For true with false and new with old
    To fight the battles of the Lord !

O brothers ! blest by partial Fate
    With power to match the will and deed,
To him your summons comes too late
Who sinks beneath his armor's weight,
    And has no answer but God-speed !

TO WILLIAM H. SEWARD

On the 12th of January, 1861, Mr. Seward
delivered in the Senate chamber a speech on
The State of the Union, in which he urged the
paramount duty of preserving the Union, and
went as far as it was possible to go, without
surrender of principles, in concessions to the
Southern party.

Statesman, I thank thee ! and, if yet dis-
    sent
Mingles, reluctant, with my large content,
I cannot censure what was nobly meant.
But, while constrained to hold even Union
    less
Than Liberty and Truth and Righteousness,
I thank thee in the sweet and holy name
Of peace, for wise calm words that put to
    shame
Passion and party.   Courage may be shown
Not in defiance of the wrong alone ;
He may be bravest who, unweaponed, bears
The olive branch, and, strong in justice,
    spares
The rash wrong-doer, giving widest scope
To Christian charity and generous hope.
If, without damage to the sacred cause
Of Freedom and the safeguard of its
    laws —
If, without yielding that for which alone
We prize the Union, thou canst save it
    now
From a baptism of blood, upon thy brow
A wreath whose flowers no earthly soil
    have known,
Woven of the beatitudes, shall rest,
And the peacemaker be forever blest !

IN WAR TIME

TO SAMUEL E. SEWALL AND
HARRIET W. SEWALL

OF MELROSE

These lines to my old friends stood as dedi-
cation in the volume which contained a collec-
tion of pieces under the general title of *In
War Time*.   The group belonging distinctly
under that title I have retained here ; the
other pieces in the volume are distributed
among the appropriate divisions.

OLOR ISCANUS queries : " Why should we
Vex at the land's ridiculous miserie ? "
So on his Usk banks, in the blood-red dawn
Of England's civil strife, did careless
         Vaughan
Bemock his times. O friends of many
         years !
Though faith and trust are stronger than
         our fears,
And the signs promise peace with liberty,
Not thus we trifle with our country's tears
And sweat of agony. The future's gain
Is certain as God's truth ; but, meanwhile,
         pain
Is bitter and tears are salt : our voices take
A sober tone ; our very household songs
Are heavy with a nation's griefs and
         wrongs ;
And innocent mirth is chastened for the
         sake
Of the brave hearts that nevermore shall
         beat,
The eyes that smile no more, the unreturn-
         ing feet !

THY WILL BE DONE

WE see not, know not ; all our way
Is night, — with Thee alone is day :
From out the torrent's troubled drift,
Above the storm our prayers we lift,
         Thy will be done !

The flesh may fail, the heart may faint,
But who are we to make complaint,
Or dare to plead, in times like these,
The weakness of our love of ease ?
         Thy will be done !

We take with solemn thankfulness
Our burden up, nor ask it less,
And count it joy that even we
May suffer, serve, or wait for Thee,
         Whose will be done !

Though dim as yet in tint and line,
We trace Thy picture's wise design,
And thank Thee that our age supplies
Its dark relief of sacrifice.
         Thy will be done !

And if, in our unworthiness,
Thy sacrificial wine we press ;
If from Thy ordeal's heated bars

Our feet are seamed with crimson scars,
         Thy will be done !

If, for the age to come, this hour
Of trial hath vicarious power,
And, blest by Thee, our present pain
Be Liberty's eternal gain,
         Thy will be done !

Strike, Thou the Master, we Thy keys,
The anthem of the destinies !
The minor of Thy loftier strain,
Our hearts shall breathe the old refrain,
         Thy will be done !

A WORD FOR THE HOUR

THE firmament breaks up. In black eclipse
Light after light goes out. One evil star,
Luridly glaring through the smoke of war,
As in the dream of the Apocalypse,
Drags others down. Let us not weakly
         weep
Nor rashly threaten. Give us grace to keep
Our faith and patience ; wherefore should
         we leap
On one hand into fratricidal fight,
Or, on the other, yield eternal right,
Frame lies of law, and good and ill con-
         found ?
What fear we ? Safe on freedom's vantage-
         ground
Our feet are planted : let us there remain
In unrevengeful calm, no means untried
Which truth can sanction, no just claim
         denied,
The sad spectators of a suicide !
They break the links of Union : shall we
         light
The fires of hell to weld anew the chain
On that red anvil where each blow is pain ?
Draw we not even now a freer breath,
As from our shoulders falls a load of death
Loathsome as that the Tuscan's victim bore
When keen with life to a dead horror bound?
Why take we up the accursed thing again ?
Pity, forgive, but urge them back no more
Who, drunk with passion, flaunt disunion's
         rag
With its vile reptile-blazon. Let us press
The golden cluster on our brave old flag
In closer union, and, if numbering less,
Brighter shall shine the stars which still
         remain.

"EIN FESTE BURG IST UNSER GOTT"

LUTHER'S HYMN

WE wait beneath the furnace-blast
  The pangs of transformation ;
Not painlessly doth God recast
And mould anew the nation.
    Hot burns the fire
    Where wrongs expire ;
    Nor spares the hand
    That from the land
Uproots the ancient evil.

The hand-breadth cloud the sages feared
  Its bloody rain is dropping ;
The poison plant the fathers spared
  All else is overtopping.
    East, West, South, North,
    It curses the earth ;
    All justice dies,
    And fraud and lies
Live only in its shadow.

What gives the wheat-field blades of steel ?
  What points the rebel cannon ?
What sets the roaring rabble's heel
  On the old star-spangled pennon ?
    What breaks the oath
    Of the men o' the South ?
    What whets the knife
    For the Union's life ? —
Hark to the answer : Slavery !

Then waste no blows on lesser foes
  In strife unworthy freemen.
God lifts to-day the veil, and shows
  The features of the demon !
    O North and South,
    Its victims both,
    Can ye not cry,
    " Let slavery die ! "
And union find in freedom ?

What though the cast-out spirit tear
  The nation in his going ?
We who have shared the guilt must share
  The pang of his o'erthrowing !
    Whate'er the loss,
    Whate'er the cross,
    Shall they complain
    Of present pain
Who trust in God's hereafter ?

For who that leans on His right arm
  Was ever yet forsaken ?
What righteous cause can suffer harm
  If He its part has taken ?
    Though wild and loud,
    And dark the cloud,
    Behind its folds
    His hand upholds
The calm sky of to-morrow !

Above the maddening cry for blood,
  Above the wild war-drumming,
Let Freedom's voice be heard, with good
  The evil overcoming.
    Give prayer and purse
    To stay the Curse
    Whose wrong we share,
    Whose shame we, bear,
Whose end shall gladden Heaven !

In vain the bells of war shall ring
  Of triumphs and revenges,
While still is spared the evil thing
  That severs and estranges.
    But blest the ear
    That yet shall hear
    The jubilant bell
    That rings the knell
Of Slavery forever !

Then let the selfish lip be dumb,
  And hushed the breath of sighing ;
Before the joy of peace must come
  The pains of purifying.
    God give us grace
    Each in his place
    To bear his lot,
    And, murmuring not,
Endure and wait and labor !

TO JOHN C. FRÉMONT

On the 31st of August, 1861, General Fré-
mont, then in charge of the Western Depart-
ment, issued a proclamation which contained a
clause, famous as the first announcement of
emancipation: "The property," it declared,
"real and personal, of all persons in the State
of Missouri, who shall take up arms against the
United States, or who shall be directly proven
to have taken active part with their enemies in
the field, is declared to be confiscated to the
public use ; and their slaves, if any they have,
are hereby declared free men." Mr. Lincoln

regarded the proclamation as premature and
countermanded it, after vainly endeavoring to
persuade Frémont of his own motion to re-
voke it.

THY error, Frémont, simply was to act
A brave man's part, without the statesman's
tact,
And, taking counsel but of common sense,
To strike at cause as well as consequence.
Oh, never yet since Roland wound his horn
At Roncesvalles, has a blast been blown
Far-heard, wide-echoed, startling as thine
own,
Heard from the van of freedom's hope for-
lorn !
It had been safer, doubtless, for the time,
To flatter treason, and avoid offence
To that Dark Power whose underlying
crime
Heaves upward its perpetual turbulence.
But if thine be the fate of all who break
The ground for truth's seed, or forerun
their years
Till lost in distance, or with stout hearts
make
A lane for freedom through the level spears,
Still take thou courage ! God has spoken
through thee,
Irrevocable, the mighty words, Be free !
The land shakes with them, and the slave's
dull ear
Turns from the rice-swamp stealthily to
hear.
Who would recall them now must first ar-
rest
The winds that blow down from the free
Northwest,
Ruffling the Gulf ; or like a scroll roll back
The Mississippi to its upper springs.
Such words fulfil their prophecy, and lack
But the full time to harden into things.

THE WATCHERS

BESIDE a stricken field I stood ;
On the torn turf, on grass and wood,
Hung heavily the dew of blood.

Still in their fresh mounds lay the slain,
But all the air was quick with pain
And gusty sighs and tearful rain.

Two angels, each with drooping head
And folded wings and noiseless tread,
Watched by that valley of the dead.

The one, with forehead saintly bland
And lips of blessing, not command,
Leaned, weeping, on her olive wand.

The other's brows were scarred and knit,
His restless eyes were watch-fires lit,
His hands for battle-gauntlets fit.

"How long !" — I knew the voice of
Peace, —
"Is there no respite ? no release ?
When shall the hopeless quarrel cease ?

"O Lord, how long ! One human soul
Is more than any parchment scroll,
Or any flag thy winds unroll.

"What price was Ellsworth's, young and
brave ?
How weigh the gift that Lyon gave,
Or count the cost of Winthrop's grave ?

"O brother ! if thine eye can see,
Tell how and when the end shall be,
What hope remains for thee and me."

Then Freedom sternly said : "I shun
No strife nor pang beneath the sun,
When human rights are staked and won.

"I knelt with Ziska's hunted flock,
I watched in Toussaint's cell of rock,
I walked with Sidney to the block.

"The moor of Marston felt my tread,
Through Jersey snows the march I led,
My voice Magenta's charges sped.

"But now, through weary day and night,
I watch a vague and aimless fight
For leave to strike one blow aright.

"On either side my foe they own :
One guards through love his ghastly throne,
And one through fear to reverence grown.

"Why wait we longer, mocked, betrayed,
By open foes, or those afraid
To speed thy coming through my aid ?

" Why watch to see who win or fall ?
I shake the dust against them all,
I leave them to their senseless brawl."

" Nay," Peace implored : " yet longer wait ;
The doom is near, the stake is great :
God knoweth if it be too late.

" Still wait and watch ; the way prepare
Where I with folded wings of prayer
May follow, weaponless and bare."

" Too late ! " the stern, sad voice replied,
"Too late ! " its mournful echo sighed.
In low lament the answer died.

A rustling as of wings in flight,
An upward gleam of lessening white,
So passed the vision, sound and sight.

But round me, like a silver bell
Rung down the listening sky to tell
Of holy help, a sweet voice fell.

" Still hope and trust," it sang ; " the rod
Must fall, the wine-press must be trod,
But all is possible with God ! "

TO ENGLISHMEN

Written when, in the stress of our terrible
war, the English ruling class, with few excep-
tions, were either coldly indifferent or hostile to
the party of freedom. Their attitude was illus-
trated by caricatures of America, among which
was one of a slaveholder and cowhide, with
the motto, " Have n't I a right to wallop my
nigger ? "

You flung your taunt across the wave ;
  We bore it as became us,
Well knowing that the fettered slave
Left friendly lips no option save
  To pity or to blame us.

You scoffed our plea.   " Mere lack of
    will,
  Not lack of power," you told us :
We showed our free-state records ; still
You mocked, confounding good and ill,
  Slave-haters and slaveholders.

We struck at Slavery ; to the verge
  Of power and means we checked it ;

Lo ! — presto, change ! its claims you
    urge,
Send greetings to it o'er the surge,
  And comfort and protect it.

But yesterday you scarce could shake,
  In slave-abhorring rigor,
Our Northern palms for conscience' sake :
To-day you clasp the hands that ache
  With " walloping the nigger ! "

O Englishmen ! — in hope and creed,
  In blood and tongue our brothers !
We too are heirs of Runnymede ;
And Shakespeare's fame and Cromwell's
    deed
  Are not alone our mother's.

" Thicker than water," in one rill
  Through centuries of story
Our Saxon blood has flowed, and still
We share with you its good and ill,
  The shadow and the glory.

Joint heirs and kinfolk, leagues of wave
  Nor length of years can part us :
Your right is ours to shrine and grave,
The common freehold of the brave,
  The gift of saints and martyrs.

Our very sins and follies teach
  Our kindred frail and human :
We carp at faults with bitter speech,
The while, for one unshared by each,
  We have a score in common.

We bowed the heart, if not the knee,
  To England's Queen, God bless her !
We praised you when your slaves went
    free :
We seek to unchain ours.   Will ye
  Join hands with the oppressor ?

And is it Christian England cheers
  The bruiser, not the bruisèd ?
And must she run, despite the tears
And prayers of eighteen hundred years,
  Amuck in Slavery's crusade ?

Oh, black disgrace ! Oh, shame and loss
  Too deep for tongue to phrase on !
Tear from your flag its holy cross,
And in your van of battle toss
  The pirate's skull-bone blazon !

MITHRIDATES AT CHIOS

It is recorded that the Chians, when subjugated by Mithridates of Cappadocia, were delivered up to their own slaves, to be carried away captive to Colchis. Athenæus considers this a just punishment for their wickedness in first introducing the slave-trade into Greece. From this ancient villainy of the Chians the proverb arose, "The Chian hath bought himself a master."

Know'st thou, O slave-cursed land !
How, when the Chian's cup of guilt
  Was full to overflow, there came
  God's justice in the sword of flame
That, red with slaughter to its hilt,
Blazed in the Cappadocian victor's hand ?

The heavens are still and far ;
But, not unheard of awful Jove,
  The sighing of the island slave
  Was answered, when the Ægean wave
The keels of Mithridates clove,
And the vines shrivelled in the breath of war.

" Robbers of Chios ! hark,"
The victor cried, " to Heaven's decree !
  Pluck your last cluster from the vine,
  Drain your last cup of Chian wine ;
Slaves of your slaves, your doom shall be,
In Colchian mines by Phasis rolling dark."

Then rose the long lament
From the hoar sea-god's dusky caves :
  The priestess rent her hair and cried,
  " Woe ! woe ! The gods are sleepless-eyed ! "
And, chained and scourged, the slaves of slaves,
The lords of Chios into exile went.

" The gods at last pay well,"
So Hellas sang her taunting song,
  " The fisher in his net is caught,
  The Chian hath his master bought ; "
And isle from isle, with laughter long,
Took up and sped the mocking parable.

Once more the slow, dumb years
Bring their avenging cycle round,
  And, more than Hellas taught of old,
  Our wiser lesson shall be told,

Of slaves uprising, freedom-crowned,
To break, not wield, the scourge wet with their blood and tears.

AT PORT ROYAL

In November, 1861, a Union force under Commodore Dupont and General Sherman captured Port Royal, and from this point as a basis of operations the neighboring islands between Charleston and Savannah were taken possession of. The early occupation of this district, where the negro population was greatly in excess of the white, gave an opportunity which was at once seized upon, of practically emancipating the slaves and of beginning that work of civilization which was accepted as the grave responsibility of those who had labored for freedom.

The tent-lights glimmer on the land,
  The ship-lights on the sea ;
The night-wind smooths with drifting sand
  Our track on lone Tybee.

At last our grating keels outslide,
  Our good boats forward swing ;
And while we ride the land-locked tide,
  Our negroes row and sing.

For dear the bondman holds his gifts
  Of music and of song :
The gold that kindly Nature sifts
  Among his sands of wrong ;

The power to make his toiling days
  And poor home-comforts please ;
The quaint relief of mirth that plays
  With sorrow's minor keys.

Another glow than sunset's fire
  Has filled the west with light,
Where field and garner, barn and byre,
  Are blazing through the night.

The land is wild with fear and hate,
  The rout runs mad and fast ;
From hand to hand, from gate to gate
  The flaming brand is passed.

The lurid glow falls strong across
  Dark faces broad with smiles :
Not theirs the terror, hate, and loss
  That fire yon blazing piles.

With oar-strokes timing to their song,
  They weave in simple lays
The pathos of remembered wrong,
  The hope of better days, —

The triumph-note that Miriam sung,
  The joy of uncaged birds :
Softening with Afric's mellow tongue
  Their broken Saxon words.

SONG OF THE NEGRO BOATMEN

Oh, praise an' tanks !   De Lord he come
  To set de people free ;
An' massa tink it day ob doom,
  An' we ob jubilee.
De Lord dat heap de Red Sea waves
  He jus' as 'trong as den ;
He say de word : we las' night slaves ;
  To-day, de Lord's free men.
    De yam will grow, de cotton blow,
      We 'll hab de rice an' corn ;
    Oh nebber you fear, if nebber you hear
      De driver blow his horn !

Ole massa on he trabbels gone ;
  He leaf de land behind :
De Lord's breff blow him furder on,
  Like corn-shuck in de wind.
We own de hoe, we own de plough,
  We own de hands dat hold ;
We sell de pig, we sell de cow,
  But nebber chile be sold.
    De yam will grow, de cotton blow,
      We 'll hab de rice an' corn ;
    Oh nebber you fear, if nebber you hear
      De driver blow his horn !

We pray de Lord : he gib us signs
  Dat some day we be free ;
De norf-wind tell it to de pines,
  De wild-duck to de sea ;
We tink it when de church-bell ring,
  We dream it in de dream ;
De rice-bird mean it when he sing,
  De eagle when he scream.
    De yam will grow, de cotton blow,
      We 'll hab de rice an' corn ;
    Oh nebber you fear, if nebber you hear
      De driver blow his horn !

We know de promise nebber fail,
  An' nebber lie de word ;

So, like de 'postles in de jail,
  We waited for de Lord :
An' now he open ebery door,
  An' trow away de key ;
He tink we lub him so before,
  We lub him better free.
    De yam will grow, de cotton blow,
      He 'll gib de rice an' corn ;
    Oh nebber you fear, if nebber you hear
      De driver blow his horn !

So sing our dusky gondoliers ;
  And with a secret pain,
And smiles that seem akin to tears,
  We hear the wild refrain.

We dare not share the negro's trust,
  Nor yet his hope deny ;
We only know that God is just,
  And every wrong shall die.

Rude seems the song ; each swarthy face,
  Flame-lighted, ruder still :
We start to think that hapless race
  Must shape our good or ill ;

That laws of changeless justice bind
  Oppressor with oppressed ;
And, close as sin and suffering joined,
  We march to Fate abreast.

Sing on, poor hearts ! your chant shall be
  Our sign of blight or bloom,
The Vala-song of Liberty,
  Or death-rune of our doom !

ASTRÆA AT THE CAPITOL

ABOLITION OF SLAVERY IN THE DISTRICT OF COLUMBIA, 1862

[The reference in the fourth stanza is to Dr.
Reuben Crandall of Washington, who, in 1834,
was arrested and confined in the old city prison
until his health was destroyed.   His crime was
in lending to a brother physician Whittier's
pamphlet *Justice and Expediency.*]

WHEN first I saw our banner wave
  Above the nation's council-hall,
  I heard beneath its marble wall
The clanking fetters of the slave !

In the foul market-place I stood,
  And saw the Christian mother sold,
  And childhood with its locks of gold,
Blue-eyed and fair with Saxon blood.

I shut my eyes, I held my breath,
  And, smothering down the wrath and
    shame
That set my Northern blood aflame,
Stood silent, — where to speak was death.

Beside me gloomed the prison-cell
  Where wasted one in slow decline
  For uttering simple words of mine,
And loving freedom all too well.

The flag that floated from the dome
  Flapped menace in the morning air ;
  I stood a perilled stranger where
The human broker made his home.

For crime was virtue : Gown and Sword
  And Law their threefold sanction gave,
  And to the quarry of the slave
Went hawking with our symbol-bird.

On the oppressor's side was power ;
  And yet I knew that every wrong,
  However old, however strong,
But waited God's avenging hour.

I knew that truth would crush the lie, —
  Somehow, some time, the end would be ;
  Yet scarcely dared I hope to see
The triumph with my mortal eye.

But now I see it ! In the sun
  A free flag floats from yonder dome,
  And at the nation's hearth and home
The justice long delayed is done.

Not as we hoped, in calm of prayer,
  The message of deliverance comes,
  But heralded by roll of drums
On waves of battle-troubled air !

Midst sounds that madden and appall,
  The song that Bethlehem's shepherds
    knew !
The harp of David melting through
The demon-agonies of Saul !

Not as we hoped ; but what are we ?
  Above our broken dreams and plans

God lays, with wiser hand than man's,
  The corner-stones of liberty.

I cavil not with Him : the voice
  That freedom's blessed gospel tells
  Is sweet to me as silver bells,
Rejoicing ! yea, I will rejoice !

Dear friends still toiling in the sun ;
  Ye dearer ones who, gone before,
  Are watching from the eternal shore
The slow work by your hands begun,

Rejoice with me ! The chastening rod
  Blossoms with love ; the furnace heat
  Grows cool beneath His blessed feet
Whose form is as the Son of God !

Rejoice ! Our Marah's bitter springs
  Are sweetened ; on our ground of grief
  Rise day by day in strong relief
The prophecies of better things.

Rejoice in hope ! The day and night
  Are one with God, and one with them
  Who see by faith the cloudy hem
Of Judgment fringed with Mercy's light !

THE BATTLE AUTUMN OF 1862

THE flags of war like storm-birds fly,
  The charging trumpets blow ;
Yet rolls no thunder in the sky,
  No earthquake strives below.

And, calm and patient, Nature keeps
  Her ancient promise well,
Though o'er her bloom and greenness
    sweeps
  The battle's breath of hell.

And still she walks in golden hours
  Through harvest-happy farms,
And still she wears her fruits and flowers
  Like jewels on her arms.

What mean the gladness of the plain,
  This joy of eve and morn,
The mirth that shakes the beard of grain
  And yellow locks of corn ?

Ah ! eyes may well be full of tears,
  And hearts with hate are hot ;

But even-paced come round the years,
  And Nature changes not.

She meets with smiles our bitter grief,
  With songs our groans of pain ;
She mocks with tint of flower and leaf
  The war-field's crimson stain.

Still, in the cannon's pause, we hear
  Her sweet thanksgiving-psalm ;
Too near to God for doubt or fear,
  She shares the eternal calm.

She knows the seed lies safe below
  The fires that blast and burn ;
For all the tears of blood we sow
  She waits the rich return.

She sees with clearer eye than ours
  The good of suffering born, —
The hearts that blossom like her flowers,
  And ripen like her corn.

Oh, give to us, in times like these,
  The vision of her eyes ;
And make her fields and fruited trees
  Our golden prophecies !

Oh, give to us her finer ear !
  Above this stormy din,
We too would hear the bells of cheer
  Ring peace and freedom in.

HYMN

SUNG AT CHRISTMAS BY THE SCHOLARS
  OF ST. HELENA'S ISLAND, S. C.

[Written at the request of the teacher, Miss
Charlotte Forten, now Mrs. Grimké.]

OH, none in all the world before
  Were ever glad as we !
We 're free on Carolina's shore,
  We 're all at home and free.

Thou Friend and Helper of the poor,
  Who suffered for our sake,
To open every prison door,
  And every yoke to break !

Bend low Thy pitying face and mild,
  And help us sing and pray ;
The hand that blessed the little child,
  Upon our foreheads lay.

We hear no more the driver's horn,
  No more the whip we fear,
This holy day that saw Thee born
  Was never half so dear.

The very oaks are greener clad,
  The waters brighter smile ;
Oh, never shone a day so glad
  On sweet St. Helen's Isle.

We praise Thee in our songs to-day,
  To Thee in prayer we call,
Make swift the feet and straight the way
  Of freedom unto all.

Come once again, O blessed Lord !
  Come walking on the sea !
And let the mainlands hear the word
  That sets the island free !

THE PROCLAMATION

President Lincoln's proclamation of emanci-
pation was issued January 1, 1863.

SAINT PATRICK, slave to Milcho of the
    herds
Of Ballymena, wakened with these words :
  " Arise, and flee
Out from the land of bondage, and be free ! "

Glad as a soul in pain, who hears from
    heaven
The angels singing of his sins forgiven,
    And, wondering, sees
His prison opening to their golden keys,

He rose a man who laid him down a slave,
Shook from his locks the ashes of the grave,
    And outward trod
Into the glorious liberty of God.

He cast the symbols of his shame away ;
And, passing where the sleeping Milcho
    lay,
    Though back and limb
Smarted with wrong, he prayed, " God par-
    don him ! "

So went he forth ; but in God's time he
    came
To light on Uilline's hills a holy flame ;
    And, dying, gave
The land a saint that lost him as a slave.

O dark, sad millions, patiently and dumb
Waiting for God, your hour at last has
    come,
    And freedom's song
Breaks the long silence of your night of
    wrong !

Arise and flee ! shake off the vile restraint
Of ages ; but, like Ballymena's saint,
    The oppressor spare,
Heap only on his head the coals of prayer.

Go forth, like him ! like him return again,
To bless the land whereon in bitter pain
    Ye toiled at first,
And heal with freedom what your slavery
    cursed.

ANNIVERSARY POEM

Read before the Alumni of the Friends'
Yearly Meeting School, at the Annual Meeting
at Newport, R. I., 15th 6th mo., 1863.

ONCE more, dear friends, you meet beneath
    A clouded sky :
Not yet the sword has found its sheath,
And on the sweet spring airs the breath
    Of war floats by.

Yet trouble springs not from the ground,
    Nor pain from chance ;
The Eternal order circles round,
And wave and storm find mete and bound
    In Providence.

Full long our feet the flowery ways
    Of peace have trod,
Content with creed and garb and phrase :
A harder path in earlier days
    Led up to God.

Too cheaply truths, once purchased dear,
    Are made our own ;
Too long the world has smiled to hear
Our boast of full corn in the ear
    By others sown ;

To see us stir the martyr fires
    Of long ago,
And wrap our satisfied desires
In the singed mantles that our sires
    Have dropped below.

But now the cross our worthies bore
    On us is laid ;
Profession's quiet sleep is o'er,
And in the scale of truth once more
    Our faith is weighed.

The cry of innocent blood at last
    Is calling down
An answer in the whirlwind-blast,
The thunder and the shadow cast
    From Heaven's dark frown.

The land is red with judgments.   Who
    Stands guiltless forth ?
Have we been faithful as we knew,
To God and to our brother true,
    To Heaven and Earth ?

How faint, through din of merchandise
    And count of gain,
Have seemed to us the captive's cries !
How far away the tears and sighs
    Of souls in pain !

This day the fearful reckoning comes
    To each and all ;
We hear amidst our peaceful homes
The summons of the conscript drums,
    The bugle's call.

Our path is plain ; the war-net draws
    Round us in vain,
While, faithful to the Higher Cause,
We keep our fealty to the laws
    Through patient pain.

The levelled gun, the battle-brand,
    We may not take :
But, calmly loyal, we can stand
And suffer with our suffering land
    For conscience' sake.

Why ask for ease where all is pain ?
    Shall we alone
Be left to add our gain to gain,
When over Armageddon's plain
    The trump is blown ?

To suffer well is well to serve ;
    Safe in our Lord
The rigid lines of law shall curve
To spare us ; from our heads shall swerve
    Its smiting sword.

And light is mingled with the gloom,
    And joy with grief ;
Divinest compensations come,
Through thorns of judgment mercies bloom
    In sweet relief.

Thanks for our privilege to bless,
    By word and deed,
The widow in her keen distress,
The childless and the fatherless,
    The hearts that bleed !

For fields of duty, opening wide,
    Where all our powers
Are tasked the eager steps to guide
Of millions on a path untried :
    The slave is ours !

Ours by traditions dear and old,
    Which make the race
Our wards to cherish and uphold,
And cast their freedom in the mould
    Of Christian grace.

And we may tread the sick-bed floors
    Where strong men pine,
And, down the groaning corridors,
Pour freely from our liberal stores
    The oil and wine.

Who murmurs that in these dark days
    His lot is cast ?
God's hand within the shadow lays
The stones whereon His gates of praise
    Shall rise at last.

Turn and o'erturn, O outstretched Hand !
    Nor stint, nor stay ;
The years have never dropped their sand
On mortal issue vast and grand
    As ours to-day.

Already, on the sable ground
    Of man's despair
Is Freedom's glorious picture found,
With all its dusky hands unbound
    Upraised in prayer.

Oh, small shall seem all sacrifice
    And pain and loss,
When God shall wipe the weeping eyes,
For suffering give the victor's prize,
    The crown for cross !

BARBARA FRIETCHIE

This poem was written in strict conformity
to the account of the incident as I had it from
respectable and trustworthy sources. It has
since been the subject of a good deal of con-
flicting testimony, and the story was probably
incorrect in some of its details. It is admitted
by all that Barbara Frietchie was no myth, but
a worthy and highly esteemed gentlewoman,
intensely loyal and a hater of the Slavery Re-
bellion, holding her Union flag sacred and
keeping it with her Bible ; that when the Con-
federates halted before her house, and entered
her dooryard, she denounced them in vigorous
language, shook her cane in their faces, and
drove them out ; and when General Burnside's
troops followed close upon Jackson's, she waved
her flag and cheered them. It is stated that
May Quantrell, a brave and loyal lady in an-
other part of the city, did wave her flag in
sight of the Confederates. It is possible that
there has been a blending of the two incidents.

Up from the meadows rich with corn,
Clear in the cool September morn,

The clustered spires of Frederick stand
Green-walled by the hills of Maryland.

Round about them orchards sweep,
Apple and peach tree fruited deep,

Fair as the garden of the Lord
To the eyes of the famished rebel horde,

On that pleasant morn of the early fall
When Lee marched over the mountain
    wall ;

Over the mountains winding down,
Horse and foot, into Frederick town.

Forty flags with their silver stars,
Forty flags with their crimson bars,

Flapped in the morning wind : the sun
Of noon looked down, and saw not one.

Up rose old Barbara Frietchie then,
Bowed with her fourscore years and ten ;

Bravest of all in Frederick town,
She took up the flag the men hauled down;

In her attic window the staff she set,
To show that one heart was loyal yet.

Up the street came the rebel tread,
Stonewall Jackson riding ahead.

Under his slouched hat left and right
He glanced ; the old flag met his sight.

" Halt ! " — the dust-brown ranks stood
    fast.
" Fire ! " — out blazed the rifle-blast.

It shivered the window, pane and sash ;
It rent the banner with seam and gash.

Quick, as it fell, from the broken staff
Dame Barbara snatched the silken scarf.

She leaned far out on the window-sill,
And shook it forth with a royal will.

" Shoot, if you must, this old gray head,
But spare your country's flag," she said.

A shade of sadness, a blush of shame,
Over the face of the leader came ;

The nobler nature within him stirred
To life at that woman's deed and word ;

" Who touches a hair of yon gray head
Dies like a dog ! March on ! " he said.

All day long through Frederick street
Sounded the tread of marching feet :

All day long that free flag tost
Over the heads of the rebel host.

Ever its torn folds rose and fell
On the loyal winds that loved it well ;

And through the hill-gaps sunset light
Shone over it with a warm good-night.

Barbara Frietchie's work is o'er,
And the Rebel rides on his raids no more.

Honor to her ! and let a tear
Fall, for her sake, on Stonewall's bier.

Over Barbara Frietchie's grave,
Flag of Freedom and Union, wave !

Peace and order and beauty draw
Round thy symbol of light and law ;

And ever the stars above look down
On thy stars below in Frederick town !

WHAT THE BIRDS SAID

THE birds against the April wind
    Flew northward, singing as they flew ;
They sang, " The land we leave behind
    Has swords for corn-blades, blood for
      dew."

" O wild-birds, flying from the South,
    What saw and heard ye, gazing down ? "
" We saw the mortar's upturned mouth,
    The sickened camp, the blazing town !

" Beneath the bivouac's starry lamps,
    We saw your march-worn children die ;
In shrouds of moss, in cypress swamps,
    We saw your dead uncoffined lie.

" We heard the starving prisoner's sighs
    And saw, from line and trench, your
      sons
Follow our flight with home-sick eyes
    Beyond the battery's smoking guns."

" And heard and saw ye only wrong
    And pain," I cried, " O wing - worn
      flocks ? "
" We heard," they sang, " the freedman's
      song,
    The crash of Slavery's broken locks !

" We saw from new, uprising States
    The treason-nursing mischief spurned,
As, crowding Freedom's ample gates,
    The long-estranged and lost returned.

" O'er dusky faces, seamed and old,
    And hands horn-hard with unpaid toil,
With hope in every rustling fold,
    We saw your star-dropt flag uncoil.

" And struggling up through sounds ac-
      cursed,
    A grateful murmur clomb the air ;
A whisper scarcely heard at first,
    It filled the listening heavens with
      prayer.

" And sweet and far, as from a star,
  Replied a voice which shall not cease,
Till, drowning all the noise of war,
  It sings the blessed song of peace ! "

So to me, in a doubtful day
  Of chill and slowly greening spring,
Low stooping from the cloudy gray,
  The wild-birds sang or seemed to sing.

They vanished in the misty air,
  The song went with them in their flight ;
But lo ! they left the sunset fair,
  And in the evening there was light.

THE MANTLE OF ST. JOHN DE MATHA

A LEGEND OF " THE RED, WHITE, AND BLUE," A. D. 1154–1864

A STRONG and mighty Angel,
  Calm, terrible, and bright,
The cross in blended red and blue
  Upon his mantle white !

Two captives by him kneeling,
  Each on his broken chain,
Sang praise to God who raiseth
  The dead to life again !

Dropping his cross-wrought mantle,
  " Wear this," the Angel said ;
" Take thou, O Freedom's priest, its sign, —
  The white, the blue, and red."

Then rose up John de Matha
  In the strength the Lord Christ gave,
And begged through all the land of France
  The ransom of the slave.

The gates of tower and castle
  Before him open flew,
The drawbridge at his coming fell,
  The door-bolt backward drew.

For all men owned his errand,
  And paid his righteous tax ;
And the hearts of lord and peasant
  Were in his hands as wax.

At last, outbound from Tunis,
  His bark her anchor weighed,
Freighted with seven-score Christian souls
  Whose ransom he had paid.

But, torn by Paynim hatred,
  Her sails in tatters hung ;
And on the wild waves, rudderless,
  A shattered hulk she swung

" God save us ! " cried the captain,
  " For naught can man avail ;
Oh, woe betide the ship that lacks
  Her rudder and her sail !

" Behind us are the Moormen ;
  At sea we sink or strand :
There 's death upon the water,
  There 's death upon the land ! "

Then up spake John de Matha :
  " God's errands never fail !
Take thou the mantle which I wear,
  And make of it a sail."

They raised the cross-wrought mantle
  The blue, the white, the red ;
And straight before the wind off-shore
  The ship of Freedom sped.

" God help us ! " cried the seamen,
  " For vain is mortal skill :
The good ship on a stormy sea
  Is drifting at its will. "

Then up spake John de Matha :
  " My mariners, never fear !
The Lord whose breath has filled her sail
  May well our vessel steer ! "

So on through storm and darkness
  They drove for weary hours ;
And lo ! the third gray morning shone
  On Ostia's friendly towers.

And on the walls the watchers
  The ship of mercy knew,—
They knew far off its holy cross,
  The red, the white, and blue.

And the bells in all the steeples
  Rang out in glad accord,
To welcome home to Christian soil
  The ransomed of the Lord.

So runs the ancient legend
  By bard and painter told ;
And lo ! the cycle rounds again,
  The new is as the old !

With rudder foully broken,
  And sails by traitors torn,
Our country on a midnight sea
  Is waiting for the morn.

Before her, nameless terror ;
  Behind, the pirate foe ;
The clouds are black above her,
  The sea is white below.

The hope of all who suffer,
  The dread of all who wrong,
She drifts in darkness and in storm,
  How long, O Lord ! how long ?

But courage, O my mariners !
  Ye' shall not suffer wreck,
While up to God the freedman's prayers
  Are rising from your deck.

Is not your sail the banner
  Which God hath blest anew,
The mantle that De Matha wore,
  The red, the white, the blue ?

Its hues are all of heaven, —
  The red of sunset's dye,
The whiteness of the moon-lit cloud,
  The blue of morning's sky.

Wait cheerily, then, O mariners,
  For daylight and for land ;
The breath of God is in your sail,
  Your rudder is His hand.

Sail on, sail on, deep-freighted
  With blessings and with hopes ;
The saints of old with shadowy hands
  Are pulling at your ropes.

Behind ye holy martyrs
  Uplift the palm and crown ;
Before ye unborn ages send
  Their benedictions down.

Take heart from John de Matha ! —
  God's errands never fail !
Sweep on through storm and darkness,
  The thunder and the hail !

Sail on ! The morning cometh,
  The port ye yet shall win ;
And all the bells of God shall ring
  The good ship bravely in !

LAUS DEO !

On hearing the bells ring on the passage of
the constitutional amendment abolishing slav-
ery. The resolution was adopted by Congress,
January 31, 1865. The ratification by the re-
quisite number of States was announced Decem-
ber 18, 1865. [The suggestion came to the poet
as he sat in the Friends' Meeting-house in Ames-
bury, where he was present at the regular Fifth-
day meeting. All sat in silence, but on his
return to his home, he recited a portion of the
poem, not yet committed to paper, to his house-
mates in the garden room. " It wrote itself, or
rather sang itself, while the bells rang," he
wrote to Lucy Larcom.]

  IT is done !
Clang of bell and roar of gun
Send the tidings up and down.
  How the belfries rock and reel !
  How the great guns, peal on peal,
Fling the joy from town to town !

  Ring, O bells !
Every stroke exulting tells
Of the burial hour of crime.
  Loud and long, that all may hear,
  Ring for every listening ear
Of Eternity and Time !

  Let us kneel :
God's own voice is in that peal,
And this spot is holy ground.
  Lord, forgive us ! What are we,
  That our eyes this glory see,
That our ears have heard the sound !

  For the Lord
On the whirlwind is abroad ;
In the earthquake He has spoken ;
  He has smitten with His thunder
  The iron walls asunder,
And the gates of brass are broken !

  Loud and long
Lift the old exulting song ;
Sing with Miriam by the sea,
  He has cast the mighty down ;
  Horse and rider sink and drown ;
" He hath triumphed gloriously ! "

  Did we dare,
In our agony of prayer,
Ask for more than He has done ?

When was ever His right hand
Over any time or land
Stretched as now beneath the sun ?

How they pale,
Ancient myth and song and tale,
In this wonder of our days,
When the cruel rod of war
Blossoms white with righteous law,
And the wrath of man is praise !

Blotted out !
All within and all about
Shall a fresher life begin ;
Freer breathe the universe
As it rolls its heavy curse
On the dead and buried sin !

It is done !
In the circuit of the sun
Shall the sound thereof go forth.
It shall bid the sad rejoice,
It shall give the dumb a voice,
It shall belt with joy the earth !

Ring and swing,
Bells of joy ! On morning's wing
Send the song of praise abroad !
With a sound of broken chains
Tell the nations that He reigns,
Who alone is Lord and God !

HYMN

FOR THE CELEBRATION OF EMANCIPA-
TION AT NEWBURYPORT

Not unto us who did but seek
The word that burned within to speak,
Not unto us this day belong
The triumph and exultant song.

Upon us fell in early youth
The burden of unwelcome truth,
And left us, weak and frail and few,
The censor's painful work to do.

Thenceforth our life a fight became,
The air we breathed was hot with blame ;
For not with gauged and softened tone
We made the bondman's cause our own.

We bore, as Freedom's hope forlorn,
The private hate, the public scorn ;

Yet held through all the paths we trod
Our faith in man and trust in God.

We prayed and hoped ; but still, with awe,
The coming of the sword we saw ;
We heard the nearing steps of doom,
We saw the shade of things to come.

In grief which they alone can feel
Who from a mother's wrong appeal,
With blended lines of fear and hope
We cast our country's horoscope.

For still within her house of life
We marked the lurid sign of strife,
And, poisoning and imbittering all,
We saw the star of Wormwood fall.

Deep as our love for her became
Our hate of all that wrought her shame,
And if, thereby, with tongue and pen
We erred, — we were but mortal men.

We hoped for peace ; our eyes survey
The blood-red dawn of Freedom's day :
We prayed for love to loose the chain ;
'T is shorn by battle's axe in twain !

Nor skill nor strength nor zeal of ours
Has mined and heaved the hostile towers ;
Not by our hands is turned the key
That sets the sighing captives free.

A redder sea than Egypt's wave
Is piled and parted for the slave ;
A darker cloud moves on in light ;
A fiercer fire is guide by night !

The praise, O Lord ! is Thine alone,
In Thy own way Thy work is done !
Our poor gifts at Thy feet we cast,
To whom be glory, first and last !

AFTER THE WAR

THE PEACE AUTUMN

Written for the Essex County Agricultural
Festival, 1865.

Thank God for rest, where none molest,
And none can make afraid ;
For Peace that sits as Plenty's guest
Beneath the homestead shade !

Bring pike and gun, the sword's red
 scourge,
The negro's broken chains,
And beat them at the blacksmith's forge
To ploughshares for our plains.

Alike henceforth our hills of snow,
 And vales where cotton flowers ;
All streams that flow, all winds that blow,
 Are Freedom's motive-powers.

Henceforth to Labor's chivalry
 Be knightly honors paid ;
For nobler than the sword's shall be
 The sickle's accolade.

Build up an altar to the Lord,
 O grateful hearts of ours !
And shape it of the greenest sward
 That ever drank the showers.

Lay all the bloom of gardens there,
 And there the orchard fruits ;
Bring golden grain from sun and air,
 From earth her goodly roots.

There let our banners droop and flow,
 The stars uprise and fall ;
Our roll of martyrs, sad and slow,
 Let sighing breezes call.

Their names let hands of horn and tan
 And rough-shod feet applaud,
Who died to make the slave a man,
 And link with toil reward.

There let the common heart keep time
 To such an anthem sung
As never swelled on poet's rhyme,
 Or thrilled on singer's tongue.

Song of our burden and relief,
 Of peace and long annoy ;
The passion of our mighty grief
 And our exceeding joy !

A song of praise to Him who filled
 The harvests sown in tears,
And gave each field a double yield
 To feed our battle-years !

A song of faith that trusts the end
 To match the good begun,
Nor doubts the power of Love to blend
 The hearts of men as one !

TO THE THIRTY-NINTH CONGRESS

The thirty-ninth congress was that which met in 1865, after the close of the war, when it was charged with the great question of reconstruction ; the uppermost subject in men's minds was the standing of those who had recently been in arms against the Union and their relations to the freedmen.

O PEOPLE-CHOSEN ! are ye not
 Likewise the chosen of the Lord,
 To do His will and speak His word ?

From the loud thunder-storm of war
 Not man alone hath called ye forth,
 But He, the God of all the earth !

The torch of vengeance in your hands
 He quenches ; unto Him belongs
 The solemn recompense of wrongs.

Enough of blood the land has seen,
 And not by cell or gallows-stair
 Shall ye the way of God prepare.

Say to the pardon-seekers : Keep
 Your manhood, bend no suppliant knees,
 Nor palter with unworthy pleas.

Above your voices sounds the wail
 Of starving men ; we shut in vain
 Our eyes to Pillow's ghastly stain.

What words can drown that bitter cry ?
 What tears wash out the stain of death ?
 What oaths confirm your broken faith ?

From you alone the guaranty
 Of union, freedom, peace, we claim ;
 We urge no conqueror's terms of shame.

Alas ! no victor's pride is ours ;
 We bend above our triumphs won
 Like David o'er his rebel son.

Be men, not beggars. Cancel all
 By one brave, generous action ; trust
 Your better instincts, and be just !

Make all men peers before the law,
 Take hands from off the negro's throat,
 Give black and white an equal vote.

Keep all your forfeit lives and lands,
But give the common law's redress
To labor's utter nakedness.

Revive the old heroic will ;
Be in the right as brave and strong
As ye have proved yourselves in wrong.

Defeat shall then be victory,
Your loss the wealth of full amends,
And hate be love, and foes be friends.

Then buried be the dreadful past,
Its common slain be mourned, and let
All memories soften to regret.

Then shall the Union's mother-heart
Her lost and wandering ones recall,
Forgiving and restoring all, —

And Freedom break her marble trance
Above the Capitolian dome,
Stretch hands, and bid ye welcome
home !

THE HIVE AT GETTYSBURG

In the old Hebrew myth the lion's frame,
So terrible alive,
Bleached by the desert's sun and wind, be-
came
The wandering wild bees' hive ;
And he who, lone and naked-handed, tore
Those jaws of death apart,
In after time drew forth their honeyed store
To strengthen his strong heart.

Dead seemed the legend : but it only slept
To wake beneath our sky ;
Just on the spot whence ravening Treason
crept
Back to its lair to die,
Bleeding and torn from Freedom's moun-
tain bounds,
A stained and shattered drum
Is now the hive where, on their flowery
rounds,
The wild bees go and come.

Unchallenged by a ghostly sentinel,
They wander wide and far,
Along green hillsides, sown with shot and
shell,
Through vales once choked with war.

The low reveille of their battle-drum
Disturbs no morning prayer :
With deeper peace in summer noons their
hum
Fills all the drowsy air.

And Samson's riddle is our own to-day,
Of sweetness from the strong,
Of union, peace, and freedom plucked
away
From the rent jaws of wrong.
From Treason's death we draw a purer
life,
As, from the beast he slew,
A sweetness sweeter for his bitter strife
The old-time athlete drew !

HOWARD AT ATLANTA

Right in the track where Sherman
Ploughed his red furrow,
Out of the narrow cabin,
Up from the cellar's burrow,
Gathered the little black people,
With freedom newly dowered,
Where, beside their Northern teacher,
Stood the soldier, Howard.

He listened and heard the children
Of the poor and long-enslaved
Reading the words of Jesus,
Singing the songs of David.
Behold ! — the dumb lips speaking,
The blind eyes seeing !
Bones of the Prophet's vision
Warmed into being !

Transformed he saw them passing
Their new life's portal !
Almost it seemed the mortal
Put on the immortal.
No more with the beasts of burden,
No more with stone and clod,
But crowned with glory and honor
In the image of God !

There was the human chattel
Its manhood taking ;
There, in each dark, bronze statue,
A soul was waking !
The man of many battles,
With tears his eyelids pressing,
Stretched over those dusky foreheads
His one-armed blessing.

And he said : " Who hears can never
   Fear for or doubt you ;
What shall I tell the children
   Up North about you ? "
Then ran round a whisper, a murmur,
   Some answer devising ;
And a little boy stood up : " General,
   Tell 'em we 're rising ! "

O black boy of Atlanta !
   But half was spoken :
The slave's chain and the master's
   Alike are broken.
The one curse of the races
   Held both in tether :
They are rising, — all are rising,
   The black and white together !

O brave men and fair women !
   Ill comes of hate and scorning :
Shall the dark faces only
   Be turned to morning ? —
Make Time your sole avenger,
   All-healing, all-redressing ;
Meet Fate half-way, and make it
   A joy and blessing !

THE EMANCIPATION GROUP

Moses Kimball, a citizen of Boston, pre-
sented to the city a duplicate of the Freedman's
Memorial statue erected in Lincoln Square,
Washington. The group, which stands in Park
Square, represents the figure of a slave, from
whose limbs the broken fetters have fallen,
kneeling in gratitude at the feet of Lincoln.
The group was designed by Thomas Ball, and
was unveiled December 9, 1879. These verses
were written for the occasion.

AMIDST thy sacred effigies
   Of old renown give place,
O city, Freedom-loved ! to his
   Whose hand unchained a race.

Take the worn frame, that rested not
   Save in a martyr's grave ;
The care-lined face, that none forgot,
   Bent to the kneeling slave.

Let man be free ! The mighty word
   He spake was not his own ;
An impulse from the Highest stirred
   These chiselled lips alone.

The cloudy sign, the fiery guide,
   Along his pathway ran,
And Nature, through his voice, denied
   The ownership of man.

We rest in peace where these sad eyes
   Saw peril, strife, and pain ;
His was the nation's sacrifice,
   And ours the priceless gain.

O symbol of God's will on earth
   As it is done above !
Bear witness to the cost and worth
   Of justice and of love.

Stand in thy place and testify
   To coming ages long,
That truth is stronger than a lie,
   And righteousness than wrong.

THE JUBILEE SINGERS

A number of students of Fisk University,
under the direction of one of the officers, gave
a series of concerts in the Northern States, for
the purpose of establishing the college on a
firmer financial foundation. Their hymns and
songs, mostly in a minor key, touched the
hearts of the people, and were received as pe-
culiarly expressive of a race delivered from
bondage.

VOICE of a people suffering long,
The pathos of their mournful song,
The sorrow of their night of wrong !

Their cry like that which Israel gave,
A prayer for one to guide and save,
Like Moses by the Red Sea's wave !

The stern accord her timbrel lent
To Miriam's note of triumph sent
O'er Egypt's sunken armament !

The tramp that startled camp and town,
And shook the walls of slavery down,
The spectral march of old John Brown !

The storm that swept through battle-days,
The triumph after long delays,
The bondmen giving God the praise !

Voice of a ransomed race, sing on
Till Freedom's every right is won,
And slavery's every wrong undone !

GARRISON

The earliest poem in this division was my youthful tribute to the great reformer when himself a young man he was first sounding his trumpet in Essex County. I close with the verses inscribed to him at the end of his earthly career, May 24, 1879. My poetical service in the cause of freedom is thus almost synchronous with his life of devotion to the same cause.

THE storm and peril overpast,
  The hounding hatred shamed and still,
Go, soul of freedom ! take at last
  The place which thou alone canst fill.

Confirm the lesson taught of old —
  Life saved for self is lost, while they
Who lose it in His service hold
  The lease of God's eternal day.

Not for thyself, but for the slave
  Thy words of thunder shook the world ;
No selfish griefs or hatred gave
  The strength wherewith thy bolts were
    hurled.

From lips that Sinai's trumpet blew
  We heard a tender under song ;
Thy very wrath from pity grew,
  From love of man thy hate of wrong.

Now past and present are as one ;
  The life below is life above ;
Thy mortal years have but begun
  Thy immortality of love.

With somewhat of thy lofty faith
  We lay thy outworn garment by,
Give death but what belongs to death,
  And life the life that cannot die !

Not for a soul like thine the calm
  Of selfish ease and joys of sense ;
But duty, more than crown or palm,
  Its own exceeding recompense.

Go up and on ! thy day well done,
  Its morning promise well fulfilled,
Arise to triumphs yet unwon,
  To holier tasks that God has willed.

Go, leave behind thee all that mars
  The work below of man for man ;
With the white legions of the stars
  Do service such as angels can.

Wherever wrong shall right deny
  Or suffering spirits urge their plea,
Be thine a voice to smite the lie,
  A hand to set the captive free !

SONGS OF LABOR AND REFORM

THE QUAKER OF THE OLDEN TIME

THE Quaker of the olden time!
  How calm and firm and true,
Unspotted by its wrong and crime,
  He walked the dark earth through.
The lust of power, the love of gain,
  The thousand lures of sin
Around him, had no power to stain
  The purity within.

With that deep insight which detects
  All great things in the small,
And knows how each man's life affects
  The spiritual life of all,
He walked by faith and not by sight,
  By love and not by law;
The presence of the wrong or right
  He rather felt than saw.

He felt that wrong with wrong partakes,
  That nothing stands alone,
That whoso gives the motive, makes
  His brother's sin his own.
And, pausing not for doubtful choice
  Of evils great or small,
He listened to that inward voice
  Which called away from all.

O Spirit of that early day,
  So pure and strong and true,
Be with us in the narrow way
  Our faithful fathers knew.
Give strength the evil to forsake,
  The cross of Truth to bear,
And love and reverent fear to make
  Our daily lives a prayer!

DEMOCRACY

All things whatsoever ye would that men should do to you, do ye even so to them. — Matthew vii. 12.

BEARER of Freedom's holy light,
  Breaker of Slavery's chain and rod,
The foe of all which pains the sight,
  Or wounds the generous ear of God!

Beautiful yet thy temples rise,
  Though there profaning gifts are thrown;
And fires unkindled of the skies
  Are glaring round thy altar-stone.

Still sacred, though thy name be breathed
  By those whose hearts thy truth de-
    ride;
And garlands, plucked from thee, are
    wreathed
  Around the haughty brows of Pride.

Oh, ideal of my boyhood's time!
  The faith in which my father stood,
Even when the sons of Lust and Crime
  Had stained thy peaceful courts with
    blood!

Still to those courts my footsteps turn,
  For through the mists which darken there,
I see the flame of Freedom burn, —
  The Kebla of the patriot's prayer!

The generous feeling, pure and warm,
  Which owns the right of all divine;
The pitying heart, the helping arm,
  The prompt self-sacrifice, are thine.

Beneath thy broad, impartial eye,
  How fade the lines of caste and birth!
How equal in their suffering lie
  The groaning multitudes of earth!

Still to a stricken brother true,
  Whatever clime hath nurtured him;
As stooped to heal the wounded Jew
  The worshipper of Gerizim.

By misery unrepelled, unawed
  By pomp or power, thou seest a Man
In prince or peasant, slave or lord,
  Pale priest, or swarthy artisan.

Through all disguise, form, place, or
    name,
  Beneath the flaunting robes of sin,
Through poverty and squalid shame,
  Thou lookest on the man within.

On man, as man, retaining yet,
  Howe'er debased, and soiled, and dim,
The crown upon his forehead set,
  The immortal gift of God to him.

And there is reverence in thy look ;
  For that frail form which mortals wear
The Spirit of the Holiest took,
  And veiled His perfect brightness there.

Not from the shallow babbling fount
  Of vain philosophy thou art ;
He who of old on Syria's Mount
  Thrilled, warmed, by turns, the listen-
    er's heart,

In holy words which cannot die,
  In thoughts which angels leaned to
    know,
Proclaimed thy message from on high,
  Thy mission to a world of woe.

That voice's echo hath not died !
  From the blue lake of Galilee,
And Tabor's lonely mountain-side,
  It calls a struggling world to thee.

Thy name and watchword o'er this land
  I hear in every breeze that stirs,
And round a thousand altars stand
  Thy banded party worshippers.

Not to these altars of a day,
  At party's call, my gift I bring ;
But on thy olden shrine I lay
  A freeman's dearest offering :

The voiceless utterance of his will, —
  His pledge to Freedom and to Truth,
That manhood's heart remembers still
  The homage of his generous youth.

THE GALLOWS

Written on reading pamphlets published by
clergymen against the abolition of the gallows.
[Originally entitled *Lines*.]

I

THE suns of eighteen centuries have shone
  Since the Redeemer walked with man, and
    made
The fisher's boat, the cavern's floor of stone,
  And mountain moss, a pillow for His
    head ;
And He, who wandered with the peasant
    Jew,
  And broke with publicans the bread of
    shame,
  And drank with blessings, in His Father's
    name,
The water which Samaria's outcast drew,
Hath now His temples upon every shore,
  Altar and shrine and priest ; and incense
    dim
  Evermore rising, with low prayer and
    hymn,
From lips which press the temple's marble
    floor,
Or kiss the gilded sign of the dread cross
    He bore.

II

Yet as of old, when, meekly "doing good,"
He fed a blind and selfish multitude,
And even the poor companions of His lot
With their dim earthly vision knew Him
    not,
  How ill are His high teachings under-
    stood !
Where He hath spoken Liberty, the priest
  At His own altar binds the chain anew ;
Where He hath bidden to Life's equal feast,
  The starving many wait upon the few ;
Where He hath spoken Peace, His name
    hath been
The loudest war-cry of contending men ;
Priests, pale with vigils, in His name have
    blessed
The unsheathed sword, and laid the spear
    in rest,
Wet the war-banner with their sacred wine,
And crossed its blazon with the holy sign ;
Yea, in His name who bade the erring live,
And daily taught His lesson, to forgive !
  Twisted the cord and edged the murder-
    ous steel ;
And, with His words of mercy on their
    lips,
Hung gloating o'er the pincers' burning
    grips,

And the grim horror of the straining
   wheel ;
Fed the slow flame which gnawed the vic-
   tim's limb,
Who saw before his searing eyeballs swim
   The image of their Christ in cruel zeal,
Through the black torment-smoke, held
   mockingly to him !

III

The blood which mingled with the desert
   sand,
   And beaded with its red and ghastly
     dew
The vines and olives of the Holy Land ;
   The shrieking curses of the hunted Jew ;
The white-sown bones of heretics, where'er
They sank beneath the Crusade's holy spear,
Goa's dark dungeons, Malta's sea-washed
   cell,
   Where with the hymns the ghostly fa-
     thers sung
   Mingled the groans by subtle torture
     wrung,
Heaven's anthem blending with the shriek
   of hell !
The midnight of Bartholomew, the stake
   Of Smithfield, and that thrice-accursed
     flame
Which Calvin kindled by Geneva's lake ;
New England's scaffold, and the priestly
   sneer
Which mocked its victims in that hour of
   fear,
   When guilt itself a human tear might
     claim, —
Bear witness, O Thou wronged and merci-
   ful One !
That Earth's most hateful crimes have in
   Thy name been done !

IV

Thank God ! that I have lived to see the
   time
   When the great truth begins at last to
     find
   An utterance from the deep heart of
     mankind,
Earnest and clear, that all Revenge is Crime,
That man is holier than a creed, that all
   Restraint upon him must consult his good,
Hope's sunshine linger on his prison wall,
And Love look in upon his solitude.

The beautiful lesson which our Saviour
   taught
Through long, dark centuries its way hath
   wrought
Into the common mind and popular thought ;
And words, to which by Galilee's lake shore
The humble fishers listened with hushed oar,
Have found an echo in the general heart,
And of the public faith become a living part.

V

Who shall arrest this tendency ?   Bring
   back
The cells of Venice and the bigot's rack ?
Harden the softening human heart again
To cold indifference to a brother's pain ?
Ye most unhappy men ! who, turned away
From the mild sunshine of the Gospel day,
   Grope in the shadows of Man's twilight
     time,
What mean ye, that with ghoul-like zest
   ye brood,
O'er those foul altars streaming with warm
   blood,
   Permitted in another age and clime ?
Why cite that law with which the bigot Jew
Rebuked the Pagan's mercy, when he knew
No evil in the Just One ?   Wherefore turn
To the dark, cruel past ?   Can ye not learn
From the pure Teacher's life how mildly
   free
Is the great Gospel of Humanity ?
The Flamen's knife is bloodless, and no
   more
Mexitli's altars soak with human gore,
No more the ghastly sacrifices smoke
Through the green arches of the Druid's
   oak ;
And ye of milder faith, with your high claim
Of prophet-utterance in the Holiest name,
Will ye become the Druids of our time !
Set up your scaffold-altars in our land,
And, consecrators of Law's darkest crime,
   Urge to its loathsome work the hang-
     man's hand ?
Beware, lest human nature, roused at last,
From its peeled shoulder your encumbrance
   cast,
   And, sick to loathing of your cry for
     blood,
Rank ye with those who led their victims
   round
The Celt's red altar and the Indian's mound,
   Abhorred of Earth and Heaven, a pagan
     brotherhood !

SEED–TIME AND HARVEST

As o'er his furrowed fields which lie
Beneath a coldly dropping sky,
Yet chill with winter's melted snow,
The husbandman goes forth to sow,

Thus, Freedom, on the bitter blast
The ventures of thy seed we cast,
And trust to warmer sun and rain
To swell the germs and fill the grain.

Who calls thy glorious service hard ?
Who deems it not its own reward ?
Who, for its trials, counts it less
A cause of praise and thankfulness ?

It may not be our lot to wield
The sickle in the ripened field ;
Nor ours to hear, on summer eves,
The reaper's song among the sheaves.

Yet where our duty's task is wrought
In unison with God's great thought,
The near and future blend in one,
And whatsoe'er is willed, is done !

And ours the grateful service whence
Comes day by day the recompense ;
The hope, the trust, the purpose stayed,
The fountain and the noonday shade.

And were this life the utmost span,
The only end and aim of man,
Better the toil of fields like these
Than waking dream and slothful ease.

But life, though falling like our grain,
Like that revives and springs again ;
And, early called, how blest are they
Who wait in heaven their harvest-day !

TO THE REFORMERS OF ENG-
LAND

This poem was addressed to those who like
Richard Cobden and John Bright were seeking
the reform of political evils in Great Britain by
peaceful and Christian means. It will be re-
membered that the Anti-Corn-Law League
was in the midst of its labors at this time.

GOD bless ye, brothers ! in the fight
Ye 're waging now, ye cannot fail,
For better is your sense of right
Than king-craft's triple mail.

Than tyrant's law, or bigot's ban,
More mighty is your simplest word ;
The free heart of an honest man
Than crosier or the sword.

Go, let your blinded Church rehearse
The lesson it has learned so well ;
It moves not with its prayer or curse
The gates of heaven or hell.

Let the State scaffold rise again ;
Did Freedom die when Russell died ?
Forget ye how the blood of Vane
From earth's green bosom cried ?

The great hearts of your olden time
Are beating with you, full and strong
All holy memories and sublime
And glorious round ye throng.

The bluff, bold men of Runnymede
Are with ye still in times like these ;
The shades of England's mighty dead,
Your cloud of witnesses !

The truths ye urge are borne abroad
By every wind and every tide ;
The voice of Nature and of God
Speaks out upon your side.

The weapons which your hands have found
Are those which Heaven itself has
wrought,
Light, Truth, and Love ; your battle-
ground
The free, broad field of Thought.

No partial, selfish purpose breaks
The simple beauty of your plan,
Nor lie from throne or altar shakes
Your steady faith in man.

The languid pulse of England starts
And bounds beneath your words of
power,
The beating of her million hearts
Is with you at this hour !

O ye who, with undoubting eyes,
Through present cloud and gathering
storm,

Behold the span of Freedom's skies,
  And sunshine soft and warm ;

Press bravely onward ! not in vain
  Your generous trust in human-kind ;
The good which bloodshed could not gain
  Your peaceful zeal shall find.

Press on ! the triumph shall be won
  Of common rights and equal laws,
The glorious dream of Harrington,
  And Sidney's good old cause.

Blessing the cotter and the crown,
  Sweetening worn Labor's bitter cup ;
And, plucking not the highest down,
  Lifting the lowest up.

Press on ! and we who may not share
  The toil or glory of your fight
May ask, at least, in earnest prayer,
  God's blessing on the right !

THE HUMAN SACRIFICE

Some leading sectarian papers had lately
published the letter of a clergyman, giving
an account of his attendance upon a criminal
(who had committed murder during a fit of
intoxication), at the time of his execution, in
western New York. The writer describes the
agony of the wretched being, his abortive at-
tempts at prayer, his appeal for life, his fear
of a violent death ; and, after declaring his
belief that the poor victim died without hope
of salvation, concludes with a warm eulogy
upon the gallows, being more than ever con-
vinced of its utility by the awful dread and
horror which it inspired.

I

Far from his close and noisome cell,
  By grassy lane and sunny stream,
Blown clover field and strawberry dell,
  And green and meadow freshness, fell
    The footsteps of his dream.
Again from careless feet the dew
  Of summer's misty morn he shook ;
Again with merry heart he threw
  His light line in the rippling brook.
Back crowded all his school-day joys ;
  He urged the ball and quoit again,
And heard the shout of laughing boys
  Come ringing down the walnut glen.

Again he felt the western breeze,
  With scent of flowers and crisping hay ;
And down again through wind-stirred trees
  He saw the quivering sunlight play.
An angel in home's vine-hung door,
He saw his sister smile once more ;
Once more the truant's brown-locked head
Upon his mother's knees was laid,
And sweetly lulled to slumber there,
With evening's holy hymn and prayer !

II

He woke.   At once on heart and brain
The present Terror rushed again ;
Clanked on his limbs the felon's chain !
He woke, to hear the church-tower tell
Time's footfall on the conscious bell,
And, shuddering, feel that clanging din
His life's last hour had ushered in ;
To see within his prison-yard,
Through the small window, iron barred,
The gallows shadow rising dim
Between the sunrise heaven and him ;
A horror in God's blessed air ;
A blackness in his morning light ;
Like some foul devil-altar there
  Built up by demon hands at night.
And, maddened by that evil sight,
Dark, horrible, confused, and strange,
A chaos of wild, weltering change,
All power of check and guidance gone,
Dizzy and blind, his mind swept on.
In vain he strove to breathe a prayer,
  In vain he turned the Holy Book,
He only heard the gallows-stair
  Creak as the wind its timbers shook.
No dream for him of sin forgiven,
  While still that baleful spectre stood,
With its hoarse murmur, "*Blood for
  Blood !*"
Between him and the pitying Heaven !

III

Low on his dungeon floor he knelt,
  And smote his breast, and on his chain,
Whose iron clasp he always felt,
  His hot tears fell like rain ;
And near him, with the cold, calm look
  And tone of one whose formal part,
Unwarmed, unsoftened of the heart,
Is measured out by rule and book,
With placid lip and tranquil blood,
The hangman's ghostly ally stood,
Blessing with solemn text and word
The gallows-drop and strangling cord ;

Lending the sacred Gospel's awe
And sanction to the crime of Law.

IV

He saw the victim's tortured brow,
  The sweat of anguish starting there,
The record of a nameless woe
  In the dim eye's imploring stare,
  Seen hideous through the long, damp
    hair, —
Fingers of ghastly skin and bone
Working and writhing on the stone !
And heard, by mortal terror wrung
From heaving breast and stiffened tongue,
  The choking sob and low hoarse prayer ;
As o'er his half-crazed fancy came
A vision of the eternal flame,
Its smoking cloud of agonies,
Its demon worm that never dies,
The everlasting rise and fall
Of fire-waves round the infernal wall ;
While high above that dark red flood,
Black, giant-like, the gallows stood ;
Two busy fiends attending there :
One with cold mocking rite and prayer,
The other with impatient grasp,
Tightening the death-rope's strangling
    clasp.

V

The unfelt rite at length was done,
  The prayer unheard at length was said,
An hour had passed : the noonday sun
  Smote on the features of the dead !
And he who stood the doomed beside,
Calm gauger of the swelling tide
Of mortal agony and fear,
Heeding with curious eye and ear
Whate'er revealed the keen excess
Of man's extremest wretchedness :
And who in that dark anguish saw
An earnest of the victim's fate,
The vengeful terrors of God's law,
  The kindlings of Eternal hate,
The first drops of that fiery rain
Which beats the dark red realm of pain,
Did he uplift his earnest cries
  Against the crime of Law, which gave
His brother to that fearful grave,
Whereon Hope's moonlight never lies,
  And Faith's white blossoms never wave
To the soft breath of Memory's sighs ;
Which sent a spirit marred and stained,
By fiends of sin possessed, profaned,
In madness and in blindness stark,

Into the silent, unknown dark ?
No, from the wild and shrinking dread,
With which he saw the victim led
  Beneath the dark veil which divides
Ever the living from the dead,
  And Nature's solemn secret hides,
The man of prayer can only draw
New reasons for his bloody law ;
New faith in staying Murder's hand
By murder at that Law's command ;
New reverence for the gallows-rope,
As human nature's latest hope ;
Last relic of the good old time,
When Power found license for its crime,
And held a writhing world in check
By that fell cord about its neck ;
Stifled Sedition's rising shout,
Choked the young breath of Freedom out,
And timely checked the words which
    sprung
From Heresy's forbidden tongue ;
While in its noose of terror bound,
The Church its cherished union found,
Conforming, on the Moslem plan,
The motley-colored mind of man,
Not by the Koran and the Sword,
But by the Bible and the Cord !

VI

O Thou ! at whose rebuke the grave
Back to warm life its sleeper gave,
Beneath whose sad and tearful glance
The cold and changëd countenance
Broke the still horror of its trance,
And, waking, saw with joy above,
A brother's face of tenderest love ;
Thou, unto whom the blind and lame,
The sorrowing and the sin-sick came,
And from Thy very garment's hem
Drew life and healing unto them,
The burden of Thy holy faith
Was love and life, not hate and death ;
Man's demon ministers of pain,
  The fiends of his revenge, were sent
  From thy pure Gospel's element
To their dark home again.
Thy name is Love ! What, then, is he,
Who in that name the gallows rears,
An awful altar built to Thee,
  With sacrifice of blood and tears ?
Oh, once again Thy healing lay
  On the blind eyes which knew **Thee**
    not,
And let the light of Thy pure day
  Melt in upon his darkened thought.

Soften his hard, cold heart, and show
  The power which in forbearance lies,
And let him feel that mercy now
  Is better than old sacrifice !

VII

As on the White Sea's charmëd shore,
  The Parsee sees his holy hill
With dunnest smoke-clouds curtained o'er,
Yet knows beneath them, evermore,
  The low, pale fire is quivering still ;
So, underneath its clouds of sin,
  The heart of man retaineth yet
Gleams of its holy origin ;
  And half-quenched stars that never set,
Dim colors of its faded bow,
  And early beauty, linger there,
And o'er its wasted desert blow
  Faint breathings of its morning air.
Oh, never yet upon the scroll
Of the sin-stained, but priceless soul,
  Hath Heaven inscribed " Despair ! "
Cast not the clouded gem away,
Quench not the dim but living ray, —
  My brother man, Beware !
With that deep voice which from the skies
Forbade the Patriarch's sacrifice,
  God's angel cries, Forbear !

SONGS OF LABOR

DEDICATION

Prefixed to the volume of which the group
of six poems following this prelude constituted
the first portion.

I WOULD the gift I offer here
  Might graces from thy favor take,
And, seen through Friendship's atmos-
      phere,
On softened lines and coloring, wear
The unaccustomed light of beauty, for thy
      sake.

Few leaves of Fancy's spring remain :
  But what I have I give to thee,
The o'er-sunned bloom of summer's
      plain,
And paler flowers, the latter rain
Calls from the westering slope of life's
      autumnal lea.

Above the fallen groves of green,
  Where youth's enchanted forest stood,

Dry root and mossëd trunk between,
  A sober after-growth is seen,
As springs the pine where falls the gay-
      leafed maple wood !

Yet birds will sing, and breezes play
  Their leaf-harps in the sombre tree ;
And through the bleak and wintry day
It keeps its steady green alway, —
So, even my after-thoughts may have a
      charm for thee.

Art's perfect forms no moral need,
  And beauty is its own excuse ;
But for the dull and flowerless weed
Some healing virtue still must plead,
And the rough ore must find its honors in
      its use.

So haply these, my simple lays
  Of homely toil, may serve to show
The orchard bloom and tasselled maize
That skirt and gladden duty's ways,
The unsung beauty hid life's common
      things below.

Haply from them the toiler, bent
  Above his forge or plough, may gain
A manlier spirit of content,
And feel that life is wisest spent
Where the strong working hand makes
      strong the working brain.

The doom which to the guilty pair
  Without the walls of Eden came,
Transforming sinless ease to care
And rugged toil, no more shall bear
The burden of old crime, or mark of pri-
      mal shame.

A blessing now, a curse no more ;
  Since He, whose name we breathe
      with awe,
The coarse mechanic vesture wore,
A poor man toiling with the poor,
In labor, as in prayer, fulfilling the same
      law.

THE SHOEMAKERS

Ho ! workers of the old time styled
  The Gentle Craft of Leather !
Young brothers of the ancient guild,
  Stand forth once more together !

Call out again your long array,
  In the olden merry manner !
Once more, on gay St. Crispin's day,
  Fling out your blazoned banner !

Rap, rap ! upon the well-worn stone
  How falls the polished hammer !
Rap, rap ! the measured sound has grown
  A quick and merry clamor.
Now shape the sole ! now deftly curl
  The glossy vamp around it,
And bless the while the bright-eyed girl
  Whose gentle fingers bound it !

For you, along the Spanish main
  A hundred keels are ploughing ;
For you, the Indian on the plain
  His lasso-coil is throwing ;
For you, deep glens with hemlock dark
  The woodman's fire is lighting ;
For you, upon the oak's gray bark,
  The woodman's axe is smiting.

For you, from Carolina's pine
  The rosin-gum is stealing ;
For you, the dark-eyed Florentine
  Her silken skein is reeling ;
For you, the dizzy goatherd roams
  His rugged Alpine ledges ;
For you, round all her shepherd homes,
  Bloom England's thorny hedges.

The foremost still, by day or night,
  On moated mound or heather,
Where'er the need of trampled right
  Brought toiling men together ;
Where the free burghers from the wall
  Defied the mail-clad master,
Than yours, at Freedom's trumpet-call,
  No craftsmen rallied faster.

Let foplings sneer, let fools deride,
  Ye heed no idle scorner ;
Free hands and hearts are still your pride,
  And duty done your honor.
Ye dare to trust, for honest fame,
  The jury Time empanels,
And leave to truth each noble name
  Which glorifies your annals.

Thy songs, Hans Sachs, are living yet,
  In strong and hearty German ;
And Bloomfield's lay, and Gifford's wit,
  And patriot fame of Sherman ;
Still from his book, a mystic seer,

The soul of Behmen teaches,
And England's priestcraft shakes to hear
  Of Fox's leathern breeches.

The foot is yours ; where'er it falls,
  It treads your well-wrought leather,
On earthen floor, in marble halls
  On carpet, or on heather.
Still there the sweetest charm is found
  Of matron grace or vestal's,
As Hebe's foot bore nectar round
  Among the old celestials !

Rap, rap ! — your stout and bluff brogan,
  With footsteps slow and weary,
May wander where the sky's blue span
  Shuts down upon the prairie.
On Beauty's foot your slippers glance,
  By Saratoga's fountains,
Or twinkle down the summer dance
  Beneath the Crystal Mountains !

The red brick to the mason's hand,
  The brown earth to the tiller's,
The shoe in yours shall wealth command,
  Like fairy Cinderella's !
As they who shunned the household maid
  Beheld the crown upon her,
So all shall see your toil repaid
  With hearth and home and honor.

Then let the toast be freely quaffed,
  In water cool and brimming, —
" All honor to the good old Craft,
  Its merry men and women ! "
Call out again your long array,
  In the old time's pleasant manner :
Once more, on gay St. Crispin's day,
  Fling out his blazoned banner !

THE FISHERMEN

HURRAH ! the seaward breezes
  Sweep down the bay amain ;
Heave up, my lads, the anchor !
  Run up the sail again !
Leave to the lubber landsmen
  The rail-car and the steed ;
The stars of heaven shall guide us,
  The breath of heaven shall speed.

From the hill-top looks the steeple,
  And the lighthouse from the sand ;

And the scattered pines are waving
  Their farewell from the land.
One glance, my lads, behind us,
  For the homes we leave one sigh,
Ere we take the change and chances
  Of the ocean and the sky.

Now, brothers, for the icebergs
  Of frozen Labrador,
Floating spectral in the moonshine,
  Along the low, black shore !
Where like snow the gannet's feathers
  On Brador's rocks are shed,
And the noisy murr are flying,
  Like black scuds, overhead ;

Where in mist the rock is hiding,
  And the sharp reef lurks below,
And the white squall smites in summer,
  And the autumn tempests blow ;
Where, through gray and rolling vapor,
  From evening unto morn,
A thousand boats are hailing,
  Horn answering unto horn.

Hurrah ! for the Red Island,
  With the white cross on its crown !
Hurrah ! for Meccatina,
  And its mountains bare and brown !
Where the Caribou's tall antlers
  O'er the dwarf-wood freely toss,
And the footstep of the Mickmack
  Has no sound upon the moss.

There we 'll drop our lines, and gather
  Old Ocean's treasures in,
Where'er the mottled mackerel
  Turns up a steel-dark fin.
The sea 's our field of harvest,
  Its scaly tribes our grain ;
We 'll reap the teeming waters
  As at home they reap the plain !

Our wet hands spread the carpet,
  And light the hearth of home ;
From our fish, as in the old time,
  The silver coin shall come.
As the demon fled the chamber
  Where the fish of Tobit lay,
So ours from all our dwellings
  Shall frighten Want away.

Though the mist upon our jackets
  In the bitter air congeals,

And our lines wind stiff and slowly
  From off the frozen reels ;
Though the fog be dark around us,
  And the storm blow high and loud,
We will whistle down the wild wind,
  And laugh beneath the cloud !

In the darkness as in daylight,
  On the water as on land,
God's eye is looking on us,
  And beneath us is His hand !
Death will find us soon or later,
  On the deck or in the cot ;
And we cannot meet him better
  Than in working out our lot.

Hurrah ! hurrah ! the west-wind
  Comes freshening down the bay,
The rising sails are filling ;
  Give way, my lads, give way !
Leave the coward landsman clinging
  To the dull earth, like a weed ;
The stars of heaven shall guide us,
  The breath of heaven shall speed !

THE LUMBERMEN

WILDLY round our woodland quarters
  Sad-voiced Autumn grieves ;
Thickly down these swelling waters
  Float his fallen leaves.
Through the tall and naked timber,
  Column-like and old,
Gleam the sunsets of November,
  From their skies of gold.

O'er us, to the southland heading,
  Screams the gray wild-goose ;
On the night-frost sounds the treading
  Of the brindled moose.
Noiseless creeping, while we 're sleeping,
  Frost his task-work plies ;
Soon, his icy bridges heaping,
  Shall our log-piles rise.

When, with sounds of smothered thunder,
  On some night of rain,
Lake and river break asunder
  Winter's weakened chain,
Down the wild March flood shall bear them
  To the saw-mill's wheel,
Or where Steam, the slave, shall tear them
  With his teeth of steel.

Be it starlight, be it moonlight,
  In these vales below,
When the earliest beams of sunlight
  Streak the mountain's snow,
Crisps the hoar-frost, keen and early,
  To our hurrying feet,
And the forest echoes clearly
  All our blows repeat.

Where the crystal Ambijejis
  Stretches broad and clear,
And Millnoket's pine-black ridges
  Hide the browsing deer :
Where, through lakes and wide morasses,
  Or through rocky walls,
Swift and strong, Penobscot passes
  White with foamy falls ;

Where, through clouds, are glimpses given
  Of Katahdin's sides, —
Rock and forest piled to heaven,
  Torn and ploughed by slides !
Far below, the Indian trapping,
  In the sunshine warm ;
Far above, the snow-cloud wrapping
  Half the peak in storm !

Where are mossy carpets better
  Than the Persian weaves,
And than Eastern perfumes sweeter
  Seem the fading leaves ;
And a music wild and solemn,
  From the pine-tree's height,
Rolls its vast and sea-like volume
  On the wind of night ;

Make we here our camp of winter ;
  And, through sleet and snow,
Pitchy knot and beechen splinter
  On our hearth shall glow.
Here, with mirth to lighten duty,
  We shall lack alone
Woman's smile and girlhood's beauty,
  Childhood's lisping tone.

But their hearth is brighter burning
  For our toil to-day ;
And the welcome of returning
  Shall our loss repay,
When, like seamen from the waters,
  From the woods we come,
Greeting sisters, wives, and daughters,
  Angels of our home !

Not for us the measured ringing
  From the village spire,
Not for us the Sabbath singing
  Of the sweet-voiced choir ;
Ours the old, majestic temple,
  Where God's brightness shines
Down the dome so grand and ample,
  Propped by lofty pines !

Through each branch-enwoven skylight,
  Speaks He in the breeze,
As of old beneath the twilight
  Of lost Eden's trees !
For His ear, the inward feeling
  Needs no outward tongue ;
He can see the spirit kneeling
  While the axe is swung.

Heeding truth alone, and turning
  From the false and dim,
Lamp of toil or altar burning
  Are alike to Him.
Strike then, comrades !   Trade is waiting
  On our rugged toil ;
Far ships waiting for the freighting
  Of our woodland spoil !

Ships whose traffic links these highlands,
  Bleak and cold, of ours,
With the citron-planted islands
  Of a clime of flowers ;
To our frosts the tribute bringing
  Of eternal heats ;
In our lap of winter flinging
  Tropic fruits and sweets.

Cheerly, on the axe of labor,
  Let the sunbeams dance,
Better than the flash of sabre
  Or the gleam of lance !
Strike !   With every blow is given
  Freer sun and sky,
And the long-hid earth to heaven
  Looks, with wondering eye !

Loud behind us grow the murmurs
  Of the age to come ;
Clang of smiths, and tread of farmers,
  Bearing harvest home !
Here her virgin lap with treasures
  Shall the green earth fill ;
Waving wheat and golden maize-ears
  Crown each beechen hill.

Keep who will the city's alleys,
　Take the smooth-shorn plain ;
Give to us the cedarn valleys,
　Rocks and hills of Maine !
In our North-land, wild and woody,
　Let us still have part :
Rugged nurse and mother sturdy,
　Hold us to thy heart !

Oh, our free hearts beat the warmer
　For thy breath of snow ;
And our tread is all the firmer
　For thy rocks below.
Freedom, hand in hand with labor,
　Walketh strong and brave ;
On the forehead of his neighbor
　No man writeth Slave !

Lo, the day breaks ! old Katahdin's
　Pine-trees show its fires,
While from these dim forest gardens
　Rise their blackened spires.
Up, my comrades ! up and doing !
　Manhood's rugged play
Still renewing, bravely hewing
　Through the world our way !

THE SHIP–BUILDERS

THE sky is ruddy in the east,
　The earth is gray below,
And, spectral in the river-mist,
　The ship's white timbers show.
Then let the sounds of measured stroke
　And grating saw begin ;
The broad-axe to the gnarlëd oak,
　The mallet to the pin !

Hark ! roars the bellows, blast on blast,
　The sooty smithy jars,
And fire-sparks, rising far and fast,
　Are fading with the stars.
All day for us the smith shall stand
　Beside that flashing forge ;
All day for us his heavy hand
　The groaning anvil scourge.

From far-off hills, the panting team
　For us is toiling near ;
For us the raftsmen down the stream
　Their island barges steer.
Rings out for us the axe-man's stroke
　In forests old and still ;

For us the century-circled oak
　Falls crashing down his hill.

Up ! up ! in nobler toil than ours
　No craftsmen bear a part :
We make of Nature's giant powers
　The slaves of human Art.
Lay rib to rib and beam to beam,
　And drive the treenails free ;
Nor faithless joint nor yawning seam
　Shall tempt the searching sea !

Where'er the keel of our good ship
　The sea's rough field shall plough ;
Where'er her tossing spars shall drip
　With salt-spray caught below ;
That ship must heed her master's beck,
　Her helm obey his hand,
And seamen tread her reeling deck
　As if they trod the land.

Her oaken ribs the vulture-beak
　Of Northern ice may peel ;
The sunken rock and coral peak
　May grate along her keel ;
And know we well the painted shell
　We give to wind and wave,
Must float, the sailor's citadel,
　Or sink, the sailor's grave !

Ho ! strike away the bars and blocks,
　And set the good ship free !
Why lingers on these dusty rocks
　The young bride of the sea ?
Look ! how she moves adown the grooves,
　In graceful beauty now !
How lowly on the breast she loves
　Sinks down her virgin prow !

God bless her ! wheresoe'er the breeze
　Her snowy wing shall fan,
Aside the frozen Hebrides,
　Or sultry Hindostan !
Where'er, in mart or on the main,
　With peaceful flag unfurled,
She helps to wind the silken chain
　Of commerce round the world !

Speed on the ship ! But let her bear
　No merchandise of sin,
No groaning cargo of despair
　Her roomy hold within ;
No Lethean drug for Eastern lands,
　Nor poison-draught for ours ;

But honest fruits of toiling hands
  And Nature's sun and showers.

Be hers the Prairie's golden grain,
  The Desert's golden sand,
The clustered fruits of sunny Spain,
  The spice of Morning-land !
Her pathway on the open main
  May blessings follow free,
And glad hearts welcome back again
  Her white sails from the sea !

THE DROVERS

THROUGH heat and cold, and shower and
    sun,
  Still onward cheerly driving !
There 's life alone in duty done,
  And rest alone in striving.
But see ! the day is closing cool,
  The woods are dim before us ;
The white fog of the wayside pool
  Is creeping slowly o'er us.

The night is falling, comrades mine,
  Our footsore beasts are weary,
And through yon elms the tavern sign
  Looks out upon us cheery.
The landlord beckons from his door,
  His beechen fire is glowing ;
These ample barns, with feed in store,
  Are filled to overflowing.

From many a valley frowned across
  By brows of rugged mountains ;
From hillsides where, through spongy
    moss,
  Gush out the river fountains ;
From quiet farm-fields, green and low,
  And bright with blooming clover ;
From vales of corn the wandering crow
  No richer hovers over, —

Day after day our way has been
  O'er many a hill and hollow ;
By lake and stream, by wood and glen,
  Our stately drove we follow.
Through dust-clouds rising thick and dun,
  As smoke of battle o'er us,
Their white horns glisten in the sun,
  Like plumes and crests before us.

We see them slowly climb the hill,
  As slow behind it sinking ;

Or, thronging close, from roadside rill,
  Or sunny lakelet, drinking.
Now crowding in the narrow road,
  In thick and struggling masses,
They glare upon the teamster's load,
  Or rattling coach that passes.

Anon, with toss of horn and tail,
  And paw of hoof, and bellow,
They leap some farmer's broken pale,
  O'er meadow-close or fallow.
Forth comes the startled goodman ; forth
  Wife, children, house-dog, sally,
Till once more on their dusty path
  The baffled truants rally.

We drive no starvelings, scraggy grown,
  Loose-legged, and ribbed and bony,
Like those who grind their noses down
  On pastures bare and stony, —
Lank oxen, rough as Indian dogs,
  And cows too lean for shadows,
Disputing feebly with the frogs
  The crop of saw-grass meadows !

In our good drove, so sleek and fair,
  No bones of leanness rattle ;
No tottering hide-bound ghosts are there,
  Or Pharaoh's evil cattle.
Each stately beeve bespeaks the hand
  That fed him unrepining ;
The fatness of a goodly land
  In each dun hide is shining.

We 've sought them where, in warmest
    nooks,
  The freshest feed is growing,
By sweetest springs and clearest brooks
  Through honeysuckle flowing ;
Wherever hillsides, sloping south,
  Are bright with early grasses,
Or, tracking green the lowland's drouth,
  The mountain streamlet passes.

But now the day is closing cool,
  The woods are dim before us,
The white fog of the wayside pool
  Is creeping slowly o'er us.
The cricket to the frog's bassoon
  His shrillest time is keeping ;
The sickle of yon setting moon
  The meadow-mist is reaping.

The night is falling, comrades mine,
  Our footsore beasts are weary,

And through yon elms the tavern sign
  Looks out upon us cheery.
To-morrow, eastward with our charge
  We 'll go to meet the dawning,
Ere yet the pines of Kearsarge
  Have seen the sun of morning.

When snow-flakes o'er the frozen earth,
  Instead of birds, are flitting ;
When children throng the glowing hearth,
  And quiet wives are knitting ;
While in the fire-light strong and clear
  Young eyes of pleasure glisten,
To tales of all we see and hear
  The ears of home shall listen.

By many a Northern lake and hill,
  From many a mountain pasture,
Shall Fancy play the Drover still,
  And speed the long night faster.
Then let us on, through shower and sun,
  And heat and cold, be driving ;
There 's life alone in duty done,
  And rest alone in striving.

THE HUSKERS

It was late in mild October, and the long
    autumnal rain
Had left the summer harvest - fields all
    green with grass again ;
The first sharp frosts had fallen, leaving all
    the woodlands gay
With the hues of summer's rainbow, or the
    meadow-flowers of May.

Through a thin, dry mist, that morning, the
    sun rose broad and red,
At first a rayless disk of fire, he brightened
    as he sped ;
Yet even his noontide glory fell chastened
    and subdued,
On the cornfields and the orchards and
    softly pictured wood.

And all that quiet afternoon, slow sloping
    to the night,
He wove with golden shuttle the haze with
    yellow light ;
Slanting through the painted beeches, he
    glorified the hill ;
And, beneath it, pond and meadow lay
    brighter, greener still.

And shouting boys in woodland haunts
    caught glimpses of that sky,
Flecked by the many-tinted leaves, and
    laughed, they knew not why ;
And school-girls, gay with aster-flowers,
    beside the meadow brooks,
Mingled the glow of autumn with the sun-
    shine of sweet looks.

From spire and barn looked westerly the
    patient weathercocks ;
But even the birches on the hill stood mo-
    tionless as rocks.
No sound was in the woodlands, save the
    squirrel's dropping shell,
And the yellow leaves among the boughs,
    low rustling as they fell.

The summer grains were harvested ; the
    stubble-fields lay dry,
Where June winds rolled, in light and
    shade, the pale green waves of
    rye ;
But still, on gentle hill-slopes, in valleys
    fringed with wood,
Ungathered, bleaching in the sun, the
    heavy corn crop stood.

Bent low, by autumn's wind and rain,
    through husks that, dry and sere,
Unfolded from their ripened charge, shone
    out the yellow ear ;
Beneath, the turnip lay concealed, in many
    a verdant fold,
And glistened in the slanting light the
    pumpkin's sphere of gold.

There wrought the busy harvesters ; and
    many a creaking wain
Bore slowly to the long barn-floor its load
    of husk and grain ;
Till broad and red, as when he rose, the sun
    sank down, at last,
And like a merry guest's farewell, the day
    in brightness passed.

And lo ! as through the western pines, on
    meadow, stream, and pond,
Flamed the red radiance of a sky, set all
    afire beyond,
Slowly o'er the eastern sea-bluffs a milder
    glory shone,
And the sunset and the moonrise were min-
    gled into one !

As thus into the quiet night the twilight
    lapsed away,
And deeper in the brightening moon the
    tranquil shadows lay ;
From many a brown old farm-house, and
    hamlet without name,
Their milking and their home-tasks done,
    the merry huskers came.

Swung o'er the heaped-up harvest, from
    pitchforks in the mow,
Shone dimly down the lanterns on the
    pleasant scene below ;
The growing pile of husks behind, the
    golden ears before,
And laughing eyes and busy hands and
    brown cheeks glimmering o'er.

Half hidden, in a quiet nook, serene of
    look and heart,
Talking their old times over, the old men
    sat apart ;
While up and down the unhusked pile,
    or nestling in its shade,
At hide-and-seek, with laugh and shout,
    the happy children played.

Urged by the good host's daughter, a
    maiden young and fair,
Lifting to light her sweet blue eyes and
    pride of soft brown hair,
The master of the village school, sleek of
    hair and smooth of tongue,
To the quaint tune of some old psalm, a
    husking-ballad sung.

THE CORN-SONG

Heap high the farmer's wintry hoard !
    Heap high the golden corn !
No richer gift has Autumn poured
    From out her lavish horn !

Let other lands, exulting, glean
    The apple from the pine,
The orange from its glossy green,
    The cluster from the vine ;

We better love the hardy gift
    Our rugged vales bestow,
To cheer us when the storm shall drift
    Our harvest-fields with snow.

Through vales of grass and meads of flowers
    Our ploughs their furrows made,

While on the hills the sun and showers
    Of changeful April played.

We dropped the seed o'er hill and plain
    Beneath the sun of May,
And frightened from our sprouting grain
    The robber crows away.

All through the long, bright days of June
    Its leaves grew green and fair,
And waved in hot midsummer's noon
    Its soft and yellow hair.

And now, with autumn's moonlit eves,
    Its harvest-time has come,
We pluck away the frosted leaves,
    And bear the treasure home.

There, when the snows about us drift,
    And winter winds are cold,
Fair hands the broken grain shall sift,
    And knead its meal of gold.

Let vapid idlers loll in silk
    Around their costly board ;
Give us the bowl of samp and milk,
    By homespun beauty poured !

Where'er the wide old kitchen hearth
    Sends up its smoky curls,
Who will not thank the kindly earth,
    And bless our farmer girls !

Then shame on all the proud and vain,
    Whose folly laughs to scorn
The blessing of our hardy grain,
    Our wealth of golden corn !

Let earth withhold her goodly root,
    Let mildew blight the rye,
Give to the worm the orchard's fruit,
    The wheat-field to the fly :

But let the good old crop adorn
    The hills our fathers trod ;
Still let us, for his golden corn,
    Send up our thanks to God !

THE REFORMER

ALL grim and soiled and brown with tan,
    I saw a Strong One, in his wrath,
Smiting the godless shrines of man
    Along his path.

The Church, beneath her trembling dome,
  Essayed in vain her ghostly charm :
Wealth shook within his gilded home
    With strange alarm.

Fraud from his secret chambers fled
  Before the sunlight bursting in :
Sloth drew her pillow o'er her head
    To drown the din.

"Spare," Art implored, "yon holy pile ;
  That grand, old, time-worn turret spare ; "
Meek Reverence, kneeling in the aisle,
    Cried out, " Forbear ! "

Gray-bearded Use, who, deaf and blind,
  Groped for his old accustomed stone,
Leaned on his staff, and wept to find
    His seat o'erthrown.

Young Romance raised his dreamy eyes,
  O'erhung with paly locks of gold, —
" Why smite," he asked in sad surprise,
    " The fair, the old ? "

Yet louder rang the Strong One's stroke,
  Yet nearer flashed his axe's gleam ;
Shuddering and sick of heart I woke,
    As from a dream.

I looked : aside the dust-cloud rolled,
  The Waster seemed the Builder too ;
Upspringing from the ruined Old
    I saw the New.

'T was but the ruin of the bad, —
  The wasting of the wrong and ill ;
Whate'er of good the old time had
    Was living still.

Calm grew the brows of him I feared ;
  The frown which awed me passed away,
And left behind a smile which cheered
    Like breaking day.

The grain grew green on battle-plains,
  O'er swarded war-mounds grazed the
    cow ;
The slave stood forging from his chains
    The spade and plough.

Where frowned the fort, pavilions gay
  And cottage windows, flower-entwined,
Looked out upon the peaceful bay
    And hills behind.

Through vine-wreathed cups with wine once
    red,
  The lights on brimming crystal fell,
Drawn, sparkling, from the rivulet head
    And mossy well.

Through prison walls, like Heaven-sent
    hope,
  Fresh breezes blew, and sunbeams
    strayed,
And with the idle gallows-rope
    The young child played.

Where the doomed victim in his cell
  Had counted o'er the weary hours,
Glad school-girls, answering to the bell,
    Came crowned with flowers.

Grown wiser for the lesson given,
  I fear no longer, for I know
That, where the share is deepest driven,
    The best fruits grow.

The outworn rite, the old abuse,
  The pious fraud transparent grown,
The good held captive in the use
    Of wrong alone, —

These wait their doom, from that great law
  Which makes the past time serve to-day ;
And fresher life the world shall draw
    From their decay.

Oh, backward-looking son of time !
  The new is old, the old is new,
The cycle of a change sublime
    Still sweeping through.

So wisely taught the Indian seer ;
  Destroying Seva, forming Brahm,
Who wake by turns Earth's love and fear,
    Are one, the same.

Idly as thou, in that old day
  Thou mournest, did thy sire repine ;
So, in his time, thy child grown gray
    Shall sigh for thine.

But life shall on and upward go ;
  Th' eternal step of Progress beats
To that great anthem, calm and slow,
    Which God repeats.

Take heart ! the Waster builds again, —
  A charmèd life old Goodness hath ;

The tares may perish, but the grain
  Is not for death.

God works in all things ; all obey
  His first propulsion from the night :
Wake thou and watch ! the world is gray
  With morning light !

THE PEACE CONVENTION AT BRUSSELS

STILL in thy streets, O Paris ! doth the stain
Of blood defy the cleansing autumn rain ;
Still breaks the smoke Messina's ruins
  through,
And Naples mourns that new Bartholomew,
When squalid beggary, for a dole of bread,
At a crowned murderer's beck of license,
  fed
The yawning trenches with her noble dead ;
Still, doomed Vienna, through thy stately
  halls
The shell goes crashing and the red shot
  falls,
And, leagued to crush thee, on the Danube's
  side,
The bearded Croat and Bosniak spearman
  ride ;
Still in that vale where Himalaya's snow
Melts round the cornfields and the vines
  below,
The Sikh's hot cannon, answering ball for
  ball,
Flames in the breach of Moultan's shattered
  wall ;
On Chenab's side the vulture seeks the slain,
And Sutlej paints with blood its banks again.

"What folly, then," the faithless critic
  cries,
With sneering lip, and wise world-knowing
  eyes,
"While fort to fort, and post to post, repeat
The ceaseless challenge of the war-drum's
  beat,
And round the green earth, to the church-
  bell's chime,
The morning drum-roll of the camp keeps
  time,
To dream of peace amidst a world in arms,
Of swords to ploughshares changed by
  Scriptural charms,
Of nations, drunken with the wine of blood,

Staggering to take the Pledge of Brother-
  hood,
Like tipplers answering Father Mathew's
  call ;
The sullen Spaniard, and the mad-cap Gaul,
The bull-dog Briton, yielding but with life,
The Yankee swaggering with his bowie-
  knife,
The Russ, from banquets with the vulture
  shared,
The blood still dripping from his amber
  beard,
Quitting their mad Berserker dance to hear
The dull, meek droning of a drab-coat seer ;
Leaving the sport of Presidents and Kings,
Where men for dice each titled gambler
  flings,
To meet alternate on the Seine and Thames,
For tea and gossip, like old country dames !
No ! let the cravens plead the weakling's
  cant,
Let Cobden cipher, and let Vincent rant,
Let Sturge preach peace to democratic
  throngs,
And Burritt, stammering through his hun-
  dred tongues,
Repeat, in all, his ghostly lessons o'er,
Timed to the pauses of the battery's roar ;
Check Ban or Kaiser with the barricade
Of ' Olive-leaves ' and Resolutions made,
Spike guns with pointed Scripture-texts,
  and hope
To capsize navies with a windy trope ;
Still shall the glory and the pomp of War
Along their train the shouting millions
  draw ;
Still dusty Labor to the passing Brave
His cap shall doff, and Beauty's kerchief
  wave ;
Still shall the bard to Valor tune his song,
Still Hero-worship kneel before the Strong ;
Rosy and sleek, the sable-gowned divine,
O'er his third bottle of suggestive wine,
To plumed and sworded auditors, shall
  prove
Their trade accordant with the Law of
  Love ;
And Church for State, and State for
  Church, shall fight,
And both agree, that Might alone is
  Right !"
Despite of sneers like these, O faithful few,
Who dare to hold God's word and witness
  true,

Whose clear-eyed faith transcends our evil
time,
And o'er the present wilderness of crime
Sees the calm future, with its robes of
green,
Its fleece-flecked mountains, and soft
streams between, —
Still keep the path which duty bids ye tread
Though worldly wisdom shake the cautious
head ;
No truth from Heaven descends upon our
sphere,
Without the greeting of the skeptic's sneer ;
Denied and mocked at, till its blessings fall,
Common as dew and sunshine, over all.

Then, o'er Earth's war-field, till the
strife shall cease,
Like Morven's harpers, sing your song of
peace ;
As in old fable rang the Thracian's lyre,
Midst howl of fiends and roar of penal fire,
Till the fierce din to pleasing murmurs fell,
And love subdued the maddened heart of
hell.
Lend, once again, that holy song a tongue,
Which the glad angels of the Advent sung,
Their cradle-anthem for the Saviour's birth,
Glory to God, and peace unto the earth !
Through the mad discord send that calming
word
Which wind and wave on wild Gennesareth
heard,
Lift in Christ's name his Cross against the
Sword !
Not vain the vision which the prophets saw,
Skirting with green the fiery waste of war,
Through the hot sand-gleam, looming soft
and calm
On the sky's rim, the fountain-shading
palm.
Still lives for Earth, which fiends so long
have trod,
The great hope resting on the truth of
God, —
Evil shall cease and Violence pass away,
And the tired world breathe free through
a long Sabbath day.

THE PRISONER FOR DEBT

Before the law authorizing imprisonment for
debt had been abolished in Massachusetts, a
revolutionary pensioner was confined in Charles-
town jail for a debt of fourteen dollars, and
on the fourth of July was seen waving a hand-
kerchief from the bars of his cell in honor of
the day.

Look on him ! through his dungeon grate,
Feebly and cold, the morning light
Comes stealing round him, dim and late,
As if it loathed the sight.
Reclining on his strawy bed,
His hand upholds his drooping head ;
His bloodless cheek is seamed and hard,
Unshorn his gray, neglected beard ;
And o'er his bony fingers flow
His long, dishevelled locks of snow.

No grateful fire before him glows,
And yet the winter's breath is chill ;
And o'er his half-clad person goes
The frequent ague thrill !
Silent, save ever and anon,
A sound, half murmur and half groan,
Forces apart the painful grip
Of the old sufferer's bearded lip ;
Oh, sad and crushing is the fate
Of old age chained and desolate !

Just God ! why lies that old man there ?
A murderer shares his prison bed,
Whose eyeballs, through his horrid hair,
Gleam on him, fierce and red ;
And the rude oath and heartless jeer
Fall ever on his loathing ear,
And, or in wakefulness or sleep,
Nerve, flesh, and pulses thrill and creep
Whene'er that ruffian's tossing limb,
Crimson with murder, touches him !

What has the gray-haired prisoner done ?
Has murder stained his hands with gore ?
Not so ; his crime 's a fouler one ;
God made the old man poor !
For this he shares a felon's cell,
The fittest earthly type of hell !
For this, the boon for which he poured
His young blood on the invader's sword,
And counted light the fearful cost,
His blood-gained liberty is lost !

And so, for such a place of rest,
Old prisoner, dropped thy blood as rain
On Concord's field, and Bunker's crest,
And Saratoga's plain ?
Look forth, thou man of many scars,
Through thy dim dungeon's iron bars ;

It must be joy, in sooth, to see
Yon monument upreared to thee ;
Piled granite and a prison cell, —
The land repays thy service well !

Go, ring the bells and fire the guns,
    And fling the starry banner out ;
Shout " Freedom ! " till your lisping ones
    Give back their cradle-shout ;
Let boastful eloquence declaim
Of honor, liberty, and fame ;
Still let the poet's strain be heard,
With glory for each second word,
And everything with breath agree
To praise " our glorious liberty " !

But when the patron cannon jars
    That prison's cold and gloomy wall,
And through its grates the stripes and stars
    Rise on the wind, and fall,
Think ye that prisoner's aged ear
Rejoices in the general cheer ?
Think ye his dim and failing eye
Is kindled at your pageantry ?
Sorrowing of soul, and chained of limb,
What is your carnival to him ?

Down with the law that binds him thus !
    Unworthy freemen, let it find
No refuge from the withering curse
    Of god and human-kind !
Open the prison's living tomb,
And usher from its brooding gloom
The victims of your savage code
To the free sun and air of God ;
No longer dare as crime to brand
The chastening of the Almighty's hand.

THE CHRISTIAN TOURISTS

The reader of the biography of William
Allen, the philanthropic associate of Clarkson
and Romilly, cannot fail to admire his simple
and beautiful record of a tour through Europe,
in the years 1818 and 1819, in the company of
his American friend, Stephen Grellett.

No aimless wanderers, by the fiend Unrest
    Goaded from shore to shore ;
No schoolmen, turning, in their classic
    quest,
    The leaves of empire o'er.
Simple of faith, and bearing in their hearts
    The love of man and God,

Isles of old song, the Moslem's ancient
    marts,
    And Scythia's steppes, they trod.

Where the long shadows of the fir and pine
    In the night sun are cast,
And the deep heart of many a Norland
    mine
    Quakes at each riving blast ;
Where, in barbaric grandeur, Moskwa
    stands,
    A baptized Scythian queen,
With Europe's arts and Asia's jewelled
    hands,
    The North and East between !

Where still, through vales of Grecian fable
    stray
    The classic forms of yore,
And beauty smiles, new risen from the
    spray,
    And Dian weeps once more ;
Where every tongue in Smyrna's mart re-
    sounds ;
    And Stamboul from the sea
Lifts her tall minarets over burial-grounds
    Black with the cypress-tree !

From Malta's temples to the gates of Rome,
    Following the track of Paul,
And where the Alps gird round the Switz-
    er's home
    Their vast, eternal wall ;
They paused not by the ruins of old time,
    They scanned no pictures rare,
Nor lingered where the snow-locked moun-
    tains climb
    The cold abyss of air !

But unto prisons, where men lay in chains,
    To haunts where Hunger pined,
To kings and courts forgetful of the pains
    And wants of human-kind,
Scattering sweet words, and quiet deeds of
    good,
    Along their way, like flowers,
Or pleading, as Christ's freemen only could.
    With princes and with powers ;

Their single aim the purpose to fulfil
    Of Truth, from day to day,
Simply obedient to its guiding will,
    They held their pilgrim way.
Yet dream not, hence, the beautiful and old
    Were wasted on their sight,

Who in the school of Christ had learned to
    hold
    All outward things aright.

Not less to them the breath of vineyards
    blown
    From off the Cyprian shore,
Not less for them the Alps in sunset shone,
    That man they valued more.
A life of beauty lends to all it sees
    The beauty of its thought ;
And fairest forms and sweetest harmonies
    Make glad its way, unsought.

In sweet accordancy of praise and love,
    The singing waters run ;
And sunset mountains wear in light above
    The smile of duty done ;
Sure stands the promise, — ever to the
    meek
    A heritage is given ;
Nor lose they Earth who, single-hearted,
    seek
    The righteousness of Heaven !

THE MEN OF OLD

WELL speed thy mission, bold Iconoclast !
    Yet all unworthy of its trust thou art,
    If, with dry eye, and cold, unloving
    heart,
Thou tread'st the solemn Pantheon of the
    Past,
    By the great Future's dazzling hope
    made blind
    To all the beauty, power, and truth be-
    hind.
Not without reverent awe shouldst thou
    put by
    The cypress branches and the amaranth
    blooms,
    Where, with clasped hands of prayer,
    upon their tombs
The effigies of old confessors lie,
God's witnesses ; the voices of His will,
Heard in the slow march of the centuries
    still !
Such were the men at whose rebuking
    frown,
    Dark with God's wrath, the tyrant's knee
    went down ;
Such from the terrors of the guilty drew
The vassal's freedom and the poor man's
    due.

St. Anselm (may he rest forevermore
    In Heaven's sweet peace !) forbade, of
    old, the sale
    Of men as slaves, and from the sacred
    pale
Hurled the Northumbrian buyers of the
    poor.
To ransom souls from bonds and evil fate
St. Ambrose melted down the sacred
    plate, —
Image of saint, the chalice, and the pix,
Crosses of gold, and silver candlesticks.
" Man is worth more than temples ! " he
    replied
To such as came his holy work to chide.
And brave Cesarius, stripping altars bare,
    And coining from the Abbey's golden
    hoard
The captive's freedom, answered to the
    prayer
    Or threat of those whose fierce zeal for
    the Lord
Stifled their love of man, — " An earthen
    dish
    The last sad supper of the Master bore :
Most miserable sinners ! do ye wish
    More than your Lord, and grudge His
    dying poor
What your own pride and not His need
    requires ?
    Souls, than these shining gauds, He
    values more :
Mercy, not sacrifice, His heart desires ! "
O faithful worthies ! resting far behind
In your dark ages, since ye fell asleep,
Much has been done for truth and human-
    kind ;
Shadows are scattered wherein ye groped
    blind ;
Man claims his birthright, freer pulses
    leap
Through peoples driven in your day like
    sheep ;
Yet, like your own, our age's sphere of
    light,
Though widening still, is walled around by
    night ;
With slow, reluctant eye, the Church has
    read,
Skeptic at heart, the lessons of its Head ;
Counting, too oft, its living members less
Than the wall's garnish and the pulpit's
    dress ;
World-moving zeal, with power to bless
    and feed

Life's fainting pilgrims, to their utter
      need,
Instead of bread, holds out the stone of
      creed;
Sect builds and worships where its wealth
      and pride
And vanity stand shrined and deified,
Careless that in the shadow of its walls
God's living temple into ruin falls.
We need, methinks, the prophet-hero still,
Saints true of life, and martyrs strong of
      will,
To tread the land, even now, as Xavier
      trod
      The streets of Goa, barefoot, with his
      bell,
Proclaiming freedom in the name of God,
      And startling tyrants with the fear of
      hell!
      Soft words, smooth prophecies, are
      doubtless well;
But to rebuke the age's popular crime,
We need the souls of fire, the hearts of
      that old time!

TO PIUS IX

The writer of these lines is no enemy of
Catholics. He has, on more than one occa-
sion, exposed himself to the censures of his
Protestant brethren, by his strenuous endea-
vors to procure indemnification for the own-
ers of the convent destroyed near Boston.
He defended the cause of the Irish patriots
long before it had become popular in this
country; and he was one of the first to urge
the most liberal aid to the suffering and starv-
ing population of the Catholic island. The
severity of his language finds its ample apol-
ogy in the reluctant confession of one of the
most eminent Romish priests, the eloquent
and devoted Father Ventura.

THE cannon's brazen lips are cold;
   No red shell blazes down the air;
And street and tower, and temple old,
   Are silent as despair.

The Lombard stands no more at bay,
   Rome's fresh young life has bled in vain;
The ravens scattered by the day
   Come back with night again.

Now, while the fratricides of France
   Are treading on the neck of Rome,

Hider at Gaeta, seize thy chance!
   Coward and cruel, come!

Creep now from Naples' bloody skirt;
   Thy mummer's part was acted well,
While Rome, with steel and fire begirt,
   Before thy crusade fell!

Her death-groans answered to thy prayer;
   Thy chant, the drum and bugle-call;
Thy lights, the burning villa's glare;
   Thy beads, the shell and ball!

Let Austria clear thy way, with hands
   Foul from Ancona's cruel sack,
And Naples, with his dastard bands
   Of murderers, lead thee back!

Rome's lips are dumb; the orphan's wail,
   The mother's shriek, thou mayst not hear
Above the faithless Frenchman's hail,
   The unsexed shaveling's cheer!

Go, bind on Rome her cast-off weight,
   The double curse of crook and crown,
Though woman's scorn and manhood's hate
   From wall and roof flash down!

Nor heed those blood-stains on the wall,
   Not Tiber's flood can wash away,
Where, in thy stately Quirinal,
   Thy mangled victims lay!

Let the world murmur; let its cry
   Of horror and disgust be heard;
Truth stands alone; thy coward lie
   Is backed by lance and sword!

The cannon of St. Angelo,
   And chanting priest and clanging bell,
And beat of drum and bugle blow,
   Shall greet thy coming well!

Let lips of iron and tongues of slaves
   Fit welcome give thee; for her part,
Rome, frowning o'er her new-made graves,
   Shall curse thee from her heart!

No wreaths of sad Campagna's flowers
   Shall childhood in thy pathway fling;
No garlands from their ravaged bowers
   Shall Terni's maidens bring;

But, hateful as that tyrant old,
   The mocking witness of his crime,

In thee shall loathing eyes behold
  The Nero of our time !

Stand where Rome's blood was freest shed,
  Mock Heaven with impious thanks and call
Its curses on the patriot dead,
  Its blessings on the Gaul !

Or sit upon thy throne of lies,
  A poor, mean idol, blood-besmeared,
Whom even its worshippers despise,
  Unhonored, unrevered !

Yet, Scandal of the World ! from thee
  One needful truth mankind shall learn :
That kings and priests to Liberty
  And God are false in turn.

Earth wearies of them ; and the long
  Meek sufferance of the Heavens doth fail :
Woe for weak tyrants, when the strong
  Wake, struggle, and prevail !

Not vainly Roman hearts have bled
  To feed the Crosier and the Crown,
If, roused thereby, the world shall tread
  The twin-born vampires down !

CALEF IN BOSTON

1692

IN the solemn days of old,
  Two men met in Boston town,
One a tradesman frank and bold,
  One a preacher of renown.

Cried the last, in bitter tone :
  " Poisoner of the wells of truth !
Satan's hireling, thou hast sown
  With his tares the heart of youth ! "

Spake the simple tradesman then,
  " God be judge 'twixt thee and me ;
All thou knowest of truth hath been
  Once a lie to men like thee.

" Falsehoods which we spurn to-day
  Were the truths of long ago ;
Let the dead boughs fall away,
  Fresher shall the living grow.

" God is good and God is light,
  In this faith I rest secure ;
Evil can but serve the right,
  Over all shall love endure.

" Of your spectral puppet play
  I have traced the cunning wires ;
Come what will, I needs must say,
  God is true, and ye are liars."

When the thought of man is free,
  Error fears its lightest tones ;
So the priest cried, " Sadducee ! "
  And the people took up stones.

In the ancient burying-ground,
  Side by side the twain now lie ;
One with humble grassy mound,
  One with marbles pale and high.

But the Lord hath blest the seed
  Which that tradesman scattered then,
And the preacher's spectral creed
  Chills no more the blood of men.

Let us trust, to one is known
  Perfect love which casts out fear,
While the other's joys atone
  For the wrong he suffered here.

OUR STATE

[Originally entitled *Dedication of a School-house*. It was written for the dedication services of a new school building in Newbury, Mass.]

THE South-land boasts its teeming cane,
The prairied West its heavy grain,
And sunset's radiant gates unfold
On rising marts and sands of gold !

Rough, bleak, and hard, our little State
Is scant of soil, of limits strait ;
Her yellow sands are sands alone,
Her only mines are ice and stone !

From Autumn frost to April rain,
Too long her winter woods complain ;
From budding flower to falling leaf,
Her summer time is all too brief.

Yet, on her rocks, and on her sands,
And wintry hills, the school-house stands,

And what her rugged soil denies,
The harvest of the mind supplies.

The riches of the Commonwealth
Are free, strong minds, and hearts of health;
And more to her than gold or grain,
The cunning hand and cultured brain.

For well she keeps her ancient stock,
The stubborn strength of Pilgrim Rock ;
And still maintains, with milder laws,
And clearer light, the Good Old Cause !

Nor heeds the skeptic's puny hands,
While near her school the church - spire
  stands ;
Nor fears the blinded bigot's rule,
While near her church - spire stands the
  school.

THE PRISONERS OF NAPLES

I HAVE been thinking of the victims bound
In Naples, dying for the lack of air
And sunshine, in their close, damp cells of
  pain,
Where hope is not, and innocence in vain
Appeals against the torture and the chain !
Unfortunates ! whose crime it was to share
Our common love of freedom, and to dare,
In its behalf, Rome's harlot triple-crowned,
And her base pander, the most hateful
  thing
Who upon Christian or on Pagan ground
Makes vile the old heroic name of king.
O God most merciful ! Father just and
  kind !
Whom man hath bound let thy right hand
  unbind.
Or, if thy purposes of good behind
Their ills lie hidden, let the sufferers find
Strong consolations ; leave them not to
  doubt
Thy providential care, nor yet without
The hope which all thy attributes inspire,
That not in vain the martyr's robe of
  fire
Is worn, nor the sad prisoner's fretting
  chain ;
Since all who suffer for thy truth send
  forth,
Electrical, with every throb of pain,
Unquenchable sparks, thy own baptismal
  rain

Of fire and spirit over all the earth,
Making the dead in slavery live again.
Let this great hope be with them, as they
  lie
Shut from the light, the greenness, and the
  sky ;
From the cool waters and the pleasant
  breeze,
The smell of flowers, and shade of summer
  trees ;
Bound with the felon lepers, whom dis-
  ease
And sins abhorred make loathsome ; let
  them share
Pellico's faith, Foresti's strength to bear
Years of unutterable torment, stern and
  still,
As the chained Titan victor through his
  will !
Comfort them with thy future ; let them
  see
The day-dawn of Italian liberty ;
For that, with all good things, is hid with
  Thee,
And, perfect in thy thought, awaits its time
  to be !

I, who have spoken for freedom at the
  cost
Of some weak friendships, or some paltry
  prize
Of name or place, and more than I have
  lost
Have gained in wider reach of sympathies,
And free communion with the good and
  wise ;
May God forbid that I should ever boast
Such easy self-denial, or repine
That the strong pulse of health no more is
  mine ;
That, overworn at noonday, I must yield
To other hands the gleaning of the field ;
A tired on-looker through the day's de-
  cline.
For blest beyond deserving still, and know-
  ing
That kindly Providence its care is show-
  ing
In the withdrawal as in the bestowing,
Scarcely I dare for more or less to pray.
Beautiful yet for me this autumn day
Melts on its sunset hills ; and, far away,
For me the Ocean lifts its solemn psalm,
To me the pine-woods whisper ; and for
  me

Yon river, winding through its vales of
    calm,
By greenest banks, with asters purple-
    starred,
And gentian bloom and golden-rod made
    gay,
Flows down in silent gladness to the sea,
Like a pure spirit to its great reward !

Nor lack I friends, long-tried and near and
    dear,
Whose love is round me like this atmos-
    phere,
Warm, soft, and golden. For such gifts to
    me
What shall I render, O my God, to thee ?
Let me not dwell upon my lighter share
Of pain and ill that human life must bear ;
Save me from selfish pining ; let my heart,
Drawn from itself in sympathy, forget
The bitter longings of a vain regret,
The anguish of its own peculiar smart.
Remembering others, as I have to-day,
In their great sorrows, let me live alway
Not for myself alone, but have a part,
Such as a frail and erring spirit may,
In love which is of Thee, and which indeed
    Thou art !

THE PEACE OF EUROPE

"GREAT peace in Europe ! Order reigns
From Tiber's hills to Danube's plains ! "
So say her kings and priests ; so say
The lying prophets of our day.

Go lay to earth a listening ear ;
The tramp of measured marches hear ;
The rolling of the cannon's wheel,
The shotted musket's murderous peal,
The night alarm, the sentry's call,
The quick-eared spy in hut and hall !
From Polar sea and tropic fen
The dying-groans of exiled men !
The bolted cell, the galley's chains,
The scaffold smoking with its stains !
Order, the hush of brooding slaves !
Peace, in the dungeon-vaults and graves !

O Fisher ! of the world-wide net,
With meshes in all waters set,
Whose fabled keys of heaven and hell
Bolt hard the patriot's prison-cell,
And open wide the banquet-hall,

Where kings and priests hold carnival !
Weak vassal tricked in royal guise,
Boy Kaiser with thy lip of lies ;
Base gambler for Napoleon's crown,
Barnacle on his dead renown !
Thou, Bourbon Neapolitan,
Crowned scandal, loathed of God and man ;
And thou, fell Spider of the North !
Stretching thy giant feelers forth,
Within whose web the freedom dies
Of nations eaten up like flies !
Speak, Prince and Kaiser, Priest and
    Czar !
If this be Peace, pray what is War ?

White Angel of the Lord ! unmeet
That soil accursed for thy pure feet.
Never in Slavery's desert flows
The fountain of thy charmed repose ;
No tyrant's hand thy chaplet weaves
Of lilies and of olive-leaves ;
Not with the wicked shalt thou dwell,
Thus saith the Eternal Oracle ;
Thy home is with the pure and free !
Stern herald of thy better day,
Before thee, to prepare thy way,
The Baptist Shade of Liberty,
Gray, scarred and hairy-robed, must press
With bleeding feet the wilderness !
Oh that its voice might pierce the ear
Of princes, trembling while they hear
A cry as of the Hebrew seer :
Repent ! God's kingdom draweth near !

ASTRÆA

"Jove means to settle
Astræa in her seat again,
And let down from his golden chain
An age of better metal."
            BEN JONSON, 1615.

O POET rare and old !
  Thy words are prophecies ;
Forward the age of gold,
  The new Saturnian lies.

The universal prayer
  And hope are not in vain ;
Rise, brothers ! and prepare
  The way for Saturn's reign.

Perish shall all which takes
  From labor's board and can ;
Perish shall all which makes
  A spaniel of the man !

Free from its bonds the mind,
  The body from the rod ;
Broken all chains that bind
  The image of our God.

Just men no longer pine
  Behind their prison-bars ;
Through the rent dungeon shine
  The free sun and the stars.

Earth own, at last, untrod
  By sect, or caste, or clan,
The fatherhood of God,
  The brotherhood of man !

Fraud fail, craft perish, forth
  The money-changers driven,
And God's will done on earth,
  As now in heaven !

THE DISENTHRALLED

HE had bowed down to drunkenness,
  An abject worshipper :
The pride of manhood's pulse had grown
  Too faint and cold to stir ;
And he had given his spirit up
  To the unblessèd thrall,
And bowing to the poison cup,
  He gloried in his fall !

There came a change — the cloud rolled off,
  And light fell on his brain —
And like the passing of a dream
  That cometh not again,
The shadow of the spirit fled.
  He saw the gulf before,
He shuddered at the waste behind,
  And was a man once more.

He shook the serpent folds away,
  That gathered round his heart,
As shakes the swaying forest-oak
  Its poison vine apart ;
He stood erect ; returning pride
  Grew terrible within,
And conscience sat in judgment, on
  His most familiar sin.

The light of Intellect again
  Along his pathway shone ;
And Reason like a monarch sat
  Upon his olden throne.

The honored and the wise once more
  Within his presence came ;
And lingered oft on lovely lips
  His once forbidden name.

There may be glory in the might,
  That treadeth nations down;
Wreaths for the crimson conqueror,
  Pride for the kingly crown ;
But nobler is that triumph hour,
  The disenthralled shall find,
When evil passion boweth down
  Unto the Godlike mind !

THE POOR VOTER ON ELEC-
TION DAY

THE proudest now is but my peer,
  The highest not more high ;
To-day, of all the weary year,
  A king of men am I.
To-day alike are great and small,
  The nameless and the known ;
My palace is the people's hall,
  The ballot-box my throne !

Who serves to-day upon the list
  Beside the served shall stand ;
Alike the brown and wrinkled fist,
  The gloved and dainty hand !
The rich is level with the poor,
  The weak is strong to-day ;
And sleekest broadcloth counts no more
  Than homespun frock of gray.

To-day let pomp and vain pretence
  My stubborn right abide ;
I set a plain man's common sense
  Against the pedant's pride.
To-day shall simple manhood try
  The strength of gold and land ;
The wide world has not wealth to buy
  The power in my right hand !

While there 's a grief to seek redress,
  Or balance to adjust,
Where weighs our living manhood less
  Than Mammon 's vilest dust, —
While there 's a right to need my vote,
  A wrong to sweep away,
Up ! clouted knee and ragged coat !
  A man 's a man to-day !

THE DREAM OF PIO NONO

It chanced that while the pious troops of
      France
Fought in the crusade Pio Nono preached,
What time the holy Bourbons stayed his
      hands
(The Hur and Aaron meet for such a
      Moses),
Stretched forth from Naples towards rebel-
      lious Rome
To bless the ministry of Oudinot,
And sanctify his iron homilies
And sharp persuasions of the bayonet,
That the great pontiff fell asleep, and
      dreamed.

He stood by Lake Tiberias, in the sun
Of the bright Orient; and beheld the
      lame,
The sick, and blind, kneel at the Master's
      feet,
And rise up whole. And, sweetly over
      all,
Dropping the ladder of their hymn of praise
From heaven to earth, in silver rounds of
      song,
He heard the blessed angels sing of peace,
Good-will to man, and glory to the Lord.

Then one, with feet unshod, and leathern
      face
Hardened and darkened by fierce summer
      suns
And hot winds of the desert, closer drew
His fisher's haick, and girded up his loins,
And spake, as one who had authority :
" Come thou with me."

            Lakeside and eastern sky
And the sweet song of angels passed away,
And, with a dream's alacrity of change,
The priest, and the swart fisher by his
      side,
Beheld the Eternal City lift its domes
And solemn fanes and monumental pomp
Above the waste Campagna. On the hills
The blaze of burning villas rose and fell,
And momently the mortar's iron throat
Roared from the trenches ; and, within the
      walls,
Sharp crash of shells, low groans of human
      pain.

Shout, drum beat, and the clanging larum-
      bell,
And tramp of hosts, sent up a mingled
      sound,
Half wail and half defiance. As they passed
The gate of San Pancrazio, human blood
Flowed ankle-high about them, and dead
      men
Choked the long street with gashed and
      gory piles, —
A ghastly barricade of mangled flesh,
From which, at times, quivered a living
      hand,
And white lips moved and moaned. A
      father tore
His gray hairs, by the body of his son,
In frenzy ; and his fair young daughter
      wept
On his old bosom. Suddenly a flash
Clove the thick sulphurous air, and man
      and maid
Sank, crushed and mangled by the shatter-
      ing shell.

Then spake the Galilean : "Thou hast
      seen
The blessed Master and His works of love;
Look now on thine ! Hear'st thou the
      angels sing
Above this open hell ? Thou God's high-
      priest !
Thou the Vicegerent of the Prince of Peace !
Thou the successor of His chosen ones !
I, Peter, fisherman of Galilee,
In the dear Master's name, and for the
      love
Of His true Church, proclaim thee Anti-
      christ,
Alien and separate from His holy faith
Wide as the difference between death and
      life,
The hate of man and the great love of God !
Hence, and repent ! "

            Thereat the pontiff woke,
Trembling, and muttering o'er his fearful
      dream.
" What means he ? " cried the Bourbon.
      " Nothing more
Than that your majesty hath all too well
Catered for your poor guests, and that, in
      sooth,
The Holy Father's supper troubleth him,"
Said Cardinal Antonelli, with a smile.

THE VOICES

"Why urge the long, unequal fight,
  Since Truth has fallen in the street,
Or lift anew the trampled light,
  Quenched by the heedless million's feet?

"Give o'er the thankless task; forsake
  The fools who know not ill from good:
Eat, drink, enjoy thy own, and take
  Thine ease among the multitude.

"Live out thyself; with others share
  Thy proper life no more; assume
The unconcern of sun and air,
  For life or death, or blight or bloom.

"The mountain pine looks calmly on
  The fires that scourge the plains be-
    low,
Nor heeds the eagle in the sun
  The small birds piping in the snow!

"The world is God's, not thine; let Him
  Work out a change, if change must be:
The hand that planted best can trim
  And nurse the old unfruitful tree."

So spake the Tempter, when the light
  Of sun and stars had left the sky;
I listened, through the cloud and night,
  And heard, methought, a voice reply:

"That task may well seem over-hard,
  Who scatterest in a thankless soil
Thy life as seed, with no reward
  Save that which Duty gives to Toil.

"Not wholly is thy heart resigned
  To Heaven's benign and just decree,
Which, linking thee with all thy kind,
  Transmits their joys and griefs to thee.

"Break off that sacred chain, and turn
  Back on thyself thy love and care;
Be thou thine own mean idol, burn
  Faith, Hope, and Trust, thy children,
    there.

"Released from that fraternal law
  Which shares the common bale and bliss,
No sadder lot could Folly draw,
  Or Sin provoke from Fate, than this.

"The meal unshared is food unblest:
  Thou hoard'st in vain what love should
    spend;
Self-ease is pain; thy only rest
  Is labor for a worthy end;

"A toil that gains with what it yields,
  And scatters to its own increase,
And hears, while sowing outward fields,
  The harvest-song of inward peace.

"Free-lipped the liberal streamlets run,
  Free shines for all the healthful ray;
The still pool stagnates in the sun,
  The lurid earth-fire haunts decay!

"What is it that the crowd requite
  Thy love with hate, thy truth with lies?
And but to faith, and not to sight,
  The walls of Freedom's temple rise?

"Yet do thy work; it shall succeed
  In thine or in another's day;
And, if denied the victor's meed,
  Thou shalt not lack the toiler's pay.

"Faith shares the future's promise; Love's
  Self-offering is a triumph won;
And each good thought or action moves
  The dark world nearer to the sun.

"Then faint not, falter not, nor plead
  Thy weakness; truth itself is strong;
The lion's strength, the eagle's speed,
  Are not alone vouchsafed to wrong.

"Thy nature, which, through fire and flood,
  To place or gain finds out its way,
Hath power to seek the highest good,
  And duty's holiest call obey!

"Strivest thou in darkness?— foes with-
    out
  In league with traitor thoughts within;
Thy night-watch kept with trembling Doubt
  And pale Remorse the ghost of Sin?

"Hast thou not, on some week of storm,
  Seen the sweet Sabbath breaking fair,
And cloud and shadow, sunlit, form
  The curtains of its tent of prayer?

"So, haply, when thy task shall end,
  The wrong shall lose itself in right,

And all thy week-day darkness blend
  With the long Sabbath of the light ! "

THE NEW EXODUS

Written upon hearing that slavery had been
formally abolished in Egypt. Unhappily, the
professions and pledges of the vacillating gov-
ernment of Egypt proved unreliable.

BY fire and cloud, across the desert sand,
  And through the parted waves,
From their long bondage, with an out-
      stretched hand,
  God led the Hebrew slaves !

Dead as the letter of the Pentateuch,
  As Egypt's statues cold,
In the adytum of the sacred book
  Now stands that marvel old.

"Lo, God *is* great ! " the simple Moslem
      says.
  We seek the ancient date,
Turn the dry scroll, and make that living
      phrase
  A dead one : "God *was* great ! "

And, like the Coptic monks by Mousa's
      wells,
  We dream of wonders past,
Vague as the tales the wandering Arab
      tells,
  Each drowsier than the last.

O fools and blind ! Above the Pyramids
  Stretches once more that hand,
And trancëd Egypt, from her stony lids,
  Flings back her veil of sand.

And morning - smitten Memnon, singing,
      wakes ;
  And, listening by his Nile,
O'er Ammon's grave and awful visage
      breaks
  A sweet and human smile.

Not as before, with hail and fire, and call
  Of death for midnight graves,
But in the stillness of the noonday, fall
  The fetters of the slaves.

No longer through the Red Sea, as of old,
  The bondmen walk dry shod ;

Through human hearts, by love of Him
      controlled,
  Runs now that path of God !

THE CONQUEST OF FINLAND

" Joseph Sturge, with a companion, Thomas
Harvey, has been visiting the shores of Fin-
land, to ascertain the amount of mischief and
loss to poor and peaceable sufferers, occasioned
by the gun-boats of the allied squadrons in the
late war, with a view to obtaining relief for
them." — *Friends' Review.*

ACROSS the frozen marshes
  The winds of autumn blow,
And the fen-lands of the Wetter
  Are white with early snow.

But where the low, gray headlands
  Look o'er the Baltic brine,
A bark is sailing in the track
  Of England's battle-line.

No wares hath she to barter
  For Bothnia's fish and grain ;
She saileth not for pleasure,
  She saileth not for gain.

But still by isle or mainland
  She drops her anchor down,
Where'er the British cannon
  Rained fire on tower and town.

Outspake the ancient Amtman,
  At the gate of Helsingfors :
" Why comes this ship a-spying
  In the track of England's wars ? "

" God bless her," said the coast-guard, —
  " God bless the ship, I say.
The holy angels trim the sails
  That speed her on her way !

" Where'er she drops her anchor,
  The peasant's heart is glad ;
Where'er she spreads her parting sail,
  The peasant's heart is sad.

" Each wasted town and hamlet
  She visits to restore ;
To roof the shattered cabin,
  And feed the starving poor.

" The sunken boats of fishers,
  The foraged beeves and grain,
The spoil of flake and storehouse,
  The good ship brings again.

" And so to Finland's sorrow
  The sweet amend is made,
As if the healing hand of Christ
  Upon her wounds were laid ! "

Then said the gray old Amtman,
  " The will of God be done !
The battle lost by England's hate,
  By England's love is won !

" We braved the iron tempest
  That thundered on our shore ;
But when did kindness fail to find
  The key to Finland's door ?

" No more from Aland's ramparts
  Shall warning signal come,
Nor startled Sweaborg hear again
  The roll of midnight drum.

" Beside our fierce Black Eagle
  The Dove of Peace shall rest ;
And in the mouths of cannon
  The sea-bird make her nest.

" For Finland, looking seaward,
  No coming foe shall scan ;
And the holy bells of Abo
  Shall ring, ' Good-will to man ! '

" Then row thy boat, O fisher !
  In peace on lake and bay ;
And thou, young maiden, dance again
  Around the poles of May !

" Sit down, old men, together,
  Old wives, in quiet spin ;
Henceforth the Anglo-Saxon
  Is the brother of the Finn ! "

THE EVE OF ELECTION

FROM gold to gray
Our mild sweet day
Of Indian Summer fades too soon ;
  But tenderly
  Above the sea
Hangs, white and calm, the hunter's moon.

In its pale fire,
The village spire
Shows like the zodiac's spectral lance ;
  The painted walls
  Whereon it falls
Transfigured stand in marble trance !

O'er fallen leaves
The west-wind grieves,
Yet comes a seed-time round again ;
  And morn shall see
  The State sown free
With baleful tares or healthful grain.

Along the street
The shadows meet
Of Destiny, whose hands conceal
  The moulds of fate
  That shape the State,
And make or mar the common weal.

Around I see
The powers that be ;
I stand by Empire's primal springs ;
  And princes meet,
  In every street,
And hear the tread of uncrowned kings !

Hark ! through the crowd
The laugh runs loud,
Beneath the sad, rebuking moon.
  God save the land
  A careless hand
May shake or swerve ere morrow's noon !

No jest is this ;
One cast amiss
May blast the hope of Freedom's year.
  Oh, take me where
  Are hearts of prayer,
And foreheads bowed in reverent fear !

Not lightly fall
Beyond recall
The written scrolls a breath can float ;
  The crowning fact,
  The kingliest act
Of Freedom is the freeman's vote !

For pearls that gem
A diadem
The diver in the deep sea dies ;
  The regal right
  We boast to-night
Is ours through costlier sacrifice ;

The blood of Vane,
His prison pain
Who traced the path the Pilgrim trod,
And hers whose faith
Drew strength from death,
And prayed her Russell up to God !

Our hearts grow cold,
We lightly hold
A right which brave men died to gain ;
The stake, the cord,
The axe, the sword,
Grim nurses at its birth of pain.

The shadow rend,
And o'er us bend,
O martyrs, with your crowns and palms ;
Breathe through these throngs
Your battle songs,
Your scaffold prayers, and dungeon psalms !

Look from the sky,
Like God's great eye,
Thou solemn moon, with searching beam,
Till in the sight
Of thy pure light
Our mean self-seekings meaner seem.

Shame from our hearts
Unworthy arts,
The fraud designed, the purpose dark ;
And smite away
The hands we lay
Profanely on the sacred ark.

To party claims
And private aims,
Reveal that august face of Truth,
Whereto are given
The age of heaven,
The beauty of immortal youth.

So shall our voice
Of sovereign choice
Swell the deep bass of duty done,
And strike the key
Of time to be,
When God and man shall speak as one !

FROM PERUGIA

"The thing which has the most dissevered
the people from the Pope, — the *unforgivable*
thing, — the breaking point between him and
them, — has been the encouragement and pro-
motion he gave to the officer under whom were
executed the slaughters of Perugia. *That* made
the breaking point in many honest hearts that
had clung to him before." — HARRIET BEECH-
ER STOWE's *Letters from Italy.*

THE tall, sallow guardsmen their horsetails
    have spread,
Flaming out in their violet, yellow, and red ;
And behind go the lackeys in crimson and
    buff,
And the chamberlains gorgeous in velvet
    and ruff ;
Next, in red-legged pomp, come the cardi-
    nals forth,
Each a lord of the church and a prince of
    the earth.

What 's this squeak of the fife, and this bat-
    ter of drum ?
Lo ! the Swiss of the Church from Perugia
    come ;
The militant angels, whose sabres drive
    home
To the hearts of the malcontents, cursed
    and abhorred,
The good Father's missives, and "Thus
    saith the Lord !"
And lend to his logic the point of the sword !

O maids of Etruria, gazing forlorn
O'er dark Thrasymenus, dishevelled and
    torn !
O fathers, who pluck at your gray beards
    for shame !
O mothers, struck dumb by a woe without
    name !
Well ye know how the Holy Church hire-
    ling behaves,
And his tender compassion of prisons and
    graves !

There they stand, the hired stabbers, the
    blood-stains yet fresh,
That splashed like red wine from the vin-
    tage of flesh ;
Grim instruments, careless as pincers and
    rack
How the joints tear apart, and the strained
    sinews crack ;
But the hate that glares on them is sharp
    as their swords,
And the sneer and the scowl print the air
    with fierce words !

Off with hats, down with knees, shout your
    vivas like mad !
Here 's the Pope in his holiday righteousness
    clad,
From shorn crown to toe-nail, kiss-worn to
    the quick,
Of sainthood in purple the pattern and
    pick,
Who the *rôle* of the priest and the soldier
    unites,
And, praying like Aaron, like Joshua fights !

Is this Pio Nono the gracious, for whom
We sang our hosannas and lighted all
    Rome ;
With whose advent we dreamed the new
    era began
When the priest should be human, the monk
    be a man ?
Ah, the wolf 's with the sheep, and the fox
    with the fowl,
When freedom we trust to the crosier and
    cowl !

Stand aside, men of Rome !   Here 's a hang-
    man-faced Swiss —
(A blessing for him surely can't go amiss) —
Would kneel down the sanctified slipper to
    kiss.
Short shrift will suffice him, — he 's blest
    beyond doubt ;
But there 's blood on his hands which would
    scarcely wash out,
Though Peter himself held the baptismal
    spout !

Make way for the next !   Here 's another
    sweet son !
What 's this mastiff-jawed rascal in epaulets
    done ?
He did, whispers rumor, (its truth God for-
    bid !)
At Perugia what Herod at Bethlehem
    did.
And the mothers ?   Don't name them ! these
    humors of war
They who keep him in service must pardon
    him for.

Hist ! here 's the arch-knave in a cardinal's
    hat,
With the heart of a wolf, and the stealth
    of a cat
(As if Judas and Herod together were
    rolled),

Who keeps, all as one, the Pope's conscience
    and gold,
Mounts guard on the altar, and pilfers from
    thence,
And flatters St. Peter while stealing his
    pence !

Who doubts Antonelli ?   Have miracles
    ceased
When robbers say mass, and Barabbas is
    priest ?
When the Church eats and drinks, at its
    mystical board,
The true flesh and blood carved and shed
    by its sword,
When its martyr, unsinged, claps the crown
    on his head,
And roasts, as his proxy, his neighbor in-
    stead !

There ! the bells jow and jangle the same
    blessed way
That they did when they rang for Barthol-
    omew's day.
Hark ! the tallow-faced monsters, nor
    women nor boys,
Vex the air with a shrill, sexless horror of
    noise.
Te Deum laudamus !   All round without
    stint
The incense-pot swings with a taint of blood
    in 't !

And now for the blessing !   Of little ac-
    count,
You know, is the old one they heard on the
    Mount.
Its giver was landless, His raiment was
    poor,
No jewelled tiara His fishermen wore ;
No incense, no lackeys, no riches, no home,
No Swiss guards !   We order things better
    at Rome.

So bless us the strong hand, and curse us
    the weak ;
Let Austria's vulture have food for her
    beak ;
Let the wolf-whelp of Naples play Bomba
    again,
With his death-cap of silence, and halter,
    and chain ;
Put reason, and justice, and truth under
    ban ;
For the sin unforgiven is freedom for man !

ITALY

ACROSS the sea I heard the groans
  Of nations in the intervals
Of wind and wave. Their blood and bones
Cried out in torture, crushed by thrones,
  And sucked by priestly cannibals.

I dreamed of Freedom slowly gained
  By martyr meekness, patience, faith,
And lo ! an athlete grimly stained,
With corded muscles battle-strained,
  Shouting it from the fields of death !

I turn me, awe-struck, from the sight,
  Among the clamoring thousands mute,
I only know that God is right,
And that the children of the light
  Shall tread the darkness under foot.

I know the pent fire heaves its crust,
  That sultry skies the bolt will form
To smite them clear ; that Nature must
The balance of her powers adjust,
  Though with the earthquake and the
    storm.

God reigns, and let the earth rejoice !
  I bow before His sterner plan.
Dumb are the organs of my choice ;
He speaks in battle's stormy voice,
  His praise is in the wrath of man !

Yet, surely as He lives, the day
  Of peace He promised shall be ours,
To fold the flags of war, and lay
Its sword and spear to rust away,
  And sow its ghastly fields with flowers !

FREEDOM IN BRAZIL

WITH clearer light, Cross of the South,
    shine forth
  In blue Brazilian skies ;
And thou, O river, cleaving half the earth
  From sunset to sunrise,
From the great mountains to the Atlantic
    waves
  Thy joy's long anthem pour.
Yet a few years (God make them less !)
    and slaves
  Shall shame thy pride no more.

No fettered feet thy shaded margins press ;
  But all men shall walk free
Where thou, the high-priest of the wilder-
    ness,
  Hast wedded sea to sea.

And thou, great - hearted ruler, through
    whose mouth
  The word of God is said,
Once more, "Let there be light !"—Son
    of the South,
  Lift up thy honored head,
Wear unashamed a crown by thy desert
  More than by birth thy own,
Careless of watch and ward ; thou art
    begirt
  By grateful hearts alone.
The moated wall and battle-ship may fail,
  But safe shall justice prove ;
Stronger than greaves of brass or iron
    mail
  The panoply of love.

Crowned doubly by man's blessing and
    God's grace,
  Thy future is secure ;
Who frees a people makes his statue's place
  In Time's Valhalla sure.
Lo ! from his Neva's banks the Scythian
    Czar
  Stretches to thee his hand,
Who, with the pencil of the Northern star,
  Wrote freedom on his land.
And he whose grave is holy by our calm
  And prairied Sangamon,
From his gaunt hand shall drop the mar-
    tyr's palm
  To greet thee with "Well done !"

And thou, O Earth, with smiles thy face
    make sweet,
  And let thy wail be stilled,
To hear the Muse of prophecy repeat
  Her promise half fulfilled.
The Voice that spake at Nazareth speaks
    still,
  No sound thereof hath died ;
Alike thy hope and Heaven's eternal will
  Shall yet be satisfied.
The years are slow, the vision tarrieth
    long,
  And far the end may be ;
But, one by one, the fiends of ancient wrong
  Go out and leave thee free.

AFTER ELECTION

THE day's sharp strife is ended now,
Our work is done, God knoweth how !
As on the thronged, unrestful town
The patience of the moon looks down,
I wait to hear, beside the wire,
The voices of its tongues of fire.

Slow, doubtful, faint, they seem at first :
Be strong, my heart, to know the worst !
Hark ! there the Alleghanies spoke ;
That sound from lake and prairie broke,
That sunset-gun of triumph rent
The silence of a continent !

That signal from Nebraska sprung,
This from Nevada's mountain tongue !
Is that thy answer, strong and free,
O loyal heart of Tennessee ?
What strange, glad voice is that which calls
From Wagner's grave and Sumter's walls ?

From Mississippi's fountain-head
A sound as of the bison's tread !
There rustled freedom's Charter Oak !
In that wild burst the Ozarks spoke !
Cheer answers cheer from rise to set
Of sun.   We have a country yet !

The praise, O God, be thine alone !
Thou givest not for bread a stone ;
Thou hast not led us through the night
To blind us with returning light ;
Not through the furnace have we passed,
To perish at its mouth at last.

O night of peace, thy flight restrain !
November's moon, be slow to wane !
Shine on the freedman's cabin floor,
On brows of prayer a blessing pour ;
And give, with full assurance blest,
The weary heart of Freedom rest !

DISARMAMENT

" PUT up the sword ! " The voice of Christ
      once more
Speaks, in the pauses of the cannon's roar,
O'er fields of corn by fiery sickles reaped
And left dry ashes ; over trenches heaped
With nameless dead ; o'er cities starving
      slow

Under a rain of fire ; through wards of
      woe
Down which a groaning diapason runs
From tortured brothers, husbands, lovers,
      sons
Of desolate women in their far-off homes,
Waiting to hear the step that never
      comes !
O men and brothers ! let that voice be
      heard.
War fails, try peace ; put up the useless
      sword !

Fear not the end.   There is a story told
In Eastern tents, when autumn nights
      grow cold,
And round the fire the Mongol shepherds
      sit
With grave responses listening unto it :
Once, on the errands of his mercy bent,
Buddha, the holy and benevolent,
Met a fell monster, huge and fierce of
      look,
Whose awful voice the hills and forests
      shook.
" O son of peace ! " the giant cried, " thy
      fate
Is sealed at last, and love shall yield to
      hate."
The unarmed Buddha looking, with no
      trace
Of fear or anger, in the monster's face,
In pity said : " Poor fiend, even thee I
      love."
Lo ! as he spake the sky-tall terror sank
To hand-breadth size ; the huge abhorrence
      shrank
Into the form and fashion of a dove ;
And where the thunder of its rage was
      heard,
Circling above him sweetly sang the bird :
" Hate hath no harm for love," so ran the
      song ;
" And peace unweaponcl conquers every
      wrong ! "

THE PROBLEM

I

NOT without envy Wealth at times must
      look
On their brown strength who wield the
      reaping-hook

And scythe, or at the forge-fire shape
  the plough
Or the steel harness of the steeds of steam;
  All who, by skill and patience, anyhow
Make service noble, and the earth redeem
From savageness. By kingly accolade
Than theirs was never worthier knighthood
  made.
Well for them, if, while demagogues their
  vain
And evil counsels proffer, they maintain
  Their honest manhood unseduced, and
  wage
No war with Labor's right to Labor's gain
Of sweet home-comfort, rest of hand and
  brain,
  And softer pillow for the head of Age.

II

And well for Gain if it ungrudging yields
  Labor its just demand; and well for
  Ease
If in the uses of its own, it sees
No wrong to him who tills its pleasant
  fields
  And spreads the table of its luxuries.
The interests of the rich man and the poor
Are one and same, inseparable evermore ;
And, when scant wage or labor fail to give
Food, shelter, raiment, wherewithal to
  live,
Need has its rights, necessity its claim.
Yea, even self-wrought misery and shame
Test well the charity suffering long and
  kind.
The home-pressed question of the age can
  find
No answer in the catch-words of the blind
Leaders of blind. Solution there is none
Save in the Golden Rule of Christ alone.

OUR COUNTRY

Read at Woodstock, Conn., July 4, 1883.

WE give thy natal day to hope,
  O Country of our love and prayer !
Thy way is down no fatal slope,
  But up to freer sun and air.

Tried as by furnace-fires, and yet
  By God's grace only stronger made,
In future tasks before thee set
  Thou shalt not lack the old-time aid.

The fathers sleep, but men remain
  As wise, as true, and brave as they;
Why count the loss and not the gain ?
  The best is that we have to-day.

Whate'er of folly, shame, or crime,
  Within thy mighty bounds transpires,
With speed defying space and time,
  Comes to us on the accusing wires ;

While of thy wealth of noble deeds,
  Thy homes of peace, thy votes unsold,
The love that pleads for human needs,
  The wrong redressed, but half is told !

We read each felon's chronicle,
  His acts, his words, his gallows-mood ;
We know the single sinner well
  And not the nine and ninety good.

Yet if, on daily scandals fed,
  We seem at times to doubt thy worth,
We know thee still, when all is said,
  The best and dearest spot on earth.

From the warm Mexic Gulf, or where
  Belted with flowers Los Angeles
Basks in the semi-tropic air,
  To where Katahdin's cedar trees

Are dwarfed and bent by Northern winds,
  Thy plenty's horn is yearly filled ;
Alone, the rounding century finds
  Thy liberal soil by free hands tilled.

A refuge for the wronged and poor,
  Thy generous heart has borne the blame
That, with them, through thy open door,
  The old world's evil outcasts came.

But, with thy just and equal rule,
  And labor's need and breadth of lands,
Free press and rostrum, church and school,
  Thy sure, if slow, transforming hands,

Shall mould even them to thy design,
  Making a blessing of the ban ;
And Freedom's chemistry combine
  The alien elements of man.

The power that broke their prison bar
  And set the dusky millions free,
And welded in the flame of war
  The Union fast to Liberty,

Shall it not deal with other ills,
  Redress the red man's grievance, break
The Circean cup which shames and kills,
  And Labor full requital make ?

Alone to such as fitly bear
  Thy civic honors bid them fall ?
And call thy daughters forth to share
  The rights and duties pledged to all ?

Give every child his right of school,
  Merge private greed in public good,
And spare a treasury overfull
  The tax upon a poor man's food ?

No lack was in thy primal stock,
  No weakling founders builded here ;
Thine were the men of Plymouth Rock,
  The Huguenot and Cavalier ;

And they whose firm endurance gained
  The freedom of the souls of men,
Whose hands, unstained with blood, main-
    tained
  The swordless commonwealth of Penn.

And thine shall be the power of all
  To do the work which duty bids,
And make the people's council hall
  As lasting as the Pyramids !

Well have thy later years made good
  Thy brave-said word a century back,
The pledge of human brotherhood,
  The equal claim of white and black.

That word still echoes round the world,
  And all who hear it turn to thee,
And read upon thy flag unfurled
  The prophecies of destiny.

Thy great world-lesson all shall learn,
  The nations in thy school shall sit,
Earth's farthest mountain-tops shall burn
  With watch-fires from thy own uplit.

Great without seeking to be great
  By fraud or conquest, rich in gold,
But richer in the large estate
  Of virtue which thy children hold,

With peace that comes of purity
  And strength to simple justice due,
So runs our loyal dream of thee ;
  God of our fathers ! make it true.

O Land of lands ! to thee we give
  Our prayers, our hopes, our service free ;
For thee thy sons shall nobly live,
  And at thy need shall die for thee !

ON THE BIG HORN

In the disastrous battle on the Big Horn River, in which General Custer and his entire force were slain, the chief Rain-in-the-Face was one of the fiercest leaders of the Indians. In Longfellow's poem on the massacre, these lines will be remembered : —

" Revenge ! " cried Rain-in-the-Face,
" Revenge upon all the race
  Of the White Chief with yellow hair ! "
And the mountains dark and high
From their crags reëchoed the cry
  Of his anger and despair.

He is now a man of peace ; and the agent at Standing Rock, Dakota, writes, September 28, 1886 : " Rain-in-the-Face is very anxious to go to Hampton. I fear he is too old, but he desires very much to go." *The Southern Workman*, the organ of General Armstrong's Industrial School at Hampton, Va., says in a late number : —
" Rain-in-the-Face has applied before to come to Hampton, but his age would exclude him from the school as an ordinary student. He has shown himself very much in earnest about it, and is anxious, all say, to learn the better ways of life. It is as unusual as it is striking to see a man of his age, and one who has had such an experience, willing to give up the old way, and put himself in the position of a boy and a student."

THE years are but half a score,
And the war-whoop sounds no more
  With the blast of bugles, where
Straight into a slaughter pen,
With his doomed three hundred men,
  Rode the chief with the yellow hair.

O Hampton, down by the sea !
What voice is beseeching thee
  For the scholar's lowliest place ?
Can this be the voice of him
Who fought on the Big Horn's rim ?
  Can this be Rain-in-the-Face ?

His war-paint is washed away,
His hands have forgotten to slay ;
  He seeks for himself and his race
The arts of peace and the lore
That give to the skilled hand more
  Than the spoils of war and chase.

O chief of the Christ-like school !
Can the zeal of thy heart grow cool
  When the victor scarred with fight
Like a child for thy guidance craves,
And the faces of hunters and braves
  Are turning to thee for light ?

The hatchet lies overgrown
With grass by the Yellowstone,
  Wind River and Paw of Bear ;
And, in sign that foes are friends,
Each lodge like a peace-pipe sends
  Its smoke in the quiet air.

The hands that have done the wrong
To right the wronged are strong,
  And the voice of a nation saith :
" Enough of the war of swords,
Enough of the lying words
  And shame of a broken faith ! "

The hills that have watched afar
The valleys ablaze with war
  Shall look on the tasselled corn ;
And the dust of the grinded grain,
Instead of the blood of the slain,
  Shall sprinkle thy banks, Big Horn !

The Ute and the wandering Crow
Shall know as the white men know,
  And fare as the white men fare ;
The pale and the red shall be brothers,
One's rights shall be as another's,
  Home, School, and House of Prayer !

O mountains that climb to snow,
O river winding below,
  Through meadows by war once trod,
O wild, waste lands that await
The harvest exceeding great,
  Break forth into praise of God !

POEMS SUBJECTIVE AND REMINISCENT

MEMORIES

["It was not without thought and delibera-
tion," Whittier's biographer writes, "that in
1888 he directed this poem to be placed at the
head of his Poems Subjective and Reminiscent.
He had never before publicly acknowledged
how much of his heart was wrapped up in this
delightful play of poetic fancy. The poem was
written in 1841, and although the romance it
embalms lies far back of this date, possibly
there is a heart still beating which fully under-
stands its meaning. The biographer can do no
more than make this suggestion, which has the
sanction of the poet's explicit word. To a friend
who told him that *Memories* was her favorite
poem, he said, 'I love it too; but I hardly
knew whether to publish it, it was so personal
and near my heart.'"]

A BEAUTIFUL and happy girl,
  With step as light as summer air,
Eyes glad with smiles, and brow of pearl,
Shadowed by many a careless curl
  Of unconfined and flowing hair;
A seeming child in everything,
  Save thoughtful brow and ripening
      charms,
As Nature wears the smile of Spring
  When sinking into Summer's arms.

A mind rejoicing in the light
  Which melted through its graceful
      bower,
Leaf after leaf, dew-moist and bright,
And stainless in its holy white,
  Unfolding like a morning flower:
A heart, which, like a fine-toned lute,
  With every breath of feeling woke,
And, even when the tongue was mute,
  From eye and lip in music spoke.

How thrills once more the lengthening
    chain
Of memory, at the thought of thee!
Old hopes which long in dust have lain,
Old dreams, come thronging back again,
  And boyhood lives again in me;

I feel its glow upon my cheek,
  Its fulness of the heart is mine,
As when I leaned to hear thee speak,
  Or raised my doubtful eye to thine.

I hear again thy low replies,
  I feel thy arm within my own,
And timidly again uprise
The fringèd lids of hazel eyes,
  With soft brown tresses overblown.
Ah! memories cf sweet summer eves,
  Of moonlit wave and willowy way,
Of stars and flowers, and dewy leaves,
  And smiles and tones more dear than
      they!

Ere this, thy quiet eye hath smiled
  My picture of thy youth to see,
When, half a woman, half a child,
Thy very artlessness beguiled,
  And folly's self seemed wise in thee;
I too can smile, when o'er that hour
  The lights of memory backward stream,
Yet feel the while that manhood's power
  Is vainer than my boyhood's dream.

Years have passed on, and left their trace,
  Of graver care and deeper thought;
And unto me the calm, cold face
Of manhood, and to thee the grace
  Of woman's pensive beauty brought.
More wide, perchance, for blame than
    praise,
  The school-boy's humble name has flown;
Thine, in the green and quiet ways
  Of unobtrusive goodness known.

And wider yet in thought and deed
  Diverge our pathways, one in youth;
Thine the Genevan's sternest creed,
While answers to my spirit's need
  The Derby dalesman's simple truth.
For thee, the priestly rite and prayer,
  And holy day, and solemn psalm;
For me, the silent reverence where
  My brethren gather, slow and calm.

Yet hath thy spirit left on me
  An impress Time has worn not out,
And something of myself in thee,
A shadow from the past, I see,
  Lingering, even yet, thy way about ;
Not wholly can the heart unlearn
  That lesson of its better hours,
Not yet has Time's dull footstep worn
  To common dust that path of flowers.

Thus, while at times before our eyes
  The shadows melt, and fall apart,
And, smiling through them, round us lies
The warm light of our morning skies, —
  The Indian Summer of the heart !
In secret sympathies of mind,
  In founts of feeling which retain
Their pure, fresh flow, we yet may find
  Our early dreams not wholly vain !

RAPHAEL

Suggested by the portrait of Raphael, at the age of fifteen.

I SHALL not soon forget that sight :
  The glow of Autumn's westering day,
A hazy warmth, a dreamy light,
  On Raphael's picture lay.

It was a simple print I saw,
  The fair face of a musing boy ;
Yet, while I gazed, a sense of awe
  Seemed blending with my joy.

A single print, — the graceful flow
  Of boyhood's soft and wavy hair,
And fresh young lip and cheek, and brow
  Unmarked and clear, were there.

Yet through its sweet and calm repose
  I saw the inward spirit shine ;
It was as if before me rose
  The white veil of a shrine.

As if, as Gothland's sage has told,
  The hidden life, the man within,
Dissevered from its frame and mould,
  By mortal eye were seen.

Was it the lifting of that eye,
  The waving of that pictured hand ?
Loose as a cloud-wreath on the sky,
  I saw the walls expand.

The narrow room had vanished, — space,
  Broad, luminous, remained alone,
Through which all hues and shapes of grace
  And beauty looked or shone.

Around the mighty master came
  The marvels which his pencil wrought,
Those miracles of power whose fame
  Is wide as human thought.

There drooped thy more than mortal face,
  O Mother, beautiful and mild !
Enfolding in one dear embrace
  Thy Saviour and thy Child !

The rapt brow of the Desert John ;
  The awful glory of that day
When all the Father's brightness shone
  Through manhood's veil of clay.

And, midst gray prophet forms, and wild
  Dark visions of the days of old,
How sweetly woman's beauty smiled
  Through locks of brown and gold !

There Fornarina's fair young face
  Once more upon her lover shone,
Whose model of an angel's grace
  He borrowed from her own.

Slow passed that vision from my view,
  But not the lesson which it taught ;
The soft, calm shadows which it threw
  Still rested on my thought :

The truth, that painter, bard, and sage,
  Even in Earth's cold and changeful clime,
Plant for their deathless heritage
  The fruits and flowers of time.

We shape ourselves the joy or fear
  Of which the coming life is made,
And fill our Future's atmosphere
  With sunshine or with shade.

The tissue of the Life to be
  We weave with colors all our own,
And in the field of Destiny
  We reap as we have sown.

Still shall the soul around it call
  The shadows which it gathered here,
And, painted on the eternal wall,
  The Past shall reappear.

Think ye the notes of holy song
  On Milton's tuneful ear have died?
Think ye that Raphael's angel throng
  Has vanished from his side?

Oh no! — We live our life again;
  Or warmly touched, or coldly dim,
The pictures of the Past remain, —
  Man's works shall follow him!

EGO

WRITTEN IN THE ALBUM OF A FRIEND

[Originally entitled *Lines Written in the Book of a Friend*.]

ON page of thine I cannot trace
The cold and heartless commonplace,
A statue's fixed and marble grace.

For ever as these lines I penned,
Still with the thought of thee will blend
That of some loved and common friend,

Who in life's desert track has made
His pilgrim tent with mine, or strayed
Beneath the same remembered shade.

And hence my pen unfettered moves
In freedom which the heart approves,
The negligence which friendship loves.

And wilt thou prize my poor gift less
For simple air and rustic dress,
And sign of haste and carelessness?

Oh, more than specious counterfeit
Of sentiment or studied wit,
A heart like thine should value it.

Yet half I fear my gift will be
Unto thy book, if not to thee,
Of more than doubtful courtesy.

A banished name from Fashion's sphere,
A lay unheard of Beauty's ear,
Forbid, disowned, — what do they here?

Upon my ear not all in vain
Came the sad captive's clanking chain,
The groaning from his bed of pain.

And sadder still, I saw the woe
Which only wounded spirits know
When Pride's strong footsteps o'er them
  go.

Spurned not alone in walks abroad,
But from the temples of the Lord
Thrust out apart, like things abhorred.

Deep as I felt, and stern and strong,
In words which Prudence smothered long,
My soul spoke out against the wrong;

Not mine alone the task to speak
Of comfort to the poor and weak,
And dry the tear on Sorrow's cheek;

But, mingled in the conflict warm,
To pour the fiery breath of storm
Through the harsh trumpet of Reform;

To brave Opinion's settled frown,
From ermined robe and saintly gown,
While wrestling reverenced Error down.

Founts gushed beside my pilgrim way,
Cool shadows on the greensward lay,
Flowers swung upon the bending spray.

And, broad and bright, on either hand,
Stretched the green slopes of Fairy-land,
With Hope's eternal sunbow spanned;

Whence voices called me like the flow,
Which on the listener's ear will grow,
Of forest streamlets soft and low.

And gentle eyes, which still retain
Their picture on the heart and brain,
Smiled, beckoning from that path of pain.

In vain! nor dream, nor rest, nor pause
Remain for him who round him draws
The battered mail of Freedom's cause.

From youthful hopes, from each green
  spot
Of young Romance, and gentle Thought,
Where storm and tumult enter not;

From each fair altar, where belong
The offerings Love requires of Song
In homage to her bright-eyed throng;

With soul and strength, with heart and
  hand,
I turned to Freedom's struggling band,
To the sad Helots of our land.

What marvel then that Fame should turn
Her notes of praise to those of scorn ;
Her gifts reclaimed, her smiles with-
  drawn ?

What matters it ? a few years more,
Life's surge so restless heretofore
Shall break upon the unknown shore !

In that far land shall disappear
The shadows which we follow here,
The mist-wreaths of our atmosphere !

Before no work of mortal hand,
Of human will or strength expand
The pearl gates of the Better Land ;

Alone in that great love which gave
Life to the sleeper of the grave,
Resteth the power to seek and save.

Yet, if the spirit gazing through
The vista of the past can view
One deed to Heaven and virtue true ;

If through the wreck of wasted powers,
Of garlands wreathed from Folly's bowers,
Of idle aims and misspent hours,

The eye can note one sacred spot
By Pride and Self profanëd not,
A green place in the waste of thought,

Where deed or word hath rendered less
The sum of human wretchedness,
And Gratitude looks forth to bless ;

The simple burst of tenderest feeling
From sad hearts worn by evil-dealing,
For blessing on the hand of healing ;

Better than Glory's pomp will be
That green and blessed spot to me,
A palm-shade in Eternity !

Something of Time which may invite
The purified and spiritual sight
To rest on with a calm delight.

And when the summer winds shall sweep
With their light wings my place of sleep,
And mosses round my headstone creep ;

If still, as Freedom's rallying sign,
Upon the young heart's altars shine
The very fires they caught from mine ;

If words my lips once uttered still,
In the calm faith and steadfast will
Of other hearts, their work fulfil ;

Perchance with joy the soul may learn
These tokens, and its eye discern
The fires which on those altars burn ;

A marvellous joy that even then,
The spirit hath its life again,
In the strong hearts of mortal men.

Take, lady, then, the gift I bring,
No gay and graceful offering,
No flower-smile of the laughing spring.

Midst the green buds of Youth's fresh
  May,
With Fancy's leaf-enwoven bay,
My sad and sombre gift I lay.

And if it deepens in thy mind
A sense of suffering human-kind, —
The outcast and the spirit-blind ;

Oppressed and spoiled on every side,
By Prejudice, and Scorn, and Pride,
Life's common courtesies denied ;

Sad mothers mourning o'er their trust,
Children by want and misery nursed,
Tasting life's bitter cup at first ;

If to their strong appeals which come
From fireless hearth, and crowded room,
And the close alley's noisome gloom,—

Though dark the hands upraised to thee
In mute beseeching agony,
Thou lend'st thy woman's sympathy ;

Not vainly on thy gentle shrine,
Where Love, and Mirth, and Friendship
  twine
Their varied gifts, I offer mine.

THE PUMPKIN

OH, greenly and fair in the lands of the
    sun,
The vines of the gourd and the rich melon
    run,
And the rock and the tree and the cottage
    enfold,
With broad leaves all greenness and blos-
    soms all gold,
Like that which o'er Nineveh's prophet once
    grew,
While he waited to know that his warning
    was true,
And longed for the storm-cloud, and lis-
    tened in vain
For the rush of the whirlwind and red fire-
    rain.

On the banks of the Xenil the dark Spanish
    maiden
Comes up with the fruit of the tangled vine
    laden ;
And the Creole of Cuba laughs out to be-
    hold
Through orange-leaves shining the broad
    spheres of gold ;
Yet with dearer delight from his home in
    the North,
On the fields of his harvest the Yankee
    looks forth,
Where crook-necks are coiling and yellow
    fruit shines,
And the sun of September melts down on
    his vines.

Ah ! on Thanksgiving day, when from East
    and from West,
From North and from South come the pil-
    grim and guest,
When the gray-haired New Englander sees
    round his board
The old broken links of affection restored,
When the care-wearied man seeks his mo-
    ther once more,
And the worn matron smiles where the girl
    smiled before,
What moistens the lip and what brightens
    the eye ?
What calls back the past, like the rich
    Pumpkin pie ?

Oh, fruit loved of boyhood ! the old days
    recalling,

When wood-grapes were purpling and
    brown nuts were falling !
When wild, ugly faces we carved in its
    skin,
Glaring out through the dark with a candle
    within !
When we laughed round the corn-heap,
    with hearts all in tune,
Our chair a broad pumpkin, — our lantern
    the moon,
Telling tales of the fairy who travelled like
    steam,
In a pumpkin-shell coach, with two rats for
    her team !

Then thanks for thy present ! none sweeter
    or better
E'er smoked from an oven or circled a
    platter !
Fairer hands never wrought at a pastry
    more fine,
Brighter eyes never watched o'er its bak-
    ing, than thine !
And the prayer, which my mouth is too
    full to express,
Swells my heart that thy shadow may
    never be less,
That the days of thy lot may be length-
    ened below,
And the fame of thy worth like a pumpkin-
    vine grow,
And thy life be as sweet, and its last sun-
    set sky
Golden-tinted and fair as thy own Pumpkin
    pie !

FORGIVENESS

MY heart was heavy, for its trust had
    been
  Abused, its kindness answered with foul
    wrong ;
So, turning gloomily from my fellow-
    men,
  One summer Sabbath day I strolled
    among
The green mounds of the village burial-
    place ;
  Where, pondering how all human love
    and hate
  Find one sad level ; and how, soon or
    late,
Wronged and wrongdoer, each with meek-
    ened face,

And cold hands folded over a still heart,
Pass the green threshold of our common
    grave,
    Whither all footsteps tend, whence none
        depart,
Awed for myself, and pitying my race,
Our common sorrow, like a mighty wave,
Swept all my pride away, and trembling I
    forgave !

TO MY SISTER

WITH A COPY OF "THE SUPERNATU-
RALISM OF NEW ENGLAND"

The work referred to was a series of papers
under this title, contributed to the *Democratic
Review* and afterward collected into a volume,
in which I noted some of the superstitions and
folklore prevalent in New England. The vol-
ume has not been kept in print, but most of
its contents are distributed in my *Literary
Recreations and Miscellanies* [now scattered in
volumes v. and vi. of the Riverside edition].

DEAR Sister ! while the wise and sage
Turn coldly from my playful page,
And count it strange that ripened age
    Should stoop to boyhood's folly ;
I know that thou wilt judge aright
Of all which makes the heart more light,
Or lends one star-gleam to the night
    Of clouded Melancholy.

Away with weary cares and themes !
Swing wide the moonlit gate of dreams !
Leave free once more the land which
    teems
    With wonders and romances !
Where thou, with clear discerning eyes,
Shalt rightly read the truth which lies
Beneath the quaintly masking guise
    Of wild and wizard fancies.

Lo ! once again our feet we set
On still green wood-paths, twilight wet,
By lonely brooks, whose waters fret
    The roots of spectral beeches ;
Again the hearth-fire glimmers o'er
Home's whitewashed wall and painted
    floor,
And young eyes widening to the lore
    Of faery-folks and witches.

Dear heart ! the legend is not vain
Which lights that holy hearth again,
And calling back from care and pain,
    And death's funereal sadness,
Draws round its old familiar blaze
The clustering groups of happier days,
And lends to sober manhood's gaze
    A glimpse of childish gladness.

And, knowing how my life hath been
A weary work of tongue and pen,
A long, harsh strife with strong-willed men,
    Thou wilt not chide my turning
To con, at times, an idle rhyme,
To pluck a flower from childhood's clime,
Or listen, at Life's noonday chime,
    For the sweet bells of Morning !

MY THANKS

ACCOMPANYING MANUSCRIPTS PRE-
SENTED TO A FRIEND

[Formerly entitled *Lines*.]

'T IS said that in the Holy Land
    The angels of the place have blessed
The pilgrim's bed of desert sand,
    Like Jacob's stone of rest.

That down the hush of Syrian skies
    Some sweet-voiced saint at twilight sings
The song whose holy symphonies
    Are beat by unseen wings ;

Till starting from his sandy bed,
    The wayworn wanderer looks to see
The halo of an angel's head
    Shine through the tamarisk-tree.

So through the shadows of my way
    Thy smile hath fallen soft and clear,
So at the weary close of day
    Hath seemed thy voice of cheer.

That pilgrim pressing to his goal
    May pause not for the vision's sake,
Yet all fair things within his soul
    The thought of it shall wake :

The graceful palm-tree by the well,
    Seen on the far horizon's rim ;
The dark eyes of the fleet gazelle,
    Bent timidly on him ;

Each pictured saint, whose golden hair
  Streams sunlike through the convent's
      gloom ;
Pale shrines of martyrs young and fair,
  And loving Mary's tomb ;

And thus each tint or shade which falls,
  From sunset cloud or waving tree,
Along my pilgrim path, recalls
  The pleasant thought of thee.

Of one in sun and shade the same,
  In weal and woe my steady friend,
Whatever by that holy name
  The angels comprehend.

Not blind to faults and follies, thou
  Hast never failed the good to see,
Nor judged by one unseemly bough
  The upward-struggling tree.

These light leaves at thy feet I lay, —
  Poor common thoughts on common
      things,
Which Time is shaking, day by day,
  Like feathers from his wings ;

Chance shootings from a frail life-tree,
  To nurturing care but little known,
Their good was partly learned of thee,
  Their folly is my own.

That tree still clasps the kindly mould,
  Its leaves still drink the twilight dew,
And weaving its pale green with gold,
  Still shines the sunlight through.

There still the morning zephyrs play,
  And there at times the spring bird
      sings,
And mossy trunk and fading spray
  Are flowered with glossy wings.

Yet, even in genial sun and rain,
  Root, branch, and leaflet fail and fade ;
The wanderer on its lonely plain
  Erelong shall miss its shade.

O friend beloved, whose curious skill
  Keeps bright the last year's leaves and
      flowers,
With warm, glad, summer thoughts to
      fill
  The cold, dark, winter hours !

Pressed on thy heart, the leaves I bring
  May well defy the wintry cold,
Until, in Heaven's eternal spring,
  Life's fairer ones unfold.

REMEMBRANCE

WITH COPIES OF THE AUTHOR'S WRITINGS

FRIEND of mine ! whose lot was cast
With me in the distant past ;
Where, like shadows flitting fast,

Fact and fancy, thought and theme,
Word and work, begin to seem
Like a half-remembered dream !

Touched by change have all things been
Yet I think of thee as when
We had speech of lip and pen.

For the calm thy kindness lent
To a path of discontent,
Rough with trial and dissent ;

Gentle words where such were few,
Softening blame where blame was true,
Praising where small praise was due ;

For a waking dream made good,
For an ideal understood,
For thy Christian womanhood ;

For thy marvellous gift to cull
From our common life and dull
Whatsoe'er is beautiful ;

Thoughts and fancies, Hybla's bees
Dropping sweetness ; true heart's-ease
Of congenial sympathies ; —

Still for these I own my debt ;
Memory, with her eyelids wet,
Fain would thank thee even yet ;

And as one who scatters flowers
Where the Queen of May's sweet hours
Sits, o'ertwined with blossomed bowers,

In superfluous zeal bestowing
Gifts where gifts are overflowing,
So I pay the debt I 'm owing.

To thy full thoughts, gay or sad,
Sunny-hued or sober clad,
Something of my own I add ;

Well assured that thou wilt take
Even the offering which I make
Kindly for the giver's sake.

MY NAMESAKE

Addressed to Francis Greenleaf Allinson of
Burlington, N. J.

You scarcely need my tardy thanks,
    Who, self-rewarded, nurse and tend —
A green leaf on your own Green Banks —
    The memory of your friend.

For me, no wreath, bloom-woven, hides
    The sobered brow and lessening hair :
For aught I know, the myrtled sides
    Of Helicon are bare.

Their scallop-shells so many bring
    The fabled founts of song to try,
They 've drained, for aught I know, the
        spring
    Of Aganippe dry.

Ah well ! — The wreath the Muses braid
    Proves often Folly's cap and bell ;
Methinks, my ample beaver's shade
    May serve my turn as well.

Let Love's and Friendship's tender debt
    Be paid by those I love in life.
Why should the unborn critic whet
    For me his scalping-knife ?

Why should the stranger peer and pry
    One's vacant house of life about,
And drag for curious ear and eye
    His faults and follies out ? —

Why stuff, for fools to gaze upon,
    With chaff of words, the garb he wore,
As corn-husks when the ear is gone
    Are rustled all the more ?

Let kindly Silence close again,
    The picture vanish from the eye,
And on the dim and misty main
    Let the small ripple die.

Yet not the less I own your claim
    To grateful thanks, dear friends of mine.
Hang, if it please you so, my name
    Upon your household line.

Let Fame from brazen lips blow wide
    Her chosen names, I envy none :
A mother's love, a father's pride,
    Shall keep alive my own !

Still shall that name as now recall
    The young leaf wet with morning dew,
The glory where the sunbeams fall
    The breezy woodlands through.

That name shall be a household word,
    A spell to waken smile or sigh ;
In many an evening prayer be heard
    And cradle lullaby.

And thou, dear child, in riper days
    When asked the reason of thy name,
Shalt answer : " One 't were vain to praise
    Or censure bore the same.

" Some blamed him, some believed him
        good,
    The truth lay doubtless 'twixt the two ;
He reconciled as best he could
    Old faith and fancies new.

" In him the grave and playful mixed,
    And wisdom held with folly truce,
And Nature compromised betwixt
    Good fellow and recluse.

" He loved his friends, forgave his foes ;
    And, if his words were harsh at times,
He spared his fellow-men, — his blows
    Fell only on their crimes.

" He loved the good and wise, but found
    His human heart to all akin
Who met him on the common ground
    Of suffering and of sin.

" Whate'er his neighbors might endure
    Of pain or grief his own became ;
For all the ills he could not cure
    He held himself to blame.

" His good was mainly an intent,
    His evil not of forethought done ;
The work he wrought was rarely meant
    Or finished as begun.

" Ill served his tides of feeling strong
  To turn the common mills of use ;
And, over restless wings of song,
  His birthright garb hung loose !

" His eye was beauty's powerless slave,
  And his the ear which discord pains ;
Few guessed beneath his aspect grave
  What passions strove in chains.

" He had his share of care and pain,
  No holiday was life to him ;
Still in the heirloom cup we drain
  The bitter drop will swim.

" Yet Heaven was kind, and here a bird
  And there a flower beguiled his way ;
And cool, in summer noons, he heard
  The fountains plash and play.

" On all his sad or restless moods
  The patient peace of Nature stole ;
The quiet of the fields and woods
  Sank deep into his soul.

" He worshipped as his fathers did,
  And kept the faith of childish days,
And, howsoe'er he strayed or slid,
  He loved the good old ways.

" The simple tastes, the kindly traits,
  The tranquil air, and gentle speech,
The silence of the soul that waits
  For more than man to teach.

" The cant of party, school, and sect,
  Provoked at times his honest scorn,
And Folly, in its gray respect,
  He tossed on satire's horn.

" But still his heart was full of awe
  And reverence for all sacred things ;
And, brooding over form and law,
  He saw the Spirit's wings !

" Life's mystery wrapt him like a cloud ;
  He heard far voices mock his own,
The sweep of wings unseen, the loud,
  Long roll of waves unknown.

" The arrows of his straining sight
  Fell quenched in darkness ; priest and
    sage,
Like lost guides calling left and right,
  Perplexed his doubtful age.

" Like childhood, listening for the sound
  Of its dropped pebbles in the well,
All vainly down the dark profound
  His brief-lined plummet fell.

" So, scattering flowers with pious pains
  On old beliefs, of later creeds,
Which claimed a place in Truth's do-
    mains,
  He asked the title-deeds.

" He saw the old-time's groves and shrines
  In the long distance fair and dim ;
And heard, like sound of far-off pines,
  The century-mellowed hymn !

" He dared not mock the Dervish whirl,
  The Brahmin's rite, the Lama's spell ;
God knew the heart ; Devotion's pearl
  Might sanctify the shell.

" While others trod the altar stairs
  He faltered like the publican ;
And, while they praised as saints, his
    prayers
  Were those of sinful man.

" For, awed by Sinai's Mount of Law,
  The trembling faith alone sufficed,
That, through its cloud and flame, he
    saw
  The sweet, sad face of Christ !

" And listening, with his forehead bowed,
  Heard the Divine compassion fill
The pauses of the trump and cloud
  With whispers small and still.

" The words he spake, the thoughts he
    penned,
  Are mortal as his hand and brain,
But, if they served the Master's end,
  He has not lived in vain ! "

Heaven make thee better than thy name,
  Child of my friends ! — For thee I
    crave
What riches never bought, nor fame
  To mortal longing gave.

I pray the prayer of Plato old :
  God make thee beautiful within,
And let thine eyes the good behold
  In everything save sin !

Imagination held in check
  To serve, not rule, thy poisëd mind ;
Thy Reason, at the frown or beck
  Of Conscience, loose or bind.

No dreamer thou, but real all, —
  Strong manhood crowning vigorous youth
Life made by duty epical
  And rhythmic with the truth.

So shall that life the fruitage yield
  Which trees of healing only give,
And green-leafed in the Eternal field
  Of God, forever live !

A MEMORY

[The singer in this poem was a daughter of
Whittier's early friend, N. P. Rogers.]

HERE, while the loom of Winter weaves
  The shroud of flowers and fountains,
I think of thee and summer eves
  Among the Northern mountains.

When thunder tolled the twilight's close,
  And winds the lake were rude on,
And thou wert singing, *Ca' the Yowes,*
  The bonny yowes of Cluden !

When, close and closer, hushing breath,
  Our circle narrowed round thee,
And smiles and tears made up the wreath
  Wherewith our silence crowned thee ;

And, strangers all, we felt the ties
  Of sisters and of brothers ;
Ah ! whose of all those kindly eyes
  Now smile upon another's ?

The sport of Time, who still apart
  The waifs of life is flinging ;
Oh, nevermore shall heart to heart
  Draw nearer for that singing !

Yet when the panes are frosty-starred,
  And twilight's fire is gleaming,
I hear the songs of Scotland's bard
  Sound softly through my dreaming !

A song that lends to winter snows
  The glow of summer weather, —
Again I hear thee ca' the yowes
  To Cludən's hills of heather !

MY DREAM

IN my dream, methought I trod,
Yesternight, a mountain road ;
Narrow as Al Sirat's span,
High as eagle's flight, it ran.

Overhead, a roof of cloud
With its weight of thunder bowed ;
Underneath, to left and right,
Blankness and abysmal night.

Here and there a wild-flower blushed ;
Now and then a bird-song gushed ;
Now and then, through rifts of shade,
Stars shone out, and sunbeams played.

But the goodly company,
Walking in that path with me,
One by one the brink o'erslid,
One by one the darkness hid.

Some with wailing and lament,
Some with cheerful courage went ;
But, of all who smiled or mourned,
Never one to us returned.

Anxiously, with eye and ear,
Questioning that shadow drear,
Never hand in token stirred,
Never answering voice I heard !

Steeper, darker ! — lo ! I felt
From my feet the pathway melt,
Swallowed by the black despair,
And the hungry jaws of air,

Past the stony-throated caves,
Strangled by the wash of waves,
Past the splintered crags, I sank
On a green and flowery bank, —

Soft as fall of thistle-down,
Lightly as a cloud is blown,
Soothingly as childhood pressed
To the bosom of its rest.

Of the sharp-horned rocks instead,
Green the grassy meadows spread,
Bright with waters singing by
Trees that propped a golden sky.

Painless, trustful, sorrow-free,
Old lost faces welcomed me,

With whose sweetness of content
Still expectant hope was blent.

Waking while the dawning gray
Slowly brightened into day,
Pondering that vision fled,
Thus unto myself I said: —

"Steep and hung with clouds of strife
Is our narrow path of life;
And our death the dreaded fall
Through the dark, awaiting all.

"So, with painful steps we climb
Up the dizzy ways of time,
Ever in the shadow shed
By the forecast of our dread.

"Dread of mystery solved alone,
Of the untried and unknown;
Yet the end thereof may seem
Like the falling of my dream.

"And this heart-consuming care,
All our fears of here or there,
Change and absence, loss and death,
Prove but simple lack of faith."

Thou, O Most Compassionate!
Who didst stoop to our estate,
Drinking of the cup we drain,
Treading in our path of pain, —

Through the doubt and mystery,
Grant to us thy steps to see,
And the grace to draw from thence
Larger hope and confidence.

Show thy vacant tomb, and let,
As of old, the angels sit,
Whispering, by its open door:
"Fear not! He hath gone before!"

THE BAREFOOT BOY

BLESSINGS on thee, little man,
Barefoot boy, with cheek of tan!
With thy turned-up pantaloons,
And thy merry whistled tunes;
With thy red lip, redder still
Kissed by strawberries on the hill;
With the sunshine on thy face,
Through thy torn brim's jaunty grace;
From my heart I give thee joy, —

I was once a barefoot boy!
Prince thou art, — the grown-up man
Only is republican.
Let the million-dollared ride!
Barefoot, trudging at his side,
Thou hast more than he can buy
In the reach of ear and eye, —
Outward sunshine, inward joy:
Blessings on thee, barefoot boy!

Oh for boyhood's painless play,
Sleep that wakes in laughing day,
Health that mocks the doctor's rules,
Knowledge never learned of schools,
Of the wild bee's morning chase,
Of the wild-flower's time and place,
Flight of fowl and habitude
Of the tenants of the wood;
How the tortoise bears his shell,
How the woodchuck digs his cell,
And the ground-mole sinks his well;
How the robin feeds her young,
How the oriole's nest is hung;
Where the whitest lilies blow,
Where the freshest berries grow,
Where the ground-nut trails its vine,
Where the wood-grape's clusters shine;
Of the black wasp's cunning way,
Mason of his walls of clay,
And the architectural plans
Of gray hornet artisans!
For, eschewing books and tasks,
Nature answers all he asks;
Hand in hand with her he walks,
Face to face with her he talks,
Part and parcel of her joy, —
Blessings on the barefoot boy!

Oh for boyhood's time of June,
Crowding years in one brief moon,
When all things I heard or saw,
Me, their master, waited for.
I was rich in flowers and trees,
Humming-birds and honey-bees;
For my sport the squirrel played,
Plied the snouted mole his spade;
For my taste the blackberry cone
Purpled over hedge and stone;
Laughed the brook for my delight
Through the day and through the night,
Whispering at the garden wall,
Talked with me from fall to fall;
Mine the sand-rimmed pickerel pond,
Mine the walnut slopes beyond,
Mine, on bending orchard trees,

Apples of Hesperides !
Still as my horizon grew,
Larger grew my riches too ;
All the world I saw or knew
Seemed a complex Chinese toy,
Fashioned for a barefoot boy !

Oh for festal dainties spread,
Like my bowl of milk and bread ;
Pewter spoon and bowl of wood,
On the door-stone, gray and rude !
O'er me, like a regal tent,
Cloudy-ribbed, the sunset bent,
Purple-curtained, fringed with gold,
Looped in many a wind-swung fold ;
While for music came the play
Of the pied frogs' orchestra ;
And, to light the noisy choir,
Lit the fly his lamp of fire.
I was monarch : pomp and joy
Waited on the barefoot boy !

Cheerily, then, my little man,
Live and laugh, as boyhood can !
Though the flinty slopes be hard,
Stubble-speared the new-mown sward,
Every morn shall lead thee through
Fresh baptisms of the dew ;
Every evening from thy feet
Shall the cool wind kiss the heat :
All too soon these feet must hide
In the prison cells of pride,
Lose the freedom of the sod,
Like a colt's for work be shod,
Made to tread the mills of toil,
Up and down in ceaseless moil :
Happy if their track be found
Never on forbidden ground ;
Happy if they sink not in
Quick and treacherous sands of sin.
Ah ! that thou couldst know thy joy,
Ere it passes, barefoot boy !

MY PSALM

I MOURN no more my vanished years:
    Beneath a tender rain,
An April rain of smiles and tears,
    My heart is young again.

The west-winds blow, and, singing low,
    I hear the glad streams run ;
The windows of my soul I throw
    Wide open to the sun.

No longer forward nor behind
    I look in hope or fear ;
But, grateful, take the good I find,
    The best of now and here.

I plough no more a desert land,
    To harvest weed and tare ;
The manna dropping from God's hand
    Rebukes my painful care.

I break my pilgrim staff, I lay
    Aside the toiling oar ;
The angel sought so far away
    I welcome at my door.

The airs of spring may never play
    Among the ripening corn,
Nor freshness of the flowers of May
    Blow through the autumn morn ;

Yet shall the blue-eyed gentian look
    Through fringèd lids to heaven,
And the pale aster in the brook
    Shall see its image given ; —

The woods shall wear their robes of praise,
    The south-wind softly sigh,
And sweet, calm days in golden haze
    Melt down the amber sky.

Not less shall manly deed and word
    Rebuke an age of wrong ;
The graven flowers that wreathe the sword
    Make not the blade less strong.

But smiting hands shall learn to heal, —
    To build as to destroy ;
Nor less my heart for others feel
    That I the more enjoy.

All as God wills, who wisely heeds
    To give or to withhold,
And knoweth more of all my needs
    Than all my prayers have told !

Enough that blessings undeserved
    Have marked my erring track ;
That wheresoe'er my feet have swerved,
    His chastening turned me back ;

That more and more a Providence
    Of love is understood,
Making the springs of time and sense
    Sweet with eternal good ; —

That death seems but a covered way
    Which opens into light,
Wherein no blinded child can stray
    Beyond the Father's sight ;

That care and trial seem at last,
    Through Memory's sunset air,
Like mountain-ranges overpast,
    In purple distance fair ;

That all the jarring notes of life
    Seem blending in a psalm,
And all the angles of its strife
    Slow rounding into calm.

And so the shadows fall apart,
    And so the west-winds play ;
And all the windows of my heart
    I open to the day.

THE WAITING

I WAIT and watch : before my eyes
    Methinks the night grows thin and
        gray ;
I wait and watch the eastern skies
To see the golden spears uprise
    Beneath the oriflamme of day !

Like one whose limbs are bound in trance
    I hear the day-sounds swell and grow,
And see across the twilight glance,
Troop after troop, in swift advance,
    The shining ones with plumes of snow !

I know the errand of their feet,
    I know what mighty work is theirs ;
I can but lift up hands unmeet
The threshing-floors of God to beat,
    And speed them with unworthy prayers.

I will not dream in vain despair
    The steps of progress wait for me :
The puny leverage of a hair
The planet's impulse well may spare,
    A drop of dew the tided sea.

The loss, if loss there be, is mine,
    And yet not mine if understood ;
For one shall grasp and one resign,
One drink life's rue, and one its wine,
    And God shall make the balance good.

Oh power to do !   Oh baffled will !
    Oh prayer and action ! ye are one.
Who may not strive, may yet fulfil
The harder task of standing still,
    And good but wished with God is done !

SNOW–BOUND

A WINTER IDYL

TO THE MEMORY OF THE HOUSEHOLD IT DESCRIBES

THIS POEM IS DEDICATED BY THE AUTHOR

The inmates of the family at the Whittier homestead who are referred to in the poem were my father, mother, my brother and two sisters, and my uncle and aunt, both unmarried. In addition, there was the district school master, who boarded with us. The "not unfeared, half-welcome guest" was Harriet Livermore, daughter of Judge Livermore, of New Hampshire, a young woman of fine natural ability, enthusiastic, eccentric, with slight control over her violent temper, which sometimes made her religious profession doubtful. She was equally ready to exhort in school-house prayer-meetings and dance in a Washington ball-room, while her father was a member of congress. She early embraced the doctrine of the Second Advent, and felt it her duty to proclaim the Lord's speedy coming. With this message she crossed the Atlantic and spent the greater part of a long life in travelling over Europe and Asia. She lived some time with Lady Hester Stanhope, a woman as fantastic and mentally strained as herself, on the slope of Mt. Lebanon, but finally quarrelled with her in regard to two white horses with red marks on their backs which suggested the idea of saddles, on which her titled hostess expected to ride into Jerusalem with the Lord. A friend of mine found her, when quite an old woman, wandering in Syria with a tribe of Arabs, who with the Oriental notion that madness is inspiration, accepted her as their prophetess and leader. At the time referred to in *Snow-Bound* she was boarding at the Rocks Village, about two miles from us.

In my boyhood, in our lonely farm-house, we had scanty sources of information; few books and only a small weekly newspaper. Our only annual was the Almanac. Under such circumstances story-telling was a necessary resource in the long winter evenings. My father when a young man had traversed the wilderness to Canada, and could tell us of his adventures with Indians and wild beasts, and of his sojourn in the French villages. My uncle was ready with his record of hunting and fishing and, it must be confessed, with stories which he at least half believed, of witchcraft and apparitions. My mother, who was born in the Indian-haunted region of Somersworth, New Hampshire, between Dover and Portsmouth, told us of the inroads of the savages, and the narrow escape of her ancestors. She described strange people who lived on the Piscataqua and Cocheco, among whom was Bantam the sorcerer. I have in my possession the wizard's "conjuring book," which he solemnly opened when consulted. It is a copy of Cornelius Agrippa's *Magic*, printed in 1651, dedicated to Dr. Robert Child, who, like Michael Scott, had learned

> " the art of glammorie
> In Padua beyond the sea,"

and who is famous in the annals of Massachusetts, where he was at one time a resident, as the first man who dared petition the General Court for liberty of conscience. The full title of the book is *Three Books of Occult Philosophy, by Henry Cornelius Agrippa, Knight, Doctor of both Laws, Counsellor to Cæsar's Sacred Majesty and Judge of the Prerogative Court.*

" As the Spirits of Darkness be stronger in the dark, so Good Spirits, which be Angels of Light, are augmented not only by the Divine light of the Sun, but also by our common VVood Fire : and as the Celestial Fire drives away dark spirits, so also this our Fire of VVood doth the same." — COR. AGRIPPA, *Occult Philosophy*, Book I. ch. v.

" Announced by all the trumpets of the sky,
Arrives the snow, and, driving o'er the fields,
Seems nowhere to alight : the whited air
Hides hills and woods, the river and the heaven,
And veils the farm-house at the garden's end.
The sled and traveller stopped, the courier's feet
Delayed, all friends shut out, the housemates sit
Around the radiant fireplace, enclosed
In a tumultuous privacy of storm."
EMERSON. The Snow Storm.

THE sun that brief December day
Rose cheerless over hills of gray,
And, darkly circled, gave at noon
A sadder light than waning moon.

Slow tracing down the thickening sky
Its mute and ominous prophecy,
A portent seeming less than threat,
It sank from sight before it set.
A chill no coat, however stout,
Of homespun stuff could quite shut out,
A hard, dull bitterness of cold,
That checked, mid-vein, the circling race
Of life-blood in the sharpened face,
The coming of the snow-storm told.
The wind blew east; we heard the roar
Of Ocean on his wintry shore,
And felt the strong pulse throbbing there
Beat with low rhythm our inland air.

Meanwhile we did our nightly chores, —
Brought in the wood from out of doors,
Littered the stalls, and from the mows
Raked down the herd's-grass for the cows :
Heard the horse whinnying for his corn ;
And, sharply clashing horn on horn,
Impatient down the stanchion rows
The cattle shake their walnut bows ;
While, peering from his early perch
Upon the scaffold's pole of birch,
The cock his crested helmet bent
And down his querulous challenge sent.

Unwarmed by any sunset light
The gray day darkened into night,
A night made hoary with the swarm
And whirl-dance of the blinding storm,
As zigzag, wavering to and fro,
Crossed and recrossed the wingèd snow :
And ere the early bedtime came
The white drift piled the window-frame,
And through the glass the clothes-line posts
Looked in like tall and sheeted ghosts.

So all night long the storm roared on :
The morning broke without a sun ;
In tiny spherule traced with lines
Of Nature's geometric signs,
In starry flake, and pellicle,
All day the hoary meteor fell ;
And, when the second morning shone,
We looked upon a world unknown,
On nothing we could call our own.
Around the glistening wonder bent
The blue walls of the firmament,
No cloud above, no earth below, —
A universe of sky and snow !
The old familiar sights of ours
Took marvellous shapes ; strange domes
  and towers

Rose up where sty or corn-crib stood,
Or garden-wall, or belt of wood ;
A smooth white mound the brush - pile
  showed,
A fenceless drift what once was road ;
The bridle-post an old man sat
With loose-flung coat and high cocked hat ;
The well-curb had a Chinese roof ;
And even the long sweep, high aloof,
In its slant splendor, seemed to tell
Of Pisa's leaning miracle.

A prompt, decisive man, no breath
Our father wasted : " Boys, a path ! "
Well pleased, (for when did farmer boy
Count such a summons less than joy ?)
Our buskins on our feet we drew ;
With mittened hands, and caps drawn low,
To guard our necks and ears from snow,
We cut the solid whiteness through.
And, where the drift was deepest, made
A tunnel walled and overlaid
With dazzling crystal : we had read
Of rare Aladdin's wondrous cave,
And to our own his name we gave,
With many a wish the luck were ours
To test his lamp's supernal powers.
We reached the barn with merry din,
And roused the prisoned brutes within.
The old horse thrust his long head out,
And grave with wonder gazed about ;
The cock his lusty greeting said,
And forth his speckled harem led ;
The oxen lashed their tails, and hooked,
And mild reproach of hunger looked ;
The hornëd patriarch of the sheep,
Like Egypt's Amun roused from sleep,
Shook his sage head with gesture mute,
And emphasized with stamp of foot.

All day the gusty north-wind bore
The loosening drift its breath before ;
Low circling round its southern zone,
The sun through dazzling snow-mist shone.
No church-bell lent its Christian tone
To the savage air, no social smoke
Curled over woods of snow-hung oak.
A solitude made more intense
By dreary-voicëd elements,
The shrieking of the mindless wind,
The moaning tree-boughs swaying blind,
And on the glass the unmeaning beat
Of ghostly finger-tips of sleet.
Beyond the circle of our hearth
No welcome sound of toil or mirth

Unbound the spell, and testified
Of human life and thought outside.
We minded that the sharpest ear
The buried brooklet could not hear,
The music of whose liquid lip
Had been to us companionship,
And, in our lonely life, had grown
To have an almost human tone.

As night drew on, and, from the crest
Of wooded knolls that ridged the west,
The sun, a snow-blown traveller, sank
From sight beneath the smothering bank,
We piled, with care, our nightly stack
Of wood against the chimney-back, —
The oaken log, green, huge, and thick,
And on its top the stout back-stick;
The knotty forestick laid apart,
And filled between with curious art
The ragged brush ; then, hovering near,
We watched the first red blaze appear,
Heard the sharp crackle, caught the gleam
On whitewashed wall and sagging beam,
Until the old, rude-furnished room
Burst, flower-like, into rosy bloom ;
While radiant with a mimic flame
Outside the sparkling drift became,
And through the bare-boughed lilac-tree
Our own warm hearth seemed blazing free.
The crane and pendent trammels showed,
The Turks' heads on the andirons glowed;
While childish fancy, prompt to tell
The meaning of the miracle,
Whispered the old rhyme : " *Under the tree,*
When fire outdoors burns merrily,
There the witches are making tea."

The moon above the eastern wood
Shone at its full ; the hill-range stood
Transfigured in the silver flood,
Its blown snows flashing cold and keen,
Dead white, save where some sharp ravine
Took shadow, or the sombre green
Of hemlocks turned to pitchy black
Against the whiteness at their back.
For such a world and such a night
Most fitting that unwarming light,
Which only seemed where'er it fell
To make the coldness visible.

Shut in from all the world without,
We sat the clean-winged hearth about,
Content to let the north-wind roar
In baffled rage at pane and door,
While the red logs before us beat

The frost-line back with tropic heat ;
And ever, when a louder blast
Shook beam and rafter as it passed,
The merrier up its roaring draught
The great throat of the chimney laughed;
The house-dog on his paws outspread
Laid to the fire his drowsy head,
The cat's dark silhouette on the wall
A couchant tiger's seemed to fall ;
And, for the winter fireside meet,
Between the andirons' straddling feet,
The mug of cider simmered slow,
The apples sputtered in a row,
And, close at hand, the basket stood
With nuts from brown October's wood.

What matter how the night behaved ?
What matter how the north-wind raved ?
Blow high, blow low, not all its snow
Could quench our hearth - fire's ruddy
      glow.
O Time and Change ! — with hair as gray
As was my sire's that winter day,
How strange it seems, with so much gone
Of life and love, to still live on !
Ah, brother ! only I and thou
Are left of all that circle now, —
The dear home faces whereupon
That fitful firelight paled and shone.
Henceforward, listen as we will,
The voices of that hearth are still ;
Look where we may, the wide earth o'er,
Those lighted faces smile no more.
We tread the paths their feet have worn,
    We sit beneath their orchard trees,
    We hear, like them, the hum of bees
And rustle of the bladed corn ;
We turn the pages that they read,
    Their written words we linger o'er,
But in the sun they cast no shade,
No voice is heard, no sign is made,
    No step is on the conscious floor !
Yet Love will dream, and Faith will
      trust,
(Since He who knows our need is just,)
That somehow, somewhere, meet we must.
Alas for him who never sees
The stars shine through his cypress-trees !
Who, hopeless, lays his dead away,
Nor looks to see the breaking day
Across the mournful marbles play !
Who hath not learned, in hours of faith,
    The truth to flesh and sense unknown,
That Life is ever lord of Death,
    And Love can never lose its own !

We sped the time with stories old,
Wrought puzzles out, and riddles told,
Or stammered from our school-book lore
" The Chief of Gambia's golden shore."
How often since, when all the land
Was clay in Slavery's shaping hand,
As if a far-blown trumpet stirred
The languorous sin-sick air, I heard :
" *Does not the voice of reason cry,*
    Claim the first right which Nature gave,
From the red scourge of bondage fly,
    Nor deign to live a burdened slave ! "
Our father rode again his ride
On Memphremagog's wooded side ;
Sat down again to moose and samp
In trapper's hut and Indian camp ;
Lived o'er the old idyllic ease
Beneath St. François' hemlock-trees ;
Again for him the moonlight shone
On Norman cap and bodiced zone ;
Again he heard the violin play
Which led the village dance away.
And mingled in its merry whirl
The grandam and the laughing girl.
Or, nearer home, our steps he led
Where Salisbury's level marshes spread
    Mile-wide as flies the laden bee ;
Where merry mowers, hale and strong,
Swept, scythe on scythe, their swaths along
    The low green prairies of the sea.
We shared the fishing off Boar's Head,
    And round the rocky Isles of Shoals
    The hake-broil on the drift-wood coals ;
The chowder on the sand-beach made,
Dipped by the hungry, steaming hot,
With spoons of clam-shell from the pot.
We heard the tales of witchcraft old,
And dream and sign and marvel told
To sleepy listeners as they lay
Stretched idly on the salted hay,
Adrift along the winding shores,
When favoring breezes deigned to blow
The square sail of the gundelow
And idle lay the useless oars.

Our mother, while she turned her wheel
Or run the new-knit stocking-heel,
Told how the Indian hordes came down
At midnight on Cocheco town,
And how her own great-uncle bore
His cruel scalp-mark to fourscore.
Recalling, in her fitting phrase,
    So rich and picturesque and free,
    (The common unrhymed poetry
Of simple life and country ways,)

The story of her early days, —
She made us welcome to her home ;
Old hearths grew wide to give us room ;
We stole with her a frightened look
At the gray wizard's conjuring-book,
The fame whereof went far and wide
Through all the simple country side ;
We heard the hawks at twilight play,
The boat-horn on Piscataqua,
The loon's weird laughter far away ;
We fished her little trout-brook, knew
What flowers in wood and meadow grew,
What sunny hillsides autumn-brown
She climbed to shake the ripe nuts down,
Saw where in sheltered cove and bay
The ducks' black squadron anchored lay,
And heard the wild-geese calling loud
Beneath the gray November cloud.

Then, haply, with a look more grave,
And soberer tone, some tale she gave
From painful Sewel's ancient tome,
Beloved in every Quaker home,
Of faith fire-winged by martyrdom,
Or Chalkley's Journal, old and quaint, —
Gentlest of skippers, rare sea-saint ! —
Who, when the dreary calms prevailed,
And water-butt and bread-cask failed,
And cruel, hungry eyes pursued
His portly presence mad for food,
With dark hints muttered under breath
Of casting lots for life or death,
Offered, if Heaven withheld supplies,
To be himself the sacrifice.
Then, suddenly, as if to save
The good man from his living grave,
A ripple on the water grew,
A school of porpoise flashed in view.
"Take, eat," he said, "and be content ;
These fishes in my stead are sent
By Him who gave the tangled ram
To spare the child of Abraham."

Our uncle, innocent of books,
Was rich in lore of fields and brooks,
The ancient teachers never dumb
Of Nature's unhoused lyceum.
In moons and tides and weather wise,
He read the clouds as prophecies,
And foul or fair could well divine,
By many an occult hint and sign,
Holding the cunning-warded keys
To all the woodcraft mysteries ;
Himself to Nature's heart so near
That all her voices in his ear

Of beast or bird had meanings clear,
Like Apollonius of old,
Who knew the tales the sparrows told,
Or Hermes, who interpreted
What the sage cranes of Nilus said ;
A simple, guileless, childlike man,
Content to live where life began ;
Strong only on his native grounds,
The little world of sights and sounds
Whose girdle was the parish bounds,
Whereof his fondly partial pride
The common features magnified,
As Surrey hills to mountains grew
In White of Selborne's loving view, —
He told how teal and loon he shot,
And how the eagle's eggs he got,
The feats on pond and river done,
The prodigies of rod and gun ;
Till, warming with the tales he told,
Forgotten was the outside cold,
The bitter wind unheeded blew,
From ripening corn the pigeons flew,
The partridge drummed i' the wood, the
    mink
Went fishing down the river-brink.
In fields with bean or clover gay,
The woodchuck, like a hermit gray,
    Peered from the doorway of his cell ;
The muskrat plied the mason's trade,
And tier by tier his mud-walls laid ;
And from the shagbark overhead
    The grizzled squirrel dropped his shell.

Next, the dear aunt, whose smile of cheer
And voice in dreams I see and hear, —
The sweetest woman ever Fate
Perverse denied a household mate,
Who, lonely, homeless, not the less
Found peace in love's unselfishness,
And welcome wheresoe'er she went,
A calm and gracious element,
Whose presence seemed the sweet income
And womanly atmosphere of home, —
Called up her girlhood memories,
The huskings and the apple-bees,
The sleigh-rides and the summer sails,
Weaving through all the poor details
And homespun warp of circumstance
A golden woof-thread of romance.
For well she kept her genial mood
And simple faith of maidenhood ;
Before her still a cloud-land lay,
The mirage loomed across her way ;
The morning dew, that dries so soon
With others, glistened at her noon ;

Through years of toil and soil and care,
From glossy tress to thin gray hair,
All unprofaned she held apart
The virgin fancies of the heart.
Be shame to him of woman born
Who hath for such but thought of scorn.

There, too, our elder sister plied
Her evening task the stand beside ;
A full, rich nature, free to trust,
Truthful and almost sternly just,
Impulsive, earnest, prompt to act,
And make her generous thought a fact,
Keeping with many a light disguise
The secret of self-sacrifice.
O heart sore-tried ! thou hast the best
That Heaven itself could give thee, — rest,
Rest from all bitter thoughts and things !
    How many a poor one's blessing went
    With thee beneath the low green tent
Whose curtain never outward swings !

As one who held herself a part
Of all she saw, and let her heart
    Against the household bosom lean,
Upon the motley-braided mat
Our youngest and our dearest sat,
Lifting her large, sweet, asking eyes,
    Now bathed in the unfading green
And holy peace of Paradise.
Oh, looking from some heavenly hill,
    Or from the shade of saintly palms,
    Or silver reach of river calms,
Do those large eyes behold me still ?
With me one little year ago : —
The chill weight of the winter snow
    For months upon her grave has lain ;
And now, when summer south-winds blow
    And brier and harebell bloom again,
I tread the pleasant paths we trod,
I see the violet-sprinkled sod
Whereon she leaned, too frail and weak
The hillside flowers she loved to seek,
Yet following me where'er I went
With dark eyes full of love's content.
The birds are glad ; the brier-rose fills
The air with sweetness ; all the hills
Stretch green to June's unclouded sky ;
But still I wait with ear and eye
For something gone which should be nigh,
A loss in all familiar things,
In flower that blooms, and bird that sings.
And yet, dear heart ! remembering thee,
    Am I not richer than of old ?
Safe in thy immortality,

What change can reach the wealth I
    hold ?
What chance can mar the pearl and gold
Thy love hath left in trust with me ?
And while in life's late afternoon,
    Where cool and long the shadows grow,
I walk to meet the night that soon
    Shall shape and shadow overflow,
I cannot feel that thou art far,
Since near at need the angels are ;
And when the sunset gates unbar,
    Shall I not see thee waiting stand,
And, white against the evening star,
    The welcome of thy beckoning hand ?

Brisk wielder of the birch and rule,
The master of the district school
Held at the fire his favored place,
Its warm glow lit a laughing face
Fresh-hued and fair, where scarce appeared
The uncertain prophecy of beard.
He teased the mitten-blinded cat,
Played cross-pins on my uncle's hat,
Sang songs, and told us what befalls
In classic Dartmouth's college halls.
Born the wild Northern hills among,
From whence his yeoman father wrung
By patient toil subsistence scant,
Not competence and yet not want,
He early gained the power to pay
His cheerful, self-reliant way ;
Could doff at ease his scholar's gown
To peddle wares from town to town ;
Or through the long vacation's reach
In lonely lowland districts teach,
Where all the droll experience found
At stranger hearths in boarding round,
The moonlit skater's keen delight,
The sleigh-drive through the frosty night,
The rustic party, with its rough
Accompaniment of blind-man's-buff,
And whirling-plate, and forfeits paid,
His winter task a pastime made.
Happy the snow-locked homes wherein
He tuned his merry violin,
Or played the athlete in the barn,
Or held the good dame's winding-yarn,
Or mirth-provoking versions told
Of classic legends rare and old,
Wherein the scenes of Greece and Rome
Had all the commonplace of home,
And little seemed at best the odds
'Twixt Yankee pedlers and old gods ;
Where Pindus-born Arachthus took
The guise of any grist-mill brook,

And dread Olympus at his will
Became a huckleberry hill.

A careless boy that night he seemed ;
　But at his desk he had the look
And air of one who wisely schemed,
　And hostage from the future took
In trainëd thought and lore of book.
Large-brained, clear-eyed, of such as he
Shall Freedom's young apostles be,
Who, following in War's bloody trail,
Shall every lingering wrong assail ;
All chains from limb and spirit strike,
Uplift the black and white alike ;
Scatter before their swift advance
The darkness and the ignorance,
The pride, the lust, the squalid sloth,
Which　nurtured　Treason's　monstrous
　　growth,
Made murder pastime, and the hell
Of prison-torture possible ;
The cruel lie of caste refute,
Old forms remould, and substitute
For Slavery's lash the freeman's will,
For blind routine, wise-handed skill ;
A school-house plant on every hill,
Stretching in radiate nerve-lines thence
The quick wires of intelligence ;
Till North and South together brought
Shall own the same electric thought,
In peace a common flag salute,
And, side by side in labor's free
And unresentful rivalry,
Harvest the fields wherein they fought.

Another guest that winter night
Flashed back from lustrous eyes the light.
Unmarked by time, and yet not young,
The honeyed music of her tongue
And words of meekness scarcely told
A nature passionate and bold,
Strong, self-concentred, spurning guide,
Its milder features dwarfed beside
Her unbent will's majestic pride.
She sat among us, at the best,
A not unfeared, half-welcome guest,
Rebuking with her cultured phrase
Our homeliness of words and ways.
A certain pard-like, treacherous grace
Swayed　the　lithe　limbs　and　drooped　the
　　lash,
Lent the white teeth their dazzling flash;
And under low brows, black with night,
Rayed out at times a dangerous light;
The sharp heat-lightnings of her face

Presaging ill to him whom Fate
Condemned to share her love or hate.
A woman tropical, intense
In thought and act, in soul and sense,
She blended in a like degree
The vixen and the devotee,
Revealing with each freak or feint
　The temper of Petruchio's Kate,
The raptures of Siena's saint.
Her tapering hand and rounded wrist
Had facile power to form a fist ;
The warm, dark languish of her eyes
Was never safe from wrath's surprise.
Brows saintly calm and lips devout
Knew every change of scowl and pout;
And the sweet voice had notes more high
And shrill for social battle-cry.

Since then what old cathedral town
Has missed her pilgrim staff and gown,
What convent-gate has held its lock
Against the challenge of her knock !
Through Smyrna's plague-hushed thorough-
　　fares,
Up sea-set Malta's rocky stairs,
Gray olive slopes of hills that hem
Thy tombs and shrines, Jerusalem,
Or startling on her desert throne
The crazy Queen of Lebanon
With claims fantastic as her own,
Her tireless feet have held their way ;
And still, unrestful, bowed, and gray,
She watches under Eastern skies,
　With hope each day renewed and fresh,
　The Lord's quick coming in the flesh,
Whereof she dreams and prophesies !

Where'er her troubled path may be,
　The Lord's sweet pity with her go !
The outward wayward life we see,
　The hidden springs we may not know.
Nor is it given us to discern
　What threads the fatal sisters spun,
　Through what ancestral years has run
The sorrow with the woman born,
What forged her cruel chain of moods,
What set her feet in solitudes,
　And held the love within her mute,
What mingled madness in the blood,
　A life-long discord and annoy,
　Water of tears with oil of joy,
And hid within the folded bud
　Perversities of flower and fruit.
It is not ours to separate
The tangled skein of will and fate,

To show what metes and bounds should
    stand
Upon the soul's debatable land,
And between choice and Providence
Divide the circle of events ;
But He who knows our frame is just,
Merciful and compassionate,
And full of sweet assurances
And hope for all the language is,
That He remembereth we are dust !

At last the great logs, crumbling low,
Sent out a dull and duller glow,
The bull's-eye watch that hung in view,
Ticking its weary circuit through,
Pointed with mutely warning sign
Its black hand to the hour of nine.
That sign the pleasant circle broke :
My uncle ceased his pipe to smoke,
Knocked from its bowl the refuse gray,
And laid it tenderly away;
Then roused himself to safely cover
The dull red brands with ashes over.
And while, with care, our mother laid
The work aside, her steps she stayed
One moment, seeking to express
Her grateful sense of happiness
For food and shelter, warmth and health,
And love's contentment more than wealth,
With simple wishes (not the weak,
Vain prayers which no fulfilment seek,
But such as warm the generous heart,
O'er-prompt to do with Heaven its part)
That none might lack, that bitter night,
For bread and clothing, warmth and light.

Within our beds awhile we heard
The wind that round the gables roared,
With now and then a ruder shock,
Which made our very bedsteads rock.
We heard the loosened clapboards tost,
The board-nails snapping in the frost ;
And on us, through the unplastered wall,
Felt the light sifted snow-flakes fall.
But sleep stole on, as sleep will do
When hearts are light and life is new ;
Faint and more faint the murmurs grew,
Till in the summer-land of dreams
They softened to the sound of streams,
Low stir of leaves, and dip of oars,
And lapsing waves on quiet shores.

Next morn we wakened with the shout
Of merry voices high and clear ;

And saw the teamsters drawing near
To break the drifted highways out.
Down the long hillside treading slow
We saw the half-buried oxen go,
Shaking the snow from heads uptost,
Their straining nostrils white with frost.
Before our door the straggling train
Drew up, an added team to gain.
The elders threshed their hands a-cold,
    Passed, with the cider-mug, their jokes
    From lip to lip ; the younger folks
Down the loose snow - banks, wrestling,
    rolled,
Then toiled again the cavalcade
    O'er windy hill, through clogged ravine,
    And woodland paths that wound between
Low drooping pine-boughs winter-weighed.
From every barn a team afoot,
At every house a new recruit,
Where, drawn by Nature's subtlest law,
Haply the watchful young men saw
Sweet doorway pictures of the curls
And curious eyes of merry girls,
Lifting their hands in mock defence
Against the snow-ball's compliments,
And reading in each missive tost
The charm with Eden never lost.

We heard once more the sleigh-bells' sound ;
    And, following where the teamsters led,
The wise old Doctor went his round,
Just pausing at our door to say,
In the brief autocratic way
Of one who, prompt at Duty's call,
Was free to urge her claim on all,
That some poor neighbor sick abed
At night our mother's aid would need.
For, one in generous thought and deed,
    What mattered in the sufferer's sight
    The Quaker matron's inward light,
The Doctor's mail of Calvin's creed ?
All hearts confess the saints elect
Who, twain in faith, in love agree,
And melt not in an acid sect
    The Christian pearl of charity !

So days went on : a week had passed
Since the great world was heard from
    last.
The Almanac we studied o'er,
Read and reread our little store
Of books and pamphlets, scarce a score ;
One harmless novel, mostly hid
From younger eyes, a book forbid,

And poetry, (or good or bad,
A single book was all we had,)
Where Ellwood's meek, drab-skirted Muse,
  A stranger to the heathen Nine,
  Sang, with a somewhat nasal whine,
The wars of David and the Jews.
At last the floundering carrier bore
The village paper to our door.
Lo! broadening outward as we read,
To warmer zones the horizon spread
In panoramic length unrolled
We saw the marvels that it told.
Before us passed the painted Creeks,
  And daft McGregor on his raids
  In Costa Rica's everglades.
And up Taygetos winding slow
Rode Ypsilanti's Mainote Greeks,
A Turk's head at each saddle-bow!
Welcome to us its week-old news,
Its corner for the rustic Muse,
  Its monthly gauge of snow and rain,
Its record, mingling in a breath
The wedding bell and dirge of death:
Jest, anecdote, and love-lorn tale,
The latest culprit sent to jail;
Its hue and cry of stolen and lost,
Its vendue sales and goods at cost,
  And traffic calling loud for gain.
We felt the stir of hall and street,
The pulse of life that round us beat;
The chill embargo of the snow
Was melted in the genial glow;
Wide swung again our ice-locked door,
And all the world was ours once more!

Clasp, Angel of the backward look
  And folded wings of ashen gray
  And voice of echoes far away,
The brazen covers of thy book;
The weird palimpsest old and vast,
Wherein thou hid'st the spectral past;
Where, closely mingling, pale and glow
The characters of joy and woe;
The monographs of outlived years,
Or smile-illumed or dim with tears,
  Green hills of life that slope to death,
And haunts of home, whose vistaed trees
Shade off to mournful cypresses
  With the white amaranths underneath.
Even while I look, I can but heed
  The restless sands' incessant fall,
Importunate hours that hours succeed,
Each clamorous with its own sharp need,
  And duty keeping pace with all.
Shut down and clasp the heavy lids;

I hear again the voice that bids
The dreamer leave his dream midway
For larger hopes and graver fears:
Life greatens in these later years,
The century's aloe flowers to-day!

Yet, haply, in some lull of life,
Some Truce of God which breaks its strife,
The worldling's eyes shall gather dew,
  Dreaming in throngful city ways
Of winter joys his boyhood knew;
And dear and early friends — the few
Who yet remain — shall pause to view
  These Flemish pictures of old days;
Sit with me by the homestead hearth,
And stretch the hands of memory forth
  To warm them at the wood-fire's blaze!
And thanks untraced to lips unknown
Shall greet me like the odors blown
From unseen meadows newly mown,
Or lilies floating in some pond,
Wood-fringed, the wayside gaze beyond;
The traveller owns the grateful sense
Of sweetness near, he knows not whence,
And, pausing, takes with forehead bare
The benediction of the air.

MY TRIUMPH

THE autumn-time has come;
On woods that dream of bloom,
And over purpling vines,
The low sun fainter shines.

The aster-flower is failing,
The hazel's gold is paling;
Yet overhead more near
The eternal stars appear!

And present gratitude
Insures the future's good,
And for the things I see
I trust the things to be;

That in the paths untrod,
And the long days of God,
My feet shall still be led,
My heart be comforted.

O living friends who love me
O dear ones gone above me!
Careless of other fame,
I leave to you my name.

Hide it from idle praises,
Save it from evil phrases :
Why, when dear lips that spake it
Are dumb, should strangers wake it ?

Let the thick curtain fall ;
I better know than all
How little I have gained,
How vast the unattained.

Not by the page word-painted
Let life be banned or sainted :
Deeper than written scroll
The colors of the soul.

Sweeter than any sung
My songs that found no tongue ;
Nobler than any fact
My wish that failed of act.

Others shall sing the song,
Others shall right the wrong, —
Finish what I begin,
And all I fail of win.

What matter, I or they ?
Mine or another's day,
So the right word be said
And life the sweeter made ?

Hail to the coming singers !
Hail to the brave light-bringers !
Forward I reach and share
All that they sing and dare.

The airs of heaven blow o'er me ;
A glory shines before me
Of what mankind shall be, —
Pure, generous, brave, and free.

A dream of man and woman
Diviner but still human,
Solving the riddle old,
Shaping the Age of Gold !

The love of God and neighbor ;
An equal-handed labor ;
The richer life, where beauty
Walks hand in hand with duty.

Ring, bells in unreared steeples,
The joy of unborn peoples !
Sound, trumpets far off blown,
Your triumph is my own !

Parcel and part of all,
I keep the festival,
Fore-reach the good to be,
And share the victory.

I feel the earth move sunward,
I join the great march onward,
And take, by faith, while living,
My freehold of thanksgiving.

IN SCHOOL—DAYS

STILL sits the school-house by the road,
  A ragged beggar sleeping ;
Around it still the sumachs grow,
  And blackberry-vines are creeping.

Within, the master's desk is seen,
  Deep scarred by raps official ;
The warping floor, the battered seats,
  The jack-knife's carved initial ;

The charcoal frescos on its wall ;
  Its door's worn sill, betraying
The feet that, creeping slow to school,
  Went storming out to playing !

Long years ago a winter sun
  Shone over it at setting ;
Lit up its western window-panes,
  And low eaves' icy fretting.

It touched the tangled golden curls,
  And brown eyes full of grieving,
Of one who still her steps delayed
  When all the school were leaving.

For near her stood the little boy
  Her childish favor singled :
His cap pulled low upon a face
  Where pride and shame were mingled

Pushing with restless feet the snow
  To right and left, he lingered ; —
As restlessly her tiny hands
  The blue-checked apron fingered.

He saw her lift her eyes ; he felt
  The soft hand's light caressing,
And heard the tremble of her voice,
  As if a fault confessing.

"I 'm sorry that I spelt the word :
  I hate to go above you,

Because," — the brown eyes lower fell, —
" Because, you see, I love you ! "

Still memory to a gray-haired man
   That sweet child-face is showing.
Dear girl ! the grasses on her grave
   Have forty years been growing !

He lives to learn, in life's hard school,
   How few who pass above him
Lament their triumph and his loss,
   Like her, — because they love him.

MY BIRTHDAY

BENEATH the moonlight and the snow
   Lies dead my latest year ;
The winter winds are wailing low
   Its dirges in my ear.

I grieve not with the moaning wind
   As if a loss befell ;
Before me, even as behind,
   God is, and all is well !

His light shines on me from above,
   His low voice speaks within, —
The patience of immortal love
   Outwearying mortal sin.

Not mindless of the growing years
   Of care and loss and pain,
My eyes are wet with thankful tears
   For blessings which remain.

If dim the gold of life has grown,
   I will not count it dross,
Nor turn from treasures still my own
   To sigh for lack and loss.

The years no charm from Nature take ;
   As sweet her voices call,
As beautiful her mornings break,
   As fair her evenings fall.

Love watches o'er my quiet ways,
   Kind voices speak my name,
And lips that find it hard to praise
   Are slow, at least, to blame.

How softly ebb the tides of will !
   How fields, once lost or won,
Now lie behind me green and still
   Beneath a level sun !

How hushed the hiss of party hate,
   The clamor of the throng !
How old, harsh voices of debate
   Flow into rhythmic song !

Methinks the spirit's temper grows
   Too soft in this still air ;
Somewhat the restful heart foregoes
   Of needed watch and prayer.

The bark by tempest vainly tossed
   May founder in the calm,
And he who braved the polar frost
   Faint by the isles of balm.

Better than self-indulgent years
   The outflung heart of youth,
Than pleasant songs in idle ears
   The tumult of the truth.

Rest for the weary hands is good,
   And love for hearts that pine,
But let the manly habitude
   Of upright souls be mine.

Let winds that blow from heaven refresh.
   Dear Lord, the languid air ;
And let the weakness of the flesh
   Thy strength of spirit share.

And, if the eye must fail of light,
   The ear forget to hear,
Make clearer still the spirit's sight,
   More fine the inward ear !

Be near me in mine hours of need
   To soothe, or cheer, or warn,
And down these slopes of sunset lead
   As up the hills of morn !

RED RIDING-HOOD

ON the wide lawn the snow lay deep,
Ridged o'er with many a drifted heap ;
The wind that through the pine-trees sung
The naked elm-boughs tossed and swung ;
While, through the window, frosty-starred
Against the sunset purple barred,
We saw the sombre crow flap by,
The hawk's gray fleck along the sky,
The crested blue-jay flitting swift,
The squirrel poising on the drift,
Erect, alert, his broad gray tail
Set to the north wind like a sail.

It came to pass, our little lass,
With flattened face against the glass,
And eyes in which the tender dew
Of pity shone, stood gazing through
The narrow space her rosy lips
Had melted from the frost's eclipse :
"Oh, see," she cried, "the poor blue-jays !
What is it that the black crow says ?
The squirrel lifts his little legs
Because he has no hands, and begs;
He 's asking for my nuts, I know :
May I not feed them on the snow ? "

Half lost within her boots, her head
Warm-sheltered in her hood of red,
Her plaid skirt close about her drawn,
She floundered down the wintry lawn ;
Now struggling through the misty veil
Blown round her by the shrieking gale ;
Now sinking in a drift so low
Her scarlet hood could scarcely show
Its dash of color on the snow.

She dropped for bird and beast forlorn
Her little store of nuts and corn,
And thus her timid guests bespoke :
"Come, squirrel, from your hollow oak, —
Come, black old crow, — come, poor blue-
jay,
Before your supper 's blown away !
Don't be afraid, we all are good ;
And I 'm mamma's Red Riding-Hood ! "

O Thou whose care is over all,
Who heedest even the sparrow's fall,
Keep in the little maiden's breast
The pity which is now its guest !
Let not her cultured years make less
The childhood charm of tenderness,
But let her feel as well as know,
Nor harder with her polish grow !
Unmoved by sentimental grief
That wails along some printed leaf,
But prompt with kindly word and deed
To own the claims of all who need,
Let the grown woman's self make good
The promise of Red Riding-Hood !

RESPONSE

On the occasion of my seventieth birthday, in
1877, I was the recipient of many tokens of
esteem. The publishers of the *Atlantic Monthly*
gave a dinner in my name, and the editor of
The Literary World gathered in his paper many
affectionate messages from my associates in
literature and the cause of human progress.
The lines which follow were written in acknow-
ledgment.

BESIDE that milestone where the level sun,
    Nigh unto setting, sheds his last, low
    rays
On word and work irrevocably done,
Life's blending threads of good and ill out-
    spun,
    I hear, O friends ! your words of cheer
    and praise,
Half doubtful if myself or otherwise.
    Like him who, in the old Arabian joke,
    A beggar slept and crownëd Caliph
    woke.
Thanks not the less. With not unglad
    surprise
I see my life-work through your partial
    eyes ;
Assured, in giving to my home - taught
    songs
A higher value than of right belongs,
You do but read between the written lines
The finer grace of unfulfilled designs.

AT EVENTIDE

POOR and inadequate the shadow-play
    Of gain and loss, of waking and of
    dream,
    Against life's solemn background needs
    must seem
At this late hour. Yet, not unthankfully,
I call to mind the fountains by the way,
The breath of flowers, the bird-song on the
    spray,
Dear friends, sweet human loves, the joy of
    giving
And of receiving, the great boon of liv-
    ing
    In grand historic years when Liberty
Had need of word and work, quick sympa-
    thies
For all who fail and suffer, song's relief,
Nature's uncloying loveliness ; and chief,
    The kind restraining hand of Providence,
    The inward witness, the assuring sense
Of an Eternal Good which overlies
The sorrow of the world, Love which out-
    lives

All sin and wrong, Compassion which for-
gives
To the uttermost, and Justice whose clear
eyes
Through lapse and failure look to the in-
tent,
And judge our frailty by the life we meant.

VOYAGE OF THE JETTIE

The picturesquely situated Wayside Inn at
West Ossipee, N. H., is now in ashes; and to
its former guests these somewhat careless
rhymes may be a not unwelcome reminder of
pleasant summers and autumns on the banks
of the Bearcamp and Chocorua. To the author
himself they have a special interest from the
fact that they were written, or improvised,
under the eye and for the amusement of a be-
loved invalid friend, whose last earthly sunsets
faded from the mountain ranges of Ossipee
and Sandwich.

A SHALLOW stream, from fountains
Deep in the Sandwich mountains,
  Ran lakeward Bearcamp River;
And between its flood-torn shores,
Sped by sail or urged by oars,
  No keel had vexed it ever.

Alone the dead trees yielding
To the dull axe Time is wielding,
  The shy mink and the otter,
And golden leaves and red,
By countless autumns shed,
  Had floated down its water.

From the gray rocks of Cape Ann,
Came a skilled seafaring man,
  With his dory, to the right place;
Over hill and plain he brought her,
Where the boatless Bearcamp water
  Comes winding down from White-Face.

Quoth the skipper : " Ere she floats forth,
I'm sure my pretty boat's worth,
  At least, a name as pretty."
On her painted side he wrote it,
And the flag that o'er her floated
  Bore aloft the name of Jettie.

On a radiant morn of summer,
Elder guest and latest comer
  Saw her wed the Bearcamp water;
Heard the name the skipper gave her,

And the answer to the favor
  From the Bay State's graceful daughter

Then a singer, richly gifted,
Her charmëd voice uplifted ;
  And the wood-thrush and song-sparrow
Listened, dumb with envious pain,
To the clear and sweet refrain
  Whose notes they could not borrow.

Then the skipper plied his oar,
And from off the shelving shore,
  Glided out the strange explorer ;
Floating on, she knew not whither, —
The tawny sands beneath her,
  The great hills watching o'er her.

On, where the stream flows quiet
As the meadows' margins by it,
  Or widens out to borrow a
New life from that wild water,
The mountain giant's daughter,
  The pine-besung Chocorua.

Or, mid the tangling cumber
And pack of mountain lumber
  That spring floods downward force,
Over sunken snag, and bar
Where the grating shallows are,
  The good boat held her course.

Under the pine-dark highlands,
Around the vine-hung islands,
  She ploughed her crooked furrow ;
And her rippling and her lurches
Scared the river eels and perches,
  And the musk-rat in his burrow.

Every sober clam below her,
Every sage and grave pearl-grower,
  Shut his rusty valves the tighter ;
Crow called to crow complaining,
And old tortoises sat craning
  Their leathern necks to sight her.

So, to where the still lake glasses
The misty mountain masses
  Rising dim and distant northward,
And, with faint-drawn shadow pictures,
Low shores, and dead pine spectres,
  Blends the skyward and the earthward,

On she glided, overladen,
With merry man and maiden
  Sending back their song and laughter, —

While, perchance, a phantom crew,
In a ghostly birch canoe,
  Paddled dumb and swiftly after !

And the bear on Ossipee
Climbed the topmost crag to see
  The strange thing drifting under ;
And, through the haze of August,
Passaconaway and Paugus
  Looked down in sleepy wonder.

All the pines that o'er her hung
In mimic sea-tones sung
  The song familiar to her ;
And the maples leaned to screen her,
And the meadow-grass seemed greener,
  And the breeze more soft to woo her.

The lone stream mystery-haunted
To her the freedom granted
  To scan its every feature,
Till new and old were blended,
And round them both extended
  The loving arms of Nature.

Of these hills the little vessel
Henceforth is part and parcel ;
  And on Bearcamp shall her log
Be kept, as if by Georges
Or Grand Menan the surges
  Tossed her skipper through the fog.

And I, who, half in sadness,
Recall the morning gladness
  Of life, at evening time,
By chance, onlooking idly,
Apart from all so widely,
  Have set her voyage to rhyme.

Dies now the gay persistence
Of song and laugh, in distance ;
  Alone with me remaining
The stream, the quiet meadow,
The hills in shine and shadow,
  The sombre pines complaining.

And, musing here, I dream
Of voyagers on a stream
  From whence is no returning,
Under sealèd orders going,
Looking forward little knowing,
  Looking back with idle yearning.

And I pray that every venture
The port of peace may enter,

That, safe from snag and fall
And siren-haunted islet,
And rock, the Unseen Pilot
  May guide us one and all.

MY TRUST

A PICTURE memory brings to me :
I look across the years and see
Myself beside my mother's knee.

I feel her gentle hand restrain
My selfish moods, and know again
A child's blind sense of wrong and pain.

But wiser now, a man gray grown,
My childhood's needs are better known,
My mother's chastening love I own.

Gray grown, but in our Father's sight
A child still groping for the light
To read His works and ways aright.

I wait, in His good time to see
That as my mother dealt with me
So with His children dealeth He.

I bow myself beneath His hand':
That pain itself was wisely planned
I feel, and partly understand.

The joy that comes in sorrow's guise,
The sweet pains of self-sacrifice,
I would not have them otherwise.

And what were life and death if sin
Knew not the dread rebuke within,
The pang of merciful discipline ?

Not with thy proud despair of old,
Crowned stoic of Rome's noblest mould !
Pleasure and pain alike I hold.

I suffer with no vain pretence
Of triumph over flesh and sense,
Yet trust the grievous providence,

How dark soe'er it seems, may tend,
By ways I cannot comprehend,
To some unguessed benignant end ;

That every loss and lapse may gain
The clear-aired heights by steps of pain,
And never cross is borne in vain.

A NAME

Addressed to my grand-nephew, Greenleaf Whittier Pickard. Jonathan Greenleaf, in *A Genealogy of the Greenleaf Family*, says briefly: " From all that can be gathered, it is believed that the ancestors of the Greenleaf family were Huguenots, who left France on account of their religious principles some time in the course of the sixteenth century, and settled in England. The name was probably translated from the French Feuillevert."

THE name the Gallic exile bore,
St. Malo ! from thy ancient mart,
Became upon our Western shore
Greenleaf for Feuillevert.

A name to hear in soft accord
Of leaves by light winds overrun,
Or read, upon the greening sward
Of May, in shade and sun.

The name my infant ear first heard
Breathed softly with a mother's kiss ;
His mother's own, no tenderer word
My father spake than this.

No child have I to bear it on ;
Be thou its keeper ; let it take
From gifts well used and duty done
New beauty for thy sake.

The fair ideals that outran
My halting footsteps seek and find —
The flawless symmetry of man,
The poise of heart and mind.

Stand firmly where I felt the sway
Of every wing that fancy flew,
See clearly where I groped my way,
Nor real from seeming knew.

And wisely choose, and bravely hold
Thy faith unswerved by cross or crown,
Like the stout Huguenot of old
Whose name to thee comes down.

As Marot's songs made glad the heart
Of that lone exile, haply mine
May in life's heavy hours impart
Some strength and hope to thine.

Yet when did Age transfer to Youth
The hard-gained lessons of its day ?

Each lip must learn the taste of truth,
Each foot must feel its way.

We cannot hold the hands of choice
That touch or shun life's fateful keys ;
The whisper of the inward voice
Is more than homilies.

Dear boy ! for whom the flowers are born,
Stars shine, and happy song-birds sing,
What can my evening give to morn,
My winter to thy spring !

A life not void of pure intent,
With small desert of praise or blame,
The love I felt, the good I meant,
I leave thee with my name.

GREETING

Originally prefixed to the volume, *The King's Missive and other Poems*. [Entitled there, *The Prelude.*]

I SPREAD a scanty board too late ;
The old-time guests for whom I wait
Come few and slow, methinks, to-day.
Ah ! who could hear my messages
Across the dim unsounded seas
On which so many have sailed away !

Come, then, old friends, who linger yet,
And let us meet, as we have met,
Once more beneath this low sunshine ;
And grateful for the good we 've known,
The riddles solved, the ills outgrown,
Shake hands upon the border line.

The favor, asked too oft before,
From your indulgent ears, once more
I crave, and, if belated lays
To slower, feebler measures move,
The silent sympathy of love
To me is dearer now than praise.

And ye, O younger friends, for whom
My hearth and heart keep open room,
Come smiling through the shadows long,
Be with me while the sun goes down,
And with your cheerful voices drown
The minor of my even-song.

For, equal through the day and night,
The wise Eternal oversight
And love and power and righteous will

Remain : the law of destiny,
The best for each and all must be,
   And life its promise shall fulfil.

AN AUTOGRAPH

I WRITE my name as one,
On sands by waves o'errun
Or winter's frosted pane,
Traces a record vain.

Oblivion's blankness claims
Wiser and better names,
And well my own may pass
As from the strand or glass.

Wash on, O waves of time !
Melt, noons, the frosty rime !
Welcome the shadow vast,
The silence that shall last !

When I and all who know
And love me vanish so,
What harm to them or me
Will the lost memory be ?

If any words of mine,
Through right of life divine,
Remain, what matters it
Whose hand the message writ ?

Why should the "crowner's quest"
Sit on my worst or best ?
Why should the showman claim
The poor ghost of my name ?

Yet, as when dies a sound
Its spectre lingers round,
Haply my spent life will
Leave some faint echo still.

A whisper giving breath
Of praise or blame to death,
Soothing or saddening such
As loved the living much.

Therefore with yearnings vain
And fond I still would fain
A kindly judgment seek,
A tender thought bespeak.

And, while my words are read,
Let this at least be said :
" Whate'er his life's defeatures,
He loved his fellow-creatures.

" If, of the Law's stone table,
To hold he scarce was able
The first great precept fast,
He kept for man the last.

" Through mortal lapse and dulness
What lacks the Eternal Fulness,
If still our weakness can
Love Him in loving man ?

" Age brought him no despairing
Of the world's future faring ;
In human nature still
He found more good than ill.

" To all who dumbly suffered,
His tongue and pen he offered ;
His life was not his own,
Nor lived for self alone.

" Hater of din and riot
He lived in days unquiet ;
And, lover of all beauty,
Trod the hard ways of duty.

" He meant no wrong to any
He sought the good of many,
Yet knew both sin and folly, —
May God forgive him wholly ! "

ABRAM MORRISON

'MIDST the men and things which will
Haunt an old man's memory still,
Drollest, quaintest of them all,
With a boy's laugh I recall
   Good old Abram Morrison.

When the Grist and Rolling Mill
Ground and rumbled by Po Hill,
And the old red school-house stood
Midway in the Powow's flood,
   Here dwelt Abram Morrison.

From the Beach to far beyond
Bear-Hill, Lion's Mouth and Pond,
Marvellous to our tough old stock,
Chips o' the Anglo-Saxon block,
   Seemed the Celtic Morrison.

Mudknock, Balmawhistle, all
Only knew the Yankee drawl,
Never brogue was heard till when,

Foremost of his countrymen,
  Hither came Friend Morrison ;

Yankee born, of alien blood,
Kin of his had well withstood
Pope and King with pike and ball
Under Derry's leaguered wall,
  As became the Morrisons.

Wandering down from Nutfield woods
With his household and his goods,
Never was it clearly told
How within our quiet fold
  Came to be a Morrison.

Once a soldier, blame him not
That the Quaker he forgot,
When, to think of battles won,
And the red-coats on the run,
  Laughed aloud Friend Morrison.

From gray Lewis over sea
Bore his sires their family tree,
On the rugged boughs of it
Grafting Irish mirth and wit,
  And the brogue of Morrison.

Half a genius, quick to plan,
Blundering like an Irishman,
But with canny shrewdness lent
By his far-off Scotch descent,
  Such was Abram Morrison.

Back and forth to daily meals,
Rode his cherished pig on wheels,
And to all who came to see,
ʞ Aisier for the pig an' me,
  Sure it is," said Morrison.

Simple-hearted, boy o'ergrown,
With a humor quite his own,
Of our sober-stepping ways,
Speech and look and cautious phrase,
  Slow to learn was Morrison.

Much we loved his stories told
Of a country strange and old,
Where the fairies danced till dawn,
And the goblin Leprecaun
  Looked, we thought, like Morrison.

Or wild tales of feud and fight,
Witch and troll and second sight
Whispered still where Stornoway

Looks across its stormy bay,
  Once the home of Morrisons.

First was he to sing the praise
Of the Powow's winding ways ;
And our straggling village took
City grandeur to the look
  Of its poet Morrison.

All his words have perished.   Shame
On the saddle-bags of Fame,
That they bring not to our time
One poor couplet of the rhyme
  Made by Abram Morrison !

When, on calm and fair First Days,
Rattled down our one-horse chaise,
Through the blossomed apple-boughs
To the old brown meeting-house,
  There was Abram Morrison.

Underneath his hat's broad brim
Peered the queer old face of him ;
And with Irish jauntiness
Swung the coat-tails of the dress
  Worn by Abram Morrison.

Still, in memory, on his feet,
Leaning o'er the elders' seat,
Mingling with a solemn drone,
Celtic accents all his own,
  Rises Abram Morrison.

"Don't," he's pleading, "don't ye go,
Dear young friends, to sight and show ;
Don't run after elephants,
Learned pigs and presidents
  And the likes !" said Morrison.

On his well-worn theme intent,
Simple, child-like, innocent,
Heaven forgive the half-checked smile
Of our careless boyhood, while
  Listening to Friend Morrison !

We have learned in latter days
Truth may speak in simplest phrase ;
That the man is not the less
For quaint ways and home-spun dress,
  Thanks to Abram Morrison !

Not to pander nor to please
Come the needed homilies,
With no lofty argument

Is the fitting message sent,
   Through such lips as Morrison's.

Dead and gone ! But while its track
Powow keeps to Merrimac,
While Po Hill is still on guard,
Looking land and ocean ward,
   They shall tell of Morrison !

After half a century's lapse,
We are wiser now, perhaps,
But we miss our streets amid
Something which the past has hid,
   Lost with Abram Morrison.

Gone forever with the queer
Characters of that old year !
Now the many are as one ;
Broken is the mould that run
   Men like Abram Morrison.

A LEGACY

FRIEND of my many years !
When the great silence falls, at last, on me,

Let me not leave, to pain and sadden thee,
   A memory of tears,

   But pleasant thoughts alone
Of one who was thy friendship's honored
   guest
And drank the wine of consolation pressed
   From sorrows of thy own.

   I leave with thee a sense
Of hands upheld and trials rendered less —
The unselfish joy which is to helpfulness
   Its own great recompense ;

The knowledge that from thine,
As from the garments of the Master,
   stole
Calmness and strength, the virtue which
   makes whole
And heals without a sign ;

Yea more, the assurance strong
That love, which fails of perfect utterance
   here,
Lives on to fill the heavenly atmosphere
   With its immortal song.

RELIGIOUS POEMS

THE STAR OF BETHLEHEM

WHERE Time the measure of his hours
  By changeful bud and blossom keeps,
And, like a young bride crowned with
    flowers,
  Fair Shiraz in her garden sleeps ;

Where, to her poet's turban stone,
  The Spring her gift of flowers imparts,
Less sweet than those his thoughts have
    sown
  In the warm soil of Persian hearts :

There sat the stranger, where the shade
  Of scattered date-trees thinly lay,
While in the hot clear heaven delayed
  The long and still and weary day.

Strange trees and fruits above him hung,
  Strange odors filled the sultry air,
Strange birds upon the branches swung,
  Strange insect voices murmured there.

And strange bright blossoms shone around,
  Turned sunward from the shadowy bow-
    ers,
As if the Gheber's soul had found
  A fitting home in Iran's flowers.

Whate'er he saw, whate'er he heard,
  Awakened feelings new and sad, —
No Christian garb, nor Christian word,
  Nor church with Sabbath - bell chimes
    glad,

But Moslem graves, with turban stones,
  And mosque-spires gleaming white, in
    view,
And graybeard Mollahs in low tones
  Chanting their Koran service through.

The flowers which smiled on either hand,
  Like tempting fiends, were such as they
Which once, o'er all that Eastern land,
  As gifts on demon altars lay.

As if the burning eye of Baal
  The servant of his Conqueror knew,
From skies which knew no cloudy veil,
  The Sun's hot glances smote him through.

"Ah me ! " the lonely stranger said,
  " The hope which led my footsteps on,
And light from heaven around them shed,
  O'er weary wave and waste, is gone !

"Where are the harvest fields all white,
  For Truth to thrust her sickle in ?
Where flock the souls, like doves in flight,
  From the dark hiding-place of sin ?

" A silent horror broods o'er all, —
  The burden of a hateful spell, —
The very flowers around recall
  The hoary magi's rites of hell !

" And what am I, o'er such a land
  The banner of the Cross to bear ?
Dear Lord, uphold me with Thy hand,
  Thy strength with human weakness
    share ! "

He ceased ; for at his very feet
  In mild rebuke a floweret smiled ;
How thrilled his sinking heart to greet
  The Star-flower of the Virgin's child !

Sown by some wandering Frank, it drew
  Its life from alien air and earth,
And told to Paynim sun and dew
  The story of the Saviour's birth.

From scorching beams, in kindly mood,
  The Persian plants its beauty screened,
And on its pagan sisterhood,
  In love, the Christian floweret leaned.

With tears of joy the wanderer felt
  The darkness of his long despair
Before that hallowed symbol melt,
  Which God's dear love had nurtured
    there.

From Nature's face, that simple flower
  The lines of sin and sadness swept ;
And Magian pile and Paynim bower
  In peace like that of Eden slept.

Each Moslem tomb, and cypress old,
  Looked holy through the sunset air ;
And, angel-like, the Muezzin told
  From tower and mosque the hour of
    prayer.

With cheerful steps, the morrow's dawn
  From Shiraz saw the stranger part ;
The Star-flower of the Virgin-Born
  Still blooming in his hopeful heart !

THE CITIES OF THE PLAIN

"Get ye up from the wrath of God's ter-
    rible day !
Ungirded, unsandalled, arise and away !
'T is the vintage of blood, 't is the fulness
    of time,
And vengeance shall gather the harvest of
    crime ! "

The warning was spoken — the righteous
    had gone,
And the proud ones of Sodom were feast-
    ing alone ;
All gay was the banquet — the revel was
    long,
With the pouring of wine and the breath-
    ing of song.

'T was an evening of beauty ; the air was
    perfume,
The earth was all greenness, the trees were
    all bloom ;
And softly the delicate viol was heard,
Like the murmur of love or the notes of a
    bird.

And beautiful maidens moved down in the
    dance,
With the magic of motion and sunshine of
    glance ;
And white arms wreathed lightly, and
    tresses fell free
As the plumage of birds in some tropical
    tree.

Where the shrines of foul idols were lighted
    on high,
And wantonness tempted the lust of the
    eye ;
Midst rites of obsceneness, strange, loath-
    some, abhorred,
The blasphemer scoffed at the name of the
    Lord.

Hark ! the growl of the thunder, — the
    quaking of earth !
Woe, woe to the worship, and woe to the
    mirth !
The black sky has opened ; there 's flame
    in the air ;
The red arm of vengeance is lifted and
    bare !

Then the shriek of the dying rose wild
    where the song
And the low tone of love had been whis-
    pered along ;
For the fierce flames went lightly o'er pal-
    ace and bower,
Like the red tongues of demons, to blast
    and devour !

Down, down on the fallen the red ruin
    rained,
And the reveller sank with his wine-cup
    undrained ;
The foot of the dancer, the music's loved
    thrill,
And the shout and the laughter grew sud-
    denly still.

The last throb of anguish was fearfully
    given ;
The last eye glared forth in its madness on
    Heaven !
The last groan of horror rose wildly and
    vain,
And death brooded over the pride of the
    Plain !

THE CALL OF THE CHRISTIAN

Not always as the whirlwind's rush
  On Horeb's mount of fear,
Not always as the burning bush
  To Midian's shepherd seer,

Nor as the awful voice which came
  To Israel's prophet bards,
Nor as the tongues of cloven flame,
  Nor gift of fearful words, —

Not always thus, with outward sign
  Of fire or voice from Heaven,
The message of a truth divine,
  The call of God is given !
Awaking in the human heart
  Love for the true and right, —
Zeal for the Christian's better part,
  Strength for the Christian's fight.

Nor unto manhood's heart alone
  The holy influence steals :
Warm with a rapture not its own,
  The heart of woman feels !
As she who by Samaria's wall
  The Saviour's errand sought, —
As those who with the fervent Paul
  And meek Aquila wrought :

Or those meek ones whose martyrdom
  Rome's gathered grandeur saw :
Or those who in their Alpine home
  Braved the Crusader's war,
When the green Vaudois, trembling, heard,
  Through all its vales of death,
The martyr's song of triumph poured
  From woman's failing breath.

And gently, by a thousand things
  Which o'er our spirits pass,
Like breezes o'er the harp's fine strings,
  Or vapors o'er a glass,
Leaving their token strange and new
  Of music or of shade,
The summons to the right and true
  And merciful is made.

Oh, then, if gleams of truth and light
  Flash o'er thy waiting mind,
Unfolding to thy mental sight
  The wants of human-kind ;
If, brooding over human grief,
  The earnest wish is known
To soothe and gladden with relief
  An anguish not thine own ;

Though heralded with naught of fear,
  Or outward sign or show ;
Though only to the inward ear
  It whispers soft and low ;

Though dropping, as the manna fell,
  Unseen, yet from above,
Noiseless as dew-fall, heed it well, —
  Thy Father's call of love !

THE CRUCIFIXION

SUNLIGHT upon Judæa's hills !
  And on the waves of Galilee ;
On Jordan's stream, and on the rills
  That feed the dead and sleeping sea !
Most freshly from the green wood springs
The light breeze on its scented wings ;
And gayly quiver in the sun
The cedar tops of Lebanon !

A few more hours, — a change hath come !
  The sky is dark without a cloud !
The shouts of wrath and joy are dumb,
  And proud knees unto earth are bowed.
A change is on the hill of Death,
The helmèd watchers pant for breath,
And turn with wild and maniac eyes
From the dark scene of sacrifice !

That Sacrifice ! — the death of Him, —
  The Christ of God, the holy One !
Well may the conscious Heaven grow dim,
  And blacken the beholding Sun.
The wonted light hath fled away,
Night settles on the middle day,
And earthquake from his caverned bed
Is waking with a thrill of dread !

The dead are waking underneath !
  Their prison door is rent away !
And, ghastly with the seal of death
  They wander in the eye of day !
The temple of the Cherubim,
The House of God is cold and dim ;
A curse is on its trembling walls,
Its mighty veil asunder falls !

Well may the cavern-depths of Earth
  Be shaken, and her mountains nod ;
Well may the sheeted dead come forth
  To see the suffering son of God !
Well may the temple-shrine grow dim,
And shadows veil the Cherubim,
When He, the chosen one of Heaven,
A sacrifice for guilt is given !

And shall the sinful heart, alone,
  Behold unmoved the fearful hour,

When Nature trembled on her throne,
  And Death resigned his iron power ?
Oh, shall the heart — whose sinfulness
Gave keenness to His sore distress,
And added to His tears of blood —
Refuse its trembling gratitude ?

PALESTINE

BLEST land of Judæa ! thrice hallowed of
    song,
Where the holiest of memories pilgrim-like
    throng ;
In the shade of thy palms, by the shores of
    thy sea,
On the hills of thy beauty, my heart is with
    thee.

With the eye of a spirit I look on that
    shore
Where pilgrim and prophet have lingered
    before ;
With the glide of a spirit I traverse the
    sod
Made bright by the steps of the angels of
    God.

Blue sea of the hills ! in my spirit I hear
Thy waters, Gennesaret, chime on my
    ear ;
Where the Lowly and Just with the people
    sat down,
And thy spray on the dust of His sandals
    was thrown.

Beyond are Bethulia's mountains of green,
And the desolate hills of the wild Gada-
    rene ;
And I pause on the goat-crags of Tabor to
    see
The gleam of thy waters, O dark Galilee !

Hark, a sound in the valley ! where, swollen
    and strong,
Thy river, O Kishon, is sweeping along ;
Where the Canaanite strove with Jehovah
    in vain,
And thy torrent grew dark with the blood
    of the slain.

There down from his mountains stern Zeb-
    ulon came,
And Naphthali's stag, with his eyeballs of
    flame,

And the chariots of Jabin rolled harmlessly
    on,
For the arm of the Lord was Abinoam's
    son !

There sleep the still rocks and the caverns
    which rang
To the song which the beautiful prophetess
    sang,
When the princes of Issachar stood by her
    side,
And the shout of a host in its triumph re-
    plied.

Lo, Bethlehem's hill-site before me is seen,
With the mountains around, and the valleys
    between ;
There rested the shepherds of Judah, and
    there
The song of the angels rose sweet on the
    air.

And Bethany's palm-trees in beauty still
    throw
Their shadows at noon on the ruins below ;
But where are the sisters who hastened to
    greet
The lowly Redeemer, and sit at His feet ?

I tread where the twelve in their wayfaring
    trod ;
I stand where they stood with the chosen of
    God —
Where His blessing was heard and His les-
    sons were taught,
Where the blind were restored and the
    healing was wrought.

Oh, here with His flock the sad Wanderer
    came ;
These hills He toiled over in grief are the
    same ;
The founts where He drank by the wayside
    still flow,
And the same airs are blowing which
    breathed on His brow !

And throned on her hills sits Jerusalem
    yet,
But with dust on her forehead, and chains
    on her feet ;
For the crown of her pride to the mocker
    hath gone,
And the holy Shechinah is dark where it
    shone.

But wherefore this dream of the earthly
    abode
Of Humanity clothed in the brightness of
    God ?
Were my spirit but turned from the out-
    ward and dim,
It could gaze, even now, on the presence of
    Him !

Not in clouds and in terrors, but gentle as
    when,
In love and in meekness, He moved among
    men ;
And the voice which breathed peace to the
    waves of the sea
In the hush of my spirit would whisper to
    me !

And what if my feet may not tread where
    He stood,
Nor my ears hear the dashing of Galilee's
    flood,
Nor my eyes see the cross which He bowed
    Him to bear,
Nor my knees press Gethsemane's garden
    of prayer.

Yet, Loved of the Father, Thy Spirit is near
To the meek, and the lowly, and penitent
    here ;
And the voice of Thy love is the same even
    now
As at Bethany's tomb or on Olivet's brow.

Oh, the outward hath gone ! but in glory
    and power,
The spirit surviveth the things of an hour ;
Unchanged, undecaying, its Pentecost flame
On the heart's secret altar is burning the
    same !

HYMNS

FROM THE FRENCH OF LAMARTINE

I

" Encore un hymne, O ma lyre !
    Un hymne pour le Seigneur,
  Un hymne dans mon délire,
    Un hymne dans mon bonheur."

ONE hymn more, O my lyre !
  Praise to the God above,
  Of joy and life and love,
Sweeping its strings of fire !

Oh, who the speed of bird and wind
  And sunbeam's glance will lend to me,
That, soaring upward, I may find
  My resting-place and home in Thee ?
Thou, whom my soul, midst doubt and
    gloom,
  Adoreth with a fervent flame, —
Mysterious spirit ! unto whom
  Pertain nor sign nor name !

Swiftly my lyre's soft murmurs go
  Up from the cold and joyless earth,
Back to the God who bade them flow,
  Whose moving spirit sent them forth.
But as for me, O God ! for me,
  The lowly creature of Thy will,
Lingering and sad, I sigh to Thee,
  An earth-bound pilgrim still !

Was not my spirit born to shine
  Where yonder stars and suns are glow-
    ing ?
To breathe with them the light divine
  From God's own holy altar flowing ?
To be, indeed, whate'er the soul
  In dreams hath thirsted for so long, —
A portion of heaven's glorious whole
  Of loveliness and song ?

Oh, watchers of the stars at night,
  Who breathe their fire, as we the air, —
Suns, thunders, stars, and rays of light,
  Oh, say, is He, the Eternal, there ?
Bend there around His awful throne
  The seraph's glance, the angel's knee ?
Or are thy inmost depths His own,
  O wild and mighty sea ?

Thoughts of my soul, how swift ye go !
  Swift as the eagle's glance of fire,
Or arrows from the archer's bow,
  To the far aim of your desire !
Thought after thought, ye thronging rise,
  Like spring-doves from the startled wood,
Bearing like them your sacrifice
  Of music unto God !

And shall these thoughts of joy and love
  Come back again no more to me ?
Returning like the patriarch's dove
  Wing-weary from the eternal sea,
To bear within my longing arms
  The promise-bough of kindlier skies,
Plucked from the green, immortal palms
  Which shadow Paradise ?

All-moving spirit! freely forth
   At Thy command the strong wind goes:
Its errand to the passive earth,
   Nor art can stay, nor strength oppose,
Until it folds its weary wing
   Once more within the hand divine;
So, weary from its wandering,
   My spirit turns to Thine!

Child of the sea, the mountain stream,
   From its dark caverns, hurries on,
Ceaseless, by night and morning's beam,
   By evening's star and noontide's sun,
Until at last it sinks to rest,
   O'erwearied, in the waiting sea,
And moans upon its mother's breast, —
   So turns my soul to Thee!

O Thou who bidst the torrent flow,
   Who lendest wings unto the wind, —
Mover of all things! where art Thou?
   Oh, whither shall I go to find
The secret of Thy resting-place?
   Is there no holy wing for me,
That, soaring, I may search the space
   Of highest heaven for Thee?

Oh, would I were as free to rise
   As leaves on autumn's whirlwind borne, —
The arrowy light of sunset skies,
   Or sound, or ray, or star of morn,
Which melts in heaven at twilight's close,
   Or aught which soars unchecked and free
Through earth and heaven; that I might
     lose
   Myself in finding Thee!

II

LE CRI DE L'AME

"Quand le souffle divin qui flotte sur le monde."

When the breath divine is flowing,
Zephyr-like o'er all things going,
And, as the touch of viewless fingers,
Softly on my soul it lingers,
Open to a breath the lightest,
Conscious of a touch the slightest, —
As some calm, still lake, whereon
Sinks the snowy-bosomed swan,
And the glistening water-rings
Circle round her moving wings:
When my upward gaze is turning
Where the stars of heaven are burning

Through the deep and dark abyss, —
Flowers of midnight's wilderness,
Blowing with the evening's breath
Sweetly in their Maker's path:
When the breaking day is flushing
All the east, and light is gushing
Upward through the horizon's haze,
Sheaf-like, with its thousand rays,
Spreading, until all above
Overflows with joy and love,
And below, on earth's green bosom,
All is changed to light and blossom:

When my waking fancies over
Forms of brightness flit and hover
Holy as the seraphs are,
Who by Zion's fountains wear
On their foreheads, white and broad,
"Holiness unto the Lord!"
When, inspired with rapture high,
It would seem a single sigh
Could a world of love create;
That my life could know no date,
And my eager thoughts could fill
Heaven and Earth, o'erflowing still!

Then, O Father! Thou alone,
From the shadow of Thy throne,
To the sighing of my breast
And its rapture answerest.
All my thoughts, which, upward winging,
Bathe where Thy own light is springing, —
All my yearnings to be free
Are as echoes answering Thee!

Seldom upon lips of mine,
Father! rests that name of Thine;
Deep within my inmost breast,
In the secret place of mind,
Like an awful presence shrined,
Doth the dread idea rest!
Hushed and holy dwells it there,
Prompter of the silent prayer,
Lifting up my spirit's eye
And its faint, but earnest cry,
From its dark and cold abode,
Unto Thee, my Guide and God!

THE FAMILIST'S HYMN

The Puritans of New England, even in their
wilderness home, were not exempted from the
sectarian contentions which agitated the mo-
ther country after the downfall of Charles the

First, and of the established Episcopacy. The Quakers, Baptists, and Catholics were banished, on pain of death, from the Massachusetts Colony. One Samuel Gorton, a bold and eloquent declaimer, after preaching for a time in Boston against the doctrines of the Puritans, and declaring that their churches were mere human devices, and their sacrament and baptism an abomination, was driven out of the jurisdiction of the colony, and compelled to seek a residence among the savages. He gathered round him a considerable number of converts, who, like the primitive Christians, shared all things in common. His opinions, however, were so troublesome to the leading clergy of the colony, that they instigated an attack upon his "Family" by an armed force, which seized upon the principal men in it, and brought them into Massachusetts, where they were sentenced to be kept at hard labor in several towns (one only in each town), during the pleasure of the General Court, they being forbidden, under severe penalties, to utter any of their religious sentiments, except to such ministers as might labor for their conversion. They were unquestionably sincere in their opinions, and, whatever may have been their errors, deserve to be ranked among those who have in all ages suffered for the freedom of conscience.

FATHER ! to Thy suffering poor
　　Strength and grace and faith impart,
And with Thy own love restore
　　Comfort to the broken heart !
Oh, the failing ones confirm
　　With a holier strength of zeal !
Give Thou not the feeble worm
　　Helpless to the spoiler's heel !

Father ! for Thy holy sake
　　We are spoiled and hunted thus ;
Joyful, for Thy truth we take
　　Bonds and burthens unto us :
Poor, and weak, and robbed of all,
　　Weary with our daily task,
That Thy truth may never fall
　　Through our weakness, Lord, we ask.

Round our fired and wasted homes
　　Flits the forest-bird unscared,
And at noon the wild beast comes
　　Where our frugal meal was shared ;
For the song of praises there
　　Shrieks the crow the livelong day ;
For the sound of evening prayer
　　Howls the evil beast of prey.

Sweet the songs we loved to sing
　　Underneath Thy holy sky ;
Words and tones that used to bring
　　Tears of joy in every eye ;
Dear the wrestling hours of prayer,
　　When we gathered knee to knee,
Blameless youth and hoary hair,
　　Bowed, O God, alone to Thee.

As Thine early children, Lord,
　　Shared their wealth and daily bread,
Even so, with one accord,
　　We, in love, each other fed.
Not with us the miser's hoard,
　　Not with us his grasping hand;
Equal round a common board,
　　Drew our meek and brother band !

Safe our quiet Eden lay
　　When the war-whoop stirred the land
And the Indian turned away
　　From our home his bloody hand.
Well that forest-ranger saw,
　　That the burthen and the curse
Of the white man's cruel law
　　Rested also upon us.

Torn apart, and driven forth
　　To our toiling hard and long,
Father ! from the dust of earth
　　Lift we still our grateful song !
Grateful, that in bonds we share
　　In Thy love which maketh free ;
Joyful, that the wrongs we bear,
　　Draw us nearer, Lord, to Thee !

Grateful ! that where'er we toil, —
　　By Wachuset's wooded side,
On Nantucket's sea-worn isle,
　　Or by wild Neponset's tide, —
Still, in spirit, we are near,
　　And our evening hymns, which rise
Separate and discordant here,
　　Meet and mingle in the skies !

Let the scoffer scorn and mock,
　　Let the proud and evil priest
Rob the needy of his flock,
　　For his wine-cup and his feast, —
Redden not Thy bolts in store
　　Through the blackness of Thy skies ?
For the sighing of the poor
　　Wilt Thou not, at length, arise ?

Worn and wasted, oh ! how long
   Shall thy trodden poor complain ?
In Thy name they bear the wrong,
   In Thy cause the bonds of pain !
Melt oppression's heart of steel,
   Let the haughty priesthood see,
And their blinded followers feel,
   That in us they mock at Thee !

In Thy time, O Lord of hosts,
   Stretch abroad that hand to save
Which of old, on Egypt's coasts,
   Smote apart the Red Sea's wave !
Lead us from this evil land,
   From the spoiler set us free,
And once more our gathered band,
   Heart to heart, shall worship Thee !

EZEKIEL

Ezekiel xxxiii. 30–33.

THEY hear Thee not, O God ! nor see ;
Beneath Thy rod they mock at Thee ;
The princes of our ancient line
Lie drunken with Assyrian wine ;
The priests around Thy altar speak
The false words which their hearers seek ;
And hymns which Chaldea's wanton maids
Have sung in Dura's idol-shades
Are with the Levites' chant ascending,
With Zion's holiest anthems blending !

On Israel's bleeding bosom set,
The heathen heel is crushing yet ;
The towers upon our holy hill
Echo Chaldean footsteps still.
Our wasted shrines, — who weeps for
   them ?
Who mourneth for Jerusalem ?
Who turneth from his gains away ?
Whose knee with mine is bowed to pray ?
Who, leaving feast and purpling cup,
Takes Zion's lamentation up ?

A sad and thoughtful youth, I went
With Israel's early banishment ;
And where the sullen Chebar crept,
The ritual of my fathers kept.
The water for the trench I drew,
The firstling of the flock I slew,
And, standing at the altar's side,
I shared the Levites' lingering pride,
That still, amidst her mocking foes,
The smoke of Zion's offering rose.

In sudden whirlwind, cloud and flame,
The Spirit of the Highest came !
Before mine eyes a vision passed,
A glory terrible and vast ;
With dreadful eyes of living things,
And sounding sweep of angel wings,
With circling light and sapphire throne,
And flame-like form of One thereon,
And voice of that dread Likeness sent
Down from the crystal firmament !

The burden of a prophet's power
Fell on me in that fearful hour ;
From off unutterable woes
The curtain of the future rose ;
I saw far down the coming time
The fiery chastisement of crime ;
With noise of mingling hosts, and jar
Of falling towers and shouts of war,
I saw the nations rise and fall,
Like fire-gleams on my tent's white wall.

In dream and trance, I saw the slain
Of Egypt heaped like harvest grain.
I saw the walls of sea-born Tyre
Swept over by the spoiler's fire ;
And heard the low, expiring moan
Of Edom on his rocky throne ;
And, woe is me ! the wild lament
From Zion's desolation sent ;
And felt within my heart each blow
Which laid her holy places low.

In bonds and sorrow, day by day,
Before the pictured tile I lay ;
And there, as in a mirror, saw
The coming of Assyria's war ;
Her swarthy lines of spearmen pass
Like locusts through Bethhoron's grass ;
I saw them draw their stormy hem
Of battle round Jerusalem ;
And, listening, heard the Hebrew wail
Blend with the victor-trump of Baal !

Who trembled at my warning word ?
Who owned the prophet of the Lord ?
How mocked the rude, how scoffed the
   vile,
How stung the Levites' scornful smile,
As o'er my spirit, dark and slow,
The shadow crept of Israel's woe
As if the angel's mournful roll
Had left its record on my soul,
And traced in lines of darkness there
The picture of its great despair !

Yet ever at the hour I feel
My lips in prophecy unseal.
Prince, priest, and Levite gather near,
And Salem's daughters haste to hear,
On Chebar's waste and alien shore,
The harp of Judah swept once more.
They listen, as in Babel's throng
The Chaldeans to the dancer's song,
Or wild sabbeka's nightly play,
As careless and as vain as they.

And thus, O Prophet-bard of old,
Hast thou thy tale of sorrow told!
The same which earth's unwelcome seers
Have felt in all succeeding years.
Sport of the changeful multitude,
Nor calmly heard nor understood,
Their song has seemed a trick of art,
Their warnings but the actor's part.
With bonds, and scorn, and evil will,
The world requites its prophets still.

So was it when the Holy One
The garments of the flesh put on!
Men followed where the Highest led
For common gifts of daily bread,
And gross of ear, of vision dim,
Owned not the Godlike power of Him.
Vain as a dreamer's words to them
His wail above Jerusalem,
And meaningless the watch He kept
Through which His weak disciples slept.

Yet shrink not thou, whoe'er thou art,
For God's great purpose set apart,
Before whose far-discerning eyes,
The Future as the Present lies!
Beyond a narrow-bounded age
Stretches thy prophet-heritage,
Through Heaven's vast spaces angel-trod,
And through the eternal years of God!
Thy audience, worlds! — all things to be
The witness of the Truth in thee!

WHAT THE VOICE SAID

MADDENED by Earth's wrong and evil,
  "Lord!" I cried in sudden ire,
"From Thy right hand, clothed with thun-
    der,
  Shake the bolted fire!

"Love is lost, and Faith is dying;
  With the brute the man is sold;
And the dropping blood of labor
  Hardens into gold.

"Here the dying wail of Famine,
  There the battle's groan of pain;
And, in silence, smooth-faced Mammon
  Reaping men like grain.

"'Where is God, that we should fear
    Him?'
  Thus the earth-born Titans say;
'God! if Thou art living, hear us!'
  Thus the weak ones pray."

"Thou, the patient Heaven upbraiding,"
  Spake a solemn Voice within;
"Weary of our Lord's forbearance,
  Art thou free from sin?

"Fearless brow to Him uplifting,
  Canst thou for His thunders call,
Knowing that to guilt's attraction
  Evermore they fall?

"Know'st thou not all germs of evil
  In thy heart await their time?
Not thyself, but God's restraining,
  Stays their growth of crime.

"Couldst thou boast, O child of weakness
  O'er the sons of wrong and strife,
Were their strong temptations planted
  In thy path of life?

"Thou hast seen two streamlets gushing
  From one fountain, clear and free,
But by widely varying channels
  Searching for the sea.

"Glideth one through greenest valleys,
  Kissing them with lips still sweet;
One, mad roaring down the mountains,
  Stagnates at their feet.

"Is it choice whereby the Parsee
  Kneels before his mother's fire?
In his black tent did the Tartar
  Choose his wandering sire?

"He alone, whose hand is bounding
  Human power and human will,
Looking through each soul's surrounding,
  Knows its good or ill.

" For thyself, while wrong and sorrow
　　Make to thee their strong appeal,
Coward wert thou not to utter
　　What the heart must feel.

" Earnest words must needs be spoken
　　When the warm heart bleeds or burns
With its scorn of wrong, or pity
　　For the wronged, by turns.

" But, by all thy nature's weakness,
　　Hidden faults and follies known,
Be thou, in rebuking evil,
　　Conscious of thine own.

" Not the less shall stern-eyed Duty
　　To thy lips her trumpet set,
But with harsher blasts shall mingle
　　Wailings of regret."

Cease not, Voice of holy speaking,
　　Teacher sent of God, be near,
Whispering through the day's cool silence,
　　Let my spirit hear !

So, when thoughts of evil-doers
　　Waken scorn, or hatred move,
Shall a mournful fellow-feeling
　　Temper all with love.

THE ANGEL OF PATIENCE

A FREE PARAPHRASE OF THE GERMAN

To weary hearts, to mourning homes,
God's meekest Angel gently comes :
No power has he to banish pain,
Or give us back our lost again ;
And yet in tenderest love, our dear
And Heavenly Father sends him here.

There 's quiet in that Angel's glance,
There 's rest in his still countenance !
He mocks no grief with idle cheer,
Nor wounds with words the mourner's ear ;
But ills and woes he may not cure
He kindly trains us to endure.

Angel of Patience ! sent to calm
Our feverish brows with cooling palm ;
To lay the storms of hope and fear,
And reconcile life's smile and tear ;
The throbs of wounded pride to still,
And make our own our Father's will !

O thou who mournest on thy way,
With longings for the close of day ;
He walks with thee, that Angel kind,
And gently whispers, " Be resigned :
Bear up, bear on, the end shall tell
The dear Lord ordereth all things well ! "

THE WIFE OF MANOAH TO HER HUSBAND

AGAINST the sunset's glowing wall
The city towers rise black and tall,
Where Zorah, on its rocky height,
Stands like an armed man in the light.

Down Eshtaol's vales of ripened grain
Falls like a cloud the night amain,
And up the hillsides climbing slow
The barley reapers homeward go.

Look, dearest ! how our fair child's head
The sunset light hath hallowëd,
Where at this olive's foot he lies,
Uplooking to the tranquil skies.

Oh, while beneath the fervent heat
Thy sickle swept the bearded wheat,
I 've watched, with mingled joy and dread,
Our child upon his grassy bed.

Joy, which the mother feels alone
Whose morning hope like mine had flown,
When to her bosom, over-blessed,
A dearer life than hers is pressed.

Dread, for the future dark and still,
Which shapes our dear one to its will ;
Forever in his large calm eyes,
I read a tale of sacrifice.

The same foreboding awe I felt
When at the altar's side we knelt,
And he, who as a pilgrim came,
Rose, winged and glorious, through the
　　flame.

I slept not, though the wild bees made
A dreamlike murmuring in the shade,
And on me the warm-fingered hours
Pressed with the drowsy smell of flowers.

Before me, in a vision, rose
The hosts of Israel's scornful foes, —

Rank over rank, helm, shield, and spear,
Glittered in noon's hot atmosphere.

I heard their boast, and bitter word,
Their mockery of the Hebrew's Lord,
I saw their hands His ark assail,
Their feet profane His holy veil.

No angel down the blue space spoke,
No thunder from the still sky broke;
But in their midst, in power and awe,
Like God's waked wrath, our child I saw !

A child no more ! — harsh-browed and
     strong,
He towered a giant in the throng,
And down his shoulders, broad and bare,
Swept the black terror of his hair.

He raised his arm — he smote amain ;
As round the reaper falls the grain,
So the dark host around him fell,
So sank the foes of Israel !

Again I looked.   In sunlight shone
The towers and domes of Askelon;
Priest, warrior, slave, a mighty crowd
Within her idol temple bowed.

Yet one knelt not; stark, gaunt, and blind,
His arms the massive pillars twined, —
An eyeless captive, strong with hate,
He stood there like an evil Fate.

The red shrines smoked, — the trumpets
     pealed:
He stooped, — the giant columns reeled;
Reeled tower and fane, sank arch and wall,
And the thick dust-cloud closed o'er all!

Above the shriek, the crash, the groan
Of the fallen pride of Askelon,
I heard, sheer down the echoing sky,
A voice as of an angel cry, —

The voice of him, who at our side
Sat through the golden eventide;
Of him who, on thy altar's blaze,
Rose fire-winged, with his song of praise.

" Rejoice o'er Israel's broken chain,
Gray mother of the mighty slain!
Rejoice! " it cried, " he vanquisheth!
The strong in life is strong in death!

" To him shall Zorah's daughters raise
Through coming years their hymns of
     praise,
And gray old men at evening tell
Of all he wrought for Israel.

" And they who sing and they who hear
Alike shall hold thy memory dear,
And pour their blessings on thy head,
O mother of the mighty dead! "

It ceased ; and though a sound I heard
As if great wings the still air stirred,
I only saw the barley sheaves
And hills half hid by olive leaves.

I bowed my face, in awe and fear,
On the dear child who slumbered near ;
" With me, as with my only son,
O God," I said, " Thy will be done ! "

MY SOUL AND I

STAND still, my soul, in the silent dark
     I would question thee,
Alone in the shadow drear and stark
     With God and me !

What, my soul, was thy errand here ?
     Was it mirth or ease,
Or heaping up dust from year to year ?
     " Nay, none of these ! "

Speak, soul, aright in His holy sight
     Whose eye looks still
And steadily on thee through the night:
     " To do His will ! "

What hast thou done, O soul of mine,
     That thou tremblest so ?
Hast thou wrought His task, and kept the
     line
     He bade thee go ?

What, silent all ! art sad of cheer ?
     Art fearful now ?
When God seemed far and men were near,
     How brave wert thou !

Aha ! thou tremblest ! — well I see
     Thou 'rt craven grown.
Is it so hard with God and me
     To stand alone ?

Summon thy sunshine bravery back,
    O wretched sprite !
Let me hear thy voice through this deep
    and black
    Abysmal night.

What hast thou wrought for Right and
    Truth,
    For God and Man,
From the golden hours of bright-eyed
    youth
    To life's mid span ?

Ah, soul of mine, thy tones I hear,
    But weak and low,
Like far sad murmurs on my ear
    They come and go.

"I have wrestled stoutly with the Wrong,
    And borne the Right
From beneath the footfall of the throng
    To life and light.

"Wherever Freedom shivered a chain,
    God speed, quoth I ;
To Error amidst her shouting train
    I gave the lie."

Ah, soul of mine ! ah, soul of mine !
    Thy deeds are well :
Were they wrought for Truth's sake or for
    thine ?
    My soul, pray tell.

"Of all the work my hand hath wrought
    Beneath the sky,
Save a place in kindly human thought,
    No gain have I."

Go to, go to ! for thy very self
    Thy deeds were done :
Thou for fame, the miser for pelf,
    Your end is one !

And where art thou going, soul of mine ?
    Canst see the end ?
And whither this troubled life of thine
    Evermore doth tend ?

What daunts thee now ? what shakes thee
    so ?
    My sad soul, say.
"I see a cloud like a curtain low
    Hang o'er my way.

"Whither I go I cannot tell :
    That cloud hangs black,
High as the heaven and deep as hell
    Across my track.

"I see its shadow coldly enwrap
    The souls before.
Sadly they enter it, step by step,
    To return no more.

"They shrink, they shudder, dear God !
    they kneel
    To Thee in prayer.
They shut their eyes on the cloud, but feel
    That it still is there.

"In vain they turn from the dread Be-
    fore
    To the Known and Gone ;
For while gazing behind them evermore
    Their feet glide on.

"Yet, at times, I see upon sweet pale faces
    A light begin
To tremble, as if from holy places
    And shrines within.

"And at times methinks their cold lips
    move
    With hymn and prayer,
As if somewhat of awe, but more of love
    And hope were there.

"I call on the souls who have left the
    light
    To reveal their lot ;
I bend mine ear to that wall of night,
    And they answer not.

"But I hear around me sighs of pain
    And the cry of fear,
And a sound like the slow sad dropping of
    rain,
    Each drop a tear !

"Ah, the cloud is dark, and day by day
    I am moving thither :
I must pass beneath it on my way —
    God pity me ! — whither ?"

Ah, soul of mine ! so brave and wise
    In the life-storm loud,
Fronting so calmly all human eyes
    In the sunlit crowd !

Now standing apart with God and me
    Thou art weakness all,
Gazing vainly after the things to be
    Through Death's dread wall.

But never for this, never for this
    Was thy being lent ;
For the craven's fear is but selfishness,
    Like his merriment.

Folly and Fear are sisters twain :
    One closing her eyes,
The other peopling the dark inane
    With spectral lies.

Know well, my soul, God's hand controls
    Whate'er thou fearest ;
Round Him in calmest music rolls
    Whate'er thou hearest.

What to thee is shadow, to Him is day,
    And the end He knoweth,
And not on a blind and aimless way
    The spirit goeth.

Man sees no future, — a phantom show
    Is alone before him ;
Past Time is dead, and the grasses grow,
    And flowers bloom o'er him.

Nothing before, nothing behind ;
    The steps of Faith
Fall on the seeming void, and find
    The rock beneath.

The Present, the Present is all thou hast
    For thy sure possessing ;
Like the patriarch's angel hold it fast
    Till it gives its blessing.

Why fear the night ? why shrink from
    Death,
    That phantom wan ?
There is nothing in heaven or earth be-
    neath
    Save God and man.

Peopling the shadows we turn from Him
    And from one another ;
All is spectral and vague and dim
    Save God and our brother !

Like warp and woof all destinies
    Are woven fast,

Linked in sympathy like the keys
    Of an organ vast.

Pluck one thread, and the web ye mar ;
    Break but one
Of a thousand keys, and the paining jar
    Through all will run.

O restless spirit ! wherefore strain
    Beyond thy sphere ?
Heaven and hell, with their joy and pain,
    Are now and here.

Back to thyself is measured well
    All thou hast given ;
Thy neighbor's wrong is thy present hell,
    His bliss, thy heaven.

And in life, in death, in dark and light,
    All are in God's care :
Sound the black abyss, pierce the deep of
    night,
    And He is there !

All which is real now remaineth,
    And fadeth never :
The hand which upholds it now sustaineth
    The soul forever.

Leaning on Him, make with reverent meek-
    ness
    His own thy will,
And with strength from Him shall thy ut-
    ter weakness
    Life's task fulfil ;

And that cloud itself, which now before
    thee
    Lies dark in view,
Shall with beams of light from the inner
    glory
    Be stricken through.

And like meadow mist through autumn's
    dawn
    Uprolling thin,
Its thickest folds when about thee drawn
    Let sunlight in.

Then of what is to be, and of what is
    done,
    Why queriest thou ?
The past and the time to be are one,
    And both are now !

WORSHIP

*Pure religion and undefiled before God and the Father is this, To visit the fatherless and widows in their affliction, and to keep himself unspotted from the world.
—James i. 27.*

THE Pagan's myths through marble lips
        are spoken,
    And ghosts of old Beliefs still flit and
        moan
Round fane and altar overthrown and
        broken,
    O'er tree-grown barrow and gray ring of
        stone.

Blind Faith had martyrs in those old high
        places,
    The Syrian hill grove and the Druid's
        wood,
With mothers offering, to the Fiend's
        embraces,
    Bone of their bone, and blood of their
        own blood.

Red altars, kindling through that night of
        error,
    Smoked with warm blood beneath the
        cruel eye
Of lawless Power and sanguinary Terror,
    Throned on the circle of a pitiless sky ;

Beneath whose baleful shadow, overcasting
    All heaven above, and blighting earth
        below,
The scourge grew red, the lip grew pale
        with fasting,
    And man's oblation was his fear and
        woe !

Then through great temples swelled the
        dismal moaning
    Of   dirge-like music and sepulchral
        prayer ;
Pale wizard priests, o'er occult symbols
        droning,
    Swung their white censers in the bur-
        dened air :

As if the pomp of rituals, and the savor
    Of gums and spices could the Unseen
        One please ;
As if His ear could bend, with childish
        favor,
    To the poor flattery of the organ keys !

Feet red from war-fields trod the church
        aisles holy,
    With trembling reverence : and the op-
        pressor there,
Kneeling before his priest, abased and
        lowly,
    Crushed human hearts beneath his knee
        of prayer.

Not such the service the benignant Father
    Requireth at His earthly children's
        hands :
Not the poor offering of vain rites, but
        rather
    The simple duty man from man demands.

For Earth He asks it : the full joy of
        heaven
    Knoweth no change of waning or in-
        crease ;
The great heart of the Infinite beats even,
    Untroubled flows the river of His peace.

He asks no taper lights, on high surround-
        ing
    The priestly altar and the saintly grave,
No dolorous chant nor organ music sound-
        ing,
    Nor incense clouding up the twilight
        nave.

For he whom Jesus loved hath truly
        spoken :
    The holier worship which he deigns to
        bless
Restores the lost, and binds the spirit
        broken,
    And feeds the widow and the fatherless !

Types of our human weakness and our sor-
        row !
    Who lives unhaunted by his loved ones
        dead ?
Who, with vain longing, seeketh not to
        borrow
    From stranger eyes the home lights
        which have fled ?

O brother man ! fold to thy heart thy
        brother ;
    Where pity dwells, the peace of God is
        there ;
To worship rightly is to love each other,
    Each smile a hymn, each kindly deed a
        prayer.

Follow with reverent steps the great exam-
ple
  Of Him whose holy work was " doing
    good ; "
So shall the wide earth seem our Father's
temple,
  Each loving life a psalm of gratitude.

Then shall all shackles fall ; the stormy
clangor
  Of wild war music o'er the earth shall
    cease ;
Love shall tread out the baleful fire of anger,
  And in its ashes plant the tree of peace !

THE HOLY LAND

Paraphrased from the lines in Lamartine's
Adieu to Marseilles, beginning

    " Je n'ai pas navigué sur l'océan de sable."

I HAVE not felt, o'er seas of sand,
  The rocking of the desert bark ;
Nor laved at Hebron's fount my hand,
  By Hebron's palm-trees cool and dark;
Nor pitched my tent at even-fall,
  On dust where Job of old has lain,
Nor dreamed beneath its canvas wall
  The dream of Jacob o'er again.

One vast world-page remains unread ;
  How shine the stars in Chaldea's sky,
How sounds the reverent pilgrim's tread,
  How beats the heart with God so nigh !
How round gray arch and column lone
  The spirit of the old time broods,
And sighs in all the winds that moan
  Along the sandy solitudes !

In thy tall cedars, Lebanon,
  I have not heard the nations' cries,
Nor seen thy eagles stooping down
  Where buried Tyre in ruin lies.
The Christian's prayer I have not said
  In Tadmor's temples of decay,
Nor startled, with my dreary tread,
  The waste where Memnon's empire lay.

Nor have I, from thy hallowed tide,
  O Jordan ! heard the low lament,
Like that sad wail along thy side
  Which Israel's mournful prophet sent !
Nor thrilled within that grotto lone
  Where, deep in night, the Bard of Kings

Felt hands of fire direct his own,
  And sweep for God the conscious strings

I have not climbed to Olivet,
  Nor laid me where my Saviour lay,
And left His trace of tears as yet
  By angel eyes unwept away ;
Nor watched, at midnight's solemn time,
  The garden where His prayer and groan,
Wrung by His sorrow and our crime,
  Rose to One listening ear alone.

I have not kissed the rock-hewn grot
  Where in His mother's arms He lay,
Nor knelt upon the sacred spot
  Where last His footsteps pressed the
    clay ;
Nor looked on that sad mountain head,
  Nor smote my sinful breast, where wide
His arms to fold the world He spread,
  And bowed His head to bless — and died i

THE REWARD

WHO, looking backward from his man-
  hood's prime,
Sees not the spectre of his misspent time ?
  And, through the shade
Of funeral cypress planted thick behind,
Hears no reproachful whisper on the wind
  From his loved dead ?

Who bears no trace of passion's evil force ?
Who shuns thy sting, O terrible Remorse ?
  Who does not cast
On the thronged pages of his memory's
  book,
At times, a sad and half-reluctant look,
  Regretful of the past ?

Alas ! the evil which we fain would shun
We do, and leave the wished-for good un-
  done :
  Our strength to-day
Is but to-morrow's weakness, prone to fall ;
Poor, blind, unprofitable servants all
  Are we alway.

Yet who, thus looking backward o'er his
  years,
Feels not his eyelids wet with grateful
  tears,
  If he hath been
Permitted, weak and sinful as he was,

To cheer and aid, in some ennobling cause,
  His fellow-men ?

If he hath hidden the outcast, or let in
A ray of sunshine to the cell of sin ;
  If he hath lent
Strength to the weak, and, in an hour of
  need,
Over the suffering, mindless of his creed
  Or home, hath bent ;

He has not lived in vain, and while he gives
The praise to Him, in whom he moves and
  lives,
  With thankful heart ;
He gazes backward, and with hope before,
Knowing that from his works he never-
  more
  Can henceforth part.

THE WISH OF TO-DAY

I ASK not now for gold to gild
  With mocking shine a weary frame ;
The yearning of the mind is stilled,
  I ask not now for Fame.

A rose-cloud, dimly seen above,
  Melting in heaven's blue depths away ;
Oh, sweet, fond dream of human Love !
  For thee I may not pray.

But, bowed in lowliness of mind,
  I make my humble wishes known ;
I only ask a will resigned,
  O Father, to Thine own !

To-day, beneath Thy chastening eye
  I crave alone for peace and rest,
Submissive in Thy hand to lie,
  And feel that it is best.

A marvel seems the Universe,
  A miracle our Life and Death ;
A mystery which I cannot pierce,
  Around, above, beneath.

In vain I task my aching brain,
  In vain the sage's thought I scan,
I only feel how weak and vain,
  How poor and blind, is man.

And now my spirit sighs for home,
  And longs for light whereby to see,

And, like a weary child, would come,
  O Father, unto Thee !

Though oft, like letters traced on sand,
  My weak resolves have passed away
In mercy lend Thy helping hand
  Unto my prayer to-day !

ALL'S WELL

THE clouds, which rise with thunder, slake
  Our thirsty souls with rain ;
The blow most dreaded falls to break
  From off our limbs a chain ;
And wrongs of man to man but make
  The love of God more plain.
As through the shadowy lens of even
The eye looks farthest into heaven
On gleams of star and depths of blue
The glaring sunshine never knew !

INVOCATION

THROUGH Thy clear spaces, Lord, of old,
Formless and void the dead earth rolled ;
Deaf to Thy heaven's sweet music, blind
To the great lights which o'er it shined ;
No sound, no ray, no warmth, no breath, —
A dumb despair, a wandering death.

To that dark, weltering horror came
Thy spirit, like a subtle flame, —
A breath of life electrical,
Awakening and transforming all,
Till beat and thrilled in every part
The pulses of a living heart.

Then knew their bounds the land and sea ;
Then smiled the bloom of mead and tree ;
From flower to moth, from beast to man,
The quick creative impulse ran ;
And earth, with life from thee renewed,
Was in thy holy eyesight good.

As lost and void, as dark and cold
And formless as that earth of old ;
A wandering waste of storm and night,
Midst spheres of song and realms of light ;
A blot upon thy holy sky,
Untouched, unwarmed of thee, am I.

O Thou who movest on the deep
Of spirits, wake my own from sleep !

Its darkness melt, its coldness warm,
The lost restore, the ill transform,
That flower and fruit henceforth may be
Its grateful offering, worthy Thee.

QUESTIONS OF LIFE

And the angel that was sent unto me, whose name
was Uriel, gave me an answer,
And said, Thy heart hath gone too far in this world,
and thinkest thou to comprehend the way of the Most
High ?
Then said I, Yea, my Lord. . . .
Then said he unto me, Go thy way, weigh me the
weight of the fire or measure me the blast of the wind,
or call me again the hour that is past. — 2 *Esdras* ch. iv.

A BENDING staff I would not break,
A feeble faith I would not shake,
Nor even rashly pluck away
The error which some truth may stay,
Whose loss might leave the soul without
A shield against the shafts of doubt.

And yet, at times, when over all
A darker mystery seems to fall,
(May God forgive the child of dust,
Who seeks to know, where Faith should
        trust !)
I raise the questions, old and dark,
Of Uzdom's tempted patriarch,
And, speech-confounded, build again
The baffled tower of Shinar's plain.

I am : how little more I know !
Whence came I ?   Whither do I go ?
A centred self, which feels and is ;
A cry between the silences ;
A shadow-birth of clouds at strife
With sunshine on the hills of life ;
A shaft from Nature's quiver cast
Into the Future from the Past ;
Between the cradle and the shroud,
A meteor's flight from cloud to cloud.

Thorough the vastness, arching all,
I see the great stars rise and fall,
The rounding seasons come and go,
The tided oceans ebb and flow ;
The tokens of a central force,
Whose circles, in their widening course,
O'erlap and move the universe ;
The workings of the law whence springs
The rhythmic harmony of things,
Which shapes in earth the darkling spar,
And orbs in heaven the morning star.

Of all I see, in earth and sky, —
Star, flower, beast, bird, — what part have I ?
This conscious life, — is it the same
Which thrills the universal frame,
Whereby the caverned crystal shoots,
And mounts the sap from forest roots,
Whereby the exiled wood-bird tells
When Spring makes green her native dells ?
How feels the stone the pang of birth,
Which brings its sparkling prism forth?
The forest-tree the throb which gives
The life-blood to its new-born leaves ?
Do bird and blossom feel, like me,
Life's many-folded mystery, —
The wonder which it is to be ?
Or stand I severed and distinct,
From Nature's chain of life unlinked ?
Allied to all, yet not the less
Prisoned in separate consciousness,
Alone o'erburdened with a sense
Of life, and cause, and consequence ?

In vain to me the Sphinx propounds
The riddle of her sights and sounds ;
Back still the vaulted mystery gives
The echoed question it receives.
What sings the brook ?   What oracle
Is in the pine-tree's organ swell ?
What may the wind's low burden be ?
The meaning of the moaning sea ?
The hieroglyphics of the stars ?
Or clouded sunset's crimson bars ?
I vainly ask, for mocks my skill
The trick of Nature's cipher still.

I turn from Nature unto men,
I ask the stylus and the pen ;
What sang the bards of old ?   What mean
The prophets of the Orient ?
The rolls of buried Egypt, hid
In painted tomb and pyramid ?
What mean Idúmea's arrowy lines,
Or dusk Elora's monstrous signs ?
How speaks the primal thought of man
From the grim carvings of Copan ?
Where rests the secret ?   Where the keys
Of the old death-bolted mysteries ?
Alas ! the dead retain their trust ;
Dust hath no answer from the dust.

The great enigma still unguessed,
Unanswered the eternal quest ;
I gather up the scattered rays
Of wisdom in the early days,
Faint gleams and broken, like the light

Of meteors in a northern night,
Betraying to the darkling earth
The unseen sun which gave them birth ;
I listen to the sibyl's chant,
The voice of priest and hierophant ;
I know what Indian Kreeshna saith,
And what of life and what of death
The demon taught to Socrates ;
And what, beneath his garden-trees
Slow pacing, with a dream-like tread,
The solemn-thoughted Plato said ;
Nor lack I tokens, great or small,
Of God's clear light in each and all,
While holding with more dear regard
The scroll of Hebrew seer and bard,
The starry pages promise-lit
With Christ's Evangel over-writ,
Thy miracle of life and death,
O Holy One of Nazareth !

On Aztec ruins, gray and lone,
The circling serpent coils in stone, —
Type of the endless and unknown ;
Whereof we seek the clue to find,
With groping fingers of the blind !
Forever sought, and never found,
We trace that serpent-symbol round
Our resting-place, our starting bound !
Oh, thriftlessness of dream and guess !
Oh, wisdom which is foolishness !
Why idly seek from outward things
The answer inward silence brings ?
Why stretch beyond our proper sphere
And age, for that which lies so near ?
Why climb the far-off hills with pain,
A nearer view of heaven to gain ?
In lowliest depths of bosky dells
The hermit Contemplation dwells.
A fountain's pine-hung slope his seat,
And lotus-twined his silent feet,
Whence, piercing heaven, with screenëd
sight,
He sees at noon the stars, whose light
Shall glorify the coming night.

Here let me pause, my quest forego ;
Enough for me to feel and know
That He in whom the cause and end,
The past and future, meet and blend, —
Who, girt with his Immensities,
Our vast and star-hung system sees,
Small as the clustered Pleiades, —
Moves not alone the heavenly quires,
But waves the spring-time's grassy spires,

Guards not archangel feet alone,
But deigns to guide and keep my own ;
Speaks not alone the words of fate
Which worlds destroy, and worlds create,
But whispers in my spirit's ear,
In tones of love, or warning fear,
A language none beside may hear.

To Him, from wanderings long and wild,
I come, an over-wearied child,
In cool and shade His peace to find,
Like dew-fall settling on my mind.
Assured that all I know is best,
And humbly trusting for the rest,
I turn from Fancy's cloud-built scheme,
Dark creed, and mournful eastern dream
Of power, impersonal and cold,
Controlling all, itself controlled,
Maker and slave of iron laws,
Alike the subject and the cause ;
From vain philosophies, that try
The sevenfold gates of mystery,
And, baffled ever, babble still,
Word-prodigal of fate and will ;
From Nature, and her mockery, Art,
And book and speech of men apart,
To the still witness in my heart ;
With reverence waiting to behold
His Avatár of love untold,
The Eternal Beauty new and old !

FIRST-DAY THOUGHTS

In calm and cool and silence, once again
  I find my old accustomed place among
  My brethren, where, perchance, no hu-
    man tongue
  Shall utter words ; where never hymn
    is sung,
  Nor deep-toned organ blown, nor censer
    swung,
Nor dim light falling through the pictured
    pane !
There, syllabled by silence, let me hear
The still small voice which reached the
    prophet's ear ;
Read in my heart a still diviner law
Than Israel's leader on his tables saw !
There let me strive with each besetting sin,
  Recall my wandering fancies, and re-
    strain
  The sore disquiet of a restless brain ;
  And, as the path of duty is made plain,

May grace be given that I may walk
    therein,
  Not like the hireling, for his selfish gain,
With backward glances and reluctant tread,
Making a merit of his coward dread,
    But, cheerful, in the light around me
    thrown,
  Walking as one to pleasant service led ;
  Doing God's will as if it were my own,
Yet trusting not in mine, but in His
    strength alone !

TRUST

THE same old baffling questions ! O my
    friend,
I cannot answer them. In vain I send
My soul into the dark, where never burn
    The lamps of science, nor the natural
    light
Of Reason's sun and stars ! I cannot learn
Their great and solemn meanings, nor dis-
    cern
The awful secrets of the eyes which turn
    Evermore on us through the day and
    night
    With silent challenge and a dumb de-
    mand,
Proffering the riddles of the dread un-
    known,
Like the calm Sphinxes, with their eyes of
    stone,
    Questioning the centuries from their veils
    of sand !
I have no answer for myself or thee,
Save that I learned beside my mother's
    knee ;
" All is of God that is, and is to be ;
    And God is good." Let this suffice us
    still,
  Resting in childlike trust upon His will
Who moves to His great ends unthwarted
    by the ill.

TRINITAS

AT morn I prayed, " I fain would see
How Three are One, and One is Three ;
Read the dark riddle unto me."

I wandered forth, the sun and air
I saw bestowed with equal care
On good and evil, foul and fair.

No partial favor dropped the rain ;
Alike the righteous and profane
Rejoiced above their heading grain.

And my heart murmured, " Is it meet
That blindfold Nature thus should treat
With equal hand the tares and wheat ? "

A presence melted through my mood, —
A warmth, a light, a sense of good,
Like sunshine through a winter wood.

I saw that presence, mailed complete
In her white innocence, pause to greet
A fallen sister of the street.

Upon her bosom snowy pure
The lost one clung, as if secure
From inward guilt or outward lure.

" Beware ! " I said ; " in this I see
No gain to her, but loss to thee :
Who touches pitch defiled must be."

I passed the haunts of shame and sin,
And a voice whispered, " Who therein
Shall these lost souls to Heaven's peace
    win ?

" Who there shall hope and health dis-
    pense,
And lift the ladder up from thence
Whose rounds are prayers of penitence ? "

I said, " No higher life they know ;
These earth-worms love to have it so.
Who stoops to raise them sinks as low."

That night with painful care I read
What Hippo's saint and Calvin said ;
The living seeking to the dead !

In vain I turned, in weary quest,
Old pages, where (God give them rest !)
The poor creed-mongers dreamed and
    guessed.

And still I prayed, " Lord, let me see
How Three are One, and One is Three ;
Read the dark riddle unto me ! "

Then something whispered, " Dost thou
    pray
For what thou hast ? This very day
The Holy Three have crossed thy way.

" Did not the gifts of sun and air
To good and ill alike declare
The all-compassionate Father's care ?

" In the white soul that stooped to raise
The lost one from her evil ways,
Thou saw'st the Christ, whom angels praise !

" A bodiless Divinity,
The still small Voice that spake to thee
Was the Holy Spirit's mystery !

" O blind of sight, of faith how small !
Father, and Son, and Holy Call ;
This day thou hast denied them all !

" Revealed in love and sacrifice,
The Holiest passed before thine eyes,
One and the same, in threefold guise.

" The equal Father in rain and sun,
His Christ in the good to evil done,
His Voice in thy soul ; — and the Three are
    One ! "

I shut my grave Aquinas fast ;
The monkish gloss of ages past,
The schoolman's creed aside I cast.

And my heart answered, " Lord, I see
How Three are One, and One is Three ;
Thy riddle hath been read to me ! "

THE SISTERS

A PICTURE BY BARRY

THE shade for me, but over thee
    The lingering sunshine still ;
As, smiling, to the silent stream
    Comes down the singing rill.

So come to me, my little one, —
    My years with thee I share,
And mingle with a sister's love
    A mother's tender care.

But keep the smile upon thy lip,
    The trust upon thy brow ;
Since for the dear one God hath called
    We have an angel now.

Our mother from the fields of heaven
    Shall still her ear incline ;

Nor need we fear her human love
    Is less for love divine.

The songs are sweet they sing beneath
    The trees of life so fair,
But sweetest of the songs of heaven
    Shall be her children's prayer.

Then, darling, rest upon my breast,
    And teach my heart to lean
With thy sweet trust upon the arm
    Which folds us both unseen !

"THE ROCK" IN EL GHOR

DEAD Petra in her hill-tomb sleeps,
    Her stones of emptiness remain ;
Around her sculptured mystery sweeps
    The lonely waste of Edom's plain.

From the doomed dwellers in the cleft
    The bow of vengeance turns not back ;
Of all her myriads none are left
    Along the Wady Mousa's track.

Clear in the hot Arabian day
    Her arches spring, her statues climb ;
Unchanged, the graven wonders pay
    No tribute to the spoiler, Time !

Unchanged the awful lithograph
    Of power and glory undertrod ;
Of nations scattered like the chaff
    Blown from the threshing-floor of God.

Yet shall the thoughtful stranger turn
    From Petra's gates with deeper awe,
To mark afar the burial urn
    Of Aaron on the cliffs of Hor ;

And where upon its ancient guard
    Thy Rock, El Ghor, is standing yet, —
Looks from its turrets desertward,
    And keeps the watch that God has set.

The same as when in thunders loud
    It heard the voice of God to man,
As when it saw in fire and cloud
    The angels walk in Israel's van !

Or when from Ezion-Geber's way
    It saw the long procession file,
And heard the Hebrew timbrels play
    The music of the lordly Nile ;

Or saw the tabernacle pause,
　Cloud-bound, by Kadesh Barnea's wells,
While Moses graved the sacred laws,
　And Aaron swung his golden bells.

Rock cf the desert, prophet-sung !
　How grew its shadowing pile at length,
A symbol, in the Hebrew tongue,
　Of God's eternal love and strength.

On lip of bard and scroll of seer,
　From age to age went down the name,
Until the Shiloh's promised year,
　And Christ, the Rock of Ages, came !

The path of life we walk to-day
　Is strange as that the Hebrews trod ;
We need the shadowing rock, as they, —
　We need, like them, the guides of God.

God send His angels, Cloud and Fire,
　To lead us o'er the desert sand !
God give our hearts their long desire,
　His shadow in a weary land !

THE OVER-HEART

For of Him, and through Him, and to Him are all
things : to whom be glory forever ! — *Romans* xi. 36.

ABOVE, below, in sky and sod,
　In leaf and spar, in star and man,
　Well might the wise Athenian scan
The geometric signs of God,
　The measured order of His plan.

And India's mystics sang aright,
　Of the One Life pervading all, —
　One Being's tidal rise and fall
In soul and form, in sound and sight, —
　Eternal outflow and recall.

God is : and man in guilt and fear
　The central fact of Nature owns ;
　Kneels, trembling, by his altar stones,
And darkly dreams the ghastly smear
　Of blood appeases and atones.

Guilt shapes the Terror : deep within
　The human heart the secret lies
　Of all the hideous deities ;
And, painted on a ground of sin,
　The fabled gods of torment rise !

And what is He ?　The ripe grain nods,
　The sweet dews fall, the sweet flowers
　　blow ;
But darker signs His presence show :
The earthquake and the storm are God's,
　And good and evil interflow.

O hearts of love !　O souls that turn
　Like sunflowers to the pure and best !
　To you the truth is manifest :
For they the mind of Christ discern
　Who lean like John upon His breast !

In him of whom the sibyl told,
　For whom the prophet's harp was toned,
　Whose need the sage and magian owned,
The loving heart of God behold,
　The hope for which the ages groaned !

Fade, pomp of dreadful imagery
　Wherewith mankind have deified
　Their hate, and selfishness, and pride !
Let the scared dreamer wake to see
　The Christ of Nazareth at his side !

What doth that holy Guide require ?
　No rite of pain, nor gift of blood,
　But man a kindly brotherhood,
Looking, where duty is desire,
　To Him, the beautiful and good.

Gone be the faithlessness of fear,
　And let the pitying heaven's sweet rain
　Wash out the altar's bloody stain ;
The law of Hatred disappear,
　The law of Love alone remain.

How fall the idols false and grim !
　And lo ! their hideous wreck above
　The emblems of the Lamb and Dove !
Man turns from God, not God from him;
　And guilt, in suffering, whispers Love !

The world sits at the feet of Christ,
　Unknowing, blind, and unconsoled ;
　It yet shall touch His garment's fold,
And feel the heavenly Alchemist
　Transform its very dust to gold.

The theme befitting angel tongues
　Beyond a mortal's scope has grown.
O heart of mine ! with reverence own
The fulness which to it belongs,
　And trust the unknown for the known.

THE SHADOW AND THE LIGHT

"And I sought, whence is Evil : I set before the eye of my spirit the whole creation; whatsoever we see therein, — sea, earth, air, stars, trees, moral creatures, — yea, whatsoever there is we do not see, — angels and spiritual powers. Where is evil, and whence comes it, since God the Good hath created all things? Why made He anything at all of evil, and not rather by His Almightiness cause it not to be? These thoughts I turned in my miserable heart, overcharged with most gnawing cares." "And, admonished to return to myself, I entered even into my inmost soul, Thou being my guide, and beheld even beyond my soul and mind the Light unchangeable. He who knows the Truth knows what that Light is, and he that knows it knows Eternity! O Truth, who art Eternity! Love, who art Truth! Eternity, who art Love! And I beheld that Thou madest all things good, and to Thee is nothing whatsoever evil. From the angel to the worm, from the first motion to the last, Thou settest each in its place, and everything is good in its kind. Woe is me ! — how high art Thou in the highest, how deep in the deepest! and Thou never departest from us, and we scarcely return to Thee." — AUGUSTINE'S *Soliloquies*, Book VII.

THE fourteen centuries fall away
  Between us and the Afric saint,
And at his side we urge, to-day,
The immemorial quest and old complaint.

No outward sign to us is given, —
  From sea or earth comes no reply ;
Hushed as the warm Numidian heaven
He vainly questioned bends our frozen sky.

No victory comes of all our strife, —
  From all we grasp the meaning slips ;
The Sphinx sits at the gate of life,
With the old question on her awful lips.

In paths unknown we hear the feet
  Of fear before, and guilt behind ;
We pluck the wayside fruit, and eat
Ashes and dust beneath its golden rind.

From age to age descends unchecked
  The sad bequest of sire to son,
The body's taint, the mind's defect ;
Through every web of life the dark threads run.

Oh, why and whither ? God knows all ;
  I only know that He is good,
And that whatever may befall
Or here or there, must be the best that could.

Between the dreadful cherubim
  A Father's face I still discern,

As Moses looked of old on Him,
And saw His glory into goodness turn !

For He is merciful as just ;
  And so, by faith correcting sight,
I bow before His will, and trust
Howe'er they seem He doeth all things right ;

And dare to hope that He will make
  The rugged smooth, the doubtful plain ;
His mercy never quite forsake ;
His healing visit every realm of pain ;

That suffering is not His revenge
  Upon His creatures weak and frail,
Sent on a pathway new and strange
With feet that wander and with eyes that fail ;

That, o'er the crucible of pain,
  Watches the tender eye of Love
The slow transmuting of the chain
Whose links are iron below to gold above !

Ah me ! we doubt the shining skies,
  Seen through our shadows of offence,
And drown with our poor childish cries
The cradle-hymn of kindly Providence.

And still we love the evil cause,
  And of the just effect complain :
We tread upon life's broken laws,
And murmur at our self-inflicted pain ;

We turn us from the light, and find
  Our spectral shapes before us thrown,
As they who leave the sun behind
Walk in the shadows of themselves alone.

And scarce by will or strength of ours
  We set our faces to the day ;
Weak, wavering, blind, the Eternal Powers
Alone can turn us from ourselves away.

Our weakness is the strength of sin,
  But love must needs be stronger far,
Outreaching all and gathering in
The erring spirit and the wandering star.

A Voice grows with the growing years ;
  Earth, hushing down her bitter cry,
Looks upward from her graves, and hears,
"The Resurrection and the Life am I."

O Love Divine ! — whose constant beam
　Shines on the eyes that will not see,
And waits to bless us, while we dream
Thou leavest us because we turn from
　　thee !

All souls that struggle and aspire,
　All hearts of prayer by thee are lit ;
And, dim or clear, thy tongues of fire
On dusky tribes and twilight centuries sit.

Nor bounds, nor clime, nor creed thou
　　know'st,
　Wide as our need thy favors fall ;
The white wings of the Holy Ghost
Stoop, seen or unseen, o'er the heads of all.

O Beauty, old yet ever new !
　Eternal Voice, and Inward Word,
The Logos of the Greek and Jew,
The old sphere-music which the Samian
　　heard !

Truth which the sage and prophet saw,
　Long sought without, but found within,
The Law of Love beyond all law,
The Life o'erflooding mortal death and
　　sin !

Shine on us with the light which glowed
　Upon the trance-bound shepherd's way,
Who saw the Darkness overflowed
And drowned by tides of everlasting Day.

Shine, light of God ! — make broad thy
　　scope
　To all who sin and suffer ; more
And better than we dare to hope
With Heaven's compassion make our long-
　　ings poor !

THE CRY OF A LOST SOUL

Lieutenant Herndon's *Report of the Explo-
ration of the Amazon* has a striking description
of the peculiar and melancholy notes of a bird
heard by night on the shores of the river. The
Indian guides called it " The Cry of a Lost
Soul " ! Among the numerous translations of
this poem is one by the Emperor of Brazil.

IN that black forest, where, when day is
　　done,
With a snake's stillness glides the Amazon
Darkly from sunset to the rising sun,

A cry, as of the pained heart of the wood,
The long, despairing moan of solitude
And darkness and the absence of all good,

Startles the traveller, with a sound so drear,
So full of hopeless agony and fear,
His heart stands still and listens like his
　　ear.

The guide, as if he heard a dead-bell toll,
Starts, drops his oar against the gunwale's
　　thole,
Crosses himself, and whispers, " A lost
　　soul ! "

" No, Señor, not a bird.   I know it well, —
It is the pained soul of some infidel
Or cursëd heretic that cries from hell.

" Poor fool ! with hope still mocking his
　　despair,
He wanders, shrieking on the midnight
　　air
For human pity and for Christian prayer.

" Saints strike him dumb !   Our Holy Mo-
　　ther hath
No prayer for him who, sinning unto death,
Burns always in the furnace of God's
　　wrath ! "

Thus to the baptized pagan's cruel lie,
Lending new horror to that mournful cry,
The voyager listens, making no reply.

Dim burns the boat-lamp ; shadows deepen
　　round,
From giant trees with snake-like creepers
　　wound,
And the black water glides without a sound.

But in the traveller's heart a secret sense
Of nature plastic to benign intents,
And an eternal good in Providence,

Lifts to the starry calm of heaven his
　　eyes ;
And lo ! rebuking all earth's ominous cries,
The Cross of pardon lights the tropic
　　skies !

" Father of all ! " he urges his strong plea,
" Thou lovest all : Thy erring child may
　　be
Lost to himself, but never lost to Thee ! "

" All souls are Thine ; the wings of morn-
ing bear
None from that Presence which is every-
where,
Nor hell itself can hide, for Thou art there.

"Through sins of sense, perversities of will,
Through doubt and pain, through guilt and
shame and ill,
Thy pitying eye is on Thy creature still.

" Wilt thou not make, Eternal Source and
Goal !
In Thy long years, life's broken circle whole,
And change to praise the cry of a lost soul? "

ANDREW RYKMAN'S PRAYER

ANDREW RYKMAN 's dead and gone ;
　You can see his leaning slate
In the graveyard, and thereon
　Read his name and date.

" *Trust is truer than our fears,*"
　Runs the legend through the moss,
" *Gain is not in added years,*
　Nor in death is loss."

Still the feet that thither trod,
　All the friendly eyes are dim ;
Only Nature, now, and God
　Have a care for him.

There the dews of quiet fall,
　Singing birds and soft winds stray.
Shall the tender Heart of all
　Be less kind than they ?

What he was and what he is
　They who ask may haply find,
If they read this prayer of his
　Which he left behind.

Pardon, Lord, the lips that dare
Shape in words a mortal's prayer !
Prayer, that, when my day is done,
And I see its setting sun,
Shorn and beamless, cold and dim,
Sink beneath the horizon's rim, —
When this ball of rock and clay
Crumbles from my feet away,
And the solid shores of sense

Melt into the vague immense,
Father ! I may come to Thee
Even with the beggar's plea,
As the poorest of Thy poor,
With my needs, and nothing more.

Not as one who seeks his home
With a step assured I come ;
Still behind the tread I hear
Of my life-companion, Fear ;
Still a shadow deep and vast
From my westering feet is cast,
Wavering, doubtful, undefined,
Never shapen nor outlined :
From myself the fear has grown,
And the shadow is my own.
Yet, O Lord, through all a sense
Of Thy tender providence
Stays my failing heart on Thee,
And confirms the feeble knee ;
And, at times, my worn feet press
Spaces of cool quietness,
Lilied whiteness shone upon
Not by light of moon or sun.
Hours there be of inmost calm,
Broken but by grateful psalm,
When I love Thee more than fear Thee,
And Thy blessed Christ seems near me,
With forgiving look, as when
He beheld the Magdalen.
Well I know that all things move
To the spheral rhythm of love, —
That to Thee, O Lord of all !
Nothing can of chance befall :
Child and seraph, mote and star,
Well Thou knowest what we are !
Through Thy vast creative plan
Looking, from the worm to man,
There is pity in Thine eyes,
But no hatred nor surprise.
Not in blind caprice of will,
Not in cunning sleight of skill,
Not for show of power, was wrought
Nature's marvel in Thy thought.
Never careless hand and vain
Smites these chords of joy and pain :
No immortal selfishness
Plays the game of curse and bless :
Heaven and earth are witnesses
That Thy glory goodness is.
Not for sport of mind and force
Hast Thou made Thy universe,
But as atmosphere and zone
Of Thy loving heart alone.
Man, who walketh in a show,

Sees before him, to and fro,
Shadow and illusion go ;
All things flow and fluctuate,
Now contract and now dilate.
In the welter of this sea,
Nothing stable is but Thee ;
In this whirl of swooning trance,
Thou alone art permanence ;
All without Thee only seems,
All beside is choice of dreams.
Never yet in darkest mood
Doubted I that Thou wast good,
Nor mistook my will for fate,
Pain of sin for heavenly hate, —
Never dreamed the gates of pearl
Rise from out the burning marl,
Or that good can only live
Of the bad conservative,
And through counterpoise of hell
Heaven alone be possible.

For myself alone I doubt ;
All is well, I know, without ;
I alone the beauty mar,
I alone the music jar.
Yet, with hands by evil stained,
And an ear by discord pained,
I am groping for the keys
Of the heavenly harmonies ;
Still within my heart I bear
Love for all things good and fair.
Hands of want or souls in pain
Have not sought my door in vain ;
I have kept my fealty good
To the human brotherhood ;
Scarcely have I asked in prayer
That which others might not share.
I, who hear with secret shame
Praise that paineth more than blame,
Rich alone in favors lent,
Virtuous by accident,
Doubtful where I fain would rest,
Frailest where I seem the best,
Only strong for lack of test, —
What am I, that I should press
Special pleas of selfishness,
Coolly mounting into heaven
On my neighbor unforgiven ?
Ne'er to me, howe'er disguised,
Comes a saint unrecognized ;
Never fails my heart to greet
Noble deed with warmer beat ;
Halt and maimed, I own not less
All the grace of holiness ;
Nor, through shame or self-distrust,

Less I love the pure and just.
Lord, forgive these words of mine :
What have I that is not Thine ?
Whatsoe'er I fain would boast
Needs Thy pitying pardon most.
Thou, O Elder Brother ! who
In Thy flesh our trial knew,
Thou, who hast been touched by these
Our most sad infirmities,
Thou alone the gulf canst span
In the dual heart of man,
And between the soul and sense
Reconcile all difference,
Change the dream of me and mine
For the truth of Thee and Thine,
And, through chaos, doubt, and strife,
Interfuse Thy calm of life.
Haply, thus by Thee renewed,
In Thy borrowed goodness good,
Some sweet morning yet in God's
Dim, æonian periods,
Joyful I shall wake to see
Those I love who rest in Thee
And to them in Thee allied,
Shall my soul be satisfied.

Scarcely Hope hath shaped for me
What the future life may be.
Other lips may well be bold ;
Like the publican of old,
I can only urge the plea,
"Lord, be merciful to me ! "
Nothing of desert I claim,
Unto me belongeth shame.
Not for me the crowns of gold,
Palms, and harpings manifold ;
Not for erring eye and feet
Jasper wall and golden street.
What thou wilt, O Father, give !
All is gain that I receive.
If my voice I may not raise
In the elders' song of praise,
If I may not, sin-defiled,
Claim my birthright as a child,
Suffer it that I to Thee
As an hired servant be ;
Let the lowliest task be mine,
Grateful, so the work be Thine ;
Let me find the humblest place
In the shadow of Thy grace :
Blest to me were any spot
Where temptation whispers not.
If there be some weaker one,
Give me strength to help him on ;
If a blinder soul there be,

Let me guide him nearer Thee.
Make my mortal dreams come true
With the work I fain would do ;
Clothe with life the weak intent,
Let me be the thing I meant ;
Let me find in Thy employ
Peace that dearer is than joy ;
Out of self to love be led
And to heaven acclimated,
Until all things sweet and good
Seem my natural habitude.

So we read the prayer of him
  Who, with John of Labadie,
Trod, of old, the oozy rim
  Of the Zuyder Zee.

Thus did Andrew Rykman pray.
  Are we wiser, better grown,
That we may not, in our day,
  Make his prayer our own ?

THE ANSWER

SPARE me, dread angel of reproof,
  And let the sunshine weave to-day
Its gold-threads in the warp and woof
  Of life so poor and gray.

Spare me awhile ; the flesh is weak.
  These lingering feet, that fain would stray
Among the flowers, shall some day seek
  The strait and narrow way.

Take off thy ever-watchful eye,
  The awe of thy rebuking frown ;
The dullest slave at times must sigh
  To fling his burdens down ;

To drop his galley's straining oar,
  And press, in summer warmth and calm,
The lap of some enchanted shore
  Of blossom and of balm.

Grudge not my life its hour of bloom,
  My heart its taste of long desire ;
This day be mine : be those to come
  As duty shall require.

The deep voice answered to my own,
  Smiting my selfish prayers away ;

"To-morrow is with God alone,
  And man hath but to-day.

"Say not, thy fond, vain heart within,
  The Father's arm shall still be wide,
When from these pleasant ways of sin
  Thou turn'st at eventide.

"'Cast thyself down,' the tempter saith,
  'And angels shall thy feet upbear.'
He bids thee make a lie of faith,
  And blasphemy of prayer.

"Though God be good and free be heaven,
  No force divine can love compel ;
And, though the song of sins forgiven
  May sound through lowest hell,

"The sweet persuasion of His voice
  Respects thy sanctity of will.
He giveth day : thou hast thy choice
  To walk in darkness still ;

"As one who, turning from the light,
  Watches his own gray shadow fall,
Doubting, upon his path of night,
  If there be day at all !

"No word of doom may shut thee out,
  No wind of wrath may downward whirl,
No swords of fire keep watch about
  The open gates of pearl ;

"A tenderer light than moon or sun,
  Than song of earth a sweeter hymn,
May shine and sound forever on,
  And thou be deaf and dim.

"Forever round the Mercy-seat
  The guiding lights of Love shall burn ;
But what if, habit-bound, thy feet
  Shall lack the will to turn ?

"What if thine eye refuse to see,
  Thine ear of Heaven's free welcome
    fail,
And thou a willing captive be,
  Thyself thy own dark jail ?

"Oh, doom beyond the saddest guess,
  As the long years of God unroll,
To make thy dreary selfishness
  The prison of a soul !

"To doubt the love that fain would break
  The fetters from thy self-bound limb ;
And dream that God can thee forsake
  As thou forsakest Him ! "

THE ETERNAL GOODNESS

O FRIENDS ! with whom my feet have trod
  The quiet aisles of prayer,
Glad witness to your zeal for God
  And love of man I bear.

I trace your lines of argument ;
  Your logic linked and strong
I weigh as one who dreads dissent,
  And fears a doubt as wrong.

But still my human hands are weak
  To hold your iron creeds :
Against the words ye bid me speak
  My heart within me pleads.

Who fathoms the Eternal Thought ?
  Who talks of scheme and plan ?
The Lord is God ! He needeth not
  The poor device of man.

I walk with bare, hushed feet the ground
  Ye tread with boldness shod ;
I dare not fix with mete and bound
  The love and power of God.

Ye praise His justice ; even such
  His pitying love I deem :
Ye seek a king ; I fain would touch
  The robe that hath no seam.

Ye see the curse which overbroods
  A world of pain and loss ;
I hear our Lord's beatitudes
  And prayer upon the cross.

More than your schoolmen teach, within
  Myself, alas ! I know :
Too dark ye cannot paint the sin,
  Too small the merit show.

I bow my forehead to the dust,
  I veil mine eyes for shame,
And urge, in trembling self-distrust,
  A prayer without a claim.

I see the wrong that round me lies,
  I feel the guilt within ;

I hear, with groan and travail-cries,
  The world confess its sin.

Yet, in the maddening maze of things,
  And tossed by storm and flood,
To one fixed trust my spirit clings ;
  I know that God is good !

Not mine to look where cherubim
  And seraphs may not see,
But nothing can be good in Him
  Which evil is in me.

The wrong that pains my soul below
  I dare not throne above,
I know not of His hate, — I know
  His goodness and His love.

I dimly guess from blessings known
  Of greater out of sight,
And, with the chastened Psalmist, own
  His judgments too are right.

I long for household voices gone,
  For vanished smiles I long,
But God hath led my dear ones on,
  And He can do no wrong.

I know not what the future hath
  Of marvel or surprise,
Assured alone that life and death
  His mercy underlies.

And if my heart and flesh are weak
  To bear an untried pain,
The bruisëd reed He will not break,
  But strengthen and sustain.

No offering of my own I have,
  Nor works my faith to prove ;
I can but give the gifts He gave,
  And plead His love for love.

And so beside the Silent Sea
  I wait the muffled oar ;
No harm from Him can come to me
  On ocean or on shore.

I know not where His islands lift
  Their fronded palms in air ;
I only know I cannot drift
  Beyond His love and care.

O brothers ! if my faith is vain,
  If hopes like these betray,

Pray for me that my feet may gain
  The sure and safer way.

And Thou, O Lord! by whom are seen
  Thy creatures as they be,
Forgive me if too close I lean
  My human heart on Thee!

THE COMMON QUESTION

BEHIND us at our evening meal
  The gray bird ate his fill,
Swung downward by a single claw,
  And wiped his hookëd bill.

He shook his wings and crimson tail,
  And set his head aslant,
And, in his sharp, impatient way,
  Asked, "What does Charlie want?"

"Fie, silly bird!" I answered, "tuck
  Your head beneath your wing,
And go to sleep;" — but o'er and o'er
  He asked the self-same thing.

Then, smiling, to myself I said:
  How like are men and birds!
We all are saying what he says,
  In action or in words.

The boy with whip and top and drum,
  The girl with hoop and doll,
And men with lands and houses, ask
  The question of Poor Poll.

However full, with something more
  We fain the bag would cram;
We sigh above our crowded nets
  For fish that never swam.

No bounty of indulgent Heaven
  The vague desire can stay;
Self-love is still a Tartar mill
  For grinding prayers alway.

The dear God hears and pities all;
  He knoweth all our wants;
And what we blindly ask of Him
  His love withholds or grants.

And so I sometimes think our prayers
  Might well be merged in one;
And nest and perch and hearth and church
  Repeat, "Thy will be done."

OUR MASTER

IMMORTAL Love, forever full,
  Forever flowing free,
Forever shared, forever whole,
  A never-ebbing sea!

Our outward lips confess the name
  All other names above;
Love only knoweth whence it came
  And comprehendeth love.

Blow, winds of God, awake and blow
  The mists of earth away!
Shine out, O Light Divine, and show
  How wide and far we stray!

Hush every lip, close every book,
  The strife of tongues forbear;
Why forward reach, or backward look,
  For love that clasps like air?

We may not climb the heavenly steeps
  To bring the Lord Christ down:
In vain we search the lowest deeps,
  For Him no depths can drown.

Nor holy bread, nor blood of grape,
  The lineaments restore
Of Him we know in outward shape
  And in the flesh no more.

He cometh not a king to reign;
  The world's long hope is dim;
The weary centuries watch in vain
  The clouds of heaven for Him.

Death comes, life goes; the asking eye
  And ear are answerless;
The grave is dumb, the hollow sky
  Is sad with silentness.

The letter fails, and systems fall,
  And every symbol wanes;
The Spirit over-brooding all
  Eternal Love remains.

And not for signs in heaven above
  Or earth below they look,
Who know with John His smile of love,
  With Peter His rebuke.

In joy of inward peace, or sense
  Of sorrow over sin,

He is His own best evidence,
  His witness is within.

No fable old, nor mythic lore,
  Nor dream of bards and seers,
No dead fact stranded on the shore
  Of the oblivious years ; —

But warm, sweet, tender, even yet
  A present help is He ;
And faith has still its Olivet,
  And love its Galilee.

The healing of His seamless dress
  Is by our beds of pain ;
We touch Him in life's throng and press,
  And we are whole again.

Through Him the first fond prayers are said
  Our lips of childhood frame,
The last low whispers of our dead
  Are burdened with His name.

Our Lord and Master of us all !
  Whate'er our name or sign,
We own Thy sway, we hear Thy call,
  We test our lives by Thine.

Thou judgest us ; Thy purity
  Doth all our lusts condemn ;
The love that draws us nearer Thee
  Is hot with wrath to them.

Our thoughts lie open to Thy sight ;
  And, naked to Thy glance,
Our secret sins are in the light
  Of Thy pure countenance.

Thy healing pains, a keen distress
  Thy tender light shines in ;
Thy sweetness is the bitterness,
  Thy grace the pang of sin.

Yet, weak and blinded though we be,
  Thou dost our service own ;
We bring our varying gifts to Thee,
  And Thou rejectest none.

To Thee our full humanity,
  Its joys and pains, belong ;
The wrong of man to man on Thee
  Inflicts a deeper wrong.

Who hates, hates Thee, who loves becomes
  Therein to Thee allied ;

All sweet accords of hearts and homes
  In Thee are multiplied.

Deep strike Thy roots, O heavenly Vine,
  Within our earthly sod,
Most human and yet most divine,
  The flower of man and God !

O Love ! O Life ! Our faith and sight
  Thy presence maketh one,
As through transfigured clouds of white
  We trace the noon-day sun.

So, to our mortal eyes subdued,
  Flesh-veiled, but not concealed,
We know in Thee the fatherhood
  And heart of God revealed.

We faintly hear, we dimly see,
  In differing phrase we pray ;
But, dim or clear, we own in Thee
  The Light, the Truth, the Way !

The homage that we render Thee
  Is still our Father's own ;
No jealous claim or rivalry
  Divides the Cross and Throne.

To do Thy will is more than praise,
  As words are less than deeds,
And simple trust can find Thy ways
  We miss with chart of creeds.

No pride of self Thy service hath,
  No place for me and mine ;
Our human strength is weakness, death
  Our life, apart from Thine.

Apart from Thee all gain is loss,
  All labor vainly done ;
The solemn shadow of Thy Cross
  Is better than the sun.

Alone, O Love ineffable !
  Thy saving name is given ;
To turn aside from Thee is hell,
  To walk with Thee is heaven !

How vain, secure in all Thou art,
  Our noisy championship !
The sighing of the contrite heart
  Is more than flattering lip.

Not Thine the bigot's partial plea,
  Nor Thine the zealot's ban ;

Thou well canst spare a love of Thee
Which ends in hate of man.

Our Friend, our Brother, and our Lord,
What may Thy service be? —
Nor name, nor form, nor ritual word,
But simply following Thee.

We bring no ghastly holocaust,
We pile no graven stone ;
He serves thee best who loveth most
His brothers and Thy own.

Thy litanies, sweet offices
Of love and gratitude ;
Thy sacramental liturgies
The joy of doing good.

In vain shall waves of incense drift
The vaulted nave around,
In vain the minster turret lift
Its brazen weights of sound.

The heart must ring Thy Christmas bells,
Thy inward altars raise ;
Its faith and hope Thy canticles,
And its obedience praise !

THE MEETING

The two speakers in the meeting referred
to in this poem were Avis Keene, whose very
presence was a benediction, a woman lovely in
spirit and person, whose words seemed a mes-
sage of love and tender concern to her hearers;
and Sibyl Jones, whose inspired eloquence and
rare spirituality impressed all who knew her.
In obedience to her apprehended duty she
made visits of Christian love to various parts
of Europe, and to the West Coast of Africa and
Palestine.

THE elder folks shook hands at last,
Down seat by seat the signal passed.
To simple ways like ours unused,
Half solemnized and half amused,
With long-drawn breath and shrug, my
    guest
His sense of glad relief expressed.
Outside, the hills lay warm in sun ;
The cattle in the meadow-run
Stood half-leg deep ; a single bird
The green repose above us stirred.
" What part or lot have you," he said,
" In these dull rites of drowsy-head ?

Is silence worship ?   Seek it where
It soothes with dreams the summer air,
Not in this close and rude-benched hall,
But where soft lights and shadows fall,
And all the slow, sleep-walking hours
Glide soundless over grass and flowers !
From time and place and form apart,
Its holy ground the human heart,
Nor ritual-bound nor templeward
Walks the free spirit of the Lord !
Our common Master did not pen
His followers up from other men ;
His service liberty indeed,
He built no church, He framed no creed ;
But while the saintly Pharisee
Made broader his phylactery,
As from the synagogue was seen
The dusty-sandalled Nazarene
Through ripening cornfields lead the way
Upon the awful Sabbath day,
His sermons were the healthful talk
That shorter made the mountain-walk,
His wayside texts were flowers and birds,
Where mingled with His gracious words
The rustle of the tamarisk-tree
And ripple-wash of Galilee."

" Thy words are well, O friend," I said ;
" Unmeasured and unlimited,
With noiseless slide of stone to stone,
The mystic Church of God has grown.
Invisible and silent stands
The temple never made with hands,
Unheard the voices still and small
Of its unseen confessional.
He needs no special place of prayer
Whose hearing ear is everywhere ;
He brings not back the childish days
That ringed the earth with stones of praise,
Roofed Karnak's hall of gods, and laid
The plinths of Philæ's colonnade.
Still less He owns the selfish good
And sickly growth of solitude, —
The worthless grace that, out of sight,
Flowers in the desert anchorite ;
Dissevered from the suffering whole,
Love hath no power to save a soul.
Not out of Self, the origin
And native air and soil of sin,
The living waters spring and flow,
The trees with leaves of healing grow.

" Dream not, O friend, because I seek
This quiet shelter twice a week,
I better deem its pine-laid floor

Than breezy hill or sea-sung shore ;
But nature is not solitude :
She crowds us with her thronging wood ;
Her many hands reach out to us,
Her many tongues are garrulous ;
Perpetual riddles of surprise
She offers to our ears and eyes ;
She will not leave our senses still,
But drags them captive at her will :
And, making earth too great for heaven,
She hides the Giver in the given.

" And so I find it well to come
For deeper rest to this still room,
For here the habit of the soul
Feels less the outer world's control ;
The strength of mutual purpose pleads
More earnestly our common needs ;
And from the silence multiplied
By these still forms on either side,
The world that time and sense have known
Falls off and leaves us God alone.

" Yet rarely through the charmed repose
Unmixed the stream of motive flows,
A flavor of its many springs,
The tints of earth and sky it brings ;
In the still waters needs must be
Some shade of human sympathy ;
And here, in its accustomed place,
I look on memory's dearest face ;
The blind by-sitter guesseth not
What shadow haunts that vacant spot ;
No eyes save mine alone can see
The love wherewith it welcomes me !
And still, with those alone my kin,
In doubt and weakness, want and sin,
I bow my head, my heart I bare,
As when that face was living there,
And strive (too oft, alas ! in vain)
The peace of simple trust to gain,
Fold fancy's restless wings, and lay
The idols of my heart away.

" Welcome the silence all unbroken,
Nor less the words of fitness spoken, —
Such golden words as hers for whom
Our autumn flowers have just made room ;
Whose hopeful utterance through and
        through
The freshness of the morning blew ;
Who loved not less the earth that light
Fell on it from the heavens in sight,
But saw in all fair forms more fair
The Eternal beauty mirrored there.

Whose eighty years but added grace
And saintlier meaning to her face, —
The look of one who bore away
Glad tidings from the hills of day,
While all our hearts went forth to meet
The coming of her beautiful feet !
Or haply hers, whose pilgrim tread
Is in the paths where Jesus led ;
Who dreams her childhood's sabbath
        dream
By Jordan's willow-shaded stream,
And, of the hymns of hope and faith,
Sung by the monks of Nazareth,
Hears pious echoes, in the call
To prayer, from Moslem minarets fall,
Repeating where His works were wrought
The lesson that her Master taught,
Of whom an elder Sibyl gave,
The prophecies of Cumæ's cave !

" I ask no organ's soulless breath
To drone the themes of life and death,
No altar candle-lit by day,
No ornate wordsman's rhetoric-play,
No cool philosophy to teach
Its bland audacities of speech
To double-tasked idolaters
Themselves their gods and worshippers,
No pulpit hammered by the fist
Of loud-asserting dogmatist,
Who borrows for the Hand of love
The smoking thunderbolts of Jove.
I know how well the fathers taught,
What work the later schoolmen wrought ;
I reverence old-time faith and men,
But God is near us now as then ;
His force of love is still unspent,
His hate of sin as imminent ;
And still the measure of our needs
Outgrows the cramping bounds of creeds ;
The manna gathered yesterday
Already savors of decay ;
Doubts to the world's child-heart unknown
Question us now from star and stone ;
Too little or too much we know,
And sight is swift and faith is slow ;
The power is lost to self-deceive
With shallow forms of make-believe.
We walk at high noon, and the bells
Call to a thousand oracles,
But the sound deafens, and the light
Is stronger than our dazzled sight ;
The letters of the sacred Book
Glimmer and swim beneath our look ;
Still struggles in the Age's breast

With deepening agony of quest
The old entreaty : ' Art thou He,
Or look we for the Christ to be ? '

" God should be most where man is least :
So, where is neither church nor priest,
And never rag of form or creed
To clothe the nakedness of need, —
Where farmer-folk in silence meet, —
I turn my bell-unsummoned feet ;
I lay the critic's glass aside,
I tread upon my lettered pride,
And, lowest-seated, testify
To the oneness of humanity ;
Confess the universal want,
And share whatever Heaven may grant.
He findeth not who seeks his own,
The soul is lost that 's saved alone.
Not on one favored forehead fell
Of old the fire-tongued miracle,
But flamed o'er all the thronging host
The baptism of the Holy Ghost ;
Heart answers heart : in one desire
The blending lines of prayer aspire ;
' Where, in my name, meet two or three,
Our Lord hath said, ' I there will be ! '

" So sometimes comes to soul and sense
The feeling which is evidence
That very near about us lies
The realm of spiritual mysteries.
The sphere of the supernal powers
Impinges on this world of ours.
The low and dark horizon lifts,
To light the scenic terror shifts ;
The breath of a diviner air
Blows down the answer of a prayer :
That all our sorrow, pain, and doubt
A great compassion clasps about,
And law and goodness, love and force,
Are wedded fast beyond divorce.
Then duty leaves to love its task,
The beggar Self forgets to ask ;
With smile of trust and folded hands,
The passive soul in waiting stands
To feel, as flowers the sun and dew,
The One true Life its own renew.

" So to the calmly gathered thought
The innermost of truth is taught,
The mystery dimly understood,
That love of God is love of good,
And, chiefly, its divinest trace
In Him of Nazareth's holy face ;

That to be saved is only this, —
Salvation from our selfishness,
From more than elemental fire,
The soul's unsanctified desire,
From sin itself, and not the pain
That warns us of its chafing chain ;
That worship's deeper meaning lies
In mercy, and not sacrifice,
Not proud humilities of sense
And posturing of penitence,
But love's unforced obedience ;
That Book and Church and Day are given
For man, not God, — for earth, not
    heaven, —
The blessed means to holiest ends,
Not masters, but benignant friends ;
That the dear Christ dwells not afar,
The king of some remoter star,
Listening, at times, with flattered ear
To homage wrung from selfish fear,
But here, amidst the poor and blind,
The bound and suffering of our kind,
In works we do, in prayers we pray,
Life of our life, He lives to-day."

THE CLEAR VISION

I DID but dream.   I never knew
    What charms our sternest season wore.
Was never yet the sky so blue,
    Was never earth so white before.
Till now I never saw the glow
Of sunset on yon hills of snow,
And never learned the bough's designs
Of beauty in its leafless lines.

Did ever such a morning break
    As that my eastern windows see ?
Did ever such a moonlight take
    Weird photographs of shrub and tree ?
Rang ever bells so wild and fleet
The music of the winter street ?
Was ever yet a sound by half
So merry as yon school-boy's laugh ?

O Earth ! with gladness overfraught,
    No added charm thy face hath found ;
Within my heart the change is wrought,
    My footsteps make enchanted ground.
From couch of pain and curtained room
Forth to thy light and air I come,
To find in all that meets my eyes
The freshness of a glad surprise.

Fair seem these winter days, and soon
　Shall blow the warm west-winds of spring,
To set the unbound rills in tune
　And hither urge the bluebird's wing.
The vales shall laugh in flowers, the woods
Grow misty green with leafing buds,
And violets and wind-flowers sway
Against the throbbing heart of May.

Break forth, my lips, in praise, and own
　The wiser love severely kind ;
Since, richer for its chastening grown,
　I see, whereas I once was blind.
The world, O Father ! hath not wronged
With loss the life by Thee prolonged ;
But still, with every added year,
More beautiful Thy works appear !

As Thou hast made thy world without,
　Make Thou more fair my world within ;
Shine through its lingering clouds of doubt ;
　Rebuke its haunting shapes of sin ;
Fill, brief or long, my granted span
Of life with love to thee and man ;
Strike when thou wilt the hour of rest,
But let my last days be my best !

DIVINE COMPASSION

Long since, a dream of heaven I had,
　And still the vision haunts me oft ;
I see the saints in white robes clad,
　The martyrs with their palms aloft ;
But hearing still, in middle song,
　The ceaseless dissonance of wrong ;
And shrinking, with hid faces, from the
　　strain
Of sad, beseeching eyes, full of remorse
　and pain.

The glad song falters to a wail,
　The harping sinks to low lament ;
Before the still unlifted veil
　I see the crownèd foreheads bent,
Making more sweet the heavenly air
　With breathings of unselfish prayer ;
And a Voice saith : " O Pity which is pain,
O Love that weeps, fill up my sufferings
　　which remain !

" Shall souls redeemed by me refuse
　To share my sorrow in their turn ?
Or, sin-forgiven, my gift abuse
　Of peace with selfish unconcern ?

Has saintly ease no pitying care ?
　Has faith no work, and love no prayer ?
While sin remains, and souls in darkness
　　dwell,
Can heaven itself be heaven, and look un-
　moved on hell ? "

Then through the Gates of Pain, I dream,
　A wind of heaven blows coolly in ;
Fainter the awful discords seem,
　The smoke of torment grows more thin,
Tears quench the burning soil, and thence
　Spring sweet, pale flowers of penitence :
And through the dreary realm of man's de
　　spair,
Star-crowned an angel walks, and lo ! God's
　hope is there !

Is it a dream ?　Is heaven so high
　That pity cannot breathe its air ?
Its happy eyes forever dry,
　Its holy lips without a prayer !
My God ! my God ! if thither led
　By Thy free grace unmerited,
No crown nor palm be mine, but let me
　keep
A heart that still can feel, and eyes that still
　can weep.

THE PRAYER-SEEKER

Along the aisle where prayer was made,
A woman, all in black arrayed,
Close-veiled, between the kneeling host,
With gliding motion of a ghost,
Passed to the desk, and laid thereon
A scroll which bore these words alone,
　Pray for me !

Back from the place of worshipping
She glided like a guilty thing :
The rustle of her draperies, stirred
By hurrying feet, alone was heard ;
While, full of awe, the preacher read,
As out into the dark she sped :
　Pray for me !

Back to the night from whence she came,
To unimagined grief or shame !
Across the threshold of that door
None knew the burden that she bore ;
Alone she left the written scroll,
The legend of a troubled soul, —
　Pray for me !

Glide on, poor ghost of woe or sin !
Thou leav'st a common need within ;
Each bears, like thee, some nameless weight,
Some misery inarticulate,
Some secret sin, some shrouded dread,
Some household sorrow all unsaid.
        Pray for us !

Pass on ! The type of all thou art,
Sad witness to the common heart !
With face in veil and seal on lip,
In mute and strange companionship,
Like thee we wander to and fro,
Dumbly imploring as we go :
        Pray for us !

Ah, who shall pray, since he who pleads
Our want perchance hath greater needs ?
Yet they who make their loss the gain
Of others shall not ask in vain,
And Heaven bends low to hear the prayer
Of love from lips of self-despair :
        Pray for us !

In vain remorse and fear and hate
Beat with bruised hands against a fate
Whose walls of iron only move
And open to the touch of love.
He only feels his burdens fall
Who, taught by suffering, pities all.
        Pray for us !

He prayeth best who leaves unguessed
The mystery of another's breast.
Why cheeks grow pale, why eyes o'erflow,
Or heads are white, thou need'st not know.
Enough to note by many a sign
That every heart hath needs like thine.
        Pray for us !

THE BREWING OF SOMA

" These libations mixed with milk have been prepared
for Indra : offer Soma to the drinker of Soma." — *Va-
shista*, translated by MAX MÜLLER.

THE fagots blazed, the caldron's smoke
  Up through the green wood curled ;
" Bring honey from the hollow oak,
Bring milky sap," the brewers spoke,
  In the childhood of the world.

And brewed they well or brewed they ill,
  The priests thrust in their rods,
First tasted, and then drank their fill,

And shouted, with one voice and will,
  " Behold the drink of gods ! "

They drank, and lo ! in heart and brain
  A new, glad life began ;
The gray of hair grew young again,
The sick man laughed away his pain,
  The cripple leaped and ran.

" Drink, mortals, what the gods have sent,
  Forget your long annoy."
So sang the priests.   From tent to tent
The Soma's sacred madness went,
  A storm of drunken joy.

Then knew each rapt inebriate
  A winged and glorious birth,
Soared upward, with strange joy elate,
Beat, with dazed head, Varuna's gate,
  And, sobered, sank to earth.

The land with Soma's praises rang ;
  On Gihon's banks of shade
Its hymns the dusky maidens sang ;
In joy of life or mortal pang
  All men to Soma prayed.

The morning twilight of the race
  Sends down these matin psalms ;
And still with wondering eyes we trace
The simple prayers to Soma's grace,
  That Vedic verse embalms.

As in that child-world's early year,
  Each after age has striven
By music, incense, vigils drear,
And trance, to bring the skies more near,
  Or lift men up to heaven !

Some fever of the blood and brain,
  Some self-exalting spell,
The scourger's keen delight of pain,
The Dervish dance, the Orphic strain,
  The wild-haired Bacchant's yell, —

The desert's hair-grown hermit sunk
  The saner brute below ;
The naked Santon, hashish-drunk,
The cloister madness of the monk,
  The fakir's torture-show !

And yet the past comes round again,
  And new doth old fulfil ;
In sensual transports wild as vain

We brew in many a Christian fane
  The heathen Soma still !

Dear Lord and Father of mankind,
  Forgive our foolish ways !
Reclothe us in our rightful mind,
In purer lives Thy service find,
  In deeper reverence, praise.

In simple trust like theirs who heard
  Beside the Syrian sea
The gracious calling of the Lord,
Let us, like them, without a word,
  Rise up and follow Thee.

O Sabbath rest by Galilee !
  O calm of hills above,
Where Jesus knelt to share with Thee
The silence of eternity
  Interpreted by love !

With that deep hush subduing all
  Our words and works that drown
The tender whisper of Thy call,
As noiseless let Thy blessing fall
  As fell Thy manna down.

Drop Thy still dews of quietness,
  Till all our strivings cease ;
Take from our souls the strain and stress,
And let our ordered lives confess
  The beauty of Thy peace.

Breathe through the heats of our desire
  Thy coolness and Thy balm ;
Let sense be dumb, let flesh retire ;
Speak through the earthquake, wind, and
    fire,
  O still, small voice of calm !

A WOMAN

Oh, dwarfed and wronged, and stained with
  ill,
Behold ! thou art a woman still !
And, by that sacred name and dear,
I bid thy better self appear.
Still, through thy foul disguise, I see
  The rudimental purity,
That, spite of change and loss, makes good
Thy birthright-claim of womanhood ;
An inward loathing, deep, intense ;
A shame that is half innocence.
Cast off the grave-clothes of thy sin !

Rise from the dust thou liest in,
As Mary rose at Jesus' word,
Redeemed and white before the Lord !
Reclaim thy lost soul ! In His name,
Rise up, and break thy bonds of shame.
Art weak ? He 's strong. Art fearful ?
  Hear
The world's O'ercomer : " Be of cheer ! "
What lip shall judge when He approves ?
Who dare to scorn the child He loves ?

THE PRAYER OF AGASSIZ

  The island of Penikese in Buzzard's Bay was
given by Mr. John Anderson to Agassiz for
the uses of a summer school of natural history.
A large barn was cleared and improvised as a
lecture-room. Here, on the first morning of
the school, all the company was gathered.
" Agassiz had arranged no programme of ex-
ercises," says Mrs. Agassiz, in *Louis Agassiz;
his Life and Correspondence*, " trusting to the
interest of the occasion to suggest what might
best be said or done. But, as he looked upon
his pupils gathered there to study nature with
him, by an impulse as natural as it was un-
premeditated, he called upon them to join in
silently asking God's blessing on their work
together. The pause was broken by the first
words of an address no less fervent than its un-
spoken prelude." This was in the summer of
1873, and Agassiz died the December following.

On the isle of Penikese,
Ringed about by sapphire seas,
Fanned by breezes salt and cool,
Stood the Master with his school.
Over sails that not in vain
Wooed the west-wind's steady strain,
Line of coast that low and far
Stretched its undulating bar,
Wings aslant across the rim
Of the waves they stooped to skim,
Rock and isle and glistening bay,
Fell the beautiful white day.

Said the Master to the youth :
" We have come in search of truth,
Trying with uncertain key
Door by door of mystery ;
We are reaching, through His laws,
To the garment-hem of Cause,
Him, the endless, unbegun,
The Unnamable, the One
Light of all our light the Source,
Life of life, and Force of force.

As with fingers of the blind,
We are groping here to find
What the hieroglyphics mean
Of the Unseen in the seen,
What the Thought which underlies
Nature's masking and disguise,
What it is that hides beneath
Blight and bloom and birth and death.
By past efforts unavailing,
Doubt and error, loss and failing,
Of our weakness made aware,
On the threshold of our task
Let us light and guidance ask,
Let us pause in silent prayer ! "

Then the Master in his place
Bowed his head a little space,
And the leaves by soft airs stirred,
Lapse of wave and cry of bird,
Left the solemn hush unbroken
Of that wordless prayer unspoken,
While its wish, on earth unsaid,
Rose to heaven interpreted.
As, in life's best hours, we hear
By the spirit's finer ear
His low voice within us, thus
The All-Father heareth us ;
And His holy ear we pain
With our noisy words and vain.
Not for Him our violence
Storming at the gates of sense,
His the primal language, His
The eternal silences !

Even the careless heart was moved,
And the doubting gave assent,
With a gesture reverent,
To the Master well-beloved.
As thin mists are glorified
By the light they cannot hide,
All who gazed upon him saw,
Through its veil of tender awe,
How his face was still uplit
By the old sweet look of it,
Hopeful, trustful, full of cheer,
And the love that casts out fear.
Who the secret may declare
Of that brief, unuttered prayer ?
Did the shade before him come
Of th' inevitable doom,
Of the end of earth so near,
And Eternity's new year ?

In the lap of sheltering seas
Rests the isle of Penikese ;

But the lord of the domain
Comes not to his own again :
Where the eyes that follow fail,
On a vaster sea his sail
Drifts beyond our beck and hail.
Other lips within its bound
Shall the laws of life expound ;
Other eyes from rock and shell
Read the world's old riddles well :
But when breezes light and bland
Blow from Summer's blossomed land,
When the air is glad with wings,
And the blithe song-sparrow sings,
Many an eye with his still face
Shall the living ones displace,
Many an ear the word shall seek
He alone could fitly speak.
And one name forevermore
Shall be uttered o'er and o'er
By the waves that kiss the shore,
By the curlew's whistle sent
Down the cool, sea-scented air ;
In all voices known to her,
Nature owns her worshipper,
Half in triumph, half lament.
Thither Love shall tearful turn,
Friendship pause uncovered there,
And the wisest reverence learn
From the Master's silent prayer.

IN QUEST

HAVE I not voyaged, friend beloved, with
thee
On the great waters of the unsounded sea,
Momently listening with suspended oar
For the low rote of waves upon a shore
Changeless as heaven, where never fog-
cloud drifts
Over its windless wood, nor mirage lifts
The steadfast hills ; where never birds of
doubt
Sing to mislead, and every dream dies out,
And the dark riddles which perplex us
here
In the sharp solvent of its light are clear ?
Thou knowest how vain our quest ; how,
soon or late,
The baffling tides and circles of debate
Swept back our bark unto its starting-
place,
Where, looking forth upon the blank, gray
space,
And round about us seeing, with sad eyes,

The same old difficult hills and cloud-cold
    skies,
We said : " This outward search availeth
    not
To find Him. He is farther than we
    thought,
Or, haply, nearer. To this very spot
Whereon we wait, this commonplace of
    home,
As to the well of Jacob, He may come
And tell us all things." As I listened
    there,
Through the expectant silences of prayer,
Somewhat I seemed to hear, which hath to
    me
Been hope, strength, comfort, and I give it
    thee.

" The riddle of the world is understood
Only by him who feels that God is good,
As only he can feel who makes his love
The ladder of his faith, and climbs above
On th' rounds of his best instincts ; draws
    no line
Between mere human goodness and divine,
But, judging God by what in him is best,
With a child's trust leans on a Father's
    breast,
And hears unmoved the old creeds babble
    still
Of kingly power and dread caprice of will,
Chary of blessing, prodigal of curse,
The pitiless doomsman of the universe.
Can Hatred ask for love ? Can Selfishness
Invite to self-denial ? Is He less
Than man in kindly dealing ? Can He
    break
His own great law of fatherhood, forsake
And curse His children ? Not for earth
    and heaven
Can separate tables of the law be given.
No rule can bind which He himself denies ;
The truths of time are not eternal lies."

So heard I ; and the chaos round me spread
To light and order grew ; and, " Lord," I
    said,
" Our sins are our tormentors, worst of all
Felt in distrustful shame that dares not call
Upon Thee as our Father. We have set
A strange god up, but Thou remainest yet.
All that I feel of pity Thou hast known
Before I was ; my best is all Thy own.
From Thy great heart of goodness mine but
    drew

Wishes and prayers ; but Thou, O Lord,
    wilt do,
In Thy own time, by ways I cannot see,
All that I feel when I am nearest Thee ! "

THE FRIEND'S BURIAL

MY thoughts are all in yonder town,
    Where, wept by many tears,
To-day my mother's friend lays down
    The burden of her years.

True as in life, no poor disguise
    Of death with her is seen,
And on her simple casket lies
    No wreath of bloom and green.

Oh, not for her the florist's art,
    The mocking weeds of woe ;
Dear memories in each mourner's heart
    Like heaven's white lilies blow.

And all about the softening air
    Of new-born sweetness tells,
And the ungathered May-flowers wear
    The tints of ocean shells.

The old, assuring miracle
    Is fresh as heretofore ;
And earth takes up its parable
    Of life from death once more.

Here organ-swell and church-bell toll
    Methinks but discord were ;
The prayerful silence of the soul
    Is best befitting her.

No sound should break the quietude
    Alike of earth and sky ;
O wandering wind in Seabrook wood,
    Breathe but a half-heard sigh !

Sing softly, spring-bird, for her sake ;
    And thou not distant sea,
Lapse lightly as if Jesus spake,
    And thou wert Galilee !

For all her quiet life flowed on
    As meadow streamlets flow,
Where fresher green reveals alone
    The noiseless ways they go.

From her loved place of prayer I see
    The plain-robed mourners pass,

With slow feet treading reverently
The graveyard's springing grass.

Make room, O mourning ones, for me,
Where, like the friends of Paul,
That you no more her face shall see
You sorrow most of all.

Her path shall brighten more and more
Unto the perfect day ;
She cannot fail of peace who bore
Such peace with her away.

O sweet, calm face that seemed to wear
The look of sins forgiven !
O voice of prayer that seemed to bear
Our own needs up to heaven !

How reverent in our midst she stood,
Or knelt in grateful praise !
What grace of Christian womanhood
Was in her household ways !

For still her holy living meant
No duty left undone ;
The heavenly and the human blent
Their kindred loves in one.

And if her life small leisure found
For feasting ear and eye,
And Pleasure, on her daily round,
She passed unpausing by,

Yet with her went a secret sense
Of all things sweet and fair,
And Beauty's gracious providence
Refreshed her unaware.

She kept her line of rectitude
With love's unconscious ease ;
Her kindly instincts understood
All gentle courtesies.

An inborn charm of graciousness
Made sweet her smile and tone,
And glorified her farm-wife dress
With beauty not its own.

The dear Lord's best interpreters
Are humble human souls ;
The Gospel of a life like hers
Is more than books or scrolls.

From scheme and creed the light goes out,
The saintly fact survives ;

The blessed Master none can doubt
Revealed in holy lives.

A CHRISTMAS CARMEN

I

SOUND over all waters, reach out from all
lands,
The chorus of voices, the clasping of hands ;
Sing hymns that were sung by the stars of
the morn,
Sing songs of the angels when Jesus was
born !
With glad jubilations
Bring hope to the nations !
The dark night is ending and dawn has be-
gun :
Rise, hope of the ages, arise like the sun,
All speech flow to music, all hearts beat
as one !

II

Sing the bridal of nations ! with chorals of
love
Sing out the war-vulture and sing in the
dove,
Till the hearts of the peoples keep time in
accord,
And the voice of the world is the voice of
the Lord !
Clasp hands of the nations
In strong gratulations :
The dark night is ending and dawn has be-
gun ;
Rise, hope of the ages, arise like the sun,
All speech flow to music, all hearts beat
as one !

III

Blow, bugles of battle, the marches of
peace ;
East, west, north, and south let the long
quarrel cease :
Sing the song of great joy that the angels
began,
Sing of glory to God and of good-will to
man !
Hark ! joining in chorus
The heavens bend o'er us !
The dark night is ending and dawn has be-
gun ;
Rise, hope of the ages, arise like the sun,
All speech flow to music, all hearts beat
as one !

VESTA

O CHRIST of God ! whose life and death
  Our own have reconciled,
Most quietly, most tenderly
  Take home Thy star-named child !

Thy grace is in her patient eyes,
  Thy words are on her tongue ;
The very silence round her seems
  As if the angels sung.

Her smile is as a listening child's
  Who hears its mother call ;
The lilies of Thy perfect peace
  About her pillow fall.

She leans from out our clinging arms
  To rest herself in Thine ;
Alone to Thee, dear Lord, can we
  Our well-beloved resign !

Oh, less for her than for ourselves
  We bow our heads and pray ;
Her setting star, like Bethlehem's,
  To Thee shall point the way !

CHILD–SONGS

STILL linger in our noon of time
  And on our Saxon tongue
The echoes of the home-born hymns
  The Aryan mothers sung.

And childhood had its litanies
  In every age and clime ;
The earliest cradles of the race
  Were rocked to poet's rhyme.

Nor sky, nor wave, nor tree, nor flower,
  Nor green earth's virgin sod,
So moved the singer's heart of old
  As these small ones of God.

The mystery of unfolding life
  Was more than dawning morn,
Than opening flower or crescent moon
  The human soul new-born !

And still to childhood's sweet appeal
  The heart of genius turns,
And more than all the sages teach
  From lisping voices learns, —

The voices loved of him who sang,
  Where Tweed and Teviot glide,
That sound to-day on all the winds
  That blow from Rydal-side, —

Heard in the Teuton's household songs,
  And folk-lore of the Finn,
Where'er to holy Christmas hearths
  The Christ-child enters in !

Before life's sweetest mystery still
  The heart in reverence kneels ;
The wonder of the primal birth
  The latest mother feels.

We need love's tender lessons taught
  As only weakness can ;
God hath His small interpreters ;
  The child must teach the man.

We wander wide through evil years,
  Our eyes of faith grow dim ;
But he is freshest from His hands
  And nearest unto Him !

And haply, pleading long with Him
  For sin-sick hearts and cold,
The angels of our childhood still
  The Father's face behold.

Of such the kingdom ! — Teach Thou us,
  O Master most divine,
To feel the deep significance
  Of these wise words of Thine !

The haughty eye shall seek in vain
  What innocence beholds ;
No cunning finds the key of heaven,
  No strength its gate unfolds.

Alone to guilelessness and love
  That gate shall open fall ;
The mind of pride is nothingness,
  The childlike heart is all !

THE HEALER

TO A YOUNG PHYSICIAN, WITH DORÉ'S
PICTURE OF CHRIST HEALING THE SICK

So stood of old the holy Christ
  Amidst the suffering throng ;
With whom His lightest touch sufficed
  To make the weakest strong.

That healing gift He lends to them
  Who use it in His name ;
The power that filled His garment's hem
  Is evermore the same.

For lo ! in human hearts unseen
  The Healer dwelleth still,
And they who make His temples clean
  The best subserve His will.

The holiest task by Heaven decreed,
  An errand all divine,
The burden of our common need
  To render less is thine.

The paths of pain are thine. Go forth
  With patience, trust, and hope ;
The sufferings of a sin-sick earth
  Shall give thee ample scope.

Beside the unveiled mysteries
  Of life and death go stand,
With guarded lips and reverent eyes
  And pure of heart and hand.

So shalt thou be with power endued
  From Him who went about
The Syrian hillsides doing good,
  And casting demons out.

That Good Physician liveth yet
  Thy friend and guide to be ;
The Healer by Gennesaret
  Shall walk the rounds with thee.

THE TWO ANGELS

God called the nearest angels who dwell
    with Him above :
The tenderest one was Pity, the dearest
    one was Love.

"Arise," He said, "my angels ! a wail of
    woe and sin
Steals through the gates of heaven, and
    saddens all within.

"My harps take up the mournful strain
    that from a lost world swells,
The smoke of torment clouds the light and
    blights the asphodels.

"Fly downward to that under world, and
    on its souls of pain

Let Love drop smiles like sunshine, and
    Pity tears like rain !"

Two faces bowed before the Throne, veiled
    in their golden hair ;
Four white wings lessened swiftly down
    the dark abyss of air.

The way was strange, the flight was long ;
    at last the angels came
Where swung the lost and nether world,
    red-wrapped in rayless flame.

There Pity, shuddering, wept ; but Love,
    with faith too strong for fear,
Took heart from God's almightiness and
    smiled a smile of cheer.

And lo ! that tear of Pity quenched the
    flame whereon it fell,
And, with the sunshine of that smile, hope
    entered into hell !

Two unveiled faces full of joy looked up-
    ward to the Throne,
Four white wings folded at the feet of Him
    who sat thereon !

And deeper than the sound of seas, more
    soft than falling flake,
Amidst the hush of wing and song the
    Voice Eternal spake :

"Welcome, my angels ! ye have brought a
    holier joy to heaven ;
Henceforth its sweetest song shall be the
    song of sin forgiven !"

OVERRULED

The threads our hands in blindness spin
No self-determined plan weaves in ;
The shuttle of the unseen powers
Works out a pattern not as ours.

Ah ! small the choice of him who sings
What sound shall leave the smitten strings ;
Fate holds and guides the hand of art ;
The singer's is the servant's part.

The wind-harp chooses not the tone
That through its trembling threads is
    blown ;
The patient organ cannot guess
What hand its passive keys shall press.

Through wish, resolve, and act, our will
Is moved by undreamed forces still ;
And no man measures in advance
His strength with untried circumstance.

As streams take hue from shade and sun,
As runs the life the song must run ;
But, glad or sad, to His good end
God grant the varying notes may tend !

HYMN OF THE DUNKERS

KLOSTER KEDAR, EPHRATA, PENNSYL-
VANIA (1738)

SISTER MARIA CHRISTINA *sings.*

WAKE, sisters, wake ! the day-star shines ;
Above Ephrata's eastern pines
The dawn is breaking, cool and calm.
Wake, sisters, wake to prayer and psalm !

Praised be the Lord for shade and light,
For toil by day, for rest by night !
Praised be His name who deigns to bless
Our Kedar of the wilderness !

Our refuge when the spoiler's hand
Was heavy on our native land ;
And freedom, to her children due,
The wolf and vulture only knew.

We praised Him when to prison led,
We owned Him when the stake blazed red ;
We knew, whatever might befall,
His love and power were over all.

He heard our prayers ; with outstretched
arm
He led us forth from cruel harm ;
Still, wheresoe'er our steps were bent,
His cloud and fire before us went !

The watch of faith and prayer He set,
We kept it then, we keep it yet.
At midnight, crow of cock, or noon,
He cometh sure, He cometh soon.

He comes to chasten, not destroy,
To purge the earth from sin's alloy.
At last, at last shall all confess
His mercy as His righteousness.

The dead shall live, the sick be whole,
The scarlet sin be white as wool ;

No discord mar below, above,
The music of eternal love !

Sound, welcome trump, the last alarm !
Lord God of hosts, make bare thine arm,
Fulfil this day our long desire,
Make sweet and clean the world with fire !

Sweep, flaming besom, sweep from sight
The lies of time ; be swift to smite,
Sharp sword of God, all idols down,
Genevan creed and Roman crown.

Quake, earth, through all thy zones, till
all
The fanes of pride and priestcraft fall
And lift thou up in place of them
Thy gates of pearl, Jerusalem !

Lo ! rising from baptismal flame,
Transfigured, glorious, yet the same,
Within the heavenly city's bound
Our Kloster Kedar shall be found.

He cometh soon ! at dawn or noon
Or set of sun, He cometh soon.
Our prayers shall meet Him on His way ;
Wake, sisters, wake ! arise and pray !

GIVING AND TAKING

I have attempted to put in English verse a
prose translation of a poem by Tinnevaluva, a
Hindoo poet of the third century of our era.

WHO gives and hides the giving hand,
Nor counts on favor, fame, or praise,
Shall find his smallest gift outweighs
The burden of the sea and land.

Who gives to whom hath naught been given,
His gift in need, though small indeed
As is the grass-blade's wind-blown seed,
Is large as earth and rich as heaven.

Forget it not, O man, to whom
A gift shall fall, while yet on earth ;
Yea, even to thy seven-fold birth
Recall it in the lives to come.

Who broods above a wrong in thought
Sins much ; but greater sin is his
Who, fed and clothed with kindnesses,
Shall count the holy alms as naught.

Who dares to curse the hands that bless
  Shall know of sin the deadliest cost ;
The patience of the heavens is lost
Beholding man's unthankfulness.

For he who breaks all laws may still
  In Sivam's mercy be forgiven ;
But none can save, in earth or heaven,
The wretch who answers good with ill.

THE VISION OF ECHARD

THE Benedictine Echard
  Sat by the wayside well,
Where Marsberg sees the bridal
  Of the Sarre and the Moselle.

Fair with its sloping vineyards
  And tawny chestnut bloom,
The happy vale Ausonius sung
  For holy Treves made room.

On the shrine Helena builded
  To keep the Christ coat well,
On minster tower and kloster cross,
  The westering sunshine fell.

There, where the rock-hewn circles
  O'erlooked the Roman's game,
The veil of sleep fell on him,
  And his thought a dream became.

He felt the heart of silence
  Throb with a soundless word,
And by the inward ear alone
  A spirit's voice he heard.

And the spoken word seemed written
  On air and wave and sod,
And the bending walls of sapphire
  Blazed with the thought of God :

"What lack I, O my children ?
  All things are in my hand ;
The vast earth and the awful stars
  I hold as grains of sand.

"Need I your alms ? The silver
  And gold are mine alone ;
The gifts ye bring before me
  Were evermore my own.

"Heed I the noise of viols,
  Your pomp of masque and show ?

Have I not dawns and sunsets ?
  Have I not winds that blow ?

"Do I smell your gums of incense ?
  Is my ear with chantings fed ?
Taste I your wine of worship,
  Or eat your holy bread ?

"Of rank and name and honors
  Am I vain as ye are vain ?
What can Eternal Fulness
  From your lip-service gain ?

"Ye make me not your debtor
  Who serve yourselves alone ;
Ye boast to me of homage
  Whose gain is all your own.

"For you I gave the prophets,
  For you the Psalmist's lay :
For you the law's stone tables,
  And holy book and day.

"Ye change to weary burdens
  The helps that should uplift ;
Ye lose in form the spirit,
  The Giver in the gift.

"Who called ye to self-torment,
  To fast and penance vain ?
Dream ye Eternal Goodness
  Has joy in mortal pain ?

"For the death in life of Nitria,
  For your Chartreuse ever dumb,
What better is the neighbor,
  Or happier the home ?

"Who counts his brother's welfare
  As sacred as his own,
And loves, forgives and pities,
  He serveth me alone.

"I note each gracious purpose,
  Each kindly word and deed ;
Are ye not all my children ?
  Shall not the Father heed ?

"No prayer for light and guidance
  Is lost upon mine ear :
The child's cry in the darkness
  Shall not the Father hear ?

"I loathe your wrangling councils,
  I tread upon your creeds ;

Who made ye mine avengers,
    Or told ye of my needs ;

" I bless men and ye curse them,
    I love them and ye hate ;
Ye bite and tear each other,
    I suffer long and wait.

" Ye bow to ghastly symbols,
    To cross and scourge and thorn ;
Ye seek his Syrian manger
    Who in the heart is born.

" For the dead Christ, not the living,
    Ye watch His empty grave,
Whose life alone within you
    Has power to bless and save.

" O blind ones, outward groping,
    The idle quest forego ;
Who listens to His inward voice
    Alone of Him shall know.

" His love all love exceeding
    The heart must needs recall,
Its self-surrendering freedom,
    Its loss that gaineth all.

" Climb not the holy mountains,
    Their eagles know not me ;
Seek not the Blessed Islands,
    I dwell not in the sea.

" Gone is the mount of Meru,
    The triple gods are gone,
And, deaf to all the lama's prayers,
    The Buddha slumbers on.

" No more from rocky Horeb
    The smitten waters gush ;
Fallen is Bethel's ladder,
    Quenched is the burning bush.

" The jewels of the Urim
    And Thummim all are dim ;
The fire has left the altar,
    The sign the teraphim.

" No more in ark or hill grove
    The Holiest abides ;
Not in the scroll's dead letter
    The eternal secret hides.

" The eye shall fail that searches
    For me the hollow sky ;

The far is even as the near,
    The low is as the high.

" What if the earth is hiding
    Her old faiths, long outworn ?
What is it to the changeless truth
    That yours shall fail in turn ?

" What if the o'erturned altar
    Lays bare the ancient lie ?
What if the dreams and legends
    Of the world's childhood die ?

" Have ye not still my witness
    Within yourselves alway,
My hand that on the keys of life
    For bliss or bale I lay ?

" Still, in perpetual judgment,
    I hold assize within,
With sure reward of holiness,
    And dread rebuke of sin.

" A light, a guide, a warning,
    A presence ever near,
Through the deep silence of the flesh
    I reach the inward ear.

" My Gerizim and Ebal
    Are in each human soul,
The still, small voice of blessing,
    And Sinai's thunder-roll.

" The stern behest of duty,
    The doom-book open thrown,
The heaven ye seek, the hell ye fear,
    Are with yourselves alone."

A gold and purple sunset
    Flowed down the broad Moselle ;
On hills of vine and meadow lands
    The peace of twilight fell.

A slow, cool wind of evening
    Blew over leaf and bloom ;
And, faint and far, the Angelus
    Rang from Saint Matthew's tomb.

Then up rose Master Echard,
    And marvelled : " Can it be
That here, in dream and vision,
    The Lord hath talked with me ? "

He went his way ; behind him
    The shrines of saintly dead,

The holy coat and nail of cross,
He left unvisited.

He sought the vale of Eltzbach
His burdened soul to free,
Where the foot-hills of the Eifel
Are glassed in Laachersee.

And, in his Order's kloster,
He sat, in night-long parle,
With Tauler of the Friends of God,
And Nicolas of Basle.

And lo ! the twain made answer :
" Yea, brother, even thus
The Voice above all voices
Hath spoken unto us.

" The world will have its idols,
And flesh and sense their sign :
But the blinded eyes shall open,
And the gross ear be fine.

" What if the vision tarry ?
God's time is always best ;
The true Light shall be witnessed,
The Christ within confessed.

" In mercy or in judgment
He shall turn and overturn,
Till the heart shall be His temple
Where all of Him shall learn."

INSCRIPTIONS

ON A SUN-DIAL

FOR DR. HENRY I. BOWDITCH

WITH warning hand I mark Time's rapid
  flight
From life's glad morning to its solemn
  night ;
Yet, through the dear God's love, I also
  show
There 's Light above me by the Shade be-
  low.

ON A FOUNTAIN

FOR DOROTHEA L. DIX

STRANGER and traveller,
  Drink freely and bestow

A kindly thought on her
  Who bade this fountain flow,
Yet hath no other claim
  Than as the minister
Of blessing in God's name.
  Drink, and in His peace go !

THE MINISTER'S DAUGHTER

IN the minister's morning sermon
  He had told of the primal fall,
And how thenceforth the wrath of God
  Rested on each and all.

And how of His will and pleasure,
  All souls, save a chosen few,
Were doomed to the quenchless burning,
  And held in the way thereto.

Yet never by faith's unreason
  A saintlier soul was tried,
And never the harsh old lesson
  A tenderer heart belied.

And, after the painful service
  On that pleasant Sabbath day,
He walked with his little daughter
  Through the apple-bloom of May.

Sweet in the fresh green meadows
  Sparrow and blackbird sung ;
Above him their tinted petals
  The blossoming orchards hung.

Around on the wonderful glory
  The minister looked and smiled ;
" How good is the Lord who gives us
  These gifts from His hand, my child !

" Behold in the bloom of apples
  And the violets in the sward
A hint of the old, lost beauty
  Of the Garden of the Lord !"

Then up spake the little maiden,
  Treading on snow and pink :
" O father ! these pretty blossoms
  Are very wicked, I think.

" Had there been no Garden of Eden
  There never had been a fall ;
And if never a tree had blossomed
  God would have loved us all."

" Hush, child ! " the father answered,
" By His decree man fell ;
His ways are in clouds and darkness,
But He doeth all things well.

" And whether by His ordaining
To us cometh good or ill,
Joy or pain, or light or shadow,
We must fear and love Him still."

" Oh, I fear Him ! " said the daughter,
" And I try to love Him, too ;
But I wish He was good and gentle,
Kind and loving as you."

The minister groaned in spirit
As the tremulous lips of pain
And wide, wet eyes uplifted
Questioned his own in vain.

Bowing his head he pondered
The words of the little one ;
Had he erred in his life-long teaching ?
Had he wrong to his Master done ?

To what grim and dreadful idol
Had he lent the holiest name ?
Did his own heart, loving and human,
The God of his worship shame ?

And lo ! from the bloom and greenness,
From the tender skies above,
And the face of his little daughter,
He read a lesson of love.

No more as the cloudy terror
Of Sinai's mount of law,
But as Christ in the Syrian lilies
The vision of God he saw.

And, as when, in the clefts of Horeb,
Of old was His presence known,
The dread Ineffable Glory
Was Infinite Goodness alone.

Thereafter his hearers noted
In his prayers a tenderer strain,
And never the gospel of hatred
Burned on his lips again.

And the scoffing tongue was prayerful,
And the blinded eyes found sight,
And hearts, as flint aforetime,
Grew soft in his warmth and light.

BY THEIR WORKS

CALL him not heretic whose works attest
His faith in goodness by no creed confessed.
Whatever in love's name is truly done
To free the bound and lift the fallen one
Is done to Christ.   Whoso in deed and
      word
Is not against Him labors for our Lord.
When He, who, sad and weary, longing
      sore
For love's sweet service, sought the sisters'
      door,
One saw the heavenly, one the human guest,
But who shall say which loved the Master
      best ?

THE WORD

VOICE of the Holy Spirit, making known
   Man to himself, a witness swift and sure,
   Warning, approving, true and wise and
      pure,
Counsel and guidance that misleadeth none !
By thee the mystery of life is read ;
   The picture-writing of the world's gray
      seers,
   The myths and parables of the primal
      years,
Whose letter kills, by thee interpreted
Take healthful meanings fitted to our needs,
   And in the soul's vernacular express
   The common law of simple righteous-
      ness.
Hatred of cant and doubt of human creeds
May well be felt : the unpardonable sin
Is to deny the Word of God within !

THE BOOK

GALLERY of sacred pictures manifold,
   A minster rich in holy effigies,
   And bearing on entablature and frieze
The hieroglyphic oracles of old.
Along its transept aureoled martyrs sit ;
   And the low chancel side-lights half ac-
      quaint
   The eye with shrines of prophet, bard,
      and saint,
Their age-dimmed tablets traced in doubt-
      ful writ !

But only when on form and word obscure
  Falls from above the white supernal
    light
  We read the mystic characters aright,
And life informs the silent portraiture,
Until we pause at last, awe-held, before
The One ineffable Face, love, wonder, and
    adore.

REQUIREMENT

WE live by Faith; but Faith is not the
    slave
  Of text and legend. Reason's voice and
    God's,
Nature's and Duty's, never are at odds.
What asks our Father of His children, save
Justice and mercy and humility,
  A reasonable service of good deeds,
  Pure living, tenderness to human needs,
Reverence and trust, and prayer for light
    to see
The Master's footprints in our daily ways?
  No knotted scourge nor sacrificial knife,
  But the calm beauty of an ordered life
Whose very breathing is unworded
    praise! —
A life that stands as all true lives have
    stood,
Firm-rooted in the faith that God is Good.

HELP

DREAM not, O Soul, that easy is the task
  Thus set before thee. If it proves at
    length,
  As well it may, beyond thy natural
    strength,
Faint not, despair not. As a child may ask
A father, pray the Everlasting Good
  For light and guidance midst the subtle
    snares
  Of sin thick planted in life's thorough-
    fares,
For spiritual strength and moral hardihood;
Still listening, through the noise of time
    and sense,
  To the still whisper of the Inward Word;
  Bitter in blame, sweet in approval heard,
Itself its own confirming evidence:
To health of soul a voice to cheer and please,
To guilt the wrath of the Eumenides.

UTTERANCE

BUT what avail inadequate words to reach
  The innermost of Truth? Who shall
    essay,
  Blinded and weak, to point and lead the
    way,
Or solve the mystery in familiar speech?
Yet, if it be that something not thy own,
  Some shadow of the Thought to which
    our schemes,
  Creeds, cult, and ritual are at best but
    dreams,
Is even to thy unworthiness made known,
Thou mayst not hide what yet thou shouldst
    not dare
  To utter lightly, lest on lips of thine
  The real seem false, the beauty undi-
    vine.
So, weighing duty in the scale of prayer,
Give what seems given thee. It may prove
    a seed
Of goodness dropped in fallow-grounds of
    need.

ORIENTAL MAXIMS

PARAPHRASE OF SANSCRIT TRANSLA-
TIONS

THE INWARD JUDGE

From *Institutes of Manu.*

THE soul itself its awful witness is.
Say not in evil doing, "No one sees,"
And so offend the conscious One within,
Whose ear can hear the silences of sin
Ere they find voice, whose eyes unsleeping
    see
The secret motions of iniquity.

Nor in thy folly say, "I am alone."
For, seated in thy heart, as on a throne,
The ancient Judge and Witness liveth
    still,
To note thy act and thought; and as thy
    ill
Or good goes from thee, far beyond thy
    reach,
The solemn Doomsman's seal is set on
    each.

LAYING UP TREASURE

From the Mahàbhárata.

BEFORE the Ender comes, whose charioteer
Is swift or slow Disease, lay up each year
Thy harvests of well-doing, wealth that
      kings
Nor thieves can take away. When all the
      things
Thou callest thine, goods, pleasures, honors
      fall,
Thou in thy virtue shalt survive them all.

CONDUCT

From the Mahàbhárata.

HEED how thou livest. Do no act by day
Which from the night shall drive thy peace
      away.
In months of sun so live that months of rain
Shall still be happy. Evermore restrain
Evil and cherish good, so shall there be
Another and a happier life for thee.

AN EASTER FLOWER GIFT

O DEAREST bloom the seasons know,
Flowers of the Resurrection, blow,
   Our hope and faith restore ;
And through the bitterness of death
And loss and sorrow, breathe a breath
   Of life forevermore !

The thought of Love Immortal blends
With fond remembrances of friends ;
   In you, O sacred flowers,
By human love made doubly sweet,
The heavenly and the earthly meet,
   The heart of Christ and ours !

THE MYSTIC'S CHRISTMAS

" ALL hail ! " the bells of Christmas rang,
" All hail ! " the monks at Christmas sang,
The merry monks who kept with cheer
The gladdest day of all their year.

But still apart, unmoved thereat,
A pious elder brother sat

Silent, in his accustomed place,
With God's sweet peace upon his face.

" Why sitt'st thou thus ? " his brethren
      cried.
" It is the blessed Christmas-tide ;
The Christmas lights are all aglow,
The sacred lilies bud and blow.

" Above our heads the joy-bells ring,
Without the happy children sing,
And all God's creatures hail the morn
On which the holy Christ was born !

" Rejoice with us ; no more rebuke
Our gladness with thy quiet look."
The gray monk answered : " Keep, I pray,
Even as ye list, the Lord's birthday.

" Let heathen Yule fires flicker red
Where thronged refectory feasts are
      spread ;
With mystery-play and masque and mime
And wait-songs speed the holy time !

" The blindest faith may haply save ;
The Lord accepts the things we have ;
And reverence, howsoe'er it strays,
May find at last the shining ways.

" They needs must grope who cannot see,
The blade before the ear must be ;
As ye are feeling I have felt,
And where ye dwell I too have dwelt.

" But now, beyond the things of sense,
Beyond occasions and events,
I know, through God's exceeding grace,
Release from form and time and place.

" I listen, from no mortal tongue,
To hear the song the angels sung ;
And wait within myself to know
The Christmas lilies bud and blow.

" The outward symbols disappear
From him whose inward sight is clear ;
And small must be the choice of days
To him who fills them all with praise !

" Keep while you need it, brothers mine,
With honest zeal your Christmas sign,
But judge not him who every morn
Feels in his heart the Lord Christ born ! "

AT LAST

[Recited by one of the little group of relations, who stood by the poet's bedside, as the last moment of his life approached.]

WHEN on my day of life the night is falling,
And, in the winds from unsunned spaces blown,
I hear far voices out of darkness calling
My feet to paths unknown,

Thou who hast made my home of life so pleasant,
Leave not its tenant when its walls decay;
O Love Divine, O Helper ever present,
Be Thou my strength and stay !

Be near me when all else is from me drifting;
Earth, sky, home's pictures, days of shade and shine,
And kindly faces to my own uplifting
The love which answers mine.

I have but Thee, my Father ! let Thy spirit
Be with me then to comfort and uphold ;
No gate of pearl, no branch of palm I merit,
Nor street of shining gold.

Suffice it if — my good and ill unreckoned,
And both forgiven through Thy abounding grace —
I find myself by hands familiar beckoned
Unto my fitting place.

Some humble door among Thy many mansions,
Some sheltering shade where sin and striving cease,
And flows forever through heaven's green expansions
The river of Thy peace.

There, from the music round about me stealing,
I fain would learn the new and holy song,
And find at last, beneath Thy trees of healing,
The life for which I long.

WHAT THE TRAVELLER SAID AT SUNSET

THE shadows grow and deepen round me,
I feel the dew-fall in the air ;
The muezzin of the darkening thicket,
I hear the night-thrush call to prayer.

The evening wind is sad with farewells,
And loving hands unclasp from mine ;
Alone I go to meet the darkness
Across an awful boundary-line.

As from the lighted hearths behind me
I pass with slow, reluctant feet,
What waits me in the land of strangeness ?
What face shall smile, what voice shall greet ?

What space shall awe, what brightness blind me ?
What thunder-roll of music stun ?
What vast processions sweep before me
Of shapes unknown beneath the sun ?

I shrink from unaccustomed glory,
I dread the myriad-voicëd strain ;
Give me the unforgotten faces,
And let my lost ones speak again.

He will not chide my mortal yearning
Who is our Brother and our Friend ;
In whose full life, divine and human,
The heavenly and the earthly blend.

Mine be the joy of soul-communion,
The sense of spiritual strength renewed,
The reverence for the pure and holy,
The dear delight of doing good.

No fitting ear is mine to listen
An endless anthem's rise and fall ;
No curious eye is mine to measure
The pearl gate and the jasper wall.

For love must needs be more than knowledge :
What matter if I never know
Why Aldebaran's star is ruddy,
Or warmer Sirius white as snow !

Forgive my human words, O Father !
I go Thy larger truth to prove ;

Thy mercy shall transcend my longing :
　I seek but love, and Thou art Love !

I go to find my lost and mourned for
　Safe in Thy sheltering goodness still,
And all that hope and faith foreshadow
　Made perfect in Thy holy will !

"THE STORY OF IDA"

Francesca Alexander, whose pen and pencil
have so reverently transcribed the simple faith
and life of the Italian peasantry, wrote the
narrative published with John Ruskin's intro-
duction under the title, *The Story of Ida*.

WEARY of jangling noises never stilled,
　The skeptic's sneer, the bigot's hate, the
　　din
　Of clashing texts, the webs of creed
　　men spin
Round simple truth, the children grown
　who build
With gilded cards their new Jerusalem,
　Busy, with sacerdotal tailorings
And tinsel gauds, bedizening holy things,
I turn, with glad and grateful heart, from
　them
To the sweet story of the Florentine
　Immortal in her blameless maidenhood,
　Beautiful as God's angels and as good ;
Feeling that life, even now, may be divine
With love no wrong can ever change to
　hate,
No sin make less than all-compassionate !

THE LIGHT THAT IS FELT

A TENDER child of summers three,
　Seeking her little bed at night,
Paused on the dark stair timidly.
"Oh, mother !　Take my hand," said she,
　" And then the dark will all be light."

We older children grope our way
　From dark behind to dark before ;
And only when our hands we lay,
Dear Lord, in Thine, the night is day,
　And there is darkness nevermore.

Reach downward to the sunless days
　Wherein our guides are blind as we,
And faith is small and hope delays ;

Take Thou the hands of prayer we raise,
　And let us feel the light of Thee !

THE TWO LOVES

SMOOTHING soft the nestling head
Of a maiden fancy-led,
Thus a grave-eyed woman said :

" Richest gifts are those we make,
Dearer than the love we take
That we give for love's own sake.

" Well I know the heart's unrest ;
Mine has been the common quest,
To be loved and therefore blest.

" Favors undeserved were mine ;
At my feet as on a shrine
Love has laid its gifts divine.

" Sweet the offerings seemed, and yet
With their sweetness came regret,
And a sense of unpaid debt.

" Heart of mine unsatisfied,
Was it vanity or pride
That a deeper joy denied ?

" Hands that ope but to receive
Empty close ; they only live
Richly who can richly give.

" Still," she sighed, with moistening eyes
" Love is sweet in any guise ;
But its best is sacrifice !

" He who, giving, does not crave
Likest is to Him who gave
Life itself the loved to save.

" Love, that self-forgetful gives,
Sows surprise of ripened sheaves,
Late or soon its own receives."

ADJUSTMENT

THE tree of Faith its bare, dry boughs must
　shed
　That nearer heaven the living ones may
　　climb ;
　The false must fail, though from our
　　shores of time

The old lament be heard, "Great Pan is dead!"
That wail is Error's, from his high place hurled;
 This sharp recoil is Evil undertrod;
 Our time's unrest, an angel sent of God
Troubling w'th life the waters of the world.
Even as they list the winds of the Spirit blow
 To turn or break our century - rusted vanes;
 Sands shift and waste; the rock alone remains
Where, led of Heaven, the strong tides come and go,
And storm-clouds, rent by thunderbolt and wind,
Leave, free of mist, the permanent stars behind.

Therefore I trust, although to outward sense
 Both true and false seem shaken; I will hold
 With newer light my reverence for the old
And calmly wait the births of Providence.
No gain is lost; the clear-eyed saints look down
 Untroubled on the wreck of schemes and creeds;
 Love yet remains, its rosary of good deeds
Counting in task-field and o'erpeopled town.
Truth has charmed life; the Inward Word survives,
 And, day by day, its revelation brings;
 Faith, hope, and charity, whatsoever things
Which cannot be shaken, stand. Still holy lives
Reveal the Christ of whom the letter told,
And the new gospel verifies the old.

HYMNS OF THE BRAHMO SOMAJ

I have attempted this paraphrase of the Hymns of the Brahmo Somaj of India, as I find them in Mozoomdar's account of the devotional exercises of that remarkable religious development which has attracted far less attention and sympathy from the Christian world than it deserves, as a fresh revelation of the direct action of the Divine Spirit upon the human heart.

I

THE mercy, O Eternal One!
 By man unmeasured yet,
In joy or grief, in shade or sun,
 I never will forget.
I give the whole, and not a part,
 Of all Thou gavest me;
My goods, my life, my soul and heart,
 I yield them all to Thee!

II

We fast and plead, we weep and pray,
 From morning until even;
We feel to find the holy way,
 We knock at the gate of heaven!
And when in silent awe we wait,
 And word and sign forbear,
The hinges of the golden gate
 Move, soundless, to our prayer!
Who hears the eternal harmonies
 Can heed no outward word;
Blind to all else is he who sees
 The vision of the Lord!

III

O soul, be patient, restrain thy tears,
 Have hope, and not despair;
As a tender mother heareth her child
 God hears the penitent prayer.
And not forever shall grief be thine;
 On the Heavenly Mother's breast,
Washed clean and white in waters of joy
 Shall His seeking child find rest.
Console thyself with His word of grace,
 And cease thy wail of woe,
For His mercy never an equal hath,
 And His love no bounds can know.
Lean close unto Him in faith and hope;
 How many like thee have found
In Him a shelter and home of peace,
 By His mercy compassed round!
There, safe from sin and the sorrow it brings,
 They sing their grateful psalms,
And rest, at noon, by the wells of God,
 In the shade of His holy palms!

REVELATION

" And I went into the Vale of Beavor, and as I went I preached repentance to the people. And one morning sitting by the fire, a great cloud came over me, and a temptation beset me. And it was said: *All things come by Nature*; and the Elements and the Stars came over me. And as I sat still and let it alone, a living hope arose in me, and a true Voice which said: *There is a living God who made all things.* And immediately the cloud and the temptation vanished, and Life rose over all, and my heart was glad and I praised the living God."— *Journal of George Fox*, 1690.

STILL, as of old, in Beavor's Vale,
  O man of God! our hope and faith
The Elements and Stars assail,
  And the awed spirit holds its breath,
  Blown over by a wind of death.

Takes Nature thought for such as we,
  What place her human atom fills,
The weed-drift of her careless sea,
  The mist on her unheeding hills?
  What recks she of our helpless wills?

Strange god of Force, with fear, not love,
  Its trembling worshipper! Can prayer
Reach the shut ear of Fate, or move
  Unpitying Energy to spare?
  What doth the cosmic Vastness care?

In vain to this dread Unconcern
  For the All-Father's love we look;
In vain, in quest of it, we turn
  The storied leaves of Nature's book,
  The prints her rocky tablets took.

I pray for faith, I long to trust;
  I listen with my heart, and hear
A Voice without a sound: "Be just,
  Be true, be merciful, revere
  The Word within thee: God is near!

"A light to sky and earth unknown
  Pales all their lights: a mightier force

Than theirs the powers of Nature own,
  And, to its goal as at its source,
  His Spirit moves the Universe.

"Believe and trust. Through stars and
    suns,
  Through life and death, through soul and
    sense,
His wise, paternal purpose runs;
  The darkness of His providence
  Is star-lit with benign intents."

O joy supreme! I know the Voice,
  Like none beside on earth or sea;
Yea, more, O soul of mine, rejoice,
  By all that He requires of me,
  I know what God himself must be.

No picture to my aid I call,
  I shape no image in my prayer;
I only know in Him is all
  Of life, light, beauty, everywhere,
  Eternal Goodness here and there!

I know He is, and what He is,
  Whose one great purpose is the good
Of all. I rest my soul on His
  Immortal Love and Fatherhood;
  And trust Him, as His children should.

I fear no more. The clouded face
  Of Nature smiles; through all her things
Of time and space and sense I trace
  The moving of the Spirit's wings,
  And hear the song of hope she sings.

AT SUNDOWN

TO E. C. S.

Poet and friend of poets, if thy glass
Detects no flower in winter's tuft of grass,
Let this slight token of the debt I owe
    Outlive for thee December's frozen day,
And, like the arbutus budding under snow,
    Take bloom and fragrance from some morn
        of May
When he who gives it shall have gone the way
Where faith shall see and reverent trust shall
    know.

THE CHRISTMAS OF 1888

Low in the east, against a white, cold
    dawn,
The black-lined silhouette of the woods was
    drawn,
    And on a wintry waste
Of frosted streams and hillsides bare and
    brown,
Through thin cloud-films a pallid ghost
    looked down,
    The waning moon half-faced !

In that pale sky and sere, snow-waiting
    earth,
What sign was there of the immortal birth ?
    What herald of the One ?
Lo ! swift as thought the heavenly radiance
    came,
A rose-red splendor swept the sky like
    flame,
    Up rolled the round, bright sun !

And all was changed.   From a transfigured
    world
The moon's ghost fled, the smoke of home-
    hearths curled
    Up the still air unblown.
In Orient warmth and brightness, did that
    morn
O'er Nain and Nazareth, when the Christ
    was born,
    Break fairer than our own ?

The morning's promise noon and eve ful-
    filled
In warm, soft sky and landscape hazy-hilled
    And sunset fair as they ;
A sweet reminder of His holiest time,
A summer-miracle in our winter clime,
    God gave a perfect day.

The near was blended with the old and far,
And Bethlehem's hillside and the Magi's
    star
    Seemed here, as there and then, —
Our homestead pine-tree was the Syrian
    palm,
Our heart's desire the angels' midnight
    psalm,
    Peace, and good-will to men !

THE VOW OF WASHINGTON

Read in New York, April 30, 1889, at the
Centennial Celebration of the Inauguration of
George Washington as the first President of the
United States.

The sword was sheathed : in April's sun
    Lay green the fields by Freedom won ;
And severed sections, weary of debates,
Joined hands at last and were United
    States.

O City sitting by the Sea !
How proud the day that dawned on thee,
When the new era, long desired, began,
And, in its need, the hour had found the
    man !

One thought the cannon salvos spoke,
    The resonant bell-tower's vibrant stroke,
The voiceful streets, the plaudit-echoing
    halls,
And prayer and hymn borne heavenward
    from St. Paul's !

How felt the land in every part
The strong throb of a nation's heart,

As its great leader gave, with reverent awe,
His pledge to Union, Liberty, and Law !

That pledge the heavens above him
    heard,
That vow the sleep of centuries stirred ;
In world-wide wonder listening peoples
    bent
Their gaze on Freedom's great experiment.

Could it succeed ?   Of honor sold
And hopes deceived all history told.
Above the wrecks that strewed the mourn-
    ful past,
Was the long dream of ages true at last ?

Thank God ! the people's choice was just,
The one man equal to his trust,
Wise beyond lore, and without weakness
    good,
Calm in the strength of flawless rectitude !

His rule of justice, order, peace,
Made possible the world's release ;
Taught prince and serf that power is but a
    trust,
And rule alone, which serves the ruled, is
    just ;

That Freedom generous is, but strong
In hate of fraud and selfish wrong,
Pretence that turns her holy truth to lies,
And lawless license masking in her guise.

Land of his love ! with one glad voice
Let thy great sisterhood rejoice ;
A century's suns o'er thee have risen and set,
And, God be praised, we are one nation yet.

And still we trust the years to be
Shall prove his hope was destiny,
Leaving our flag, with all its added stars,
Unrent by faction and unstained by wars.

Lo ! where with patient toil he nursed
And trained the new-set plant at first,
The widening branches of a stately tree
Stretch from the sunrise to the sunset sea.

And in its broad and sheltering shade,
Sitting with none to make afraid,
Were we now silent, through each mighty
    limb,
The winds of heaven would sing the praise
    of him.

Our first and best ! — his ashes lie
Beneath his own Virginian sky.
Forgive, forget, O true and just and brave,
The storm that swept above thy sacred
    grave !

For, ever in the awful strife
And dark hours of the nation's life,
Through the fierce tumult pierced his
    warning word,
Their father's voice his erring children
    heard !

The change for which he prayed and
    sought
In that sharp agony was wrought ;
No partial interest draws its alien line
'Twixt North and South, the cypress and
    the pine !

One people now, all doubt beyond,
His name shall be our Union-bond ;
We lift our hands to Heaven, and here and
    now
Take on our lips the old Centennial vow.

For rule and trust must needs be ours ;
Chooser and chosen both are powers
Equal in service as in rights ; the claim
Of Duty rests on each and all the same.

Then let the sovereign millions, where
Our banner floats in sun and air,
From the warm palm-lands to Alaska's
    cold,
Repeat with us the pledge a century old !

THE CAPTAIN'S WELL

The story of the shipwreck of Captain Val-
entine Bagley, on the coast of Arabia, and his
sufferings in the desert, has been familiar from
my childhood.   It has been partially told in the
singularly beautiful lines of my friend, Har-
riet Prescott Spofford, on the occasion of a pub-
lic celebration at the Newburyport Library.
To the charm and felicity of her verse, as far
as it goes, nothing can be added ; but in the
following ballad I have endeavored to give a
fuller detail of the touching incident upon
which it is founded.

FROM pain and peril, by land and main,
The shipwrecked sailor came back again ;

And like one from the dead, the threshold
    crossed
Of his wondering home, that had mourned
    him lost,

Where he sat once more with his kith and
    kin,
And welcomed his neighbors thronging in.

But when morning came he called for his
    spade.
"I must pay my debt to the Lord," he said.

"Why dig you here ? " asked the passer-
    by ;
"Is there gold or silver the road so
    nigh ? "

"No, friend," he answered : " but under
    this sod
Is the blessed water, the wine of God."

"Water ! the Powow is at your back,
And right before you the Merrimac,

"And look you up, or look you down,
There 's a well-sweep at every door in
    town."

"True," he said, "we have wells of our
    own ;
But this I dig for the Lord alone."

Said the other : "This soil is dry, you
    know,
I doubt if a spring can be found below ;

"You had better consult, before you dig,
Some water-witch, with a hazel twig."

"No, wet or dry, I will dig it here,
Shallow or deep, if it takes a year.

"In the Arab desert, where shade is none,
The waterless land of sand and sun,

"Under the pitiless, brazen sky
My burning throat as the sand was dry ;

"My crazed brain listened in fever dreams
For plash of buckets and ripple of streams;

"And opening my eyes to the blinding glare,
And my lips to the breath of the blistering
    air,

"Tortured alike by the heavens and earth,
I cursed, like Job, the day of my birth.

"Then something tender, and sad, and mild
As a mother's voice to her wandering child,

"Rebuked my frenzy ; and bowing my
    head,
I prayed as I never before had prayed :

"*Pity me, God ! for I die of thirst ;*
Take me out of this land accurst ;

"*And if ever I reach my home again,*
Where earth has springs, and the sky has
    rain,

"*I will dig a well for the passers-by,*
And none shall suffer from thirst as I.

"I saw, as I prayed, my home once more,
The house, the barn, the elms by the door,

"The grass - lined road, that riverward
    wound,
The tall slate stones of the burying-ground,

"The belfry and steeple on meeting-house
    hill,
The brook with its dam, and gray grist mill,

"And I knew in that vision beyond the
    sea,
The very place where my well must be.

"God heard my prayer in that evil day ;
He led my feet in their homeward way,

"From false mirage and dried-up well,
And the hot sand storms of a land of hell,

"Till I saw at last through the coast-hill's
    gap,
A city held in its stony lap,

"The mosques and the domes of scorched
    Muscat,
And my heart leaped up with joy thereat ;

"For there was a ship at anchor lying,
A Christian flag at its mast-head flying,

"And sweetest of sounds to my homesick
    ear
Was my native tongue in the sailor's cheer.

"Now the Lord be thanked, I am back again,
Where earth has springs, and the skies have rain,

"And the well I promised by Oman's Sea,
I am digging for him in Amesbury."

His kindred wept, and his neighbors said :
"The poor old captain is out of his head."

But from morn to noon, and from noon to night,
He toiled at his task with main and might ;

And when at last, from the loosened earth,
Under his spade the stream gushed forth,

And fast as he climbed to his deep well's brim,
The water he dug for followed him,

He shouted for joy : "I have kept my word,
And here is the well I promised the Lord !"

The long years came and the long years went,
And he sat by his roadside well content ;

He watched the travellers, heat-oppressed,
Pause by the way to drink and rest,

And the sweltering horses dip, as they drank,
Their nostrils deep in the cool, sweet tank,

And grateful at heart, his memory went
Back to that waterless Orient,

And the blessed answer of prayer, which came
To the earth of iron and sky of flame.

And when a wayfarer weary and hot,
Kept to the mid road, pausing not

For the well's refreshing, he shook his head;
"He don't know the value of water," he said ;

"Had he prayed for a drop, as I have done,
In the desert circle of sand and sun,

"He would drink and rest, and go home to tell
That God's best gift is the wayside well !"

AN OUTDOOR RECEPTION

The substance of these lines, hastily pencilled several years ago, I find among such of my unprinted scraps as have escaped the waste-basket and the fire. In transcribing it I have made some changes, additions, and omissions.

On these green banks, where falls too soon
The shade of Autumn's afternoon,
The south wind blowing soft and sweet,
The water gliding at my feet,
The distant northern range uplit
By the slant sunshine over it,
With changes of the mountain mist
From tender blush to amethyst,
The valley's stretch of shade and gleam
Fair as in Mirza's Bagdad dream,
With glad young faces smiling near
And merry voices in my ear,
I sit, methinks, as Hafiz might
In Iran's Garden of Delight.
For Persian roses blushing red,
Aster and gentian bloom instead ;
For Shiraz wine, this mountain air ;
For feast, the blueberries which I share
With one who proffers with stained hands
Her gleanings from yon pasture lands,
Wild fruit that art and culture spoil,
The harvest of an untilled soil;
And with her one whose tender eyes
Reflect the change of April skies,
Midway 'twixt child and maiden yet,
Fresh as Spring's earliest violet ;
And one whose look and voice and ways
Make where she goes idyllic days ;
And one whose sweet, still countenance
Seems dreamful of a child's romance ;
And others, welcome as are these,
Like and unlike, varieties
Of pearls on nature's chaplet strung,
And all are fair, for all are young.
Gathered from seaside cities old,
From midland prairie, lake, and wold,
From the great wheat-fields, which might feed
The hunger of a world at need,
In healthful change of rest and play
Their school-vacations glide away.

No critics these : they only see
An old and kindly friend in me,
In whose amused, indulgent look
Their innocent mirth has no rebuke.
They scarce can know my rugged rhymes,
The harsher songs of evil times,
Nor graver themes in minor keys
Of life's and death's solemnities :
But haply, as they bear in mind
Some verse of lighter, happier kind, —
Hints of the boyhood of the man,
Youth viewed from life's meridian,
Half seriously and half in play
My pleasant interviewers pay
Their visit, with no fell intent
Of taking notes and punishment.

As yonder solitary pine
Is ringed below with flower and vine,
More favored than that lonely tree,
The bloom of girlhood circles me.
In such an atmosphere of youth
I half forget my age's truth ;
The shadow of my life's long date
Runs backward on the dial-plate,
Until it seems a step might span
The gulf between the boy and man.

My young friends smile, as if some jay
On bleak December's leafless spray
Essayed to sing the songs of May.
Well, let them smile, and live to know,
When their brown locks are flecked with
         snow,
'T is tedious to be always sage
And pose the dignity of age,
While so much of our early lives
On memory's playground still survives,
And owns, as at the present hour,
The spell of youth's magnetic power.

But though I feel, with Solomon,
'T is pleasant to behold the sun,
I would not if I could repeat
A life which still is good and sweet ;
I keep in age, as in my prime,
A not uncheerful step with time,
And, grateful for all blessings sent,
I go the common way, content
To make no new experiment.
On easy terms with law and fate,
For what must be I calmly wait,
And trust the path I cannot see, —
That God is good sufficeth me.
And when at last on life's strange play

The curtain falls, I only pray
That hope may lose itself in truth,
And age in Heaven's immortal youth.
And all our loves and longing prove
The foretaste of diviner love !

The day is done. Its afterglow
Along the west is burning low.
My visitors, like birds, have flown ;
I hear their voices, fainter grown,
And dimly through the dusk I see
Their kerchiefs wave good-night to me,
Light hearts of girlhood, knowing naught
Of all the cheer their coming brought ;
And, in their going, unaware
Of silent-following feet of prayer :
Heaven make their budding promise good
With flowers of gracious womanhood !

R. S. S. AT DEER ISLAND ON THE MERRIMAC

MAKE, for he loved thee well, our Merri-
    mac,
    From wave and shore a low and long
        lament
    For him whose last look sought thee, as
        he went
The unknown way from which no step
    comes back.
And ye, O ancient pine-trees, at whose
    feet
    He watched in life the sunset's redden-
        ing glow,
    Let the soft south wind through your
        needles blow
A fitting requiem tenderly and sweet !
No fonder lover of all lovely things
    Shall walk where once he walked, no
        smile more glad
    Greet friends than his who friends in all
        men had,
Whose pleasant memory to that Island
    clings,
Where a dear mourner in the home he left
Of love's sweet solace cannot be bereft.

BURNING DRIFT-WOOD

BEFORE my drift-wood fire I sit,
    And see, with every waif I burn,
Old dreams and fancies coloring it,
    And folly's unlaid ghosts return.

O ships of mine, whose swift keels cleft
　The enchanted sea on which they sailed,
Are these poor fragments only left
　Of vain desires and hopes that failed ?

Did I not watch from them the light
　Of sunset on my towers in Spain,
And see, far off, uploom in sight
　The Fortunate Isles I might not gain ?

Did sudden lift of fog reveal
　Arcadia's vales of song and spring,
And did I pass, with grazing keel,
　The rocks whereon the sirens sing ?

Have I not drifted hard upon
　The unmapped regions lost to man,
The cloud-pitched tents of Prester John,
　The palace domes of Kubla Khan ?

Did land winds blow from jasmine flowers,
　Where Youth the ageless Fountain fills ?
Did Love make sign from rose blown bow-
　ers,
　And gold from Eldorado's hills ?

Alas ! the gallant ships, that sailed
　On blind Adventure's errand sent,
Howe'er they laid their courses, failed
　To reach the haven of Content.

And of my ventures, those alone
　Which Love had freighted, safely sped,
Seeking a good beyond my own,
　By clear-eyed Duty piloted.

O mariners, hoping still to meet
　The luck Arabian voyagers met,
And find in Bagdad's moonlit street,
　Haroun al Raschid walking yet,

Take with you, on your Sea of Dreams,
　The fair, fond fancies dear to youth.
I turn from all that only seems,
　And seek the sober grounds of truth.

What matter that it is not May,
　That birds have flown, and trees are
　　bare,
That darker grows the shortening day,
　And colder blows the wintry air !

The wrecks of passion and desire,
　The castles I no more rebuild,

May fitly feed my drift-wood fire,
　And warm the hands that age has chilled.

Whatever perished with my ships,
　I only know the best remains ;
A song of praise is on my lips
　For losses which are now my gains.

Heap high my hearth ! No worth is lost ;
　No wisdom with the folly dies.
Burn on, poor shreds, your holocaust
　Shall be my evening sacrifice !

Far more than all I dared to dream,
　Unsought before my door I see ;
On wings of fire and steeds of steam
　The world's great wonders come to me,

And holier signs, unmarked before,
　Of Love to seek and Power to save, —
The righting of the wronged and poor,
　The man evolving from the slave ;

And life, no longer chance or fate,
　Safe in the gracious Fatherhood.
I fold o'er-wearied hands and wait,
　In full assurance of the good.

And well the waiting time must be,
　Though brief or long its granted days,
If Faith and Hope and Charity
　Sit by my evening hearth-fire's blaze.

And with them, friends whom Heaven has
　　spared,
　Whose love my heart has comforted,
And, sharing all my joys, has shared
　My tender memories of the dead, —

Dear souls who left us lonely here,
　Bound on their last, long voyage, to
　　whom
We, day by day, are drawing near,
　Where every bark has sailing room.

I know the solemn monotone
　Of waters calling unto me ;
I know from whence the airs have blown
　That whisper of the Eternal Sea.

As low my fires of drift-wood burn,
　I hear that sea's deep sounds increase,
And, fair in sunset light, discern
　Its mirage-lifted Isles of Peace.

O. W. HOLMES ON HIS EIGHTI-
ETH BIRTHDAY

CLIMBING a path which leads back never
    more
  We heard behind his footsteps and his
    cheer ;
Now, face to face, we greet him standing
    here
Upon the lonely summit of Fourscore !
Welcome to us, o'er whom the lengthened
    day
  Is closing and the shadows colder grow,
  His genial presence, like an afterglow,
Following the one just vanishing away.
Long be it ere the table shall be set
  For the last breakfast of the Autocrat,
  And love repeat with smiles and tears
    thereat
His own sweet songs that time shall not
    forget.
Waiting with us the call to come up higher,
Life is not less, the heavens are only nigher !

JAMES RUSSELL LOWELL

FROM purest wells of English undefiled
None deeper drank than he, the New
    World's child,
Who in the language of their farm-fields
    spoke
The wit and wisdom of New England folk,
Shaming a monstrous wrong. The world-
    wide laugh
Provoked thereby might well have shaken
    half
The walls of Slavery down, ere yet the ball
And mine of battle overthrew them all.

HAVERHILL

1640–1890

Read at the Celebration of the Two Hun-
dred and Fiftieth Anniversary of the City,
July 2, 1890.

O RIVER winding to the sea !
  We call the old time back to thee ;
  From forest paths and water-ways
  The century-woven veil we raise.

The voices of to-day are dumb,
Unheard its sounds that go and come ;
We listen, through long-lapsing years,
To footsteps of the pioneers.

Gone steepled town and cultured plain,
The wilderness returns again,
The drear, untrodden solitude,
The gloom and mystery of the wood !

Once more the bear and panther prowl,
The wolf repeats his hungry howl,
And, peering through his leafy screen,
The Indian's copper face is seen.

We see, their rude-built huts beside,
Grave men and women anxious-eyed,
And wistful youth remembering still
Dear homes in England's Haverhill.

We summon forth to mortal view
Dark Passaquo and Saggahew, —
Wild chiefs, who owned the mighty sway
Of wizard Passaconaway.

Weird memories of the border town,
By old tradition handed down,
In chance and change before us pass
Like pictures in a magic glass, —

The terror of the midnight raid,
The death-concealing ambuscade,
The winter march, through deserts wild,
Of captive mother, wife, and child.

Ah ! bleeding hands alone subdued
And tamed the savage habitude
Of forests hiding beasts of prey,
And human shapes as fierce as they.

Slow from the plough the woods withdrew,
Slowly each year the corn-lands grew ;
Nor fire, nor frost, nor foe could kill
The Saxon energy of will.

And never in the hamlet's bound
Was lack of sturdy manhood found,
And never failed the kindred good
Of brave and helpful womanhood.

That hamlet now a city is,
Its log-built huts are palaces ;
The wood-path of the settler's cow
Is Traffic's crowded highway now.

And far and wide it stretches still,
Along its southward sloping hill,
And overlooks on either hand
A rich and many-watered land.

And, gladdening all the landscape, fair
As Pison was to Eden's pair,
Our river to its valley brings
The blessing of its mountain springs.

And Nature holds with narrowing space,
From mart and crowd, her old - time
        grace,
And guards with fondly jealous arms
The wild growths of outlying farms.

Her sunsets on Kenoza fall,
Her autumn leaves by Saltonstall ;
No lavished gold can richer make
Her opulence of hill and lake.

Wise was the choice which led our sires
To kindle here their household fires,
And share the large content of all
Whose lines in pleasant places fall.

More dear, as years on years advance,
We prize the old inheritance,
And feel, as far and wide we roam,
That all we seek we leave at home.

Our palms are pines, our oranges
Are apples on our orchard trees ;
Our thrushes are our nightingales,
Our larks the blackbirds of our vales.

No incense which the Orient burns
Is sweeter than our hillside ferns ;
What tropic splendor can outvie
Our autumn woods, our sunset sky ?

If, where the slow years came and went,
And left not affluence, but content,
Now flashes in our dazzled eyes
The electric light of enterprise ;

And if the old idyllic ease
Seems lost in keen activities,
And crowded workshops now replace
The hearth's and farm-field's rustic grace ;

No dull, mechanic round of toil
Life's morning charm can quite despoil ;
And youth and beauty, hand in hand,
Will always find enchanted land.

No task is ill where hand and brain
And skill and strength have equal gain,
And each shall each in honor hold,
And simple manhood outweigh gold.

Earth shall be near to Heaven when all
That severs man from man shall fall,
For, here or there, salvation's plan
Alone is love of God and man.

O dwellers by the Merrimac,
The heirs of centuries at your back,
Still reaping where you have not sown,
A broader field is now your own.

Hold fast your Puritan heritage,
But let the free thought of the age
Its light and hope and sweetness add
To the stern faith the fathers had.

Adrift on Time's returnless tide,
As waves that follow waves, we glide.
God grant we leave upon the shore
Some waif of good it lacked before ;

Some seed, or flower, or plant of worth,
Some added beauty to the earth ;
Some larger hope, some thought to make
The sad world happier for its sake.

As tenants of uncertain stay,
So may we live our little day
That only grateful hearts shall fill
The homes we leave in Haverhill.

The singer of a farewell rhyme,
Upon whose outmost verge of time
The shades of night are falling down,
I pray, God bless the good old town !

TO G. G.

AN AUTOGRAPH

The daughter of Daniel Gurteen, Esq., dele-
gate from Haverhill, England, to the two hun-
dred and fiftieth anniversary celebration of Ha-
verhill, Massachusetts. The Rev. John Ward
of the former place and many of his old par-
ishioners were the pioneer settlers of the new
town on the Merrimac.

GRACEFUL in name and in thyself, our
        river
  None fairer saw in John Ward's pilgrim
        flock,

Proof that upon their century-rooted
stock
The English roses bloom as fresh as ever.

Take the warm welcome of new friends
with thee,
And listening to thy home's familiar
chime
Dream that thou hearest, with it keep-
ing time,
The bells on Merrimac sound across the
sea.

Think of our thrushes, when the lark sings
clear,
Of our sweet Mayflowers when the dai-
sies bloom ;
And bear to our and thy ancestral home
The kindly greeting of its children here.

Say that our love survives the severing
strain ;
That the New England, with the Old,
holds fast
The proud, fond memories of a common
past ;
Unbroken still the ties of blood remain !

INSCRIPTION

For the bass-relief by Preston Powers, carved
upon the huge boulder in Denver Park, Col.,
and representing the Last Indian and the Last
Bison.

THE eagle, stooping from yon snow-blown
peaks,
For the wild hunter and the bison seeks,
In the changed world below ; and finds
alone
Their graven semblance in the eternal
stone.

LYDIA H. SIGOURNEY

Inscription on her Memorial Tablet in Christ
Church at Hartford, Conn.

SHE sang alone, ere womanhood had known
The gift of song which fills the air to-
day :
Tender and sweet, a music all her own
May fitly linger where she knelt to pray.

MILTON

Inscription on the Memorial Window in St.
Margaret's Church, Westminster, the gift of
George W. Childs, of America.

THE new world honors him whose lofty
plea
For England's freedom made her own
more sure,
Whose song, immortal as its theme, shall
be
Their common freehold while both worlds
endure.

THE BIRTHDAY WREATH

December 17, 1891.

BLOSSOM and greenness, making all
The winter birthday tropical
And the plain Quaker parlors gay,
Have gone from bracket, stand, and wall ;
We saw them fade, and droop, and fall,
And laid them tenderly away.

White virgin lilies, mignonette,
Blown rose, and pink, and violet,
A breath of fragrance passing by ;
Visions of beauty and decay.
Colors and shapes that could not stay,
The fairest, sweetest, first to die.

But still this rustic wreath of mine,
Of acorned oak and needled pine,
And lighter growths of forest lands,
Woven and wound with careful pains,
And tender thoughts and prayers, remains,
As when it dropped from love's dear
hands.

And not unfitly garlanded,
Is he, who, country-born and bred,
Welcomes the sylvan ring which gives
A feeling of old summer days,
The wild delight of woodland ways,
The glory of the autumn leaves.

And, if the flowery meed of song
To other bards may well belong,
Be his, who from the farm-field spoke
A word for Freedom when her need
Was not of dulcimer and reed,
This Isthmian wreath of pine and oak.

THE WIND OF MARCH

Up from the sea the wild north wind is
blowing
Under the sky's gray arch ;
Smiling, I watch the shaken elm-boughs,
knowing
It is the wind of March.

Between the passing and the coming season,
This stormy interlude
Gives to our winter-wearied hearts a reason
For trustful gratitude.

Welcome to waiting ears its harsh fore-
warning
Of light and warmth to come,
The longed-for joy of Nature's Easter
morning,
The earth arisen in bloom !

In the loud tumult winter's strength is
breaking ;
I listen to the sound,
As to a voice of resurrection, waking
To life the dead, cold ground.

Between these gusts, to the soft lapse I
hearken
Of rivulets on their way ;
I see these tossed and naked tree-tops
darken
With the fresh leaves of May.

This roar of storm, this sky so gray and
lowering
Invite the airs of Spring,
A warmer sunshine over fields of flowering,
The bluebird's song and wing.

Closely behind, the Gulf's warm breezes
follow
This northern hurricane,
And, borne thereon, the bobolink and swal-
low
Shall visit us again.

And, in green wood-paths, in the kine-fed
pasture
And by the whispering rills,
Shall flowers repeat the lesson of the Mas-
ter,
Taught on his Syrian hills.

Blow, then, wild wind ! thy roar shall end
in singing,
Thy chill in blossoming ;
Come, like Bethesda's troubling angel,
bringing
The healing of the Spring.

BETWEEN THE GATES

Between the gates of birth and death
An old and saintly pilgrim passed,
With look of one who witnesseth
The long-sought goal at last.

"O thou whose reverent feet have found
The Master's footprints in thy way
And walked thereon as holy ground,
A boon of thee I pray.

"My lack would borrow thy excess,
My feeble faith the strength of thine ;
I need thy soul's white saintliness
To hide the stains of mine.

"The grace and favor else denied
May well be granted for thy sake."
So, tempted, doubting, sorely tried,
A younger pilgrim spake.

"Thy prayer, my son, transcends my gift ;
No power is mine," the sage replied,
"The burden of a soul to lift
Or stain of sin to hide.

"Howe'er the outward life may seem,
For pardoning grace we all must pray ;
No man his brother can redeem
Or a soul's ransom pay.

"Not always age is growth of good ;
Its years have losses with their gain ;
Against some evil youth withstood
Weak hands may strive in vain.

"With deeper voice than any speech
Of mortal lips from man to man,
What earth's unwisdom may not teach
The Spirit only can.

"Make thou that holy guide thine own,
And following where it leads the way,
The known shall lapse in the unknown
As twilight into day.

" The best of earth shall still remain,
    And heaven's eternal years shall prove
That life and death, and joy and pain,
    Are ministers of Love."

THE LAST EVE OF SUMMER

SUMMER's last sun nigh unto setting shines
    Through yon columnar pines,
And on the deepening shadows of the
        lawn
    Its golden lines are drawn.

Dreaming of long gone summer days like
        this,
    Feeling the wind's soft kiss,
Grateful and glad that failing ear and sight
    Have still their old delight,

I sit alone, and watch the warm, sweet
        day
    Lapse tenderly away ;
And, wistful, with a feeling of forecast,
    I ask, " Is this the last ?

" Will nevermore for me the seasons run
    Their round, and will the sun
Of ardent summers yet to come forget
    For me to rise and set ? "

Thou shouldst be here, or I should be with
        thee
    Wherever thou mayst be,
Lips mute, hands clasped, in silences of
        speech
    Each answering unto each.

For this still hour, this sense of mystery
        far
    Beyond the evening star,
No words outworn suffice on lip or scroll :
    The soul would fain with soul

Wait, while these few swift-passing days
        fulfil
    The wise-disposing Will,
And, in the evening as at morning, trust
    The All-Merciful and Just.

The solemn joy that soul-communion feels
    Immortal life reveals ;
And human love, its prophecy and sign,
    Interprets love divine.

Come then, in thought, if that alone may be,
    O friend ! and bring with thee
Thy calm assurance of transcendent Spheres
    And the Eternal Years !

TO OLIVER WENDELL HOLMES

8TH MO. 29TH, 1892

[This, the last of Mr. Whittier's poems, was
written but a few weeks before his death.]

AMONG the thousands who with hail and
        cheer
    Will welcome thy new year,
How few of all have passed, as thou and I,
    So many milestones by !

We have grown old together ; we have
        seen,
    Our youth and age between,
Two generations leave us, and to-day
    We with the third hold way,

Loving and loved. If thought must back-
        ward run
    To those who, one by one,
In the great silence and the dark beyond
    Vanished with farewells fond,

Unseen, not lost ; our grateful memories
        still
    Their vacant places fill,
And with the full-voiced greeting of new
        friends
    A tenderer whisper blends.

Linked close in a pathetic brotherhood
    Of mingled ill and good,
Of joy and grief, of grandeur and of shame,
    For pity more than blame, —

The gift is thine the weary world to make
    More cheerful for thy sake,
Soothing the ears its Miserere pains,
    With the old Hellenic strains,

Lighting the sullen face of discontent
    With smiles for blessing sent.
Enough of selfish wailing has been had,
    Thank God ! for notes more glad.

Life is indeed no holiday ; therein
    Are want, and woe, and sin,

Death and its nameless fears, and over all
  Our pitying tears must fall.

Sorrow is real ; but the counterfeit
  Which folly brings to it,
We need thy wit and wisdom to resist,
  O rarest Optimist !

Thy hand, old friend ! the service of our
    days,
  In differing moods and ways
May prove to those who follow in our train
  Not valueless nor vain.

Far off, and faint as echoes of a dream,
  The songs of boyhood seem,

Yet on our autumn boughs, unflown with
    spring,
  The evening thrushes sing.

The hour draws near, howe'er delayed and
    late,
  When at the Eternal Gate
We leave the words and works we call our
    own,
  And lift void hands alone

For love to fill.   Our nakedness of soul
  Brings to that Gate no toll ;
Giftless we come to Him, who all things
    gives,
  And live because He lives.

POEMS BY ELIZABETH H. WHITTIER

Originally published in the volume entitled *Hazel Blossoms*, and accompanied by the following prefatory note : —

I have ventured, in compliance with the desire of dear friends of my beloved sister, ELIZABETH H. WHITTIER, to add to this little volume the few poetical pieces which she left behind her. . . . These poems, with perhaps two or three exceptions, afford but slight indications of the inward life of the writer, who had an almost morbid dread of spiritual and intellectual egotism, or of her tenderness of sympathy, chastened mirthfulness, and pleasant play of thought and fancy, when her shy, beautiful soul opened like a flower in the warmth of social communion. In the lines on Dr. Kane her friends will see something of her fine individuality, — the rare mingling of delicacy and intensity of feeling which made her dear to them. This little poem reached Cuba while the great explorer lay on his death-bed, and we are told that he listened with grateful tears while it was read to him by his mother.

I am tempted to say more, but I write as under the eye of her who, while with us, shrank with painful deprecation from the praise or mention of performances which seemed so far below her ideal of excellence. To those who best knew her, the beloved circle of her intimate friends, I dedicate this slight memorial.

J. G. W.

AMESBURY, 9th mo., 1874.

THE DREAM OF ARGYLE

EARTHLY arms no more uphold him
On his prison's stony floor ;
Waiting death in his last slumber,
Lies the doomed MacCallum More.

And he dreams a dream of boyhood ;
Rise again his heathery hills,
Sound again the hound's long baying,
Cry of moor-fowl, laugh of rills.

Now he stands amidst his clansmen
In the low, long banquet-hall,
Over grim ancestral armor
Sees the ruddy firelight fall.

Once again, with pulses beating,
Hears the wandering minstrel tell
How Montrose on Inverary
Thief-like from his mountains fell.

Down the glen, beyond the castle,
Where the linn's swift waters shine,
Round the youthful heir of Argyle
Shy feet glide and white arms twine.

Fairest of the rustic dancers,
Blue-eyed Effie smiles once more,
Bends to him her snooded tresses,
Treads with him the grassy floor.

Now he hears the pipes lamenting,
Harpers for his mother mourn,
Slow, with sable plume and pennon,
To her cairn of burial borne.

Then anon his dreams are darker,
Sounds of battle fill his ears,
And the pibroch's mournful wailing
For his father's fall he hears.

Wild Lochaber's mountain echoes
Wail in concert for the dead,
And Loch Awe's deep waters murmur
For the Campbell's glory fled !

Fierce and strong the godless tyrants
Trample the apostate land,
While her poor and faithful remnant
Wait for the Avenger's hand.

Once again at Inverary,
Years of weary exile o'er,
Armed to lead his scattered clansmen,
Stands the bold MacCallum More.

Once again to battle calling
Sound the war-pipes through the glen ;

And the court-yard of Dunstaffnage
　　Rings with tread of armëd men.

All is lost !　The godless triumph,
　　And the faithful ones and true
From the scaffold and the prison
　　Covenant with God anew.

On the darkness of his dreaming
　　Great and sudden glory shone ;
Over bonds and death victorious
　　Stands he by the Father's throne !

From the radiant ranks of martyrs
　　Notes of joy and praise he hears,
Songs of his poor land's deliverance
　　Sounding from the future years.

Lo, he wakes ! but airs celestial
　　Bathe him in immortal rest,
And he sees with unsealed vision
　　Scotland's cause with victory blest.

Shining hosts attend and guard him
　　As he leaves his prison door ;
And to death as to a triumph
　　Walks the great MacCallum More !

LINES

Written on the departure of Joseph Sturge,
after his visit to the abolitionists of the United
States.

FAIR islands of the sunny sea ! midst all
　　rejoicing things,
No more the wailing of the slave a wild
　　discordance brings ;
On the lifted brows of freemen the tropic
　　breezes blow,
The mildew of the bondman's toil the land
　　no more shall know.

How swells from those green islands,
　　where bird and leaf and flower
Are praising in their own sweet way the
　　dawn of freedom's hour,
The glorious resurrection song from hearts
　　rejoicing poured,
Thanksgiving for the priceless gift, — man's
　　regal crown restored !

How beautiful through all the green and
　　tranquil summer land,

Uplifted, as by miracle, the solemn churches
　　stand !
The grass is trodden from the paths where
　　waiting freemen throng,
Athirst and fainting for the cup of life de-
　　nied so long.

Oh, blessed were the feet of him whose
　　generous errand here
Was to unloose the captive's chain and dry
　　the mourner's tear ;
To lift again the fallen ones a brother's
　　robber hand
Had left in pain and wretchedness by the
　　waysides of the land.

The islands of the sea rejoice ; the harvest
　　anthems rise ;
The sower of the seed must own 't is mar-
　　vellous in his eyes ;
The old waste places are rebuilt, — the
　　broken walls restored, —
And the wilderness is blooming like the
　　garden of the Lord !

Thanksgiving for the holy fruit ! should
　　not the laborer rest,
His earnest faith and works of love have
　　been so richly blest ?
The pride of all fair England shall her
　　ocean islands be,
And their peasantry with joyful hearts
　　keep ceaseless jubilee.

Rest, never ! while his countrymen have
　　trampled hearts to bleed,
The stifled murmur of their wrongs his
　　listening ear shall heed,
Where England's far dependencies her
　　might, not *mercy*, know,
To all the crushed and suffering there his
　　pitying love shall flow.

The friend of freedom everywhere, how
　　mourns he for our land,
The brand of whose hypocrisy burns on
　　her guilty hand !
Her thrift a theft, the robber's greed and
　　cunning in her eye,
Her glory shame, her flaunting flag on all
　　the winds a lie !

For us with steady strength of heart and
　　zeal forever true,

The champion of the island slave the con-
flict doth renew,
His labor here hath been to point the
Pharisaic eye
Away from empty creed and form to where
the wounded lie.

How beautiful to us should seem the com-
ing feet of such !
Their garments of self-sacrifice have heal-
ing in their touch ;
Their gospel mission none may doubt, for
they heed the Master's call,
Who here walked with the multitude, and
sat at meat with all !

JOHN QUINCY ADAMS

HE rests with the immortals ; his journey
has been long :
For him no wail of sorrow, but a pæan full
and strong !
So well and bravely has he done the work
he found to do,
To justice, freedom, duty, God, and man
forever true.

Strong to the end, a man of men, from out
the strife he passed ;
The grandest hour of all his life was that
of earth the last.
Now midst his snowy hills of home to the
grave they bear him down,
The glory of his fourscore years resting on
him like a crown.

The mourning of the many bells, the
drooping flags, all seem
Like some dim, unreal pageant passing on-
ward in a dream ;
And following with the living to his last
and narrow bed,
Methinks I see a shadowy band, a train of
noble dead.

'T is a strange and weird procession that is
slowly moving on,
The phantom patriots gathered to the fu-
neral of their son !
In shadowy guise they move along, brave
Otis with hushed tread,
And Warren walking reverently by the
father of the dead.

Gliding foremost in the misty band a gentle
form is there,
In the white robes of the angels and their
glory round her hair.
She hovers near and bends above her world-
wide honored child,
And the joy that heaven alone can know
beams on her features mild.

And so they bear him to his grave in the
fulness of his years,
True sage and prophet, leaving us in a time
of many fears.
Nevermore amid the darkness of our wild
and evil day
Shall his voice be heard to cheer us, shall
his finger point the way.

DR. KANE IN CUBA

A NOBLE life is in thy care,
A sacred trust to thee is given ;
Bright Island ! let thy healing air
Be to him as the breath of Heaven.

The marvel of his daring life —
The self-forgetting leader bold —
Stirs, like the trumpet's call to strife,
A million hearts of meaner mould.

Eyes that shall never meet his own
Look dim with tears across the sea,
Where from the dark and icy zone,
Sweet Isle of Flowers ! he comes to thee

Fold him in rest, O pitying clime !
Give back his wasted strength again ;
Soothe, with thy endless summer time,
His winter-wearied heart and brain.

Sing soft and low, thou tropic bird,
From out the fragrant, flowery tree, —
The ear that hears thee now has heard
The ice-break of the winter sea.

Through his long watch of awful night,
He saw the Bear in Northern skies ;
Now, to the Southern Cross of light
He lifts in hope his weary eyes.

Prayers from the hearts that watched in fear
When the dark North no answer gave,
Rise, trembling, to the Father's ear,
That still His love may help and save.

LADY FRANKLIN

FOLD thy hands, thy work is over ;
  Cool thy watching eyes with tears ;
Let thy poor heart, over-wearied,
  Rest alike from hopes and fears, —

Hopes, that saw with sleepless vision
  One sad picture fading slow ;
Fears, that followed, vague and nameless,
  Lifting back the veils of snow.

For thy brave one, for thy lost one,
  Truest heart of woman, weep !
Owning still the love that granted
  Unto thy beloved sleep.

Not for him that hour of terror
  When, the long ice-battle o'er,
In the sunless day his comrades
  Deathward trod the Polar shore.

Spared the cruel cold and famine,
  Spared the fainting heart's despair,
What but that could mercy grant him ?
  What but that has been thy prayer ?

Dear to thee that last memorial
  From the cairn beside the sea ;
Evermore the month of roses
  Shall be sacred time to thee.

Sad it is the mournful yew-tree
  O'er his slumbers may not wave ;
Sad it is the English daisy
  May not blossom on his grave.

But his tomb shall storm and winter
  Shape and fashion year by year,
Pile his mighty mausoleum,
  Block by block, and tier on tier.

Guardian of its gleaming portal
  Shall his stainless honor be,
While thy love, a sweet immortal,
  Hovers o'er the winter sea.

NIGHT AND DEATH

THE storm-wind is howling
  Through old pines afar ;
The drear night is falling
  Without moon or star.

The roused sea is lashing
  The bold shore behind,
And the moan of its ebbing
  Keeps time with the wind.

On, on through the darkness,
  A spectre, I pass
Where, like moaning of broken hearts
  Surges the grass !

I see her lone head-stone, —
  'T is white as a shroud ;
Like a pall hangs above it
  The low drooping cloud.

Who speaks through the dark night
  And lull of the wind ?
'T is the sound of the pine-leaves
  And sea-waves behind.

The dead girl is silent, —
  I stand by her now ;
And her pulse beats no quicker,
  Nor crimsons her brow.

The small hand that trembled,
  When last in my own,
Lies patient and folded,
  And colder than stone.

Like the white blossoms falling
  To-night in the gale,
So she in her beauty
  Sank mournful and pale.

Yet I loved her ! I utter
  Such words by her grave,
As I would not have spoken
  Her last breath to save.

Of her love the angels
  In heaven might tell,
While mine would be whispered
  With shudders in hell !

'T was well that the white ones
  Who bore her to bliss
Shut out from her new life
  The vision of this ;

Else, sure as I stand here,
  And speak of my love,
She would leave for my darkness
  Her glory above.

THE MEETING WATERS

CLOSE beside the meeting waters,
  Long I stood as in a dream,
Watching how the little river
  Fell into the broader stream.

Calm and still the mingled current
  Glided to the waiting sea ;
On its breast serenely pictured
  Floating cloud and skirting tree.

And I thought, " O human spirit !
  Strong and deep and pure and blest,
Let the stream of my existence
  Blend with thine, and find its rest ! "

I could die as dies the river,
  In that current deep and wide ;
I would live as live its waters,
  Flashing from a stronger tide !

THE WEDDING VEIL

DEAR Anna, when I brought her veil,
  Her white veil, on her wedding night,
Threw o'er my thin brown hair its folds,
  And, laughing, turned me to the light.

" See, Bessie, see ! you wear at last
  The bridal veil, forsworn for years ! "
She saw my face, — her laugh was hushed,
  Her happy eyes were filled with tears.

With kindly haste and trembling hand
  She drew away the gauzy mist ;
" Forgive, dear heart ! " her sweet voice
    said :
  Her loving lips my forehead kissed.

We passed from out the searching light ;
  The summer night was calm and fair :
I did not see her pitying eyes,
  I felt her soft hand smooth my hair.

Her tender love unlocked my heart ;
  Mid falling tears, at last I said,
" Forsworn indeed to me that veil
  Because I only love the dead ! "

She stood one moment statue-still,
  And, musing, spake, in undertone,
" The living love may colder grow ;
  The dead is safe with God alone ! "

CHARITY

THE pilgrim and stranger who through the
    day
Holds over the desert his trackless way,
Where the terrible sands no shade have
    known,
No sound of life save his camel's moan,
Hears, at last, through the mercy of Allah
    to all,
From his tent-door at evening the Bedouin's
    call :
" *Whoever thou art whose need is great,*
In the name of God, the Compassionate
And Merciful One, for thee I wait ! "

For gifts in His name of food and rest
The tents of Islam of God are blest ;
Thou who hast faith in the Christ above,
Shall the Koran teach thee the Law of
    Love ? —
O Christian ! open thy heart and door,
Cry east and west to the wandering poor :
" *Whoever thou art whose need is great,*
In the name of Christ, the Compassionate
And Merciful One, for thee I wait ! "

APPENDIX

I. EARLY AND UNCOLLECTED VERSES

I AM yielding to what seems, under the circumstances, almost a necessity, in adding to the pieces assigned for one reason or another to the limbo of an appendix, some of my very earliest attempts at verse, which have been kept alive in the newspapers for the last half century. A few of them have even been printed in book form without my consent, and greatly to my annoyance, with all their accumulated errors of the press added to their original defects and crudity. I suppose they should have died a natural death long ago, but their feline tenacity of life seems to contradict the theory of the "survival of the fittest." I have consented, at my publishers' request, to take the poor vagrants home and give them a more presentable appearance, in the hope that they may at least be of some interest to those who are curious enough to note the weak beginnings of the graduate of a small country district school, sixty years ago. That they met with some degree of favor at that time may be accounted for by the fact that the makers of verse were then few in number, with little competition in their unprofitable vocation, and that the standard of criticism was not discouragingly high.

The earliest of the author's verses that found their way into print were published in the Newburyport *Free Press*, edited by William Lloyd Garrison, in 1826. [The poems here collected, with the exception of the last, were written during the years 1825–1833.]

THE EXILE'S DEPARTURE

FOND scenes, which delighted my youthful existence,
  With feelings of sorrow I bid ye adieu —
A lasting adieu! for now, dim in the distance,
  The shores of Hibernia recede from my view.
Farewell to the cliffs, tempest-beaten and gray,
  Which guard the lov'd shores of my own native land;
Farewell to the village and sail-shadow'd bay,
  The forest-crown'd hill and the water-wash'd strand.

I 've fought for my country — I 've brav'd all the dangers
  That throng round the path of the warrior in strife;
I now must depart to a nation of strangers,
  And pass in seclusion the remnant of life;
Far, far from the friends to my bosom most dear,
  With none to support me in peril and pain,
And none but the stranger to drop the sad tear
  On the grave where the heart-broken Exile is lain.

Friends of my youth! I must leave you forever,
  And hasten to dwell in a region unknown: —
Yet time cannot change, nor the broad ocean sever,
  Hearts firmly united and tried as our own.
Ah, no! though I wander, all sad and forlorn,
  In a far distant land, yet shall memory trace,
When far o'er the ocean's white surges I 'm borne,
  The scene of past pleasures, — my own native place.

Farewell, shores of Erin, green land of my fathers: —
  Once more, and forever, a mournful adieu!
For round thy dim headlands the ocean-mist gathers,
  And shrouds the fair isle I no longer can view.
I go — but wherever my footsteps I bend,
  For freedom and peace to my own native isle,
And contentment and joy to each warm-hearted friend
  Shall be the heart's prayer of the lonely Exile!

THE DEITY

                    THE Prophet stood
On the high mount, and saw the tempest cloud
Pour the fierce whirlwind from its reservoir
Of congregated gloom. The mountain oak,
Torn from the earth, heaved high its roots where once
Its branches waved. The fir-tree's shapely form,
Smote by the tempest, lashed the mountain's side.
Yet, calm in conscious purity, the Seer
Beheld the awful desolation, for
The Eternal Spirit moved not in the storm.

The tempest ceased. The caverned earthquake burst
Forth from its prison, and the mountain rocked
Even to its base. The topmost crags were thrown,
With fearful crashing, down its shuddering sides.
Unawed, the Prophet saw and heard; he felt
Not in the earthquake moved the God of Heaven.
The murmur died away; and from the height,
Torn by the storm and shattered by the shock,
Rose far and clear a pyramid of flame
Mighty and vast; the startled mountain deer
Shrank from its glare, and cowered within the shade;
The wild fowl shrieked — but even then the Seer
Untrembling stood and marked the fearful glow,
For Israel's God came not within the flame!

The fiery beacon sank. A still, small voice,
Unlike to human sound, at once conveyed
Deep awe and reverence to his pious heart.
Then bowed the holy man; his face he veiled
Within his mantle — and in meekness owned
The presence of his God, discerned not in
The storm, the earthquake, or the mighty flame.

THE VALE OF THE MERRIMAC

THERE are streams which are famous in history's story,
  Whose names are familiar to pen and to tongue,
Renowned in the records of love and of glory,
  Where knighthood has ridden and minstrels have sung: —
Fair streams thro' more populous regions are gliding,
  Tower, temple, and palace their borders adorning,
With tall-masted ships on their broad bosoms riding,
  Their banners stretch'd out in the breezes of morning;
And their vales may be lovely and pleasant — but never
Was skiff ever wafted, or wav'd a white sail
O'er a lovelier wave than my dear native river,
  Or brighter tides roll'd than in Merrimac's vale!

And fair streams may glide where the climate is milder,
  Where winter ne'er gathers and spring ever blooms,
And others may roll where the region is wilder,
  Their dark waters hid in some forest's deep gloom,
Where the thunder-scath'd peaks of Helvetia are frowning,
  And the Rhine's rapid waters encircle their bases,

Where the snows of long years are the hoary Alps crowning,
  And the tempest-charg'd vapor their tall tops embraces: —
There sure might be fix'd, amid scenery so frightful,
  The region of romance and wild fairy-tale, —
But such scenes could not be to my heart so delightful
  As the home of my fathers, — fair Merrimac's vale!

There are streams where the bounty of Providence musters
  The fairest of fruits by their warm sunny sides,
The vine bending low with the grape's heavy clusters,
  And the orange-tree waving its fruit o'er their tides: —
But I envy not him whose lot has been cast there,
  For oppression is there — and the hand of the spoiler,
Regardless of justice or mercy, has past there,
  And made him a wretched and indigent toiler.
No — dearer to me are the scenes of my childhood,
  The moss-cover'd bank and the breeze-wafted sail,
The age-stinted oak and the green groves of wild-wood
  That wave round the borders of Merrimac's vale!

Oh, lovely the scene, when the gray misty vapor
  Of morning is lifted from Merrimac's shore;
When the fire-fly, lighting his wild gleaming taper,
  Thy dimly seen lowlands comes glimmering o'er;
When on thy calm surface the moonbeam falls brightly,
  And the dull bird of night is his covert forsaking,
When the whippoorwill's notes from thy margin sound lightly,
  And break on the sound which thy small waves are making,
O brightest of visions! my heart shall forever,
  Till memory shall perish and reason shall fail,
Still preference give to my own native river,
  The home of my fathers, and Merrimac's vale!

BENEVOLENCE

HAIL, heavenly gift! within the human breast,
Germ of unnumber'd virtues — by thy aid
The fainting heart, with riving grief opprest,
  Survives the ruin adverse scenes have made:
Woes that have wrung the bosom, cares that preyed
  Long on the spirit, are dissolv'd by thee —
Misfortune's frown, despair's disastrous shade.

Ghastly disease, and pining poverty,
Thy influence dread, and at thy approach they
  flee.

Thy spirit led th' immortal Howard on;
  Nurtur'd by thee, on many a foreign shore
Imperishable fame, by virtue won,
  Adorns his memory, tho' his course is o'er;
Thy animating smile his aspect wore,
  To cheer the sorrow-desolated soul,
Compassion's balm in grief-worn hearts to pour,
  And snatch the prisoner from despair's con-
    trol,
Steal half his woes away, and lighter make the
  whole.

Green be the sod on Cherson's honor'd field,
  Where wraps the turf around his mouldering
    clay;
There let the earth her choicest beauties yield,
  And there the breeze in gentlest murmurs
    play;
There let the widow and the orphan stray,
  To wet with tears their benefactor's tomb;
There let the rescued prisoner bend his way,
  And mourn o'er him, who in the dungeon's
    gloom
Had sought him and averted misery's fearful
  doom.

His grave perfum'd with heartfelt sighs of
    grief,
  And moistened by the tear of gratitude, —
Oh, how unlike the spot where war's grim chief
  Sinks on the field, in sanguine waves im-
    brued!
Who mourns for him, whose footsteps can be
    viewed
  With reverential awe imprinted near
The monument rear'd o'er the man of blood?
  Or who waste on it sorrow's balmy tear?
None! shame and misery rest alone upon his
  bier.

Offspring of heaven! Benevolence, thy pow'r
  Bade Wilberforce its mighty champion be,
And taught a Clarkson's ardent mind to soar
  O'er every obstacle, when serving thee: —
Theirs was the task to set the sufferer free,
  To break the bonds which bound th' unwill-
    ing slave,
To shed abroad the light of liberty,
  And leave to all the rights their Maker gave,
To bid the world rejoice o'er hated slavery's
  grave.

Diffuse thy charms, Benevolence! let thy light
  Pierce the dark clouds which ages past have
    thrown
Before the beams of truth — and nature's right,
  Inborn, let every hardened tyrant own;
On our fair shore be thy mild presence known;
  And every portion of Columbia's land
Be as God's garden with thy blessings sown;
  Yea, o'er Earth's regions let thy love expand
Till all united are in friendship's sacred band!

Then in that hour of joy will be fulfilled
  The prophet's heart-consoling prophecy;
Then war's commotion shall on earth be stilled,
  And men their swords to other use apply;
Then Afric's injured sons no more shall try
  The bitterness of slavery's toil and pain,
Nor pride nor love of gain direct the eye
  Of stern oppression to their homes again;
But peace, a lasting peace, throughout the
  world shall reign.

OCEAN

UNFATHOMED deep, unfetter'd waste
    Of never-silent waves,
Each by its rushing follower chas'd,
    Through unillumin'd caves,
And o'er the rocks whose turrets rude,
    E'en since the birth of time,
Have heard amid thy solitude
    The billow's ceaseless chime.

O'er what recesses, depths unknown,
    Dost thou thy waves impel,
Where never yet a sunbeam shone,
    Or gleam of moonlight fell?
For never yet did mortal eyes
    Thy gloom-wrapt deeps behold,
And naught of thy dread mysteries
    The tongue of man hath told.

What, though proud man presume to hold
    His course upon thy tide,
O'er thy dark billows uncontroll'd
    His fragile bark to guide —
Yet who, upon thy mountain waves,
    Can feel himself secure
While sweeping o'er thy yawning caves,
    Deep, awful, and obscure?

But thou art mild and tranquil now —
    Thy wrathful spirits sleep,
And gentle billows, calm and slow,
    Across thy bosom sweep.
Yet where the dim horizon's bound
    Rests on thy sparkling bed,
The tempest-cloud, in gloom profound,
    Prepares its wrath to shed.

Thus, mild and calm in youth's bright hour
    The tide of life appears,
When fancy paints, with magic spell,
    The bliss of coming years;
But clouds will rise, and darkness bring
    O'er life's deceitful way,
And cruel disappointment fling
    Its shade on hope's dim ray.

THE SICILIAN VESPERS

SILENCE o'er sea and earth
    With the veil of evening fell,
Till the convent-tower sent deeply forth
    The chime of its vesper bell.

One moment — and that solemn sound
  Fell heavy on the ear;
But a sterner echo passed around,
  And the boldest shook to hear.

The startled monks thronged up,
  In the torchlight cold and dim;
And the priest let fall his incense-cup,
  And the virgin hushed her hymn,
For a boding clash, and a clanging tramp,
  And a summoning voice were heard,
And fretted wall, and dungeon damp,
  To the fearful echo stirred.

The peasant heard the sound,
  As he sat beside his hearth;
And the song and the dance were hushed around,
  With the fire-side tale of mirth.
The chieftain shook in his banner'd hall,
  As the sound of fear drew nigh,
And the warder shrank from the castle wall,
  As the gleam of spears went by.

Woe! woe! to the stranger, then,
  At the feast and flow of wine,
In the red array of mailëd men,
  Or bowed at the holy shrine;
For the wakened pride of an injured land
  Had burst its iron thrall,
From the plumëd chief to the pilgrim band;
  Woe! woe! to the sons of Gaul!

Proud beings fell that hour,
  With the young and passing fair,
And the flame went up from dome and tower,
  The avenger's arm was there!
The stranger priest at the altar stood,
  And clasped his beads in prayer,
But the holy shrine grew dim with blood,
  The avenger found him there!

Woe! woe! to the sons of Gaul,
  To the serf and mailëd lord;
They were gathered darkly, one and all,
  To the harvest of the sword:
And the morning sun, with a quiet smile,
  Shone out o'er hill and glen,
On ruined temple and smouldering pile,
  And the ghastly forms of men.

Ay, the sunshine sweetly smiled,
  As its early glance came forth,
It had no sympathy with the wild
  And terrible things of earth.
And the man of blood that day might read,
  In a language freely given,
How ill his dark and midnight deed
  Became the calm of Heaven.

THE SPIRIT OF THE NORTH

SPIRIT of the frozen North,
  Where the wave is chained and still,
And the savage bear looks forth
  Nightly from his caverned hill!

Down from thy eternal throne,
  From thy land of cloud and storm,
Where the meeting icebergs groan,
  Sweepeth on thy wrathful form.

Spirit of the frozen wing!
  Dweller of a voiceless clime,
Where no coming on of spring
  Gilds the weary course of time!
Monarch of a realm untrod
  By the restless feet of men,
Where alone the hand of God
  'Mid his mighty works hath been!

Throned amid the ancient hills,
  Piled with undecaying snow,
Flashing with the path of rills,
  Frozen in their first glad flow;
Thou hast seen the gloomy north,
  Gleaming with unearthly light,
Spreading its pale banners forth,
  Checkered with the stars of night.

Thou hast gazed untrembling, where
  Giant forms of flame were driven,
Like the spirits of the air,
  Striding up the vault of heaven!
Thou hast seen that midnight glow,
  Hiding moon and star and sky,
And the icy hills below
  Reddening to the fearful dye.

Dark and desolate and lone,
  Curtained with the tempest-cloud,
Drawn around thy ancient throne
  Like oblivion's moveless shroud,
Dim and distantly the sun
  Glances on thy palace walls,
But a shadow cold and dun
  Broods along its pillared halls.

Lord of sunless depths and cold!
  Chainer of the northern sea!
At whose feet the storm is rolled,
  Who hath power to humble thee?
Spirit of the stormy north!
  Bow thee to thy Maker's nod;
Bend to him who sent thee forth,
  Servant of the living God.

THE EARTHQUAKE

CALMLY the night came down
  O'er Scylla's shatter'd walls;
How desolate that silent town!
  How tenantless the halls,
Where yesterday her thousands trod,
And princes graced their proud abode!

Low, on the wet sea sand,
  Humbled in anguish now,
The despot, midst his menial band,
  Bent down his kingly brow;
And prince and peasant knelt in prayer,
For grief had made them equal there.

Again as at the morn,
  The earthquake roll'd its car :
Lowly the castle-towers were borne,
  That mock'd the storms of war ;
The mountain reeled, its shiver'd brow
Went down among the waves below.

Up rose the kneelers then,
  As the wave's rush was heard :
The horror of those fated men
  Was uttered by no word.
But closer still the mother prest
The infant to her faithful breast.

One long, wild shriek went up,
  Full mighty in despair ;
As bow'd to drink death's bitter cup,
  The thousands gathered there ;
And man's strong wail and woman's cry
Blent as the waters hurried by.

On swept the whelming sea ;
  The mountains felt its shock,
As the long cry of agony
  Thrills thro' their towers of rock ;
An echo round that fatal shore
The death wail of the sufferers bore.

The morning sun shed forth
  Its light upon the scene,
Where tower and palace strew'd the earth
  With wrecks of what had been.
But of the thousands who were gone,
No trace was left, no vestige shown.

JUDITH AT THE TENT OF HOLO-
FERNES

Night was down among the mountains,
  In her dim and quiet manner,
Where Bethulia's silver fountains
  Gushed beneath the Assyrian banner.
Moonlight, o'er her meek dominion,
  As a mighty flag unfurled,
Like an angel's snowy pinion
  Resting on a darkened world !

Faintly rose the city's murmur,
  But the crowded camp was calm ;
Girded in their battle armor,
  Each a falchion at his arm,
Lordly chief and weary vassal
  In the arms of slumber fell ;
It had been a day of wassail,
  And the wine had circled well.

Underneath his proud pavilion
  Lay Assyria's champion,
Where the ruby's rich vermilion
  Shone beside the beryl-stone.
With imperial purple laden,
  Breathing in the perfumed air,
Dreams he of the Jewish maiden,
  With her dark and jewelled hair.

Who is she, the pale-browed stranger,
  Bending o'er that son of slaughter ?

God be with thee in thy danger,
  Israel's lone and peerless daughter !
She hath bared her queenly beauty
  To the dark Assyrian's glance ;
Now a high and sterner duty
  Bids her to his couch advance.

Beautiful and pale she bendeth
  In her earnest prayer to Heaven ;
Look again, that maiden standeth
  In the strength her God has given !
Strangely is her dark eye kindled,
  Hot blood through her cheek is poured ;
Lo, her every fear hath dwindled,
  And her hand is on the sword !

Upward to the flashing curtain,
  See, that mighty blade is driven,
And its fall ! — 'tis swift and certain
  As the cloud-fire's track in heaven !
Down, as with a power supernal,
  Twice the lifted weapon fell ;
Twice, his slumber is eternal —
  Who shall wake the infidel ?

Sunlight on the mountains streameth
  Like an air-borne wave of gold ;
And Bethulia's armor gleameth
  Round Judea's banner-fold.
Down they go, the mailëd warriors,
  As the upper torrents sally
Headlong from their mountain-barriers
  Down upon the sleeping valley.

Rouse thee from thy couch, Assyrian !
  Dream no more of woman's smile ;
Fiercer than the leaguered Tyrian,
  Or the dark-browed sons of Nile,
Foes are on thy slumber breaking,
  Chieftain, to thy battle rise !
Vain the call — he will not waken —
  Headless on his couch he lies.

Who hath dimmed your boasted glory ?
  What hath woman's weakness done ?
Whose dark brow is up before ye,
  Blackening in the fierce-haired sun ?
Lo ! an eye that never slumbers
  Looketh in its vengeance down ;
And the thronged and mailëd numbers
  Wither at Jehovah's frown !

METACOM

Metacom, or Philip, the chief of the Wam-
panoags, was the most powerful and sagacious
Sachem who ever made war upon the English.

Red as the banner which enshrouds
  The warrior-dead, when strife is done,
A broken mass of crimson clouds
  Hung over the departed sun.
The shadow of the western hill
Crept swiftly down, and darkly still,
As if a sullen wave of night
Were rushing on the pale twilight ;

The forest-openings grew more dim,
  As glimpses of the arching blue
  And waking stars came softly through
The rifts of many a giant limb.
Above the wet and tangled swamp
White vapors gathered thick and damp,
And through their cloudy curtaining
Flapped many a brown and dusky wing —
Pinions that fan the moonless dun,
But fold them at the rising sun !

Beneath the closing veil of night,
  And leafy bough and curling fog,
With his few warriors ranged in sight —
Scarred relics of his latest fight —
  Rested the fiery Wampanoag.
He leaned upon his loaded gun,
Warm with its recent work of death,
And, save the struggling of his breath,
That, slow and hard and long-repressed,
Shook the damp folds around his breast,
An eye that was unused to scan
The sterner moods of that dark man
Had deemed his tall and silent form
With hidden passion fierce and warm,
With that fixed eye, as still and dark
As clouds which veil their lightning spark,
That of some forest-champion,
Whom sudden death had passed upon —
A giant frozen into stone !
Son of the thronëd Sachem ! — Thou,
The sternest of the forest kings, —
Shall the scorned pale-one trample now,
Unambushed on thy mountain's brow,
Yea, drive his vile and hated plough
  Among thy nation's holy things,
Crushing the warrior-skeleton
In scorn beneath his armëd heel,
And not a hand be left to deal
A kindred vengeance fiercely back,
And cross in blood the Spoiler's track ?

He turned him to his trustiest one,
The old and war-tried Annawon —
" Brother ! " — The favored warrior stood
In hushed and listening attitude —
" This night the Vision-Spirit hath
  Unrolled the scroll of fate before me ;
And ere the sunrise cometh, Death
  Will wave his dusky pinion o'er me !
Nay, start not — well I know thy faith —
Thy weapon now may keep its sheath ;
But, when the bodeful morning breaks,
And the green forest widely wakes
Unto the roar of English thunder,
Then trusted brother, be it thine
To burst upon the foeman's line,
And rend his serried strength asunder.
Perchance thyself and yet a few
Of faithful ones may struggle through,
And, rallying on the wooded plain,
Strike deep for vengeance once again,
And offer up in pale-face blood
An offering to the Indian's God."

A musket shot — a sharp, quick yell —
  And then the stifled groan of pain,

Told that another red man fell, —
  And blazed a sudden light again
Across that kingly brow and eye,
Like lightning on a clouded sky, —
And a low growl, like that which thrills
The hunter of the Eastern hills,
  Burst through clenched teeth and rigid lip —
And, when the great chief spoke again
His deep voice shook beneath its rein,
  As wrath and grief held fellowship.

" Brother ! methought when as but now
  I pondered on my nation's wrong,
With sadness on his shadowy brow
  My father's spirit passed along !
He pointed to the far south-west,
  Where sunset's gold was growing dim,
  And seemed to beckon me to him,
And to the forests of the blest ! —
My father loved the white men, when
They were but children, shelterless,
For his great spirit at distress
Melted to woman's tenderness —
Nor was it given him to know
  That children whom he cherished then
  Would rise at length, like armëd men,
To work his people's overthrow.
Yet thus it is ; — the God before
Whose awful shrine the pale ones bow
Hath frowned upon, and given o'er
The red man to the stranger now !
A few more moons, and there will be
No gathering to the council tree ;
The scorchëd earth — the blackened log —
  The naked bones of warriors slain,
  Be the sole relics which remain
Of the once mighty Wampanoag !
The forests of our hunting-land,
  With all their old and solemn green,
Will bow before the Spoiler's axe —
The plough displace the hunter's tracks,
And the tall prayer-house steeple stand
Where the Great Spirit's shrine hath been!

" Yet, brother, from this awful hour
  The dying curse of Metacom
Shall linger with abiding power
  Upon the spoilers of my home.
The fearful veil of things to come,
By Kitchtan's hand is lifted from
The shadows of the embryo years ;
  And I can see more clearly through
Than ever visioned Powwaw did,
For all the future comes unbid
  Yet welcome to my trancëd view,
As battle-yell to warrior-ears !
From stream and lake and hunting-hill
  Our tribes may vanish like a dream,
  And even my dark curse may seem
Like idle winds when Heaven is still,
  No bodeful harbinger of ill ;
But, fiercer than the downright thunder,
When yawns the mountain-rock asunder,
And riven pine and knotted oak
Are reeling to the fearful stroke,
  That curse shall work its master's will !
The bed of yon blue mountain stream

Shall pour a darker tide than rain —
The sea shall catch its blood-red stain,
And broadly on its banks shall gleam
　　The steel of those who should be brothers ;
Yea, those whom one fond parent nursed
Shall meet in strife, like fiends accursed,
And trample down the once loved form,
While yet with breathing passion warm,
　　As fiercely as they would another's ! "

The morning star sat dimly on
The lighted eastern horizon —
The deadly glare of levelled gun
　　Came streaking through the twilight haze
　　And naked to its reddest blaze,
A hundred warriors sprang in view ;
　　One dark red arm was tossed on high,
One giant shout came hoarsely through
　　The clangor and the charging cry,
Just as across the scattering gloom,
Red as the naked hand of Doom,
　　The English volley hurtled by —
The arm — the voice of Metacom ! —
One piercing shriek — one vengeful yell,
Sent like an arrow to the sky,
　　Told when the hunter-monarch fell !

MOUNT AGIOCHOOK

The Indians supposed the White Mountains
were the residence of powerful spirits, and in
consequence rarely ascended them.

GRAY searcher of the upper air,
　　There 's sunshine on thy ancient walls,
A crown upon thy forehead bare,
　　A flash upon thy waterfalls,
A rainbow glory in the cloud
　　Upon thine awful summit bowed,
The radiant ghost of a dead storm !
　　And music from the leafy shroud
Which swathes in green thy giant form,
　　Mellowed and softened from above
Steals downward to the lowland ear,
　　Sweet as the first, fond dream of love
That melts upon the maiden's ear.

The time has been, white giant, when
　　Thy shadows veiled the red man's home,
And over crag and serpent den,
And wild gorge where the steps of men
　　In chase or battle might not come,
The mountain eagle bore on high
　　The emblem of the free of soul,
And, midway in the fearful sky,
Sent back the Indian battle cry,
　　And answered to the thunder's roll.

The wigwam fires have all burned out,
　　The moccasin has left no track ;
Nor wolf nor panther roam about
　　The Saco and the Merrimac.
And thou, that liftest up on high
Thy mighty barriers to the sky,
　　Art not the haunted mount of old,
Where on each crag of blasted stone

Some dreadful spirit found his throne,
　　And hid within the thick cloud fold,
Heard only in the thunder's crash,
Seen only in the lightning's flash,
When crumbled rock and riven branch
Went down before the avalanche !

No more that spirit moveth there ;
　　The dwellers of the vale are dead ;
No hunter's arrow cleaves the air ;
　　No dry leaf rustles to his tread.
The pale-face climbs thy tallest rock,
His hands thy crystal gates unlock ;
From steep to steep his maidens call,
Light laughing, like the streams that fall
In music down thy rocky wall,
And only when their careless tread
Lays bare an Indian arrow-head,
Spent and forgetful of the deer,
Think of the race that perished here.

Oh, sacred to the Indian seer,
　　Gray altar of the men of old !
Not vainly to the listening ear
　　The legends of thy past are told, —
Tales of the downward sweeping flood,
When bowed like reeds thy ancient wood ;
Of armëd hands, and spectral forms ;
Of giants in their leafy shroud,
And voices calling long and loud
In the dread pauses of thy storms.
For still within their caverned home
Dwell the strange gods of heathendom !

THE DRUNKARD TO HIS BOTTLE

I was thinking of the temperance lyrics the
great poet of Scotland might have written had
he put his name to a pledge of abstinence, a
thing unhappily unknown in his day. The
result of my cogitation was this poor imitation
of his dialect.

HOOT ! — daur ye shaw ye're face again,
Ye auld black thief o' purse an' brain ?
For foul disgrace, for dool an' pain
　　An' shame I ban ye :
Wae 's me, that e'er my lips have ta'en
　　Your kiss uncanny !

Nae mair, auld knave, without a shillin'
To keep a starvin' wight frae stealin'
Ye 'll sen' me hameward, blin' and reelin',
　　Frae nightly swagger,
By wall an' post my pathway feelin',
　　Wi' mony a stagger.

Nae mair o' fights that bruise an' mangle,
Nae mair o' nets my feet to tangle,
Nae mair o' senseless brawl an' wrangle,
　　Wi' frien' an' wife too,
Nae mair o' deavin' din an' jangle
　　My feckless life through.

Ye thievin', cheatin' auld Cheap Jack,
Peddlin' your poison brose, I crack

Your banes against my ingle-back
  Wi' meikle pleasure.
Deil mend ye i' his workshop black,
  E'en at his leisure !

I 'll brak ye're neck, ye foul auld sinner,
I 'll spill ye're bluid, ye vile beginner
O' a' the ills an' aches that winna
  Quat saul an' body !
Gie me hale breeks an' weel-spread dinner —
  Deil tak' ye're toddy !

Nae mair wi' witches' broo gane gyte,
Gie me ance mair the auld delight
O' sittin' wi' my bairns in sight,
  The gude wife near,
The weel-spent day, the peacefu' night,
  The mornin' cheer !

Cock a' ye're heids, my bairns fu' gleg,
My winsome Robin, Jean, an' Meg,
For food and claes ye shall na beg
  A doited daddie.
Dance, auld wife, on your girl-day leg,
  Ye 've foun' your laddie !

THE FAIR QUAKERESS

SHE was a fair young girl, yet on her brow
No pale pearl shone, a blemish on the pure
And snowy lustre of its living light,
No radiant gem shone beautifully through
The shadowing of her tresses, as a star
Through the dark sky of midnight; and no wreath
Of coral circled on her queenly neck,
In mockery of the glowing cheek and lip,
Whose hue the fairy guardian of the flowers
Might never rival when her delicate touch
Tinges the rose of springtime.

               Unadorned,
Save by her youthful charms, and with a garb
Simple as Nature's self, why turn to her
The proud and gifted, and the versed in all
The pageantry of fashion ?

              She hath not
Moved down the dance to music, when the hall
Is lighted up like sunshine, and the thrill
Of the light viol and the mellow flute,
And the deep tones of manhood, softened down
To very music melt upon the ear. —
She has not mingled with the hollow world
Nor tampered with its mockeries, until all
The delicate perceptions of the heart,
The innate modesty, the watchful sense
Of maiden dignity, are lost within
The maze of fashion and the din of crowds.

Yet Beauty hath its homage. Kings have bowed
From the tall majesty of ancient thrones
With a prostrated knee, yea, cast aside
The awfulness of time-created power

For the regardful glances of a child.
Yea, the high ones and powerful of Earth,
The helmëd sons of victory, the grave
And schooled philosophers, the giant men
Of overmastering intellect, have turned
Each from the separate idol of his high
And vehement ambition for the low
Idolatry of human loveliness ;
And bartered the sublimity of mind,
The godlike and commanding intellect
Which nations knelt to, for a woman's tear,
A soft-toned answer, or a wanton's smile.

And in the chastened beauty of that eye,
And in the beautiful play of that red lip,
And in the quiet smile, and in the voice
Sweet as the tuneful greeting of a bird
To the first flowers of springtime, there is more
Than the perfection of the painter's skill
Or statuary's moulding. *Mind* is there,
The pure and holy attributes of soul,
The seal of virtue, the exceeding grace
Of meekness blended with a maiden pride ;
Nor deem ye that beneath the gentle smile,
And the calm temper of a chastened mind
No warmth of passion kindles, and no tide
Of quick and earnest feeling courses on
From the warm heart's pulsations. There are springs
Of deep and pure affection, hidden now,
Within that quiet bosom, which but wait
The thrilling of some kindly touch, to flow
Like waters from the Desert-rock of old.

BOLIVAR

A DIRGE is wailing from the Gulf of storm-vexed Mexico,
To where through Pampas' solitudes the mighty rivers flow ;
The dark Sierras hear the sound, and from each mountain rift,
Where Andes and Cordilleras their awful summits lift,
Where Cotopaxi's fiery eye glares redly upon heaven,
And Chimborazo's shattered peak the upper sky has riven ;
From mount to mount, from wave to wave, a wild and long lament,
A sob that shakes like her earthquakes the startled continent !

A light dies out, a life is sped — the hero's at whose word
The nations started as from sleep, and girded on the sword ;
The victor of a hundred fields where blood was poured like rain,
And Freedom's loosened avalanche hurled down the hosts of Spain,
The eagle soul on Junin's slope who showed his shouting men
A grander sight than Balboa saw from wave-washed Darien,

As from the snows with battle red died out the
    sinking sun,
And broad and vast beneath him lay a world
    for freedom won.

How died that victor? In the field with ban-
    ners o'er him thrown,
With trumpets in his failing ear, by charging
    squadrons blown,
With scattered foemen flying fast and fearfully
    before him,
With shouts of triumph swelling round and
    brave men bending o'er him?
Not on his fields of victory, nor in his council
    hall,
The worn and sorrowing leader heard the inev-
    itable call.
Alone he perished in the land he saved from
    slavery's ban,
Maligned and doubted and denied, a broken-
    hearted man!

Now let the New World's banners droop above
    the fallen chief,
And let the mountaineer's dark eyes be wet
    with tears of grief!
For slander's sting, for envy's hiss, for friend-
    ship hatred grown,
Can funeral pomp, and tolling bell, and priestly
    mass atone?
Better to leave unmourned the dead than wrong
    men while they live;
What if the strong man failed or erred, could
    not his own forgive?
O people freed by him, repent above your hero's
    bier:
The sole resource of late remorse is now his
    tomb to rear!

ISABELLA OF AUSTRIA

Isabella, Infanta of Parma, and consort of
Joseph of Austria, predicted her own death,
immediately after her marriage with the Em-
peror. Amidst the gayety and splendor of
Vienna and Presburg, she was reserved and
melancholy; she believed that Heaven had
given her a view of the future, and that her
child, the namesake of the great Maria The-
resa, would perish with her. Her prediction
was fulfilled.

'MIDST the palace bowers of Hungary, imperial
    Presburg's pride,
With the noble born and beautiful assembled
    at her side,
She stood beneath the summer heavens, the soft
    wind sighing on,
Stirring the green and arching boughs like
    dancers in the sun.
The beautiful pomegranate flower, the snowy
    orange bloom,
The lotus and the trailing vine, the rose's
    meek perfume,

The willow crossing with its green some statue's
    marble hair,
All that might charm the fresh young sense, or
    light the soul, was there!

But she, a monarch's treasured one, leaned
    gloomily apart,
With her dark eyes tearfully cast down; and
    a shadow on her heart.
Young, beautiful, and dearly loved, what sorrow
    hath she known?
Are not the hearts and swords of all held
    sacred as her own?
Is not her lord the kingliest in battle-field or
    tower?
The wisest in the council-hall, the gayest in
    the bower?
Is not his love as full and deep as his own
    Danube's tide?
And wherefore in her princely home weeps
    Isabel, his bride?

She raised her jewelled hand, and flung her
    veiling tresses back,
Bathing its snowy tapering within their glossy
    black.
A tear fell on the orange leaves, rich gem and
    mimic blossom,
And fringëd robe shook fearfully upon her
    sighing bosom.
"Smile on, smile on," she murmured low,
    "for all is joy around,
Shadow and sunshine, stainless sky, soft airs,
    and blossomed ground.
'T is meet the light of heart should smile,
    when nature's smile is fair,
And melody and fragrance meet, twin sisters
    of the air.

"But ask me not to share with you the beauty
    of the scene,
The fountain-fall, mosaic walk, and breadths
    of tender green;
And point not to the mild blue sky, or glorious
    summer sun,
I know how very fair is all the hand of God
    has done.
The hills, the sky, the sunlit cloud, the waters
    leaping forth,
The swaying trees, the scented flowers, the
    dark green robes of earth, —
I love them well, but I have learned to turn
    aside from all,
And nevermore my heart must own their
    sweet but fatal thrall.

"And I could love the noble one whose mighty
    name I bear,
And closer to my breaking heart his princely
    image wear,
And I could love our sweet young flower, un-
    folding day by day,
And taste of that unearthly joy which mothers
    only may, —
But what am I to cling to these? — A voice is
    in my ear,

A shadow lingers at my side, the death-wail
    and the bier !
The cold and starless night of Death where
    day may never beam,
The silence and forgetfulness, the sleep that
    hath no dream !

"O God, to leave this fair bright world, and
    more than all to know
The moment when the Spectral One shall
    strike his fearful blow ;
To know the day, the very hour, to feel the
    tide roll on,
To shudder at the gloom before and weep the
    sunshine gone ;
To count the days, the few short days, of light
    and love and breath
Between me and the noisome grave, the voice-
    less home of death !
Alas ! — if feeling, knowing this, I murmur at
    my doom,
Let not thy frowning, O my God ! lend dark-
    ness to the tomb.

"Oh, I have borne my spirit up, and smiled
    amidst the chill
Remembrance of my certain doom which lin-
    gers with me still ;
I would not cloud my fair child's brow, nor let
    a tear-drop dim
The eye that met my wedded lord's, lest it
    should sadden him ;
But there are moments when the strength of
    feeling must have way ;
That hidden tide of unnamed woe nor fear nor
    love can stay.
Smile on, smile on, light-hearted ones ! Your
    sun of joy is high :
Smile on, and leave the doomed of Heaven
    alone to weep and die ! "

A funeral chant was wailing through Vienna's
    holy pile,
A coffin with its gorgeous pall was borne along
    the aisle ;
The drooping flags of many lands waved slow
    above the dead,
A mighty band of mourners came, a king was
    at its head, —
A youthful king, with mournful tread, and
    dim and tearful eye ;
He scarce had dreamed that one so pure as his
    fair bride could die.
And sad and long above the throng the funeral
    anthem rung :
"Mourn for the hope of Austria ! Mourn for
    the loved and young ! "

The wail went up from other lands, the valleys
    of the Hun,
Fair Parma with its orange bowers, and hills of
    vine and sun :
The lilies of imperial France drooped as the
    sound went by,
The long lament of cloistered Spain was min-
    gled with the cry.

The dwellers in Colorno's halls, the Slowak at
    his cave,
The bowed at the Escurial, the Magyar stoutly
    brave,
All wept the early stricken flower ; and still
    the anthem rung :
"Mourn for the pride of Austria ! Mourn for
    the loved and young ! "

THE FRATRICIDE

HE stood on the brow of the well-known hill,
Its few gray oaks moan'd over him still ;
The last of that forest which cast the gloom
Of its shadow at eve o'er his childhood's home ;
And the beautiful valley beneath him lay
With its quivering leaves, and its streams at
    play,
And the sunshine over it all the while
Like the golden shower of the Eastern isle.

He knew the rock with its fingering vine,
And its gray top touch'd by the slant sunshine,
And the delicate stream which crept beneath
Soft as the flow of an infant's breath ;
And the flowers which lean'd to the West
    wind's sigh,
Kissing each ripple which glided by ;
And he knew every valley and wooded swell,
For the visions of childhood are treasured well.

Why shook the old man as his eye glanced down
That narrow ravine where the rude cliffs frown,
With their shaggy brows and their teeth of
    stone,
And their grim shade back from the sunlight
    thrown ?
What saw he there save the dreary glen,
Where the shy fox crept from the eye of men,
And the great owl sat on the leafy limb
That the hateful sun might not look on him ?

Fix'd, glassy, and strange was that old man's
    eye,
As if a spectre were stealing by,
And glared it still on that narrow dell
Where thicker and browner the twilight fell ;
Yet at every sigh of the fitful wind,
Or stirring of leaves in the wood behind,
His wild glance wander'd the landscape o'er,
Then fix'd on that desolate dell once more.

Oh, who shall tell of the thoughts which ran
Through the dizzied brain of that gray old
    man ?
His childhood's home, and his father's toil,
And his sister's kiss, and his mother's smile,
And his brother's laughter and gamesome mirth,
At the village school and the winter hearth ;
The beautiful thoughts of his early time,
Ere his heart grew dark with its later crime.

And darker and wilder his visions came
Of the deadly feud and the midnight flame,
Of the Indian's knife with its slaughter red,
Of the ghastly forms of the scalpless dead,

Of his own fierce deeds in that fearful hour
When the terrible Brandt was forth in power,
And he clasp'd his hands o'er his burning eye
To shadow the vision which glided by.

It came with the rush of the battle-storm —
With a brother's shaken and kneeling form,
And his prayer for life when a brother's arm
Was lifted above him for mortal harm,
And the fiendish curse, and the groan of death,
And the welling of blood, and the gurgling
    breath,
And the scalp torn off while each nerve could
    feel
The wrenching hand and the jagged steel!

And the old man groan'd — for he saw, again,
The mangled corse of his kinsman slain,
As it lay where his hand had hurl'd it then,
At the shadow'd foot of that fearful glen!
And it rose erect, with the death-pang grim,
And pointed its bloodied finger at him!
And his heart grew cold — and the curse of
    Cain
Burn'd like a fire in the old man's brain.

Oh, had he not seen that spectre rise
On the blue of the cold Canadian skies?
From the lakes which sleep in the ancient
    wood,
It had risen to whisper its tale of blood,
And follow'd his bark to the sombre shore,
And glared by night through the wigwam door;
And here, on his own familiar hill,
It rose on his haunted vision still!

Whose corse was that which the morrow's
    sun,
Through the opening boughs, look'd calmly
    on?
There were those who bent o'er that rigid face
Who well in its darken'd lines might trace
The features of him who, a traitor, fled
From a brother whose blood himself had shed,
And there, on the spot where he strangely died,
They made the grave of the Fratricide!

ISABEL

I do not love thee, Isabel, and yet thou art
    most fair!
I know the tempting of thy lips, the witchcraft
    of thy hair,
The winsome smile that might beguile the shy
    bird from his tree;
But from their spell I know so well, I shake my
    manhood free.

I might have loved thee, Isabel; I know I
    should if aught
Of all thy words and ways had told of one un-
    selfish thought;
If through the cloud of fashion, the pictured
    veil of art,
One casual flash had broken warm, earnest
    from the heart.

But words are idle, Isabel, and if I praise or
    blame,
Or cheer or warn, it matters not; thy life will
    be the same;
Still free to use, and still abuse, unmindful of
    the harm,
The fatal gift of beauty, the power to choose
    and charm.

Then go thy way, fair Isabel, nor heed that
    from thy train
A doubtful follower falls away, enough will still
    remain.
But what the long-rebuking years may bring to
    them or thee
No prophet and no prophet's son am I to guess
    or see.

I do not love thee, Isabel; I would as soon put
    on
A crown of slender frost - work beneath the
    heated sun,
Or chase the winds of summer, or trust the
    sleeping sea,
Or lean upon a shadow as think of loving thee.

STANZAS

Bind up thy tresses, thou beautiful one,
Of brown in the shadow and gold in the sun!
Free should their delicate lustre be thrown
O'er a forehead more pure than the Parian
    stone;
Shaming the light of those Orient pearls
Which bind o'er its whiteness thy soft wreath-
    ing curls.

Smile, for thy glance on the mirror is thrown,
And the face of an angel is meeting thine
    own!
Beautiful creature, I marvel not
That thy cheek a lovelier tint hath caught;
And the kindling light of thine eye hath told
Of a dearer wealth than the miser's gold.

Away, away, there is danger here!
A terrible phantom is bending near:
Ghastly and sunken, his rayless eye
Scowls on thy loveliness scornfully,
With no human look, with no human breath,
He stands beside thee, the haunter, Death!

Fly! but, alas! he will follow still,
Like a moonlight shadow, beyond thy will;
In thy noonday walk, in thy midnight sleep,
Close at thy hand will that phantom keep;
Still in thine ear shall his whispers be;
Woe, that such phantom should follow thee!

In the lighted hall where the dancers go,
Like beautiful spirits, to and fro;
When thy fair arms glance in their stainless
    white,
Like ivory bathed in still moonlight;
And not one star in the holy sky
Hath a clearer light than thine own blue eye!

Oh, then, even then, he will follow thee,
As the ripple follows the bark at sea;
In the soften'd light, in the turning dance,
He will fix on thine dead, cold glance;
The chill of his breath on thy cheek shall linger,
And thy warm blood shrink from his icy finger!

And yet there is hope. Embrace it now,
While thy soul is open as thy brow;
While thy heart is fresh, while its feelings still
Gush clear as the unsoil'd mountain-rill;
And thy smiles are free as the airs of spring,
Greeting and blessing each breathing thing.

When the after cares of thy life shall come,
When the bud shall wither before its bloom;
When thy soul is sick of the emptiness
And changeful fashion of human bliss;
When the weary torpor of blighted feeling
Over thy heart as ice is stealing;

Then, when thy spirit is turn'd above,
By the mild rebuke of the Chastener's love;
When the hope of that joy in thy heart is stirr'd,
Which eye hath not seen, nor ear hath heard,
Then will that phantom of darkness be
Gladness, and promise, and bliss to thee.

MOGG MEGONE

This poem was commenced in 1830, but
did not assume its present shape until four
years after. It deals with the border strife of
the early settlers of eastern New England and
their savage neighbors; but its personages
and incidents are mainly fictitious. Looking
at it, at the present time, it suggests the idea
of a big Indian in his war-paint strutting
about in Sir Walter Scott's plaid.

PART I

WHO stands on that cliff, like a figure of stone,
  Unmoving and tall in the light of the sky,
  Where the spray of the cataract sparkles on
    high,
Lonely and sternly, save Mogg Megone?
Close to the verge of the rock is he,
  While beneath him the Saco its work is do-
    ing,
Hurrying down to its grave, the sea,
  And slow through the rock its pathway hew-
    ing!
Far down, through the mist of the falling river,
Which rises up like an incense ever,
The splintered points of the crags are seen,
With water howling and vexed between,
While the scooping whirl of the pool beneath
Seems an open throat, with its granite teeth!

But Mogg Megone never trembled yet
Wherever his eye or his foot was set.
He is watchful: each form in the moonlight
    dim,
Of rock or of tree, is seen of him:

He listens; each sound from afar is caught,
The faintest shiver of leaf and limb:
But he sees not the waters, which foam and
    fret,
Whose moonlit spray has his moccasin wet, —
And the roar of their rushing, he hears it not.

The moonlight, through the open bough
  Of the gnarl'd beech, whose naked root
  Coils like a serpent at his foot,
Falls, checkered, on the Indian's brow.
His head is bare, save only where
Waves in the wind one lock of hair,
  Reserved for him, whoe'er he be,
More mighty than Megone in strife,
  When breast to breast and knee to knee,
Above the fallen warrior's life
Gleams, quick and keen, the scalping-knife.

Megone hath his knife and hatchet and gun,
And his gaudy and tasselled blanket on:
His knife hath a handle with gold inlaid,
And magic words on its polished blade, —
'T was the gift of Castine to Mogg Megone,
For a scalp or twain from the Yengees torn:
His gun was the gift of the Tarrantine,
  And Modocawando's wives had strung
The brass and the beads, which tinkle and shine
On the polished breech, and broad bright line
  Of beaded wampum around it hung.

What seeks Megone? His foes are near, —
  Grey Jocelyn's eye is never sleeping,
And the garrison lights are burning clear,
  Where Phillips' men their watch are keeping.
Let him hie him away through the dank river
    fog,
  Never rustling the boughs nor displacing the
    rocks,
For the eyes and the ears which are watching
    for Mogg
  Are keener than those of the wolf or the fox.

He starts, — there 's a rustle among the leaves:
  Another, — the click of his gun is heard!
A footstep, — is it the step of Cleaves,
  With Indian blood on his English sword?
Steals Harmon down from the sands of York,
With hand of iron and foot of cork?
Has Scamman, versed in Indian wile,
For vengeance left his vine-hung isle?
Hark! at that whistle, soft and low,
  How lights the eye of Mogg Megone!
A smile gleams o'er his dusky brow, —
  "Boon welcome, Johnny Boniton!"

Out steps, with cautious foot and slow,
And quick, keen glances to and fro,
  The hunted outlaw, Boniton!
A low, lean, swarthy man is he,
With blanket-garb and buskined knee,
  And naught of English fashion on;
For he hates the race from whence he sprung,
And he couches his words in the Indian tongue.

"Hush, — let the Sachem's voice be weak;
The water-rat shall hear him speak, —

The owl shall whoop in the white man's ear,
That Mogg Megone, with his scalps, is here!"
He pauses, — dark, over cheek and brow,
A flush, as of shame, is stealing now:
"Sachem!" he says, "let me have the land,
Which stretches away upon either hand,
As far about as my feet can stray
In the half of a gentle summer's day,
  From the leaping brook to the Saco river, —
And the fair-haired girl thou hast sought of me
Shall sit in the Sachem's wigwam, and be
  The wife of Mogg Megone forever."

There's a sudden light in the Indian's glance,
  A moment's trace of powerful feeling,
Of love or triumph, or both perchance,
  Over his proud, calm features stealing.
"The words of my father are very good;
He shall have the land, and water, and wood;
And he who harms the Sagamore John,
Shall feel the knife of Mogg Megone;
But the fawn of the Yengees shall sleep on my breast,
And the bird of the clearing shall sing in my nest."

"But, father!" — and the Indian's hand
  Falls gently on the white man's arm,
And with a smile as shrewdly bland
  As the deep voice is slow and calm, —
"Where is my father's singing-bird,
  The sunny eye, and sunset hair?
I know I have my father's word
  And that his word is good and fair;
But will my father tell me where
Megone shall go and look for his bride? —
For he sees her not by her father's side."

The dark, stern eye of Boniton
Flashes over the features of Mogg Megone,
In one of those glances which search within;
But the stolid calm of the Indian alone
Remains where the trace of emotion has been.
"Does the Sachem doubt? Let him go with me,
And the eyes of the Sachem his bride shall see."

Cautious and slow, with pauses oft,
And watchful eyes and whispers soft,
The twain are stealing through the wood,
Leaving the downward-rushing flood,
Whose deep and solemn roar behind
Grows fainter on the evening wind.

  Hark! — is that the angry howl
    Of the wolf, the hills among? —
  Or the hooting of the owl,
    On his leafy cradle swung? —
  Quickly glancing, to and fro,
  Listening to each sound they go
  Round the columns of the pine,
    Indistinct, in shadow, seeming
  Like some old and pillared shrine;
  With the soft and white moonshine,
  Round the foliage-tracery shed
  Of each column's branching head,

For its lamps of worship gleaming!
And the sounds awakened there,
  In the pine-leaves fine and small,
  Soft and sweetly musical,
By the fingers of the air,
For the anthem's dying fall
Lingering round some temple's wall!
Niche and cornice round and round
Wailing like the ghost of sound!
Is not Nature's worship thus,
  Ceaseless ever, going on?
Hath it not a voice for us
  In the thunder, or the tone
Of the leaf-harp faint and small,
  Speaking to the unsealed ear
  Words of blended love and fear,
Of the mighty Soul of all?

Naught had the twain of thoughts like these
As they wound along through the crowded trees,
Where never had rung the axeman's stroke
On the gnarlèd trunk of the rough-barked oak; —
Climbing the dead tree's mossy log,
  Breaking the mesh of the bramble fine,
  Turning aside the wild grapevine,
And lightly crossing the quaking bog
Whose surface shakes at the leap of the frog,
And out of whose pools the ghostly fog
  Creeps into the chill moonshine!

Yet, even that Indian's ear had heard
The preaching of the Holy Word:
Sanchekantacket's isle of sand
Was once his father's hunting land,
Where zealous Hiaccomes stood, —
The wild apostle of the wood,
Shook from his soul the fear of harm,
And trampled on the Powwaw's charm;
Until the wizard's curses hung
Suspended on his palsying tongue,
And the fierce warrior, grim and tall,
Trembled before the forest Paul!

A cottage hidden in the wood, —
  Red through its seams a light is glowing,
On rock and bough and tree-trunk rude,
  A narrow lustre throwing.
"Who's there?" a clear, firm voice demands;
  "Hold, Ruth, — 'tis I, the Sagamore!"
Quick, at the summons, hasty hands
  Unclose the bolted door;
And on the outlaw's daughter shine
The flashes of the kindled pine.

Tall and erect the maiden stands,
  Like some young priestess of the wood,
The freeborn child of Solitude,
  And bearing still the wild and rude,
Yet noble trace of Nature's hands.
Her dark brown cheek has caught its stain
More from the sunshine than the rain;
Yet, where her long fair hair is parting,
A pure white brow into light is starting;
And, where the folds of her blanket sever,
Are neck and a bosom as white as ever
The foam-wreaths rise on the leaping river.

But in the convulsive quiver and grip
Of the muscles around her bloodless lip,
  There is something painful and sad to see;
And her eye has a glance more sternly wild
Than even that of a forest child
  In its fearless and untamed freedom should
  be.
Yet, seldom in hall or court are seen
So queenly a form and so noble a mien,
  As freely and smiling she welcomes them
  there, —
Her outlawed sire and Mogg Megone:
  "Pray, father, how does thy hunting fare?
  And, Sachem, say, — does Scamman wear,
In spite of thy promise, a scalp of his own?"
Hurried and light is the maiden's tone;
  But a fearful meaning lurks within
Her glance, as it questions the eye of Me-
  gone, —
  An awful meaning of guilt and sin! —
The Indian hath opened his blanket, and there
Hangs a human scalp by its long damp hair!
With hand upraised, with quick-drawn breath,
She meets that ghastly sign of death.
In one long, glassy, spectral stare
The enlarging eye is fastened there,
As if that mesh of pale brown hair
  Had power to change at sight alone,
Even as the fearful locks which wound
Medusa's fatal forehead round,
  The gazer into stone.
With such a look Herodias read
The features of the bleeding head,
So looked the mad Moor on his dead,
Or the young Cenci as she stood,
O'er-dabbled with a father's blood!

Look! — feeling melts that frozen glance,
It moves that marble countenance,
  As if at once within her strove
Pity with shame, and hate with love.
The Past recalls its joy and pain,
Old memories rise before her brain, —
The lips which love's embraces met,
The hand her tears of parting wet,
The voice whose pleading tones beguiled
The pleased ear of the forest-child, —
And tears she may no more repress
Reveal her lingering tenderness.

Oh, woman wronged can cherish hate
  More deep and dark than manhood may;
But when the mockery of Fate
  Hath left Revenge its chosen way,
And the fell curse, which years have nursed,
Full on the spoiler's head hath burst, —
When all her wrong, and shame, and pain,
Burns fiercely on his heart and brain, —
Still lingers something of the spell
  Which bound her to the traitor's bosom, —
Still, midst the vengeful fires of hell,
  Some flowers of old affection blossom.

John Boniton's eyebrows together are drawn
With a fierce expression of wrath and scorn, —
He hoarsely whispers, "Ruth, beware!
  Is this the time to be playing the fool, —

Crying over a paltry lock of hair,
  Like a love-sick girl at school? —
Curse on it! — an Indian can see and hear;
Away, — and prepare our evening cheer!"

How keenly the Indian is watching now
Her tearful eye and her varying brow, —
  With a serpent eye, which kindles and burns,
  Like a fiery star in the upper air:
On sire and daughter his fierce glance turns: —
  "Has my old white father a scalp to spare?
  For his young one loves the pale brown hair
Of the scalp of an English dog far more
Than Mogg Megone, or his wigwam floor;
  Go, — Mogg is wise: he will keep his land, —
  And Sagamore John, when he feels with his
  hand,
Shall miss his scalp where it grew before."

The moment's gust of grief is gone, —
  The lip is clenched, — the tears are still, —
God pity thee, Ruth Boniton!
  With what a strength of will
Are nature's feelings in thy breast,
As with an iron hand, repressed!
And how, upon that nameless woe,
Quick as the pulse can come and go,
While shakes the unsteadfast knee, and yet
The bosom heaves, — the eye is wet, —
Has thy dark spirit power to stay
The heart's wild current on its way?
  And whence that baleful strength of guile,
Which over that still working brow
And tearful eye and cheek can throw
  The mockery of a smile?
Warned by her father's blackening frown,
With one strong effort crushing down
Grief, hate, remorse, she meets again
  The savage murderer's sullen gaze,
  And scarcely look or tone betrays
How the heart strives beneath its chain.

"Is the Sachem angry, — angry with Ruth,
Because she cries with an ache in her tooth,
Which would make a Sagamore jump and cry,
And look about with a woman's eye?
No, — Ruth will sit in the Sachem's door
And braid the mats for his wigwam floor,
And broil his fish and tender fawn,
And weave his wampum, and grind his corn,
For she loves the brave and the wise, and none
Are braver and wiser than Mogg Megone!"

The Indian's brow is clear once more:
  With grave, calm face, and half-shut eye,
He sits upon the wigwam floor,
  And watches Ruth go by,
Intent upon her household care;
  And ever and anon, the while,
Or on the maiden, or her fare,
Which smokes in grateful promise there,
  Bestows his quiet smile.

Ah, Mogg Megone! — what dreams are thine,
  But those which love's own fancies dress, —
The sum of Indian happiness! —

A wigwam, where the warm sunshine
Looks in among the groves of pine, —
A stream, where, round thy light canoe,
The trout and salmon dart in view,
And the fair girl, before thee now,
Spreading thy mat with hand of snow,
Or plying, in the dews of morn,
Her hoe amidst thy patch of corn,
Or offering up, at eve, to thee,
Thy birchen dish of hominy!

From the rude board of Boniton,
Venison and succotash have gone, —
For long these dwellers of the wood
Have felt the gnawing want of food.
But untasted of Ruth is the frugal cheer, —
With head averted, yet ready ear,
She stands by the side of her austere sire,
Feeding, at times, the unequal fire
With the yellow knots of the pitch-pine tree,
Whose flaring light, as they kindle, falls
On the cottage-roof, and its black log walls,
And over its inmates three.

From Sagamore Boniton's hunting flask
    The fire-water burns at the lip of Megone :
" Will the Sachem hear what his father shall
    ask ?
Will he make his mark, that it may be known,
On the speaking-leaf, that he gives the land,
From the Sachem's own, to his father's hand ? "
The fire-water shines in the Indian's eyes,
    As he rises, the white man's bidding to do :
" Wuttamuttata — weekan ! Mogg is wise, —
    For the water he drinks is strong and new, —
Mogg's heart is great ! — will he shut his hand,
When his father asks for a little land ? " —
With unsteady fingers, the Indian has drawn
    On the parchment the shape of a hunter's
        bow,
" Boon water, — boon water, — Sagamore John !
Wuttamuttata, — weekan ! our hearts will
        grow ! "
He drinks yet deeper, — he mutters low, —
He reels on his bear-skin to and fro, —
His head falls down on his naked breast, —
He struggles, and sinks to a drunken rest.

" Humph — drunk as a beast ! " — and Boni-
        ton's brow
Is darker than ever with evil thought —
" The fool has signed his warrant ; but how
And when shall the deed be wrought ?
Speak, Ruth ! why, what the devil is there,
To fix thy gaze in that empty air ? —
Speak, Ruth ! by my soul, if I thought that tear
Which shames thyself and our purpose here,
Were shed for that cursed and pale-faced dog,
Whose green scalp hangs from the belt of Mogg,
    And whose beastly soul is in Satan's keeping ;
This — this ! " — he dashes his hand upon
The rattling stock of his loaded gun, —
    " Should send thee with him to do thy weep-
        ing ! "

" Father ! " — the eye of Boniton
Sinks at that low, sepulchral tone,

Hollow and deep, as it were spoken
    By the unmoving tongue of death, —
Or from some statue's lips had broken, —
    A sound without a breath !
" Father ! — my life I value less
Than yonder fool his gaudy dress ;
And how it ends it matters not,
By heart-break or by rifle-shot ;
But spare awhile the scoff and threat, —
Our business is not finished yet."

" True, true, my girl, — I only meant
To draw up again the bow unbent.
Harm thee, my Ruth ! I only sought
To frighten off thy gloomy thought ;
Come, — let 's be friends ! " He seeks to clasp
His daughter's cold, damp hand in his.
Ruth startles from her father's grasp,
As if each nerve and muscle felt,
Instinctively, the touch of guilt
Through all their subtle sympathies.

He points her to the sleeping Mogg :
" What shall be done with yonder dog ?
Scamman is dead, and revenge is thine, —
The deed is signed and the land is mine ;
And this drunken fool is of use no more,
Save as thy hopeful bridegroom, and sooth,
'T were Christian mercy to finish him, Ruth,
Now, while he lies like a beast on our floor, —
If not for thine, at least for his sake,
Rather than let the poor dog awake
To drain my flask, and claim as his bride
Such a forest devil to run by his side, —
Such a Wetuomanit as thou wouldst make ! "

He laughs at his jest. Hush — what is there ?—
    The sleeping Indian is striving to rise,
    With his knife in his hand, and glaring eyes !—
" Wagh ! — Mogg will have the pale-face's hair,
    For his knife is sharp, and his fingers can help
The hair to pull and the skin to peel, —
Let him cry like a woman and twist like an eel,
    The great Captain Scamman must lose his
        scalp !
And Ruth, when she sees it, shall dance with
        Mogg."
His eyes are fixed, — but his lips draw in, —
With a low, hoarse chuckle, and fiendish grin, —
    And he sinks again, like a senseless log.

Ruth does not speak, — she does not stir ;
But she gazes down on the murderer,
Whose broken and dreamful slumbers tell
Too much for her ear of that deed of hell.
She sees the knife, with its slaughter red,
And the dark fingers clenching the bearskin
        bed !
What thoughts of horror and madness whirl
Through the burning brain of that fallen girl !

John Boniton lifts his gun to his eye,
    Its muzzle is close to the Indian's ear, —
But he drops it again. " Some one may be
        nigh,
    And I would not that even the wolves should
        hear."

He draws his knife from his deer-skin belt, —
Its edge with his fingers is slowly felt ; —
Kneeling down on one knee, by the Indian's
    side,
From his throat he opens the blanket wide ;
And twice or thrice he feebly essays
A trembling hand with the knife to raise.

" I cannot," — he mutters, — " did he not save
My life from a cold and wintry grave,
When the storm came down from Agiochook,
And the north-wind howled, and the tree-tops
    shook, —
And I strove, in the drifts of the rushing snow,
Till my knees grew weak and I could not go,
And I felt the cold to my vitals creep,
And my heart's blood stiffen, and pulses sleep !
I cannot strike him — Ruth Boniton !
In the Devil's name, tell me — what 's to be
    done ? "

·Oh, when the soul, once pure and high,
Is stricken down from Virtue's sky,
As, with the downcast star of morn,
Some gems of light are with it drawn,
And, through its night of darkness, play
Some tokens of its primal day,
Some lofty feelings linger still, —
    The strength to dare, the nerve to meet
    Whatever threatens with defeat
Its all-indomitable will ! —
But lacks the mean of mind and heart,
Though eager for the gains of crime,
Or, at his chosen place and time,
The strength to bear his evil part ;
And, shielded by his very Vice,
Escapes from Crime by Cowardice.

Ruth starts erect, — with bloodshot eye,
    And lips drawn tight across her teeth
Showing their locked embrace beneath,
In the red firelight : '' Mogg must die !
Give me the knife ! " The outlaw turns,
    Shuddering in heart and limb away,
But, fitfully there, the hearth-fire burns,
    And he sees on the wall strange shadows
        play.
A lifted arm, a tremulous blade,
Are dimly pictured in light and shade,
    Plunging down in the darkness. Hark, that
        cry
Again — and again — he sees it fall,
That shadowy arm down the lighted wall !
    He hears quick footsteps — a shape flits by —
The door on its rusted hinges creaks : —
"Ruth — daughter Ruth ! " the outlaw shrieks.
But no sound comes back, — he is standing
    alone
By the mangled corse of Mogg Megone !

PART II

'T is morning over Norridgewock, —
On tree and wigwam, wave and rock,
Bathed in the autumnal sunshine, stirred
At intervals by breeze and bird,

And wearing all the hues which glow
In heaven's own pure and perfect bow,
    That glorious picture of the air,
Which summer's light-robed angel forms
On the dark ground of fading storms,
    With pencil dipped in sunbeams there, —
And, stretching out, on either hand,
O'er all that wide and unshorn land,
Till, weary of its gorgeousness,
The aching and the dazzled eye
Rests, gladdened, on the calm blue sky, —
Slumbers the mighty wilderness !
The oak, upon the windy hill,
    Its dark green burthen upward heaves —
The hemlock broods above its rill,
Its cone-like foliage darker still,
    Against the birch's graceful stem,
And the rough walnut-bough receives
The sun upon its crowded leaves,
    Each colored like a topaz gem ;
    And the tall maple wears with them
The coronal, which autumn gives,
    The brief, bright sign of ruin near,
    The hectic of a dying year !

The hermit priest, who lingers now
On the Bald Mountain's shrubless brow,
    The gray and thunder-smitten pile
Which marks afar the Desert Isle,
While gazing on the scene below,
May half forget the dreams of home,
That nightly with his slumbers come, —
The tranquil skies of sunny France,
The peasant's harvest song and dance,
The vines around the hillsides wreathing,
The soft airs midst their clusters breathing,
The wings which dipped, the stars which shone
Within thy bosom, blue Garonne !
And round the Abbey's shadowed wall,
At morning spring and even-fall,
    Sweet voices in the still air singing, —
The chant of many a holy hymn, —
    The solemn bell of vespers ringing, —
And hallowed torchlight falling dim
On pictured saint and seraphim !
For here beneath him lies unrolled,
Bathed deep in morning's flood of gold,
A vision gorgeous as the dream
Of the beatified may seem,
    When, as his Church's legends say,
Born upward in ecstatic bliss,
    The rapt enthusiast soars away
Unto a brighter world than this :
A mortal's glimpse beyond the pale, —
A moment's lifting of the veil !

Far eastward o'er the lovely bay,
Penobscot's clustered wigwams lay ;
And gently from that Indian town
The verdant hillside slopes adown,
To where the sparkling waters play
    Upon the yellow sands below ;
And shooting round the winding shores
    Of narrow capes, and isles which lie
    Slumbering to ocean's lullaby, —
With birchen boat and glancing oars,
The red men to their fishing go ;

While from their planting ground is borne
The treasure of the golden corn,
By laughing girls, whose dark eyes glow
Wild through the locks which o'er them flow.
The wrinkled squaw, whose toil is done,
Sits on her bear-skin in the sun,
Watching the huskers, with a smile
For each full ear which swells the pile ;
And the old chief, who nevermore
May bend the bow or pull the oar,
Smokes gravely in his wigwam door,
Or slowly shapes, with axe of stone,
The arrow-head from flint and bone.

Beneath the westward turning eye
A thousand wooded islands lie,
Gems of the waters ! with each hue
Of brightness set in ocean's blue.
Each bears aloft its tuft of trees
　　Touched by the pencil of the frost,
And, with the motion of each breeze,
　　A moment seen, a moment lost,
　　Changing and blent, confused and tossed,
　　The brighter with the darker crossed,
Their thousand tints of beauty glow
Down in the restless waves below,
　　And tremble in the sunny skies,
As if, from waving bough to bough,
　　Flitted the birds of paradise.
There sleep Placentia's group, and there
Père Breteaux marks the hour of prayer ;
And there, beneath the sea-worn cliff,
　　On which the Father's hut is seen,
The Indian stays his rocking skiff,
　　And peers the hemlock-boughs between,
Half trembling, as he seeks to look
Upon the Jesuit's Cross and Book.
There, gloomily against the sky
The Dark Isles rear their summits high ;
And Desert Rock, abrupt and bare,
Lifts its gray turrets in the air,
Seen from afar, like some stronghold
Built by the ocean kings of old ;
And, faint as smoke-wreath white and thin,
Swells in the north vast Katahdin :
And, wandering from its marshy feet,
The broad Penobscot comes to meet
　　And mingle with his own bright bay.
Slow sweep his dark and gathering floods,
Arched over by the ancient woods,
Which Time, in those dim solitudes,
　　Wielding the dull axe of Decay,
　　Alone hath ever shorn away.

Not thus, within the woods which hide
The beauty of thy azure tide,
　　And with their falling timbers block
Thy broken currents, Kennebec !
Gazes the white man on the wreck
Of the down-trodden Norridgewock ;
In one lone village hemmed at length,
In battle shorn of half their strength,
Turned, like the panther in his lair,
　　With his fast-flowing life-blood wet,
For one last struggle of despair,
　　Wounded and faint, but tameless yet !
Unreaped, upon the planting lands,

The scant, neglected harvest stands :
　　No shout is there, no dance, no song :
The aspect of the very child
Scowls with a meaning sad and wild
　　Of bitterness and wrong.
The almost infant Norridgewock
Essays to lift the tomahawk ;
And plucks his father's knife away,
To mimic, in his frightful play,
　　The scalping of an English foe :
Wreathes on his lip a horrid smile,
Burns, like a snake's, his small eye, while
　　Some bough or sapling meets his blow.
The fisher, as he drops his line,
Starts, when he sees the hazels quiver
Along the margin of the river,
Looks up and down the rippling tide,
And grasps the firelock at his side.
For Bomazeen from Tacconock
Has sent his runners to Norridgewock,
With tidings that Moulton and Harmon of
　　York
　　Far up the river have come :
They have left their boats, they have entered
　　the wood,
And filled the depths of the solitude
　　With the sound of the ranger's drum.

On the brow of a hill, which slopes to meet
The flowing river, and bathe its feet ;
The bare-washed rock, and the drooping grass,
And the creeping vine, as the waters pass,
A rude and unshapely chapel stands,
Built up in that wild by unskilled hands,
Yet the traveller knows it a place of prayer,
For the holy sign of the cross is there :
And should he chance at that place to be,
　　Of a Sabbath morn, or some hallowed day,
When prayers are made and masses are said,
Some for the living and some for the dead,
Well might that traveller start to see
　　The tall dark forms, that take their way
From the birch canoe, on the river shore,
And the forest paths, to that chapel door ;
And marvel to mark the naked knees
　　And the dusky foreheads bending there,
While, in coarse white vesture, over these
　　In blessing or in prayer,
Stretching abroad his thin pale hands,
Like a shrouded ghost, the Jesuit stands.

Two forms are now in that chapel dim,
　　The Jesuit, silent and sad and pale,
　　Anxiously heeding some fearful tale,
Which a stranger is telling him.
That stranger's garb is soiled and torn,
And wet with dew and loosely worn ;
Her fair neglected hair falls down
O'er cheeks with wind and sunshine brown ;
Yet still, in that disordered face,
The Jesuit's cautious eye can trace
Those elements of former grace
Which, half effaced, seem scarcely less,
Even now, than perfect loveliness.

With drooping head, and voice so low
　　That scarce it meets the Jesuit's ears,

While through her claspëd fingers flow,
From the heart's fountain, hot and slow,
  Her penitential tears, —
She tells the story of the woe
  And evil of her years.

" O father, bear with me ; my heart
  Is sick and death-like, and my brain
  Seems girdled with a fiery chain,
Whose scorching links will never part,
  And never cool again.
Bear with me while I speak, but turn
  Away that gentle eye, the while ;
The fires of guilt more fiercely burn
  Beneath its holy smile ;
For half I fancy I can see
My mother's sainted look in thee.

" My dear lost mother ! sad and pale,
  Mournfully sinking day by day,
And with a hold on life as frail
  As frosted leaves, that, thin and gray,
  Hang feebly on their parent spray,
And tremble in the gale ;
Yet watching o'er my childishness
With patient fondness, not the less
For all the agony which kept
Her blue eye wakeful, while I slept ;
And checking every tear and groan
That haply might have waked my own,
And bearing still, without offence,
My idle words, and petulance ;
  Reproving with a tear, and, while
The tooth of pain was keenly preying
Upon her very heart, repaying
  My brief repentance with a smile.

" Oh, in her meek, forgiving eye
  There was a brightness not of mirth,
A light whose clear intensity
  Was borrowed not of earth.
Along her cheek a deepening red
Told where the feverish hectic fed ;
  And yet, each fatal token gave
To the mild beauty of her face
A newer and a dearer grace,
  Unwarning of the grave.
'T was like the hue which Autumn gives
To yonder changed and dying leaves,
  Breathed over by his frosty breath ;
Scarce can the gazer feel that this
Is but the spoiler's treacherous kiss,
  The mocking-smile of Death !

Sweet were the tales she used to tell
  When summer's eve was dear to us,
And, fading from the darkening dell,
The glory of the sunset fell
  On wooded Agamenticus, —
When, sitting by our cottage wall,
The murmur of the Saco's fall,
  And the south-wind's expiring sighs,
Came, softly blending, on my ear
With the low tones I loved to hear:
  Tales of the pure, the good, the wise,
The holy men and maids of old,
In the all-sacred pages told ;

Of Rachel, stooped at Haran's fountains,
Amid her father's thirsty flock,
Beautiful to her kinsman seeming
As the bright angels of his dreaming,
  On Padan-aran's holy rock ;
Of gentle Ruth, and her who kept
  Her awful vigil on the mountains,
By Israel's virgin daughters wept ;
Of Miriam, with her maidens, singing
  The song for grateful Israel meet,
While every crimson wave was bringing
  The spoils of Egypt at her feet ;
Of her, Samaria's humble daughter,
  Who paused to hear, beside her well,
  Lessons of love and truth, which fell
Softly as Shiloh's flowing water ;
  And saw, beneath his pilgrim guise,
The Promised One, so long foretold
By holy seer and bard of old,
  Revealed before her wondering eyes !

" Slowly she faded.   Day by day
Her step grew weaker in our hall,
And fainter, at each even-fall,
  Her sad voice died away.
Yet on her thin, pale lip, the while,
Sat Resignation's holy smile :
And even my father checked his tread,
And hushed his voice, beside her bed :
Beneath the calm and sad rebuke
Of her meek eye's imploring look,
The scowl of hate his brow forsook,
  And in his stern and gloomy eye,
At times, a few unwonted tears
Wet the dark lashes, which for years
Hatred and pride had kept so dry.

" Calm as a child to slumber soothed,
As if an angel's hand had smoothed
  The still, white features into rest,
Silent and cold, without a breath
  To stir the drapery on her breast,
Pain, with its keen and poisoned fang,
The horror of the mortal pang,
The suffering look her brow had worn,
The fear, the strife, the anguish gone,
  She slept at last in death !

" Oh, tell me, father, *can* the dead
  Walk on the earth, and look on us,
And lay upon the living's head
  Their blessing or their curse ?
For, oh, last night she stood by me,
As I lay beneath the woodland tree ! "

The Jesuit crosses himself in awe, —
" Jesu ! what was it my daughter saw ? "

" *She* came to me last night.
  The dried leaves did not feel her tread ;
She stood by me in the wan moonlight,
  In the white robes of the dead !
Pale, and very mournfully
She bent her light form over me.
I heard no sound, I felt no breath
Breathe o'er me from that face of death :
Its blue eyes rested on my own,

Rayless and cold as eyes of stone ;
Yet, in their fixed, unchanging gaze,
Something, which spoke of early days, —
A sadness in their quiet glare,
As if love's smile were frozen there, —
Came o'er me with an icy thrill ;
O God ! I feel its presence still ! ''

The Jesuit makes the holy sign, —
" How passed the vision, daughter mine ? "

" All dimly in the wan moonshine,
As a wreath of mist will twist and twine,
And scatter, and melt into the light ;
So scattering, melting on my sight,
  The pale, cold vision passed ;
But those sad eyes were fixed on mine
  Mournfully to the last."

" God help thee, daughter, tell me why
That spirit passed before thine eye ! "

" Father, I know not, save it be
That deeds of mine have summoned her
  From the unbreathing sepulchre,
To leave her last rebuke with me.
Ah, woe for me ! my mother died
Just at the moment when I stood
Close on the verge of womanhood,
A child in everything beside ;
And when my wild heart needed most
Her gentle counsels, they were lost.

" My father lived a stormy life,
Of frequent change and daily strife ;
And — God forgive him ! left his child
To feel, like him, a freedom wild ;
To love the red man's dwelling-place,
  The birch boat on his shaded floods,
The wild excitement of the chase
  Sweeping the ancient woods,
The camp-fire, blazing on the shore
  Of the still lakes, the clear stream where
  The idle fisher sets his weir,
Or angles in the shade, far more
  Than that restraining awe I felt
Beneath my gentle mother's care,
  When nightly at her knee I knelt,
With childhood's simple prayer.

" There came a change. The wild, glad mood
  Of unchecked freedom passed.
Amid the ancient solitude
Of unshorn grass and waving wood
  And waters glancing bright and fast,
A softened voice was in my ear,
Sweet as those lulling sounds and fine
The hunter lifts his head to hear,
Now far and faint, now full and near —
  The murmur of the wind-swept pine.
A manly form was ever nigh,
A bold, free hunter, with an eye
  Whose dark, keen glance had power to wake
Both fear and love, to awe and charm ;
  'T was as the wizard rattlesnake,
Whose evil glances lure to harm —
Whose cold and small and glittering eye,

And brilliant coil, and changing dye,
Draw, step by step, the gazer near,
With drooping wing and cry of fear,
Yet powerless all to turn away,
A conscious, but a willing prey !

" Fear, doubt, thought, life itself, erelong
Merged in one feeling deep and strong.
Faded the world which I had known,
  A poor vain shadow, cold and waste ;
In the warm present bliss alone
  Seemed I of actual life to taste.
Fond longings dimly understood,
The glow of passion's quickening blood,
And cherished fantasies which press
The young lip with a dream's caress ;
The heart's forecast and prophecy
Took form and life before my eye,
Seen in the glance which met my own,
Heard in the soft and pleading tone,
Felt in the arms around me cast,
And warm heart-pulses beating fast.
Ah ! scarcely yet to God above
With deeper trust, with stronger love,
Has prayerful saint his meek heart lent,
Or cloistered nun at twilight bent,
Than I, before a human shrine,
As mortal and as frail as mine,
With heart, and soul, and mind, and form,
Knelt madly to a fellow-worm.

" Full soon, upon that dream of sin,
An awful light came bursting in.
The shrine was cold at which I knelt,
  The idol of that shrine was gone ;
A humbled thing of shame and guilt,
  Outcast, and spurned and lone,
Wrapt in the shadows of my crime,
  With withering heart and burning brain,
  And tears that fell like fiery rain,
I passed a fearful time.

" There came a voice — it checked the tear,
  In heart and soul it wrought a change ;
My father's voice was in my ears ;
  It whispered of revenge !
A new and fiercer feeling swept
  All lingering tenderness away ;
And tiger passions, which had slept
  In childhood's better day,
Unknown, unfelt, arose at length
In all their own demoniac strength.

" A youthful warrior of the wild,
By words deceived, by smiles beguiled,
Of crime the cheated instrument,
Upon our fatal errands went.
  Through camp and town and wilderness
He tracked his victim ; and at last,
Just when the tide of hate had passed,
And milder thoughts came warm and fast,
Exulting, at my feet he cast
  The bloody token of success.

" O God ! with what an awful power
  I saw the buried past uprise,
And gather, in a single hour,

Its ghost-like memories!
And then I felt, alas! too late,
  That underneath the mask of hate,
That shame and guilt and wrong had thrown
O'er feelings which they might not own,
  The heart's wild love had known no change;
And still that deep and hidden love,
With its first fondness, wept above
  The victim of its own revenge!
There lay the fearful scalp, and there
The blood was on its pale brown hair!
I thought not of the victim's scorn,
  I thought not of his baleful guile,
My deadly wrong, my outcast name,
The characters of sin and shame
On heart and forehead drawn;
  I only saw that victim's smile,
The still green places where we met, —
The moonlit branches, dewy wet;
I only felt, I only heard,
The greeting and the parting word, —
The smile, the embrace, the tone, which made
  An Eden of the forest shade.

" And oh, with what a loathing eye,
  With what a deadly hate, and deep,
I saw that Indian murderer lie
  Before me, in his drunken sleep!
What though for me the deed was done,
And words of mine had sped him on!
Yet when he murmured, as he slept,
  The horrors of that deed of blood,
The tide of utter madness swept
  O'er brain and bosom, like a flood,
And, father, with this hand of mine " —
  " Ha! what didst thou ? " the Jesuit cries,
Shuddering, as smitten with sudden pain,
  And shading, with one thin hand, his eyes,
With the other he makes the holy sign.
" — I smote him as I would a worm;
With hate as steeled, with nerves as firm:
  He never woke again! "

" Woman of sin and blood and shame,
Speak, I would know that victim's name."

"Father," she gasped, " a chieftain, known
As Saco's Sachem, — Mogg Megone! "

Pale priest! What proud and lofty dreams,
What keen desires, what cherished schemes,
What hopes, that time may not recall,
Are darkened by that chieftain's fall!
Was he not pledged, by cross and vow,
  To lift the hatchet of his sire,
And, round his own, the Church's foe,
  To light the avenging fire ?
Who now the Tarrantine shall wake,
For thine and for the Church's sake ?
  Who summon to the scene
Of conquest and unsparing strife,
And vengeance dearer than his life,
  The fiery-souled Castine ?
Three backward steps the Jesuit takes,
His long, thin frame as ague shakes;
  And loathing hate is in his eye,
As from his lips these words of fear

Fall hoarsely on the maiden's ear, —
  " The soul that sinneth shall surely die ! "

She stands, as stands the stricken deer,
  Checked midway in the fearful chase,
When bursts, upon his eye and ear,
  The gaunt, gray robber, baying near,
  Between him and his hiding-place;
While still behind, with yell and blow,
Sweeps, like a storm, the coming foe.
" Save me, O holy man ! " her cry
  Fills all the void, as if a tongue
  Unseen, from rib and rafter hung,
Thrilling with mortal agony;
Her hands are clasping the Jesuit's knee,
  And her eye looks fearfully into his own ; —
" Off, woman of sin ! nay, touch not me
  With the fingers of blood; begone ! "
With a gesture of horror, he spurns the form
That writhes at his feet like a trodden worm.

Ever thus the spirit must,
  Guilty in the sight of Heaven,
  With a keener woe be riven,
For its weak and sinful trust
In the strength of human dust;
  And its anguish thrill afresh,
For each vain reliance given
  To the failing arm of flesh.

PART III

AH, weary Priest! with pale hands pressed
  On thy throbbing brow of pain,
Baffled in thy life-long quest,
  Overworn with toiling vain,
How ill thy troubled musings fit
  The holy quiet of a breast
  With the Dove of Peace at rest,
Sweetly brooding over it.
Thoughts are thine which have no part
With the meek and pure of heart,
Undisturbed by outward things,
Resting in the heavenly shade,
By the overspreading wings
Of the Blessed Spirit made.
Thoughts of strife and hate and wrong
Sweep thy heated brain along,
Fading hopes for whose success
  It were sin to breathe a prayer ; —
Schemes which Heaven may never bless,
  Fears which darken to despair.
Hoary priest! thy dream is done
Of a hundred red tribes won
  To the pale of Holy Church ;
And the heretic o'erthrown,
And his name no longer known,
And thy weary brethren turning,
Joyful from their years of mourning
'Twixt the altar and the porch.
Hark ! what sudden sound is heard
  In the wood and in the sky,
Shriller than the scream of bird,
  Than the trumpet's clang more high!
Every wolf-cave of the hills,
  Forest arch and mountain gorge,

Rock and dell, and river verge,
With an answering echo thrills.
Well does the Jesuit know that cry,
Which summons the Norridgewock to die,
And tells that the foe of his flock is nigh.
He listens, and hears the rangers come,
With loud hurrah, and jar of drum,
And hurrying feet (for the chase is hot),
And the short, sharp sound of rifle shot,
And taunt and menace, — answered well
By the Indians' mocking cry and yell, —
The bark of dogs, — the squaw's mad scream,
The dash of paddles along the stream,
The whistle of shot as it cuts the leaves
Of the maples around the church's eaves,
And the gride of hatchets fiercely thrown
On wigwam-log and tree and stone.
Black with the grime of paint and dust,
    Spotted and streaked with human gore,
A grim and naked head is thrust
    Within the chapel-door.
"Ha — Bomazeen! In God's name say,
What mean these sounds of bloody fray?"
Silent, the Indian points his hand
    To where across the echoing glen
Sweep Harmon's dreaded ranger-band,
    And Moulton with his men.
"Where are thy warriors, Bomazeen?
Where are De Rouville and Castine,
And where the braves of Sawga's queen?"
"Let my father find the winter snow
Which the sun drank up long moons ago!
Under the falls of Tacconock,
The wolves are eating the Norridgewock;
Castine with his wives lies closely hid
Like a fox in the woods of Pemaquid!
On Sawga's banks the man of war
Sits in his wigwam like a squaw;
Squando has fled, and Mogg Megone,
    Struck by the knife of Sagamore John,
Lies stiff and stark and cold as a stone."

Fearfully over the Jesuit's face,
Of a thousand thoughts, trace after trace,
Like swift cloud-shadows, each other chase.
One instant, his fingers grasp his knife,
For a last vain struggle for cherished life, —
The next, he hurls the blade away,
And kneels at his altar's foot to pray;
Over his beads his fingers stray,
And he kisses the cross, and calls aloud
On the Virgin and her Son;
For terrible thoughts his memory crowd
    Of evil seen and done,
Of scalps brought home by his savage flock
From Casco and Sawga and Sagadahock
    In the Church's service won.

No shrift the gloomy savage brooks,
As scowling on the priest he looks:
"Cowesass — cowesass — tawhich wessa seen?
Let my father look upon Bomazeen, —
My father's heart is the heart of a squaw,
But mine is so hard that it does not thaw;
Let my father ask his God to make
    A dance and a feast for a great sagamore,
When he paddles across the western lake,

With his dogs and his squaws to the spirit's
    shore.
Cowesass — cowesass — tawhich wessa seen?
Let my father die like Bomazeen!"

Through the chapel's narrow doors,
    And through each window in the walls,
Round the priest and warrior pours
    The deadly shower of English balls.
Low on his cross the Jesuit falls;
While at his side the Norridgewock,
With failing breath, essays to mock
And menace yet the hated foe,
Shakes his scalp-trophies to and fro
    Exultingly before their eyes,
Till, cleft and torn by shot and blow,
    Defiant still, he dies.

"So fare all eaters of the frog!
Death to the Babylonish dog!
Down with the beast of Rome!"
With shouts like these, around the dead,
Unconscious on his bloody bed,
    The rangers crowding come.
Brave men! the dead priest cannot hear
The unfeeling taunt, — the brutal jeer;
Spurn — for he sees ye not — in wrath,
The symbol of your Saviour's death;
    Tear from his death-grasp, in your zeal,
And trample, as a thing accursed,
The cross he cherished in the dust:
    The dead man cannot feel!

Brutal alike in deed and word,
    With callous heart and hand of strife,
How like a fiend may man be made,
Plying the foul and monstrous trade
    Whose harvest-field is human life,
Whose sickle is the reeking sword!
Quenching, with reckless hand in blood,
Sparks kindled by the breath of God;
Urging the deathless soul, unshriven,
    Of open guilt or secret sin,
Before the bar of that pure Heaven
    The holy only enter in!
Oh, by the widow's sore distress,
The orphan's wailing wretchedness,
By Virtue struggling in the accursed
Embraces of polluting Lust,
By the fell discord of the Pit,
And the pained souls that people it,
And by the blessed peace which fills
    The Paradise of God forever,
Resting on all its holy hills,
    And flowing with its crystal river, —
Let Christian hands no longer bear
    In triumph on his crimson car
    The foul and idol god of war;
No more the purple wreaths prepare
To bind amid his snaky hair;
Nor Christian bards his glories tell,
Nor Christian tongues his praises swell.

Through the gun-smoke wreathing white,
Glimpses on the soldier's sight
A thing of human shape I ween,
For a moment only seen,

With its loose hair backward streaming,
And its eyeballs madly gleaming,
Shrieking, like a soul in pain,
From the world of light and breath,
Hurrying to its place again,
Spectre-like it vanisheth !

Wretched girl ! one eye alone
Notes the way which thou hast gone.
That great Eye, which slumbers never,
Watching o'er a lost world ever,
Tracks thee over vale and mountain,
By the gushing forest-fountain,
Plucking from the vine its fruit,
Searching for the ground-nut's root,
Peering in the she-wolf's den,
Wading through the marshy fen,
Where the sluggish water-snake
Basks beside the sunny brake,
Coiling in his slimy bed,
Smooth and cold against thy tread ;
Purposeless, thy mazy way
Threading through the lingering day,
And at night securely sleeping
Where the dogwood's dews are weeping !
Still, though earth and man discard thee,
Doth thy Heavenly Father guard thee :
He who spared the guilty Cain,
Even when a brother's blood,
Crying in the ear of God,
Gave the earth its primal stain ;
He whose mercy ever liveth,
Who repenting guilt forgiveth,
And the broken heart receiveth ;
Wanderer of the wilderness,
Haunted, guilty, crazed and wild,
He regardeth thy distress,
And careth for His sinful child !

'T is springtime on the eastern hills !
Like torrents gush the summer rills ;
Through winter's moss and dry dead leaves
The bladed grass revives and lives,
Pushes the mouldering waste away,
For glimpses to the April day.
In kindly shower and sunshine bud
The branches of the dull gray wood ;
Out from its sunned and sheltered nooks
The blue eye of the violet looks ;
The southwest wind is warmly blowing,
And odors from the springing grass,
The pine-tree and the sassafras,
Are with it on its errands going.

A band is marching through the wood
Where rolls the Kennebec his flood ;
The warriors of the wilderness,
Painted, and in their battle dress ;
And with them one whose bearded cheek,
And white and wrinkled brow, bespeak
A wanderer from the shores of France.
A few long locks of scattering snow
Beneath a battered morion flow,
And from the rivets of the vest
Which girds in steel his ample breast,
The slanted sunbeams glance.

In the harsh outlines of his face
Passion and sin have left their trace ;
Yet, save worn brow and thin gray hair,
No signs of weary age are there.
His step is firm, his eye is keen,
Nor years in broil and battle spent,
Nor toil, nor wounds, nor pain have bent
The lordly frame of old Castine.

No purpose now of strife and blood
Urges the hoary veteran on :
The fire of conquest and the mood
Of chivalry have gone.
A mournful task is his, — to lay
Within the earth the bones of those
Who perished in that fearful day,
When Norridgewock became the prey
Of all unsparing foes.
Sadly and still, dark thoughts between,
Of coming vengeance mused Castine,
Of the fallen chieftain Bomazeen,
Who bade for him the Norridgewocks
Dig up their buried tomahawks
For firm defence or swift attack ;
And him whose friendship formed the tie
Which held the stern self-exile back
From lapsing into savagery ;
Whose garb and tone and kindly glance
Recalled a younger, happier day,
And prompted memory's fond essay,
To bridge the mighty waste which lay
Between his wild home and that gray,
Tall chateau of his native France :
Whose chapel bell, with far-heard din,
Ushered his birth-hour gayly in,
And counted with its solemn toll
The masses for his father's soul.

Hark ! from the foremost of the band
Suddenly bursts the Indian yell ;
For now on the very spot they stand
Where the Norridgewocks fighting fell.
No wigwam smoke is curling there ;
The very earth is scorched and bare :
And they pause and listen to catch a sound
Of breathing life, — but there comes not one,
Save the fox's bark and the rabbit's bound ;
But here and there, on the blackened ground,
White bones are glistening in the sun.
And where the house of prayer arose,
And the holy hymn, at daylight's close,
And the aged priest stood up to bless
The children of the wilderness,
There is naught save ashes sodden and dank ;
And the birchen boats of the Norridgewock,
Tethered to tree and stump and rock,
Rotting along the river bank !

Blessed Mary ! who is she
Leaning against that maple-tree ?
The sun upon her face burns hot,
But the fixed eyelid moveth not ;
The squirrel's chirp is shrill and clear
From the dry bough above her ear ;
Dashing from rock and root its spray,
Close at her feet the river rushes ;
The blackbird's wing against her brushes,

And sweetly through the hazel-bushes
The robin's mellow music gushes ;
God save her ! will she sleep alway ?

Castine hath bent him over the sleeper :
"Wake, daughter, — wake !" but she stirs
  no limb :
The eye that looks on him is fixed and dim ;
And the sleep she is sleeping shall be no deeper,
Until the angel's oath is said,
And the final blast of the trump goes forth
To the graves of the sea and the graves of
  earth.
Ruth Boniton is dead !

THE PAST AND COMING YEAR

WAVE of an awful torrent, thronging down,
With all the wealth of centuries, and the cold
Embraces of eternity, o'erstrown
With the great wrecks of empire, and the old
Magnificence of nations, who are gone ;
Thy last, faint murmur — thy departing sigh,
Along the shore of being, like a tone
Thrilling on broken harp-strings, or the swell
Of the chained winds' last whisper, hath gone
  by,
And thou hast floated from the world of
  breath
To the still guidance of o'ermastering Death,
Thy pilot to eternity. Farewell !

Go, swell the throngful past. Go, blend with
  all
The garnered things of Death ; and bear with
  thee
The treasures of thy pilgrimage, the tall
And beautiful dreams of Hope, the ministry
Of Love and high Ambition. Man remains
To dream again as idly ; and the stains
Of passion will be visible once more.
The wingèd spirit will not be confined
By the experience of thy journey. Mind
Will struggle in its prison-house, and still,
With Earth's strong fetters binding it to ill,
Unfurl the pinions fitted but to soar
In that pure atmosphere, where spirits range —
The home of high existences — where change
And blighting may not enter. Love again
Will bloom, a fickle flower, upon the grave
Of old affections ; and Ambition wave
His eagle-plume most proudly, for the rein
Of Conscience will be loosened from the soul
To give his purpose freedom. The control
Of reason will be changeful, and the ties
Which gather hearts together, and make up
The romance of existence, will be rent :
Yea, poison will be poured in Friendship's cup ;
And for Earth's low familiar element,
Even Love itself forsake its kindred skies.

But not alone dark visions ! happier things
Will float above existence, like the wings
Of the starred bird of paradise ; and Love
Will not be all a dream, or rather prove
A dream — a sweet forgetfulness — that hath

No wakeful changes, ending but in Death.
Yea, pure hearts shall be pledged beneath the
  eyes
Of the beholding heaven, and in the light
Of the love-hallowed moon. The quiet Night
Shall hear that language underneath the skies
Which whispereth above them, as the prayer
And the deep vow are spoken. Passing fair
And gifted creatures, with the light of truth
And undebarred affection, as a crown,
Resting upon the beautiful brow of youth,
Shall smile on stately manhood, kneeling down
Before them, as to Idols. Friendship's hand
Shall clasp its brothers ; and Affection's tear
Be sanctified with sympathy. The bier
Of stricken love shall lose the fears, which
  Death
Giveth his awful work, and earnest Faith
Shall look beyond the shadow of the clay,
The pulseless sepulchre, the cold decay ;
And to the quiet of the spirit-land
Follow the mourned and lovely. Gifted ones
Lighting the Heaven of Intellect, like suns,
Shall wrestle well with circumstance, and bear
The agony of scorn, the preying care,
Wedded to burning bosoms ; and go down
In sorrow to the noteless sepulchre,
With one lone hope embracing like a crown
The cold and death-like forehead of Despair,
That after times shall treasure up their fame
Even as a proud inheritance and high ;
And beautiful beings love to breathe their name
With the recorded things that never die.

And thou, gray voyager to the breezeless sea
Of infinite Oblivion — speed thou on;
Another gift of time succeedeth thee
Fresh from the hand of God ; for thou hast done
The errand of thy destiny ; and none
May dream of thy returning. Go, and bear
Mortality's frail records to thy cold,
Eternal prison-house ; the midnight prayer
Of suffering bosoms, and the fevered care
Of worldly hearts ; the miser's dream of gold ;
Ambition's grasp at greatness ; the quenched
  light
Of broken spirits ; the forgiven wrong
And the abiding curse — ay, bear along
These wrecks of thy own making. Lo, thy knell
Gathers upon the windy breath of night,
Its last and faintest echo. Fare thee well !

THE MISSIONARY

"It is an awful, an arduous thing to root out
every affection for earthly things, so as to live
only for another world. I am now far, very
far. from you all ; and as often as I look around
and see the Indian scenery, I sigh to think of
the distance which separates us." — *Letters of
Henry Martyn, from India.*

"SAY, whose is this fair picture, which the light
  From the unshutter'd window rests upon
Even as a lingering halo ? Beautiful !

The keen, fine eye of manhood, and a lip
Lovely as that of Hylas, and impressed
With the bright signet of some brilliant thought;
That broad expanse of forehead, clear and high,
Marked visibly with the characters of mind,
And the free locks around it, raven black,
Luxuriant and unsilver'd! — who was he?"

A friend, a more than brother. In the spring
And glory of his being he went forth
From the embraces of devoted friends,
From ease and quiet happiness, from more —
From the warm heart that loved him with a love
Holier than earthly passion, and to whom
The beauty of his spirit shone above
The charms of perishing nature. He went forth
Strengthened to suffer, gifted to subdue
The might of human passion, to pass on
Quietly to the sacrifice of all
The lofty hopes of boyhood, and to turn
The high ambition written on that brow,
From its first dream of power and human fame,
Unto a task of seeming lowliness,
Yet God-like in its purpose. He went forth
To bind the broken spirit, to pluck back
The heathen from the wheel of Juggernaut;
To place the spiritual image of a God
Holy and just and true, before the eye
Of the dark-minded Brahmin, and unseal
The holy pages of the Book of Life,
Fraught with sublimer mysteries than all
The sacred tomes of Vedas, to unbind
The widow from her sacrifice, and save
The perishing infant from the worshipped river!

"And, lady, where is he?" He slumbers well
Beneath the shadow of an Indian palm.
There is no stone above his grave. The wind,
Hot from the desert, as it stirs the leaves
Heavy and long above him, sighs alone
Over his place of slumber.

        "God forbid
That he should die alone!" Nay, not alone.
His God was with him in that last dread hour;
His great arm underneath him, and His smile
Melting into a spirit full of peace.
And one kind friend, a human friend, was
    near —
One whom his teachings and his earnest prayers
Had snatch'd as from the burning. He alone
Felt the last pressure of his failing hand,
Caught the last glimpse of his closing eye,
And laid the green turf over him with tears,
And left him with his God.

        "And was it well,
Dear lady, that this noble mind should cast
Its rich gifts on the waters? That a heart
Full of all gentleness and truth and love
Should wither on the suicidal shrine
Of a mistaken duty? If I read
Aright the fine intelligence which fills
That amplitude of brow, and gazes out
Like an indwelling spirit from that eye,
He might have borne him loftily among
The proudest of his land, and with a step

Unfaltering ever, steadfast and secure,
Gone up the paths of greatness, — bearing still
A sister spirit with him, as some star,
Preëminent in Heaven, leads steadily up
A kindred watcher, with its fainter beams
Baptized in its great glory. Was it well
That all this promise of the heart and mind
Should perish from the earth, and leave no
    trace,
Unfolding like the Cereus of the clime
Which hath its sepulchre, but in the night
Of pagan desolation — was it well?"

Thy will be done, O Father! — it *was* well.
What are the honors of a perishing world
Grasp'd by a palsied finger? the applause
Of the unthoughtful multitude which greets
The dull ear of decay? the wealth that loads
The bier with costly drapery, and shines
In tinsel on the coffin, and builds up
The cold substantial monument? Can these
Bear up the sinking spirit in that hour
When heart and flesh are failing, and the grave
Is opening under us? Oh, dearer then
The memory of a kind deed done to him
Who was our enemy, one grateful tear
In the meek eye of virtuous suffering,
One smile call'd up by unseen charity
On the wan lips of hunger, or one prayer
Breathed from the bosom of the penitent —
The stain'd with crime and outcast, unto whom
Our mild rebuke and tenderness of love
A merciful God hath bless'd.

        "But, lady, say,
Did he not sometimes almost sink beneath
The burden of his toil, and turn aside
To weep above his sacrifice, and cast
A sorrowing glance upon his childhood's home,
Still green in memory? Clung not to his heart
Something of earthly hope uncrucified,
Of earthly thought unchastened? Did he bring
Life's warm affections to the sacrifice —
Its loves, hopes, sorrows — and become as one
Knowing no kindred but a perishing world,
No love but of the sin-endangered soul,
No hope but of the winning back to life
Of the dead nations, and no passing thought
Save of the errand wherewith he was sent
As to a martyrdom?"

        Nay, though the heart
Be consecrated to the holiest work
Vouchsafed to mortal effort, there will be
Ties of the earth around it, and, through all
Its perilous devotion, it must keep
Its own humanity. And it is well.
Else why wept He, who with our nature veiled
The spirit of a God, o'er lost Jerusalem,
And the cold grave of Lazarus? And why
In the dim garden rose his earnest prayer,
That from his lips the cup of suffering
Might pass, if it were possible?

        My friend
Was of a gentle nature, and his heart
Gushed like a river-fountain of the hills,

Ceaseless and lavish, at a kindly smile,
A word of welcome, or a tone of love.
Freely his letters to his friends disclosed
His yearnings for the quiet haunts of home,
For love and its companionship, and all
The blessings left behind him ; yet above
Its sorrows and its clouds his spirit rose,
Tearful and yet triumphant, taking hold
Of the eternal promises of God,
And steadfast in its faith.

     Here are some lines
Penned in his lonely mission-house and sent
To a dear friend at home who even now
Lingers above them with a mournful joy,
Holding them well-nigh sacred as a leaf
Plucked from the record of a breaking heart.

EVENING IN BURMAH

A night of wonder ! piled afar
 With ebon feet and crests of snow,
Like Himalaya's peaks, which bar
The sunset and the sunset's star
 From half the shadowed vale below,
Volumed and vast the dense clouds lie,
And over them, and down the sky,
 Paled in the moon, the lightnings go.

And what a strength of light and shade
 Is chequering all the earth below !
And, through the jungle's verdant braid,
Of tangled vine and wild reed made,
 What blossoms in the moonlight glow !
The Indian rose's loveliness,
The ceiba with its crimson dress,
 The twining myrtle dropped with snow.

And flitting in the fragrant air,
 Or nestling in the shadowy trees,
A thousand bright-hued birds are there —
Strange plumage, quivering wild and rare,
 With every faintly breathing breeze ;
And, wet with dew from roses shed,
The bulbul droops her weary head,
 Forgetful of her melodies.

Uprising from the orange-leaves,
 The tall pagoda's turrets glow ;
O'er graceful shaft and fretted eaves,
Its verdant web the myrtle weaves,
 And hangs in flowering wreaths below ;
And where the clustered palms eclipse
The moonbeams, from its marble lips
 The fountain's silver waters flow.

Strange beauty fills the earth and air,
 The fragrant grove and flowering tree,
And yet my thoughts are wandering where
My native rocks lie bleak and bare,
 A weary way beyond the sea.
The yearning spirit is not here ;
It lingers on a spot more dear
 Than India's brightest bowers to me.

Methinks I tread the well-known street —
 The tree my childhood loved is there,

Its bare-worn roots are at my feet,
And through its open boughs I meet
 White glimpses of the place of prayer
And unforgotten eyes again
Are glancing through the cottage pane,
 Than Asia's lustrous eyes more fair.

Oh, holy haunts ! oh, childhood's home !
 Where, now, my wandering heart, is thine
Here, where the dusky heathen come
To bow before the deaf and dumb,
 Dead idols of their own design ;
Where in their worshipped river's tide
The infant sinks, and on its side
 The widow's funeral altars shine !

Here, where, mid light and song and flowers,
 The priceless soul in ruin lies ;
Lost, dead to all those better powers
Which link this fallen world of ours
 To God's clear-shining Paradise ;
And wrong and shame and hideous crime
Are like the foliage of their clime,
 The unshorn growth of centuries !

Turn, then, my heart ; thy home is here ;
 No other now remains for thee :
The smile of love, and friendship's tear,
The tones that melted on thine ear,
 The mutual thrill of sympathy,
The welcome of the household band,
The pressure of the lip and hand,
 Thou mayst not hear, nor feel, nor see.

God of my spirit ! Thou, alone,
 Who watchest o'er my pillowed head,
Whose ear is open to the moan
And sorrowing of thy child, hast known
 The grief which at my heart has fed ;
The struggle of my soul to rise
Above its earth-born sympathies ;
 The tears of many a sleepless bed !

Oh ! be Thine arm, as it hath been,
 In every test of heart and faith, —
The tempter's doubt, the wiles of men,
The heathen's scoff, the bosom sin, —
 A helper and a stay beneath ;
A strength in weakness, through the strife
And anguish of my wasting life —
 My solace and my hope, in death !

MASSACHUSETTS

Written on hearing that the Resolutions of
the Legislature of Massachusetts on the subject
of Slavery, presented by Hon. C. Cushing to the
House of Representatives of the United States
[in 1837] had been laid on the table unread and
unreferred, under the infamous rule of "Pat-
ton's Resolution."

AND have they spurned thy word,
 Thou of the old Thirteen !

Whose soil, where Freedom's blood first poured,
　　Hath yet a darker green?
To outworn patience suffering long
Is insult added to the wrong?

And have they closed thy mouth,
　　And fixed the padlock fast?
Dumb as the black slave of the South!
　　Is this thy fate at last?
Oh shame! thy honored seal and sign
Trod under hoofs so asinine!

Call from the Capitol
　　Thy chosen ones again,
Unmeet for them the base control
Of Slavery's curbing rein!
Unmeet for men like them to feel
The spurring of a rider's heel.

When votes are things of trade
　　And force is argument,
Call back to Quincy's shade
　　Thy old man eloquent.
Why leave him longer striving thus
With the wild beasts of Ephesus!

Back from the Capitol —
　　It is no place for thee!
Beneath the arch of Heaven's blue wall,
　　Thy voice may still be free!
What power shall chain thy utterance there,
In God's free sun and freer air?

A voice is calling thee,
　　From all the martyr graves
Of those stern men, in death made free,
　　Who could not live as slaves.
The slumberings of thy honored dead
Are for thy sake disquieted.

So let thy Faneuil Hall
　　By freemen's feet be trod,
And give the echoes of its wall
　　Once more to Freedom's God!
And in the midst unseen shall stand
The mighty fathers of thy land.

Thy gathered sons shall feel
　　The soul of Adams near,
And Otis with his fiery zeal,
　　And Warren's onward cheer;
And heart to heart shall thrill as when
They moved and spake as living men.

Not on Potomac's side,
　　With treason in thy rear,
Can Freedom's holy cause be tried:
　　Not there, my State, but here.
Here must thy needed work be done,
The battle at thy hearth-stone won.

Proclaim a new crusade
　　Against the foes within;
From bar and pulpit, press and trade,
　　Cast out the shame and sin.
Then speak thy now-unheeded word,
Its lightest whisper shall be heard.

II. POEMS PRINTED IN THE "LIFE OF WHITTIER"

THE HOME-COMING OF THE BRIDE

[The home of Sarah Greenleaf was upon the Newbury shore of the Merrimac, nearly opposite the home of the Whittiers. The house was standing until a recent date. Among Mr. Whittier's papers was found the following fragment of a ballad about the home-coming, as a bride, of his grandmother, Sarah Greenleaf, now first published.]

SARAH GREENLEAF, of eighteen years,
　　Stepped lightly her bridegroom's boat within,
Waving mid-river, through smiles and tears,
　　A farewell back to her kith and kin.
With her sweet blue eyes and her new gold gown,
　　She sat by her stalwart lover's side —
Oh, never was brought to Haverhill town
　　By land or water so fair a bride.
Glad as the glad autumnal weather,
　　The Indian summer so soft and warm,
They walked through the golden woods together,
　　His arm the girdle about her form.

They passed the dam and the gray gristmill,
　　Whose walls with the jar of grinding shook,
And crossed, for the moment awed and still,
　　The haunted bridge of the Country Brook.
The great oaks seemed on Job's Hill crown
　　To wave in welcome their branches strong,
And an upland streamlet came rippling down
　　Over root and rock, like a bridal song.
And lo! in the midst of a clearing stood
　　The rough-built farmhouse, low and lone,
While all about it the unhewn wood
　　Seemed drawing closer to claim its own.

But the red apples dropped from orchard trees,
　　The red cock crowed on the low fence rail,
From the garden hives came the sound of bees,
　　On the barn floor pealed the smiting flail.
·　·　·　·　·　·　·　·

THE SONG OF THE VERMONTERS, 1779

[Written during school-days, and published anonymously in 1833. The secret of authorship was not discovered for sixty years.]

Ho — all to the borders! Vermonters, come down,
With your breeches of deerskin and jackets of brown;
With your red woollen caps, and your moccasins, come,
To the gathering summons of trumpet and drum.

Come down with your rifles! Let gray wolf and fox
Howl on in the shade of their primitive rocks;

Let the bear feed securely from pig-pen and
    stall;
Here 's two-legged game for your powder and
    ball.

On our south came the Dutchmen, enveloped in
    grease;
And arming for battle while canting of peace;
On our east, crafty Meshech has gathered his
    band
To hang up our leaders and eat up our land.

Ho — all to the rescue! For Satan shall work
No gain for his legions of Hampshire and York!
They claim our possessions — the pitiful
    knaves —
The tribute we pay shall be prisons and graves!

Let Clinton and Ten Broek, with bribes in their
    hands,
Still seek to divide and parcel our lands;
We 've coats for our traitors, whoever they are;
The warp is of feathers — the filling of tar:

Does the "old Bay State" threaten? Does
    Congress complain?
Swarms Hampshire in arms on our borders
    again?
Bark the war-dogs of Britain aloud on the
    lake —
Let 'em come; what they can they are welcome
    to take.

What seek they among us? The pride of our
    wealth
Is comfort, contentment, and labor, and health,
And lands which, as Freemen, we only have
    trod,
Independent of all, save the mercies of God.

Yet we owe no allegiance, we bow to no throne,
Our ruler is law, and the law is our own;
Our leaders themselves are our own fellow-men,
Who can handle the sword, or the scythe, or the
    pen.

Our wives are all true, and our daughters are
    fair,
With their blue eyes of smiles and their light
    flowing hair,
All brisk at their wheels till the dark even-fall,
Then blithe at the sleigh-ride, the husking, and
    ball!

We 've sheep on the hillsides, we 've cows on
    the plain,
And gay-tasselled corn-fields and rank-growing
    grain;
There are deer on the mountains, and wood-
    pigeons fly
From the crack of our muskets, like clouds on
    the sky.

And there 's fish in our streamlets and rivers
    which take
Their course from the hills to our broad-bosomed
    lake;

Through rock-arched Winooski the salmon leaps
    free,
And the portly shad follows all fresh from the
    sea.

Like a sunbeam the pickerel glides through the
    pool,
And the spotted trout sleeps where the water
    is cool,
Or darts from his shelter of rock and of root
At the beaver's quick plunge, or the angler's
    pursuit.

And ours are the mountains, which awfully rise,
Till they rest their green heads on the blue of
    the skies;
And ours are the forests unwasted, unshorn,
Save where the wild path of the tempest is torn.

And though savage and wild be this climate of
    ours,
And brief be our season of fruits and of flowers,
Far dearer the blast round our mountains which
    raves,
Than the sweet summer zephyr which breathes
    over slaves!

Hurrah for Vermont! For the land which we
    till
Must have sons to defend her from valley and
    hill;
Leave the harvest to rot on the fields where it
    grows,
And the reaping of wheat for the reaping of
    foes.

From far Michiscom's wild valley, to where
Poosoonsuck steals down from his wood-circled
    lair,
From Shocticook River to Lutterlock town —
Ho — all to the rescue! Vermonters, come
    down!

Come York or come Hampshire, come traitors
    or knaves,
If ye rule o'er our land, ye shall rule o'er our
    graves;
Our vow is recorded — our banner unfurled,
In the name of Vermont we defy all the world!

TO A POETICAL TRIO IN THE CITY OF GOTHAM

[This *jeu d'esprit* was written by Whittier in
1832. The notes are his own. The authorship
was not discovered till after his death.]

    Three wise men of Gotham
    Went to sea in a bowl.

BARDS of the island city! — where of old
    The Dutchman smoked beneath his favorite
    tree,
And the wild eyes of Indian hunters rolled
    On Hudson plunging in the Tappaan Zee,
Scene of Stuyvesant's might and chivalry,

The voices of human duty
Smote on his ear like pain.

In vain over island and water
The curtains of sunset swung;
In vain on the beautiful mountains
The pictures of God were hung.

The wretched years crept onward,
Each sadder than the last;
All the bloom of life fell from him,
All the freshness and greenness past.

But deep in his heart forever
And unprofaned he kept
The love of his saintly mother,
Who in the graveyard slept.

His house had no pleasant pictures;
Its comfortless walls were bare:
But the riches of earth and ocean
Could not purchase his mother's chair.

The old chair, quaintly carven,
With oaken arms outspread,
Whereby, in the long gone twilights,
His childish prayers were said.

For thence in his long night watches,
By moon or starlight dim,
A face full of love and pity
And tenderness looked on him.

And oft, as the grieving presence
Sat in his mother's chair,
The groan of his self-upbraiding
Grew into wordless prayer.

At last, in the moonless midnight,
The summoning angel came,
Severe in his pity, touching
The house with fingers of flame.

The red light flashed from its windows
And flared from its sinking roof;
And baffled and awed before it
The villagers stood aloof.

They shrank from the falling rafters,
They turned from the furnace glare;
But its tenant cried, "God help me!
I must save my mother's chair."

Under the blazing portal,
Over the floor of fire,
He seemed, in the terrible splendor,
A martyr on his pyre.

In his face the mad flames smote him,
And stung him on either side;
But he clung to the sacred relic, —
By his mother's chair he died!

O mother, with human yearnings!
O saint, by the altar stairs!
Shall not the dear God give thee
The child of thy many prayers?

O Christ! by whom the loving,
Though erring, are forgiven,
Hast thou for him no refuge,
No quiet place in heaven?

Give palms to thy strong martyrs,
And crown thy saints with gold,
But let the mother welcome
Her lost one to thy fold!

LETTER TO LUCY LARCOM

25th 3d mo., 1866.

BELIEVE me, Lucy Larcom, it gives me real sorrow
That I cannot take my carpet-bag and go to town to-morrow;
But I'm "snow-bound," and cold on cold, like layers of an onion,
Have piled my back and weighed me down as with the pack of Bunyan.
The north-east wind is damper and the north-west wind is colder,
Or else the matter simply is that I am growing older.
And then I dare not trust a moon seen over one's left shoulder,
As I saw this with slender horns caught in a west hill-pine,
As on a Stamboul minaret curves the arch-impostor's sign, —
So I must stay in Amesbury, and let you go your way,
And guess what colors greet your eyes, what shapes your steps delay;
What pictured forms of heathen lore, of god and goddess please you,
What idol graven images you bend your wicked knees to.
But why should I of evil dream, well knowing at your head goes
That flower of Christian womanhood, our dear good Anna Meadows.
She'll be discreet, I'm sure, although once, in a freak romantic,
She flung the Doge's bridal ring, and married "The Atlantic"!
And spite of all appearances, like the woman in a shoe,
She's got so many "Young Folks" now, she don't know what to do.
But I must say I think it strange that thee and Mrs. Spaulding,
Whose lives with Calvin's five-railed creed have been so tightly walled in,
Should quit your Puritan homes, and ... pains to go
So far, with malice aforethought ... a vain show"!
Did Emmons hunt for pictures ... Edwards peeping
Into the chambers of im... Tammuz weeping
Ah well! the times ... myself am fe...

And Knickerbocker's fame, — I have made bold
To come before ye, at the present time,
And *reason* with ye in the way of *rhyme*.

Time was when poets kept the quiet tenor
Of their green pathway through th' Arcadian vale, —
Chiming their music in the low sweet manner
Of song-birds warbling to the "Soft South" gale;
Wooing the Muse where gentle zephyrs fan her,
Where all is peace and earth may not assail;
Telling of lutes and flowers, of love and fear,
Of shepherds, sheep and lambs, and "such small deer."

But ye! lost recreants — straying from the green
And pleasant vista of your early time,
With broken lutes and crownless skulls — are seen
Spattering your neighbors with abhorrent slime
Of the low world's pollution![1] Ye have been
So long apostates from the Heaven of rhyme,
That of the Muses, every mother's daughter
Blushes to own such graceless bards e'er sought her.

"*Hurrah for Jackson!*" is the music now
Which your cracked lutes have learned alone to utter,
As, crouching in Corruption's shadow low,
Ye daily sweep them for your bread and butter,[2]
Cheered by the applauses of the friends who show
Their heads above the offal of the gutter,
And, like the trees which Orpheus moved at will,
Reel, as in token of your matchless skill!

Thou son of Scotia![3] — nursed beside the grave
Of the proud peasant-minstrel, and to whom
The wild muse of thy mountain-dwelling gave
A portion of its spirit, — if the tomb
Could burst its silence, o'er the Atlantic's wave,
To thee his voice of stern rebuke would come,
Who dared to waken with a master's hand
The lyre of freedom in a fettered land.

And thou! — once treading firmly the proud deck
O'er which thy country's honored flag was sleeping,
Calmly in peace, or to the hostile beck

Of coming foes in starry splendor sweeping, —
Thy graphic tales of battle or of wreck,
Or lone night-watch in middle ocean keeping,
Have made thy "Leisure Hours" more prized by far
Than those now spent in Party's wordy war.[4]

And last, not least, thou! — now nurtured in the land
Where thy bold-hearted fathers long ago
Rocked Freedom's cradle, till its infant hand
Strangled the serpent fierceness of its foe, —
Thou, whose clear brow in early time was fanned
By the soft airs which from Castalia flow![5] —
Where art thou now? feeding with hickory ladle
The curs of Faction with thy daily twaddle!

Men have looked up to thee, as one to be
A portion of our glory; and the light
And fairy hands of woman beckoned thee
On to thy laurel guerdon; and those bright
And gifted spirits, whom the broad blue sea
Hath shut from thy communion, bid thee,
"*Write*,"
Like John of Patmos. Is all this forgotten,
For Yankee brawls and Carolina cotton?

Are autumn's rainbow hues no longer seen?
Flows the "Green River" through its vale no more?
Steals not thy "Rivulet" by its banks of green?
Wheels upward from its dark and sedgy shore
Thy "Water Fowl" no longer? — that the mean
And vulgar strife, the ranting and the *roar*
Extempore, like Bottom's should be thine, —
Thou feeblest truck-horse in the Hero's line!

Lost trio! — turn ye to the minstrel pride
Of classic Britain. Even effeminate Moore
Has cast the wine-cup and the lute aside
For Erin and O'Connell; and before
His country's altar, Bulwer breasts the tide
Of old oppression. Sadly brooding o'er
The fate of heroes struggling to be free,
Even Campbell speaks for Poland. *Where are ye?*

Hirelings of traitors! — know ye not that men
Are rousing up around ye to retrieve
Our country's honor, which too long has been
Debased by those for whom ye daily weave

[1] Editors of the *Mercantile Advertiser* and the *Evening Post* in New York, — the present organs of Jacksonism.

[2] Perhaps, after all, they get something better; inasmuch as the Heroites have for some time had exclusive possession of the Hall of St. Tammany, and we have the authority of Halleck that

"There's a barrel of porter in Tammany hall
And the Bucktails are swigging it all the night long."

[3] James Lawson, Esq., of the *Mercantile*. A fine, warm-hearted Scotchman, who, having unfortunately blundered into Jacksonism, is wondering "how i' the Deil's name" he got there. He is the author of a volume entitled *Tales and Sketches*, and of the tragedy of *Giordano*.

[4] William Leggett, Esq., of the *Post*, a gentleman of good talents, favorably known as the editor of the *New York Critic*, etc.

[5] William C. Bryant, Esq., well known to the public at large as a poet of acknowledged excellence; and as a very dull editor to the people of New York.

Your web of fustian; that from tongue and
    pen
Of those who o'er our tarnished honor grieve,
Of the pure-hearted and the gifted, come
Hourly the tokens of your master's doom?

Turn from their ruin! Dash your chains
    aside!
  Stand up like men for Liberty and Law,
And free opinion. Check Corruption's pride,
  Soothe the loud storm of fratricidal war, —
And the bright honors of your eventide
  Shall share the glory which your morning
    saw;
The patriot's heart shall gladden at your name,
Ye shall be blessed with, and not "damned to
    fame"!

ALBUM VERSES

[Written in the album of May Pillsbury of
West Newbury, in the fall of 1838, when
Whittier was at home on a visit from Phila-
delphia, where he was engaged in editorial
work.]

PARDON a stranger hand that gives
Its impress to these gilded leaves.
As one who graves in idle mood
An idler's name on rock or wood,
So in a careless hour I claim
A page to leave my humble name.
Accept it; and when o'er my head
A Pennsylvanian sky is spread,
And but in dreams my eye looks back
On broad and lovely Merrimac,
And on my ear no longer breaks
The murmuring music which it makes,
When but in dreams I look again
On Salisbury beach — Grasshopper plain —
Or Powow stream — or Amesbury mills,
Or old Crane neck, or Pipestave hills,
Think of me then as one who keeps,
Where Delaware's broad current sweeps,
And down its rugged limestone-bed
The Schuylkill's arrowy flight is sped,
Deep in his heart the scenes which grace
And glorify his "native place;"
Loves every spot to childhood dear,
And leaves his heart "untraveled" here;
Longs, midst the Dutchman's kraut and greens,
For pumpkin-pie and pork and beans,
And sighs to think when, sweetly near,
The soft piano greets his ear,
That the fair hands which, small and white,
Glance on its ivory polished light,
Have ne'er an Indian pudding made,
Nor fashioned rye and Indian bread.
And oh! whene'er his footsteps turn,
Whatever stars above him burn,
Though dwelling where a Yankee's name
Is coupled with reproach or shame,
Still true to his New England birth,
Still faithful to his home and hearth,
Even 'midst the scornful stranger band
His boast shall be of YANKEE LAND.

WHAT STATE STREET SAID TO SOUTH CAROLINA, AND WHAT SOUTH CAROLINA SAID TO STATE STREET

[Published in *The National Era*, May 22, 1851.]

MUTTERING "fine upland staple," "prime Sea
    Island finer,"
With cotton bales pictured on either retina,
"Your pardon!" said State Street to South
    Carolina;
"We feel and acknowledge your laws are di-
    viner
Than any promulgated by the thunders of
    Sinai!
Sorely pricked in the sensitive conscience of
    business
We own and repent of our sins of remissness:
Our honor we 've yielded, our words we have
    swallowed;
And quenching the lights which our forefathers
    followed,
And turning from graves by their memories
    hallowed,
With teeth on ball-cartridge, and finger on trig-
    ger,
Reversed Boston Notions, and sent back a nig-
    ger!"

"Get away!" cried the Chivalry, busy a-drum-
    ming,
And fifing and drilling, and such Quattle-bum-
    ming,
"With your April-fool slave hunt! Just wait
    till December
Shall see your new Senator stalk through the
    Chamber,
And Puritan heresy prove neither dumb nor
Blind in that pestilent Anakim, Sumner!"

A FRÉMONT CAMPAIGN SONG

SOUND now the trumpet warningly!
  The storm is rolling nearer,
  The hour is striking clearer,
    In the dusky dome of sky.
If dark and wild the morning be,
  A darker morn before us
  Shall fling its shadows o'er us
    If we let the hour go by.
Sound we then the trumpet chorus!
  Sound the onset wild and nigh!
    Country and Liberty!
    Freedom and Victory!
  These words shall be our cry, —
    Frémont and Victory!

Sound, sound the trumpet fearlessly!
  Each arm its vigor lending,
  Bravely with wrong contending,
    And shouting Freedom's cry!
The Kansas homes stand cheerlessly,
  The sky with flame is ruddy,
  The prairie turf is bloody,
    Where the brave and gentle die.

Sound the trumpet stern and steady!
  Sound the trumpet strong and high!
    Country and Liberty!
    Freedom and Victory!
  These words shall be our cry, —
    Frémont and Victory!

Sound now the trumpet cheerily!
  Nor dream of Heaven's forsaking
  The issue of its making,
    That Right with Wrong must try.
The cloud that hung so drearily
  The Northern winds are breaking;
  The Northern Lights are shaking
    Their fire-flags in the sky.
Sound the signal of awaking;
  Sound the onset wild and high!
    Country and Liberty!
    Freedom and Victory!
  These words shall be our cry, —
    Frémont and Victory!

THE QUAKERS ARE OUT

[A campaign song written to be sung at a
Republican Mass Meeting held in Newbury-
port, Mass., October 11, 1860.]

NOT vainly we waited and counted the hours,
The buds of our hope have all burst into flowers.
No room for misgiving — no loop-hole of
    doubt, —
We 've heard from the Keystone! The Qua-
    kers are out.

The plot has exploded — we 've found out the
    trick;
The bribe goes a-begging; the fusion won't
    stick.
When the Wide-awake lanterns are shining
    about,
The rogues stay at home, and the true men are
    out!

The good State has broken the cords for her
    spun;
Her oil-springs and water won't fuse into one;
The Dutchman has seasoned with Freedom his
    krout,
And slow, late, but certain, the Quakers are
    out!

Give the flags to the winds! set the hills all
    aflame!
Make way for the man with the Patriarch's
    name!
Away with misgiving — away with all doubt,
For Lincoln goes in, when the Quakers are out!

A LEGEND OF THE LAKE

[This poem, originally printed in the "At-
lantic Monthly," was withheld from publica-
tion in his volumes by Mr. Whittier, in defer-
ence to living relatives of the hero of the poem.
He finally removed the restriction.]

SHOULD you go to Centre Harbor,
  As haply you some time may,
Sailing up the Winnepesaukee
  From the hills of Alton Bay, —

Into the heart of the highlands,
  Into the north wind free,
Through the rising and vanishing islands
  Over the mountain sea, —

To the little hamlet lying
  White in its mountain fold,
Asleep by the lake and dreaming
  A dream that is never told, —

And in the Red Hill's shadow
  Your pilgrim home you make,
Where the chambers open to sunrise,
  The mountains, and the lake, —

If the pleasant picture wearies,
  As the fairest sometimes will,
And the weight of the hills lies on you
  And the water is all too still, —

If in vain the peaks of Gunstock
  Redden with sunrise fire,
And the sky and the purple mountains
  And the sunset islands tire, —

If you turn from in-door thrumming
  And the clatter of bowls without,
And the folly that goes on its travels,
  Bearing the city about, —

And the cares you left behind you
  Come hunting along your track,
As Blue-Cap in German fable
  Rode on the traveller's pack, —

Let me tell you a tender story
  Of one who is now no more,
A tale to haunt like a spirit
  The Winnepesaukee shore, —

Of one who was brave and gentle,
  And strong for manly strife,
Riding with cheering and music
  Into the tourney of life.

Faltering and failing midway
  In the Tempter's subtle snare,
The chains of an evil habit
  He bowed himself to bear.

Over his fresh young manhood
  The bestial veil was flung,
The curse of the wine of Circe,
  The spell her weavers sung.

Yearly did hill and lakeside
  Their summer idyls frame;
Alone in his darkened dwelling
  He hid his face for shame.

The music of life's great marches
  Sounded for him in vain;

The wicked world my Quaker coat from off my
  shoulders peeling.
God grant that in the strange new sea of change
  wherein we swim,
We still may keep the good old plank, of simple
  faith in Him!

LINES ON LEAVING APPLEDORE

[Sent in a letter to Celia Thaxter.]

UNDER the shadow of a cloud, the light
Died out upon the waters, like a smile
Chased from a face by grief. Following the
    flight
Of a lone bird that, scudding with the breeze,
Dipped its crank wing in leaden-colored seas,
I saw in sunshine lifted, clear and bright,
On the horizon's rim the Fortunate Isle
That claims thee as its fair inhabitant,
And glad of heart I whispered, "Be to her,
Bird of the summer sea, my messenger;
Tell her, if Heaven a fervent prayer will grant,
This light that falls her island home above
Making its slopes of rock and greenness gay,
A partial glory midst surrounding gray,
Shall prove an earnest of our Father's love,
More and more shining to the perfect day."

MRS. CHOATE'S HOUSE-WARMING

[" His washerwoman, Mrs. Choate, by indus-
try and thrift had been enabled to build for
her family a comfortable house. When it was
ready for occupancy, there was a house-warm-
ing, attended by all the neighbors, who brought
substantial tokens of their good-will, including
all the furniture needed in her new parlor.
Mr. Whittier's hand was to be seen in the
whole movement; he was present at the festiv-
ity, and made a little speech, congratulating
Mrs. Choate upon her well-deserved success in
life, and said he would read a piece of machine
poetry which had been intrusted to him for the
occasion. These are the lines, which were, of
course, of his own composition." — S. T. PICK-
ARD, *Life and Letters of John Greenleaf Whit-
tier.*]

OF rights and of wrongs
Let the feminine tongues
    Talk on — none forbid it.
Our hostess best knew
What her hands found to do,
    Asked no questions, but DID IT.

Here the lesson of work,
Which so many folks shirk,
    Is so plain all may learn it;
Each brick in this dwelling,
Each timber is telling,
    If you want a home, EARN IT.

The question of labor
Is solved by our neighbor,
    The old riddle guessed out:
The wisdom sore needed,
The truth long unheeded,
    Her flat-iron 's pressed out!

Thanks, then, to Kate Choate!
Let the idle take note
    What their fingers were made for:
She, cheerful and jolly,
Worked on late and early,
    And bought — what she paid for!

Never vainly repining,
Nor begging, nor whining;
    The morning-star twinkles
On no heart that 's lighter
As she makes the world whiter
    And smooths out its wrinkles.

So, long life to Kate!
May her heirs have to wait
    Till they 're gray in attendance;
And her flat-iron press on,
    Still teaching its lesson
    Of brave independence!

AN AUTOGRAPH

[Written for an old friend, Rev. S. H. Em-
ery, of Quincy, Ill., who revisited Whittier in
1868.]

THE years that since we met have flown
Leave as they found me, still alone:
No wife, nor child, nor grandchild dear,
Are mine the heart of age to cheer.
More favored thou, with hair less gray
Than mine, canst let thy fancy stray
To where thy little Constance sees
The prairie ripple in the breeze;
For one like her to lisp thy name
Is better than the voice of fame.

TO LUCY LARCOM

3d mo., 1870.

* * * * * *

PRAY give the "Atlantic"
A brief unpedantic
Review of Miss Phelps' book,
Which teaches and helps folk
To deal with the offenders
In love which surrenders
All pride unforgiving,
The lost one receiving
With truthful believing
That she like all others,
Our sisters and brothers,
Is only a sinner
Whom God's love within her
Can change to the whiteness
Of heaven's own brightness.
For who shall see tarnish
If He sweep and garnish?

When He is the cleanser
Shall *we* dare to censure?
Say to Fields, if he ask of it,
I can't take the task of it.

. . . . . .

P. S. — For myself, if I'm able,
And half comfortable,
I shall run for the seashore
To some place as before,
Where blunt we at least find
The teeth of the East wind,
And spring does not tarry
As it does at Amesbury;
But where it will be to
I cannot yet see to.

A FAREWELL

[Written for Mr. and Mrs. Claflin as they
were about to sail to Europe.]

WHAT shall I say, dear friends, to whom I owe
The choicest blessings, dropping from the hands
Of trustful love and friendship, as you go
Forth on your journey to those older lands,
By saint and sage and bard and hero trod?
Scarcely the simple farewell of the Friends
Sufficeth; after you my full heart sends
Such benediction as the pilgrim hears
Where the Greek faith its golden dome uprears,
From Crimea's roses to Archangel snows,
The fittest prayer of parting: "Go with God!"

ON A FLY-LEAF OF LONGFELLOW'S POEMS

[Written at the Asquam House in the summer of 1882.]

HUSHED now the sweet consoling tongue
Of him whose lyre the Muses strung;
His last low swan-song has been sung!

His last! And ours, dear friend, is near;
As clouds that rake the mountains here,
We too shall pass and disappear.

Yet howsoever changed or tost,
Not even a wreath of mist is lost,
No atom can itself exhaust.

So shall the soul's superior force
Live on and run its endless course
In God's unlimited universe.

And we, whose brief reflections seem
To fade like clouds from lake and stream,
Shall brighten in a holier beam.

SAMUEL E. SEWALL

[An inscription for a marble bust, modelled
by Anne Whitney, and placed in the Cary Library, Lexington, Mass., May, 1884.]

LIKE that ancestral judge who bore his name,
Faithful to Freedom and to Truth, he gave,
When all the air was hot with wrath and blame,
His youth and manhood to the fettered slave.

And never Woman in her suffering saw
A helper tender, wise, and brave as he;
Lifting her burden of unrighteous law,
He shamed the boasts of ancient chivalry.

Noiseless as light that melts the darkness is,
He wrought as duty led and honor bid,
No trumpet heralds victories like his, —
The unselfish worker in his work is hid.

LINES WRITTEN IN AN ALBUM

[The album belonged to the grandson of
Whittier's life-long friend, Theodore D. Weld,
and the lines were written in April, 1 84.]

WHAT shall I wish him? Strength and health
May be abused, and so may wealth.
Even fame itself may come to be
But wearying notoriety.

What better can I ask than this? —
A life of brave unselfishness,
Wisdom for council, eloquence
For Freedom's need, for Truth's defence,
The championship of all that's good,
The manliest faith in womanhood,
The steadfast friendship changing not
With change of time or place or lot,
Hatred of sin, but not the less
A heart of pitying tenderness
And charity, that, suffering long,
Shames the wrong-doer from his wrong:
One wish expresses all — that he
May even as his grandsire be!

A DAY'S JOURNEY

[Written in 1886, for the tenth anniversary
of the wedding of his niece.]

AFTER your pleasant morning travel
You pause as at a wayside inn,
And take with grateful hearts your breakfast
Though served in dishes all of TIN.

Then go, while years as hours are counted,
Until the dial's hand at noon
Invites you to a dinner table
Garnished with SILVER fork and spoon.

And when the vesper bell to supper
Is calling, and the day is old,
May love transmute the tin of morning
And noonday's silver into GOLD.

A FRAGMENT

[Found among Mr. Whittier's papers, in his
handwriting, but undated.]

THE dreadful burden of our sins we feel,
The pain of wounds which Thou alone canst
  heal,
To whom our weakness is our strong appeal.

From the black depths, the ashes, and the dross
Of our waste lives, we reach out to Thy cross,
And by its fullness measure all our loss!

That holy sign reveals Thee : throned above
No Moloch sits, no false, vindictive Jove —
Thou art our Father, and Thy name is Love![1]

III. NOTES

Page 5. *Sole Pythoness of Ancient Lynn.*
The Pythoness of ancient Lynn was the re-
doubtable Moll Pitcher, who lived under the
shadow of High Rock in that town, and was
sought far and wide for her supposed powers of
divination. She died about 1810. Mr. Upham,
in his *Salem Witchcraft*, has given an account
of her.

Page 12. *St. John.*
[Dr. Francis Parkman has given a detailed
account of this episode in New England history
in *The Feudal Chiefs of Acadia*, published in
The Atlantic Monthly, January, February, 1893.
The same series of incidents forms the basis of
the romance by Mrs. Mary Hartwell Cather-
wood, entitled *The Lady of Fort St. John.*]

Page 21. *The New Wife and the Old.*
[General Moulton's mansion may still be seen
[1894] from the train, a hip-roofed house, stand-
ing on the right-hand side of the track, just be-
fore reaching the Hampton station as one comes
from Boston. Twenty-five years after writing
the poem, Mr. Whittier received a letter from
a lady who had been spending a summer in the
Moulton house, in which she said : "I remem-
ber my mother's repeating to me her recollec-
tions of the exorcising of the ghosts of General
Moulton and his wife by a parson Milton or
Bodily [the Rev. John Boddily, who died in
1802, and is buried in a Newburyport burying-
ground]. My grandfather Whipple being ab-
sent, the servants (several of them had been
slaves in Newport) insisted that General Moul-
ton and his wife disturbed the house so much at
night, he thumping with his cane, and her dress
'a-rustling up and down the stairs,' that nothing
could allay their terror ; and one Mrs. Williams,
the housekeeper, persisted so strongly that she
frequently saw them both, he in a snuff-colored
suit and enormous wig, holding a gold-headed
cane, that nothing could induce them to remain
in the house. Many persons in the vicinity came
to the exorcising, or 'laying the ghosts' as they
termed it. My mother said the scene was very
impressive to her as a child, and she could never

[1] This is an alternative reading which has been can-
celled : —

  "No lawless Terror dwells in light above,
  Cruel as Moloch, deaf and false as Jove —
  Thou art our Father, and Thy name is Love!"

forget the white and black servants and neigh-
bors, standing in solemn awe, and the abjuring
of the minister. The servants, I believe, never
afterwards complained of being disturbed or of
seeing the ghosts, after this ceremony."
In his work on *The Supernaturalism of
New England*, published in 1847, Mr. Whittier
relates the legend of the ancient house. "Gen-
eral Moulton's house was once burned in re-
venge, it is said, by the fiend, whom the former
had outwitted. He had agreed, it seems, to
furnish the general with a boot full of gold and
silver, poured annually down the chimney. The
shrewd Yankee cut off on one occasion the foot
of the boot, and the Devil kept pouring down
the coin from the chimney top, in a vain at-
tempt to fill it, until the room was literally
packed with the precious metal. When the
general died, he was laid out, and put in a coffin
as usual; but on the day of the funeral it was
whispered about that his body was missing,
and the neighbors came to the charitable con-
clusion that the enemy had got his own at
last."]

Page 26. *Here the mighty Bashaba.*
Bashaba was the name which the Indians of
New England gave to two or three of their prin-
cipal chiefs, to whom all their inferior sagamores
acknowledged allegiance. Passaconaway seems
to have been one of these chiefs. His residence
was at Pennacook. (*Mass. Hist. Coll.*, vol. iii.
pp. 21, 22.) "He was regarded," says Hub-
bard, "as a great sorcerer, and his fame was
widely spread. It was said of him that he could
cause a green leaf to grow in winter, trees to
dance, water to burn, etc. He was, undoubt-
edly, one of those shrewd and powerful men
whose achievements are always regarded by a
barbarous people as the result of supernatural
aid. The Indians gave to such the names of
Powahs or Panisees."
"The Panisees are men of great courage and
wisdom, and to these the Devill appeareth more
familiarly than to others." — Winslow's *Rela-
tion.*

Page 28. *Thus o'er the heart of Weetamoo.*
"The Indians," says Roger Williams, "have
a god whom they call Wetuomanit, who pre-
sides over the household."

Page 29. *Drawn from that great stone vase.*
There are rocks in the river at the Falls of
Amoskeag, in the cavities of which, tradition
says, the Indians formerly stored and concealed
their corn.

Page 31. *Aukeetamit.*
The Spring God. — See Roger Williams's *Key
to the Indian Language.*

Page 33. *Mat wonck kunna-monee.*
We shall see thee or her no more. — See
Roger Williams's *Key.*

Page 33. *Sowanna.*
"The Great South West God." — See Roger
Williams's *Observations*, etc.

Page 34. *As we charged on Tilly's line.*
The barbarities of Count De Tilly after the
siege of Magdeburg made such an impression
upon our forefathers that the phrase "like old

Tilly " is still heard sometimes in New England of any piece of special ferocity.

Page 42.   *A fire-mount in a frozen zone.*

Dr. Hooker, who accompanied Sir James Ross in his expedition of 1841, thus describes the appearance of that unknown land of frost and fire which was seen in latitude 77° south, — a stupendous chain of mountains, the whole mass of which, from its highest point to the ocean, was covered with everlasting snow and ice : —

"The water and the sky were both as blue, or rather more intensely blue, than I have ever seen them in the tropics, and all the coast was one mass of dazzlingly beautiful peaks of snow, which, when the sun approached the horizon, reflected the most brilliant tints of golden yellow and scarlet ; and then, to see the dark cloud of smoke, tinged with flame, rising from the volcano in a perfect unbroken column, one side jet-black, the other giving back the colors of the sun, sometimes turning off at a right angle by some current of wind, and stretching many miles to leeward ! This was a sight so surpassing everything that can be imagined, and so heightened by the consciousness that we had penetrated, under the guidance of our commander, into regions far beyond what was ever deemed practicable, that it caused a feeling of awe to steal over us at the consideration of our own comparative insignificance and helplessness, and at the same time an indescribable feeling of the greatness of the Creator in the works of his hand."

Page 59.   *Here is the place.*

["The place Whittier had in mind was his birthplace. There were bee-hives on the garden terrace near the well-sweep, occupied perhaps by the descendants of Thomas Whittier's bees. The approach to the house from over the northern shoulder of Job's Hill by a path that was in constant use in his boyhood and still in existence, is accurately described in the poem. The ' gap in the old wall ' is still to be seen, and ' the stepping stones in the shallow brook ' are still in use. His sister's garden was down by the brook-side in front of the house, and her daffodils are perpetuated and may now be found in their season each year in that place. The red-barred gate, the poplars, the cattle yard with ' the white horns tossing above the wall,' were all part of Whittier's boy life on the old farm. Even the touch of ' the sundown's blaze on her window pane ' is realistic. The only place from which the blaze of the setting sun could be seen reflected in the windows of the old mansion is from the path so perfectly described. . . . All the story about Mary and her lover is wholly imaginative." S. T. Pickard in his *Life and Letters of John Greenleaf Whittier.*

Page 67.   *Of the fast which the good man lifelong kept.*

It was the custom in Sewall's time for churches and individuals to hold fasts whenever any public or private need suggested the fitness ; and as state and church were very closely connected, the General Court sometimes ordered a fast. Out of this custom sprang the annual fast in spring, now observed [1888], but it is of comparatively recent date. Such a fast was ordered on the 14th of January, 1697, when Sewall made his special confession of guilt in condemning innocent persons under the supposition that they were witches. He is said to have observed the day privately on each annual return thereafter.

Page 68.   *His burden of prophecy yet remains.*

[In point of fact the "old man wise and good," "propped on his staff of age," was forty-five years old when he uttered his prophecy.]

Page 69.   *The Red River Voyageur.*

[The church of St. Boniface was burned in 1860, the year after *The Red River Voyageur* was printed. The bells were broken in their fall, and the fragments were sent to London, recast by their original founder, and restored to their place in the new cathedral of St. Boniface.]

Page 77.   *Cobbler Keezar's Vision.*

[For a fuller account of Cobbler Keezar, see Whittier's paper on *The Border War of 1708* in his *Prose Works*, volume II. pp. 375, 376. Cobbler Keezar was wont to pitch his tent on Po Hill and mend the foot-gear of the Amesbury people. The old towns of Amesbury and Salisbury, within a few years consolidated, were divided by the Powow River. The falls described in the poem are concealed from view now by the factories and the arches which span the river.]

Page 78.   *Or the stone of Dr. Dee.*

Dr. John Dee was a man of erudition, who had an extensive museum, library, and apparatus ; he claimed to be an astrologer, and had acquired the reputation of having dealings with evil spirits, and a mob was raised which destroyed the greater part of his possessions. He professed to raise the dead and had a magic crystal. He died a pauper in 1608.

Page 81.   *The Countess.*

[There is a slight inaccuracy in Whittier's head note to *The Countess*. According to Miss Rebecca I. Davis, *Gleanings from the Valley of the Merrimac*, where she gives her authorities, the marriage took place March 21, 1805. The Countess died January 5, 1807. Count Vipart returned to Guadaloupe whence he had come to this country at the time of the insurrection ; there he married again, and there he died and was buried, but his remains were afterward removed to the family tomb in Bordeaux, France. Mr. Matthew Whittier, the poet's only brother, married Abby, daughter of Joseph Rochemont de Poyen.]

Page 103.   *The Pennsylvania Pilgrim.*

[The following long note originally was used as an introduction to the poem.] The beginning of German emigration to America may be traced to the personal influence of William Penn, who in 1677 visited the Continent, and made the acquaintance of an intelligent and highly cultivated circle of Pietists, or Mystics, who, reviving in the seventeenth century the spiritual faith and worship of Tauler and the "Friends of God" in the fourteenth, gathered about the pastor Spener, and the young and beautiful Eleonora Johanna Von Merlau. In this circle originated the Frankfort Land Company, which bought of William Penn, the Governor of Pennsylvania, a tract of land near the new city of Philadelphia.

The company's agent in the New World was a rising young lawyer, Francis Daniel Pastorius, son of Judge Pastorius, of Windsheim, who, at the age of seventeen, entered the University of Altorf. He studied law at Strasburg, Basle, and Jena, and at Ratisbon, the seat of the Imperial Government, obtained a practical knowledge of international polity. Successful in all his examinations and disputations, he received the degree of Doctor of Law at Nuremberg in 1676. In 1679 he was a law-lecturer at Frankfort, where he became deeply interested in the teachings of Dr. Spener. In 1680–81 he travelled in France, England, Ireland, and Italy with his friend Herr Von Rodeck. "I was," he says, "glad to enjoy again the company of my Christian friends, rather than be with Von Rodeck, feasting and dancing." In 1683, in company with a small number of German Friends, he emigrated to America, settling upon the Frankfort Company's tract between the Schuylkill and the Delaware rivers. The township was divided into four hamlets, namely, Germantown, Krisheim, Crefield, and Sommerhausen. Soon after his arrival he united himself with the Society of Friends, and became one of its most able and devoted members, as well as the recognized head and lawgiver of the settlement. He married, two years after his arrival, Anneke (Anna), daughter of Dr. Klosterman, of Muhlheim.

In the year 1688 he drew up a memorial against slaveholding, which was adopted by the Germantown Friends and sent up to the Monthly Meeting, and thence to the Yearly Meeting at Philadelphia. It is noteworthy as the first protest made by a religious body against Negro Slavery. The original document was discovered in 1844 by the Philadelphia antiquarian, Nathan Kite, and published in *The Friend* (Vol. XVIII. No. 16). It is a bold and direct appeal to the best instincts of the heart. "Have not," he asks, "these negroes as much right to fight for their freedom as you have to keep them slaves?"

Under the wise direction of Pastorius, the Germantown settlement grew and prospered. The inhabitants planted orchards and vineyards, and surrounded themselves with souvenirs of their old home. A large number of them were linen-weavers, as well as small farmers. The Quakers were the principal sect, but men of all religions were tolerated, and lived together in harmony. In 1692 Richard Frame published, in what he called verse, a *Description of Pennsylvania*, in which he alludes to the settlement : —

> "The German town of which I spoke before,
> Which is at least in length one mile or more,
> Where lives High German people and Low Dutch,
> Whose trade in weaving linen cloth is much, —
> There grows the flax, as also you may know
> That from the same they do divide the tow.
> Their trade suits well their habitation,
> We find convenience for their occupation."

Pastorius seems to have been on intimate terms with William Penn, Thomas Lloyd, Chief Justice Logan, Thomas Story, and other leading men in the Province belonging to his own religious society, as also with Kelpius, the learned Mystic of the Wissahickon, with the pastor of the Swedes' church, and the leaders of the Mennonites. He wrote a description of Pennsylvania, which was published at Frankfort and Leipsic in 1700 and 1701. His *Lives of the Saints*, etc., written in German and dedicated to Professor Schurmberg, his old teacher, was published in 1690. He left behind him many unpublished manuscripts covering a very wide range of subjects, most of which are now lost. One huge manuscript folio, entitled *Hive Beestock, Melliotropheum Alucar, or Rusca Apium*, still remains, containing one thousand pages with about one hundred lines to a page. It is a medley of knowledge and fancy, history, philosophy, and poetry, written in seven languages. A large portion of his poetry is devoted to the pleasures of gardening, the description of flowers, and the care of bees. The following specimen of his punning Latin is addressed to an orchard-pilferer : —

> "Quisquis in hæc furtim reptas viridaria nostra
> Tangere fallaci poma caveto manu,
> Si non obsequeris faxit Deus omne quod opto,
> Cum malis nostris ut mala cuncta feras."

Professor Oswald Seidensticker, to whose papers in *Der Deutsche Pioneer* and that able periodical *The Penn Monthly*, of Philadelphia, I am indebted for many of the foregoing facts in regard to the German pilgrims of the New World, thus closes his notice of Pastorius : —

"No tombstone, not even a record of burial, indicates where his remains have found their last resting-place, and the pardonable desire to associate the homage due to this distinguished man with some visible memento cannot be gratified. There is no reason to suppose that he was interred in any other place than the Friends' old burying-ground in Germantown, though the fact is not attested by any definite source of information. After all, this obliteration of the last trace of his earthly existence is but typical of what has overtaken the times which he represents; *that* Germantown which he founded, which saw him live and move, is at present but a quaint idyl of the past, almost a myth, barely remembered and little cared for by the keener race that has succeeded."

The Pilgrims of Plymouth have not lacked historian and poet. Justice has been done to their faith, courage, and self-sacrifice and to the mighty influence of their endeavors to establish righteousness on the earth. The Quaker pilgrims of Pennsylvania, seeking the same object by different means, have not been equally fortunate. The power of their testimony for truth and holiness, peace and freedom, enforced only by what Milton calls "the unresistible might of meekness," has been felt through two centuries in the amelioration of penal severities, the abolition of slavery, the reform of the erring, the relief of the poor and suffering, — felt, in brief, in every step of human progress. But of the men themselves, with the single exception of William Penn, scarcely anything is known. Contrasted, from the outset, with the stern, aggressive Puritans of New England, they have come to be regarded as "a feeble folk," with a personality as doubtful as their unrecorded graves. They were not soldiers, like Miles Standish ; they had no figure so picturesque as Vane, no leader so rashly brave and haughty as Endicott. No Cotton Mather wrote their *Magnalia ;* they had no awful drama of supernaturalism in which Satan and his angels were actors ; and the only witch mentioned in their simple annals was a poor old Swedish woman, who, on complaint of her countrywomen, was tried and acquitted of everything but imbecility and folly. Nothing but commonplace offices of civility came to pass between them and the Indians ; indeed, their enemies taunted them with the fact that the savages did not regard them as Christians, but just such men as themselves. Yet it must be apparent to every careful observer of the progress of American civilization that its two principal currents had their sources in the entirely opposite directions of the Puritan and Quaker colonies. To use the words of a late writer :[1] "The historical forces, with which no others may be compared in their influence on the people, have been those of the Puritan and the Quaker. The strength of the one was in the confession of an invisible Presence, a righteous, eternal Will, which would establish righteousness on earth ; and thence arose the conviction of a direct personal responsibility, which could be tempted by no eternal splendor and could be shaken by no internal agitation, and could not be evaded or transferred. The strength of the other was the witness in the human spirit to an eternal Word, an Inner Voice which spoke to each alone, while yet it spoke to every man ; a Light which each was to follow, and which yet was the light of the world ; and all other voices were silent before this, and the solitary path whither it led was more sacred than the worn ways of cathedral-aisles."

It will be sufficiently apparent to the reader that, in the poem which follows, I have attempted nothing beyond a study of the life and times of the Pennsylvania colonist, — a simple picture of a noteworthy man and his locality. The colors of my sketch are all very sober, toned down to the quiet and dreamy atmosphere through which its subject is visible. Whether, in the glare and tumult of the pres-

ent time, such a picture will find favor may well be questioned. I only know that it has beguiled for me some hours of weariness, and that, whatever may be its measure of public appreciation, it has been to me its own reward.

Page 104. *As once he heard in sweet Von Merlau's bowers.*

Eleonora Johanna Von Merlau, or, as Sewall the Quaker Historian gives it, Von Merlane, a noble young lady of Frankfort, seems to have held among the Mystics of that city very much such a position as Anna Maria Schurmaus did among the Labadists of Holland. William Penn appears to have shared the admiration of her own immediate circle for this accomplished and gifted lady.

Page 106. *Or painful Kelpius from his hermit den.*

Magister Johann Kelpius, a graduate of the University of Helmstadt, came to Pennsylvania in 1694, with a company of German Mystics. They made their home in the woods on the Wissahickon, a little west of the Quaker settlement of Germantown. Kelpius was a believer in the near approach of the Millennium, and was a devout student of the Book of Revelation, and the *Morgen-Rothe* of Jacob Behmen. He called his settlement "The Woman in the Wilderness" (*Das Weib in der Wueste*). He was only twenty-four years of age when he came to America, but his gravity, learning, and devotion placed him at the head of the settlement. He disliked the Quakers, because he thought they were too exclusive in the matter of ministers. He was, like most of the Mystics, opposed to the severe doctrinal views of Calvin and even Luther, declaring "that he could as little agree with the *Damnamus* of the Augsburg Confession as with the *Anathema* of the Council of Trent."

He died in 1704, sitting in his little garden surrounded by his grieving disciples. Previous to his death it is said that he cast his famous "Stone of Wisdom" into the river, where that mystic souvenir of the times of Van Helmont, Paracelsus, and Agrippa has lain ever since, undisturbed.

Page 106. *Or Sluyter, saintly familist, whose word.*

Peter Sluyter, or Schluter, a native of Wesel, united himself with the sect of Labadists, who believed in the Divine commission of John De Labadie, a Roman Catholic priest converted to Protestantism, enthusiastic, eloquent, and evidently sincere in his special calling and election to separate the true and living members of the Church of Christ from the formalism and hypocrisy of the ruling sects. George Keith and Robert Barclay visited him at Amsterdam, and afterward at the communities of Herford and Wieward ; and, according to Gerard Croes, found him so near to them on some points, that they offered to take him into the Society of Friends. This offer, if it was really made, which is certainly doubtful, was, happily for the Friends at least, declined. Invited to Herford in West-phalia by Elizabeth, daughter of the Elector

[1] Mulford's *The Nation*, pp. 267, 268.

Palatine, De Labadie and his followers preached incessantly, and succeeded in arousing a wild enthusiasm among the people, who neglected their business and gave way to excitements and strange practices. Men and women, it was said, at the Communion drank and danced together, and private marriages, or spiritual unions, were formed. Labadie died in 1674 at Altona, in Denmark, maintaining his testimonies to the last. "Nothing remains for me," he said, "except to go to my God. Death is merely ascending from a lower and narrower chamber to one higher and holier."

In 1679, Peter Sluyter and Jasper Dankers were sent to America by the community at the Castle of Wieward. Their journal, translated from the Dutch and edited by Henry C. Murphy, has been recently [1872] published by the Long Island Historical Society. They made some converts, and among them was the eldest son of Hermanns, the proprietor of a rich tract of land at the head of Chesapeake Bay, known as Bohemia Manor. Sluyter obtained a grant of this tract, and established upon it a community numbering at one time a hundred souls. Very contradictory statements are on record regarding his headship of this spiritual family, the discipline of which seems to have been of more than monastic severity. Certain it is that he bought and sold slaves, and manifested more interest in the world's goods than became a believer in the near Millennium. He evinces in his journal an overweening spiritual pride, and speaks contemptuously of other professors, especially the Quakers whom he met in his travels. The latter, on the contrary, seem to have looked favorably upon the Labadists, and uniformly speak of them courteously and kindly. His journal shows him to have been destitute of common gratitude and Christian charity. He threw himself upon the generous hospitality of the Friends wherever he went, and repaid their kindness by the coarsest abuse and misrepresentation.

Page 107. *His long-disused and half-forgotten lore.*

Among the pioneer Friends were many men of learning and broad and liberal views. Penn was conversant with every department of literature and philosophy. Thomas Lloyd was a ripe and rare scholar. The great Loganian Library of Philadelphia bears witness to the varied learning and classical taste of its donor, James Logan. Thomas Story, member of the Council of State, Master of the Rolls and Commissioner of Claims under William Penn, and an able minister of his Society, took a deep interest in scientific questions, and in a letter to his friend Logan, written while on a religious visit to Great Britain, seems to have anticipated the conclusion of modern geologists. "I spent," he says, "some months, especially at Scarborough, during the season attending meetings, at whose high cliffs and the variety of strata therein and their several positions I further learned and was confirmed in some things, — that the earth is of much older date as to the beginning of it than the time assigned in the Holy Scriptures as commonly understood, which is suited to the common capacities of mankind, as to six days of progressive work, by which I understand certain long and competent periods of time, and not natural days." It was sometimes made a matter of reproach by the Anabaptists and other sects, that the Quakers read profane writings and philosophies, and that they quoted heathen moralists in support of their views. Sluyter and Dankers, in their journal of American travels, visiting a Quaker preacher's house at Burlington, on the Delaware, found "a volume of Virgil lying on the window, as if it were a common hand-book; also Helmont's book on Medicine (*Ortus Medicinæ, id est Initia Physica inaudita progressus medicinæ novus in morborum ultionam ad vitam longam*), whom, in an introduction they have made to it, they make to pass for one of their own sect, although in his lifetime he did not know anything about Quakers." It would appear from this that the half-mystical, half-scientific writings of the alchemist and philosopher of Vilverde had not escaped the notice of Friends, and that they had included him in their broad eclecticism.

Page 107. *As still in Hemskerck's Quaker Meeting.*

"The Quaker's Meeting," a painting by E. Hemskerck (supposed to be Egbert Hemskerck the younger, son of Egbert Hemskerck the old), in which William Penn and others — among them Charles II., or the Duke of York — are represented along with the rudest and most stolid class of the British rural population at that period. Hemskerck came to London from Holland with King William in 1689. He delighted in wild, grotesque subjects, such as the nocturnal intercourse of witches and the temptation of St. Anthony. Whatever was strange and uncommon attracted his free pencil. Judging from the portrait of Penn, he must have drawn his faces, figures, and costumes from life, although there may be something of caricature in the convulsed attitudes of two or three of the figures.

Page 109. *The Indian from his face washed all his war-paint off.*

In one of his letters addressed to German Friends, Pastorius says : "These wild men, who never in their life heard Christ's teachings about temperance and contentment, herein far surpass the Christians. They live far more contented and unconcerned for the morrow. They do not overreach in trade. They know nothing of our everlasting pomp and stylishness. They neither curse nor swear, are temperate in food and drink, and if any of them get drunk, the mouth - Christians are at fault, who, for the sake of accursed lucre, sell them strong drink."

Again he wrote in 1698 to his father that he finds the Indians reasonable people, willing to accept good teaching and manners, evincing an inward piety toward God, and more eager, in fact, to understand things divine than many among those who in the pulpit teach Christ in word, but by ungodly life deny him.

"It is evident," says Professor Seidensticker, "Pastorius holds up the Indian as Nature's unspoiled child to the eyes of the 'European Babel,' somewhat after the same manner in which Tacitus used the barbarian *Germani* to shame his degenerate countrymen."

As believers in the universality of the Saving Light, the outlook of early Friends upon the heathen was a very cheerful and hopeful one. God was as near to them as to Jew or Anglo-Saxon; as accessible at Timbuctoo as at Rome or Geneva. Not the letter of Scripture, but the spirit which dictated it, was of saving efficacy. Robert Barclay is nowhere more powerful than in his argument for the salvation of the heathen, who live according to their light, without knowing even the name of Christ. William Penn thought Socrates as good a Christian as Richard Baxter. Early Fathers of the Church, as Origen and Justin Martyr, held broader views on this point than modern Evangelicals. Even Augustine, from whom Calvin borrowed his theology, admits that he has no controversy with the admirable philosophers Plato and Plotinus. "Nor do I think," he says in *De Civ. Dei*, lib. xviii., cap. 47, "that the Jews dare affirm that none belonged unto God but the Israelites."

Page 112. *To-morrow shall bring another day.*

A common saying of Valdemar; hence his sobriquet *Alterdag.*

Page 117. *The Witch of Wenham.*

[The house referred to in the head-note is that known as the old Prince house, near Oak Knoll, on the estate now owned by the Xaverian Brothers. In sending the poem to *The Atlantic*, where it was first published, Whittier wrote to the editor: "I do not know how it may strike thee; to me (who am no good judge) it seems one of my best."]

Page 135. *The Homestead.*

[In a letter written after the appearance of *The Homestead*, Whittier wrote: "I saw in the country several of these melancholy spectacles of abandoned homes. I think the farmers of New England are better off as a class, on their hard soil, than those who are on the rich lands of the West. They are not rich, but they are not poor; they live comfortably, and as a rule own their farms clear of mortgage. If they were content to live and toil as the poorer farmers in the West do, they would double their deposits in the savings banks."]

Page 138. *And led by Him, nor man nor devils I fear.*

"He [Macy] shook the dust from off his feet, and departed with all his worldly goods and his family. He encountered a severe storm, and his wife, influenced by some omens of disaster, besought him to put back. He told her not to fear, for his faith was perfect. But she entreated him again. Then the spirit that impelled him broke forth: 'Woman, go below and seek thy God. I fear not the witches on earth, or the devils in hell!'" — *Life of Robert Pike*, page 55.

Page 142. *The hardy Anglo-Saxon stood.*

The celebrated Captain Smith, after resigning the government of the Colony in Virginia, in his capacity of "Admiral of New England," made a careful survey of the coast from Penobscot to Cape Cod, in the summer of 1614.

Page 142. *The sweetest name in all his story.*

Captain Smith gave to the promontory, now called Cape Ann, the name of Tragabizanda, in memory of his young and beautiful mistress of that name, who, while he was a captive at Constantinople, like Desdemona, "loved him for the dangers he had passed."

Page 153. *The Old Burying-Ground.*

[This poem was written with a thought of the ancient cemetery at East Haverhill, near Rocks Village. "The entire piece," Whittier wrote to Lowell, "has now to me a deep and solemn significance. It was written in part while watching at the sick-bed of my dear mother — now no longer with us. She passed away a few days ago, in the beautiful serenity of a Christian faith, a quiet and peaceful dismissal."]

Page 155. *The River Path.*

[To a friend who inquired as to the origin of this poem, Whittier wrote: "The poem was suggested by an evening on the Merrimac River in company with my dear sister, who is no longer with me, having crossed the river (as I fervently hope), to the glorified hill of God."]

Page 157. *The Vanishers.*

[This was the first poem written by Whittier after the death of his sister Elizabeth. In a letter to Mr. Fields he says: "If thee have read Schoolcraft thee will remember what he says of the Packwud-jinnies or 'little vanishers.'" The reference is to *History, Condition and Prospects of the American Indians*, pp. 122, 123.]

Page 160. *I see the gray fort's broken wall.*

[The place that was in the mind of the poet when he wrote this stanza was on the rocks at Marblehead, where he had spent an early morning more than forty years before.]

Page 171. *Over Sibmah's vine.*

"O vine of Sibmah! I will weep for thee with the weeping of Jazer!" *Jeremiah*, xlviii. 32.

Page 172.

Even as the great Augustine
Questioned earth and sea and sky.

"Interrogavi Terram," etc. August. *Soliloq.* Cap. xxxi.

Page 173. *To a Friend.*

[The friend was Elizabeth Neall, afterward Mrs. Sydney Howard Gay.]

Page 174. *Lucy Hooper.*

[It was in the summer of 1837, while residing in New York, that Whittier made the acquaintance of Lucy Hooper. She was a native of Essex County, and was at that time living with her parents in Brooklyn. Whittier encouraged her literary ambition, for she had given promise of poetic excellence, and was considering the advisability of publishing a volume. When Whittier shortly afterward was editing *The Pennsylvania Freeman*, he printed several of her poems. Later in 1839 he was with her by the Merrimac one August afternoon.]

Page 190.

> *And the goodman's voice, at strife*
> *With his shrill and tipsy wife.*

[When Whittier first went to school with his sister Mary, the school-house was undergoing repairs, and the school was held in a dwelling house, the other part of which was occupied by a tipsy and quarrelsome couple.]

Page 192. *Homilies from Oldbug hear.*

Dr. Withington, author of *The Puritan*, under the name of Jonathan Oldbug.

Page 192. *The holy monk of Kempen spake.*

Thomas à Kempis in *De Imitatione Christi*.

Page 196. *When, years ago, beside the summer sea.*

[In the great political contest of 1850, in Massachusetts, when the United States senatorship was in question, Whittier took an active part in forming the coalition between the Free Soilers and the Democrats. He went to Phillips Beach, Swampscott, to see Sumner and induce him to accept the nomination.]

Page 226. *I thank you for sweet summer days.*

[At one of the Laurel festivals the guests who had so often enjoyed the hospitality of Mr. and Mrs. Ashby presented them with an album containing photographs and other tokens of their appreciation. Upon the first page were written these lines by Whittier : —

DEAR FRIENDS : —

> Accept this book whose pages hold
> The sun-traced shadows manifold
> Of friends, who 've known you long and well
> At city hearth, in sylvan dell,
> Enjoying under roof and tree
> Your liberal hospitality ;
> Who grateful own that while you gave
> Your life-long labor to the slave,
> (A labor crowned with more success
> Than hope could dream, or wisdom guess)
> You kept warm hearts, and opened wide
> Your windows on life's sunny side.
> Take, then, the volume with our thanks,
> And long upon your river banks
> When in azalea-gladdened woods
> The June sun swells the laurel buds,
> May we still meet as we have met,
> And larger make to you our debt.]

Page 228. *Hymn for the House of Worship at Georgetown.*

[Whittier published the following card in the Boston *Transcript*, January 30, 1868: "In writing the *Hymn for the Memorial Church at Georgetown*, the author, as his verses indicate, has sole reference to the tribute of a brother and sister to the memory of a departed mother, — a tribute which seemed, and still seems to him in itself considered, very beautiful and appropriate ; but he has since seen with surprise and sorrow a letter read at the dedication, imposing certain extraordinary restrictions upon the society which is to occupy the house. It is due to himself, as a simple act of justice, to say

that had he known of the existence of that letter previously, the Hymn would never have been written, nor his name in any way connected with the proceedings." The restrictions imposed were designed to prevent the use of the building for any lecture or discussion on political subjects or other matters inconsistent with the preaching of the gospel.]

Page 245. *Fie on the witch !*

Goody Cole was brought before the Quarter Sessions in 1680 to answer to the charge of being a witch. The court could not find satisfactory evidence of witchcraft, but so strong was the feeling against her that Major Waldron, the presiding magistrate, ordered her to be imprisoned, with a " lock kept on her leg," at the pleasure of the Court. In such judicial action one can read the fear and vindictive spirit of the community at large.

Page 246. *" Amen ! " said Father Bachiler.*

[Evidence found in favor of the Rev. Stephen Bachiler, an ancestor of the poet, after the poem was first printed, led Whittier to modify lines which implied the guilt of the clergyman.]

Page 249. *His Crimean camp-song hints to us.*

The reference is to Bayard Taylor's poem, *The Song of the Camp*.

Page 258. *The Palatine.*

[The legend on which this ballad is founded was told to Mr. Whittier by his friend, Joseph P. Hazard, of Newport, R. I., two years before the poem was written. About two years after it was published, he received a curious letter from Mr. Benjamin Corydon, of Napoli, N. Y., then in the ninety-second year of his age, who wrote : —

" The Palatine was a ship that was driven upon Block Island, in a storm, more than a hundred years ago. Her people had just got ashore, and were on their knees thanking God for saving them from drowning, when the Islanders rushed upon them and murdered them all. That was a little more than the Almighty could stand, so he sent the Fire or Phantom Ship, to let them know He had not forgotten their wickedness. She was seen once a year on the same night of the year on which the murders occurred, as long as any of the wreckers were living ; but never after all were dead. I must have seen her eight or ten times — perhaps more — in my early days. It is seventy years or more since she was last seen. My father lived right opposite Block Island, on the mainland, so we had a fair view of her as she passed down by the island, then she would disappear. She resembled a full-rigged ship, with her sails all set and all ablaze. It was the grandest sight I ever saw in all my life. I know of only two living who ever saw her, — Benjamin L. Knowles, of Rhode Island, now ninety-four years old, and myself, now in my ninety-second year."]

Page 262. *Toussaint L'Ouverture.*

The reader may, perhaps, call to mind the beautiful sonnet of William Wordsworth, addressed to Toussaint L'Ouverture, during his confinement in France : —

Toussaint ! — thou most unhappy man of men !
  Whether the whistling rustic tends his plough
  Within thy hearing, or thou liest now
Buried in some deep dungeon's earless den ;
O miserable chieftain ! — where and when
  Wilt thou find patience ? — Yet, die not, do thou
  Wear rather in thy bonds a cheerful brow ;
Though fallen thyself, never to rise again,
Live and take comfort. Thou hast left behind
  Powers that will work for thee ; air, earth, and
    skies, —
There 's not a breathing of the common wind
  That will forget thee ; thou hast great allies.
  Thy friends are exultations, agonies,
And love, and man's unconquerable mind.

Page 282. *And he, the basest of the base.*
The Northern author of the Congressional rule against receiving petitions of the people on the subject of Slavery.

Page 289.
  So shalt thou deftly raise
    The market price of human flesh.
There was at the time when this poem was written an Association in Liberty County, Georgia, for the religious instruction of negroes. One of their annual reports contains an address by the Rev. Josiah Spry Law, in which the following passage occurs : "There is a growing interest in this community in the religious instruction of Negroes. There is a conviction that religious instruction promotes the quiet and order of the people, and the pecuniary interest of the owners."

Page 293. *The Pine-Tree.*
[Whittier wrote this poem immediately upon reading the proceedings of the convention. He enclosed it in the following note to Charles Sumner : "I have just read the proceedings of your Whig convention and the lines enclosed are a feeble expression of my feelings. I look upon the rejection of Stephen C. Phillips's resolutions as an evidence that the end and aim of the managers of the convention was to go just far enough to scare the party and no farther. All thanks for the free voices of thyself, Phillips, Allen, and Adams. Notwithstanding the result you have not spoken in vain. If thee thinks well enough of these verses, hand them to the *Whig* or *Chronotype.*"]

Page 298. *I hear the Free-Wills singing.*
The book-establishment of the Free-Will Baptists in Dover was refused the act of incorporation by the New Hampshire Legislature, for the reason that the newspaper organ of that sect and its leading preachers favored abolition.

Page 299. *Our Belknap brother heard with awe.*
The senatorial editor of the *Belknap Gazette* all along manifested a peculiar horror of "niggers" and "nigger parties."

Page 299. *At Pittsfield, Reuben Leavitt saw.*
The justice before whom Elder Storrs was brought for preaching abolition on a writ drawn by Hon. M. N., Jr., of Pittsfield. The sheriff served the writ while the elder was praying.

Page 299. *The schoolhouse, out of Canaan hauled.*
The academy at Canaan, N. H., received one

or two colored scholars, and was in consequence dragged off into a swamp by Democratic teams.

Page 299.
  What boots it that we pelted out
    The anti-slavery women.
The Female Anti-Slavery Society, at its first meeting in Concord, was assailed with stones and brickbats.

Page 299.
  For this did shifty Atherton
    Make gag rules for the great House !
"Papers and memorials touching the subject of slavery shall be laid on the table without reading, debate, or reference." So read the gag-law, as it was called, introduced into the House by Mr. Atherton.

Page 315.
  The first great triumph won
    In Freedom's name.
The election of Charles Sumner to the United States Senate "followed hard upon " the rendition of the fugitive Sims by the United States officials and the armed police of Boston.

Page 332. *To William H. Seward.*
[" Tell Mr. Seward," Whittier wrote to A. W. Thayer, February 1, 1861, " I have bound him to good behavior in my verse, and that if he yields the ground upon which the election was carried and consents to the further extension of slavery he will compromise *me*, as well as the country and himself."]

Page 350. *Garrison.*
[Whittier's tribute to "Garrison " was published in the *Independent*, June 5, 1879, and was accompanied by the following letter to the editor : —
" At the solemn and impressive funeral of my beloved and early friend, William Lloyd Garrison, one of the speakers read a part of the following poem, which I now send, asking a place for it in thy paper, although after the surpassingly beautiful tribute of Wendell Phillips, and the perhaps still more touchingly eloquent words of Theodore D. Weld, it may seem almost superfluous. Something on my part seems due to the intimate friendship of more than fifty years, unbroken and undisturbed by any differences of opinion and action during the long anti-slavery struggle."]

Page 357. *And beauty is its own excuse.*
For the idea of this line, I am indebted to Emerson, in his inimitable sonnet to the Rhodora, —

  If eyes were made for seeing,
  Then Beauty is its own excuse for being.

Page 400.
    No social smoke
  Curled over woods of snow-hung oak.
So isolated was the Whittier homestead that from the date of its erection to the present time no neighbor's roof has been in sight.]

Page 401. *Ah, brother ! only I and thou.*
[Matthew Franklin Whittier, born July 4, 1812, died January 7, 1883. In middle life, during his residence in Portland, he took a deep interest in the anti-slavery movement, and wrote

a series of caustic letters under the signature Ethan Spike of Hornby.]

Page 401.

The African Chief was the title of a poem by Mrs. Sarah Wentworth Morton, wife of the Hon. Perez Morton, a former attorney-general of Massachusetts. Mrs. Morton's *nom de plume* was *Philenia*. The school book in which *The African Chief* was printed was Caleb Bingham's *The American Preceptor*, and the poem contained fifteen stanzas, of which the first four were as follows : —

See how the black ship cleaves the main
  High-bounding o'er the violet wave,
Remurmuring with the groans of pain,
  Deep freighted with the princely slave.

Did all the gods of Afric sleep,
  Forgetful of their guardian love,
When the white traitors of the deep
  Betrayed him in the palmy grove?

A chief of Gambia's golden shore,
  Whose arm the band of warriors led,
Perhaps the lord of boundless power,
  By whom the foodless poor were fed.

Does not the voice of reason cry,
  " Claim the first right which nature gave;
From the red scourge of bondage fly,
  Nor deign to live a burdened slave " ?

Page 402. *Or Chalkley's Journal old and quaint.*

Chalkley's own narrative of this incident, as given in his *Journal*, is as follows : " To stop their murmuring, I told them they should not need to cast lots, which was usual in such cases, which of us should die first, for I would freely offer up my life to do them good. One said, 'God bless you! I will not eat any of you.' Another said, 'He would die before he would eat any of me,' and so said several. I can truly say, on that occasion, at that time, my life was not dear to me, and that I was serious and ingenuous in my proposition : and as I was leaning over the side of the vessel, thoughtfully considering my proposal to the company, and looking in my mind to Him that made me, a very large dolphin came up towards the top or surface of the water, and looked me in the face; and I called the people to put a hook into the sea, and take him, for here is one come to redeem me (I said to them). And they put a hook into the sea, and the fish readily took it and they caught him. He was longer than myself. I think he was about six feet long, and the largest that ever I saw. This plainly showed us that we ought not to distrust the providence of the Almighty. The people were quieted by this act of Providence, and murmured no more. We caught enough to eat plentifully of, till we got into the capes of Delaware."

Page 402. *Our uncle, innocent of books.*

[For further account of Whittier's uncle Moses, the reader is referred to Whittier's *Prose Works*, volume I. p. 323.]

Page 403. *There, too, our elder sister plied.*

[Mary Whittier, born September 3, 1806, married Jacob Caldwell of Haverhill, had two children, Lewis Henry and Mary Elizabeth, and died January 7, 1860.]

Page 403. *Our youngest and our dearest sat.*

[Elizabeth Hussey Whittier, born December 7, 1815, was to her brother John what Dorothy Wordsworth was to William. It was her brother's opinion that "had her health, sense of duty, and almost morbid dread of spiritual and intellectual egotism permitted, she might have taken a high place among lyrical singers." Some of her poems are given in this volume. She died September 3, 1864.]

Page 403. *The master of the district school.*

[Until near the end of his life, Whittier was unable to recall the name of the schoolmaster who stood for this figure in *Snow-Bound*. At last he remembered his name as Haskell, and from this clue the person was traced. He was George Haskell from Waterford, Maine, a Dartmouth student, who studied medicine, and died in Vineland, New Jersey, in 1876.]

Page 404. *Another guest that winter night.*

[In his introductory note, Whittier adds somewhat to his characterization of Harriet Livermore. At the time when *Snow-Bound* was written he did not know that she was living, or he might not have introduced her. She died in 1867.]

Page 404. *The crazy Queen of Lebanon.*

An interesting account of Lady Hester Stanhope may be found in Kinglake's *Eothen*, chap. viii.

Page 406. *These Flemish pictures of old days.*

[In 1888 Whittier wrote the following lines on the fly-leaf of a copy of the first edition of *Snow-Bound* : —

Twenty years have taken flight
Since these pages saw the light.
  All home loves are gone,
But not all with sadness, still,
Do the eyes of memory fill
  As I gaze thereon.

Lone and weary life seemed when
First these pictures of the pen
  Grew upon my page;
But I still have loving friends
And the peace our Father sends
  Cheers the heart of age.

Page 410. *From the Bay State's graceful daughter.*

[The late Mrs. Jettie Morrill Wason, daughter of the late Hon. George Morrill of Amesbury.

Page 438. *O Beauty, old yet ever new.*

"Too late I loved Thee, O Beauty of ancient days, yet ever new! And lo! Thou wert within, and I abroad searching for thee. Thou wert with me, but I was not with Thee." — August. *Soliloq.,* Book X.

Page 438. *Who saw the Darkness overflowed.*

"And I saw that there was an Ocean of Darkness and Death: but an infinite Ocean of Light and Love flowed over the Ocean of Darkness: And in that I saw the infinite Love of God." — George Fox's *Journal*.

Page 438. *The Cry of a Lost Soul.*

The story of the origin of this name, *El alma perdida*, is thus related by Lieut. Herndon. "An Indian and his wife went out from the village to work their chacra, carrying their infant with them. The woman went to the spring to get water, leaving the man in charge of the child, with many cautions to take good care of it. When she arrived at the spring, she found it dried up, and went further to look for another. The husband, alarmed at her long absence, left the child and went in search. When they returned the child was gone; and to their repeated cries, as they wandered through the woods in search, they could get no response save the wailing cry of this little bird heard for the first time, whose notes their anxious and excited imagination syllabled into *pa-pa, ma-ma* (the present Quichua name of the bird). I suppose the Spaniards heard this story, and with that religious poetic turn of thought which seems peculiar to this people, called the bird 'The Lost Soul.'" — *Exploration of the Valley of the Amazon made under direction of the Navy Department.* By William Lewis Herndon and Lardner Gibbon, Part I. p. 156.

Page 464. *The Light that is felt.*

[The origin of this poem is explained in the following letter from Mrs. George A. Palmer, of Elmira, N. Y. —

"When my oldest daughter was two and a half years old she knew Whittier's *Barefoot Boy* by heart, thus: when I would repeat it to her the omission of a line would be instantly corrected, as one day she said to me, 'Mamma, you skipted out "apples of Cusperides."' Once, in going ahead of me in a dark hall, she turned with sudden fear, and said, 'Mamma, take hold of my hand, so it will not be so dark.' This incident and the fact of her affection for Mr. Whittier's poetry was reported to him by a friend of the family. My surprise and delight were great when, in April, 1884, I received a kind letter from the poet and a manuscript copy of the poem, which was afterward published in the Christmas number of *St. Nicholas*. In his letter Mr. Whittier said, "I am glad to have such a friend in thy little girl. Her good opinion of my verses is worth more to me than that of a learned reviewer. I send a rhymed paraphrase of her own beautiful thought."]

Page 495. *Mogg Megone.*

Mogg Megone, or Hegone, was a leader among the Saco Indians, in the bloody war of 1677. He attacked and captured the garrison at Black Point, October 12th of that year; and cut off, at the same time, a party of Englishmen near Saco River. From a deed signed by this Indian in 1664, and from other circumstances, it seems that, previous to the war, he had mingled much with the colonists. On this account, he was probably selected by the principal sachems as

their agent in the treaty signed in November, 1676.

Page 495. *'T was the gift of Castine to Mogg Megone.*

Baron de St. Castine came to Canada in 1644. Leaving his civilized companions, he plunged into the great wilderness, and settled among the Penobscot Indians, near the mouth of their noble river. He here took for his wives the daughters of the great Modocawando, — the most powerful sachem of the East. His castle was plundered by Governor Andros, during his reckless administration; and the enraged Baron is supposed to have excited the Indians into open hostility to the English.

Page 495. *Grey Jocelyn's eye is never sleeping.*

The owner and commander of the garrison at Black Point, which Mogg attacked and plundered. He was an old man at the period to which the tale relates.

Page 495. *Where Phillips' men their watch are keeping.*

Major Phillips, one of the principal men of the Colony. His garrison sustained a long and terrible siege by the savages. As a magistrate and a gentleman, he exacted of his plebeian neighbors a remarkable degree of deference. The Court Records of the settlement inform us that an individual was fined for the heinous offence of saying that "Major Phillips's mare was as lean as an Indian dog."

Page 495. *Steals Harmon down from the sands of York.*

Captain Harmon, of Georgeana, now York, was for many years the terror of the Eastern Indians. In one of his expeditions up the Kennebec River, at the head of a party of rangers, he discovered twenty of the savages asleep by a large fire. Cautiously creeping towards them until he was certain of his aim, he ordered his men to single out their objects. The first discharge killed or mortally wounded the whole number of the unconscious sleepers.

Page 495. *For vengeance left his vine-hung isle.*

Wood Island, near the mouth of the Saco. It was visited by the Sieur de Monts and Champlain, in 1603. The following extract, from the journal of the latter, relates to it: "Having left the Kennebec, we ran along the coast to the westward, and cast anchor under a small island, near the mainland, where we saw twenty or more natives. I here visited an island, beautifully clothed with a fine growth of forest trees, particularly of the oak and walnut; and over spread with vines, that, in their season, produce excellent grapes. We named it the island of Bacchus." — *Les Voyages de Sieur Champlain*, liv. 2, c. 8.

Page 495. *The hunted outlaw, Bonython.*

John Bonython was the son of Richard Bonython, Gent., one of the most efficient and able magistrates of the Colony. John proved to be "a degenerate plant." In 1635, we find by the Court Records that, for some offence, he was fined 40s. In 1640, he was fined for abuse toward R. Gibson, the minister, and Mary, his wife. Soon after he was fined for disorderly conduct in the house of his father. In 1645, the "Great and General Court adjudged John Bonython outlawed, and incapable of any of his Majesty's laws, and proclaimed him a rebel." (*Court Records of the Province*, 1645.) In 1651, he bade defiance to the laws of Massachusetts, and was again outlawed. He acted independently of all law and authority; and hence, doubtless, his burlesque title of "the Sagamore of Saco," which has come down to the present generation in the following epitaph: —

Here lies Bonython, the Sagamore of Saco;
He lived a rogue, and died a knave, and went to Hobomoko.

By some means or other, he obtained a large estate. In this poem, I have taken some liberties with him, not strictly warranted by historical facts, although the conduct imputed to him is in keeping with his general character. Over the last years of his life lingers a deep obscurity. Even the manner of his death is uncertain. He was supposed to have been killed by the Indians; but this is doubted by the able and indefatigable author of the *History of Saco and Biddeford*. — Part I. p. 115.

Page 496. *From the leaping brook to the Saco River*.
Foxwell's Brook flows from a marsh or bog, called the "Heath," in Saco, containing thirteen hundred acres. In this brook, and surrounded by wild and romantic scenery, is a beautiful waterfall, of more than sixty feet.

Page 496. *Where zealous Hiacoomes stood*.
Hiacoomes, the first Christian preacher on Martha's Vineyard; for a biography of whom the reader is referred to Increase Mayhew's account of the Praying Indians, 1726. The following is related of him: "One Lord's day, after meeting, where Hiacoomes had been preaching, there came in a Powwaw very angry, and said, 'I know all the meeting Indians are liars. You say you don't care for the Powwaws;' then calling two or three of them by name, he railed at them, and told them they were deceived, for the Powwaws could kill all the meeting Indians, if they set about it. But Hiacoomes told him that he would be in the midst of all the Powwaws in the island, and they should do the utmost they could against him; and when they should do their worst by their witchcraft to kill him, he would without fear set himself against them, by remembering Jehovah. He told them also he did put all the Powwaws under his heel. Such was the faith of this good man. Nor were these Powwaws ever able to do these Christian Indians any hurt, though others were frequently hurt and killed by them." — Mayhew, pp. 6, 7, c. 1.

Page 497. *Because she cries with an ache in her tooth*.
"The tooth-ache," says Roger Williams in his observations upon the language and customs of the New England tribes, "is the only paine which will force their stoute hearts to cry." He afterwards remarks that even the Indian women

never cry as he has heard "some of their men in this paine."

Page 498. *Wuttamuttata*, "Let us drink." *Weekan*, "It is sweet." *Vide* Roger Williams's *Key to the Indian Language*, "in that parte of America called New England." — London, 1643, p. 35.

Page 498. *Wetuomanit*, — a house god, or demon. "They — the Indians — have given me the names of thirty-seven gods which I have, all which in their solemne Worships they invocate!" — R. Williams's *Briefe Observations of the Customs, Manners, Worships, etc., of the Natives, in Peace and Warre, in Life and Death*: on all which is added Spiritual Observations, General and Particular, of Chiefe and Special use — upon all occasions — to all the English inhabiting these parts; yet Pleasant and Profitable to the view of all Mene: p. 110, c. 21.

Page 499. *Which marks afar the desert isle*.
Mt. Desert Island, the Bald Mountain upon which overlooks Frenchman's and Penobscot Bay. It was upon this island that the Jesuits made their earliest settlement.

Page 500. *Half trembling, as he seeks to look*.
Father Hennepin, a missionary among the Iroquois, mentions that the Indians believed him to be a conjurer, and that they were particularly afraid of a bright silver chalice which he had in his possession. "The Indians," says Père Jerome Lallamant, "fear us as the greatest sorcerers on earth."

Page 500. *For Bomazeen from Tacconock*.
Bomazeen is spoken of by Penhallow as "the famous warrior and chieftain of Norridgewock." He was killed in the attack of the English upon Norridgewock, in 1724.

Page 500. *Like a shrouded ghost the Jesuit stands*.
Père Ralle, or Rasles, was one of the most zealous and indefatigable of that band of Jesuit missionaries who at the beginning of the seventeenth century penetrated the forests of America, with the avowed object of converting the heathen. The first religious mission of the Jesuits to the savages in North America was in 1611. The zeal of the fathers for the conversion of the Indians to the Catholic faith knew no bounds. For this they plunged into the depths of the wilderness; habituated themselves to all the hardships and privations of the natives; suffered cold, hunger, and some of them death itself, by the extremest tortures. Père Brebeuf, after laboring in the cause of his mission for twenty years, together with his companion, Père Lallamant, was burned alive. To these might be added the names of those Jesuits who were put to death by the Iroquois, — Daniel, Garnier, Buteaux, La Riborerde, Goupil, Constantin, and Liegeouis. "For bed," says Father Lallamant, in his *Relation de ce qui s'est dans le pays des Hurons*, 1640, c. 3, "we have nothing but a miserable piece of bark of a tree; for nourishment, a handful or two of corn, either roasted or soaked in water, which seldom satisfies our hunger; and after all, not venturing to perform even the ceremonies of

our religion without being considered as sorcerers." Their success among the natives, however, by no means equalled their exertions. Père Lallamant says: "With respect to adult persons, in good health, there is little apparent success; on the contrary, there have been nothing but storms and whirlwinds from that quarter."

Sebastian Ralle established himself, some time about the year 1670, at Norridgewock, where he continued more than forty years. He was accused, and perhaps not without justice, of exciting his Praying Indians against the English, whom he looked upon as the enemies not only of his king, but also of the Catholic religion. He was killed by the English in 1724, at the foot of the cross which his own hands had planted. His Indian church was broken up, and its members either killed outright or dispersed.

In a letter written by Ralle to his nephew he gives the following account of his church and his own labors: "All my converts repair to the church regularly twice every day: first, very early in the morning, to attend mass, and again in the evening, to assist in the prayers at sunset. As it is necessary to fix the imagination of savages, whose attention is easily distracted, I have composed prayers, calculated to inspire them with just sentiments of the august sacrifice of our altars: they chant, or at least recite them aloud, during mass. Besides preaching to them on Sundays and saints' days, I seldom let a working-day pass without making a concise exhortation, for the purpose of inspiring them with horror at those vices to which they are most addicted, or to confirm them in the practice of some particular virtue." — Vide *Lettres Edifiantes et Cur.*, vol. vi. p. 127.

Page 503. *Pale priest! what proud and lofty dreams.*

The character of Ralle has probably never been correctly delineated. By his brethren of the Romish Church, he has been nearly apotheosized. On the other hand, our Puritan historians have represented him as a demon in human form. He was undoubtedly sincere in his devotion to the interests of his church, and not over-scrupulous as to the means of advancing those interests. "The French," says the author of the *History of Saco and Biddeford*, "after the peace of 1713, secretly promised to supply the Indians with arms and ammunition, if they would renew hostilities. Their principal agent was the celebrated Ralle, the French Jesuit." — p. 215.

Page 504. *Where are De Rouville and Castine.*

Hertel de Rouville was an active and unsparing enemy of the English. He was the leader of the combined French and Indian forces which destroyed Deerfield and massacred its inhabitants, in 1703. He was afterwards killed in the attack upon Haverhill. Tradition says that, on examining his dead body, his head and face were found to be perfectly smooth, without the slightest appearance of hair or beard.

Page 504. *Cowesass? — tawhich wessaseen? Are you afraid? — why fear you?*

INDEX OF FIRST LINES

INDEX OF TITLES